Legacy of Letters

By

Patsy Gilbert

authorHOUSE™

1663 LIBERTY DRIVE, SUITE 200
BLOOMINGTON, INDIANA 47403
(800) 839-8640
WWW.AUTHORHOUSE.COM

First published by AuthorHouse 02/03/05

ISBN: 1-4208-0256-9 (e)
ISBN: 1-4208-0257-7 (sc)
ISBN: 1-4208-0258-5 (dj)

Library of Congress Control Number: 2004098037

Printed in the United States of America
Bloomington, Indiana

This book is printed on acid-free paper.

Cover photograph and author photograph by Michael Cairns at www.michaelcairns.com

A letter always seemed to me like immortality.
Emily Dickinson

A Southern family: Sammie, John, Baby Rickey, Wilba, John Randolph, and Patsy.

Lines of Descent

Circa 1865–1987

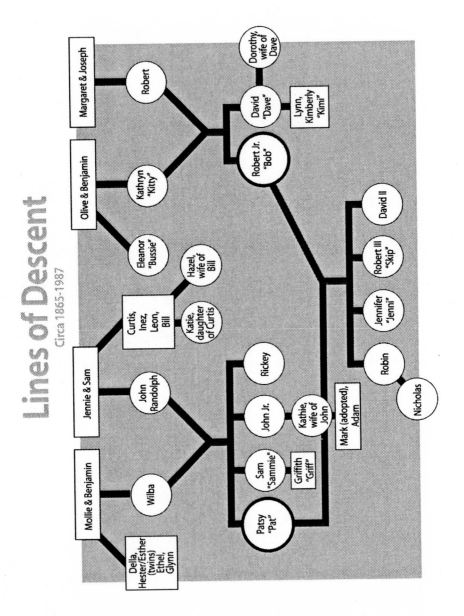

Call it a clan, call it a network, call it a tribe, call it a family.
Whatever you call it, wherever you are, you need one.
Jane Howard

Dedication

Since before any of us were born, God planned for us to share our lives with each other. He knew exactly how our strengths and weaknesses would balance one another, and the depth of love, understanding, and commitment we would learn to feel. He knew that the richness of our separate characters would be developed through the hard times, and that mutual trust and respect would be born as a result of overcoming the trials together. He knew that we would laugh together; and cry together. He knew we needed each other... to hug, to help, to teach, to serve ... to love.

We Are a Family – G. Copeland

I share *Legacy of Letters* and its sweet memories of love with three special families that form a cherished circle whose members enrich life, lessen pain, and bring joy: My Family of Origin, my Family of Marriage, Children and Grandchildren, and my Family of Friends of the World.

And with deepest love I dedicate this book to Robin, Jenni, Skip and David. It is my legacy to you, offered with a most grateful heart for the joy of being your mother.

Table of Contents

Wilba at age 16 in Mississippi

The way I walk I see my mother walking,
The feet secure and firm upon the ground.
The way I talk I hear my daughters talking,
And hear my mother's echo in the sound.
The way she thought, I find myself now thinking,
The generations linking in a firm continuum of mind.
The bridge of immortality I'm walking
The voice before me echoing behind.

Author Unknown

Dear Readers,

This first letter is to welcome you as you join me in a journey through life by way of informal personal letters and diaries. My wish is that you will be inspired to reminisce, and in so doing be reminded of and rejoice in the miracle of your own life story.

I picture life as an ever-expanding magical circle wherein smaller circles spin in a fascinating orbit into which each of us leaps for an unknown, indefinite period of time, to take our turn.

My story follows the experiences of a simple Southern country girl living a seemingly ordinary life. Except, of course, no one's life is ordinary. How could it be anything but extraordinary? Life is a precious gift … live it fully!

I am so grateful to my late mother who placed the first seed of an idea that eventually became a family history. Unbeknownst to me, she began saving all of my letters in 1953, the year I first moved away from the family home as a brand new bride. By the time her lovely secret was revealed, I too was already a keeper of cards, notes, letters, and daily personal journals.

Add to our combined collection the sporadic entries from my worn little red childhood diary, and the bundles of crinkled old treasured letters between newlyweds separated by the U.S. Navy, plus other correspondence from family members and friends over the years, and a story seemed to simply unfold from the pages. A story continuing even as it is being written.

To ensure easier readability, some letters and diary entries used in the book have been edited for length and clarity.

I hope you all enjoy the read … and the journey.

Best Wishes,
Patsy Gilbert

Sometime in your life you will go on a journey.
It will be the longest journey you have ever taken.
It is the journey to find yourself.
Katherine Sharp

Prologue

Pat as a young bride in Mobile, Alabama

January 1, 1986
Orlando, Florida
Dear Diary,

I often feel as if I am on a journey with no destination, simply stumbling along an endless, winding road, zigzagging among the forks. It's terribly scary, always wondering which path to take, which will be the right one *this* time.

In August I'll turn 54 although I look in the mirror and still see the soul of a fresh-faced young Pat on the brink of life's adventure. What happened to all the time? I'm hoping this year I'll find new direction and the fulfillment of some of my dreams. Life is such a mystery ... do others have this same deep longing to understand the unfolding of their lives?

What I *can* figure out so far is that this gift of life seems to carry with it an implied agreement to be involved in a series of learning experiences. A process of soaring through the ups and surviving the downs. Of searching for ways to gain more love, to give purer love, and to feel an ever-deepening connection to our world.

I find there are times when joy reigns supreme. It could happen on any day, feeling a *joie de vivre* for no particular reason. Or in the midst of happy celebrations. Or in moments alone with cherished memories.

And there are those piercingly painful periods fraught perhaps with illness, grief, loss, or regret over things done or not done, or even apathy.

It seems, too, that during the course of the unfolding there are sometimes long stretches of placidly coasting along in the flow of life's daily routines, with events occurring just as expected or planned.

I've recognized that in some way or another, whether smoothly sailing along or mired in moments of fear and confusion, I'm usually still aware of and touched by the beauty all around. My senses are stirred to new aliveness by myriad sights and sounds ... blue skies on a balmy day, when the sunshine sparkles on water like a scattering of diamonds. A little sliver of crescent moon moored in a midnight sky. Rolling ocean waves, quiet ripples on a lake. Stately old tree giants or tiny new rosebuds. Healthy children with laughing eyes. The fleeting glimpse of a brilliant red cardinal, a bevy of butterflies landing gracefully in a bed of flowers. The sweet-love smiles of an old couple as their eyes meet and their age-worn hands gently touch. Lively foot-tapping music or a slow, haunting guitar solo. The cooing of a dove, or of a baby. ...

There are other blessings as I travel on through the twists and turns of the path. I meet folks with wisdom and warmth who guide me in my search for the rainbow's mysterious end, and I delight in their generous spirit. They sun my soul.

Sometimes I connect with fellow seekers embarking on their own journeys, and when I stop to listen and share, a mutual caring is born that helps each of us along the path. Then too, I encounter individuals reluctant to leave the safety and security of the familiar and take that risk into the unknown to examine the deepest self. To those I strive always to impart kindness and understanding, but soon find I am eager to continue on my way.

I have so many places to go, more to explore, and much to learn. I dare not linger.

Shoot for the moon. Even if you miss, you'll land among the stars.
Les Brown

Prelude

A New Look at Life

Pat and cousin Katie at age 7

January 28, 1986
Orlando, Florida
Dear Diary,

Today the launch of the U.S.'s 25th space shuttle ended in tragedy. Only minutes after liftoff from Kennedy Space Center at Cape Canaveral, the *Challenger* exploded. The shuttle and its precious cargo of seven were no more. So horrific ... seen by millions, in person and on television. Once again, in an instant, we are made aware of just how fragile is life.

                                        Pat

February 16, 1986
Deer Valley, Utah
Dear Diary,

I've made it halfway through the weeklong interview here in a part of the country that's new to me. ... It's beautiful, and *cold*. I haven't seen snow like this since the 1950s and '60s in Connecticut, back when each snowfall seemed to offer yet another challenge for this newly transplanted Southerner. Now, looking out at nature's fleecy blanket from the picture window of a luxurious condominium, I am able to simply appreciate its pristine beauty.

The days are full, getting to know and taking care of the little ones, keeping detailed notes of questions and ideas to discuss with the parents, and visiting with the family's friends who drop in throughout the day for a cup of good hot coffee, tea or cocoa before hitting the slopes again. It's quiet in the evenings, though, and there's time to rest and to think about everything facing me. ... Could I really get used to traveling all over the world as a nanny? This fascinating couple with two young children is eager to have me join the family in their Arizona home and also accompany them as they conduct seminars and take vacations in Hawaii, Japan, Australia and other faraway places I haven't seen. ...

It's amazing where I've been and the people I've met this past month. While visiting my brother Sam out in San Francisco, I was approached about an interview with well-known author Danielle Steele, and also with a member of one of the legendary Getty families. Initially both opportunities sounded exciting, but with more information, I decided the positions that were open would not be right for me.

Later, in Los Angeles, there was an interview scheduled with Burt Bacharach and his wife, Carol Bayer Sager, but I got a call from the agency that a Scottish nanny had already been hired. That was disappointing, as were a couple more possibilities that fell through, but I figured there *would* be a spot for me. Someplace!

Staying at the Beverly Rodeo hotel a few days, and seeing Rodeo Drive … oh, ho, what a thrill, pretty heady surroundings for this country girl! Another treat while I was in the area was a few hours' visit with my new friend Victoria, who works for Richard Chamberlain. She is such a delight. We talked for hours about everything from pursuing our spiritual quests to propelling sexy new men into our lives!

But first, I have to settle on a job. And there is a lot to consider before I make any final decisions. Right now I have two other great-sounding offers. One is with an Orlando surgeon and his wife, who are expecting a baby soon. They asked me to *please* not accept another job. Then there's the lure of California again – the agency called about a position in Hollywood with a popular young actor and his family, and it turns out to be Pierce Brosnan! He and his wife want me to meet them in New York City for an interview.

Hmmm … I wonder *where* I'll be at this time next month?

Sunday, March 23, 1986
The Orlando Sentinel

A DREAM COME TRUE
FOR A SPECIAL NANNY

Nine years ago, after 25 years of marriage, Pat was divorced. The reasons for the marriage breakup at this point are irrelevant. "The main thing I had to do," she said the other day, "was decide which way to go from there. I needed to work. I'd been a legal secretary at one time but had no desire to take that up again.

"Instead, I declared myself a nanny for hire."

A nanny? Well, why not? She was 44 at the time, had raised two daughters and two sons, and certainly could manage a household.

"My three older children, Robin, Jenni and Skip, were working or in college," she said. "I felt I would not only enjoy being a nanny, but the position would allow me more flexibility as far as caring for my 7-year old, David. He's a special boy. Well, all my children are special, the best references I could possibly have."

On the strength of those and ensuing references she found fulfilling work as a nanny and household manager with two families in Winter Park, another in Orlando. All the jobs ended amicably, and early last week she left to join her new family for a 10-day Caribbean cruise.

After the cruise they will probably go on to the family home in Hollywood Hills, California, or they might all head for a film location in Finland. The head of her new family, you see, is Pierce Brosnan, star of the television series *Remington Steele*.

Brosnan, who has been mentioned as a frontrunner to take over the James Bond movie roles, and his wife, Cassie, have a teenage daughter and son and a 2-year-old son.

"I'm so excited. I can't tell you," she said before leaving Orlando. "I haven't seen their home, or met their older children yet." She flew to New York City for the interview. "But I think I'll like living in California. I have a brother out there. I hate leaving Orlando, it's wonderful, but I *have* been wanting to travel."

She feels free to take on this adventure now that David is 16 and living with his 31-year-old married sister, Robin.

"Everybody's excited for me," said the petite mother. "That includes my parents in Mobile, Alabama.

7

"You have to set your goals. I'm very particular, wanted great things, an exciting lifestyle. I registered with an agency in Beverly Hills and told them not to call me unless it was special. They said I wasn't realistic, but you have to plant your dreams. I believe in mysterious forces that bring you to the right people."

April 20, 1986
Los Angeles, California

Orlando, Florida
My dearest David,

I telephoned Robin Saturday alerting her to the possibility of my coming back home to Orlando since, unfortunately, the job and the move to California have not worked out.

These past weeks I've learned a lot about myself, more of what I want and don't want and can and cannot do, really important knowledge when considering my future and further changes. Sadly, I've realized my physical health is not as excellent as in the past and that with nearly constant back pain I simply can't continue lifting and tending young children – newborns maybe, but not hefty 30-pound toddlers. In the position here, the erratic lifestyle and extensive traveling with a small child have clearly shown me that I have limits. A somewhat creaky, jet-lagged nanny and a cranky, sleepless toddler make a rough combination.

I just can't regret following the dream I had, though, David. What interesting, exciting experiences the past few months! But now I want to start over in Orlando … and I like the idea of living at our old apartment complex again. My plan is that when I leave California I'll first go to Mobile for some R&R while visiting with Mom and Daddy and deciding just how to proceed with my life.

That's exactly what I want for you, too, sweetie, for you to figure out how to proceed with your own life. You are a unique, wonderful being, David, with a fine physical body, a brilliant mind and a very special "old soul." Please always do everything in your power to nurture yourself and be the best you can be in every way, physically, intellectually and spiritually. And remember, your own power is awesome.

With so much love,
Mom

April 21, 1986
Hollywood, California

Orlando, Florida
Dear Pat,

Thank you so much for your letter. These are exciting times we live in, particularly if our points of view resonate to the light and love of the God above and the light and love of the God within.

Every seemingly tragic event that occurs in our lives occurs for a reason: the purposeful good of our own growth. If we can constantly remember that we choose to experience what we are living in order to realize the God within us, the way we relate to "tragedy" alters and life will become glorious.

The way we perceive life is everything. In other words, we are not the victims of the world we see, we are the victims of the way we see the world. We are our own teachers. Our free will is the path of understanding – the realization of the God within us.

Trust yourself and trust your inherent love and light and your life will manifest in the same way.

Much love and light from me – and thank you again for your sweet letter.

Sincerely,
Shirley MacLaine

April 22, 1986
Woodbury, Connecticut

Mobile, Alabama
Pat dear,

It was really distressing to learn about your back problem. I'll be eager to hear the results of the lab work and bone scan. And I'm sure that you will get "revived" as you call it, because it seems to me there are people especially selected for all kinds of stages their life long – and they are the ones strong enough to always see it through and come up smiling. I know, Pat, how easy it is to get down when you feel alone and relatively helpless. I've been there more than once. But you and I have what it takes to snap back. I'm betting on you.

Much love,
Auntie Bussie

May 25, 1986
Charlotte, North Carolina

Mobile, Alabama
Dear Pat,

I know it's been a long time since you heard from this old friend but I've been thinking about you. I thoroughly enjoyed the newspaper article. Your career as a nanny certainly developed into a life filled with tremendous experiences. Who would have thought it when you first started? I'd like to read your resume as you certainly have done a superior job of selling yourself. Unlike me, you've been very selective with your job choices.

Is there any treatment that would be helpful at the present stage of your condition? My mother has talked of living with pain on a continuous basis and says it is wearing as well as depressing.

Pat, you have overcome so many big obstacles in your life since Jack and I left Orlando. I firmly believe good will come to you and that your life is destined to swing upward. You have conquered lots of disappointments and hurts – I don't know if I could have done as well – and I'm not a bit worried about you working things out.

Love,
Sally

May 29, 1986
Mobile, Alabama

The Orlando Sentinel
Orlando, Florida
Dear Ed,

You will no doubt be surprised at my news, but I wanted you to know about the change in my plans since you wrote the lovely nanny article about me for the *Orlando Sentinel* in March. I followed my dream all the way, but it seems it wasn't meant to be.

The position in Hollywood and my career as a nanny ended abruptly when there was a sudden, drastic change in my health. The back pain that had been a concern for some time worsened and tests revealed three fractured, collapsed vertebrae.

The physical and emotional stress of traveling and caring for another 2-year-old actually put the whole of me into a state of collapse. The culprit has been identified as osteoporosis, the bone disease often referred to as "the silent stalker" since generally there are no warning symptoms before a fracture. New strong pain medication has helped somewhat, I'm on hormone therapy and take high doses of calcium, and I also walk some each day (weight-bearing exercise is highly recommended to strengthen bones). In all honesty, the entire experience has left me feeling extremely fragile. So although it's hard to say goodbye to my nanny career, I know the lifting and awkward moves required in caring for a small child are things I can no longer do with ease and joy.

You can be sure I've had occasional moments of despair and feelings of fear for the future and sadness for yet another ending. As I recently read in my *Daily Word*, though, "There are no endings, only beginnings," and I do still believe those mysterious forces are at work, leading me to whatever it is I am supposed to do. Through all the upheaval, Cassie and Pierce Brosnan were wonderful to me and I wouldn't want to have missed knowing them.

In the future, besides continuing work on a "how to" book on child care, I plan to explore areas in which I might be able to use my experience and knowledge of nannying in ways other than actually handling children – perhaps through seminars for parents and parents-to-be, explaining my methods of child care, or offering my services as a nanny consultant. In the meantime, I'll be looking for a part-time job when I get back to Orlando.

Sincerely,

Pat

June 21, 1986
Mobile, Alabama

Marietta, Georgia
Dear Katie,

Hey, my sweet cousin. I hope you're doing okay. I worry about you because I know how hard you work. I won't "preach," but I wish it were easier for you to relax and take a day off now and then!

Our last phone call was kind of rushed, and I still had so much to tell you. I always feel better when I can share my ups and downs with you.

I think I mentioned to you that earlier this year my brother Sam's neighbor in Berkeley seemed really interested in the nanny book I'm writing. Well, she discussed it with her editor friend at Harcourt, Brace & Jovanovich, who asked to see the outline and a few chapters. I sent them a while ago and was so excited when the editor responded with a telephone call.

First she questioned whether there was enough material for a book, and I told her I envisioned a small one, easy to pick up and reference during a child's different stages. Then she really boosted my ego! Said she, "You have a delightful writing style, easy, entertaining, informal, reminiscent of Peg Bracken. I wonder if you might want to consider writing magazine articles, or a newspaper child care advice column, or with such a delightful style, your memoirs."

What a compliment – I love Peg Bracken's work. She's the one who wrote the *I Hate to Cook Cookbook* and *I Hate to Housekeep*, both of which are just great. I began to think, Hmm, maybe I'll make a switch from the subject of my method of child care to ME.

Actually, though, I had recently made good progress on the little nanny book …writing at my brother John's in Mississippi. He had come to Mobile for a visit and suggested I go back home with him and use to my advantage his and Kathie's office setup. It was fantastic: a computer, printer, copier, dictionaries, reference books, plenty of paper, pens, pencils, in fact everything I could possibly need. And they not only provided the perfect workplace, but both being great cooks, they nourished my somewhat battered ol' body with delicious meals. Also, each morning I went for a healthy bone-building walk and after lunch enjoyed a restorative "lie-down" on a moist heating pad for my back. A three-week oasis of rest, recuperation and productivity combined, and I was buoyed by it. Then it was time to head back to Mobile. …

When we arrived at the folks' house, John and I took the brown grocery bags containing all of my book materials from the car and set them on the floor just inside the den. The next morning I noticed they weren't there and assumed someone had moved the bags to another spot in the big house. But, oh, Katie, as I went from room to room searching, I got more frantic by the minute – they had simply disappeared.

It was a complete mystery, still is, always will be, I guess. Nobody remembered seeing or moving them. My first thought was that Daddy, being such a stickler for taking out trash right away, had just automatically grabbed the bags by mistake to put outside for pickup, but he said he hadn't. Of course, how it happened doesn't matter, anyway. They are still gone.

I felt sick to my stomach for about three days. Not wanting the folks to see my anguish, I mostly hold back the tears until I go on my long solitary walks. I know I'll have to accept the loss; I *don't* know if I'll attempt the book again. Although there are a few chapters on disks, the years' worth of saved articles, records of children's schedules, and all my notes relating to the project are irreplaceable. During these months of traveling I've been *so* careful to store the material safely, always with a prayer that nothing would happen to it. But, you know, the best laid plans. …

Thanks for listening, Katie. Take care of yourself. I love you.

Pat

June 23, 1986
Dear Diary,

News with good possibilities in a call from Robin early this morning. It concerns La Costa Brava, the apartment complex where over the years every member of our family except Skip has lived at one time or another. It's the homey place David and I moved to following the separation – then "gave over" our apartment to Bob when I took the job at the mansion for that unexpectedly short period, and then got back again. Later, Jenni lived there, and just recently Robin, Nicholas and David transferred from a two- to a three-bedroom apartment in the complex, and I'm now on the waiting list again. "Miss Mabel," the wonderful manager, knows the family well and has always been helpful and understanding through our many upheavals and moves to and from LCBA.

So ... Mabel told Robin she'll be retiring soon and she wondered if I'd be interested in her position. When Robin brought up my lack of experience, Mabel said, "I wouldn't consider doing this – or recommending anyone else in the world – except for your mother." She said the big out-of-state company managers will do the hiring but have asked for her advice and recommendations, and that if I'd be interested she would like to see me as the new manager. And she'd be happy to stay and train me. *What* a vote of confidence. Oh, my goodness, I can't help but get excited over this turn of events.

July 2, 1986
Dear Diary,

I'm in Orlando, cat-sitting Lucy and Kitty and staying at Jenni and Bill's apartment while they're vacationing and visiting friends in Colorado.

I had an interview with the management company's top guy yesterday, and Mabel called to tell me I was the first choice until this morning when a very experienced young woman beat me out. But they'd like me to take the position of assistant manager – and I am pleased about that. *Maybe* everything is going to work out well. ... I pray so.

July 4, 1986
Dear Diary,

Today these United States of America celebrate the 210th anniversary of their independence. And this year France's 1886 gift of the Statue of Liberty on Ellis Island, New York Harbor, which has been refurbished and restored, was rededicated as a great monument to freedom. There were fantastic celebrations all during "Liberty Weekend." I'm so lucky to live in America, this land of freedom and opportunity!

It's wonderful to see my Orlando kids (and adorable Nicholas) again. I couldn't get enough of hugging David. He looks devastatingly handsome, lean, tan, tall, with that beautiful blond hair. He has been saving his money for a long time, just bought Jenni's '79 Mustang, and is presently intoxicated with his own brand of freedom: wheels! Skip called today, such a sweet son, always checking up on his mom, wanting to hear me sounding perky. There's no fooling any of the children, and I've tried – they can always tell by my voice how I feel.

July 5, 1986
Orlando, Florida

Mobile, Alabama
Dearest Mom and Daddy,

Good news: I'm ready to start the job as assistant manager of La Costa Brava – and move into my new apartment. Things are looking up again.

This weekend I spent a few hours in the most beautiful home I've seen lately visiting with old friend Corrine, who is still as cute, bubbly, caring, and pretty as I remembered. And funny – she was telling me about two women she knows, each one of whom wrote a prompt sympathy note to a different widower. Now one of the ladies is dating the widower she consoled and the other is already married to hers! Even as we chuckled about it she urged me to be ready to send my own note of sympathy as soon as any opportunity should arise!

Along those lines, I attended the "Adams and Eves" bowling banquet last night. That's the league Bob and I started about 14 years ago, and it was lovely seeing lots of old friends again. The group wants me to re-join but, alas, I'd have to first attach myself to an "Adam," so everyone is going to look out for a partner for me – I said tall, dark, handsome, rich, and unentangled would do for a start!

Much love,
Pat

July 20, 1986
Dear Diary,

I guess I need to do a catch-up entry after a spell of no writing of any kind. Another shock, another period of disappointment and questioning. … My situation looked so good only two weeks ago, but from the first day on the job there were problems. The new manager's personality and methods of managing presented real challenges, especially for a fairly gentle soul like me, learning on the job. I found her to be unrelentingly aggressive, loud-spoken and brash, the complete antithesis of Mabel, who was so capable and firm in her managing style, but handled everyone and every situation with such class.

There's no need to examine what went wrong … thinking back, I'm convinced she simply didn't want me there and fired me, suddenly, unexpectedly and quite coldly. It took my breath away for a few moments, but I held myself in control until I could get out of the office. Walking back to my apartment, I tearfully asked, "God? I thought this was where I was divinely led. What now?" I only knew one thing for sure, I'd try to have NO further dealings whatsoever with that person. Not God, the manager!

Coming back here and having things go so wrong, I'm experiencing some of those same crazy emotions I grappled with in 1981 when I moved from Orlando to Mobile: feeling that I'm back where I had been before and all the years in between never happened. I have to get off that kind of treadmill. And look for ways to keep gliding forward, never doubting that the years *have been* and that they contained lots of good along with the not-so-good.

August 30, 1986
Orlando, Florida

Mobile, Alabama
Dearest Folks,

I'll catch y'all up on some of what has been going on since our couple of brief phone visits. Skip came down and the whole gang gathered for our annual family vacation in New Smyrna Beach. It was wonderful, good weather, delicious eats, walks on the beach, refreshing swims in the ocean, fun games, and lots of shared love and laughter. We all hope our week-at-the-beach tradition continues forever!

Back in Orlando Skip, David and I spent a day in the land of fantasy, courtesy of an old friend who works at Disney World. Recalling our excursion there five years ago, we wondered if we could possibly have as much fun as we did that day. We did. I think the most fun, again, was the ride on "Thunder Mountain," when I went slightly crazy with the thrill of if, laughing so much I hurt – while the boys laughed so hard at me they were wheezing! Both guys liked the much more extreme "Space Mountain" ride, too, and teased that maybe next time I should try that one. I don't think so!

Sandwiched in the middle of these enjoyable family activities, I've also answered classified ads for a motley assortment of jobs and had a few interviews. One paid off, at least temporarily – for three months I'm going to be a newborn night nanny for the baby girl of another one of Orlando's prominent families, working five or six nights a week, from 10 p.m. to 7 a.m. I'll still be available to do some daytime babysitting.

And also, as another means to increase my meager finances, I have found a roommate for the next few months. Sophie, an adorable young French woman, is here for a course of study in international hospitality. She's from Normandy, speaks fluent French, English, Spanish, quite a bit of Italian and German, and is presently studying Portuguese. Would that I could absorb by osmosis some of her amazing ability in languages, particularly since I recently registered to take classes in Conversational Spanish through Boone High School's Adult Education program.

I must say, Sophie and I immediately felt like close friends – she's one of those special old souls that I always connect so deeply with – and quite naturally started to kiss each other on both cheeks for every hello, good morning, goodnight, and bye-bye!

I saw my darling lil' Filipina "adopted" sis, Terri, and her Donald when they treated me to dinner on my 54th birthday last week. And the highlight of the next day was five hours spent visiting with Dave and Dorothy, always a special time. I love those two.

And I love you,
Pat

September 6, 1986
Woodbury, Connecticut

Orlando, Florida
Pat dear,

You've no idea how relieved I was to get your long, newsy letter. I was getting worried about you and was wondering how you were getting along.

I'm sorry you've not found a real position that you like. It seems awful that when it's almost impossible to find anyone who wants to work, anyone who does can't get it. Good luck in the hunt.

I had forgotten about your early menopausal problems. What a mess. I guess the Lord tests hardest those of us who are the toughest. When I see how some people who've never had real trouble build up the picayune little problems they have, it makes me laugh – and bores me. I am familiar with osteoarthritis but osteoporosis baffles me. I've consulted two dictionaries and can't find it. Please elucidate.

Much love,
Auntie Bussie

September 21, 1986
Dear Diary,

The last day of summer, with a definite touch of autumn in the breeze. And that huge, beautiful golden Harvest Moon seems almost close enough to hitch a ride on.

The night nanny job is a pleasure, really. Being with a precious baby is my favorite thing in the world. I'm lucky that Carrie is a contented little one, which makes it possible for me to get a fairly decent night's sleep. When baby wakes I change her and tap on the door to alert mommy. While she's nursing, I fetch a big glass of juice or milk for Nicole and a bowl of always-prepared colorful, delicious fresh fruit for myself. When baby's fed, mommy goes back to bed, and I do the burping-settling-baby-down routine, then doze again until the next call from cute little Carrie.

There are times I feel discouraged over the difficulty of finding a regular full-time job, but I just won't let myself stay down. Instead, my days are filled with all sorts of activities. I walk, swim when it's not too cool, practice Spanish, take yoga classes from a beautiful young woman I met at Unity Church with the lovely name of Noor – and study all the Silva Mind Techniques material between classes. I negotiated a trade for this course: By assisting the instructor in my class and the one following, I've earned a partial "scholarship."

News flash: Robin has met a young man who lives here at the complex. So far she and Rick are enjoying each other's company. Developments reported as they occur. ...

November 15, 1986
Dear Diary,

Ugh, a weepy week I've had, crying about different things, everything … and nothing in particular. It's been weepy weather, too, lots of rain and dark clouds creating a dreary atmosphere that fits right in with feelings of disappointment and depression. But I've been in this place before. I'll come out of it and perk up again

December 27, 1986
Dear Diary,

The Christmas holidays have been good. Katie rode down from Georgia with Skip and we loved the chance to be together for a week. I gave a great party on the 21st – an informal spaghetti supper for family and a few friends. David brought his cute new girlfriend, and Rick came with Robin. Those two are seeing each other often and seem to be growing closer.

The five hours of opening gifts on Christmas day were interspersed with numerous breaks and many good laughs. Skip always teases and "cuts up" in such a funny, endearing way, and David is beginning to follow right along in his big brother's footsteps. Katie remarked, after receiving so many little presents, "I think I'll come back here next year!" And dear Sophie, who loved being in the midst of our family gathering, said she'd think about all of us enjoying our traditions and each other from wherever she happens to be next Christmas. Oh, my goodness, am I going to miss her when she returns to France in a couple of weeks.

Another year ending, I can hardly believe it. Wonder what in the world 1988 holds in store for me? I *try* to keep the image of all positive happenings and to hold on to my faith that they *will* become reality. …

January 3, 1987
Atlanta, Georgia

Orlando, Florida
Dear Mom,

We kids don't tell you this often enough … but I am proud of you for all you've accomplished since striking out on your own. You may not have a great deal of material goods to show for your efforts, however your spiritual accomplishments are certainly *magnificent*! I always envision the best for you. You deserve it and you will have it! I love you so much.

All my love,
Skip

February 3, 1987
Saint Lo, France

Orlando, Florida

My dear Pat,

I received your letter yesterday and was very happy to have some news. In fact I tried to phone this weekend but first your line was busy and later on the international phone network was overloaded.

In about 10 days I will go to Paris with my mother and my sister for a fashion exhibition. My parents did not show any garments since 1984. I hope that we will have some customers. Their business is still very bad, it makes me sick to have seen my mother working all her life for such a result.

There's no wonder my sister Anne has been depressed, with this situation the atmosphere is not very "healthy" at home and I think I had better go somewhere else again – I worry too much about the other ones and it doesn't help anybody! So I should be in Germany from end of March till end of June.

As I told you, one of my brothers, Yonec, is studying medicine. He is very nice, always smilling and in a good mood. Today he just comes back from Caen where he is studying during the week. He has been taking exams and thinks everything went well. He is leaving soon again to spend his other days off with his girl-friend. They are together since 3 years now and though my mother thinks that they still are rather young, they go on very well together.

The two last ones, Petronille and Loic are still at school. Loic is playing a lot of music with his group. They have already been at a local radio station. Yonec is playing music, too, but a different kind. Last week we attended a jazz orchestra where he was playing the piano.

You remember Aurora from Brazil – we are also writing to each other. She sometimes stays in Rio and sometimes in Italy. If one day I have the opportunity (and money) to visit her in Brazil, I will try to plan to stop in Orlando. I also hope you will be able to come here one day!

I hope you have find a job. I wish you all the best. It is best to try to keep busy and not think too much about the future, about earning a living, about life!

How is Robin? I think about her and also wish her well. Tell David I will make his birth chart and join it with the next letter. I send you love from Normandie and a kiss to all your children.

Sophie

19

February 22, 1987
Saint Lo, France

Orlando, Florida
My dear Pat,

I am just back from Paris where my mother and Anne and I worked during a new fashion Expo. My brother Loic was on school holiday and came with us so he had an opportunity to see Paris. He came back home delighted and we came back tired!

Beginning of April I will go to Germany to teach French and to learn more German, and this till July 10. My time-table will be very busy but I like it. In the meantime I am invited to go skiing for one week. I will miss three birthdays at home but that's life! I begin to get used to be always somewhere else when there is a special day home.

Thank you very much for your last letter with the two pictures. I miss you and your children – and I still think of Katie who I enjoyed so much in December when she was with us for one week.

Bye bye Pat,
I send you all my love,
Sophie

March 11, 1987
Orlando, Florida

Woodbury, Connecticut
Dear Auntie Bussie,

Just a quick note this morning before I dive into all the work that awaits me here at the office. It's good that this is probably a fairly temporary position because I feel like I am down in a hole and might never find my way out. Mortgages, interest rates, amortizations, building codes, banking procedures, big money deals, legal lingo … ad infinitum. It should be no surprise; I always thought I was better suited to "googoo, gaga" baby babble than business jargon. Now I am convinced.

So glad you enjoyed the Christmas pictures of our gang. I'll take some more when you are here in April, too.

Okay, back into the hole. Bye for now. I love you.

Pat

P.S. – Here's a copy of an essay I wrote on osteoporosis. I'm considering sending it to *Prevention* health magazine, but whether or not I do, I wanted to write something of my experience with the disease.

CHANGES

I remember the sound. Three cracks, a muffled crunch. In an instant a life irrevocably altered. I recall, too, how quiet it was otherwise. No voice – I had none. Nor barely breath. The drowsy child on my shoulder I released very carefully, letting him slowly slide along the length of my body to the safety of the floor. I steadied him with only the tips of my fingers before he toddled over to a pile of books and plopped down to look at his favorite pictures. Bent over, leaning, but still on my feet, I was in acute pain, wondering how to move, whether to even try, puzzled at what seemed a kind of ambush by an unknown and unsuspected foe. Thankfully, in that moment I realized the telephone on the kitchen counter was close enough to pick up and dial for help. ...

Later x-rays and bone scans revealed not the expected familiar skeletal figure one sees during Halloween, only eerie, fragmented white shadows. Besides the clearly evident multiple compression fractures of the spine, at just 53, I was informed that my bones were similar to those of a person nearer 90. Often called "The Silent Crippler," my enemy had long been preparing for the assault, with teams of osteoclasts stealthily outnumbering osteoblasts until brittle, porous vertebrae had weakened to an easily crushable state.

With the devastating diagnosis of osteoporosis, a frightening new reality lay ahead. Before: Unsuspecting; feeling fit and agile. Afterward: Knowing; a lifelong burden on my back; a sense of fragility, as if I might break, literally, should someone touch me.

My successful career as a children's nanny came to an abrupt end. Lifting, bending, squatting – all the actions necessary in caring for a young child – were no longer safe for me to do. Even the simplest everyday sort of tasks, from tying my shoes to making a bed, so taken for granted in the past, would now present new challenges. Of course, during the first few months following the fractures, there was little I could do. The gentlest of movements – *breathing* – caused excruciating pain.

As healing of the fractures progressed, I expected to recover – to be careful, to make many changes, yes, but to feel well again. However, with the passage of time, the pain, not as debilitating but always present, the inability to find satisfactory employment, and the isolation that resulted from my limitations left me bereft. Needless to say, I sorely missed the daily interaction with "my" babies, and rarely could find pleasure even in simple experiences I had previously relished ... the feeling of joy and aliveness on a clear, crisp autumn day, or the sight of a roomful of rainbows created by sunlight striking my favorite window crystal, or the sound of a Scott Joplin rendition of ragtime. Finally I sought professional counseling for the depression and sense of helplessness and, although I said little and mostly sat quietly crying throughout two or three sessions, that seemed to be what I needed to fortify myself for positive action.

Becoming a sleuth, I pursued every avenue to discover more about osteoporosis; it was not a common topic of discussion. I was fortunate to find a specialist at Emory, a teaching hospital in Atlanta, Georgia, whose clinical trials were being concluded with excellent results. He immediately prescribed a new bone-building medication and hormone therapy, and started me on a regimen of gentle stretching exercises and walking, plus regular use of muscle relaxants and frequent brief rests lying on a moist heating pad for the ever-present muscle spasms. Just as importantly, this tenderly caring physician, who knew and understood so well the overall effect of the disease, helped immensely in restoring my belief that I could learn to cope with the changes and again find enjoyment in life.

That life-changing sound is well-remembered. ... And when I see another victim of this silent crippler – often one viewing the world from underneath a back and neck curved completely forward – I want to gently embrace the vulnerable, stooped frame and say I understand.

For me, the pain, sometimes only a grumble, sometimes a persistent howl, is ever present. As is my awareness each moment of no more flat belly, no more waist length sufficient for a span of hands, no more shoulders squared with strength and confidence or back straight and without muscle spasms, no more easy comfort in sitting or standing.

And, sadly, no more completely carefree spirit ... swinging a child up in my arms exuberantly for a hug or a dance of ring-around-the-rosies-pocket-full-of-posies-ashes-ashes-all-fall-down. No more.

Only the silent reminder: Careful ... Careful.

March 13th (Friday!), 1987
Orlando, Florida

Atlanta, Georgia

Dear Skip,

Isn't it crazy how one's emotions can run the gamut from despair to joy repeatedly within the space of an hour, a day, a week, a month? Mine do, anyway. Half the time I feel like I'm on a seesaw.

I'm going up and down now, wrestling with two of the main problems on my mind. One is the desire for a special person in my life and how to go about making him happen! The other is what to do to fulfill my creative urges. I'm not asking for too much, am I?

I know that a 9-to-5 job doesn't do much to satisfy my creativity. Even a challenging position such as the one I have now leaves me feeling empty in my deepest being. I'm not unhappy, just unfulfilled, restless, and my emotions are wavering more than usual.

I suppose it could be, too, that chronic pain and plain old physical tiredness have me feeling out of balance. Amazing how the body, mind and spirit are so intertwined, isn't it? I've just *got* to get all three of mine in sync.

My two-month anniversary at this job passed yesterday, and I requested a moment of silence. Even though my head is full of new knowledge, I am overwhelmed at how much of the work is still completely confusing. My young boss asked recently, "How can I get five years' worth of this business into your head real quick?" Wilting already under the pressure, I quipped, "There *is* no way, sorry!" If he just knew … it would be the same as his trying to learn everything about babies, schedules, training, discipline, the terrible twos, teenage turmoil, etc., in a couple of months – ha!

You know your ol' mom, though, Skip. I *am* learning and will continue to hang in there and do my best, right?

Love,
Mom

March 27, 1987

Dear Diary,

I just dread facing the death of dreams – whether they happen to be big life-altering dreams or foolish little everyday reveries. There's always a feeling of sadness and loss, and I have to go through a kind of grieving process before I can recover some measure of optimism and the belief that I am going to be even better able to go on with whatever life holds. How often the old cliché "sadder but wiser" seems to fit.

23

Sometimes I wonder about all the glorious possibilities that might have existed for me beyond Stonewall, Mississippi, and Prichard, Alabama, if I had possessed the knowledge, vision and courage to investigate more widely when I was young. Back then my only dream was to get married and have babies ... a good dream, one that came true in a wonderful reality. And I am deeply thankful for those blessings. At the same time I do think there was a well of creativity simply left untapped ... and that I regret.

Oh, maybe I'm just a bit depressed again from being in pain and inactive from another back flare-up ... and feeling isolated ... and thinking too much.

April 3, 1987
Dear Diary,

Well, after last month's treatise on dreams and loss and sadness – LIFE in capital letters – now it's on with daily life. And yet another old adage comes to mind: "Life is what happens while you're waiting."

Spring has burst forth in all its glory, perking up most everything, including me to some degree. The office stint is behind me, and I'm happy to be back in a position I feel more comfortable with. I'm not a nanny, but in some ways I *am* taking care of someone again and, as a Personal Assistant, I'm challenged with a variety of responsibilities. I enjoy working with the lady of the manor in all manner of ways – from cataloging famous paintings, objets d'art and items in the large Tiffany collection in the museum, and helping with inventory at the gift shops, to interviewing potential personal chefs or choosing a special gift for her godson, a young Eisenhower.

I feel as if I've suddenly become one with nature, ensconced as I am in a rustic little boathouse on the estate, where the acres and acres of woods are ablaze with beauty and color, redolent with enticing aromas. Where I am an enthusiastic albeit usually lone audience for the sound and sight of over 50 peacocks honking for mates and preening to show off their gorgeous palettes. Ah, spring, a new season, a new look at life.

Winter Park, Florida
June 13, 1987

Orlando, Florida
Dearest Robin,

When I had another fracture a few weeks ago, forcing me to just be still, I took a journey back in time by way of re-reading hundreds of old letters and diary entries. Fearing for months they had been lost in one of the many moves of recent years, I was thrilled when they turned up in

24

boxes at the back of a closet. Oh, Robin, it has been the most transforming, rewarding, revealing, healing, inspiring, sweetest experience for me.

I wish everyone whose spirit is present in the letters could have traveled the pages with me. You and Jenni, Skip, David, your dad, Nana GeeGee and Granddaddy, Nana Kitty and Granddad, Auntie Bussie, Uncles Dave, Sam, John, Rickey, and other kinfolk and dear old friends, all of you who are so much a part of my life in this cherished collection. In spite of some missing letters, our family's history unfolds just like a novel!

This recapturing of precious lost memories has brought me to a depth of understanding I hadn't fully recognized or acknowledged before: I have had a *wonderful* life, so filled with love and with warm, caring, special people. There was a period when I angrily questioned, even seemed to devalue many parts of it. But I am now clearly aware that no matter what, above all things, I prize the life I have.

As soon as I felt well enough, I started to spend a part of each day walking along the peacock path out here in these beautiful woods, letting both my body and my soul be soothed by the sunlight and fresh air, allowing myself to dream about what I really want ... and I'm still trying to sort *that* out.

In the meantime, I know you and your sister and brothers will treasure these letters and diary musings – and all they embody throughout so many years – for the story they tell. And perhaps for answers to some of your own questions about life and love and family and friends and faith.

I love you,
Mom

Other things may change us, but we start and end with family.
Anthony Brandt

Chapter One
Leaping In
1932-51

Baby Patsy in Stonewall, Mississippi

September 27, 1932
River Road
Stonewall, Mississippi

York, Alabama
c/o Railroad Depot
Dear Della,

Don't know if Papa or Mama was able to get word to you yet but the baby finally did come. It's a girl and she was born about 1:30 in the morning on August 23. We named her Patsy, and she was a big one, 12 lbs. on the kitchen scale. I had no help til near bout the end when Randolph's mama flagged down the docter coming from across the river. It was real bad. Randolph was aholding onto me while the docter pulled the baby out with some forseps and he told me later on he was just plumb scared to death. Then the worst part was it was too dark to see good so the docter come back after daylite and turned me round to the window to sew me up where I tore. I sure was wishing for more than the few sniffs of whatever it was he give me.

But anyways we got our baby and all the bruses are gone now so she's looking a lot better. I swanee, Della, she all ready looks like 4 months old at least. The baby clothes was too little and so was the dresser drawer we planed to use for awhile til we got her a bed. Randolph is just crazy about Patsy and sweet as he can be with her. He helps me all he can but he's still got to go work with Mr. Sam planting and all, plus keeping up his doffing job at the mill. When I go back to work in the spinning room his mama will keep the baby all day. Did you hear, Randolph's brother Curtis and Eva's baby is due around October 2? That is the same day Randolph will be 20 years old. You know what he said last week, Sugar, what in the world we doing with a baby, we just babies ourself! I mean this baby is *always* hungry and its about time to nurse her, so I better hurry on and get this letter done.

Tell Mildred and Billy about ther new cousin, and hug them real good for me. Is any chance y'all can get down this way before long? I just been wondering how everthing is going for y'all. This Depression sure makes it hard to get by, don't it, Della. Randolph said the other day his daddy was telling about seeing the owner of that lumber mill in town who told Mr. Sam he liked him, and had real respect for his opinun, so he wanted to ask him just what *he* thought about the situaton in these bad times. Mr Sam told him he *thought* things was looking better and the fella said Good Lord man what makes you think that. And so Mr. Sam told him about one day down in the swamp when he saw a rabbit and it was just three men chasing that rabbit 'stead of a dozen, he took that for a real good sign. I sure hope

27

Mr. Sam is right. I hope Mr. Rosevelt is right, too, promising us happy days are here again.

Love,
Wilba

April 25, 1937
Stonewall, Mississippi

Silas, Alabama

Dear Esther,

I sure don't get round to writing to you and Della like I intended to after y'all moved away from Stonewall. And I don't hardly see Hester and Ethel or Glynn even when we all still live here. It just seems like we always busy working at something. I reckon everbody else is too. But it's a good thing for us all to keep in touch anytime we can, with Mama and Papa too.

Well, you are aunt to another one, Esther. Since the last letter I wrote you I had a boy, named Sammie after Mr. Sam. He was nearly as fat as Patsy, close to 11 pounds. This time I went to the hospital in Meridian but having these big babies is not easy where ever you are. I guess you know that because wasn't your first ones pretty big too?

Patsy is getting on to 5 years old now and she's the best big sister you ever saw, just loves the baby and helps me alot. She is a real little mama already. A favorite thing she likes to do is wash dishes. I put the pan down on the oven door so it is just perfect for her to reach. And nowdays when I need to wash baby cloths she totes water from the artesun well across the road in old 4-pound lard and molasses cans. It takes lots of trips but she is happy as she can be.

The other day Randolph was sawing on some wood to build a smoke house and Patsy was on the back porch with him talking and talking and asking questions, Daddy this and Daddy that and then she told him Daddy-lo, I love you. About that time he called out Sugar, I 'spect you better come get this girl before I eat her up.

Esther I sure do feel lucky these days to have Randolph and Patsy and this baby boy. There's one thing about this little bitty place where we live now that I would change if I could, tho. Its got a tin roof and when it rains and storms the racket is pure scarey, specialy if Randolph is gone to the mill at night to work the 3rd shift. Sometime I think if the racket don't wake Patsy and the baby up, I'll go wake them up to keep me company.

Write me when you can. I hope everbody in the family is doing real good.

Love,
Wilba

May 14, 1941
Stonewall, Mississippi

Swainsboro, Georgia
Dear Katie,

Guess what, you have another new little cousin. Mama had our baby on April 28. She said this time it was easy as shelling peas. I think that sounds so funny, don't you? The baby is a boy, named John Randolph Junior after Daddy. He is pretty and so sweet I could eat him up! I really do *love* babies. Remember one day when we promised we would always be just like real sisters, well we have two brothers now! Sammie says he likes to be a BIG brother and John is just a LITTLE baby.

Last week Grandma Jennie let me help fix a cake for Mama's birthday. I like making biscuits more than cakes, but it is fun when I learn to cook different things, too. In August when I am 9 Grandma Jennie said she will let me help her cook chicken and dumplings.

I have some more news because we are going to move up to Georgia pretty soon when Daddy goes to work at the mill in a place called Royston. Ask your daddy is that close to where y'all live. I HOPE so.

I have to go now, the rolling store is coming by our house today and I can buy some candy with my pennies. I miss you lots, Katie. Write me a letter back very soon

Love,
Patsy

January 15, 1942
Royston, Georgia

Stonewall, Mississippi
Dear Grandma Jennie,

How is everybody getting along? We are allright but it is so cold here. Our Christmas was good because Katie and Uncle Curt stayed three days and nights with us. It's sad that her mama and daddy are not going to be married anymore. I wish she could come live in our house with us. You know what I still like best about our house, Grandma, the bathroom! Sammie plays like the bathtub is a swimming pool and holds his head under water, kicking and splashing. It makes a big mess but he is funny and makes us laugh.

I am not cooking very much up here because my big job is to help mama wash all the clothes and John's baby diapers. Some neighbor ladies told mama they like to watch me shake out all the clothes real good, especially the diapers, before I hang them on the line just perfect.

29

How are your chickens, Grandma, the Reds and Dominicks? Have you got any new baby chicks? When I come down there can I help you feed them, and get the eggs out of the nests? But if we make chicken and dumplings for supper, I *don't* want to help you catch the chicken and wring its neck! No siree. Can we make me a blackberry jam cake, it is so good!

I can't wait to sleep in your soft bed again, Grandma, I love to sink way down in the feathers where it feels good and cozy. I still remember that time I slept with you and we got so scared because real early in the morning a big BOOM of thunder made us jump up so fast we bumped heads!

I miss y'all a LOT. Kiss Grandpa Sam for me. I know you will like to do that, won't you? Tell Uncle Leon I said hey and tell Uncle Bill I sure do hope I get to see him before he goes away to the Army.

Lots of hugs and kisses,
Patsy (OOOXXXXO)

May 7, 1942
Royston, Georgia

Stonewall, Mississippi
c/o Grist Mill
Dear Grandma Mollie,

And you, too, Grandpa, I would not forget you! I bet you remember what day this is because it is Mama's birthday. She is 28 years old and I am almost 10 now. Daddy and me made Mama a sweet potato pie, that's what she likes best.

Grandma, do you remember one time you told me you thought I was real smart and I would work for the Lord someday? Well I never did forget that. And you know what I did this year? I learned the names of all the books in the Bible and I can say them forward *and* backward real fast! I can't wait to show you how I do it when we get back!

Love,
Patsy

My Autobiography

Grade 5   By Patsy
Prichard Elementary School   March 1943
Prichard, Alabama

I was born in Stonewall, Mississippi, on River Road, in a house with two rooms. It was called a shotgun house. My birthday is August 23, 1932. There are five people in my family. My mother's name is Wilba and she is married to Randolph. I am a big sister to Sammie and John and help take care of them. I love babies and children and hope I can have four or five, boys and girls, when I grow up.

When I was 5 years old I started to go to school, and every year I am happy with school and like my teachers and friends. A girl named Frances was my best friend in Stonewall. Sometimes we would pick ears of corn to make into funny little dolls, or we would play dress up with her grandma's pretty shoes. When I was really young I loved to play tea party, and this is what I would say:

> I had a little tea party
> this afternoon at three.
> It was very small,
> three guests in all –
> I, myself and me.
> Myself ate up the candy,
> while I drank the tea.
> It was also I who ate the pie,
> and passed the cake to me!

In 1941 my daddy got a new job in the cotton mill at Royston, Georgia. Our house there was very nice, with a bathroom and stairs and even a telephone. We never had any of those things before. Our telephone number was 66J.

Something very exciting happened to me in the fourth grade. I won my class spelling contest, then I won for the school, and next for the whole county. So I got to go to Atlanta and be in the State Spelling Bee. My teacher went with me. We stayed at a big hotel and went out to places to eat. It was a little scary because I had not done things like that, but she told me I was smart and sweet and did not need to be worried about anything at all. That helped me feel better. I was the youngest person but I stayed in the contest a long time. Then I spelled "medison" for medicine and had to sit down. But even if I did not win my teacher was so proud of me, and Mama and Daddy, too. That is a trip I will remember forever.

31

The year after the Japanese planes dropped bombs in Pearl Harbor, Daddy decided to move our family to Alabama so he could work in the shipyard in Mobile and be helping America in the war. Before we left Georgia, for many days and nights big army trucks full of soldiers passed by our house and the soldiers laughed and waved and shouted to us, and sometimes they would throw us candy kisses. It was so exciting, and we had lots of fun. But then one day I saw tears in Daddy's eyes so I knew it was something sad and scary, too. Two of my uncles went into the army. I miss them and pray for God to keep them safe. I wish the world did not have war.

I like to help my mother wash dishes and wash the clothes, dust and polish the furniture, tend to my brothers, and also cook a little bit sometimes. I like to read, play games and go to see picture shows. My life is very good and happy.

March 20, 1945
Dear Diary,

A letter came from Aunt Inez's husband, Uncle Harmon. He was wounded in his left chest in Germany February 21. He is better now. I love Uncle Harmon and Uncle Bill so much. They are so sweet and fun.

April 12, 1945
Dear Diary,

The President of the United States, President Franklin Delano Roosevelt, died today at Warm Springs, Georgia, at 3:35 p.m. of a hemoraghe. President Harry S. Truman was made president today.

April 21, 1945
Dear Diary,

Mommie and I went to town and she bought me a sanitary belt and a box of sanitary napkins. She gave me 21 napkins and said they are mine when I need them.

April 25, 1945
Dear Diary,

Today is important. Leaders from all over the world met in San Francisco, and they wrote the Charter for the United Nations. It is to try to help keep peace.

I've been elected to be in the May Pole Dance on May Day. We will wear white dresses.

May 5, 1945
Dear Diary,

Elwood climbed up the tree in our neighbor's yard and carved "PG + ES," and I don't know if I like that or not!

May 7, 1945
Dear Diary,

Mommie got a wedding and engagement ring for her birthday. She is 33. Daddy did not have enough money to buy her nice rings when they got married. These are real pretty!

June 9, 1945
Prichard, Alabama

Kosciusko, Mississippi
c/o Textile Mills
Dear Hazel,

I'm writing as an unacquainted friend, although I feel I know you, and I hope to get acquainted with you soon. My name is Patsy, and I am Bill's niece. I will be 13 years of age August 23, and I graduated from Grammar School, the seventh grade, Friday, the 1st of June. We graduated in evening dresses and it was my first. I'm sending you a picture of myself.

We live in Prichard, close to town, and I go to movies for past time. I also go swimming in the Municipal Swimming Pool, and the first time I went I really blistered because I stayed in the sun too long.

Daddy bought a little grocery store in our neighborhood. It's on the corner, not very far from our house and sometimes I go and help out at the cash register. That's fun.

I have two brothers, Sammie and John, both younger than me. All the family and I are planning on a visit from you if it is convenient for you.

Well I hope to hear from you very soon.

Yours truly,
Patsy

June 26, 1945
Dear Diary,

Uncle Bill brought Hazel to see us. I just love Hazel. She is so sweet and kind. (I bet they get married!) The United Nations Charter was signed today, and everybody hopes it will help countries learn how to be more peaceful now.

August 14, 1945
Dear Diary,

The war is over! We closed the store today. Daddy said he knew nobody in the neighborhood would mind. I saw *30 Seconds Over Tokyo* at The Rex Theater.

September 2, 1945
Dear Diary,

Today is V-J Day. I saw *Hotel Berlin* and *Cowboy and the Lady* at The Rex.

November 20, 1945
Dear Diary,

Lamar kinda acts like he likes me a tiny bit. I like him but I like Jack, too. I'm going to wink at them one day.

February 18, 1946
Dear Diary,

I worked a long time on my theme paper titled "Racial and Religious Tolerance as a Means to Lasting Peace" and got a high mark. Then the class discussed it, and everyone wished there would always be peace.

February 21, 1946
Dear Diary,

We bought a house! It has gas heaters and a stove and a bathroom and a telephone! Our telephone number is 6-3619.

April 7, 1946
Dear Diary,

The assistant principal told me there had been such good reports about my work the teachers wanted me to make a speech for the assembly on "Why We Have Vigor Day." I am nervous but happy, too.

September 7, 1946
Dear Diary,

I have started 9th grade at Murphy High School in downtown Mobile. It's so big, and there are so many people I feel lost, and I don't know if I am going to like it. I will be taking English, Civics, Biology, Latin, Advanced Algebra and Physical Education (which I already *know* I don't like).

October 30, 1946
Dear Diary,

I'm running for president of the sophomore class!

April 10, 1947
Dear Diary,

I have been really sick – I have the mumps. And look ridiculous. I just can't wait to get better.

December 15, 1947
Prichard, Alabama

Quitman, Mississippi
Dear Aunt Hazel,

So much has happened, bad and good. Now, close to Christmas, we are very glad Mommie is starting to feel a little bit better and that baby Rickey, our "Littlest Angel," is finally home with us. He had to stay in an incubator at the hospital for over a month.

A few weeks before the baby was supposed to be born Mommie had something awful, called a "placenta previa" (I asked the nurse to spell it for me). It was sudden and she lost too much blood before the ambulance could get to our house. I have never been so scared in my life, Aunt Hazel. I thought she was going to die, and the baby, too. Mommie told me later she felt sure she was going to die and when she looked at my anxious face, all she could think of was how sorry she was that I was going to be left as the mama of the family at just 15 years old. She is still very weak and the baby is so tiny. He is like a perfect little doll, though, a wonderful Christmas present for us.

Happy news about school this year. I am a junior now, love my homeroom class and teacher, and I got inducted into the National Honor Society!

A Merry Christmas to you and Uncle Bill! Kiss baby Janis for me.
Much love,
Patsy

August 30, 1949
Prichard, Alabama

Quitman, Mississippi
Dear Aunt Inez,

Life is exciting. In June I graduated with my class of 700 students from Murphy High School in Mobile. As a senior I was in the National Honor Society (for the second year), was Section Leader of my great homeroom class, and also belonged to a few clubs, though not to the "clique" of popular girls from Old Mobile families. There are some beautiful girls in that circle and sometimes I envy them, but then I try to remember and do what Mommie says, "Don't look at the people who have more than you, but always think of the ones who are not as lucky as you are."

Being 17 is pretty amazing, Aunt Inez, and I like it, well, most of the time, anyway. No party this birthday since I had that great "Sweet Sixteen" last year, swimming and a picnic in Fairhope with lots of friends.

Earlier this summer I had *so* much fun going out with a very handsome Tab Hunter look-alike Air Force Radio Operator I met at Carrie's Lake! He was in Mobile on two weeks' leave to visit family before going to Goosebay, Labrador, for 18 months (oh, boo hoo). We met the day before my graduation and he asked to take me out for a special celebration after the ceremony. First he came to the house and met Mommie and Daddy, who thought he was very nice and said I could go, so we went out – on the best date of my life! There's a nightclub in Mobile I had never been to, of course, but oh boy did I enjoy it that night. We danced and danced and had our picture taken by a photographer who came to the table, and we laughed a lot and told each other about ourselves. He is such a good dancer (and kisser!). I even had a Tom Collins to drink! Since he left we have been writing to each other, and I think there will be a reunion when he comes back.

Mommie and the boys are fine, and Daddy says "hello" to his sister. All of us sure are enjoying our little Rickey. He's so cute, almost 2 now, which is hard to believe. We all send love to you and the family. Please write with all your news. And try to come see us one of these days, hear?

Love,
Patsy

December 17, 1951
Prichard, Alabama

Athens, Georgia
Dear Katie,

Oh, my goodness, it has been so long since my last letter to you. I hardly know where to start. Well, maybe with news of my job and my brighter outlook on life! I left the transportation company and have a much more satisfying secretarial position at Brookley Air Force Base, where I really like the work atmosphere and my great co-workers. I've met lots of new friends, both military and civilian, and my social life has taken a real upward swing – my mood, too, after a long spell spent recovering from my broken heart. Now I just want to have fun dates, go dancing and to the beach and movies, *no* serious stuff.

Let me tell you the sad tale. … About the same time I graduated, I met such a handsome, fun-loving Air Force guy. We only dated two weeks before he left for an 18-month tour of duty as a radio operator in Labrador. But we wrote often – his letters were sweet and funny, and even our mailman enjoyed the cute picture of a drooling AF "doggie" on every envelope. I was still dating casually, of course, and nobody else touched my heart … until eight months later.

It was on the last night of Mardi Gras, my favorite celebration in Mobile, when the street parades are noisy and crowded and crazy. Cousin Mildred and I were thoroughly enjoying friendly flirting with lots of guys (that's most of the fun!) when two cadets from Pensacola Naval Air Station crossed our path, and lingered! The four of us ended up spending the evening and having a late-night snack together. "My" cadet was handsome, sexy, with a good sense of humor and, get this, after a gentle goodnight kiss, said he thought he was going to fall in love with me. BUT, as he quickly warned, he planned to be a jet pilot and couldn't think of getting married for a *long* time. (Do you suppose I looked so ripe for marriage?)

I would've saved myself a lot of grief if I'd heeded that warning, but we began dating and fell in love. And were alternately happy and frustrated. Of course, I was slightly confused, anyway, being in a muddle in the middle of two fantastic guys, the USAF and USN rivals, who knew about one another. The cadet and I had been going together around 9 or 10 months but he "retreated" when the AF "doggie" came back, so that I could test my feelings. Well, it looked like the AF would win when he swept me off my feet and we got unofficially engaged! We came to our senses pretty quickly, though, and knew we liked each other but weren't really in love. He soon left to go to another AF assignment …and the cadet returned, happily for both of us. But, alas, after only a few more months we had to face the fact that there was no future for us – he wanted to be a free Navy jet pilot, and marriage was not in his plan. As he had told me that first night. Thought I'd never get over him, Katie, but Mommie and Daddy kept assuring me everything *would* work out. And so it has.

Here I am, going on and on about lost loves and not wanting to fall in love again while you are basking in the bliss of new love and wedding plans. I am so happy for you, dear Katie – best wishes and congratulations to you and your groom-to-be!

Lots of love,
Pat

And when two lovers woo, they still say I love you.
On that you can rely, no matter what the future brings,
As time goes by.

Herman Hupfield

Chapter Two
Lace
1952-53

Pat and baby brother Rickey in Prichard, Alabama

November 23, 1952
Prichard, Alabama

Quitman, Mississippi
Dear Aunt Inez,

Just a quick note to say hello and send you the clipping from yesterday's newspaper. Yep, your niece is entered in the 5th Annual Miss Brookley Contest. Naturally after not winning the title last year, I had no thought of being in the 1952 contest (losing once was enough!), but friends and co-workers went right ahead and put me in the running so I can't help being pleased. I'll do my best – keep your fingers crossed.

Better sign off now and get to bed because this week especially I need *all* the beauty sleep I can get! Happy Thanksgiving!

Love,
Patsy

23 November 1952
Bachelor Officers Quarters
Naval Air Station
Pensacola, Florida

Prichard, Alabama
Dear Patsy,

I was reading the Mobile Sunday paper this morning after church and noticed the "Miss Brookley" picture. A person can't help but be his own judge in something like this, so I decided, after looking over all the gals, that you were sure to win the contest. We'll soon see how good a picker I am, won't we?

Actually the word "Brookley" first hit my eye. I had left my ship in Venice, Italy, to fly back to the States and duty here. We got as far as the Azores okay, then I got a ride in a MATS (Air Force) C-124 that was supposed to land in Westover Field, Massachusetts, not too far from my home in Riverside, Connecticut (near Greenwich). But once off the ground at Lages Field, Azores, the crew told us that they "might" land instead at Brookley Field, in Alabama. I'd never even heard of Brookley Field, and it sure seemed like a long way from Connecticut! Well, needless to say, we *did* land in Mobile very unexpectedly, and I had to put out hard cash for an Eastern Air Lines hop to New York. So you see, my estimation of the Air Force and Brookley Field dropped slightly.

40

Am I all wrong? Tell me if I am. Maybe you're the one to make me feel that Brookley and the Air Force aren't so bad after all. I'd like to hear from you, Patsy. Please write.

Sincerely,
Bob

November 27, 1952
Prichard, Alabama

Pensacola, Florida
Dear Bob,

I was so surprised when your letter came! The contestants were off work Thanksgiving Eve day (to give us plenty of time to get beautiful!) so I was at home when the mail was delivered. My mother and I were puzzled at first by the unfamiliar name in the return address. But since our house is a popular spot for good food and genuine warm Southern hospitality and we are quite used to my friends dropping by with various Navy guys, we thought the letter might be a thank-you from one of the cadets in a group that had been here recently. It was your nice letter, though.

Imagine your seeing the Mobile Press picture of the Miss Brookley contestants and picking me out of the 15 as the one you thought should win. Naturally I was tickled, and even though I didn't win I want to thank you for the compliment! It was exciting to be in the contest and I had a great time at the Brookley Ball.

I'm sorry you had such an unpleasant introduction to Brookley Air Force Base, Bob, but maybe I *can* change your first impression. Actually, although I work there and enjoy all my AF friends, I really like the Navy, too – and playing at Pensacola Beach! My best friend Celia's boyfriend is training to be a helicopter pilot at the Naval Air Station, so we girls often go over for a day of fun and sun.

Did you have a turkey-and-trimmings feast at the base yesterday? We had a delicious one here, and now today I'm just hanging around the house being lazy, a nice change from the busyness of the last few days.

Well … I have enjoyed meeting you via letter, Ensign Bob, and would like to hear from you again!

Sincerely,
Pat

29 November 1952
Pensacola, Florida

Prichard, Alabama
Dear Pat,

Thanks for your nice letter. Sorry you didn't win the contest, but I still think you should have had it! How did they select the girls to compete for the final pickings?

I'll tell you about me if you promise to tell me all about you ... agreed? My home is now in Riverside, Connecticut, although I lived in Waterbury, Connecticut, most of my life. I went to the United States Naval Academy at Annapolis, Maryland, and was graduated in June 1951. Since then I have been in the Mediterranean on a destroyer, and finally down here for flight training.

I am 24 years old, 5 feet, 11 inches, 165 pounds. The only picture I could dig up for you is this one taken about 3½ years ago by my younger brother, Dave. I guess the thing about me of which I'm most proud at the present is my new Pontiac convertible. I had a 1951 Ford, but just couldn't say no to this Pontiac, which is *really* beautiful. I call it "Splurge," because I figure I went all the way when I bought it.

By the way, where is Prichard? Is that a suburb of Mobile? And what do you do at Brookley Field? And, yes, you've boosted my estimation of the Air Force. The funny part about it is that I almost went into the Air Force. You know that 25% of all the Annapolis and West Point classes go into the Air Force. I had the chance to take it, and at the last minute decided to stay in the Navy. And, if you will excuse me, I have never regretted staying with the Blue and Gold. ... If you'll come over some weekend, Pat, I'll show you why I like the Navy.

Game's over, and Navy came out on top, 7-0! And ended up at the final gun on Army's 2-foot line. (Are you much of a football fan?)

Love,
Bob

December 1, 1952
Prichard, Alabama

Pensacola, Florida
Dear Bob,

Thanks for your prompt newsy letter, and the snapshot. (And yes, I'll send you a picture that's clearer than the newspaper photo.)

I've never met a Naval Academy graduate before – congratulations! And on your new Pontiac convertible, too, which sounds like a dream, all right.

Now for some information about me. In my family there are Mommie and Daddy plus three younger brothers: Sammie, 15, John 11, and Rickey, 5. I badly wanted a sister, too, but got a brother every time. They are sweet, though, and little Rickey is fun for all of us. I also have lots of aunts and uncles, and cousins by the dozens. Mommie has an unbelievable number of first cousins (about 90, I think). I was born in Stonewall, Mississippi, August 23, 1932, lived there until I was 9, then in Georgia for a year before moving to Prichard, about five miles out of Mobile. I've never been farther north than one brief trip to North Carolina. I am 5'3½" tall, weigh 128, have greenish-hazel eyes.

About the contest – girls are nominated and voted on by friends and co-workers, and then 15 finalists compete at the annual Thanksgiving Eve Ball, where a panel of judges selects the winner. Voila, another Miss Brookley reigns!

What do I do at BAFB? I am a secretary in the Materiel Division. Football? Not an avid fan, though I am planning to go to the Senior Bowl in Mobile next month.

I enjoyed hearing from you, Bob, please write again. And, hey, I'm glad I boosted your estimation of the Air Force!

Sincerely,

Pat

5 December 1952
Pensacola, Florida

Prichard, Alabama

Dear Pat,

Thanks to you, too, for being so prompt in writing. And I sure liked the pictures you sent me. Excuse me if my writing isn't too good right now. I've been turning up an aircraft engine for the last two hours and my hands (and the rest of me, too) are still cold!

I thought I might drive over to Mobile next Friday, 12 December. Could we get together that night? If you could be ready about 7 or 8 o'clock, we could go dancing or something. Tell me how I can find your house and I can pick you up, or else meet me someplace. Okay? Whether you can or not, please write me soon, Pat, because I am being transferred out to Whiting Field near Milton, Florida, late next week and don't know my mailing address yet. By the way, do you have a phone?

> Love,
> Bob

December 8, 1952
Prichard, Alabama

Pensacola, Florida
Hi, Bob,

You asked if we could get together here in Mobile next Friday. I would like to. In fact, that evening I'm going to a dinner/dance/party in honor of one of the colonels I work with. How would you like to go with me? (You could meet *all* of the Miss Brookley contestants!) I do hope we can connect in person before you go to Connecticut on Christmas leave. ...

My phone number is 6-3619, and I'll be waiting to hear from you.

> Love,
> Pat

December 18, 1952
Prichard, Alabama

Riverside, Connecticut
Dear Bob,

Since you'll soon be leaving for the long drive to Connecticut, I'm sending this letter there. It was exciting to meet you in person last Friday. Sorry my directions to the house were confusing. I guess I was a little nervous. I had a wonderful time at the dance – all my friends were quite impressed with you! A few cornered me at work Monday to hear the details of our most unusual meeting. We did get along well, didn't we?

I am glad you came back over Sunday for dinner so we could get better acquainted before you head "up No'th" for two weeks. You told me you'd try to call before you left, so I'm halfway expecting to hear from you tonight. Hope so!

> Love,
> Pat

P.S. – Now you drive Splurge ver-r-ry carefully, hear?

44

23 December 1952
Riverside, Connecticut

Prichard, Alabama
Dear Pat,

Thanks for your letter sent here. Not much news today from way up here in Connecticut. ... I'll be thinking of you enjoying the Senior Bowl game in Mobile when I listen to it driving back down to Florida.

Pat, would you like me to come over Saturday night, 10 January? I do want to see you again, and the sooner the better as far as I'm concerned.

Love,
Bob

December 25, 1952
Prichard, Alabama

Riverside, Connecticut
Dear Bob,

Merry Christmas ... although by the time you receive this letter, Happy New Year might be more fitting! Was it a white Christmas in Connecticut? Was Santa good to you? We had a wonderful day, with gift opening in the morning and a dee-licious dinner at 2 o'clock. Later, some kinfolk dropped by and we indulged in eggnog, fruitcake and coffee. I'm still stuffed! I wonder if traditional Christmas dinners in New England are the same as ours in Alabama?

As for your coming over January 10, yes, I'd like to see you! And how could I possibly resist your lovely invitation the following weekend in Pensacola for Happy Hour at your friends' home and dinner at the Officers' Club?

No big celebration on my calendar for New Year's Eve this year, but it will be fun just to be awake and usher in 1953, which is sure to be an exciting year for me. I am going to reach that all-important age of 21!

Love,
Pat

19 January 1953
Whiting Field
Milton, Florida

Prichard, Alabama
Pat, dearest,

I love you! We haven't even been apart 24 hours yet, and I miss you a heck of a lot already. Caught myself thinking of you during the Navigation quiz today and had to force myself to quit it. (Didn't finish the quiz, either!) See what you do to me, sweetie?

Bob

February 2, 1953
Prichard, Alabama

Milton, Florida
Hi, sweetheart,

Oh my, here I am, just one day since I saw you. It seems ages already and I can't wait to be with you again. ...

I guess I have to give up the idea of ever getting to bed early on Mondays. My friends Celia and Betty had planned to see a movie tonight after first stopping by for Celia to trim my hair, but instead they stayed to hear the latest in our moving-right-along romantic saga!

If you thought we heard a lot of wedding talk yesterday, you should have been here tonight. I'm beginning to learn just *some* of the headaches of a church wedding, and am thinking we might be tempted to elope. No, not really, like most girls I dream of having that fairy tale wedding. And so ... we'd better start our lists of relatives and friends who'll be getting an invitation! That makes it *real*, huh?

I found out this morning that I'm going to ride on the float in the Valentine's Day parade. I'll be off work Wednesday when the official base photographer is scheduled to take pictures of nine of the Miss Brookley contestants in their evening dresses on the float – for a photo on the cover of the *Welfarer*, Brookley Field's newspaper. I'll save you a copy, and then you'll have two newspaper pictures of me!

Oh, you'll laugh at this, honey. Tonight Daddy heard me saying, "When I get married ..." and he quipped, "Wait a minute, Bob hasn't asked me for you yet, so you're still mine!"

He dearly loves to tease me. The cutest thing is that he is already practicing his part for the wedding! He crooks his arm for my hand, walks slowly and in a very stately manner and, after a few steps, comes to a stop, waits just a beat, pretending to listen, then answers the minister's scheduled ceremonial question, "Who giveth this woman...?" with a firm "I DO." It gets even funnier when he tries out different tones and inflections for the two little words.

Of course, all four men of the household tease me often and with glee about one thing. They say they won't miss me ... they'll be getting a bathroom!

All my love – can't wait to see you.

Pat

February 28, 1953
Lansdowne, Pennsylvania

Prichard, Alabama
Dear Pat,

When you fall in love so suddenly, you bring all sorts of strange experiences upon yourself. You probably didn't even know that Bob had an aunt (his mother's sister) who is very much devoted to him and vitally interested in all that is important to him. Nevertheless, he does have – and he wrote me a letter telling me about you.

Since I love him so much, I am prone to be biased toward anyone who makes him happy. And I understand that you have been making him very, very happy recently. So, without even knowing you, I have a very high opinion of you.

Bob has asked me to come to your wedding. If I can't, it will be the most difficult refusal of an invitation I ever had to make. However, if I do have to refuse, I will be wishing you the best every minute; and I will be hoping you both will be able to come North at the first possible moment so I can greet the newlyweds.

The very best of wishes for a long and happy life together.

Sincerely,
"Auntie Bussie"

March 10, 1953
Prichard, Alabama

Lansdowne, Pennsylvania
Dear Auntie Bussie,

I did know about Bob's favorite aunt – he told me all about you on our second or third date and I was eager to meet you even then. Now, after your very sweet letter, I can hardly wait!

47

As you can well imagine, I have many, many things to do between now and the 1st of May, *the big day*, but I am so very happy, so much in love, and walking so high in the clouds it's difficult to come down to earth long enough to make plans for the wedding. Bob and I do get a few things accomplished on the weekends when we are together, that is, when we can manage to think about anything other than the joy of just being together.

Auntie Bussie, I didn't think there was anyone else in the world as wonderful as my Bob, but now I realize that all of his folks must be just as special as he is. His mother and dad and Dave are driving down in about three weeks, and you can guess how excited I am about meeting them. I will be very disappointed if you can't come to the wedding, but I do understand how hard it is for you to get away at that time. Anyway, we'll keep our fingers crossed until the last minute, hoping you *will* be able to come, okay?

I started writing this letter during my lunch hour and now must close and get back to work. It's hard to focus on my job, though, when I can think of nothing but Bob!

I'm sending you a snapshot of the two of us taken last weekend – and looking forward to another letter from you soon.

Love,

Pat

March 10, 1953

Riverside, Connecticut

Prichard, Alabama

Dear Pat,

First let me thank you for your thought in sending Dad a birthday card. We celebrated Saturday with a real spree in New York – shopping, luncheon at a French restaurant, good seats at a new musical comedy hit, cocktails at a lovely place 65 stories above the city, and then dinner at one of our favorite seafood places. If you have never been to New York, I hope it won't be too long before Bob can bring you, for there is certainly no place like it.

I think it would be very nice for Celia to plan her shower for you to include me. What kind of shower will it be? Also, what patterns and makes of china and crystal did you choose, and what about silver?

Dad and I don't want you and Bob to decide on the Ponte Vedra Club for a honeymoon just because we were so crazy about it, but it is a beautiful spot, and the sort we like. From our cottage – which, by the way, was the "Sea Horse" – it was just a few yards to the beach and we usually spent mornings and afternoons there alone. If for a change we wanted to be with other people we could go to the Beach Club, where there is a swimming pool and your luncheon can be served without changing from bathing suits. Just writing about it makes me long to go back!

Dave was in the infirmary at college a few days last week with a strep throat and seemed to react strangely to penicillin. The doctor there decided a specialist from Portland should see him and we have been anxious to hear results. Yesterday a postcard came from Dave announcing very briefly that the doctor couldn't find a thing wrong with him and now all he had was a sprained wrist! No explanation of that! He's quite a guy.

Keep the news coming. …

Love from us both,
"Mother Kitty"

March 16, 1953
Bowdoin College
Brunswick, Maine

Milton, Florida
Dear Bob,

Is it possible that a brother could be as excited and anxious as this one is?! Is it normal?! I'm so happy for you, Bob, and so eager to meet Pat. Since the folks first started talking about going to Alabama during my spring vacation I've been excited about it. After all, I only have one brother so I've got to really live it up this one time! As for my coming down for the wedding, it looks as though I'm going to be able – and I am up in a cloud about being your best man.

The folks have forwarded Pat's letters, and to say the least they are wonderful, priceless. She can't help but be great, and I know we'll all love her. I have the picture of her from the newspaper standing up right in front of me at my desk. Right out in the open for all to see and admire and envy. This all has happened so fast, but then you two seem so very certain and who's to know better than you. It's strange but I feel as though I already know Pat.

Your flying *must* be really suffering these days!

See you in two weeks,
Dave

April 12, 1953
Quitman, Mississippi

Prichard, Alabama
Dearest Pat,

I guess you won't be surprised to hear a few words about marriage from your Aunt Inez. It's a real exciting time for you, and for all the people who love you, too.

Know you are looking forward to the great day in your life. I'm happy for you and Bob, wishing you two all the happiness in the world. The wedding is just the beginning. There will be other days in your married life that will be full of happiness with a deeper meaning as the days and years go by. No one can tell you the true meaning of marriage, you have to grow into it. You will know what I mean in 15 or 20 years. Seems like a long time doesn't it? But the years will fly especially after you have children. Sometimes I would like to reach out and stop time, it is flying so fast, and each day grows sweeter and more dear as you grow older, thinking back over your own life. But I guess that is life, growing and learning as you go along.

Would like for you and Bob to come see us before or after the wedding. Sue is so excited about being a flower girl, with Janis and Mendy. Those three little cousins will be precious – and Rickey, too, bearing the ring. I know you will be such a beautiful, sweet bride, honey. … We'll see you in less than three weeks.

Love,
Aunt Inez

April 13, 1953
Lansdowne, Pennsylvania

Prichard, Alabama
Dear Bob and Pat,

I hope you will forgive your dear Auntie Bussie, but I have bad news. It is not going to be possible for me to get down for the wedding. Although my colleagues at the university had been wonderful about offering to take over my classes for me – and I had accepted their offers – it just so happened that advising for the fall term rostering had to be scheduled during that week.

I don't know if you understand just what this means. But the fact is that I have over 30 students who are dependent upon me to make up their rosters that week so they not only get in the proper number of credits but also all the required courses – so they may be able to graduate when they

50

become seniors. It is a very complicated mathematical problem which students can't solve by themselves. So, I am rather caught!

However, in spite of my personal disappointment, my absence from your wedding will have absolutely no influence on the future happiness of your marriage. I console myself with that fact, since it matters very little who attends the ceremony.

Old people always get "preachy" when young people get married. It is a horrible habit. When you are old folks, you will do the same thing. I just want to say that I hope you manage to develop (if you don't happen to have already) the same likes and interests: in the same people, the same activities, the same hobbies, and even in the same ways of equipping and managing a home and of working, playing and eating therein.

If I have learned anything from about 20 years of studying marriage in my profession (and also 20 years of living it), it has been that what we commonly think of as "love," in the crudest sense, is something we can experience with a number of people while we are still young. But it is also something which fades away very rapidly during the humdrum situations of everyday life unless we have all these other less-spectacular things in common.

As I tell my classes, it is pretty hard to have even a good "love" relationship when a man comes home from work and his wife is annoyed with his preoccupation with the business she knows nothing about and when the husband is annoyed because his wife doesn't realize how hungry he is and what kinds of food he likes and how he likes his home to look when he finally gets to it, tired – and when, with all this, you have nothing to talk about that really interests you both. It is under such circumstances that people get so hurt and annoyed and irritated that they just don't even feel like loving each other.

Now forgive me for preaching and just put it down to the fact that I do love you so much and wish so much for you. I hope the first of May is everything you want it to be. The best of luck in all the world to both of you.

Much, much love,
Auntie Bussie

51

Life is a voyage.
Victor Hugo

Chapter Three
Learning the Ropes
1953-54

Pat and Splurge at The Cloister on Sea Island, Georgia

May 3, 1953
The Cloister
Sea Island, Georgia

Prichard, Alabama
Dearest Mommie, Daddy and Boys,

We arrived about 11:30 last night worn out after the long hot drive from Pensacola. Sea Island is a beautiful place, but we haven't seen much of it as it is 3 p.m. and we haven't been out yet. … I'll tell you more about the place when we see you.

Folks, we are so *completely* happy. Bob is the sweetest thing in the world! Remember the deal about the double bed? They didn't mean *double* – this is the biggest darn bed I have ever seen! Bob said it was as big as left field and maybe part of right field, too! I know at least six people could sleep comfortably on it.

How are the boys? Do y'all miss me very much? I miss all of you but am too happy to be sad about anything. Everybody kiss everybody for me. Bob will write a note on the back of this. Oh, Mom, be sure to save the write-up of the wedding in next Sunday's paper, okay?

All my love,
Pat

My dear "brand new parents,"

Just want to tell you again how happy we are, and to thank you for all you did in the busy days before the wedding. We must get out soon and at least look the place over. By the way, we are the 9,500[th] couple to have honeymooned at The Cloister since June 1940! See you soon. Say hello to my new brothers for me.

Love,
Bob

3 May 1953
Sea Island, Georgia

Lansdowne, Pennsylvania
Dear Auntie Bussie,

We arrived here last night, very much in love and very happy. We'll be here until Friday. The wedding was very successful, but I *am* glad it's over with! I sure appreciated your call during the reception. Sorry if I sounded excited or confused – you understand, I'm certain. When we get home I'll write you a long letter about the wedding. All is fine now with Pat and me.

That book *Ideal Marriage* helped *immeasurably*! We have referred to it time and time again since the wedding, and it has solved every little problem so far.

I love you,
Bob

Hi, Auntie Bussie!

I just want to tell you how wonderfully happy we are. This nephew of yours is the *sweetest* person in the world, as you already know. I, too, will write when we get settled in our new home. Bye for now.

Lots of love,
Pat

May 11, 1953
Warrington, Florida

Prichard, Alabama

Dearest family,

I'm writing another thank-you note for the toaster and all the groceries and just everything! Bob and I both can't *ever* forget how wonderful you were to give us all those things. They have really come in handy.

Mommie and Daddy, thank you for giving me such a beautiful wedding. I know it was hard for you to do but you made me *very happy*. I think you are the dearest parents in the world – don't ever forget that, hear?

All my love,
Pat (and Bob)

May 12, 1953
Warrington, Florida

Mobile, Alabama

Dear Celia,

Well, here we are – I an old married lady of nearly two weeks and you the brand new mother of a precious daughter. Can't wait for us to have a visit and talk about the details of both. Bob and I will be coming over soon and are so eager to meet little Miss Debbie. In the meantime I want to tell you again, Celia, what an honor it was to wear your beautiful wedding gown for my own wedding. A wonderful gift from a sweet and generous friend. Thank you!

Now, take care of you and kiss the baby for me. See you soon.

Love,

Pat

July 29, 1953

Warrington, Florida

Prichard, Alabama

Dearest Folks,

Gee, am I ever lonely today – I sure do miss that Rickey! Rickey boy, don't you want to come and live with Bob and me?

Bob left for work at 11:00 this morning. I've cleaned the house real good, washed quite a few clothes, and now am doing my letter-writing for the week. We're pretty sure Bob is going to get out of the flying program. There are a couple of reasons, the main one being his reluctance to add two more years to the four he is committed to serve in the Navy. If he decides to drop flight school we will probably take leave and visit his folks, and then I would like to stay with y'all while he is at sea if he isn't lucky enough to get shore duty. We'll let you know the minute we decide.

I love all of you!

Pat

August 27, 1953

Riverside, Connecticut

Prichard, Alabama

Dearest Mom, Dad and Boys,

Well, we finally made it. Here I am WAY up in Connecticut. It really is beautiful country.

Wow, folks, you just can't imagine what a thrill I had on the trip, seeing all the different states for the first time, and the big cities – especially Washington and New York. In D.C., Bob and I saw the Jefferson Memorial, the Lincoln Memorial, the White House, the Pentagon, and all the department buildings. Oh, I loved stopping in Annapolis, too, where Bob pointed out all the old familiar places from his four years there and we saw a very inspiring march by some of the Naval Academy cadets.

We drove into New York with the top down on the Pontiac and I about broke my neck looking up at the skyscrapers. So many tall buildings – and tall trucks all around us. Amazing, too, the masses of humanity, and the noise and busyness were overwhelming.

Daddy, you should see the highways – six and eight lanes, with cars going in every direction. We got lost in Washington and in New York, and what a time we had getting unlost. The thing is, when you get on the wrong road up here, you have to travel to Kalamazoo to get back on the right one. Oh, goodness, I'm afraid everything in both cities is too crazy and fast for little ol' me. I wouldn't want to live in either one.

But visiting New York City is nice. One day we had tickets to a big Broadway hit, *Me and Juliet,* and tomorrow we're going back for a baseball game between the Milwaukee Braves and New York Giants – how about that, Sam and John?

Loads of love,
Pat

September 1, 1953
Riverside, Connecticut

Prichard, Alabama

Dearest Mommie, Daddy, Sam, John and Rickey,

I'm a little homesick to see all of you, but I try not to dwell on it because I am having a wonderful time. I really miss you, though, and so does Bob.

First, I'll mention the most talked-about subject here, the hot weather. Everyone is teasing us about bringing it up with us as they had been sleeping under blankets at night. But from the day we arrived the temperature has been almost 100 degrees *all the time* – the South was never like this! With such hot weather, though, we've enjoyed going to the beach to swim practically every day

Auntie Bussie drove up from Pennsylvania yesterday for a few days. It has been wonderful to meet her in person. You should see her – honestly, she looks only about 29 or 30, very attractive and very, very sweet. I love her already – y'all would, too.

Dave, Bob and I went to the ball game I mentioned, and it was exciting to see the famous ball players. (The manager of the New York Giants, Leo Durocher, is married to Lorraine Day, one of our favorite actresses, Mom.) Saturday evening all of us went to a cocktail party and buffet supper following the piano recital given by a beautiful girl in Dave's group of friends. Tomorrow we're going in to New York City to see Eddie Fisher's television program, then another Broadway show.

Miss you and love you!
Pat and Bob

September 9, 1953
Riverside, Connecticut

Prichard, Alabama
Dearest Folks,

I'm writing this while watching the Arthur Godfrey show on TV. Read your letter last night after we got back from a nice day in Waterbury. Dad needed to see the dentist and Mother Kitty was desperate for a new perm – they like to go back to Waterbury for certain appointments. Bob and I went to visit an old family friend of theirs, and on to the Country Club to see one of his best friends play tennis. He took me to see both of his family's former Waterbury homes, their church and the schools he and Dave attended. We all met up again for lunch, after which we went to see their longtime family doctor. That was fun because he enjoyed kidding me, just like Dad does, since I am so gullible! On the way back to Riverside we visited the home of some other family friends. Remind me to tell you all about it – wow, three stories, filled with beautiful furniture, acres of land, even their own tennis court. Later we stopped at a lovely place in the country for dinner.

Last Sunday we went out on another friend's yacht for a long ride, swimming, cocktails and dinner. This family friend is very nice, too – and very rich. I'll fill in more of the details about everything later, in person.

Oh, Mommie and Daddy, I must tell you the funny twin bed story. The first night here with the folks we walked into the guest room and saw that the beds were pretty far apart with a table between them. So my cute Bob proceeded to push the two beds *very* close and went looking for a piece of rope to tie them together. Of course, in the process all of the tables and chairs were shoved out of place, too. The next morning I called to his mother to come up and see. She practically went into hysterics, and we've had a lot more laughs about it since.

Well, I think I've told you most of the news. Now I have some ironing to do, and then we have to pack and be ready to leave early tomorrow. We miss you and are sending a big hug and kiss to Mom, Daddy, Rickey, Sam and John.

Love,
Pat

September 18, 1953
Coronado, California

Prichard, Alabama
Dearest Folks,

Don't mind this stationery from the motel in Flagstaff, Arizona …we are finally in California. Hooray!

We drove into San Diego city limits at 9 a.m. yesterday but didn't stop until about 12:30. It's a *big* city and very confusing. When we were looking for a certain motel and discovered we were many miles off track, I suggested we go on over to Coronado and try to find a place since that's where we wanted to be anyway. We started to go across on the ferry – Coronado is sort of an island – and the fare was 45 cents and all we had was 40 cents in change and a $50 bill. So we had to turn around, go back into the confusion of the city, get the bill cashed, go back to the ferry entrance and pay the 45 cents for the ride over. All worth it, though. Coronado is beautiful.

There's a big convention here this weekend and part of next week and it was almost impossible to find a place. We're staying at the Coronado Hotel Apartments until Saturday, when we have another one lined up. It's cute, with a bedroom, kitchen, bath, TV and nice furnishings. The rent is $125 a month, which sounds high, but all the utilities are included, plus linens, dishes, cooking utensils, etc. Other places we checked had apartments renting for $150 to more than $200 a month, so I guess we are lucky to get this. It's expensive out here. I've already noticed grocery prices being much higher.

Well, let me tell you about Arizona. We traveled over *very* high mountains and through miles and miles of desert, and when we finally arrived in Yuma the temperature was 120 degrees. And we got lost looking for a motel. We kept driving around and before we knew it had crossed the Colorado River, which is the state line between Arizona and California. So first the California Inspection Station worker stopped us, and since we had to turn right around and go *back* into Arizona, the Arizona Inspection Station stopped us and inspected the car (again, because we'd already crossed into Arizona once). When that inspection was finished, he handed me a little booklet proclaiming "Welcome to Arizona!" By that time I was hot and tired and tempted to throw it back at him.

I also want to also tell you about Jerome, the "Ghost City." We were driving way up high in the mountains and still could look up above us and see buildings and houses practically hanging on the edge of the mountain. I was thinking how crazy the people must be to live in such houses. Then we got to the city limit sign and saw this notice: "Population 20,000, 10,000, 5,000." Eerily, one after the other, the numbers were crossed out, and the words "GHOST CITY" displayed. We thought it was a joke and kept on driving – we'd planned to eat breakfast in Jerome. But all the buildings there were dilapidated and deserted, and we saw only *one* woman in the whole place! Pretty creepy and weird.

Bob just got home from the base, which is about a mile from the apartment. He heard a rumor that the Diachenko, the ship he is to serve on, is leaving in four weeks to go to Japan until April. Oh, pray it's not true.

Well, I haven't even asked about y'all. Please write *immediately* if possible – we're anxious to hear.

All love,
Pat and Bob

September 27, 1953
Coronado, California

Prichard, Alabama
My dearest folks,

We went to Los Angeles for the weekend and spent the night in a motel right on Sunset Boulevard. Had a wonderful time. First we took a tour of Beverly Hills and saw many of the movie stars' homes. As we drove past Joan Bennett's home, her husband, Walter Wanger, pulled out of the driveway and we saw him perfectly. Later we spotted one of Robert Mitchum's sons coming out of their home.

Saturday evening we had reservations for dinner and a show at Ciro's, the famous Hollywood nightclub. As we were walking in, we saw a girl in blue jeans and a man in sport clothes come out of the building right ahead of us and get into a car. It was Rosemary Clooney and her new husband, Jose Ferrer! They were so close we could have touched them. In the club we were seated next to Joan Vohs, a new movie starlet. Then later, such excitement when Lucille Ball and Desi Arnaz walked in! There was a terrific floorshow featuring The Martha Graham Dance Company. We were there about six hours, I think, all of them enjoyable.

Sunday morning we went by Grauman's Chinese Theatre to see all the handprints and footprints of famous stars. Afterward we drove past the picture studios (Paramount, RKO, Columbia). I kept gasping each time another celebrity came into view, and I think Bob was amused – and borderline embarrassed – by my excitement! The trip was Bob's birthday present to himself, but I sure did enjoy it, too.

Now I'll tell you the bad news. The lieutenant Bob is replacing told us the Diachenko is scheduled to sail October 19 and arrive back in San

Diego about May 16 of *next* year. And the last two weeks in port, Bob is scheduled for ship duty except on weekends. All this makes us so sad, as you can imagine. Since we don't know all the facts yet, I'll just say you can expect me anytime after next weekend.

Rickey, honey, your schoolwork that Mommie sent us was just wonderful! You sure are a smart little guy, you know that? Mom, we enjoyed your letter so much.

All our love,
Pat and Bob

WESTERN UNION TELEGRAM

OCTOBER 17 1953
MOBILE ALABAMA

CORONADO CALIFORNIA
HAD FINE TRIP LOVE FLYING   MISS YOU TERRIBLY
LOVE YOU PAT

17 October 1953
U.S.S. Diachenko

Prichard, Alabama
My darling,

I already miss you so much it feels as if my right arm is gone. It was so lonely in the room last night. Lying there I had the first tears I've had since I was a little boy.

I waited around and watched your flight take off. Did you see me there? I couldn't see the faces inside the plane. Be sure to tell me all about your trip, doll.

I think it would be a good idea for our old-age enjoyment to keep these letters written while we're apart. Let's number them on the envelopes, okay? Then we can look back on our letters to each other these months apart (and the *only* months, I hope!).

Please, please take care of yourself for me!

Always,
Your Bob

October 20, 1953
Prichard, Alabama

U.S.S. Diachenko
Hello, darling,

Well, the days are gradually going by and I miss you more and more. I really believe the first two or three weeks will be the hardest, especially if it's that long before I hear from you. But so far, my time has been pretty well occupied.

Sunday, we watched TV, which was kind of a lifesaver for me. Yesterday I went with Mommie to get Rickey from school and had a swell time. Rickey had told *everyone*, "Today my sister is coming to get me." All of the kids performed for us. They sang and recited poems and skipped to music – so cute, lots of fun to watch. And this morning Mom and I went to Mobile for a bit of shopping.

Honey, I just had the most wonderful surprise – your first letter! You can tell by what I wrote in the first paragraph that I didn't expect one for quite a while. Oh, it is the sweetest letter ever! I love your suggestion of keeping all of our letters. I know we will enjoy reading them again a couple of years from now and maybe later on, too, when we are old and gray.

All my love, always,
Pat

25 October 1953
U.S.S. Diachenko

Prichard, Alabama
Dearest Pat,

We got into Pearl Harbor this morning about 11:00 and I received three wonderful letters from you! They were postmarked October 19, 21, and 22, so the last one got here in *three days*. Pretty good! Mac says it takes about a week to get a letter in Japan. This is my fifth letter to you. All these last four will be mailed here in Hawaii, and the next ones in Midway.

The captain let me bring the ship in this morning up to near the dock, and then he took it over. They have a monument in the water and an American flag right where the Arkansas was sunk by the Japanese on December 7, 1941. There are always planes taking off for the States and Japan from the field right near here. Wish I could get on board one of them! (I mean one going EAST, of course!)

We will leave Pearl about Tuesday noon and get to Midway 31 October, I think. We probably won't stay at Midway very long. Next stop will be Yokoska or Yokosuka, Japan, depending on how you pronounce it.

I'm glad you're getting things done like driving, sewing, cooking, etc. Keep it up, sweetheart, and keep yourself busy. Don't forget to send some snapshots if you can.

Always yours,
Bob

November 26, 1953
Prichard, Alabama

U.S.S. Diachenko
My darling Bob,

Exactly a year ago, Thanksgiving Day, 1952, I wrote my *first* letter to you, answering the one I had received from you the day before. I didn't even know you existed before that letter, and certainly had no idea that I'd be your wife of seven months by the time Thanksgiving of 1953 came around! I want to tell you again what a wonderful year I had with you – dating, being engaged and, best of all, being your wife.

Always,
Your Pat

28 November 1953
U.S.S. Diachenko

Prichard, Alabama
My darling Pat,

Today (although it isn't time for it yet back in the States) they're playing the Army-Navy game in Philadelphia. Wouldn't it be wonderful if we could be shivering in the stands at Municipal Stadium together? We sure could have fun, but there I go dreaming again!

We arrived in Sasebo (southern Japan, you all) this morning and we'll be here until 1 December, when we leave for Inchon, Korea, and some more operations. Not having heard from you in over two weeks, I was three feet off the ground when I was handed 10 letters from you, and then six from the folks, including two from Dave and one from my good old friend Al.

I just can't tell you how much I *loved* your letters. You should write every day, then I would get all the more letters from you. Your latest, #18, was dated November 20. So this puts me even with you, or almost so. Thanks a million for the clippings, snapshots and news, but most of all for loving me so much and just being so downright wonderful yourself. I can't wait till I can hold you in my arms again and sque-e-e-ze you!

All my dearest love, Your Bob

62

December 6, 1953
Prichard, Alabama

U.S.S. Diachenko
Dear Bob,

It's neat having a "big brother" on the other side of the world, but my sister misses you a lot. I want to thank you for the money. I haven't been able to do much stamp collecting lately because I've been so busy. Such as painting the house and getting ready for Christmas.

Sorry Navy didn't win, but you can't all the time. I guess you heard about Alabama getting to play in the Cotton Bowl. They are going to play Rice. Notre Dame tied Iowa and Maryland took first place.

Rickey is sending you a note and a picture he drew of a Christmas tree and toys.

With love,
John

DEAR BOB. I LOVE YOU. HURRY HOME.
RICKEY

December 11, 1953
Prichard, Alabama

U.S.S. Diachenko
Dearest Bob,

About a year ago, December 12, on a Friday night like this, I was in a state of excitement because you were on your way to meet me for the very first time. In fact, my whole family was excited, wondering what sort of person you were and how you'd look. We went to that party dance for a colonel at Brookley Field. You told me a few of the things you liked in girls (blond hair, long fingernails, not-too-thin figure being among them), and later kissed me for the first time. That evening was the beginning of "us," though we didn't know it at the time.

Oh, darling, you mean *everything* to me. I'm so unhappy without you. Will these next five months *ever* pass?

Your very own,
Pat

WESTERN UNION TELEGRAM

DECEMBER 23 1953
MOBILE ALABAMA

USS DIACHENKO
MERRY CHRISTMAS DARLING   I LOVE YOU WITH ALL MY
HEART
YOUR PAT

1 January 1954
U.S.S. Diachenko

Prichard, Alabama

Happy New Year, sweetheart,

Now at least three of the days I was dreading without you have passed: Thanksgiving, Christmas and New Year's Eve. Only Easter and our first anniversary to go. What made today a lot brighter was the fact that I got letter #40 from you, doll. It was awfully sweet – just like the 39 that came before it. You are just too wonderful for words! I've almost caught up to you in letters, though.

Honey, do you write down the numbers 1 thru 50 like I did and check them off when you number a letter to me? I'm still missing #32 and #36 from you. Maybe they'll get here yet. … Could you have forgotten to use those two numbers and skipped on to #33 from #31 and #37 from #35? Losing your mail is a *catastrophe* to me!

Your very own Bob

What cannot letters inspire? They have souls; they can speak;
they have in them all that force which expresses
the transports of the heart; they have all the fire of our passions.
Heloise to Abelard

Chapter Four
Long Distance
1954

Pat's first foray into Connecticut snow

January 16, 1954
Riverside, Connecticut

U.S.S. Diachenko
My dearest Bob,

Here I am back up North, typing on your dad's cute little typewriter and looking out the window at the beautiful snow everywhere! Last night I told the folks I wanted to see it falling, so this morning they called up the stairs for me to open the curtain and take a look. I put on an old coat of your mother's and a pair of Dad's size 15 galoshes and we went outside and had a snowball fight. It was so much fun, and I longed for you to be here to enjoy it, too. Dad took a couple of "snowy" snapshots for you.

Let me tell you about my trip up here, which was a bit confusing. I had a plane reservation for midnight Thursday, Mom and Sammie took me to the airport, my bags were checked, and then I was told that because of bad weather all flights might be canceled. They were, so we went back home and I called your parents with the news that I wouldn't be arriving in New York at 6 o'clock Friday morning after all.

I was hoping for better weather the next day, when I could use my ticket on the 9:05 a.m. flight. It was still foggy early Friday, I checked with the airlines, and although there were no promises of a flight we went to the airport again. The plane was still in New Orleans and wouldn't get to Mobile until 11:00 at the earliest. When it finally came, I asked Mommie to send a wire to Riverside with my new arrival time of 5:40 p.m., then gave goodbye hugs and boarded the plane. The flight to New York was smooth, but the pilot told us the previous day had been the worst flying weather he had experienced all year.

Right now there's a fire in the fireplace (with the wood you chopped last summer) and it's so warm and cozy inside. But, sweetheart, you know I'm never completely relaxed and warm and cozy when you're far away from me.

Always,
Your Pat

January 21, 1954
United Nations
New York, New York

U.S.S. Diachenko
Hi, honey!

We're in the beautiful U.N. Building with a friend of your dad's as our guide. We had lunch in the Delegates' Dining Room and just came from observing a meeting of the Security Council – a very, very exciting experience! The folks and Captain Gaines are waiting for me now. I'll write you all about this later – just wanted to mail you a postcard from here today. I love you, darling, with all my heart. Take care.

Your Pat

January 22, 1954
Riverside, Connecticut

U.S.S. Diachenko
My darling Bob,

I have lots to tell you about our day in New York yesterday. First we went to "Motorama," an interesting, different kind of experience. Admittance to the affair was strictly by engraved invitation, which I didn't have, so I halfway expected to be thrown out of the Waldorf-Astoria immediately! You know your dad, though, he told me to walk in as if I owned the place and we'd bluff 'em. I did, and we did – and the next thing I knew, I was shaking hands with Mr. Harlow Curtice, the president of General Motors.

At 1:15 p.m., we met up with Captain Dick Gaines. He and your dad were in the Naval Academy class of 1925 together. His chauffeur took care of our car while Captain Gaines showed us around the United Nations Building, which is fabulous and filled with beautiful furnishings. Then he took us to lunch in the Delegates' Dining Room, a real privilege since it isn't open to the general public.

In the Security Council meeting room, the seats were equipped with earphones and a switch that can be used to hear a speech in *five* different languages. I was especially fascinated by that and kept flipping the switch back and forth, just having a great time.

We heard Andrei Vishinsky speak – he used to be the Foreign Minister of Russia but is now the permanent Soviet delegate to the United Nations. We didn't know too much about the question being discussed but found it interesting just the same. We met so many people – all along during our personal tour, the captain introduced us to various ambassadors and other VIPs.

Your mother and dad and I thought how much you would have enjoyed everything, honey, and it made us a little sad. Someday maybe we can go back for you to see it all.

Love from your Pat

10 February 1954
U.S.S. Diachenko

Riverside, Connecticut
Pat, my dearest,

I just came back from seeing a wonderful movie. It was made in 1951 and maybe you remember it, "The Blue Veil" starring Jane Wyman. It sure was sad, but it had quite a story and moral. She was a woman who went through life taking care of other people's children, never having any of her own – just heartaches. It certainly made me think of how very lucky we are to have each other.

Tonight is beautiful. Very clear, lots of moon and stars, and very calm seas for a change. I was up there on the bridge on watch. It was so peaceful. I looked out over the sea toward the east, wishing I could see thousands of miles right to you, sweetheart.

Your Bob

13 February 1954
U.S.S. Diachenko

Riverside, Connecticut
Pat, darling,

I usually sit down as soon as we get into a port where we receive mail and write a long letter to you and the folks. The ship got in yesterday morning and the mailman brought me back several letters, among them #57 and #62 through #67. They were *so* good, dearest, you do write the most heavenly letters. They're chock full of love and news. I hope you got my flowers on time, honey. All my deepest love went with them.

I'm pleased more than you know that you're having such a gay and busy time in Riverside. It sure gives me a comfortable feeling to know you are being loved and cared for and are happy. Your welfare while I'm unable to take care of you is awfully, awfully important to me! I'm glad, too, that you've met and gotten to know some of my old friends up in Connecticut.

Forever yours,
Bob

February 14, 1954
Floral Creations

Riverside, Connecticut
My dearest Pat,

For the sweetest Valentine's Day gal a guy ever had – on the first anniversary of our engagement, just one year ago, 14 February 1953. May we never be separated on another Valentine's Day. I love you.

Your Bob

February 18, 1954
Riverside, Connecticut

U.S.S. Diachenko
My dearest Bob,

Gee, but I'm blue and lonely, missing you tonight. Your letter #64 came today and it was a wee bit sad. I can understand why, though, with no mail for a long while, the sad movie, and Jack's leaving. Oh, darn, in our present situation it's not difficult to feel blue, is it? It's terrible to be separated when we're so in love. But I must stop dwelling on these things ... and instead, I'll tell you all about another one of our trips to New York.

Yesterday your mother and I planned to take the 8:30 a.m. train from Riverside, and at 7 o'clock we woke to mass confusion. It was pouring rain and the electricity was off – no heat, no lights, no water for coffee. But we quickly dressed, caught the train, and arrived at New York's Grand Central at 9:30.

First we went to an early movie, then to the famous "21" club for a drink and lunch. That was *really* an impressive experience, sweetheart. Next we attended the matinee performance of *Wonderful Town* on Broadway. Sat in perfect seats just 11 rows back. The show was out of this world and Rosalind Russell was great.

We window-shopped after the show and stopped in Schrafts for an orangeade. We'd done a lot of walking and were beginning to feel tired, and when we finally sat down we completely fell apart. Had to take a taxi to Grand Central for the 6:25 train back to Riverside. We two gals had fun but wished for our guys the whole day. I know the day was really expensive but your folks won't let me pay for anything. I'll never be able to repay them for the good times they've shown me.

I love you,
Your Pat

February 23, 1954
Riverside, Connecticut

U.S.S. Diachenko
Dearest Bob,

I really hit the jackpot with mail today! Your letters #65, 66 and 67 came and they were absolutely wonderful. You write a most heavenly letter, too, just perfect.

Yes, I am having a busy, happy time, and it has been exciting to meet so many of your friends here, plus some of my new relatives in Pennsylvania. We had a fine trip to Chambersburg over the long Washington's Birthday holiday weekend. I loved meeting your dad's mother, Nana Ellen, and his sister Margie and all her family. It was another unique experience for lil'ol' me. As you know, they live in a great big old house, and when we started to bed, Mother Kitty and Dad told me I shouldn't hesitate to come sleep in their room if I felt lonely or afraid in the night, way up in my bedroom on the third floor. It *was* kind of scary, but I was a brave girl and slept in my room alone.

Your mother also warned me that everyone in the household is always dressed at breakfast, even on holidays, so I shouldn't come down in a robe as we do every day in Riverside. Well, I was simply fascinated at breakfast. The Judge was *dressed* to the hilt (including the addition of the most impressive, eye-catching gold pocket watch and chain I've ever seen) in everything but his judicial robe and gavel, and the ladies were decked out as if for tea with royalty. And although the Judge didn't wield a gavel, Aunt Margie's little silver bell pealed fairly often to summon the maid.

Goodness gracious, I wondered whether I had been transported to another world during the night! Of course, ever since I left the South, honey, the worlds I've seen have been so different, so far from the life I've known. Your "kinfolk" were so sweet to me, though, and I learned more about your dad's boyhood in Pennsylvania. There are no better informants than a man's mother and his 15-years-older sister.

After the long weekend trip, it was kind of nice to be back home here with just the three of us. Your mother and dad are wonderful to me, sweetheart, and I've told them I am going to miss them terribly after I leave because I've *really* gotten to know and love them during this visit. Of course, we girls have been together nearly every minute and are the best of pals. When I mentioned missing them, your mother said she couldn't bear the thought of my leaving, that she didn't know what she would do without me.

So I think this visit has been good for all of us. She certainly has been helpful to me. Whatever I want to discuss, I can be sure Mother Kitty will

70

be right there to listen and say something to help me feel good. And she's always on her toes to see that I don't have time to brood too much. For instance, some evenings when I'm pretending to read but really feeling blue and missing you terribly, she immediately suspects what's going on and perks me up with a tempting "Hey, how about letting me beat you at a game of Scrabble?" She knows I love to play, so we get into a game and I forget my loneliness for a while.

Oh, it will be *paradise* to be together again, won't it, honey?

Forever yours,
Pat

9 March 1954
Dad's Birthday
U.S.S. Diachenko, at sea

Riverside, Connecticut
Darling Pat,

Hong Kong, what we saw of it in the three days we had ashore, is certainly a fascinating and fabulous place. It's like the crossroads of the world, an international city. Of all the places I've seen, I think Hong Kong is the most different and intriguing. We all would have liked to spend more time there.

I bought myself some tailor-made clothes at bargains you just couldn't match in the States. For you I got only a white camel's hair three-quarter-length coat. I decided not to buy anything else for you in clothes until we could talk it over.

Darling, I've gotten your letters through #79 and they continue to be just marvelous. I don't know for sure where to send this one, but I'll take a chance the folks talked you into staying over a little longer. I realize you miss your family when you're away from them, but I know Mother and Dad love to have you up in Riverside, too.

Always,
Your own Bob

March 11, 1954
Riverside, Connecticut

U.S.S. Diachenko
Hi, Bob honey,

Your parents and I took a trip to New York on your dad's birthday. We drove down about 1:30 p.m., parked the car and took a bus all the way up

71

Fifth Avenue to Radio City Music Hall. Dad said he wanted us to do some of the things I hadn't yet experienced in New York City.

Before going into the Music Hall, we went to an Automat, where I got a tremendous kick out of putting nickels in slots and seeing little doors open and food pop out. At Radio City, we first saw the movie *The Long, Long Trailer* with Lucille Ball and Desi Arnaz, and then a *beautiful* stage show featuring the Rockettes. After the show we went to the Roosevelt Grill for dinner and some of Guy Lombardo's "Sweetest Music This Side of Heaven." And it was ... you know he is one of my favorites.

I had two big martinis and felt really good! We ladies took turns dancing with our one gentleman and practically wore the poor guy out. During one dance Dad and I were near the bandstand and I requested "All the Things You Are" in honor of my husband overseas. It was beautiful, but the song and the whole evening made me miss you so badly. Later, when Mr. Lombardo passed by our table, I asked for his autograph. As he obliged, he asked if I'd heard my song. Nice that he had remembered me.

We stayed on into the evening, enjoying ourselves, and then rode the subway back to the car – another new experience. What a fun birthday party!

Your very own Pat

11 March 1954
U.S.S. Diachenko

Riverside, Connecticut
My dearest Pat,

Only a few lines before I hit the sack. We had a pretty rough trip from Hong Kong. In fact we haven't seen the sun for about two weeks. We've heard it has rained a lot in Yokosuka, and it's still raining here tonight.

Mother says you've matured quite a bit but that you are still the same sweet girl I left. She says you've met hundreds of new people up in the North with apparent ease and that you're a finer woman every day.

Your own man forever,
Bob

March 24, 1954
Riverside, Connecticut

U.S.S. Diachenko
Darling Bob,

I have only one more week here then it's back to Alabama. I'm really going to miss your parents and all my new friends here, but it'll be nice to be with my family and friends in Prichard for a while, too, before heading west again in May.

We spent another day in New York, the most exciting part of which was seeing "Cinerama." Do you know what that is, honey? There are only three theaters in the United States equipped to show it, and, believe me, it *is* breathtaking! The movie began with a ride on a rollercoaster – I lost my breath and my tummy turned over just exactly as if I were in a real one. Then came an airplane ride over parts of the United States and a gondola ride through Venice, both so real I almost got airsick, then could actually feel the breeze off the water. What a lot of new experiences I'm enjoying during these months up here with your folks!

I'm sorry, honey, this short letter doesn't mean I'm thinking of you less, only that I am so sleepy tonight.

Yours always,
Pat

25 March 1954
U.S.S. Diachenko

Riverside, Connecticut
Pat, darling,

I guess I can tell you now where we've been since 14 March. We went on a *big* mission called "Operation Flaghoist" at Iwo Jima. We practice-landed the whole Third Marine Division on the same beaches and same island that are still bloody from those terrible battles of World War II. We were stationed just 4,000 yards away from Mount Surabacki, where those Marines raised the flag during the war. From where we were we could see the monument with a flag flying from it.

It was a lot of hard work, but I can only be thankful this was just a practice training exercise and not the real thing as back during the war. We got released early by the admiral and are now proceeding to Yokosuka.

Goodnight, my love.
Your hubby

March 29, 1954
Riverside, Connecticut

U.S.S. Diachenko
My dearest Bob,

Whew! I'm completely exhausted. It's beautiful weather today, warm and sunny, and your adorable brother and I decided to go out and run some laps around the house for exercise. So great to have Dave here, home from Bowdoin during spring break.

I beat Dave the first go-round but lost my shoes, and it was so warm I left them off. Soon the "old folks" came outside and proposed a contest: Dave and I were to race to a certain tree in the yard and back. I started off great, jet-propelled, but before I knew it, I had fallen and was just kind of rolling down the hill. You can imagine how funny I must have looked with feet up in the air and hair down in my face. When we finally quit laughing and rested awhile, I attempted to imitate Dave and walk on my hands, but I'm afraid I flopped completely at that trick – the verb is quite descriptive! No doubt with all the exercise I'll be a little stiff and sore tomorrow. Worth it, though, for the fun I had.

Come late afternoon we had even more reason for laughter when old friend Al came for a weekend visit and kept us amused with stories of when you and he were in flight school in Pensacola. I loved being with Al again, and your family was delighted to see him. He could hardly believe I had voluntarily stayed away from my folks for almost three months, which actually is the longest I've ever been separated from them. I've missed all of them very much, but here I'm with "my family," too. Right?

By the way, Saturday night when we were all relaxing in the living room, Al, with a big grin, suddenly piped, "Say, I don't know if I should bring up things like this in front of mixed company, but I want to be a godfather!"

Your Pat

1 April 1954
U.S.S. Diachenko

Prichard, Alabama
My darling Pat,

This crazy Navy. You just can't plan on a thing! For us to try to make arrangements about when I get back to San Diego is almost impossible, as the picture changed again today. We leave for the States just 19 days from now so you'd better start planning on flying to California about 11 May, or maybe a couple of days before, just in case we should roll in early.

Take care of my Pat. Don't let anything happen to her, now. (By the way, love, what are your latest views on having a baby when I get back?)
Always your own Bob

April 7, 1954
Prichard, Alabama

U.S.S. Diachenko
My darling Bob,

For three days before I left Riverside friends kept dropping in to say goodbye, which was wonderful but sad, too. It was especially hard to leave your folks after three months but the reunion with mine was good. So were your letters waiting here for me!

It's now a few days later ... and letter #84 with the news that you'll be back in San Diego a week earlier than scheduled has cheered me up. The reason for my sadness is that Grandma Jennie died. I had called her as soon as I got back in town and knew she wasn't feeling well, but seeing her was a shock, and I must say I had a strong feeling she wouldn't live much longer. As it happened she went into the hospital that same evening. I was in the room when she died a few hours later – that was hard.

The family immediately made plans to drive to Stonewall where the funeral was held. It was a sorrowful occasion, and Daddy's grief over losing his mother was heartbreaking. It brought back the memory of when I was 9 and saw Daddy cry for the first time. After a phone call that Grandpa Sam was very sick, our family had started out on a challenging car trip from Royston, Georgia, to Stonewall in the dead of winter in a small Willys that for mile after mile seemed to bounce all over the road in the high winds and flurries of snow-mixed-with-icy-rain. I remember feeling cold and scared and sensing Mommie and Daddy's anxiety. When we finally arrived at the hospital, just Daddy went in ... and came back to the car crying because Grandpa had already died. Grandpa Sam was the sweetest, gentlest man, so loved. ... Now we like to think of him and Grandma being together again. They loved each other deeply and she had really missed his "petting" these last 13 years. Grandma Jennie was so cute, so petite. I was her first grandchild and we were close and always enjoyed each other. I loved her a lot and will miss her, but I'll keep the good memories of our talks and times together.

Hmm ... about a baby ... did I tell you your mother gave me one of your baby pictures? You were so cute. I hope we have a baby who looks just like his or her daddy! Oh, Rickey asked the other day, "Patsy, when you and

75

Bob have a little boy or girl, will I be its cousin or what?" He was tickled pink when I told him he'd be Uncle Rickey!

Always,
Your Pat

April 13, 1954
Prichard, Alabama

U.S.S. Diachenko
Dearest Bob,

I've written thank-you notes to all my new Connecticut friends ... now a love letter to my one-and-only. Your letter #90 came today, also one from our friend Bonnie in Coronado, who found a perfect place for us. Her description: garage apartment with a fenced-in patio and a yard abloom with bougainvillea, furnished beautifully and completely. It has a living room, Pullman kitchen, bedroom and bath, and rents for $90 a month, utilities included. Sounds dreamy, doesn't it? I can't wait for *us* to be *in* it. Have a Happy Easter, darling ... we'll save our first anniversary cards and celebration until May 7 when your ship comes cruising into port. Ed and Jim are cruel to tease you about pestering us on our first night back together. Tell them our welcome sign will *not* be out. And threaten that I won't be fixing them any good home-cooked meals if they misbehave, either!

I love you,
Pat

April 19, 1954
Prichard, Alabama

U.S.S. Diachenko
Sweetheart,

You are so thoughtful. The Easter corsage was delivered – red-tipped white carnations with a tiny white pink-eared bunny peeking out. Your folks sent me a dressy evening bag with a pretty compact tucked inside. I'd say the Easter bunny was good to me. After church and lunch we just relaxed until some of the kinfolk joined us for an egg hunt out in the woods. Rickey and the little cousins were awfully cute. Of course, we reminisced about last year when you and I, my family, and your parents and Dave had such a wonderful Easter day together while they were in Alabama to meet me for the first time.

I had a workday and a fun day this week. A nurse friend of ours asked for help during the Mobile Health Association free chest X-ray clinic.

Mommie and I and another volunteer registered 494 people in three hours. Then on Saturday I went with a few friends to Pensacola Beach. Had the best time watching the girls and cadets flirting with each other. No flirting for me, though, I'm taken!

Your bride,
Pat

28 April 1954
U.S.S. Diachenko

Prichard, Alabama
My own darling Pat,

The sea has been pretty rough today, so this writing may be quite jiggled but I want to get letter #100 off to you. What a grand feeling it is to realize this is the LAST letter I'll have to write to you in months, maybe *ever*, I hope!

You have a good, safe trip and a pleasant one, and take care of you and our new apartment in Coronado until I arrive. As I said, if you aren't on the dock, I'll hurry to the apartment as fast as I can.

Your very, very own Bob

May 1, 1954

Main Street Florist
Coronado, California
My darling,

All my deepest love and devotion go with these flowers on our very first anniversary. May we have 99 more and never, never be apart again. I love you so much, Pat.

Always,
Your Bob

The decision to have a child is to accept
that your heart will forever walk about outside of your body.
Katherine Hadley

Chapter Five
New Life
1954-55

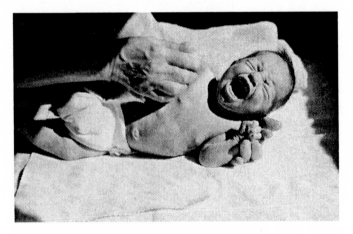

Robin arrives in Coronado, California

July 24, 1954
Lansdowne, Pennsylvania

Coronado, California
Dear kids,

I really shouldn't call you that anymore, should I? I just can't get over your news and am so excited I don't know what to do with myself. Also, I think it was sweet of you to write to me so soon to tell me about it.

My sister was very good about leaving it up to you to spring the news first. The wretch! She didn't even *hint*! And I'll have you know we are now addressing each other as "Nana" and "Great-Auntie" – we are that proud (not that we had anything to do with it).

As long as there are such definite sides as to the baby's sex, I think there should be at least one person in the family who stays neutral. I'll take that role because I just plain don't care what he or she is. "It" couldn't help being a wonderful baby.

I once thought only little girls were grand, and that boys were most uninteresting. But I got very well cured of that notion by watching my two nephews grow up. I thought I wouldn't like them much after they got over being babies, but I have kept on liking them more and more, even when they got to be great big hairy, ungainly men!

So, pink or blue, I'll be the nuttiest Great-Auntie you ever saw.

The best of luck, and very much love. Bless you both!

Auntie Bussie

14 September 1954
Coronado, California

Prichard, Alabama
Dear Folks,

Pat is doing a little housecleaning this morning, so I'll start the letter. As you probably know, I'm taking four days' leave this week while the ship is at sea. This morning when we finally could lie in bed late, we were both *wide* awake at 8:00! But the telephone man came soon after, so I guess it's just as well we were up.

Dad, Mother and Dave are having a wonderful time on their vacation here. The weather has been just beautiful every day. They'll be with us another week, and I know they hate to think the year's vacation is almost over and they must go back to the "grind." Dave plans to leave next Monday and is going to try to get a military flight back East.

I am glad to hear Sam is back in school. He will surely never regret it. In fact, I had urged him to get some college in one way or another. These days there are so many ways a young man can get help: a scholarship, G.I. Bill, or work his way through college. I'll bet Rickey is prouder than ever of his big brother Sam now. How is Rickey's new "flame" coming? Wow, when I was 7 years old I don't think I even knew the difference between a girl and a boy!

I've sent for our household effects from Pensacola and have been told they will get here between 12 and 40 days from now. The new place is certainly roomier but a little bare compared to all the furnishings we had in the old bungalow.

I've talked on and on – better let the little mother-to-be say hello, huh?

Loads of love to all,
Bob

Hi!

I just finished housecleaning and had a nice warm bath. I'm enjoying having a bathtub here. In fact, I love the whole house – it is *so* nice to have a bigger, prettier place.

Gee, it was a relief to get your letter yesterday, Mommie. I had been worried. We're sure glad Sam's home okay and back in school again. Study hard now, Sammie, and come through this school year with flying colors, okay? Rickey boy, you keep doing well in school, too, and send me a note and some drawings once in awhile. Is your new girlfriend pretty? And John, are you enjoying being a teenager for the first time this year?

I probably have loads more to ask and to tell you, but I've neglected Bob and his folks terribly this morning, so I'd better sign off and catch you up on the news after they've left. Take care of the sweetest family in the world. I love you very much Mommie, Daddy, Sam, John, Rickey – Tartar too, woof!

Pat

P.S. – Think we'd better not plan on my coming to Mobile next month for the few weeks Bob will be at sea. A flight is just too expensive.

14 October 1954
U.S.S. Diachenko

Coronado, California
My darling Pat,

Only four days away from you, and it sure seems like a year! I've been pretty busy, though, which helps. I hope you have, too, honey. If you keep real busy you just don't have so much time to think, and the time *does* go by faster. ... If my writing isn't too good it's because the Dirty-D is tossing around quite a bit as usual. The first couple of days out are normally pretty rough. It will probably soon calm down considerably and should stay nice until we get two days out of San Diego again about 6 November.

Take the best care of Pat and Baby. I love you both with all of my heart.

All my love forever,
Your Bob

October 27, 1954
Coronado, California

U.S.S. Diachenko
My dearest Bob,

Ooooh, what a sweet letter I got from you today. I bet I've read it five or six times already. I'm glad you aren't worrying about me, because I'm really getting along fine.

Just while I have been sitting here I've had to loosen my skirt so I *know* that Baby is growing and gaining weight! By the way, last night I dreamed you were here and my labor pains started, we rushed to the hospital and I had the baby – a boy – without any trouble. The dream was so real that when I woke up and saw I still had a tummy, I couldn't believe it. I've heard of other girls having similar "pregnancy dreams."

Take care of my love and hurry to me!
Your Pat

November 27, 1954
Coronado, California

Prichard, Alabama
Dearest Folks,

Please forgive me for neglecting you lately. ... I think this past week has been the busiest I *ever* had. Even today I doubt I'll have enough time

81

to write in detail about our activities, but at least you'll know we are both okay.

The Army-Navy Game has just ended and I thoroughly enjoyed it. Navy won and my honey was so excited I was afraid he'd collapse!

Things started popping Monday. I had to clean house, polish silver and wash the crystal in preparation for our Thanksgiving dinner. Tuesday, I went shopping at the commissary for a turkey and loads of other groceries, and that afternoon when Bob got home, we started to make the Japanese fruitcake. Bob was so cute, in an apron, stirring the batter like mad for me.

I soon realized we were in trouble, though, when I discovered that my flour wasn't the self-rising kind and that people out here have *no* idea what self-rising flour is! I didn't know how much baking powder to use – or exactly what to do – so I started calling friends and looking through cookbooks. Bob took off to the A&P grocery to see what he could find out from the lady who works in the bakery. She couldn't help us until after 8:15 when she got home to look at some of her recipes. That meant even though the fruitcake batter was ready for the oven at 6 o'clock, the baking had to be delayed.

We anxiously awaited her call … the instructions were to add three teaspoons of baking powder to the batter. I did that and then suddenly remembered I had only two cake pans, with batter for *three* layers, so baking had to be done in shifts. It was midnight when the cake-making marathon was finally over, and I slowly crawled into bed. The next morning the calls began, asking how the cake had turned out. It seemed like half the people in Coronado were involved in the project. But it was worth all the trouble – a perfect *dream* cake, and it's almost gone since everyone wanted a taste.

We had planned to go to church Thursday, but with our Navy friends Ed and Jim coming out, and the big dinner to prepare, we gave up that idea. Still we got up real early and I started on the 12-pound monster of a turkey, trying to get it cleaned and stuffed and in the oven in time to be bronzed and succulent for a two o'clock meal. Bob was helping and we took turns wrestling with the turkey – literally, so as to keep a good hold on it! – and cutting up onions and celery for the dressing. Before we finished we were even occasionally "cutting" at each other. We would get frustrated, then mad, then tickled. And both of us nicked our hands in a couple of places. Can you picture us doing kitchen duty together?

But, as with the cake, the dinner was worth every bit of our trouble. Everything was delicious, and the four of us ate and ate and ate. We had the beautiful golden brown turkey, good cornbread dressing (my first try), green peas, mashed potatoes, cranberry sauce, rolls, a carrot-radish-celery plate for nibbling, and then coffee and the famous Japanese fruitcake for dessert. And, Mommie, let me beg you, here and now, to please forgive me for all the times I was less than enthusiastic about helping you fix a big dinner. It's hard work!

We love you ever so much,
Pat and Bob

14 December 1954
Commanding Officer
U.S.S. Diachenko
Subject: Unqualified Resignation from the Naval Service
I hereby submit my resignation from the naval service of the United States, and request that the same be accepted in time to permit me to be discharged from the naval service on 1 June 1955, the day on which I will have completed four years of active commissioned service.

January 7, 1955
Coronado, California

Prichard, Alabama
Dearest Mommie, Daddy, John and Rickey,
I guess once again we have to leave ol' Sammie out, huh? I think the news that he had joined the Army didn't really hit me until after the phone call last night, then it was quite a shock. I know you're all depressed over Sam's leaving and miss him so much. Being the chronic worrier I am, I'll no doubt die a thousand deaths over Sammie during his Army career, especially if he should go overseas.

Daddy, will you be able to hire someone at least part-time to help you in the grocery store in Sam's place, or will you and Mom and John try to manage alone?

I can't tell you how disappointed I am that you can't come out here next month, Mommie. Of course, your physical help would have been wonderful with all the work involved in caring for a new baby, but I was counting on your emotional strength to get me through the birth, too. I'd planned to greet you and then completely relax, thinking, "Oh goody, now Mommie's here, she'll take care of everything!" Being you and such a special mother, I know you'll understand what I mean and how I feel. But this way I'll grow up a little bit more and maybe be a better person because of it. Right? So, as much as I'd like to have you here, the family and the store need you there more, and that's where you should be. I really mean it. We'll be fine – all three of us.

Tons of love,
Pat

Hello, Folks,

Yes, we were surprised and quite disappointed after your call, but I like to think that everything will turn out for the best in the end. Take good care of yourselves, now. And don't worry about Pat – I'll take very good care of her. I'll take leave for two weeks so I can be with her.

Loads of love from us,
Bob

February 2, 1955
Coronado, California

Prichard, Alabama

Dearest Mommie, Daddy, John and Rickey,

Yep, here it is a little after noon February 2, and I am still waddling around, "pregnanter" than ever. Every call from one of our friends begins with "Are you still at home?" One of these days I'm going to fool them.

When I went in for my weekly checkup yesterday, "Doctor Danny" looked so tired. He had been at the hospital for hours and delivered a bouncing baby girl due the same day as our baby. He walked in, took one look at me, grinned and asked, "So, how do you feel – pregnant?" YES, I heartily agreed!

Here is the report: I had lost a pound, I am in fine health, I had dilated a little bit, and things could start popping any minute. The doctor said, laughing, "There's just one thing about it, something has got to happen soon because this can't go on forever. You are about as pregnant as you can possibly be!" I've been having all sorts of crazy pains – none regular enough to be timed yet – and my poor back, how it ached last night and today. So, from all these signs, it just can't be too far off.

Your long good letter came Monday, Mommie, and we enjoyed it very much, as always. I also got a note from Phyllis in Oakland. She can't imagine that I am about to become a mother, still thinks of me as a young girl. She wrote that her hair is so gray now she should be able to realize just how many years have passed since I was her student in seventh grade at Prichard Elementary.

Please take real good care of yourselves – we love all of you sooooo much and still miss you all the time. (The enclosed photo of Bob is one of the prints he encloses with his letters of application for work. Pretty handsome guy I married, huh?)

All love,
Pat and Bob

P.S. – Oh, folks, since "He's in the Army now!" please keep me updated on Sammie's whereabouts and how things are going with him. …

February 9, 1955
Coronado, California

Prichard, Alabama
Riverside, Connecticut
Dear Grandparents!

She's here! On the due date, at 4:46 this afternoon. Her name is Robin, she weighs a little over 7 pounds, is almost 20 inches long, has lots of dark hair – and she's beautiful. More details later. Loads of love from all three.

Daddy Bob

As long as there are postmen, life will have zest.
William James

Chapter Six
Links to Home
1955

First home purchase in Hamden, Connecticut

13 February 1955
Fort Jackson, South Carolina

Prichard, Alabama

Dear Folks,

I'm sorry about not writing, but time is scarce here in the Army for your number one son. We've been pretty busy lately but next week, aha, next week is, I fear, going to be a bitch. We have three night problems plus preparation for an important inspection Wednesday. One of the problems is Tuesday night, and it consists of this: We'll be divided into three-man groups and given a point or location to find in a wooded area within Fort Jackson. We then strike out with compass, pack, rifle, and various other s--t.

Sleep is truly a virtue.

Went to see Jerry a few minutes ago. His unit had just been issued equipment. I felt like an old salt among them. He starts training tomorrow, my rookie cousin.

I went into Columbia last night with another guy. We went to the U.S.O. and took about a 30-minute shower, then went to eat – and I mean eat. Then we went to a club for a couple of beers. While we were out, we saw women. Ahaaaaaa ... I flipped. It was all I could do to keep from reaching out and grabbing one. But I didn't.

We will be classified around the end of the week. I should know something pretty definite after that concerning assignment, leave, etc.

I got your package Thursday, Mom. Great. Great. Great. Only I erred. I opened the wrong end first and gave away all the better brownies. Were they delicious. Every Yankee who tasted them thinks tremendously more of Southern cooking than before. In fact, they worship you.

We had a cold wave Friday and the temperature dropped to around zero degrees. Naturally we had all kinds of heat. Haha. The furnaces haven't been fired since Wednesday or Thursday. Right now it's kinda warm in the barracks, about 30 degrees, and my hands are a little stiff. There is one advantage, though. When we go on a week-long bivouac in a couple of weeks we will be used to the cold.

Write when you can,
Sammie

February 16, 1955
Coronado, California

Prichard, Alabama
Dear Folks,

Pat still doesn't feel much like writing a long letter, so I'll take that burden off her for a while longer.

Little Robin is eating like a glutton right now – wish you could see it. The nurse just got back from about four hours off to get a few things done, and everything went great while she was gone.

Robin sleeps so soundly and long. We had to wake her up for her 6 o'clock feeding. I'm already so proud of my little daughter, Miss America of 1973! By the way, she's a week old today. And her cord dropped off earlier this afternoon.

There's so much news that I can't possibly tell it all in one letter. It's a shame you aren't nearby and able to be in on all the developments. But everything is coming along fine, and we are all very, very happy. Our friends have been *so* good to Robin – the gifts continue to pour in, plus cards and letters.

We got a cheery note from Sammie today, and a while ago some ham radio operator called and gave us this message from him in South Carolina: "Exuberant over news of my new niece. Take excellent care of yourselves." What a guy, huh?

We call the baby's room "Robin's Nest." I carried Robin home from the hospital and have handled her remarkably well since, if I do say so myself. She's so light!

Well, I've saved the latest piece of big news, in a week of news from us, till the last. *Today my orders came!* Effective tomorrow, I am in the Naval Reserve, my resignation is accepted, and I am to be detached in June for separation and released from active duty.

All of which means I will most likely have to go over to WESTPAC with the ship, and return by air in June. It will mean about two months of separation from my girls, but the end result will be worth it. More about the orders and our plans for the coming months in the next letter.

All our best love
Bob, Pat and Robin

February 27, 1955
Coronado, California

Prichard, Alabama

Dear Folks,

I have a few spare minutes so I'll start a letter to you, but little Robin is going to yell for her 2 o'clock feeding soon. It's too bad, now that you'll want to hear from us more than ever, I probably won't have as much time to write.

Believe you me, I can sum up this past week in one word – WOW! Since the nurse left Monday morning we've had one hectic time. With her here we didn't feel like Robin was really ours, but now we strictly know she is. Robin must've known the nurse had left, because the first couple of nights she really let loose. Bob and I walked around with bloodshot eyes, just so tired and sleepy we didn't know what to do.

Everything went along surprisingly well, though, and probably would have continued to get better, but on Wednesday I got oh-so-sick. Gracious, what a madhouse then. When Bob got home that afternoon, so tired he could hardly move, I was in bed with a 101-degree temperature, chills, and one breast so painfully engorged that the thought of even just a sheet touching it gave me even more chills.

I don't know how, but we sterilized bottles and nipples and made the formula, fed Robin on schedule and took care of her in a million other ways. I'd crawl out of bed and help until I got too dizzy to stand, lie back down, then get up again. Finally, with Robin settled after a feeding, Bob fell into bed and slept for a couple of hours and got somewhat revived. He stayed home the next morning to do the baby's washing, etc., but I felt better by noon and all the work was caught up temporarily so I could stay in bed, and he went to the ship to work a few hours.

I know you're wondering about our plans, knowing now that Bob will still have to go overseas March 28 (so soon). We've discussed every angle and decided the best thing is for Robin and me to stay right here for the two months or so he'll be away. But I don't like even the thought of it

No matter what, though, he is going to get out in June. And we can't be Alabamy-bound soon enough! Oh, it'll be heavenly to see my wonderful family again after such a *long* separation. That will be a big day for y'all, too, greeting a brand new member of the family and seeing Bob after nearly two years – and me, too!

It just breaks my heart that you can't see Robin right now while she's so tiny and precious. You should see me bathing her – I feel like a big elephant handling such a tiny being. Of course, she may be tiny, but these days *everything* revolves around her!

89

We love you with all our hearts, and can't wait to be with you again – oh happy day! Keep writing those wonderful letters and I'll write every chance I get.

All our love,
Pat, Bob and Baby Robin

6 April 1955
Fort Campbell, Kentucky

Prichard, Alabama
Dear Folks,

Reasons for my delay in writing are so numerous it's futile to attempt explanation. I will say this: Pen, paper, envelopes and stamps are borrowed. I am at present being, for the lack of a better phrase, "put through the mill." Said harassment will be a couple of weeks in duration. After which things will probably settle down to the usual grind. This eight-week cycle will terminate about 27 May. Then I'll hang around awhile for jump school.

Changing from one post to another is like changing branches of service. One is confronted with a new environment to which he must adjust. As you probably noticed I am training with the 508th, the one that leaves a day or so after I finish basic.

This is funny. I left home a little over a week ago, and my memories of home and y'all are just as distant as they were after two months at Jackson.

I must tell you, Mom and Dad, how I appreciate the way you treated me while I was home. I will always remember it.

Damn, I can't for the life of me link two coherent sentences!

How in the heck are things at home? What about "Operation Robin?" How are you, Mom, Dad, John and Rick? Please write me a long and informative letter soon.

Sammie

16 April 1955
U.S.S. Diachenko

Coronado, California
Dearest Robin,

I've written Mommy two letters already and none to you, so I thought it was about your turn. You can let Mommy read this, though, like a good girl.

Only three more days to go on this trip that has seemed almost endless. Sixteen days at sea is a powerful long time! Thank goodness it's nearly over.

We are supposed to pull into Yokosuka about noon only three days from now.

The weather around Hawaii was just gorgeous, but after we got beyond the Islands, near Midway, we hit a pretty bad storm for about two days. The Dirty-D came through fine, though, as usual, and the only casualties were two guys who seem to get seasick every time a wave hits us. Today is cloudy and dreary. It would be so good to be back in the house with you and Mommy.

As you have undoubtedly heard, Robin, being in a Navy town, the new military pay increase became effective the first day of April. I get a $60 monthly boost, with $10 of it going to tax! That's quite a raise, huh?! Although it won't benefit me much in just two months, it will come into play when I am given a day's pay for every day of leave I haven't used (about 53!). Figuring roughly, I will be getting about $1,500 when I get out. My monthly pay goes something like this now:

Base pay $335.14
Subsistence 47.88
Rent 94.20
477.22
Income Tax 29.80
Total "Take home" pay 447.42

The pay increase is a great thing, for the career officers really need some benefits and recognition, but it doesn't make up for the lack of home life to me. There are some things money won't buy. You'll find that out, Robin, the older you get.

I guess I needn't go into how much and how often I've thought about my two girls, wondering how they are getting along together without Daddy. I imagine everything is going along on schedule – just a little lonely, no doubt.

That's about all for now, sweetie. You take good care of your mother now, smile at her often, and keep her happy until June. Then I'll help.

All my deepest love to you and to Mommy.

Daddy

P.S. – We have been getting the news regularly, and the brightest has been the announced effectiveness of Salk's polio vaccine. You won't like the shots, but we're going to take full advantage of all the possible shots against polio that we can get for you, darling. As one man said, Salk should get the Medal of Honor.

April 20, 1955
Coronado, California

U.S.S. Diachenko
Hi, Bob dear,

Nana GeeGee's having a wonderful time here in your little home with your girls. Now if only you were here.

Honest, Bob, Robin is just the sweetest baby ever (since my Pat and the boys were babies, anyway). I can't get over her being so good, sleeping all night and so much of the day. Also, when she's awake she's so happy and content. Today she was cooing with the sweetest expression. Little mommy and I were standing over her "oohing and aahing."

Pat and I think each day surely we won't have as much to talk about tomorrow but so far we have. I'll probably stay at least 10 more days, and then you'll be coming home soon after that.

We're really getting anxious to see you again after almost two years. So hurry home. Okay?

All best love to our Bob,
Mommie-Nana GeeGee

21 April 1955
Fort Campbell, Kentucky

Prichard, Alabama
Dad, John, Rick and Tartar, Bachelors Extraordinaire,

Well, I can tell you guys what you already know about me. What I want is a letter from you-all telling me what you're going to do and when.

This week has been spent at ease, so to speak. Every morning we all get up at 4:30, hold reveille at 6:30, and double time to the P.T. area. The day is spent on drills and cleaning equipment until chow time. Then at 1:00 we go back to training. As you can see, I'm living the life of Riley. How long this will last I don't know, but here's hoping.

I got a letter from Mom today. All she could tell me was how she and Pat had been talking nonstop. I gather she's really enjoying her trip to California. Robin is nothing short of a doll, believe me. Sure was glad to get the picture of her.

Got to close,
Sammie

3 May 1955
U.S.S. Diachenko

Coronado, California

Pat, my darling,

The F.I.C. stands for French Indo-China, and *we're here!* What a place! Why they're fighting over it, I don't know, but I'll be ready to leave anytime. … Present plans are that we will leave the port on 13 May, stay outside until about 16 May, and then head for Subic Bay again. It's a fascinating, desolate place, with the Viet Minh Communists waiting only a few miles away for us to get out so they can take over the city. … (I hope they can wait until we *do* leave!)

Anyway, I'll have a lot of interesting stories to tell you during our drive back to Mobile, so that driving time should go quickly. I guess I am really lucky to be in on this experience here, but I'll be glad when it's all over.

They say a plane is going to take our mail to Saigon, South Vietnam, tomorrow. Of course, the plane is French, and has to fly over Communist territory to get to Saigon, so it may never get there, eh?

I've read a lot about the bad Cutler Laboratories' polio vaccine, and how some children in San Diego, too, have come down with polio from it. It's a terrible thing to have happened, just when it looked as if polio was about to be conquered. Better keep Robin away from children for a while, okay?

Today was pretty humid but not quite as hot as in Subic. They say the monsoon season is about to begin and that means *lots* of rain! Well, at least maybe the rain will keep things cool.

No more news, but I'll get letters off whenever possible. Give little Sweetie a tiny hug and a big kiss from her Daddy. I sure love and miss you both. Only 34 days till I leave the ship.

Your own Bob

7 May 1955
U.S.S. Diachenko

Coronado, California

Pat, my dearest,

A lot has happened of real interest since I last wrote to you, but I won't begin to be able to put it all on paper. I would rather wait and just tell you the highlights now. By the way, the weather has been pretty nice here since we arrived, but today is hot and humid again.

I never knew much about Southeast Asia or Indo-China or what has been going on down in this hot, humid, poverty-stricken corner of the earth, but I'm learning now and learning fast! If only more people from the States could see some of this stuff with their own eyes, they wouldn't gripe so much about little unimportant things. Why, the United States is *paradise* compared to the way these Vietnamese live.

A Dr. Tom Dooley from St. Louis, who has been here for 10 months treating as many as 14,000 refugees at one time, and who has a wonderful personality and a thorough knowledge of the situation and the people, has been giving us talks at night for about an hour before the movie. And he sure is interesting. Some of the things he tells us are horrible. He hates communism with all his heart, because he has seen what it *really* is. He's telling us so that we may tell our friends and families and get the word around.

There is no liberty here – that is, none of our people can go ashore. The French and Vietnamese refugees are moving out. The Viet Minh Communists are moving in. And there's tension and sometimes violence in the city. Yesterday there were two killed and 14 injured in a riot.

But Ed and I got over there with Doctor Dooley on the pretense of picking up some canvas last Thursday. Doc drove us all around the city, and I wouldn't have missed that hour and a half for anything. The town is almost deserted, with the remaining people either believing that the Communists will be all right, or just too uninformed to know any better.

We sped around in a borrowed French car, never staying in one place too long, as you don't know which ones are Communist soldiers in street clothes. He showed us the dock area, the waterfront, the prize the Viet Minh Commies most want, and then showed us the refugee camp where as many as 14,000 people a day lived while waiting to be evacuated to free South Vietnam. He treated people with beriberi, leprosy, cholera, diphtheria, starvation, and every other kind of known and unknown disease in the world. There is no plumbing, no sewerage, no *nothing*. And he had very little to work with.

There are a few people coming through on their way to freedom, but it is almost over now, and the flow is down to a trickle. I believe about 800,000 refugees have passed through Haiphong alone. … We had a look at the French installations, and thence to the marketplace. We visited a couple of shops that were still open (most everything is desolate, cleared out and boarded up), and I picked up three little wooden statues of Vietnamese gods.

After a whirlwind tour of the city, I must say I felt a lot safer, cleaner and better when I got back aboard the ship. I have no desire to go back over, either, though it was an experience I am really thankful to have had. I will be one of the last Americans to have been in Haiphong.

I am enclosing a Viet Minh Communist 50 piaster note, "hot off the press," with the usual picture on it of their leader, Ho Chi Minh. These are flooding Haiphong now. The value? Oh about 1/4 of a U.S. cent. But save it. You won't see many of them around the States! *Viet Nam Dan Chi Cong Hoa* means "Vietnam under the benevolence of Communism."

Right now the Communists have moved in to about six miles around the city and port. On 13 May after we and the French leave, they will ride in their Russian-made trucks and take over the entire area. We hope, fervently, that all goes smoothly and there are no riots or violence that will put us in a bad situation.

And that's the body of my news, darling. We don't do much. The ship is our prison. As of today (I don't know when you'll even get this letter), I have just 30 days left aboard the Diachenko! Monday it'll be just four weeks! Bud has already started the process of relieving me and should be all set by 6 June.

Still no orders for Ed, but then the last mail we got was in Subic the end of April when I got #9, the most recent letter I have from you. We may easily not get or send off any more mail until we get back to Subic on about 20 May.

Say, dearest one, do you know what today is? Or rather what we were doing a year ago today about 5 o'clock? Yes, the ship was docking at Broadway Pier, and a luscious blonde in pink was on the pier to meet me, to take me home.

All my love,
Bob

12 May 1955
U.S.S. Diachenko

Coronado, California
Pat, my darling,

I've slowed down in my letter writing a little, but only because the mail isn't leaving the ship very often. I promise to be better as soon as we get out of here. The last letter I have from you is #11 written three weeks ago.

This morning we got under way and left Haiphong, came down the Cua Cam River and anchored off Doson Peninsula, where we'll be until we leave for Subic.

Soon we and the French will all pull out of Indo-China for good, and it will slip behind the Iron Curtain, like so many other countries have.

Before we left Haiphong we could see the well-dressed Communist soldiers with hundreds of their flags flying, red with one yellow star in the middle. They were all around the city, waiting until today to move in and take over completely. I'll tell you much more after I get home.

Enclosed is one of the press releases the correspondents are sending off, using our radio equipment for some of them. They are all here for the finale: *Life*, *Time*, Associated Press, United Press, and many others. We have met and talked to some of them, and they are awfully interesting people. I'm enclosing a sample of one of the stories, which will have already been in the papers in the States by the time you get this letter.

With luck, we should be in San Diego a month from today. You be good to yourself, now, and give yourself and our Robin some kisses and hugs from me. Soon I'll be able to take care of that delightful task in person.

Don't forget to start "closing up shop" there so we can leave San Diego at least by 20 June, which should put us in Alabama about 27 June.

All my deepest love and sincerest prayers to my two wonderful girls,
Your very own Bob

May 20, 1955
Coronado, California

U.S.S. Diachenko
My dearest Bob,

I was thrilled yesterday to get your letter #13. A wonderful letter – but it was shocking to read about the terrible conditions of those poor people in Haiphong. It's awfully hard to picture such things really happening in this world, and yet I know they are. Oh, how truly fortunate we are to be Americans, living in this paradise land.

So glad I didn't know until afterward that you went out into the city, honey. I would have been sick with worry after reading about all the violence in Haiphong.

The young Dr. Dooley you described is undoubtedly a great man – what an honor it is for you to get to know him. It is hard to imagine the horrible sights he must have witnessed during his 10 months there.

On the afternoon of May 7, I *did* remember, and relive that wonderful day of a year ago, darling, every moment of it. As you said, this time when you come home, it'll be even better because you will be a civilian with vacation time and no more reporting to a ship!

In a letter from Mommie today was the surprising news that they had sold the store – even though it hadn't been up for sale! But a friend of Daddy's produce supplier was in the market for a market, so to speak, and came to talk to Daddy when he heard what a good little neighborhood business it is. After 10 years of the long hours and hard work required to run the store, and stiff competition recently from the big grocery stores, the folks felt the timing was right and decided the fellow's offer was the chance of a lifetime. So Daddy is working temporarily at the Alabama Shipyard now but hopes to get a permanent job soon with a rayon plant near Mount Vernon, Alabama.

When I told Mommie you had enjoyed her note and asked why she didn't write more often, she lamented, "I just wish Bob could receive all the letters I've written to him in my *heart*." They all love you, honey.

Little Robin just woke up after a short nap on her pallet on the floor and I want to cuddle her … I'll love her for you, too, okay?

Your own Pat and Robin

20 May 1955
U.S.S. Diachenko

Coronado, California

Hi again, sweetheart,

We arrived in Subic Bay in the Philippines today about noon after having dropped some passengers from Haiphong at Sangley Point Naval Air Station. Sangley is right near Manila and we could see the big city very well. I was surprised at its tremendous size! It's quite a mammoth place. On the way we passed the island of Corregidor and the point called Bataan, both of World War II fame.

I just love all the information you've been sending me about how Robin is doing and all her little tricks. It makes me so proud and also so eager to be in on all the progress that I fairly burst! I do dearly love that little gal. How am I going to stand it when she smiles, coos, and now even laughs at me and reaches for me?

You remember when she cooed at me just that once before I left? Well, that was one of the supreme moments of my life. I hope my old heart can take all her sweetness after I get home. Only 17 days to go!

Always,
Your Bob

22 May 1955
U.S.S. Diachenko

Coronado, California
Pat, darling,

With some luck, I could be out of Subic Bay and back in your arms two weeks from right now! I'm longing to see you and Robin.

This afternoon being hot as usual, George, Doc Dooley, Milt and I took a boat and 35 enlisted men and went to a beach nearby. And, well, we also took five cases of cold beer. We all had a good time, drank all five cases without anyone getting the least bit looped, swam and played softball and football. It was very enjoyable even though the water was 85 degrees!

One of the guys caught a baby octopus. All of it could fit on this sheet of paper, but it was the exact copy of the larger ones you see. And the tentacles really had suction cups on them. A weird-looking thing, and sort of creepy. Not knowing what in the world we'd do with a growing octopus on an APD, though, we let it go in the water.

Give my love to both of our families and tell them I can't wait to see them again. And give a special little squeeze and extra kiss to my darling daughter, but keep a million tons of my love for yourself. I love you and miss you. See you soon!

Your own Bob

June 8, 1955
St. Francis Hotel
San Francisco, California

Prichard, Alabama
Dearest Folks,

No, you are not seeing things! I really am in San Francisco, a place I have always wanted to visit. And I won't keep you wondering any longer how I happen to be here.

When I wrote you last Friday, I fully expected to hear something from Bob within the next two days. By Monday I was in a nervous tizzy, but then he called from Pearl Harbor to tell me he would get to San Francisco about 2 a.m. Tuesday, and that if he had to stay in San Francisco to be discharged, he'd call again … Tuesday noon, a call: "Leave Robin, pack a bag and come up here because I have to stay two more days." My first thought, of course, was "I *can't* leave Robin."

I got busy, though, and with the help of all my neighbors and friends found a very reliable woman to come and take care of Robin, then packed a bag and made plane reservations for 4:30 p.m., and away I went! Met my wonderful Bob at 7:30 last night and we're having a marvelous third honeymoon.

Right now he is at the Navy base to get one more thing done in the separation process. He has to go again tomorrow for a few hours to get a final medical check *and* all the money that's coming, and then he will be a *civilian*. We'll fly back to Coronado Friday morning.

As Uncle Glynn used to say when he was feeling kind of mellow, words can't "compress" how wonderful it is to be back together again with no separation in the future, so far as we know now, anyway. It's also great for us to have this chance to be carefree lovers again for a couple of days before we dive into all the work in store.

As wonderful as it is to be with Bob, though, I can't help feeling like I lost a part of me on the way here, being without my little Robin. Bob and I both are finding it hard to believe I really am a mother because I feel like a new bride. And he says I look much too young and innocent and pretty to have had a baby already! My groom looks real good to me, too, except that he is still awfully tired from the long, drawn-out trip back.

Take care, see you soon, we love you!

Pat and Bob

July 19, 1955
Riverside, Connecticut

Prichard, Alabama

Dearest Mommie, Daddy, John and Rickey,

Loved your recent letter, Mommie, and enjoyed hearing all that has happened since our wonderful visit with you on our trek from California to Connecticut. For a few days the weather here was hot and humid with lots of thundershowers, much the same as during the time we were in Alabama, but now it's clear and pleasantly cool.

Robin is fine, and we've noticed her appetite increasing with the nicer weather. She loves the playpen Bob's parents borrowed, where she's exercising a lot more, rolling over every which way and wanting to stand up all the time. She's sleeping so well, too, day and night, and without much fussing before dropping off into dreamland.

Today Bob had an interview with a company in Greenwich and was offered a job in either of two engineering sections – starting in the morning! He told them he was fresh out of the Navy, had more appointments scheduled, and felt he couldn't accept a position so quickly. Tomorrow he's scheduled for a meeting about 50 miles from here, and the next day for another interview in Greenwich. We'll keep you posted on his progress.

We saw in the newspaper that the big airlift had been safely completed, which eased our minds about Sammie's trip. I wrote him a letter last week, but in case he doesn't answer soon, let us know what news y'all hear from him, okay?

We love you – *miss* you, too.
Pat, Bob and Robin

Hi, everyone,

It's great for me getting back after so long, meeting people in my "home" town, where I've really spent very little time since Mother and Dad moved here. The weather has been somewhat better than in Prichard, but not until today has it really been nice.

I'm well into the interview business now and hope to settle on a company before too long. I don't want to drag it out. It will be best for all three of us the sooner we're settled, wherever that might be.

Your sweet Pat and Robin are fine, and I'll take *very* good care of them. Thanks again for the wonderful time we had with you all. Take good care of yourselves.

Bob

August 10, 1955
Riverside, Connecticut

Prichard, Alabama
Dearest Folks,

Here we all sit, wondering if Hurricane Connie is going to be a hit or, hopefully, a miss. It looks awfully dismal outside.

Bob is writing thank-you-for-the-interview letters to all the companies he didn't choose, his mother is knitting, and Robin is happily chewing on her teething ring while babbling a blue streak. Big news: yesterday we discovered her first tooth! We can barely see and feel it, but it's there, and she loves to bite down on a spoon with it. Her weight is up to 17 pounds, 4 ounces. She's so sweet sleeping in different positions now, on her back, tummy or side, just like a grownup.

It was wonderful talking to you the other night, Mommie, but I felt so sad afterward I couldn't help choking up and shedding some tears. I might as well tell you, I'm not happy over Bob's decision to accept a job here in Connecticut because it's really hard to think of living so far away from y'all. I know I can make myself be satisfied after we're settled and have some nice friends in the New Haven area, but I just can't be as enthusiastic as I should be for Bob's sake. Ah, me, sometimes I wish Bob had been born in the South, too, and wanted to settle there.

Your letter written Monday came a little while ago. I hope the infection in Daddy's foot has cleared up by now. We're very proud of John, too, for helping you out around the house. John and Rickey, I was so sorry not to talk to you the other night, but I was supposed to talk only three minutes and I *always* go over. We love you just the same, you know!

A big hug and kiss from all three of us.

Pat, Bob and Robin

August 17, 1955
Riverside, Connecticut

Prichard, Alabama
Dearest Family,

Yesterday Bob went house-hunting in New Haven again and found two in nearby Hamden that looked very promising, so we all went back today. Sure enough, one was *really* a possibility and we're going to make an offer on it tomorrow.

I'll describe it for you. First off, the yard is almost too big to keep up easily – a little over half an acre – but it's so pretty, and I'm already crazy about the magnificent weeping willow tree that sweeps across half the back yard. The house is typical for New England: a two-story "barn red" and white Cape Cod enclosed by a matching red fence. The location is convenient to the bus line for Bob to get to work, yet there's a country look and feel to the neighborhood because of a convent and large wooded area across the road. It has a living room (no dining room), kitchen, den with built-in floor-to-ceiling bookcases, one bedroom and bath downstairs, and two bedrooms and a bath upstairs. Can you imagine me having *two* bathrooms?

All our love
Pat, Bob and Robin

21 August 1955
Fort Campbell, Kentucky

Prichard, Alabama
Dear Folks,

Well, tomorrow morning we are going to the top – moving, I mean, for a week. Our mission is to find the longest flat stretch of terra firma and cover up any chance artillery holes that may be present. Yup, that's right. It's our future demilitarized zone.

I'm eating like a horse and weigh only 171. Nothing but skin, bones and 30-caliber machine gun to muster up.

I know this is an old line, but I've never been as sorry over anything in my life as I was over not remembering you, Mom and Dad, on your 24th wedding anniversary. Anyway, I'll damn sure remember the silver one coming up.

It's been so long since I've written a letter, I can hardly manipulate this pen. Please forgive this vulgar ink. The pen is a borrowed one.

Only 28 more paydays. ...

Sammie

August 24, 1955
Riverside, Connecticut

Prichard, Alabama
Dearest Mommie, Daddy, and boys,

Thanks for the lovely birthday card. Auntie Bussie came up Monday morning for an overnight visit, a nice present for me. And she brought more gifts. Auntie always goes overboard in what she does – of course, she said she was just giving me second-hand stuff, and some of it was, but that was okay with me! Besides three pretty, useful bowls and a $10 bill for little things I wanted for the house, she gave me a beautiful amethyst pin that had belonged to her mother, and an amethyst ring her former husband had given her. And as if that wasn't enough, she gave me another $10 bill especially for one thing – calling my family in Alabama! (She sends her best wishes.)

Bob and his parents are giving me a dresser for our bedroom, but I haven't picked it out yet. And last night Bob and I went out to dinner and a movie to celebrate my birthday while Robin stayed with her Nana Kitty and Granddad.

I know you're wondering about the house. We did get the one I described in my last letter, and I'm sending you a picture from the Realtor so you can see how pretty it is. We got it for $16,000, which included the stove but not the refrigerator, and we think it really is a bargain. The former owners will be out the first of September and we'll move into it just as soon after that as possible.

Bob has started his new job at Southern New England Telephone and Telegraph Company (SNETCO, for short) and wonders if he'll ever learn all he is supposed to about telephone engineering. He likes the people, though, and says they're very helpful, so I'm sure he'll catch on quickly.

If y'all read about the flooding in Connecticut I hope you weren't worried, we were all right here in Riverside. Waterbury was one of the places hit worst, though, so Connecticut Light and Power crews were out in full force, and poor Dad had to be there all weekend – after working here the weekend before because of damage from the hurricane. He is bone tired from not much sleep for two full weeks now.

The things he told us about Waterbury were unbelievable and, in fact, he was in a mild state of shock Saturday after seeing all the horrible results of the flood. Now there's fear of diseases and people are being given typhoid shots. We're praying nothing else happens and that Dad can get some rest this weekend. We miss his old cheerful self. The weather has been terrible ever since we got to Connecticut, and the natives just can't get over it. They say never in history has it been so hot for so long, with so many lightning storms, hurricanes and floods. Hopefully, I'm seeing the very worst first and it'll be better in all the years to come.

Robin is getting a lot more hair every day, and I wish you could see her two cute little teeth. She still sleeps well, and even when awake will often lie in the crib for a long time, move all around, play a bit, then take another rest while she sucks on that delicious thumb! There's an occasional show of temper, but she's such a good baby. With Bob commuting to New Haven for work these days, he hardly gets to see her at all, and that makes us even more eager to get settled in Hamden.

Take good care of yourselves and remember how much we love and miss you. By the way, Mommie, would you send my news on to Sammie for a while till we get settled and I can start writing him regularly.

Pat, Bob and Robin

17 October 1955
Camp Chickamauga, Japan

Prichard, Alabama
Dear Folks,

Although I haven't received any mail for about a week, I'll try to think of something to say on my own. To begin with, things are relatively quiet on the Pacific Front. But remember, war is hell.

Dad, how about a little detailed explanation of your new job, such as how you like it. Also, how are you getting on? Do you wake up each morn with a bounce? Have you noticed any recent keenness of sight, taste, smell or hearing? Athlete's feet or anything like that? In other words, how the heck are you?

How's second grade, Rickey? And girls and all that? Are you slaying them? How about every once in awhile dropping your gravy-train-riding big brother a line or so? And John, are you learning to drive yet?

Got a letter from Pat today. I sure hate that I'm missing Robin's cutest stage, but that's the way it goes.

See you in a mere 26 months,

Love,
Sammie

October 26, 1955
Hamden, Connecticut

Prichard Alabama
Dearest family,

I knew as soon as I told you last week that I planned to write more often, I wouldn't be able to do it. WOW, WHAT A WEEK! I regret more and more all the times I just didn't realize how much work and responsibility were involved in marriage and mothering. And I'm sure there's no need to tell you this, Mommie, because you knew that someday I would understand. Anyway, again, please forgive me for everything I ever did that made things harder for you and Daddy. Sometimes now I look at Robin and think, "Oh no, I guess you'll do the same and, like your mommy, regret it someday!"

I won't try to tell you everything that went wrong, but I can tell you a bit of what made the little troubles seem worse. First of all, last week I got a "crack in my sacroiliac" and my back feels like it's out of joint – probably from lifting Robin so much and running up and down stairs. (Was I the one who always dreamed of having a two-story house?)

Next, little Robin's good habits have backfired on me since I started bragging. She used to sleep many hours a day and play contentedly in her crib after naps, and now she often sleeps less than two hours the whole day. She's also teething, bless her heart, and so she cries a lot during her awake time. On top of this, she seems to be in two new phases: "Mama's baby," crying for me when she's upset even if Bob is holding her, and being afraid of strangers. The situation was even more hectic this week because we had six people (nine if you include Bob, Robin and me) here all Saturday afternoon and evening – for dinner, too.

As long as I'm really spilling my troubles, another complaint is the cold weather, and it's not half as bad yet as it's going to be. After spending time with Bob's folks in Riverside last year, I recall telling Southern belle Celia that I didn't mind the weather. She just gave me a long look and drawled, "The No'uth is for the *birds!*" I believe I agree with her now. The thing is, when I was just visiting I didn't have to go out if I didn't want to. Now, of course, I have to stand in the freezing cold and hang out wet clothes, and bundle up Robin and myself and go out for appointments and to buy groceries, etc. The neighbors have been warning me "just wait until you hang out clothes and they freeze stiff before you even get them up!" Oh, Lordy, I can hardly bear even the thought of that.

Rickey, I want to see some of your writing now, so please don't disappoint me, hear? Hurry up and write a letter – and tell us all about your girlfriends, too.

All our love,
Pat, Bob and Robin

12 December 1955
Camp Chickamauga, Japan

Prichard, Alabama
Dear Folks,

Well, by now you undoubtedly know the regiment will be back home next June.

Thanks a lot for the letter, Dad and Mom. As for my parachute jumping, I blast as often as possible, which is panning out to about once a month. My last one was early this week. We had a slight wind, 13 knots, and I plowed up a half-acre of potatoes with my nose. Luckily there was someone around to collapse my chute or I would be halfway home by now.

Rickey, I don't believe I told you but your letter was about the cutest thing I've seen, ever. I enjoyed it to say the least.

Sammie

25 December 1955
Camp Chickamauga, Japan

Prichard, Alabama
Dear Folks,

Not too much is doing here. The weather is about the same as I remember in Mobile. It hasn't really gotten cold yet. I had an uneventful Christmas. How was yours? The sweater was a great gift – thanks a lot.

I think I mentioned something about working a little extra this month. That was an understatement. I've worked day and night for the past week.

And in the morning bright and early I will once more plunge diligently into my work, up through approximately 10 January.

I just said goodbye to one of the swellest guys I have ever known. He's going home. It seems like life is full of hellos to people you don't like and goodbyes to the ones you do.

I got your letter this morning, Dad. And a damn good letter it was. Thanks a lot.

Sammie

The universe is made of stories, not of atoms.
Muriel Rukeyser

Chapter Seven
New Landscapes
1956

Auntie Bussie's Christmas in Connecticut

January 4, 1956
Hamden, Connecticut

Chickasaw, Alabama
Dear Folks,

We loved all your gifts – thanks. Pat has told you about our Christmas. We did have a marvelous time and it would have been complete if only we all could have been together. But that is not to be, I guess. ... I took down our Christmas wreath tonight, so I guess the holidays are really over. I hate to see the season pass.

I'm tickled about your new house – it sounds just super! You sure deserve all the wonderful breaks you've been getting lately. May they continue and this new year bring many more better and bigger surprises.

All love,
Bob

P.S. – We thought you would like to have this reprint of one of the best Christmas snapshots. Auntie Bussie liked nothing better than to hold Robin, and Robin didn't complain!

February 14, 1956
Hamden, Connecticut

Chickasaw, Alabama
Dearest family,

We celebrated Valentine's Day and Robin's first birthday last Saturday. She was cute and so very well-behaved during dinner. Bob's folks joined us ... and everyone practically inhaled my good ol' Southern fried chicken! The festive red-and-white heart-shaped cake I made wasn't bad, either.

Robin and I entertained again this afternoon with a little tea party for four of the young mothers and their toddlers in the neighborhood. What a shindig! One of the more aggressive party-goers persisted in trying to hit Robin, so very soon the birthday miss was tired of the whole blamed scene and went to bed, where she stayed, happily, till everyone left!

But oh my, the other kids (all about 15 or 16 months old) really had a great time. They ate, dropped, squashed and trampled cookies, climbed up and down the stairs, scaring us half to death, spilled the trash cans all over the floor, and fought over toys without letup, during which bedlam we mommies were wiping up messes, refereeing toy tugs of war, trying to keep our tea cups balanced, chatting, and all in all having a grand get-together!

So excited about seeing y'all soon! Our flight arrives in Mobile early, at 6 a.m. on Sunday, February 26.

All our love,
Pat, Bob and Robin

P.S. – Remember the story from my visit with Bob's folks in early 1954 when we went to see "Motorama" and I sort of crashed the party – had no engraved invitation – but quickly found myself shaking hands with the president of General Motors? Well, that same Mr. Harlow Curtice was named *Time* Magazine's "Person of the Year" for 1955. Neat, huh?

April 24, 1956
Hamden, Connecticut

Chickasaw, Alabama
Dearest family,

It's just after 7 p.m. and as I told Bob, I could be asleep in five minutes if I leaned my head back. Wish I weren't so sleepy so early every night. I want to get this letter written, there are graduation and baby presents to wrap for mailing, and I try to do at least a few rows of needlepoint each evening so I can finish the vanity stool cover this year.

So good to talk to y'all Friday – I'll be glad when Robin will say something to you on the phone. Speaking of phones, our bill was really high last month with the calls between Bob and me while I was in Alabama. He said they were worth the $18 charge, though.

We went next door Saturday evening and I was looking forward to playing Scrabble or cards as had been suggested but we just watched television. There's no getting away from it, so disappointing. I think when we invite those neighbors to our house, I just won't permit the TV set to be turned on. So there!

Recently I called the Spring Glen Congregational Church to ask about nursery arrangements and the times of services. A few days later when the young minister came to call, the three of us were in for a surprise. His father is the pastor of the church in Waterbury that Bob's folks attended for more than 20 years!

We really liked him and the sound of the various church activities, and went for the first time Sunday. The minister, nicknamed Bucky, and his wife Kay welcomed us, helped get Robin situated, and introduced us all around. Robin was great in her first experience in a nursery. She played happily there and then went down for a long nap as soon as we got home. I think

109

there's no question we'll join the church – the Good Lord was probably as pleased as we were over such a successful Sunday!

Crazy weather again … we woke up to rain which soon turned to snow and ice, and that was on April 23. Everyone is pretty sick of wintry weather, but it'll probably be another month before we can turn off the heat and put away the coats. Oh, for that day I'm a-longing!

Bob has tentatively scheduled part of his vacation for the last week of August through the day after Labor Day, thinking that might be the time y'all will be able to come up. Hope it works out. …

Daddy, it's great that you are enjoying and doing so well in your correspondence course studies to become a real estate broker. And, John-boy, have a fun 15th birthday.

Much love and many hugs and kisses to Mom, Daddy, John, and Rickey.

Pat, Bob and Robin

2 May 1956
Camp Chickamauga, Japan

Chickasaw, Alabama
Dear Folks,

Sorry I haven't written in so long. Just lazy, I guess, plus the fact that I was on leave from 18 April till yesterday. I spent it in Tokyo. It's magnificent, grandiose to say the least. And I'm so financially wasted that if ducks were five cents a gross, I couldn't buy a quack. But it was worth twice what I left there.

The way I figure it, you folks had better not prepare yourself for a visit from me until possibly next year. No leave time.

The trip back to the States will take one month from the time we leave here until we reach Fort Campbell.

I am surprised to hear Dad is working nights now, but if he gets his rest and sleeps daily, it should work out OK.

Love,
Sammie

15 May 1956
Camp Chickamauga, Japan

Chickasaw, Alabama
Dear Folks,

This will probably be short, so don't be disappointed. Am in what I think to be great health although I only eat about one meal a day. I can't seem to gain any weight.

Am enclosing a few pictures. Those of the mountains and the festival were taken just before we went to Tokyo. The others about a week ago.

Well, it's raining tonight for about the eighth day straight. The rainy season has started early. I don't mind, though – fact is, I love it.

Sure hope this letter finds all of you in good health. Please remember, folks, that when I don't write there is nothing wrong and I'm not being inconsiderate. I've been working so steady since my return from Tokyo I've hardly seen sunlight after 7:30 a.m. and before 4:30 p.m. except through the window.

Next time you write Pat, tell her that although I don't write, still I think of her.

Mom, I hope you had a wonderful Mother's Day. I'm really sorry I couldn't send flowers.

Love,
Sammie

27 May 1956
Camp Chickamauga, Japan

Chickasaw, Alabama
Dear Dad,

I sure hope this letter finds you the picture of health that all the letters maintain you as being in. Whew, that was a tricky sentence. Also I hope you find this scribble easier to read than previous letters.

I'm very anxious to see you and your crew cut. I know you're wooing the women. You cad, you. Did you give up the mustache as a futile project?

To say that I'm proud of you in the way you've come along in your job is a gross understatement. I'll be looking forward to talking to you about exactly what the job consists of. All my ideas are very vague.

Maybe you would like a few details of my job. First remember that this is a small post of about 2,400 personnel. Well, every payday we issue about $280,000 to $300,000, and then for the next 29 or 30 days before the next payday I take back in all but about $5,000 to $15,000.

Of course, I have lots of humorous anecdotes to relate. One very busy day last month, about 1:30 in the afternoon when I was tired, nervous and strung tighter than a high wire, a woman approached my window, where there are signs stating "Buy Treasury checks here" and "Treasury checks sold here." The woman asked me, "Can I buy a treasury check?"

"Yes, you can buy a check here, Ma'am," I replied.

"For 600 dollars?" she asked.

"You sure can if you have 600 dollars in currency, Ma'am."

Whereupon she proceeded to pile 60 ten-dollar bills on the ledge of the window. Each one was folded individually in half. They made a stack just about 18 inches high.

I lit and smoked one-half a cigarette before she fished them all out of her carryall purse.

> Your honorable Son No. 1,
> Sammie

June 3, 1956
Hamden, Connecticut

Chickasaw, Alabama
Dearest family,

I'm so excited after the phone visit with all of you while you were at Aunt Inez's. In fact, the call brought me much closer to you, and I didn't want to put off writing another minute. I wanted to chat longer than the three minutes we could afford but writing is the next best thing. I still wish I could snap my fingers and join y'all at the little family reunion in Mississippi. Remember how much I used to love spending a couple of weeks in Quitman with Aunt Inez in the summer?

We really enjoyed your letter this week, Mommie, and also talking to you the other night, Daddy and Rickey. Oh, Rickey, honey, I loved your letter, too. I'm going to save it and show it to you when you're about 20, okay? I know how much you like swimming but I can't believe you can dive now. I keep forgetting what a big boy you are.

Mommie, I'm so excited about the new developments on Sammie. I would love to read his letters. You've sounded so much happier lately, and I'm sure this has something to do with it. Do you think he really is in love or is it more likely a passing phase? I'm going to write him a letter tonight.

I wish you could see the little missy right now. For the past 15 minutes, she has been sitting in the middle of the floor with a *Good Housekeeping* magazine spread across her lap, turning each page so carefully, occasionally making a comment on a certain picture. I usually give Robin all the mail we're finished with, too, since she loves to read a "leh-ah!" She also likes the phone. Last night out of the blue, she put her toy telephone to her ear and said, "Alo, Alo … okay … okay," pausing between words just as if she were listening to what the other party had to say.

We were sorry to hear you're on the night shift again, Daddy-dear. We thought that was all behind you and hope it won't last long this time. You certainly are having busy days, Mommie, in your new job selling Stanley Products, plus freezing fruits and vegetables, and the scads of other chores always waiting to be done. Woman's work is *never* done, right?

Forgot to tell you, next month Bob's parents are going to stay with us two weeks, until the house they've rented in Hartford is available. We're all looking forward to it.

All our love,
Pat, Bob and Robin

6 June 1956
Camp Chickamauga, Japan

Chickasaw, Alabama
Dear Folks,

To get off-post, one must wear a suit, full dress (tie, etc.), or Class A's with necktie and scarf. This wouldn't have been quite so bad a few months ago, but now in 90-degree weather, with 95 percent humidity, it just doesn't quite get it. Also it wouldn't be so bad in the big city, but here in this town, there are only two business establishments and both of them are restaurants.

I want out! Only 18 months and 28 days to go.

I received your letter, Mom. I'm very, very glad that we now, in more ways, understand ourselves and each other better. I'm also tremendously proud of you, Mom.

About the girl I met and fell for in Tokyo while I was on leave, I realized about three weeks after I got back that I had to forget it. It couldn't be worked out practically, and I had to start getting some sleep and nutrition. So that's all there was to it.

Well, I begin my trek to the land of the big P.X. (the WORLD) in a mere 36 days. And I should be in the green hills of Fort Campbell, Kentucky, in a mere 53 days. It's a great day. Raining like heck. And I feel terrific.

See you soon,
Sammie

8 June 1956
Camp Chickamauga, Japan

Chickasaw, Alabama

Dear Rickey,

Well, I guess by now you had given up any hope of getting a letter from me. I'm sorry it's been so long.

You must have been out of school for about a week now. I'll bet it's great loafing around. I know since I did it myself a very short while ago.

Say, boy, you're coming along splendidly in writing. The notes and the letter from you were very good. And they were greatly appreciated. Please write me again. I'd like a couple of sketches or drawings from you in the next letter. How is Tartar doing these days? Nobody mentions him anymore.

I haven't been swimming yet. It just got warm enough a few days ago. I also haven't jumped in ages, since the day before I left for Tokyo. But I should blast next week. Most probably between torrents of tropical rain.

Where are you planning to spend your vacation this summer?

The boss just came in so I'd better get to work.

Sammie

10 June 1956
Camp Chickamauga, Japan

Hamden, Connecticut

Dear Sis,

I wonder if the weather is one half as beautiful there as it is here. I'm speaking of today only, of course. Tomorrow torrents, no less, of rain will be released by the heavens to drench us poor mortals.

I received your letter today. Boy, I can't wait to see your Robin. She sounds every inch a doll. I'll begin my trek home in 33 days. As much as I hate to do it, I can't resist counting days.

While I'm thinking about it, the pictures enclosed were taken last week, unposed, in the last stages of a hard day at the office, that being "balancing out."

When I started this letter I thought I'd be able to write something long and informative because I felt unusually prolific. Now all I can think of is how much I want to be a civilian, see you and your family, see the folks, and start something constructive and future-ative (I don't know if Webster's lists this word or not).

I sure wish you could meet the girl I met while I was in Tokyo. Did I mention that?

I should be in Fort Campbell on or about 1 August.
I'm sorry, but this is all.

Sammie

22 June 1956
Camp Chickamauga, Japan

Chickasaw, Alabama
Dear Folks,

This is the last letter I will be able to answer in awhile. Mail to our division will be forwarded to Fort Campbell on or after the third of July. Got a request, Mom. Would you please call the airline agencies in town and find out the cheapest one-way rates from Mobile to New Haven? I want to go visit Pat. Not during my leave next month, of course, because we will have so much catching up to do in Alabama, but maybe in November.

Well, I guess you'all had better start stocking up on your steaks, pork chops, turnips, wine, tomatoes, corn pone and cucumbers (if I were a female I would think I was pregnant the way I eat 'em) because I'll be at the old homestead in a couple of months.

Rickey, I just received your letter and it was a very good one. The news of your grades was no surprise – I had figured all along they'd be good.

By the time I get home, I'll expect you to have mastered swimming. Think you'll do it? According to my calculations, you should be 9 years old in October, right? How much do you weigh now?

I've got to get this in the mail in 10 minutes so I had better close.

Just Sammie

August 1, 1956
Hamden, Connecticut

Chickasaw, Alabama
My dearest Mommie, Daddy, Sam, John and Rickey,

Couldn't resist writing *all* your names this time because I assume you are together again! Sammie, we were tickled to get the telegram yesterday announcing your arrival in the United States and the plans for your five days' leave. From the three of us, a great big WELCOME HOME. It's wonderful to have you back in this country!

We love you all so much and are getting plumb excited over seeing you soon!

Pat, Bob and Robin

August 29, 1956
Hamden, Connecticut

Chickasaw, Alabama
My dearest family,

We can't wait to hear what kind of flight you had back to Mobile last night. Hope it was smooth and that no one feels too down today.

Our drive home from La Guardia Airport was a lot shorter than your flight to Alabama, but I hope y'all didn't run into trouble like we did. Wow, it was a mess – and the only good part was that it helped me not to cry for a while! As soon as we left the airport, we noticed a lot of what at first seemed to be heat lightning, but after another few miles the closer and closer vivid flashes, accompanied by violent crashes of thunder, became terrifying, and the clouds just burst wide open. It rained so hard we couldn't see well enough to pull off, and since some nutty people didn't want to stop we couldn't just idle there in the middle of the road. Luckily, about the time the brakes were giving away completely, we were able to spot a place to stop on the side of the parkway. We stayed there about 15 minutes until the rain let up a little, and then started out again, *very* slowly, headed for home. We arrived safely at 11 o'clock, thankful, weary and ready for bed.

I haven't really boo-hooed since you left. But I also haven't been without that grapefruit-size lump in my throat, the one holding a bucket of unshed tears. Oh, it's *awful* not to have y'all here still. I think having to say goodbye this time was worse than ever before. I'm not sure I'll be okay again even by *next* week

Pat, Bob and Robin

September 8, 1956
Hamden, Connecticut

Chickasaw, Alabama
My dearest family,

Today feels very Septemberish, and you know how nostalgic I get in the fall. I was interested in a recent newspaper article about "autumn fever" and how it tends to cause some people to wish they could be someone, or somewhere, else. Anyway, it's cool and sunny – and my honey is outside getting yard chores done.

Mommie, your long letter came yesterday and after I thoroughly enjoyed it Bob read it and remarked what a wonderful, newsy one it was. Letters sure do give a lift to the spirit, don't they? Oh, and thanks for the compliment that I write good letters … your comment that one of these days I would " roll out from between the pages" was so cute!

A few weeks ago I told Bob how much I've missed friends just casually stopping by for short visits like they do in the South. Well, lo and behold, wouldn't you know that since then it seems we've had people literally "dropping in" from the skies? Honestly, it's the dadgummedest thing – and I love it!

On Thursday, Mother Kitty, Auntie Bussie, and Dave and Joni came for lunch with Robin and me, and that evening they and Bob and I went out to dinner. We had a wonderful time. It was great to see Auntie again, and she so enjoyed the time with family. Soon after they arrived she walked outside to look at the landscaping and Robin looked up at me with a frown and a slightly demanding, "*Where* Bussie go?" You can guess how that tickled Auntie Bussie. Everyone is still in agreement, Robin is a doll!

Ever so much love,
Pat, Bob and Robin

September 17, 1956
University of Pennsylvania
Philadelphia, Pennsylvania

Hamden, Connecticut

Pat dear,

Would you be interested in becoming a "case"? The University has given me a small grant to pay 21 mothers $25 apiece for their materials to help me with a study of the functions of the modern American mother. You know, the books all say they have so many efficiency gadgets and ready-prepared foods that they really don't do much but relax! So, I am trying to get factual day-by-day accounts of what some mothers really do.

I will send participants a notebook in which they will write a diary-like list of their days' activities (roughly hour by hour) for two weeks, from October 22 to November 5. This should take 15 to 30 minutes a day. Along with the notebook will be sent a questionnaire, which should take about 15 minutes to fill out. There is nothing of a private nature in the questionnaire except an income question. If you think this too personal, leave it blank. Upon receipt of notebook and questionnaire, we mail out the check.

I do hope you can do this. I know how busy you are, but our chief problem is that the mothers who do the most don't have the time to tell us what they do. That's one reason why what the books say is so warped.

Much love,
Auntie Bussie

September 19, 1956
Hamden, Connecticut

Chickasaw, Alabama
Dear Folks,

As I write this I am watching President Eisenhower give the first of his campaign speeches on TV. Certainly is a sincere man! And he sure seems convinced that he can live through another four years in the White House. Hope he's right. … Pat and I will register in Town Hall a week from Saturday. This will be the first presidential vote for your daughter.

Pat's out tonight at a meeting of the Hamden Women's Club. If she likes it, I guess she can join. But with all her activities lately, I don't know if she can take it on.

These are busy days for me in the office. Can't quite keep up with all the work they're throwing at me. But I know I'd rather have it that way than have too little to do.

It seemed awfully lonely around here after you left. I don't have to tell you how much we enjoyed having you with us. We did thoroughly enjoy your visit. I think everything went very smoothly indeed. We were all so impressed with John, in particular, for the way he has turned into a fine young gentleman.

Hope you had as good a time in the North as we did in having you here. And I look forward to the day when we can have another such visit.

You have company as far as letter-writing goes, Pop. I'm a real bum correspondent, I'm sorry to say. This is the first letter I've written in many months!

With that I'll say goodnight. Thanks again for your visit. We love you, think of you a great deal, and hope your days continue to be full of happiness and good luck.

Love,
Bob

October 12, 1956
Chickasaw, Alabama

Hamden, Connecticut
Dear Sis, Bob and Robin,

Thanks a lot for writing so often, Pat, I sure 'preciate it. Sorry I don't answer more often.

I am very much surprised at you, Sis. Here the boy has been halfway around the world and back and you are worried about his taking a 100-mile jaunt on his own. Of course I can manage easily and will not mind if

118

you're not present at my arrival in New York. I stand a good chance of not arriving until Monday morning anyway. Just be sure that anytime you're away from the house Sunday or Monday, you leave a way I can enter, a fire in the hearth, and food in the fridge!

Incidentally, what's the temperature in that there part of the hills nowadays? And what do you think it will be next month?

Love,
Sammie

October 22, 1956
Hamden, Connecticut

Prichard, Alabama
My dearest family,

7:00-7:10, got up, went to bathroom; 7:10-7:30, got breakfast; 7:30-7:40, got Robin up and dressed; 7:40-8:00, ate breakfast and helped feed Robin; 8:00-8:15, washed dishes – yep, that's what I'm doing every day for the next two weeks. You remember Auntie's survey of young mothers – well, the material came Saturday. Of course, I don't have a single dental or medical appointment, or many busy evenings this week, but I'll guarantee you I can still fill up that notebook for Auntie Bussie and prove that mothers do have *quite* a bit to do, even with all the fancy appliances in this fast, modern world.

Robin update: Lately she has been using her own name a lot – for instance, she'll hand me something and say "take deese sings away for Wobin," or, in reverse, "give dose sings to Wobin." Another phrase, used to explain scads of different things – she'll say "Wobin hab a hat on, Mommy hab no hat, Daddy hab no hat" and on and on for everybody around. Same thing about "Daddy go to work, Wobin no go to work, Mommy no go to work." (I don't GO to work, maybe!) These days she wants to tell everything in great detail. And what a lark to hear her sing Doris Day's "Que Sera Sera" – "Kay sa wa, sa wa, whatta will BE," holding that last note.

We had her baptized yesterday. She was utterly intrigued with the baptismal rite, her only misgivings being during the prayer. She doesn't like Mommy silent, with closed eyes. So when I prayed, she started reaching out to me from Bob, saying "Mommy?" in a very concerned voice. I took her then – and the prayer ended about the same time – so everything was fine again. She looked adorable in a new pink corduroy dress adorned with delicate little embroidered flowers in front and a saucy sash in back.

We send lots of love,
Pat, Bob and Robin

October 23, 1956
Chickasaw, Alabama

Hamden, Connecticut
Dear Pat, Bob and Robin,

I do my homework at school. We have four things to do – spelling-arithmetic-languages-sinces. Me and a boy named Richard make the same grades in arithmetic.

I guess you know Murphy football team has beat Vigor wolves all these years. But this year Vigor wolves beat Murphy 18 to 6. It was a happy day for Vigor.

Tell Robin I hope her and Sammie have a grand time.

With all my love,
Rickey

October 31, 1956
Hamden, Connecticut

Chickasaw, Alabama
Dear Mommie, Daddy, John and Rickey,

I've got the television on right now, listening to a report on the trouble in the Middle East. Oh, I'm so scared of what might happen. I do wish it could be settled before things get worse. Our neighbor from Israel is frantic because her parents are there, and her two brothers who are in the army, and she doesn't know what's happening to any of them. How I count my blessings when I think of her. I miss y'all so much, but I do know that you are safe and not in a country where there's fighting.

Update on Robin: Lately, for any small accident of mine, like bumping into a chair, she runs over to pat the "injury" and kiss me, then turns that little head practically upside down to look right in my face and ask sympathetically, "Feel all better?" She reminds me of how little Rickey always soothed me when I was sick or had hurt myself. I'll never forget his way of taking care of me by gently powdering my feet. Remember how seriously he took that responsibility and how precious he was?

Robin still amazes not only the family but others wherever she goes. … Last night at a church meeting, a lady who sees Robin in the nursery said to me in front of the group "Pat has a genius in Robin. That little one is *so* bright and speaks more distinctly than any toddler you've ever heard." I beamed … of course!

120

Right now Robin is "habing a tea party" and it's time for me to take my place as her guest. By the way, Bob's parents and Auntie Bussie loved their pictures of the boys.

All our love,
Pat, Bob and Robin

November 6, 1956
Hamden, Connecticut

Prichard, Alabama

Dearest Mommie, Daddy, John and Rickey,

Well, here we sit, Bob and I *and* Sammie, listening to the election returns, and it looks like "Ike" is going in again. I know you've been eager to hear that Sambo is actually here with us. Right now he is lying on the floor on his tummy practically at my feet and seems to be enjoying life. We're certainly enjoying him!

It was wonderful talking to y'all Friday night and sure enough, we did start looking for Sammie early Saturday. Although we didn't know it then, we still had quite a wait. By Sunday afternoon, after going to church, doing some work and taking a walk, we were really getting anxious for him to arrive.

All Sunday evening we expected a call that he was somewhere near, needing to be picked up. But no call came so we went to bed at 11 o'clock. The next morning I woke around 6, restless, and suddenly sat up in bed, not sure exactly what had startled me. I waited a minute, nothing happened, lay down again. The next instant there was a loud sound from below – and in a wink I knew, and said to Bob, "I bet that's Sammie trying to wake us up!" I jumped out of bed, opened the window … saw Sam looking up at me. The poor guy got to New Haven about 4 a.m. but wouldn't come to the house and disturb us till 6.

Of course, I had planned to look real sharp when I saw Sam after almost a year and a half, and instead looked pretty much like a wilted weed, I'm sure, sleepy-eyed with messy, uncombed hair. Nobody cared, though, because it was just wonderful to welcome him at last. Bob soon came downstairs and we had a few minutes to talk over breakfast before he was off to work.

Earlier, when Robin woke up, Sam had gone upstairs with us to get her and she started to cry, but three minutes later (and I'm not exaggerating) she was in his arms, coaching her beloved stuffed toy: "Kitty, say halo at Sammie!" Since then the little missy has been in his arms, in his lap or right at his heels practically every minute she's awake. She *really* is enjoying her Uncle Sam.

We haven't done much but talk so far, but I want to get something perking soon so Sam won't get bored. The only definite plan we have now is to go to Bob's parents' house for dinner and a visit Friday, leave Robin there for the weekend, and go into New York City early Saturday. As it stands now, Sam may stay over in New York a couple more days before heading south again, but we'll come back home that evening.

Daddy, we were tickled to hear about your raise, it sounds wonderful! Hope y'all are getting along fine in every way these days, all four of you. Sam may write tomorrow, he said – and he sends his love. We send buckets of ours, too.

Pat, Bob and Robin

November 11, 1956
Hamden, Connecticut

Chickasaw, Alabama

My dearest family,

I ought to be crawling into bed right this minute but decided to at least start a letter. Sambo has taken our favorite baby sitter to the movies again. They went last week, too – Sam says she's a pretty nice date. She's the sister of our back-door neighbor who works at the telephone company with Bob. Sam and Bob and I are planning to eat dinner out and go to a movie Tuesday night. Hope nothing comes up to change those plans since Wednesday morning Sam will be going to New York to spend the rest of his leave.

What a conversation we all had Friday night, huh? Boy, that was a scream – I don't think everybody knew what was going on half the time, but it was fun talking to you just the same!

On election night we sat up till 2 a.m. listening to the results. So, Dwight D. Eisenhower is the next U.S. president – and I helped to elect him with my first-time-ever vote! Are y'all pleased with the outcome?

The sitter kept Robin Thursday while Sam and I went into New Haven so I could take the driving test, which I passed with flying colors, thank you very much! I scored 100 percent on the written test. Since then I've driven quite a bit and am not as nervous as usual.

What a character Sam is. The other day, sporting his good-looking new glasses to correct his nearsightedness, he was so funny in his amazement at how much better he sees, especially looking at girls.

122

Robin has had a fever for a couple of days. We still don't know the cause, and I'll call the doctor if she doesn't bounce back to her perky self in another day or two.

We love you all ever, ever so much, Mommie, Daddy, John and Rickey.

Pat, Bob, Robin and Sam

December 5, 1956
Hamden, Connecticut

Chickasaw, Alabama
Dearest Folks,

Friday morning we got up, got packed, dressed, gathered all manner of stuff and took Robin and all the baggage to Hartford to stay with Bob's parents. After lunch at a drive-in near here, we actually got started on the four-hour trip to Auntie Bussie's in Devon. We arrived around 4:30 and from that minute till we left Sunday noon we enjoyed ourselves so very much. I can't wait to visit her again! Honestly, we could see she just ate it up, having family visit in her own little home.

Of course, we hardly saw Auntie Saturday since we left at 10 a.m. to go into Philadelphia and meet Al and Sarah for the game, and we didn't get back to Devon until 5:45. It was a real thrill to see the Army-Navy game and the parades of cadets and midshipmen before it started, but jeepers, it was cold. I was dressed in layers of warm clothing and still freezing – my poor frozen feet had absolutely not one speck of feeling in them by the time we left the stadium.

Dr. Jim made a special trip out to Auntie Bussie's to meet us Sunday morning and we were tickled over that. He is quite a character, and we both adored him. One of his and Auntie's new books is not the usual textbook but will be sold in regular bookstores. The title is *One Marriage, Two Faiths* – sounds interesting, I want to read it.

Ever so much love,
Pat, Bob and Robin

December 5, 1956
Devon, Pennsylvania

Hartford, Connecticut
Sister dear,

Although I know I can't tell you any news – you will have heard it all from the kids – I just can't help but write a note to tell you how very thoroughly I have enjoyed your family these past two weekends. I've been telling you for years what wonderful boys you have in Bob and Dave, but I never quite appreciated how absolutely unique they are. Frankly, I'm nuts about them. They've both got everything and are the best companions. I'm so proud of them I could burst, and I don't know how you can stand it.

And that little Pat! I'm afraid you'll just have to send her back here. I can't get along without her. Next to you, she is just the nicest little lady in the world to have around. She fits in like fingers in a glove.

When they drove away, I felt as if half my heart were being torn out. It is a good thing Dr. Jim was here. He mopped up a few tears and got me to thinking about something else or I would probably have indulged myself in a period of self-pity.

Jim was really smitten with Bob and Pat. I know him too well for him to fool me. He said he would have expected anyone in our family to be nice but that he had not been prepared for what he saw. Among other things, he remarked on Bob's beautiful eyes (and Pat and I had just been discussing them) and said Bob was a young man he'd gamble 100 percent on in business, friendship or anything else as being completely dependable. And, of course, Pat had Dr. Jim wrapped right around her little finger. Now, why wasn't *I* born and reared in the South?

With much love,
Bussie

December 13, 1956
Hamden, Connecticut

Chickasaw, Alabama
Dearest Folks,

The other day I took Robin in for an appointment with our wonderful pediatrician – I often think I couldn't raise her without his care of her and comfort to me. While we were in the waiting room everyone was intrigued, listening to our little miss who was talking to beat the band. Among other conversational gems, she told a petite elderly lady, "Next to me, my Mommy yikes Tide keen coes " – you know, Tide clean clothes, from that TV commercial? The lady was amazed, especially when she asked Robin's age and discovered that she wasn't even 2 years old.

Anyway, Robin did still have red ears, but the doctor didn't prescribe an antibiotic when I told him she seemed much better that day. She's a little "getting-into-trouble gal" now, so I guess she's almost well. He did give me some cream for her skin, which is still inclined to eczema, itchy and so dry. Growth report: she weighs 24½ pounds and is 32½ inches tall.

When I left, he said to me very nicely and calmly, "Now, Mother, you can't train that baby till she gets ready, you can't *make* her eat or drink more, you can't *make* her gain weight, and so forth – so just relax and enjoy life. She's *all right!*" See what I mean about his being a comfort?

All our love,
Pat, Bob and Robin

December 20, 1956
Hamden, Connecticut

Chickasaw, Alabama
My dearest family,

Wonder of wonders, it isn't quite 7 o'clock and here I am already beginning a letter, having finished with supper, the dishes, packing Bob's lunch for tomorrow, and putting Robin to bed. I like evenings like this, when I have a little extra time and can really relax. Of course, I'll probably have to stop soon for a cup of coffee or I'll have relaxed into an unthinking blob of protoplasm!

Your box arrived today and the gifts are ready to go under the tree – when we get a tree. All the gaily wrapped presents sure do look interesting – thank you!

How I loved talking to y'all last week. Please forgive me, though, for seeming to put a damper on your excitement over Daddy's new job, but the news was so unexpected. It really does sound like a wonderful opportunity, and I can't believe that at last, Daddy, you will get to sit at a desk and tell somebody else how to do the work. That's been my dream for you for ages, and we're really happy about it. Of course, I'm not kidding myself, I'm sure as manager of so many apartments and houses, there will be plenty of work and problems, too. But the important thing is you'll probably be happier at this type of job than some you've had in the past. And I know you'll be good at it.

Last Friday I spent the whole day in the kitchen baking one of the famous Japanese fruitcakes and preparing 52 meatballs and a bushel of sauce for a dinner party the next evening. We had invited two couples who are especially fun and a good time was had by all. After dinner we were in hysterics, most of the time talking about funny incidents involving, or revolving around, having babies.

Merry, Merry Christmas, y'all – and to all a goodnight!

Your loving children,
Pat, Bob and Robin

December 27, 1956
Hamden, Connecticut

Chickasaw, Alabama
My dearest family,

First I want to say how sorry we were to miss talking with and saying "Merry Christmas" to Daddy and the boys last Friday night, but we did love the phone visit with you, Mommie. It bothered me all Christmas Day that I had forgotten to ask how y'all planned to spend the 25th and I couldn't picture what you were doing. So, we'll look forward to hearing all about your holiday. Was Santa good to everybody? Did you like your presents, Rickey?

Thank you for all of ours. Everyone liked everything! And here's a sweet story to convey Robin's appreciation. Just before naptime, I told her she could try on the two "bew-ful" dresses you made for her, Mom. I wish you could've been watching as she stood still and let me put on her petticoat and fuss ever so much with the blue dress. When I finished she said, "Take me mirrow, let me see how poor-ty." We walked to my full-length mirror where she looked at herself, smiled really big and held her hands out just so, turned first one way, then the other, reveling in her own beautiful reflection.

With the coral dress it was the same, and then she asked to "tie on 'nother dress." I told her there weren't any more and she said, "Apper supper, we can tie on dress, okay?" That was funny to me because that's what she'll say when she wants candy or cookies and I've said no. Without fail, it's, "apper supper we hab a candy, okay?" So you see how she loves the dresses – they're in the same category as candy!

Now, I've saved some news till last. I bet if I gave you three chances, you'd guess what it is. ... You may be grandparents again sometime next summer! I am already having waves of nausea, with that dark look around the eyes I get when I don't feel up to par. In fact, during our holiday visit with Bob's folks his mother said, "When you walked in the door, Pat, I knew by your eyes that you must be pregnant." That observation, plus the firm refusal of my favorite grapefruit sections for breakfast Christmas morning, and a more formal announcement was hardly needed! We also had planned two break-the-news gifts: a little book titled *Blessed Event* to Bob from me, and from the two of us to Robin, *The New Baby,* with a request that Auntie Bussie help her open it. Seeing the title Auntie admitted with a chuckle, "The minute I saw Pat Monday when I got into the car, I had my suspicions!"

So … another precious baby on the way, due almost exactly 2½ years after Robin. *Good* news, huh?

All our love,
Pat, Bob Robin (and … ?)

Chapter Eight
A Little Laughter
1957

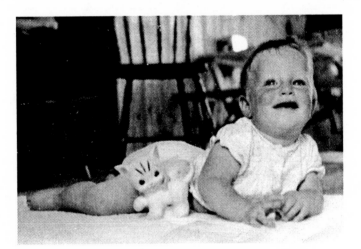

Jenni and kitty toy

January 3, 1957
Hamden, Connecticut

Chickasaw, Alabama

Dear Mom, Pop, John and Rickey,

I guess Pat will be going to the doctor soon to see if we are really to be parents again – and you, grandparents and uncles. We're very excited because we were beginning to wonder. We're both eager to have another baby. The most we can expect and hope for is another as perfect as Robin. (A boy this time, of course!)

The holiday season is over and it's quite a letdown. In one stretch I had five days off, worked two days and then had four days off. But now I have to settle down to the work ahead. Back in the Naval Academy we used to call these months between New Year's Day and springtime the "Dark Ages." Maybe it won't be so bad, though.

Thanks for all your thoughtful gifts to the three of us this Christmas – good choices!

Much love,
Bob

January 8, 1957
Hamden, Connecticut

Chickasaw, Alabama

My dearest folks,

Little widget Robin is asleep and I probably should be taking a nap, but I've just got to stay awake long enough to write a letter.

I had everything all ready to write last night at 7:30, and, well, I just couldn't. I was so sleepy and lay down on the couch – heard Bob say, as he put a blanket over me, "Oh dear, it's exactly like last time." I certainly can't complain much, though, because I really have easy pregnancies – just a tired feeling much of the time, sleepy *all the time*, and waves of nausea and dizziness.

Well, looking at the enclosed newspaper clipping and photo … how do you like having a celebrity in the family? Remember when y'all were here Bob began that big job involving a new type of phone service of Southern New England Telephone & Telegraph Company. The Station Equipment section of the engineering department developed the emergency telephone call box system described in the article for the City of New Haven. It's nice recognition for Bob's good work as the project manager.

Last evening Bob said, "Why don't you read the paper now, honey?" I had a couple of things to do and told him I'd read it later. You know me,

129

sometimes it takes a bomb-like explosion to make me catch on. ... By the time I finally picked up the paper, Bob had finished his chores and was sitting nearby to watch for my reaction. He said later he thought I was deliberately teasing him since I looked at all the other sections of the paper first, finally picked up "the one" – which he had carefully placed on top to begin with! – read every page but the important one, and then every article on that page before at last discovering his picture. When I saw it I didn't say a word, just looked up to find him grinning to beat the band. He had already shown it to Robin, who recognized him immediately – "Is dat Daddy?"

We had three inches of snow Sunday, which hasn't melted yet. And I still get madder'n old Dan Tucker over the dressing-for-outdoors routine required every time we venture out. One of the neighbors called this morning with an invitation for coffee, and to go just down the street meant getting dressed in the approximately 25 items of clothing needed for Robin and me in this weather. For Robin there are cumbersome snow pants, boots, jacket, scarf, hat and gloves – she can hardly walk when everything is finally on. And just to make it a bit more of a challenge, during the process of getting her little body satisfactorily stuffed into each garment, she is often either running away from me or lying on the floor kicking! I guess I'm doing okay, though, considering my Southern background and the fact that I never even *saw* a child's snowsuit or pair of boots until the winter of my 23rd year. Pray tell, how will I ever get *two* munchkins dressed? (Friends also warn me that once the kids are potty trained, it can be even more frustrating because invariably when they're all snug, snapped, tied and zippered into the snowsuit – with only the eyes still showing – they have to go pee or poop!)

You know, I had almost an obsession all day Sunday that I had to see y'all – not take a plane, I just wanted to get in the car, drive a few blocks and drop in on you. I felt sad knowing I couldn't possibly do such a thing. I pray that someday we'll live closer.

Hugs and kisses and tons of love to Mommie, Daddy, John and Rickey. Loved talking to you last week!

Pat

January 13, 1957
Hamden, Connecticut

Chickasaw, Alabama

My dearest family,

Friday morning at 7:30 the temperature here was a minus three – *three degrees below zero*! Later on, when it was somewhat warmer, I had another session of trying to hang out the laundry.

The cellar was running over with diapers, gowns, underwear, shirts, etc., plus two big wet sheets, so I decided I'd be brave and hang everything outside. Unfortunately I had started the second load of wash before I fully realized exactly what that might entail. (Actually, I'm being a bit brave right now attempting to write a coherent letter while Robin is screaming as loud as she can, about everything and nothing, and Bob and I are glaring at each other. He's annoyed with me and I'm mad at him because he won't give me any sympathy about my dislike of the cold weather!)

Anyway, back to my tale of torture. … Donning assorted layers of clothing and confronting the cold, I went out onto the back porch to get the reels at the proper place to start hanging up the sheets. The reels wouldn't budge. I tugged, I cussed, I got so-o-o cold. Finally I was able to get one to move – but the other never did. The clothesline was completely covered with ice so I ducked into the kitchen for a sponge to wipe it off – and the sponge immediately stuck to the line, frozen solid. I pried it loose, said to heck with cleanliness and laid it down on top of the milk box. When I tried to pick it up again later, it was frozen like a rock right to the box.

I reached for a sheet – well, maybe a mass of ice would be more descriptive – and began the fight to get the frozen-stiff length of muslin attached to the line. Got one corner pinned and then, guess what, the reel refused to budge. My hands were numb by this time, so I cussed some more, left that sheet hanging the best, the only, way I could manage, and came inside and practically threw the other sheet down the cellar stairs. Actually, I flung it over top of all the diapers… and it took *days* for everything to dry.

When Bob came home around dinnertime, he mentioned, quite innocently, that my sheet was still out on the line and asked why. In a few clipped words, I informed him, "Mister, as of this morning, that's *your* sheet, and if you want it inside, *you* bring it in. *I* am not touching it again while it's wet or cold!"

After the experience outside with the laundry, I was so upset I was shaking like a leaf. It seems nothing but the cold, ice and snowstorms can make me get so frustrated and angry, and that makes me dislike them even more.

But I'm all right again now. I've had a chance to spout off, Robin is playing contentedly, and I'm ready to start preparing dinner. *Thanks* for listening. …

Always,
Pat, Bob and Robin

January 18, 1957
Hamden, Connecticut

Chickasaw, Alabama
Dearest family,

Decided not to use the typewriter today because not for anything do I want to risk waking up little missy, oh no. She has led me on a merry chase all morning and I need this peace and quiet, believe me.

While still fresh in my mind, let me tell you a few of her latest acts of mischief. She now climbs everywhere – today I've brought her down from the kitchen table and from the little desk, where she was stranded after the chair she'd used for climbing had slipped out of her reach. She has poured borax into the roasting pan, taken labels off some cans, and unwrapped all the chewing gum she found in a drawer. After scolding her, I was dusting and straightening the drawer and she walked over to me and, with a mighty scowl, warned, "You heah me, I *told* you, don't bodder dat."

Yesterday when I caught her just as she lifted a foot to climb from the chair to the kitchen table, my stern look and firm "Robin, I said NO" brought only her prompt retort, "But I say YES." We went back and forth a bit, and I continued, "Robin, I am the boss and I said NO, and I *mean* it." She, as prissily as could be, with even a little wiggle of the fanny, said, "I de boss, I say YES!" I'm assuming we've hit the "Terrible Twos" – what am I going to do with her?

Now for the latest news. Over the weekend I had some "spotting" and an awful backache. Early Monday morning I called the doctor who ordered at least a couple of days of bed rest. What a blow. Bob's mother dropped everything and came, and I stayed in bed, except for trips to the bathroom, from Monday noon till Wednesday, when I began doing light chores. I was weak from just those two days of inactivity but wanted to get back on my feet so Mother Kitty could go home, where her "boys," Dad and Dave, were about to go crazy without her. The doctor advised me to take it easy until he examines me next week to see what's going on and whether or not I am actually pregnant. So don't worry, I'll be well taken care of – and I really feel okay.

Time to sign off writing. Robin is piling toys on top of me and I can hardly see what I'm doing!

>We love you all so very much.
>Pat, Bob and Robin

>January 28, 1957
>Devon, Pennsylvania

Suffield, Connecticut
Sister dear,

I was sort of worried over the news about Pat. I sure hope everything has settled down by now and that she is taking good care of herself. Do tell her I'm looking forward very much to having a grandnephew or another grandniece and don't want it put off! Let me know about her, will you?

I'm going shopping for Robin's birthday. I can hardly believe she is nearly 2! I just hate the way time flies. Before we know it, Dave will be having babies.

Take care of yourself and I'll be seeing you at the wedding in only a few weeks now. Is Dave getting nervous?

>With love to you all,
>Bussie

>February 16, 1957
>Hamden, Connecticut

Chickasaw, Alabama
My dearest family,

Just a few lines – oh, how hard it was to say goodbye tonight, only about five minutes ago, but I know we do have to limit the minutes of our phone conversations or our bill will be sky high.

Bob has tentatively scheduled a week of vacation April 22-26, which includes Good Friday, so we're planning our trip then if everything else works out.

I was going to write more but am so sleepy (what else is new?), I have to close this little postscript to our phone chat – and my eyes, too!

>Much love,
>Pat

February 27, 1957
Hamden, Connecticut

Chickasaw, Alabama
My dearest family,

We loved talking to y'all Sunday night but the three minutes were too short, as always! It was especially nice to find your letter in the mailbox on Monday, Mommie. It gave me such a lift. Mondays can be "blah" anyway, and this one was especially so, along with being kind of sad-like. You know, after the excitement and activity at a wedding, it's a letdown to have it all over – to everyone but the bride and groom, that is. Robin has been saying, "Day and Doni on honeymoon" and then verifying it by calling Dave and Joni on her toy telephone to ask them again.

It's time to feed my little missy, so I have to scoot. Be good. We'll talk again soon and I'll write, of course.

Pat, Bob and Robin

March 25, 1957
Hamden, Connecticut

Chickasaw, Alabama
Dearest Folks,

I hope you could understand Robin the other evening. She was a bit shy about singing over the telephone, but she can really belt out a tune around here, often even closing her eyes for emphasis.

The other night Bob called me out of the bathroom so I wouldn't miss a goody: She was patting her chest – "Look, Mommy and Daddy, my baby is wite here." We talk about her baby brother or sister but hadn't yet told her the baby is inside my tummy.

Yesterday she asked for a pencil, which she knows I am hesitant to give her, so she got an angelic look on her face and said, "Oh, Mommy, I wanna wite to Nana GeeGee." Now, could I resist *that*? But then after she scribbled on the paper, she continued her letter on the kitchen floor.

Sending loads of love to all of you.

Pat, Bob and Robin

April 6, 1957
Hamden, Connecticut

Chickasaw, Alabama
Dear Folks,

The skies opened up last night with pouring rain and lots of thunder and lightning, and this morning's surprise was a pool in the cellar. What a mess. Bob will have to set up a sump-pump to remove the water, then it'll take days to completely dry out.

The rain seemed strange after snow and ice only a couple of days before. One of my friends picked me up to go to a church group meeting the other evening, so I wasn't driving, thank goodness, but we slipped and slid all over the roads. On one hill, she had to let the car roll back three times, trying to get a better start to go all the way to the top.

I can't wait to get home to Alabama and away from this crazy weather. See you in a couple weeks.

Love,
Pat

April 21, 1957
Chickasaw, Alabama

Hamden, Connecticut
Hi, Bob honey,

Oh, I wish it had worked out that you could've come with us. Here I am in Alabama, hardly even settled, and I miss you so much already I've wanted to turn around and head back to Hamden. It's maddening, I'm forever missing loved ones!

The trip didn't continue as smoothly as it began – guess that was too good to be true. As you know, the plane took off on time at 5 o'clock, but almost immediately it developed engine trouble. We went through some long minutes of fright while heading back to La Guardia, where it seemed like about a million people were stranded because Idlewild and Newark airports had been closed due to fog. Robin was already tired and hard to hold onto as she wanted to explore, and your Pat felt pretty sorry for herself.

We were told the plane would be ready to depart in about two hours and that dinner vouchers were available. When I went to the counter to pick one up, two little ancient, sweet, scared ladies tugged on my arm to get my attention and began to ask all kinds of questions. Bless their hearts, they were confused. They had never been anywhere outside the state of Maine before and really didn't know where they were. I took them under my wing – and carrying Robin and her Kitty and Dolly, the diaper bag, my handbag ... and unborn Junior – led them to the coffee shop, settled them in, and took care of getting all of us some food. I was kept so busy there wasn't time to worry or fret!

We boarded the plane at 7:30 and waited in line another hour for our turn to take off, so we arrived in Mobile three hours late. Robin was good, she went to sleep as soon as we boarded and slept till Atlanta but was awake from there to Mobile. No doubt you can guess I'm not too fond of flying right at this moment.

Miss you and love you,
Your girls

MEMORANDUM
To: Pat
From: Bob

Tasks I Finished While You Were Gone

1) 4-21 – "Ajaxed" pencil scribblings off bathroom toilet seat.
2) 4-27 – Cut front lawn.
3) 4-27 – Wired den telephone.
4) 4-28 – Cut half back lawn.
5) 4-28 – Cleaned entire house.
6) 4-28 – Painted front and back doorsteps.
7) 4-28 – Fixed Robin's doorknob slippage.
8) 5-3 – Fixed kitchen sink power outlet.
9) 5-4 – Fixed under kitchen sink drain.
10) 5-4 – Fixed leaks in kitchen sink faucets. (Not quite)
11) Others (got tired of writing everything down).

Notes to Pat
1) Sewing box measuring tape is NOT accurate at all.
2) DON'T turn off kitchen and upstairs faucets with force. Just enough to stop water. Their washers are new and no pressure is needed. (This goes for any faucet, really.)
3) Please, keep around the sink dry, especially in back of it.

Houses at Which I Ate While You Were Gone

Date	Hosts	Food	Anyone Else There?
4-21	Joni	lamb & Easter trimmings	Mother, Dad (Dave was sick)
4-25	Ruth and Jack	pot roast & fruit delight	Nope ...

June 20, 1957
Hamden, Connecticut

Chickasaw, Alabama

Dear Folks,

I guess Pat filled me in on everything about the trip to Chickasaw. They had a wonderful time. I'll bet you all really enjoyed that little gal Robin. It's just too darn bad she had to get so sick with measles during the last part of the visit, though.

From what Pat tells me and from your letters, you all are just as busy as you can be. John is certainly changing all the time. Last year when you were up here I was amazed at how much he had matured in 12 months. But Pat was just as surprised at the change over last year. So he really must be a man by now. I guess you're pretty proud of him. Keep it up, John!

Well, it won't be long now till you have a new grandchild. Hope it's a grandson, but we'll be happy as long as the baby's healthy and sound. Pat is still taking good care of herself, under my watchful eye, and is as pretty as ever.

One of our neighbors had a baby boy last week, and Robin held the baby when he was less than six days old! Big thrill for our little girl.

Loads of love,
Bob

July 6, 1957
Hamden, Connecticut

Chickasaw, Alabama

Dearest family,

It sure was good talking to y'all Friday night when we called from Devon. I was so glad Auntie Bussie happened to be right by the phone so you could finally meet each other. I can't possibly tell you all about our trip except that we had the most *wonderful* time. Robin adored Auntie Bussie and followed her around chatting up a storm during most of the visit. Of course, Auntie was in heaven!

Soon after we got home Monday afternoon, surprise visitors arrived, but just for a quick "pit stop." It's always great to see adorable old Navy friend Al and his wife Sarah, and this time we met their little Allen, a real doll. We want one just like him!

Robin went along for my checkup today and watched, intrigued, as the doctor examined my tummy and gave me my last "ponio" (polio) shot. I'd gained 3½ pounds. The baby has turned and is in a head-down position now but, alas, there's no relief yet from pressure on the old bladder.

Bob's mother and Joni came for a short visit this afternoon, and I talked myself into a sweat (literally!) telling them all the news of the past couple of weeks. They thought Robin had grown by inches and had changed so much. I'm sure you'd see a big difference in her already, too.

Must close – love you bushels!
Pat, Bob and Robin

P.S. – Please tell Aunt Hazel and Aunt Della everybody adores the dresses they made for Robin.

July 17, 1957
Hamden, Connecticut

Chickasaw, Alabama

Dearest Folks,

Yesterday Robin woke up from a short nap feverish and fussy, and although she slept fairly well last night, she's had a high temperature and felt badly all day. Our wonderful pediatrician is away but the doctor on call said there are many children with unexplained fever and a red throat. We'll just treat the symptoms, watch and comfort her, and hope she is as good as new again by tomorrow, which often is the case.

Today, right out of the clear sky (and it was clear, we've had gorgeous weather for a couple of days), Robin said, "Mommy, I *love* John and Rickey, and I love Nana GeeGee and Granddaddy, too!" I asked who else in the family she loved – "Sammie!"

Hope y'all have had at least some relief from the heat since we talked last week.

Take care,
Pat, Bob and Robin

August 4, 1957
Hamden, Connecticut

Chickasaw, Alabama

My dearest family,

We just finished lunch and Bob is reading *The New Baby* to Robin before she takes a nap. He's changing his voice for each of the characters and I am practically in hysterics, as is Robin! This makes about the hundredth time one of us has read the book to her. Her other favorite book these days features the characters from the TV program "Romper Room," the "Do Bees" (cheerful little girls who mind their mommies, etc.) and "Don't Bees" (grouchy girls and boys).

It was wonderful talking to you Friday and getting your letter yesterday, Mommie – I've read it time and time again. There were some surprises for us, all right. Aunt Della having her very long hair cut really short was almost enough of a shock to send me into labor! And Rickey, you handled a boat all by yourself? Wow, that's hard to believe! You know, every time your name is mentioned, Robin says, "And Rickey catches de *fish*, Mommy," squealing the words in her excitement over such a wondrous feat.

Feels like Baby has the hiccups right now. I sure am having a lot of vague aches and pains, just like I did a few weeks before Robin arrived. Hear this, one day recently I kept a record of how many trips I made to the bathroom to pee – 23!

I was thinking it'd be nice if the baby arrived on August 9. It's a kind of a family pattern – both of Bob's parents, Auntie Bussie, and Robin all have birthdays on the 9th day of a month. Oh, what did you think of the list of names? Here are more girls' names to ponder: Nina, Leigh, Anne. We are really in a dither about this baby's name!

Now, I must close and get a few minutes of lying-down rest. Write soon. ...

So much love,
Pat, Bob, Robin, and ?

August 7, 1957
Hamden, Connecticut

Chickasaw, Alabama

Dearest family,

Robin, bless her heart, is in seventh heaven right now because yesterday I bought her a new plaything: a little dishpan exactly the shape and color of mine, along with a dish drainer and assorted items like Brillo pads, sponges, a plastic apron and Tide, all in small-fry sizes. This morning I put the oven door down, set the pan on it and let her wash her tea set dishes to her heart's content. She was a perfect picture, just a'washing dishes and grinning from ear to ear. She's her mother's daughter, washing dishes in a pan on the oven door like I used to.

The other night, after a "no-no," I had a stern look on my face and Robin wanted me to laugh, but I told her I didn't feel like laughing. She just kept looking at me until I did smile, then, beaming, she cajoled, "*Now*, you *do* feel like laughing, don't you, Mommy?" Before I said anything, she continued, "Mommy doesn't like to laugh when Robin is naughty, but she laughs when Robin is a good gel." Yesterday, tired and frustrated, I yelled at her when she misbehaved yet again, only to nearly laugh out loud at her immediate (and rather astute) suggestion: "You better go take a *mean* pill, Mommy!"

Went for my checkup yesterday and was disappointed that I hadn't dilated any more, still the same as three weeks ago. That probably means I'll go on to August 23. If only I survive!

Take care of the dearest-in-the-world Mommie and Daddy and John-boy and Rickey for your kids up here. We *love* you, always.

Pat, Bob, Robin, and ?

August 14, 1957
Hamden, Connecticut

Chickasaw, Alabama
Dearest family,

In October Bob's parents are going by boat to Bermuda for a wonderful two or three weeks of vacation! Ah, the life of some lucky people, huh? They are as excited as two children over a birthday party. ...

One of the neighbors drove me into New Haven to see the doctor yesterday. He said everything looked about the same. I've been partially dilated for some weeks now and have come to the conclusion that pregnancy is to be my permanent state.

We love you so much, always. ... Happy Anniversary, Mommie and Daddy!

Pat, Bob, Robin
And "almost-here?"

August 24, 1957
Yale-New Haven Hospital
New Haven, Connecticut

Chickasaw, Alabama
My dearest family,

I'm the original lady of leisure today. I've had a bath, my bed is all freshly made and I'm propped up here taking life easy. Just called my honey a few minutes ago to chat, but he couldn't take time. I got so tickled at his "Now, honey, I need to get some work done. I have to go out and buy Pet Milk and Karo syrup and get the sterilizer out and clean the house. ..."

I had a wonderful 25th birthday yesterday and felt quite proud of all my accomplishments. There were cards from family and friends and neighbors, some lovely gifts, even a card and a cute little birthday cake from the hospital staff.

Of course, my most wonderful gift, two days before the due date of my birthday, was the brand-new, tiny bit of heaven – Little Miss Jennifer! She is a dream, just like her big sister. When I first saw her, I was so pleased, but so utterly exhausted I couldn't feel much of anything except blessed relief that I was through working to get her here! After some rest, though, I was ready to get to know baby Jenni. (How I wish Grandma Jennie could meet her namesake, but maybe she'll know about her and be Jenni's guardian angel on high.)

Bob probably told you something about the birth, except, oh brother, he didn't know all of it. It seems my babies like to get into strange positions to be born. The doctor said my pelvis is large, giving a baby room to move into more unnatural positions.

Jenni came, not like Robin, whose face was turned up toward the ceiling completely (posterior position, requiring "Bill's Maneuvers" with forceps to turn her), but in another position called "face presentation," in which her head faced downward but her nose was up in the air, so to speak! Instead of seeing the top of the head first, a portion of her face appeared – and was the main attraction. I heard the doctor call out to nurses and an intern nearby to come and watch the somewhat unusual birth – face presentations occur in maybe 1 out of 200 births.

I had "natural childbirth" – well, one hypo and a couple of whiffs of something just a few minutes before Jenni was born. When things got to really popping (actually while the baby was temporarily stuck in that funny position) I, who had intended to be so brave and quiet, started begging for a bit of help. I was aware of being noisy and kept trying to apologize for making a fuss. And the doctor just kept at his job: "That's a good girl. Give me another long hard push – that's fine, no, don't waste your breath now, just push!"

During the last few contractions before the head was born, when I was nauseated, gagging, pushing and crying, he asked a nurse to get an anesthetist. She came back and said no one was available. When I heard that, I thought, "Well, just shoot me because I'll never live through this."

Of course, by that time, seeing the baby's position and realizing I would definitely need something, the doctor called more urgently for an anesthetist. To tell the truth, though, I didn't notice much difference after I'd been given something except for wanting to push harder with those last contractions. I was definitely wide awake, felt the head emerge, was told to give another push for the shoulders and felt each one ever so clearly just before being suddenly aware of the most euphoric relief as the rest of the little body wiggled and slipped out with a slight swoosh. Then came the pleased voice of the doctor: "Your baby's here. It's a little girl."

Before he showed the baby to me, he explained what had happened and said she had a puffed, blue face from the pressure but that the bruising would be temporary. For a while, every contraction had pushed the part of her little face around the nose and mouth against the rim of my pelvis, which resulted in blood congesting there.

The doctor explained that the episiotomy was quite large because of the unusual position, and I did feel every stitch as he was sewing. But when he asked if it was bothering me, both he and the intern laughed at my cavalier answer: "Oh no, I could stand this all day – it's so mild compared to what I just went through!"

You should have seen me. I was soaking wet, hair and all. I tell you, that was the hardest work I've ever done in my life – whew!

When I saw my doctor the following day, I told him I was so sorry to have made such a fuss, but he complimented my "good work," especially under the circumstances. He said he has had to do emergency Caesareans for face presentations and that it was only through my hard work the baby was finally born naturally. Did I ever feel better about my actions then!

With bushels of love,
Pat

August 31, 1957
Hamden, Connecticut

Chickasaw, Alabama

Dear Folks,

Pat's really doing well. The only trouble now is that I'll have to be firm not to let her *overdo*! I'll let her tell you about her plumbing 'cause I don't know anything about all that female stuff. All I know is that she looks good to me and is recovering fast.

My mother, our "private nurse," just left and we are now on our own. Last time, with Robin, when the hired nurse left it just about killed us; this time I'm sure we are a little more prepared and experienced. And Pat is certainly in better shape. She's now in the kitchen washing bottles in preparation for sterilizing.

Robin's in the den playing with her toys and Jenni's at her usual occupation – sleeping. That Jenni really amazes me! Honestly, all she does is sleep and eat. She has cried *very* little and even when she's waiting for a bottle to warm she's as patient as can be. She does love to be held, though, especially on someone's shoulder. That will keep her happy almost any time.

As an example of how long little Jenni sleeps between feedings, last night she had a bottle about 10:30 and then went sound asleep. I woke up at 6 a.m. and was a little worried about her. So I went into the den and found her just beginning to wake up. Of course, she was in a mess, but she patiently waited to be changed before her bottle. Never cried once.

The enclosed picture is yours. It was taken by the hospital photographer when Jenni was one or two days old. It really doesn't do her justice, you can notice how bruised she was all around the mouth. That has cleared up and she is getting prettier every day. (I think she looks like your side of the family!)

I'll let Pat finish this letter. Take care of yourselves, and our best love to you *all.*

Bob

Hi, dearest family,

I would love to sit down and write 25 pages of details of everything, but the thought of that scares me, so I'll just add a note to Bob's newsy letter instead. Both girls are napping and I sat for a little while, but I can't rest too long, thinking of things to be done. Of course, I'm lucky because Bob cleaned the house beautifully this morning. There are still many small

143

chores, though – and it always bothers me if I can't get my thank-you notes written promptly.

I *loved* talking to you last night, Mommie, and am so sorry I didn't realize you were on the phone, too, John-boy. As Bob would say, "You wouldn't have had a chance, anyway!" Not with us two gabbers on the line, huh?

Just a quickie about Robin – she is wonderful with Jenni so far. When we've let her hold the baby, she says, "Oh, look, Mommy, my baby's looking at her big sister. Isn't he sweet?" (Yep, she still calls her a he.)

Mommie, we are thrilled to pieces that you want to make Jenni a christening dress!

We love you, always,
Pat, Bob, Robin and Jenni

September 15, 1957
Devon, Pennsylvania

Hamden, Connecticut

Pat dear,

It certainly was good of you to let me come (self-invited) to lunch the other day, when you were just fresh home from the hospital and involved with a new baby. The lunch was good, and I had a wonderful time. Thanks so much. I do hope my sister and I didn't wear you out with our yakking.

It was such fun to meet Jenni. You know, it is really a great thrill for an old one like me to have a new member of the family. I consider it a personal favor to me when you have babies – although I appreciate that that isn't your prime reason for doing so. Families and babies are both so wonderful, and I don't seem to be able to do anything about producing them myself, so I sure am tickled when you do. And you do such a good job of it. Robin, of course, is perfect. And that new little one I could just eat right up. Don't let her grow too fast before Christmas – they are so nice when they are little and cuddly.

Needless to say, I enjoyed my vacation enormously. And I can't tell you how much I appreciated the boys taking a precious day off so we could all be together on Thursday. That really hit the jackpot for me.

My dearest love to all four of you,
Auntie Bussie

September 21, 1957
Hamden, Connecticut

Chickasaw, Alabama

My dearest family,

On Wednesday a package came from Phyllis in California. It was a gift for Jenni – a pretty silver baby spoon similar to the one she sent to Robin. Also enclosed were some cute little-girl socks for the big sister. Isn't it something that all these years later, my seventh-grade schoolteacher is sending gifts for my babies?

Robin has acted up a bit this week, especially when I'm feeding the baby. Also, she has said a few times, "If I mash Jenni (or pull her hair, tip the basket over, etc.), you will take her back to the hospital, *won't* you, Mommy?" Finally it dawned on me that it was jealousy showing through, and I asked if she wanted me to take her back. She nodded, and very seriously admitted, "Unh huh." I explained that God had given us Jenni, who wouldn't have anyone to take care of her if we sent her back. I'm sure Robin is reacting very normally – most of the time she's just sweet about this new addition to our lives.

We love you all, Mommie, Daddy, Sam, John, Rickey – and Tartar, Bow-wow!

All of us – Pat, Bob,
Robin and Jenni

October 24, 1957
Hamden, Connecticut

Chickasaw, Alabama

Dearest Folks,

I am running around like fury again, trying to clean the house a bit, waiting for the sterilizer to finish so I can make formula, and scooting back and forth to where Robin is "cleaning the bathroom so you won't have to do it, Mommy." She keeps calling me to see, and although it's a little discouraging to see the actual mess, I give her high praise for good work. Oops, here she is – and this time, after another check, the bathroom does look pretty good! Now she has found the decks of cards and is scattering them all around the living room. Too bad it's raining. She misses being able to play outside in the sandbox.

Bob is *really* enjoying the baby these days. You might be surprised if you could see him with Jenni. He reminds me of Daddy with babies, and I never thought of Bob in that way. But you know, he missed this period with Robin, the cooing and first smiles. It's all new and delightful to him, so I think part of it is that he is fascinated with "babyness." He was saying last night how wonderful it was to have another tiny baby. I warned him to get that gleam out of his eye!

The other day I held Jenni up to a mirror and didn't smile or say anything and within two seconds her little face erupted into one huge smile at her reflection. Robin did that real young, too. Smart children we have, don't you agree?

Earlier today Robin wanted to hold Jenni, and instead of letting her hold the baby lying across her arms I put Jenni on her shoulder where Robin could pat her and feel Jenni's head and face close to hers. That made such a hit! Robin just beamed and felt very important, so we had to do it again and again.

We've had 24- and 26-degree weather some days recently. Can you imagine weather so cold already in October? Brrr. My Southern blood does present a problem up here in the cold No'th. The trees are really beautiful now, such brilliant colors, but alas, all the leaves will soon be gone and once again the limbs will be bare – or covered with snow.

We love you,
Pat, Bob, Robin and Jenni

P.S. – Hey, what did y'all think of the news earlier this month (on your 10th birthday, Rickey) that Russia had launched *Sputnik*? They're calling it the start of the "Space Age" – and no doubt also the beginning of a race between Russia and the United States. It's pert 'nigh beyond belief that anything could go from Earth into space, huh? I still don't understand the mysterious workings of radio or telephone, never mind space-traveling vehicles.

November 4, 1957
Hamden, Connecticut

Chickasaw, Alabama

Dearest family,

Where has this year gone? And to think there used to be periods when I wished time would pass by faster. Last night Bob and I were talking about nursery school for Robin next year, and I told him I'd decided a big No on that subject since she'll start to school in less than two years. If she didn't have lots of playmates, I would want to send her. But as it is, I want to cherish these next two years. So this morning, Bob said, "Now remember, honey, the first time today you feel like pulling your hair out, *these* are the days you are cherishing!"

Jenni just woke up and she and I had a nice chat. She is such a sweet little bundle. When she looks at me so bright-eyed and starts that "aaah, ooooh, gur-glee-se, aah" business, I could eat her up!

This morning Robin breezed in from playing and crawled up onto the bed beside Jenni, and I wish y'all could've seen the big smile and all the waving and kicking and gurgling Jenni did.

On Halloween night we were all set to take Robin trick-or-treating when the first masked children came to our door, catapulting Robin into hysteria. The entire evening was a nightmare (actually quite fitting for Halloween!), with her simply scared to death. She kept saying, "Dose funny kids, I don't like dose funny kids." Believe me, when the last little goblin had come and gone, we breathed a giant sigh of relief until next year.

Thanks for the article about the "Miss Brookley" contest. Oh, it does bring back memories. … Daddy, Robin *sure* did enjoy your letter, the part of it that was especially to her. When I read it to her, she grinned and said, "Talk it some more."

Bob was out last night, checking on Naval Reserve activities. The unit wants him badly and I think he is going to join. It would mean two hours every Monday night and two weeks in the summer, but for each Monday night's work he'd receive almost $12, which we can really use.

Oh, by the way, Daddy, how about Russia's second *Sputnik* now? Guess we're already running behind in the space race. Think the United States will catch up?

We love y'all ever so much, always,
Pat, Bob, Robin and Jenni

November 12, 1957
Hamden, Connecticut

Chickasaw, Alabama
Dearest Folks,

I'm waiting awhile for Jenni's tummy to settle before giving her a bottle. She's as quiet as can be, sucking her fingers and looking around. She is undoubtedly the best, most contented baby there ever was.

You know how appreciative Robin is of every tiny thing? Well, it seems Jenni may be the same. She will lie in the crib for so long that I begin to feel guilty. When I walk in she just beams, lighting up like a Christmas tree, and seems to appreciate a few words more than she can possibly let me know. Sometimes I put dolls beside her and she coos so sweetly to them.

Got a couple of Robin quotes to relay. This morning she was upstairs with Bob while he was getting dressed, and when he told her he thought he'd wear "this tie" (a certain one that he had worn the day before), all she said, with attitude, was, "*Again*?"

Last night she was feeding her baby doll (the one she named Bussie) while I fed Jenni, and we proceeded with our new game: She came to me and very adult-like asked, "How is your baby doing today, Mom?" I said Jenni was eating very nicely, thank you, and she continued, "Baby Bussie, too, she already took 'free' ounces, and she not gonna spit up, either, I 'sink'"!

She's good entertainment. Later she was burping her baby and after a long while I made a sound (thinking I was helping!) and told Robin that her baby had burped. She looked at me like I was addled and quipped, "No, my *baby* didn't burp yet, *you* did"!

Mommie, your venture into the used clothes business sounds really good. I'll keep everything worthwhile that I no longer use and send a box to you occasionally. All the luck in the world to you.

Sammie, I do believe Miss Jenni looks a bit like you, with some of Rickey mixed in. Wish y'all could see her. John, how are you doing? Dating many good-looking girls, or just concentrating on the *book* part of school?

Take care of everyone. We love y'all with all our hearts.

Pat, Bob and "the girls"

November 29, 1957
Suffield, Connecticut

Chickasaw, Alabama
My dearest family,

As you can see from the address, and the typewritten letter, we are spending a few days with Bob's folks. Bob got off early Wednesday and we decided to surprise them by coming on up. When we walked out to get into the car at 4 o'clock, *we* were the ones surprised as a car stopped in front of our house. It was Al, Sarah and little Allen, who were on their way to Maine for the holiday (which Robin calls "Thanks-for-giving" – isn't that perfect?). They had been counting on the stop at our place for going to the bathroom, changing the baby, etc., so we insisted they come in, and we wanted them to stay longer but they were off again within half an hour. We grabbed a package of crackers to take with us in case anyone got hungry on the way, which turned out to be a wise move since the traffic tie-up – or "tractor tie-up," as little missy calls it – resulted in a much longer trip than usual and we didn't arrive in Suffield until after 7:30.

Robin got a little fidgety and we were all thirsty from the dry crackers, but bless baby Jenni, she was a dream. Just as we came upon the worst stretch, when all we could see was a line of cars, bumper to bumper, she woke up and started to cry, and we thought, Oh no, but right away she settled into sleep again. I wish you could have seen her when we got here – I looked back in the car bed and there seemed to be no baby! It was a funny sight: Jenni's hat had come off and was covering her face, but she was under it, wide awake, sucking those two favorite fingers, perfectly peaceful, even though it was already at least 30 minutes past her regular feeding time.

We had a very nice day yesterday. After my usual routine – making formula, doing laundry, bathing Jenni, etc. – and Mother Kitty's do-ahead kitchen chores, we just took it easy right up until time for the last-minute turkey dinner preparations.

Take real good care of Mommie, Daddy, Sammie, John and Rickey-boy for we love all of you with all our hearts.

Pat, Bob, Robin and Jenni

P.S. – Almost forgot to tell you a scary thing: Up until Wednesday I was in a state of *panic*, shocked, because even though I felt it was impossible, I thought we were going to have another little one next August! I'd never been so late before, except the two times I was pregnant, and was really worried.

But, imagine, Bob was tickled! I couldn't believe it, he really would have been happy to have another that soon. As I told him (while quickly considering that ours might have to be a platonic relationship forever after!), it wasn't even that a third baby so soon would be completely overwhelming, or that I wouldn't have planned it that way, it was the fact that if it seemed impossible for it to have happened, but it *had*, it was the fourth, fifth and sixth that really "worrified" me!

No more worries, though, apparently everything is back to normal.

December 27, 1957
Suffield, Connecticut

Chickasaw, Alabama
My dearest family,

I'm much more in the mood for talking to y'all than writing, but am afraid that if I call station-to-station tonight somebody won't be there. We tried to call Christmas night but the operator said it would probably be midnight our time before a call could get through, and as I was pooped and had been ready for bed since 9 o'clock, I asked her to cancel the call.

We all had a nice Christmas day together here in Suffield with the folks, but we were exhausted by the time we finished dinner.

For days Robin has been acting as if she might be coming down with something – crying so much, not agreeing on anything, looking pale – but she eats like a young filly and has no fever, so I guess she is all right.

She sure has given us a hard time, though. On Tuesday she was so unhappy and disagreeable about everything that to distract her I let her open one of the gifts from you. Luckily, it was the cute little Santa Claus. She fell in love with him, carried him about, calling him darling, and was kept amused long enough for me to get caught up on the many chores I needed to do before leaving to spend a few days here. Thanks an extra heap for him, Rickey! And thanks to all for so many pretty and practical presents.

You would find it hard to believe how sweet and wonderful Jenni-baby has been during our holiday visit. We are really blessed. I haven't seen Auntie Bussie so completely taken with anyone as she was with Jenni. You know, she is not one to even halfway push herself on children of any age – and she did finally say she had better let up a little or she would spoil Jenni for us – but "Great Auntie" would sit for the longest periods of time just gazing at the baby with a look of utter adoration on her face, talking softly to her. Oh, I think dear Auntie Bussie would have been a wonderful mother. …

Again, thanks for everything – and remember how much we love you.
Happy New Year!
Pat, Bob, Robin and Jenni

I get up, I walk, I fall down.
Meanwhile, I keep dancing.
Hillel

Chapter Nine
Lunacy
1958

Bob's dad Robert showing off Hula Hoop

January 5, 1958
Hamden, Connecticut

Chickasaw, Alabama
Dearest Folks,

Well, you should have seen your daughter today. Pat was on ice skates! For her first try at a winter sport she did very well. I really didn't expect her to keep at it like she did, and she definitely surprised me and her northern friends. I guess I hadn't ice-skated for about 15 years, and it came back to me pretty quickly. We may go again next Sunday.

Hope you get that scholarship, John. Good luck and keep it up, pal!

Much, much love to you all, and have a great 1958!

Bob

January 8, 1958
Hamden, Connecticut

Chickasaw, Alabama
My dearest family,

You should see us, near 'bout buried in white stuff. A snowstorm began early yesterday afternoon and this morning we have 14½ inches dumped over everything, plus three-foot drifts here and there.

Knowing my sentiments on this kind of weather, two of my best friends have phoned, somewhat timidly inquiring "Do you feel like swearing at me?" and "Are you cussing?" I said I suppose I'm becoming resigned to my fate. Naturally, as usually happens, a dentist appointment made months ago for today had to be canceled. And tomorrow night is likely to present a problem – I'm scheduled to provide cookies, help serve, and wash dishes at my church group meeting. It's predicted that some of the snow will melt into slush today and the temperature will dip into the 10s and 20s tonight and tomorrow, freezing everything and making driving even worse. Why do snowstorms always come when I have to go places? Wonder if I'll ever *really* get used to it. ...

I told Bob after reading his letter to y'all that he writes a very nice letter but doesn't give much information – I still have two weeks of details to report! He didn't tell you that while ice skating I had a few falls that left me with a bruised thigh and swollen hand and wrist. I enjoyed it, though, even with the spills.

Not long after Jenni's vaccination last week she developed a tight cough and runny nose, and we're so hoping she won't get sicker when the vaccination takes effect in another few days. This morning Robin woke up with a cold, too, sighing, "I guess I got too close to Jenni, huh, Mommy?"

152

Folks, I can't seem to come to a decision about making a trip to Alabama, but there is another possibility. It wouldn't be the same, of course, but if we paid your fare, Mommie, would you come up here for a couple of weeks? Daddy, I know you and the boys want to see the children and me, too, but let's at least consider that alternative.

It's almost 7:30 and I just got both girls dosed and into bed in their steamy room. Bob had already started the vaporizer ... now he's out shoveling what seems like tons of snow from the driveway. Since he took the bus to work this morning and didn't dig out, the snow was undisturbed, still waiting for him.

We love you all so much,
Pat, Bob, Robin and Jenni

January 17, 1958
Hamden, Connecticut

Chickasaw, Alabama
Dearest Folks,

Just a note with the flight information. This time next week we'll be getting ready for the drive into New York to the airport. Sure do hope we're not as tired then as we are at 10 o'clock tonight.

Will arrive in Mobile at 6 a.m. Saturday, hopefully on time after a smooth trip.

All love,
Pat

March 19, 1958
Hamden, Connecticut

Chickasaw, Alabama
My dearest family,

The girls and I miss you *ever* so much. It sure was nice to spend those relaxing weeks with y'all. We had such a good time. ... We are still feeling sad that Tartar is gone, but Robin consoles by reminding us he's happy in doggie heaven.

She isn't too happy these days, though, in yet another phase, one that's trying my patience to the limit. So I'm grateful that her little friend Teddy came a few minutes ago to escort her down the street to play at his house for a while ... and that Jenni is taking a short nap. The quiet is wonderful. I don't get many peaceful moments – my life is a whirlwind most of the time.

153

Today's schedule began at 7 a.m. with breakfast, feeding Jenni, doing dishes, starting the laundry, getting dressed, stopping to change and burp Jenni and get Robin interested in something, answering the phone, etc., etc., and I didn't see the light of day till 9:30.

I shivered through hanging out one load of wash before starting on a monstrous pile of ironing. Just then the phone rang again – and Robin began one of her crying fits, which woke Jenni from her nap and scared her out of her wits. It was Dave calling, but our conversation was pretty unsuccessful. I had to leave the phone three times to put Robin in another room so I could hear Dave, and she just kept crying and coming back. In all this I had forgotten about the iron and went to turn it off before I sat down with Robin on my lap to comfort her. As I soothed her, I began to notice a smell and got up to investigate. I had turned the dial on the iron not to Off but to High – oh my!

And it continued … I fed Jenni a favorite fruit and put her in the playpen and tried to tempt Robin with the idea of getting dressed and going outside. This brought on another full-fledged fit, followed by another soothing session. Then I ironed a few more pieces, scorched a couple, answered the phone, etc. Next on the agenda was a bath and bottle for Jenni.

Later I finished the ironing, hung out another load of clothes, fixed our lunch, got Robin to bed for a nap, answered the phone again, began the job of cleaning out kitchen shelves, stopped to change and give another bottle to Jenni, went back and finished wiping the shelves and washing dusty dishes. Changed Jenni's diaper again and gave her a baby food lunch of meat and pudding.

Baked some cookies from the dough I had made up and frozen last week, emptied all garbage and trash cans, took some of the laundry off the line, made the bed (yes, late!), got Robin ready to go with Teddy, put Jenni down, and slurped a life-saving cup of coffee. And here I present the remains of me.

And you see, the darnedest part is that with all of that hubbub and more, I really haven't accomplished a lot. The house is still as messy as it has been for days, supper is to be planned and cooked, the week's groceries bought tonight, and on and on and on it goes. Holy Toledo, it's overwhelming at times.

Guess I will seriously consider getting vitamins – or a shot of atomic hydrogen, or electronic power! – else I might just keel over pretty soon. Last night about 7:00, sitting down for almost the first time all day, I thought I would die I was so tired and sleepy. And I'm not pregnant.

Your Hamden Kids,
Pat, Bob, Robin, Jenni

154

Chickasaw, Alabama

My dearest family,

I don't know how I'm writing this morning since I have no energy, not much mental ability and, to tell the truth, possibly am only half conscious. I need to perk up, though, because today is our fifth anniversary and Bob is taking me out to dinner. He got the sitter, made reservations, and arranged it all as a surprise.

Not only that, I've already discovered two hidden presents from him. I got the dishpan out to wash the breakfast dishes and found a small gift box and Bob's card: "5 years – my how time flies!" Inside was a charm for my bracelet – a darling miniature hourglass with rosy-beige sand that flows back and forth. Later on, opening a closet to put away clothes, I spotted two pretty Hummel figurines, "Feeding Time" and "The Little Shopper." Remember, he also gave me a figurine when each of the girls was born. They're special.

I didn't send Bob a card at the office and, in fact, have led him to believe I have nothing for him but my love! But he'll have a big surprise when he gets home. Last week when the Naval Academy captain's chair I'd ordered arrived, Mother Kitty was here for the day and helped me put it in the neighbor's garage. Today Ed brought it back, uncrated, and placed it upstairs in our bedroom, where I'll send Bob to "get something for me" as soon as he comes in from work.

Much later. … Well, this has been a nice day in lots of ways, as shown by the first part of the letter, but in others … THAT ROBIN! It began when, in her brand new sneakers, she played in the wet sandbox and had to have a head-to-toe change of clothing. At 11:00 she left to play and eat lunch with a friend down the street, but next thing I knew she was waddling home, before lunch, with wet, sandy pants – this time in her soaked Sunday shoes. I just sighed and again changed her into clean, dry clothes. Darned if she didn't then go back upstairs and promptly throw both pairs of wet shoes out the window!

All that wasn't so bad, but then came the last straw. In two minutes' time when my back was turned, she got my beautiful new hourglass charm and had it in the bathroom running water over it. Of course, moisture seeped in and now the sand is a tiny blob of wet mud and the glue of the whole thing is oozing out. I just cried.

Saturday at 5, a particularly busy time, I was getting Jenni ready for supper and bed when Bob called to me from outside that I'd better check on Robin upstairs. I shouted back that she was okay, just playing in her room

155

with some dolls, which is what she had been doing a couple of minutes before. He insisted, though, so I ran up to look in on her and, oh dear, what I found. Missy Robin was using Desitin, a white, water-repellent, sticky, gooey ointment for diaper rash, to paint the windows. Yep, and if that wasn't a *mess* to clean up. The stuff sticks just about like your Stanley glue, Mommie!

Recently she has also broken or spilled a couple of bottles of lotion, and periodically I find some piece of furniture – my antique rocker, for instance – completely lotioned or powdered. Then there's the darn water business – she's forever not only making a mess on the bathroom floor, but toting sopping wet rags here and there, streaming water all over the house, and laying them on furniture or the bed. Oh the joys of motherhood!

Our love always, to all of you,

Pat

May 1, 1958
DEAR NANA GEEGEE,
I HOPE YOU ARE HAVING FUN DOWN THERE. HAVE YOU FOUND A DOG JUST LIKE TARTAR? I LOVE YOU ALL IT IS SUNNY TO DAY.
ROBIN

July 2, 1958
Cape Cod, Massachusetts

Chickasaw, Alabama
Dearest Folks,

Hmm ... while enjoying this pleasant vacation life, I really have to stay after myself to get anything done, including writing.

Oh my, have we lived it up! We just got back a little while ago from eating out, kids and all. There's a great place, Lobster-in-the-Rough, with picnic tables and a playground for children. Bob and his mother were literally up to their elbows cracking and picking out lobster meat – while Robin and I sampled the fried chicken and Jenni gnawed on her piece of Zwieback. A nice treat for all of us.

From our rental house it's only a short walk to the beach, so we go down whenever we feel like it during the day. All of us look very healthy with our nice suntans. Food always tastes especially good at the shore so, of course, we're eating like pigs at every meal. And evenings are really pleasant, either the folks and Bob and I play bridge or he and I enjoy a night out.

Monday night Bob and I went to a charming little theater to see a movie, *The Bridge on the River Kwai,* stopped for hamburgers at a drive-in

156

afterward, and ended the evening with a moonlight ride along the beach. We felt almost like daters again. Tomorrow night we have plans to see a musical play at a summer theatre, The Cape Play House, and Saturday we're going out dining (and dancing!) at a famous old inn about 30 miles from here.

One day we're going to leave the kids with his parents for the day and drive around the Cape to sightsee and browse through a few of the hundreds of shops. The folks began insisting way back in winter that we take advantage of their baby-sitting services during this vacation. We are, and it's wonderful!

This is absolutely beautiful country. Wish y'all could see it with us.

All love,
Bob, Pat, Robin, Jenni

August 25, 1958
Hamden, Connecticut

Chickasaw, Alabama
Dearest Folks,

We are so glad you had a good time up here with us, Mommie, in spite of the confusion of our moving during your visit. It would be wonderful to have you back now that we're settled and everything in the new house is in good operating order.

Mom, our friends have said such nice things about you, how pretty and sweet you are. I certainly agree! And, of course, nobody could believe you are old enough to have *me*.

Robin has had two bad nights, probably as a result of the move to a different house and being in her unfamiliar new room. Although there *is* another possible cause for her disturbed crying spells at night. Friday afternoon we started out for a walk with several neighbor mothers and their children, and the pet dog of one of the families. Just as we came to Whitney Avenue, the little dog ran out into the busy street and was run over by a car right before our eyes. Robin became almost hysterical and tried to run out to him, screaming, "Oh, is he dead, is he dead, Mommy?" I didn't realize she understood anything about death yet, but she does.

There was the most awful thud when he was hit, and when one of the mothers was able to move him over to the side of the road it was plain to see he was dead. I couldn't keep Robin from looking, and she cried out, "See the big hole in the doggie. Why did he get runned over, Lori? I'll take care of you. Lori, aren't you sorry your dog is dead?"

Truth is, I didn't sleep quite as restfully myself that night. All I could think of was Robin will be crossing that same street when she goes to school next year.

Love you,
Pat

September 30, 1958
Hamden, Connecticut

Chickasaw, Alabama
Dearest Folks,

Well the big party came off as a *complete* surprise to Bob, just as I'd hoped! What a day Saturday was. It seemed that every conversation we had took concentration on my part to keep from spilling the secret. One funny example: We had the new drapes and Bob worked hard to get them up in the living room. A couple of times I gently suggested maybe he could hang those for the dining room, too, but he said no, he'd wait till Sunday. Later, of course, he realized *why* I wanted them up on Saturday!

My ploy was for Bob to go to Hartford with our friend Jack to help move a carload of stuff for a neighbor. They planned to leave at 4:30, which meant I'd have three hours to get everything ready for the party. Bob thought all of us were going to another friend's for dinner and, with Jack's warning that they might run late getting back, he dressed for the evening before going to Hartford. As Bob laughingly admitted later, he thought Jack was nuts, not only for dressing up to move somebody's stuff, *in the rain*, but for taking a passenger when he could have been using all the space in the car for the boxes! But all the crazy plans made sense to him afterward.

When they got back and walked in our front door, there were shouts of "Surprise, Surprise!" from Mother Kitty, Dad, Dave, and lots of our friends. Everyone brought funny gifts, the most popular of which was a Hula-Hoop, the newest craze. What a hilarious sight as we all took turns wildly twisting and turning various body parts in the challenge to keep the hoop going around. I'm already sore from practicing with the darn thing. After dinner we played charades, which was even more fun than usual with two dozen enthusiastic participants. The evening was a roaring success, and Bob thoroughly enjoyed his 30th birthday celebration.

Gotta go – Love you!
Pat, Bob, Robin, Jenni

October 6, 1958
Hamden, Connecticut

Chickasaw, Alabama
Dear Folks,

A package arrived this week: an autographed copy of Dr. Jim and Auntie Bussie's newest book *Why Marriages Go Wrong*. It's dedicated to "The Third Generation of our families" (with names listed), and the written inscription from Dr. Jim reads: "For Robin and Jennifer and their Mommy and Daddy, whom I like very much." Isn't that sweet?

I'd thought we might receive a copy from Auntie Bussie, but this weekend Bob's mother had a letter from her in which Auntie wrote that Dr. Jim "was so pleased Pat had sent him a birthday card for his 70th birthday that he sat right down and got off a copy of the new book to her!"

We got to bed early last night but this morning I turned off the alarm, snuggled in again, and slept right on till Bob jumped up at 7:20! It was so cold outside (26°) and so warm and cozy in bed.

Love to all,
Pat

November 8, 1958
Hamden, Connecticut

Chickasaw, Alabama
Dearest Mommie and guys,

Every day I've planned to write in the afternoon or evening, and every day I have gone to sleep instead. Just can't seem to stay awake if I sit down.

I am so excited waiting for Daddy to arrive. A few minutes ago when I heard dogs barking, Bob's and another male voice at the back door and Bob's, "Honey, there's a friend here," I just knew it was Daddy. I went running with my arms opened wide – and surprised a friend of Bob's from the company who almost got hugged!

Saturday, 2:45 p.m. – Daddy is here but he's pooped so we put him to bed for a nap. Robin had told us, with her usual dramatic flair, how she was going to love her Granddaddy *so tight* when he got here – and she did. Jenni wasn't too sure about sitting on his lap, but soon did, and in no time was laughing as Daddy teased with her.

There were good reasons why I didn't write last week. Sunday afternoon I was napping with Robin on her bed when the persistent ringing of the phone woke me. I waited for Bob to answer it, not knowing he had gone outside, and when he didn't, I jumped up quickly to get to the phone. With

159

only socks on my feet, the minute I touched the hardwood floor I slipped and literally went down in a three-point landing – on my poor nose, right hand and right knee. My nose immediately started bleeding profusely, my heart was pounding from the adrenaline rush, and I seemed to suddenly be hurting everywhere. What a rude awakening – I was relieved that Bob came in soon and let me cry on his shoulder. The three landing points are still black, blue and purple.

During the week I worked as hard as I could, cleaning, ironing, grocery shopping and getting ready for Daddy's visit. Friday afternoon I was planning to make homemade applesauce and fry some chicken for supper on his first night here.

Before I got the table cleared from lunch, though, the mishaps started. In the garage I reached to get the playpen to bring inside and inadvertently put my left hand down on a wasp. It stung the living daylights out of me. (You remember – I think I wrote you – that about four weeks ago I was stung by a wasp that somehow had ended up nestled in my already-sprinkled pile of ironing.)

Well, again, I seemed to be hurting everywhere and went calling on "Mama Rose" next door for moral support. Soon my hand swelled up like a balloon and I broke out with hives all over my body. I was itching and nauseated, feeling simply miserable; Rose was scared to death. She didn't want to let me out of her sight, but I *had* to lie down. So she took care of the girls and I went home and lay down, but only for a few minutes because the handyman arrived to fix the storm doors.

I'd taken a healthy dose of Benadryl, which relieved most of the symptoms, and I soon went back to Rose's to see about Robin and Jenni. They were playing happily so I sat down for a cup of coffee with Rose and Ruth, who had just walked over to visit. We were discussing my run-ins with wasps when all of a sudden I shot up off my chair, went running to Rose, pulling at my collar. I took my hand away and there on the floor lay another wasp. It had stung me on the neck not once, but *twice*!

I just let the tears flow for a few minutes, it hurt so much. And my nerves were shot. Luckily, though, the hives and nausea didn't return, probably because there was still Benadryl in my system. For days I was afraid to make a move, thinking, How can I be sure there's not a wasp on me right this minute? As usual my wonderful neighbors couldn't do enough for me, and I sure was grateful.

Well, after reading about those incidents you'll enjoy some good news concerning my appointment with the doctor yesterday. He said, "Yes, you are definitely pregnant – due date, early June." I really had no doubts before, but now it is official. Are you surprised? Well, me, too! We're very happy about it, though. Jenni and the new baby will be less than two years apart, like we wanted the first two. Of course, this time, I *really* will have my hands full – I can only imagine!

All our love – from Daddy, too,
Bob, Pat, Robin, Jenni, and "?"

Chapter Ten
Lousy Weather
1959

Jenni, Pat and Robin in wintry Connecticut

January 6, 1959
DEAR NANA GEEGEE,
I WILL COME DOWN SOON. I LOVE YOU NANA. IT IS BAD
WEATHER DOWN HERE. NANA YOUR SWEET. FROM ROBIN

January 7, 1959
Hamden, Connecticut

Chickasaw, Alabama
Dearest Folks,

Our weather has been COLD. For a few days, it has even hurt to breathe in the outside air. The days are sunny and clear but the temperature goes below zero at night. The howling wind has been scary, with gusts of up to 60 miles an hour. We lost our garbage can cover, shingles blew from other houses onto our lawn, and the front storm door was ripped from its lock. It was awful to be out in the elements yesterday, going to New Haven in the morning for a prenatal checkup and then back out that afternoon buying and lugging groceries around. At least I wasn't shepherding little ones, too, as Ruth watched the girls when I went to the store.

What a dear friend Ruth is, and how great to know she's just across the street. And the best news, she has offered all her services when the baby comes. She will probably just move over here and cook and take care of Robin and Jenni the week I am in the hospital, and then come during the day to help out after I'm home.

Tell John we wish so much he could've come up to see us during Christmas – and not to give up hope that he, and maybe Sam, too, can come this summer or next Christmas, even though they are in college. I've been thinking a lot lately about my grown-up brothers and how nice it would be if we could count on visits from them often. (And Rickey, you, too, will be plumb grown-up before I know what's happening!)
We love all of you,
Pat

February 10, 1959
Hamden, Connecticut

Chickasaw, Alabama
Dearest Folks,

Well, the girls are snug in their beds and Bob and I are settled in the den on this very wet, rainy, icy evening. Ugh, what weather! About noon yesterday it started snowing, then raining, then sleeting, and today it's icy in spots and slushy in others. As a matter of fact all the area around the back door has been frozen solid, so finally about 10:30 a.m., after four attempts and no success getting out, I called Bob and asked, "How in the (fill in the blank!) am I supposed to get the milk in today?" We both had a good laugh, but I didn't get the milk till Ruth came over at 3 o'clock and kicked off the ice from the door! Now isn't that plumb ridiculous? Knowing how clumsy I am now, Bob had given me orders not to set foot out today, and I had to agree. We just hope the weather will be clear for the trip to Auntie Bussie's this weekend. I want to be able to drive in to New Haven for the refresher Natural Childbirth class on Thursday, too.

It was wonderful talking to you both on Sunday, Mommie and Daddy. Oh, but I was so struck with homesickness afterward. All day, every time I looked at Jenni and Robin, I felt sad because y'all couldn't see them. They were both so cute for Robin's birthday celebration. And Jenni's "Hah-Bir-Day-Yoo" was adorable, especially since she would grin at Robin as she said it.

Take care of all our sweet Alabama family – we love you.

Pat, Bob Robin, Jenni

February 16, 1959
Hamden, Connecticut

Chickasaw, Alabama
My dearest family,

It's Tuesday, 9:30 a.m. You'd never guess what time I went to bed last night – 8:15! I was in bed for 10½ hours and should feel absolutely great, but that "pregnancy weakness" has set in again and I've been gobbling up food all morning. What am I going to do? I have already gained about 19 pounds.

You should see what a mess the whole house is, especially this playroom, and I feel weaker just looking at it. Oh me, what I'd give to have a maid for a while … or I'd settle for the plan Bob's folks have – they're leaving Friday for three weeks of sunshine and swimming in Florida.

I guess it's only natural that we really would like to have a son this time, but Bob had a funny story about that last night. His co-worker, the father of a new baby boy, told him how much it costs these days to use the operating room for circumcision, and also how little boys pee in your face and all over the walls. After that conversation, Bob allowed as how he was thinking maybe another little girl would be okay!

All our love,
Pat, Bob Robin, Jenni

February 23, 1959
Hamden, Connecticut

Chickasaw, Alabama
Dearest family,

What a nice feeling, I am all through with work for the evening except for putting Robin to bed. With Bob on a holiday today, we had an early, easy supper of leftovers. Not one of us ate the same thing, but now I have lots more room in the refrigerator.

There was a sudden snowstorm this afternoon just as I was leaving for my prenatal appointment. I was nervous with such hazardous driving conditions but managed to get there and back safely. I asked the doctor to check really well for twins, but he said it felt like only one. I had gained eight pounds in three weeks and was discouraged. He said some of it is fluid retention and that I need to cut down on salt.

Last Tuesday morning right after I sealed the letter to you, the phone rang and I almost had heart failure when I heard Uncle Bill's voice. Of course, thinking he was in Alabama and had bad news that something horrible had happened to all of you, I was panicked. He assured me y'all were fine – and said he was in New York on a business trip. It was wonderful talking to him and we wished he could've come here to see us. The next day a florist delivered the most beautiful bouquet of spring-like flowers, with a note: "Sorry to miss you but there wasn't enough time – Love, Bill."

Yesterday we went into New Haven with our neighbors Ruth and Jack and had pizza. It was such fun. The children had a ball – Robin talked over the back of the booth to two young couples and was soon sitting with them. Jenni jabbered to them, too. One of the young women asked Robin if she knew where she was born, and we were all tickled when Robin was quick to respond, "Oh yes, I do know. I was born in a hospital!"

Last week I was sitting in a chair and Robin walked up close, looked at me real seriously, put her hand on my stomach and blurted out, "You got another baby in there?" When I said yes, she continued, "Are you keeping it warm?" The questions continued and we really had a good conversation. She wanted to know how the baby was going to come out, was the doctor going to cut a hole in my tummy, was it a girl or boy. She then said, "Well, I want this baby you got in there and then I want another one cause I want to be the big one of free (three) little ones."

All our love,
Pat, Bob, Robin and Jenni

February 27, 1959
Hamden, Connecticut

Chickasaw, Alabama

My dearest family,

Robin just went out to play. She'll be a mess afterward, I know, because there's slush all over the place. But for now she's occupied, and Jenni is busy taking the last of what seems to be one million toys out of the box and piling them up on the desk, so I'll see if I can dash off a short note.

I was feeling somewhat down this morning, but since then have read your letter, Mommie, and given myself a small talking-to, which I have to do periodically, and now I do feel better! I was interested in your thoughts about it being harder to carry a third child – that's what I had figured out for myself. The feeling of pressure is tremendous, and sometimes I seem to be completely paralyzed for nearly five minutes at a time with all sorts of pains, contractions and cramps. It's agonizing. Also, I wonder if my back and bladder have gotten weaker with the carrying and birthing of each child.

But enough about pregnancy ... I was thinking the other day that I wanted to tell you what a nice stage of marriage Bob and I have reached. I guess the best way to describe it is that we are so comfortable together now. We haven't had any disagreements in ages, and former "sore" subjects don't bother us as much because they are spoken of in a teasing manner. That way no one is as apt to get mad. Maybe it's just that we have finally accepted and/or forgotten (or forgiven!) one another's faults and instead dwell on each other's very good traits, and appreciate them to the fullest extent. 'Tis nice. ...

All our love to our wonderful family.

Pat, Bob, Robin, Jenni and "Lulu"
(Robin's idea)

March 13, 1959
Hamden, Connecticut

Chickasaw, Alabama

My dearest family,

While Robin and I were resting we had a "Mother-Big Daughter Talk!" We have those often now and I wish you could listen in sometimes. We talk of visiting the dentist and doctor, and maybe getting a shot like a big girl, of the new baby and how Robin is going to help, about school, and lots of other subjects. She always ends by telling me how much she loves me, and showing such deep affection that I'm all aglow!

One thing we have planned is that when warm weather comes, Jenni will go into panties and Robin will be in charge of training her. She told me recently that Jenni had to "tee-tee" and proceeded to get out the potty and put Jenni on it. It was such a cute sight, that's when I got the idea. Jenni, of course, adores her big sister, copies her actions and does anything Robin asks. She will let Robin "put her to bed" on the sofa, cover her up, and play mother and baby for the longest time.

Jenni often picks up a doll or animal, runs over and sets it on the stair steps, then stands there pointing her finger at it while jabbering on and on about "fall down, boo boo, no no." It's so cute. I can talk a lot, and Robin almost as much, now Jenni is in the running. (Even more competition for you and me, Mom!) Last night Bob came in and got snow on the rug, and Jenni scolded, "Oh, cold Daddy, cold no (snow)." After he walked off, she went straight to the kitchen wastebasket, picked out a used napkin, scooted back to the rug and wiped up the snow, mumbling the whole time.

We had awakened yesterday to a real March blizzard. There was a foot of snow, sleet, rain, lightning and rolling thunder, and it was 25 degrees. Ruth called to tell me all her plans for the day had been canceled, leaving her free to come over if I'd like that. She got here about noon and we visited, made a pie, played with the little ones, and "celebrated" the storm. (What a difference from my first winters here!) Later, after Jack and Bob were home safely and had shoveled snow from each of the driveways, we continued to celebrate with a glass of sherry and a steak dinner for our two families.

Bob's folks, the vacationers, got back Monday and stopped here for about half an hour on their way home. They were very tan and said they'd had a really nice time but had caught terrible head colds as they headed north. And the snow was a shock to them after sunny Florida!

All our love,
Pat, Bob, Robin, Jenni

May 18, 1959
Hamden, Connecticut

Chickasaw, Alabama
My dearest family,

Here I sit, panting for breath, eyes drooping, tummy protruding. I'll admit I am wishing away the moments now until Baby arrives. Really, I don't recall ever having been so-o-o-o uncomfortable. I think maybe when you start to dilate early, it makes for an easier, or at least quicker, delivery but, oh my, it is much more distressing beforehand. Every movement of the (very active) baby causes nearly unbearable pain and pressure, and I am forever involuntarily jumping and groaning, and waddling to the bathroom.

We all thought Saturday night was *the* time because I had so much pain and, for a while, regular hard contractions spaced 10 minutes apart – more of those Braxton-Hicks contractions, I guess. Then things quieted down, I went to sleep, and I am still here. I'm thinking at this point three children will be a perfectly lovely family. ...

One day I heard Robin coming up the stairs very slowly, groaning loudly. I asked her what was the matter and she patiently explained, "I'm pretending I'm Pat, and I have a big tummy, with a new baby, so it's hard to get around!" She kept it up for a long while and, honestly, it was so true to life I had to laugh. She has been especially affectionate lately, and a very good girl about almost everything. But Jenni has gotten perkier and more mischievous than ever, always laughing off a scolding!

Sunday – what a day – you know, the doctor said I shouldn't go out of town now so all the folks, including Joni's mother, came here for a family gathering. Dave and Joni's new baby Lynnie is an absolute *doll* and we all dearly love the precious little one already. Robin and Jenni were really sweet with the baby. They were intrigued and ever, ever so gentle with her. I feel sure they'll be good little mommies for our baby.

Pat, Bob, Robin, Jenni
(and ? … thinking of names tonight)

May 22, 1959
Yale New Haven Hospital
New Haven, Connecticut

Chickasaw, Alabama
My dearest folks,

Well, how do you like having a little grandson to join your "grandgirls"? He weighed in at 6 pounds, 8½ ounces on the 20th of May at 8:50 a.m. – two weeks early.

Everybody is *quite* excited – me more than anyone else, I'm sure! At the moment I am lounging in bed waiting for a delicious dinner to be served to me. After I eat, "Little Joe" (as Robin has insisted on calling the baby since she heard it's a boy) will be brought to me for a feeding and a lot of cuddling, and then my hubby is coming to pay me a visit. Sound like fun? It is, even though there are a few discomforts along with it. But the worst is over, and we have another healthy, beautiful (oops, handsome) baby. I have never felt more blessed. ...

> Lots of love,
> Pat, Bob, Robin, Jenni
> (And ?? – still!)

> June 3, 1959
> Hamden, Connecticut

Chickasaw, Alabama
My dearest family,

I'm going to try to write a short note while sitting outside – with Robin and a little friend playing in back, Jenni running loose all over the place but "checking in" with me frequently, and Skippy sleeping in the carriage. What do you think – isn't Skippy, or Skip, a clever nickname for "the third" when both senior and junior were Naval Academy men? We can't take the credit, though. Joni's mother had made a blanket for the baby and waited to hear the name and gender, then embroidered on it "For the New Little Skipper."

Jenni just walked up to the carriage, pulled the netting away and piped, "I wanna see Kippy, okay?" Then she picked up the Hula Hoop, put it over her head and said, "I wanna do de oola-oop!" Now she's teasing me, peeking around a corner to say, "Gonna poot in de mout" (anything and everything) and then running off where I can't see her!

Oh my goodness, Mommie, we are thrilled over the possibility that you might visit soon! How I wish all of you could come – I wish it with all my heart.

> Loads of love,
> Pat

> August 28, 1959
> Westport, Connecticut

Prichard, Alabama
Dearest Folks,

It's near the end of our vacation here with Bob's parents and we thought today was going to be ruined by rain, but now the sun is peeking through and it's hot and humid.

Bob and I and the two girls went down to the beach yesterday morning, where we discovered on the late side that Jenni is like a duck in the water. She said, "nice water" over and over. She loved it, even went under a few times and didn't cry. But Robin will have nothing to do with it. We bought all sorts of rafts, rings and toys for water play but she went in only once, the first day. The rest of us have had fun with her toys, though. Mostly we go swimming off the dock, which is so convenient, and have been to the beach only two or three times since it's quite a production.

This has been a nice vacation, and I sort of dread going back to the routine. The best part for me has been no meal planning or kitchen duty of any kind – Mother Kitty is adamant about that. Of course, the children require as much work, vacation or not, but I guess I've got that ahead of me for years yet.

I'm back to the letter after taking a break to bathe Skippy. He is such an agreeable little guy … eats three meals a day, sleeps till around 7:00 each morning, and coos all the time. I'm having a hard time with his daddy, though. Every time I get Skippy's cute little top curl combed just right, Bob plasters it down and parts the hair to make him look more like a boy. Nana Kitty and I nag him continuously to leave it alone. Robin just came in to report to us that he'd done it again and quite seriously asked, "Are you going to be mad with my Daddy? Skippy's hair is *flat!*"

We've been out to the movies twice this week, and to a play at the Ivorytown Summer Theatre to see Gloria Swanson and Buddy Rogers in *Red Letter Day.*

I must scoot now and will write next week from home, after I get my bearings. Have y'all found *your* bearings in your new home yet? Can't wait to see it!

We love you all,
Pat

P.S. – The other night Robin's bedtime prayer, all on her own, went as follows:

> God, thank You for Skippy
> Thank You for making my fanny get better
> Thank You for letting Daddy get me a jump rope
> Thank You for my nice family
> Thank You for my friends and Lori's new baby
> Thank You for my dolly's pretty clothes and my kitty
> (Lo-o-o-ng pause)
> Thank You for *everything.* (Ending breathlessly!)

September 12, 1959
Hamden, Connecticut

Prichard, Alabama
Dearest Folks,

I am a wreck from "our" first week at school. Robin loves kindergarten, but it's hard on Mommy, although I've just about accepted what my routine will be. I'm going to have to drive her to school and pick up every day – with the two little ones – and in winter I imagine that will be a challenge and a half. This week I've been walking back and forth to school – and have lost four pounds in as many days.

Bob has taken on another activity one night a week for the next nine months. He's going to teach a three-hour math class at a technical school for $15 per night (about $11 clear). He says he's going to use the money to take me out more – to dinner, movies, and shows at the Shubert Theatre. But looking at me one evening recently, he just about decided it wouldn't work because I might not be physically *able* to go out!

This week, in addition to the drama of school, I've worked hard in the house, scrubbing all tile floors, cleaning some cupboards, and sorting clothes – time to bring out the warm ones since it's close to freezing at night all of a sudden. Last evening I went shopping for some more clothes for Robin, $40 worth, and this is only kindergarten.

I can't think coherently, or write legibly, but at least you'll know from this scribbled note that we are still here, and are okay. We love you.

Pat

September 17, 1959
Hamden, Connecticut

Prichard, Alabama
Dearest Mommie, Daddy, and Rickey,

Needless to say, your last letter shocked us with its news of John's emergency operation for appendicitis. Thank goodness he's much better already. Oh, y'all must have felt terrible for poor John, his being new in college and away from home for the first time. I got goose pimples when I read that Sam had said he "couldn't stand it" when he knew John had been in enough pain to cry. It's wonderful the way the brothers show their love for one another. I'm so glad they could begin college together.

I happened to look out the window today as a neighbor at the top of the hill said goodbye to her third college-bound offspring. She looked completely forlorn, so I called to her to come down and sit with me for a few minutes. She did, and said she was okay, but I thought she still looked pretty lost when she left.

I think I have a few gray hairs since Robin started kindergarten. (But she looks real cute with her short haircut and new clothes – prissy as can be!) It's hard to have enough faith to let her go out into the big world where I feel I can't protect her. She loves school, though, and has priceless stories to tell. She and another little girl took a letter to the principal's office for the teacher today, and Robin was so pleased! Can't you see the two peanuts going along the hall on a responsible errand? She comes home asking if I know what a square is, or a crossbar, and then carefully explains it. She absorbs it all.

It worries me that I have less time to write now. I don't like this not having time to do half the things I should, or to fully enjoy the things I do.

Love you,
Pat

October 1, 1959
Hamden, Connecticut

Prichard, Alabama
Dearest Folks,

We're having some effects from the latest storm, Gracie, which is bringing in lots of wind and rain. I hope it doesn't begin to pour just as we're ready to leave for school this morning. Crazy weather … we were wearing fall clothes two or three weeks ago and now it's warm and humid and we've had to bring out summer outfits again.

Hey, guess what, I have a big announcement: AT LAST, there is a beautiful new dryer in the cellar – but it doesn't work yet! An electrician is coming soon to do the wiring and connecting. Wish he would come today because I can't dry clothes outside and there are loads of dirty laundry, as usual. The dryer, named "Wizard," which I hope it will be, is manufactured by Whirlpool. It's a $239 floor sample that we got for $139. Oh Happy Day.

We love you ever so much,
Pat

October 2, 1959
University of Alabama
Tuscaloosa, Alabama

Prichard, Alabama

Hi, Folks,

I was planning to come home this weekend, but I failed a math test and decided I had better stay here and study. If I do fail the course, it won't be too bad because I have the fastest instructor in the school. He has covered twice as much material as any other instructor. Sam is on Page 55 and I am on Page 95 as of today.

I am doing all right in the rest of my subjects. The only one I can brag on is my non-credit English because I am on TOP of the class. I don't think I will have any trouble getting in English next semester.

I must say I was surprised to hear Dad has traded the Chevrolet. I hope he got a good deal. Is it a powerglide or a standard shift? Do both cars have heaters? Remember I have a new '55 Chevy heater in the garage that I bought for the '51 and it didn't fit.

Our roommate Tom and Sam and I got out of class today at 11 a.m. and I went to town with Sam. When we got home, Tom had the furniture scattered all over the place and said he was going to make some more room. We worked for two hard hours and the place looks 50 percent better, and we have much more room.

Happy Birthday, Dad and Rick! I will definitely be home on October 16. Sam said he might come, too, if he happened to catch a good ride. You had better mail the next letter to him. He mentioned that he hadn't received one in three weeks.

See you in 14 days,
John

November 2, 1959
Hamden, Connecticut

Chickasaw, Alabama

My dear family,

It's good to hear you're still doing so well in real estate, Daddy, and that the college boys are together and having good luck.

I was just thinking how little ambition I have left for anything else after I finish my work. Then I wondered why I'd ever use the word "finish" in connection with my work anyway! At this moment, for instance, looking over at the sofa, I see the usual dozens of diapers waiting to be folded. Bob and I have had many a chuckle in the evenings when he will glance over

173

at me around 9:30 and see just my eyeballs as I sit enveloped in piles of diapers and baby clothes. He says, "Now, honey, aren't you going to miss all this if we ever get through having babies?"

There's just too much to keep up with even when I stay busy constantly, all day *and* all evening, and I feel so tired most mornings. I'm kind of grouchy, too. At breakfast yesterday, I apologized to Bob after he said I sure was mean to him in the mornings (although he told me I was really "a good kid" most of the time). I thought it over and made a suggestion: Said I, "How about this? I know I have a prickly personality in the early a.m. You know it. The children know it. So just let me have my few minutes of being mean, then I'll practice being sweet and smiley!"

Wish me luck!

Smiley Pat

November 11, 1959
Hotel Commodore
New York City

Prichard, Alabama

Dearest Folks,

The heavy traffic and rain were so bad I almost didn't catch the train I was supposed to take into the city yesterday. Bob's dad, with Robin, drove me to the New Haven station and I jumped out of the car, running to the platform to meet Bob before the train pulled out. We just made it. As I was settling into my seat I started to laugh when I noticed the extra item I'd brought along. There I was, headed for a weekend in New York City, dressed to the nines and looking very spiffy in a fancy black dress, white evening hat, white gloves, and Mother Kitty's borrowed beautiful black Persian Lamb fur jacket – hanging onto Robin's slightly worn little old red sweater!

What a weekend. It poured the whole time, the kind of rain that's cold and raw and threatens to leave a gloomy pall over everything. And it was just plumb frustrating trying to look glamorous but ending up with limp, straggly hair, damp, wrinkled clothes, and soaking wet feet and legs every time we stepped out of the hotel. Even so, we had fun, especially with our friends, Florence and Fred, who had joined us for the weekend.

The four of us went to an evening performance of the wonderful Broadway play, *Music Man*. The stars, Robert Preston and Barbara Cook, were fantastic, and the singing and dancing just thrilling. The only not-so-great part was the soggy condition we were in. Our clothes were sticky, our shoes squishy … and what do you do with dripping raincoats and umbrellas, sitting in a theater? But the show was good enough that we could almost forget our physical discomfort. The next afternoon Flo and I braved the rain again and went out shopping without the guys. I don't know why but we chose not to wear our glasses for nearsightedness, and had the most fun imaginable. Operating from our blurred view of the whirlwind that is New York City, we created a lot of craziness for ourselves and laughed till we cried. People probably stared and thought we were slightly tipsy or just plain nutty but we didn't care, and couldn't have seen them clearly, anyway!

When Bob and I got home we had to agree with the grandparents – the enthusiastic sitters – as they raved that our three children are the greatest! Oh, and Granddad gave Skippy a new name. He said we had a Bob, a Bob junior, a Robin, and a "Blob" (Skip). He is lazy, happy, the most beautiful and the sweetest baby in the world!

Loved your letter on Monday, Mommie. Sorry this is short, but there's so much to get done. By the way, what are the sweater sizes for Sam and John? I have a box ready to send soon – Christmas presents and used clothes for your shop.

Much love to all,
Pat

November 17, 1959
Hamden, Connecticut

Prichard, Alabama
Dearest Folks,

Please excuse the pencil but I just don't feel like fooling with the fountain pen – filling it, and likely spilling and getting ink on my hands.

We've had another busy week, as usual, with sickness included. At 4 a.m. Friday, Robin woke me up kind of moaning, "Mommy, my teeth are tired; I feel like I'm going to break all over," sure signs that within seconds she'd be vomiting, which she was, and it continued on and off for the next three hours. She was so brave, trying to get to the bathroom or over a basin, but not always making it in time, so there were quite a few messes to clean up.

Nothing like the ones after Jenni got the bug, too, though. She cried out softly at 9 o'clock Sunday night, and when I went up I was truly *panicked* at what I found. Of course, everything had to be changed and washed, and I even had to wash her hair. Bob and I took turns holding her for about two hours while she vomited four or five more times. It was terrible, seeing both girls so sick, knowing they didn't understand why we couldn't make the awful feeling go away. Jenni would tremble after each session, look up at me and say, "Mommy, I didn't 'ike it – no!" And once she said, "Mommy, take care of Jenni."

Skippy didn't catch the intestinal bug but has quite a bad cough, which has hung on since his last cold a couple of weeks ago. He looks fine, though, and seems to feel well, and is as beautiful as ever and almost as lazy! Honestly, if you could get hold of him right now when he is so sweet, soft and cuddly, you wouldn't be able to stand it. So I'll just cuddle and kiss him *for* y'all. Right now. …

We love you so much,
Pat

*Never get so fascinated by the extraordinary
that you forget the ordinary.*
Magdalen Nabb

Chapter Eleven
No Lollygagging
1959-61

Skip sowing his oats

December 8, 1959
University of Alabama
Tuscaloosa, Alabama

Prichard, Alabama
Dear Folks,

You are right – We have been studying hard.

You are wrong – We don't mind saying we are very happy Pat and her family are coming down. Very pleased.

I trust everybody is fine?

Sammie

Dear Folks,

Sorry I haven't written, but things are jumping – especially me. I have definitely decided to drop engineering next semester and major in mathematics instead. It's a good field, and I think I will like it.

We wrote Pat and Bob a line and told them we would be glad to see them but we do not have a single holiday in February. Better chance if they come in April.

John

January 4, 1960
Hamden, Connecticut

Prichard, Alabama
My dearest family,

Boy, I am pooped tonight, but then that's nothing new. After my regular day's work I began ironing at 7:30. Just finished that and had dessert to pep me up. I've also been doing loads of laundry and soon will have dozens of diapers and other assorted clothing to fold.

I'm not complaining, though, because I am so thankful to have my wonderful, dear dryer – how I love that piece of machinery! The only frustrating thing about using it is that with my dry skin, the cold weather, and static electricity, I get zapped when I begin removing the clothes. Once a diaper "grabbed" and clung to my leg, and the charge came out with a loud pop on the bottom of my foot. Ouch!

That Jenni – what a surprise the other day when she walked up and handed me the little basket that came with Robin's "Tiny Tears" doll (there is a companion doll, too, named "Toodles") and very politely asked, "Mom, would you wead de in-stwuck-chuns por Tiny Tears and Toodles?" Then she lisped, "I disth a happy lil Jenni!"

178

It really was such a special treat Friday when I picked up the phone and heard your voices. Oh, it was good to talk to you, Mommie and Daddy. I told Robin you had called and she sadly and dramatically lamented, "Oh, dear, and I didn't tell my Nana GeeGee and Granddaddy thank you for all those beautiful presents – could you call them again, Mommy, and just let me talk to them. I love them so!"

I wish you could get hold of Skippy, who is the sweetest bundle of baby boy you'll ever see! He laughs out loud if you just look at him with a funny face – or he'll sit in his little chair and play with a toy, then rock back and forth for a while, then he'll find his feet and be delighted with them. He may sit for one or two hours happy as can be. About the only time he cries is when he is really hungry.

It's 11 o'clock, I've got to get to bed and rest up for the morrow! (Isn't Robin's note cute?)

All our love,
Pat and gang

DEAR NANA GEEGEE,
DID YOU GET A NEW PUPPY YET. THANK YOU FOR THE DOLL CLOTHES AT CHRISTMAS. PLEASE COME SOON. I LOVE YOU.
ROBIN

February 6, 1960
Hamden, Connecticut

Prichard, Alabama
Dearest Folks,

I must be out of my mind to think I can concentrate enough to write. The three kids are livelier than ever – oh, their shrieks go right through me. Robin has been a fresh young miss and both girls have been into forbidden areas and activities and made so many messes that I have just about had it. Today I told Robin it might be a really good idea to read her "Do Bee" or "Ten Commandments" books, but she protested with a loud groan, "I don't want to read *any* of those books about goodness." A typical mess: One evening we found the girls, already fed, bathed, and in pajamas for the night, practically awash in the bathroom, playing happily amid wet toys and towels – Jenni had even rubbed bar soap in her hair!

Cute sayings this week: Jenni walked up to me, gently rubbed then patted my leg and said, "I luff you. You de gatest Mom!" Later she announced, "Daddy, we gonna see Nana GeeGee in Alabama in Apil!" Evidently she has been paying close attention to our conversations about the trip. And Robin, who remembers TV commercials, never misses a chance for a perfectly placed phrase – as I poured soup into cups for both girls the other day, she sighed, "Oh, smell that wonderful *deroma*."

Here's another Robin story: Remember how much she loves *The Wizard of Oz* but always gets so scared? The last time she watched it, crying her heart out yet again, she started babbling, "I feel like I'm *in* it. Jenni is a little girl and she's supposed to be afraid and I'm a big girl and I'm not supposed to be afraid but I'm afraid and Jenni's not afraid. I am all mixed up." When we suggested it might help if she didn't sit too close to the television set, she patiently explained her dilemma: "*I* don't move too close to TV, *myself* moves, I don't know I'm moving."

Bob's mother called Monday with a report of the sad weekend in Devon. Auntie Bussie was physically sick from the shock of losing Dr. Jim. Apparently the cause of his death was an aneurysm in the intestines – sudden, quick, fatal. She said Auntie was just devastated, but was already beginning to accept everything – what else is one to do? She will miss Dr. Jim so much. They and their families knew each other well, and the two of them had worked together for more than a quarter of a century. Dr. Jim's wife died after years of being an invalid, and over time his and Auntie Bussie's friendship and admiration blossomed into a deep love. They were planning to be married June 15, Bob's folks' 33rd wedding anniversary. My heart just breaks for her.

Well, I must close. Skippy wants his supper, and all of the kids need their baths.

All our love,
Pat and the gang

DEAR NANA GEEGEE
DID YOU GET A NEW PUPPY YET. DID YOU GET A NEW DOG
YET NANA. I LOVE YOU VERY VERY MUCH NANA. I AM EXCITED
ABOUT MY BIRCHDAY PARTY.
ROBIN

February 13, 1960
Hamden, Connecticut

Prichard, Alabama
Dearest Folks,

Bob has taken his two little gals for a ride out to Barker's, a huge discount place, to buy our first record album. His folks passed their old record player on to us when Dad got a new Hi-Fi set for Christmas, and with a few assorted old telephone company pieces Bob had here, we now have a fairly good system. We'll have to change records often but we'll buy the LPs, so at least it won't mean a change every five minutes.

Skippy and I are holding down the fort here. While I write he is in the playpen, making growling noises at some toy and every so often turning to smile and flirt with me. He is so cute, folks, I'm awfully glad you'll be seeing him soon. Oh, he got his first hair trim this morning. Bob was tired of the piece of hair that hung over Skip's left ear and he got out the scissors and snipped. It was actually quite a major family production, with Mommy holding baby, Daddy very intently and almost expertly snipping, and two big sisters looking on, wide-eyed, chatting a mile a minute.

We had some more sickness this week, though not serious. The children had fairly bad colds, and then Bob caught a dilly of one and felt so miserable he missed two days of work. We also missed the monthly couples' bridge party, which we always enjoy.

Oops, here comes the gang – yippee. You ought to hear the noise now! Bob is just bubbling over telling me what a kick he got out of the girls. Jenni, especially, tickled him and I knew what he meant. She has been cooped up in the playroom most of her young life, you know, and is so tiny and adorable and funny when she hits the big outside world. Just now she put a dolly's blanket around her shoulders and said, "Skippy, Mommy's writing and I'm going to be Susie Snowflake, okay?" Skippy loves to hang over the side of the high chair to watch and egg her on! Funny how both girls like to drape various pieces of clothing around their necks or shoulders. Remember Robin as a toddler, walking around nearly all day with one of Bob's socks lying neatly across the back of her neck?

Mommie, I know you'll love the note from Robin. She labored over it, and was worn out by the time it was finished, but oh what a labor of love. When I printed the word "beautiful" for her to copy, (she chose it) she looked slightly dismayed, "Oh, no, that's the *longest* thing." This is her very first thank-you note – at age 5!

Now for a report on her big day. She hardly ate a bite all day, she was so excited. You can't imagine what this birthday meant to her. As soon as she got up she ran to me, bubbling over, "Oh, Mom, am I really 5 years old

181

now?" Yes! I assured her. She went to her daddy with the same question, then back to me, laughing, and said, "Oh, I'd better go look!" She sprinted over to the full-length mirror, stopped close to it and stared at herself and, seconds later, in disbelief, moaned, "Oh-o-h, no, I still look *four*!"

I had written a card to the radio program we listen to in the mornings, and when we heard the announcement, "Robin, who attends Mount Carmel kindergarten, is 5 years old today and the leader of our band – Happy Birthday!" her eyes got bigger and bigger. She was thrilled.

Nana Kitty came, bearing presents and cards and a birthday cake, for an early lunch before Robin left for the afternoon kindergarten session. I had made cookies and took those and little cups of valentine candies for her school party. She told us the children sang "Happy Birthday" to her and the teacher tapped her five times.

Wondering what to fix for dinner, I suddenly had a bright idea. Why not begin a tradition of having the birthday girl or boy choose the menu for their special day? Robin has excellent taste – steak, salad, rolls, raw carrots, birthday cake ... that's what we had!

Pat

DEAR NANA GEEGEE
   THANK YOU FOR THE BEAUTIFUL SHOES. I LOVE YOU.
      ROBIN

March 8, 1960
Hamden, Connecticut

Prichard, Alabama
Dearest Folks,

It has been over a week since I've written – and, wow, what a week! The whole family sick, one nearly hospitalized, a snowstorm that dumped 14.2 inches, with drifts a couple of feet high, a bridge party-shower almost canceled but then moved to another house, another dinner date postponed – and this lil ol' Mommy really pooped and on her last leg. ...

When I wrote on Monday, Robin was awfully weak but drinking a bit of diluted tea off and on so I was encouraged. But Tuesday morning she still had some diarrhea and would not touch anything, and by afternoon just lay on her bed, looking almost unconscious. I was scared, and the doctor, too, was concerned, and asked me to keep him informed.

We began giving her Lyten, a supplement we had tried before when she was dehydrated. She resisted and cried so pitifully. I tried to entice her by

182

playing tea party, hoping she'd drink from the tiny cup, then I talked firmly, and after an hour she'd taken only two ounces. I was so glad to have gotten some liquids into her, but suddenly she began vomiting again. I cried then and was even more scared.

When I called in, the doctor told me to begin all over again with Dramamine, coke syrup and ice chips every 10 minutes to stop the vomiting. Then he called me that evening to see how she was and suggested I get her up in the night to try and get some liquids into her. He mentioned hospitalization but said, "We'll wait a bit more and probably just when we get desperate, she'll perk right out of it, I imagine." He said some children seem to be violently susceptible to diarrhea and she must be one of them. The next morning, Robin got up looking a little better and ready to accept more liquids, so the danger was past.

Wednesday, I was so relieved of the fear that Robin might need to be hospitalized – had a few minutes of feeling good – and then right after Bob left for work, Jenni started the vomiting and diarrhea. By the time I got around to poor little Skippy, he was covered with diarrhea. I ran from one to the other, cleaning up mess after mess, on the rug, in chairs, in the bathrooms – putting another wash into the machine every little while – and pretty soon Skippy was vomiting, too.

Then all of a sudden, I felt *awful*. I thought at first it was just that I had been up to my neck, *literally*, in upchucking and diarrhea, but soon *I* had diarrhea. Luckily, with my constitution like that of a horse, I was only mildly affected by the bug and never went to bed during the day, but I sure did drag.

Thursday, Robin was still improving, Jenni perked up quite a bit after lying around looking unconscious in between her sicknesses the day before, but Skippy was miserable. He cried and cried and cried. He still had diarrhea so the doctor had me start him on Lyten to help prevent dehydration.

With all of this going on I hardly looked out all day and when I did, I saw only that it was snowing something terrible, a real blizzard. I fell into bed at 8 p.m., was up off and on with the children and my own tummy distress. The next morning, peeking outside, *so* much snow – one drift up to the halfway point of our front door.

And inside, pure exhaustion. ... Robin had another brief siege of diarrhea, Jenni began vomiting again, and Skippy's diarrhea got worse, and he cried continuously. The doctor, at this point, felt sorry for me but told me to try not to be discouraged. He said with three children in the family, they were probably bouncing the bug back and forth. At least by the end of the day, though, everyone was eating and drinking small amounts. Granted, it was coming right through them but they were free from vomiting and had some appetite.

And what a week, an exciting one, for Auntie Bussie – she received an engraved invitation from the President of the United States! Yes, isn't that something? She was asked to be a technical consultant for a one-week White House conference on youth and children. It's really a fine tribute and we are *so* proud of her.

Oh, I'm tired, gotta go – we love you all.

Pat

March 31, 1960
University of Alabama
Tuscaloosa, Alabama

Prichard, Alabama
Dear Folks,

Well, I guess it's high time we wrote. We've received no letter since Monday so are assuming everything turned out OK on your hospital reports, Dad.

I suppose our grades have arrived there by now. At the risk of this sounding like a "likely story," I want to say that the "N" on the report means my chemistry professor didn't get the tests graded in time to turn them in. In fact, I don't think he's graded them yet. Anyway, he said Monday that he was gong to disregard the two tests we've taken to date since the scores were so bad.

Well, Mom, the days are fairly tearing by and it will be DSB&N Day before you know it (daughter, sister, brother-in-law and nieces).

Rickey, I guess you did me in on report cards this time, BUT this is my last semester of English, and once it's over I'm going to take off like a big bird. So don't get too confident with your lead.

Sammie

Hi,

Just thought I would drop a line, too. Sam didn't mention it, but when we went to Uncle Aubrey's funeral in Stonewall, we saw everyone from Clark County, Mississippi. There were 200 or 300 people in the small church. I guess we saw 50 people we knew but didn't remember their faces.

We were late getting to the funeral and stood in the back of the church. When we went down to the casket, I heard all the aunts and uncles saying,

"Why, there's Sammie and John!" Of course, the best part of the trip was seeing Dad.

The boy who is moving in next door is a chemistry major and Sam said he feels better now about the future of his own chemistry grades.

Love,
John

May 4, 1960
Hamden, Connecticut

Prichard, Alabama

Hi, dear ones,

I'm just sitting here reliving, for a few minutes, the wonderful time we had with you last month. And as always, wishing there were fewer miles – and more visits – between us. ...

Tonight not one single child, male or female, wanted to give in to bedtime. All three have colds again, and I spent nearly two hours on baths, cleaning noses, giving medicine, wiping tears, picking Skippy up "just one more time" for burps, and what-have-you. Now Robin has come downstairs to report that she and Jenni can't get to sleep. And no wonder, they haven't been quiet or still long enough!

There has been a switch in the girls' behavior – Robin is in a good mode now and Jenni is getting harder to handle, the little imp. Yesterday she smeared a mess of powder and "goop" on a chair and I was huffin' and puffin' as I cleaned it up, scolding, "Just look at this mess. What do you think of it?" She grinned and sighed, "I des 'sink about Robin." And later in the yard, when she kept trampling the flowers, I commanded, quietly and with clenched jaw, "Get - out - of - the - flowers." She simply chuckled ... "*If* you say pease (please)."

Thought I had lost Skippy the other day. For just a minute I left him sitting in the stroller in the garage, and when I came back – no Skippy! But before I got too frantic, I found him happily crawling around on the other side of the garage, not crying or hurt. Evidently he had just slid out of the front of the stroller. Never a dull moment.

Since this evening's quick, early supper, Bob has been outside planting two nice young maple trees in the back yard. We've had two days of perfect weather – 70 degrees, clear and sunny – so I've been outside whenever I could manage, and took the children for a walk both days.

Gotta go now. We love you all so much. Have a happy birthday, Mommie!

Pat and gang

185

May 22, 1960
Hamden, Connecticut

Prichard, Alabama
Dearest Folks,

All three children are clustered around me bombarding me with questions, wants, don't-wants, etc. I just gave up trying for a light nap. I kept dozing and then jumping like I was falling, so I'm not sure if it hurt or helped.

Robin awoke with a cold and cough this morning, and now she and Jenni both are feverish and feeling miserable. It just doesn't seem to end, huh?

Skippy is well so far, and he is he sowing some wild oats, thinks he's pretty big stuff now, at age 1. He's not sleeping much during the day, and resists bedtime with really furious, turning-blue crying. He keeps busy getting into mischief, crawling over or pulling up to explore wastebaskets, ashtrays, electrical outlets, the television set – and has banged up the coffee table and the door of the antique dry sink.

He doesn't think much of carrots, green beans and spinach, and today had me in hysterics with his funny faces. Seeing a bite of carrots coming Skip would squint his eyes shut, put both hands up in front of his face and close his teeth together, but for a little taste of ice cream, a big grin and open mouth!

Funny little clown, he'll sit on the floor and lift hands and feet up and nearly go over backward as he gets to really rocking, and then he'll squeal and clap his hands. He gives us sweet kisses and we still think he is the most beautiful little hunk of lightly tanned skin, blue eyes, fat legs and honey-colored curly hair you could find anywhere!

For his first birthday, Skippy, Robin, Jenni and I had Coca-Cola and snowball cakes – his with a lighted candle – and the girls opened his presents. Thanks for the pretty yellow outfit you sent.

Friday night Bob and I went to a church Couples Club picnic. It was the first time we'd been out together without the kids in a long time. About two weeks ago, following a "cool" period, we had "a talk" and I told Bob I was tired of getting just a peck on the cheek instead of a real kiss. The next morning I figured the ice had been broken and he had gotten the message – walking into the kitchen at breakfast time he came at me with a devilish gleam in his eye and I knew exactly what was coming. And he knew that I knew so we both burst out laughing. He swept me into his arms and leaned me over halfway to the floor and *kissed* me! Since then things have been quite wonderful.

Take care of yourselves – we love you so much.

Pat and the gang

June 9, 1960
Hamden, Connecticut

Prichard, Alabama
Dearest Folks,

I can't even remember when I wrote to you last – and I'm not in very good condition to write tonight, either. Like you, Mommie, I'm pooped, but things keep popping. I really worked today – cleaned the stove, the oven, and the refrigerator, scrubbed all wastebaskets and the big trash can, washed and ironed curtains and did other laundry, cleaned the bathroom thoroughly, waxed floors, and polished silver – all "extras." Along with the usual job of taking care of the children, which now includes the challenge of potty-training Jenni and trying to break Skippy of a few of his new habits.

Speaking of my busy schedule reminds me to tell you that Auntie Bussie gave us a copy of her new book, *The Girl That You Marry*. It's so exciting, not only is Skippy one of the children named in the dedication (along with Dr. Jim's latest grandchildren), I am in the book! She didn't tell me ahead of time, and I was reading along and suddenly came across one of my days outlined in a chapter. Remember about four years ago when she recruited me for the project and I was paid to keep a schedule of my activities for two weeks? Of course, a typical day back then, with only the one child, sounds like a dream now – I had a *nap*!

Mommie, the book is so interesting. It's written for boys, to help them better understand girls. I hope Sam and John read it. As I wrote Auntie, "Bob is wonderful in so many ways but sometimes he just doesn't know what makes me tick, and with this book you tell him so well." As planned, Dr. Jim wrote the first chapter, and she wrote the rest. She had wanted to surprise him and have him read her manuscript only after the book was published. Sadly, though, he died before that happened.

Auntie Bussie is coming up Monday and may stay overnight with us. We haven't seen her in a year and are really looking forward to seeing her again, as always.

We love you all so very much,
Pat and crew

August 5, 1960
Hamden, Connecticut

Prichard, Alabama
Dearest family,

We're having one of those dreary, cold, rainy days, reminding me all too much of winter. I can't stand to think summer is nearly over and winter will soon follow.

I just scooped ol' Skipper-doodle up and out of the bathroom – again! After we found him twice unrolling all the toilet tissue and splashing in the toilet, we've tried to keep him away from those two things. The other night the girls yelled, "Look at Skippy!" and we found him standing on the toilet seat lid, swaying this way and that, having a grand time. He also likes to climb into the rocking chair and stand up to rock. Soon he'll be walking and discovering even more entertaining activities.

Little did I know when I took Jenni for a haircut recently that I was in for such a battle. I had to half drag her up a flight of stairs, with her screaming like a banshee, without dropping Skippy, who was hanging on my hip while keeping a tight hold on my shoulder and an eagle eye on the shaky situation. As soon as we reached the shop, I practically dropped him into the lap of an agreeable stranger sitting there so that I could manage Jenni. I held her as still as I could and told the barber to just trim her bangs and forget the rest. It was a hot, humid day and the whole episode was – if you'll pardon the pun – a pretty hairy experience.

In the midst of Jenni's screams and kicks, I looked at the barber and with a raised eyebrow confided, "And sometimes my husband wonders why I am so exhausted. It's *small* battles like this that use up all my strength."

At the moment, though, all is well. The girls are dancing together to rock 'n' roll music and Skippy is jumping and cheering them on. This trio keeps me on my toes.

Now on to more chores. We love you all so much!
Pat and brood

October 3, 1960
Hamden, Connecticut

Prichard, Alabama
Dearest Folks,

For the second time in about a year, both Jenni and Skippy have napped at the same time. I hear Jenni waking up now but she may be happy in the crib a while longer. The peace and quiet – and 1½ hours of no "Mommy do this, Mommy I want that" – are heavenly, oh yes.

Your sweet letter with the boys' note included came on Saturday, Mommie. I was interested in all the news, especially tidbits about Sam and John's dating life!

But news that Celia's husband is seriously ill is so distressing I can hardly sleep thinking of their situation. It was the same when I heard that the young son of Bob's old friend from Waterbury had leukemia. Knowing it's incurable and how quickly it takes lives is very frightening.

Last week when I took Jenni to the doctor, secretly worried about the possibility of leukemia, I asked how would I know the symptoms. He told me that to be cold-blooded about it, it didn't do any good to know, but that he *had* examined her spleen first thing. Apparently the spleen becomes enlarged with the disease. He said, "It's a horrible disease but still quite rare, and Jenni doesn't have any signs of it." And added, "Johnny's mother will never get over his death – every time his two sisters have a sniffle, she rushes them down here and holds her breath till I check their spleens." Oh, how sad, how sad.

We are so blessed. And we love you.

Pat and brood

December 21, 1960
Hamden, Connecticut

Prichard, Alabama
Dearest Folks – all five,

A bulletin: Saturday, the whole family bundled up and went downtown for "Jenni's treat." We celebrated her new "toilet talents" with big cones of chocolate ice cream. At 10:30 a.m. On the first day of winter!

Both boxes from Mobile have arrived, and it looks exciting around here with all the gaily wrapped gifts. Oh, you'll laugh over my little secret – guess what I had for lunch today? PECANS and more PECANS! Yep, the package arrived before lunch and I nearly lost my mind when I saw all those beautiful nuts. Thieves must get that same feeling when they see a stash of jewels!

Have a wonderful Christmas, Mommie, Daddy, Sam, John and Rickey. We love you and miss you.

Pat

March 31, 1961
Hamden, Connecticut

Prichard, Alabama
Dear Folks,

It seems such a long time since I've written a letter to you … well, actually it *has been* a long time. When I was feeling so depressed those first few weeks after Christmas, being able to talk to you frequently on the phone was more of a lifeline to me than letters. It was probably the first time in my life that communicating by letters wasn't easy for me.

And talk about a lifeline, a new lease on life, the extended visit the children and I had with y'all in Alabama last month was invaluable in helping me recover a more positive spirit. Not only was it good to have a break from some of the worst of winter weather, but the respite from my hectic, sometimes overwhelming routine was healing. Your taking care of the children – and my knowing how mutually satisfying that was for both sides – so that I could get more rest, peace and quiet was a gift without price. Bob really missed us, naturally, but he knew the change would be good for me – and sees the results already. So he thanks y'all, too.

I think you know how much I love you, Mom and Daddy, how much I appreciate you as loving and supportive parents. I am a lucky daughter.

Hugs from all of us,
Pat

May 15, 1961
Hamden, Connecticut

Prichard, Alabama
My dearest family,

Friday Ruth and I ignored the pouring rain and went into New Haven for a nice shopping trip and lunch. It's fun and a real treat to get out with a friend for a little spree once in a while. In fact, I was so happy when Bob came home he remembers and has mentioned it quite a few times since. I told him that when he and I are getting along well and I have one day a week to halfway call my own, I feel more contented and realize I'm easier to get along with … which makes life much nicer for all of us.

Oh, do I have a funny incident to tell you involving Ruth and Jenni and our very tall, very elderly, almost deaf neighbor, "Mr. Willie." Those three and I were out front, the grownups chatting, Jenni playing quietly in the grass, not paying us much mind, when suddenly Jenni craned her neck to look way up toward his face and tugged on his pants calling, "Mr. Willie? Mr. Willie?"

190

He was oblivious to her, so Ruth fairly shouted, "Mr. Willie, Jenni wants to tell you something!" He smiled down at her, waiting. Little Miss Jenni stared up at him and, with the wisdom of her nearly four years, proclaimed, "Mr. Willie, you're so old you're gonna die." He smiled good-naturedly, still without a clue as to what Jenni had said, we were pretty sure. We hoped. Ruth turned rosy red and tried to smile, and I took Jenni by the hand, waving cheerily as we hightailed it home. Ruth says she'll think twice before coming to Jenni's aid again.

Over the weekend, we visited Bob's folks in Suffield. They seemed fine except for being discouraged over all the chores that haven't gotten done since Dad broke his back. He looks good and feels well but can't do much yet. Mother Kitty has to bathe and shampoo him, dress him, put his shoes on, all the steps in the daily routine, plus extras like cutting his toenails, etc. The grass is long and the yard covered with dandelions, and the storm windows need to be replaced with screens. (Bob did some of those this trip.)

They thoroughly enjoyed the children and were especially tickled over Skippy, who wore his red baseball hat cocked to one side the whole day and looked so all boy!

We love you all very much, always. Take care.

Pat

August 15, 1961
Hamden, Connecticut

Prichard, Alabama
Dearest Folks,

Been thinking of you today. Happy 30th Anniversary, Mommie and Daddy – wish we could celebrate with you. ...

I've been busy getting organized to leave on Saturday for our vacation in Westport. This year I have to take all the bedding, towels, food, washing powders, paper products, etc., plus our clean clothes and all kinds of personal items.

Thank goodness I shopped for Jenni's birthday, wrapped the gifts and took them to Suffield last week. That way, when the folks and Auntie Bussie come on Sunday, they will bring the presents – a birthday cake, too, since I would hardly have time to bake one there. We'll get to Westport at noon but have to get unpacked, make beds and shop for groceries before vacation *really* starts.

Thinking of all the work to be done reminds me of what that smart Robin has just figured out. She was making her bed one morning, ranting how unfair it was that Jenni didn't have to do that chore yet. I said when Jenni got to be 6 years old, she too would make her bed. As if a light suddenly dawned, Robin lamented, "O-h-h-h, I see, then *I'll* be doing *more* work. Now I know the secret of oldness."

Much, much love to Mommie, Daddy, Sam, John and Rickey.

From Pat and her brood

August 23, 1961
Westport, Connecticut

Prichard, Alabama
Dearest Folks,

My special day again, and I'm already thinking about next year when I'll turn 30. It's a dreary, rainy, cool day, and Auntie Bussie left early this morning, so we feel a wee bit down in the dumps. Four days we've been here and only two have been nice.

We certainly enjoyed Auntie and she had a good time being with all the family. We ate, slept and gabbed for three days. (She asked me to give y'all her best.) Skippy is really a sentimental little guy. When she was ready to leave today, he said, "Auntie Bussie, you kin (can't) go bye bye, peas don go bye bye."

The folks drove down for dinner last night to surprise us and also have another visit with Auntie, and Skip was so darn sweet when they left, too. His lip trembled as he said, "You run back." They said they would, he smiled and said "aw-wight." I remember, Mommie, how John was always sad over leaving your papa. Skip loves the relatives and, just like his Mommy, would like to have all of them around all the time. Auntie Bussie said that was her idea of heaven, too.

Will write more later. We love you all so much.

Pat

September 9, 1961
Hamden, Connecticut

Prichard, Alabama
My dearest family,

This will be the last time I'll write to all five of you for a while since Sam and John will be going back to college next week. You two young men have certainly done well, and all our good wishes will be with you this coming year for success in all ways. Please know that even though I don't write to

192

you very often, I think of you, Sam and John, and speak of you more than you know.

Rickey, lots of good luck to you, too, in this school year. Before we know it you will be going off to college, too. A couple of years ago I wouldn't have been able to picture it, but I've been feeling old lately and so can very well and easily believe that you are nearly grown up.

We love you 5!

Pat + 4

October 21, 1961

Hamden, Connecticut

Prichard, Alabama

Dearest Folks,

Gracious, I had a rough few days this week following dental surgery. When the dentist removed that top permanent front tooth that had never come through, we saw it was perfect and pretty. It's too bad the dentist in Mobile years ago didn't guide it down into the space when he extracted my baby tooth instead of leaving this one in the gum and filling in the "capping bridge" with a false tooth.

I took penicillin, and codeine one day, and used an icepack for a couple of days. Wednesday my nose and cheeks began to swell, and by Thursday morning there was so much swelling my left eye was nearly shut.

I had felt lousy and hadn't eaten much, so when I did perk up on the weekend we went to McDonald's for hamburgers and milkshakes. Everything tasted so good to me. But in the car afterward, to our horror, Robin suddenly began to throw up. Oh, glory, what a mess. We rushed home, hauled everybody inside, and I began bathing all the little bodies while Bob went back out and bathed the car.

Robin seemed fine and went right to bed. She slept well all night, got up and ate breakfast the next morning, went downstairs to the playroom and a few seconds later, with no warning, oops, up came her breakfast all over the place. A virus, I guess. We kept her home and gave her Dramamine that day and now she's all right.

I have started a cold, though, and the scratchy throat and runny nose added to the discomfort of my still slightly swollen, sore face from the tooth ordeal makes for one miserable being.

Did I tell you that I'm going to try Enovid, the new contraceptive pill? My friends think I'm crazy to put my faith in a little pill, but I guess I trust science more than the others do. They're all expecting me to soon be expecting!

193

I definitely would not be ready for another baby, though. … Most of the time now I'm happy, and able to accept things with a more mature attitude. Ready to rise above the confusion connected with raising a family and *be aware* of truly being thankful for having healthy, wonderful children. And, too, I find myself more appreciative of Bob and all his many good qualities. Guess I'm just getting older, and mellowing with age. Good!

Take care and remember that we love you – all 5 of you.

Pat

November 18, 1961
Hamden, Connecticut

Prichard, Alabama
Dearest Folks,

I have a few minutes before we leave for the Shubert Theatre to see *Nine O'Clock Revue* with Lena Horne. We've had the tickets for weeks then, unexpectedly, Dave and Joni wanted to stop here overnight on their way home from Greenwich. We have to leave before they arrive but our sitter will be here, and there are beds made up all over the place, notes posted inside the front door, and hot and cold drinks and brownies waiting.

I gave them a choice of sleeping on the playroom sofa bed or in the master bedroom – until yesterday when Skippy-doodle learned to climb out of his crib, our bedroom was fairly private. Now there's apt to be a little person wandering in. Skip is so delighted to be able to hop out of bed, but a bit confused because we're all mad at him when he does! Sometimes he will call out, "Is it mornin' time yet? Is mornin' time, yay, girls, is mornin' time, we can get up." Little peanut Jenni came into our room at 6 o'clock this morning holding Skip by the hand – "Look what I found in my room!" Oh brother!

It's Sunday evening and I'm back to finish the letter. We loved the show last night. Lena Horne is amazing, so beautiful, such a marvelous voice. She's probably 40 and looks 20!

Everyone was in bed when we got home. Little Lynn had a croupy cough and they slept in the playroom so as not to disturb our sleep. We had time for a nice visit with Dave and Joni before they headed home in the afternoon.

This week will seem short. The children are out of school from Wednesday noon till the following Monday, and we'll be with Bob's folks in Suffield for most of the Thanksgiving holidays. That's always a treat. …

Oh, Robin brought her report card home last week. She had three A's (reading, writing and 'rithmetic) and nine B's. Teacher, with a grin, said, "Robin likes to talk!" Chip off the old block, huh, Mommie?

Take care of all of you – we love you so much.

Pat and brood

December 5, 1961
Hamden, Connecticut

Prichard, Alabama
Dearest Folks,

The job of getting organized here at home after our trip to Philadelphia is driving me nuts. Returning from a weekend away can be a bit of a shock. The house is a mess, dirty laundry is piled up, and the children require extra attention. And this time, with the Christmas holidays so near, there are fruitcakes to bake and presents to buy, and the house needs to be decorated before our party in two weeks. By the way, Mom, how many marshmallows are called for in your Ice Box Fruitcake recipe? Let me know soon, okay?

The children made out fine all weekend, the sitter, too. And we enjoyed every minute of our getaway. The visit with Auntie Bussie in her warm, welcoming home was such a treat, and we had lots of fun with our friends Al and Sarah at the Army-Navy game on Saturday. There were two exciting happenings: We saw President Kennedy at the game, and Navy won!

Robin's teacher said she should send some of her lovely papers to her Nana GeeGee and Granddaddy in Alabama, so here you are. She's doing beautifully in school and is so excited that she can now read.

We love you so much and miss you – especially on days like today!

Pat

BY ROBIN

THE STORY ABOUT TED AND SALLY. TED AND SALLY LIKE TO PLAY. THEY LIKE TO RUN. THEY LIKE TO JUMP. DO YOU LIKE TO JUMP.

BOOTS AND TUFFY. TUFFY LIKES TO RUN. BOOTS LIKES TO RUN TOO. THEY LIKE TO PLAY. GOOD-BY.

195

December 27, 1961
Hamden, Connecticut

Prichard, Alabama
My dearest family – all 5!

Oh, I was sad last night after talking to everyone (except Rickey – where were you, honey?). I put the phone down, went back to my chair in front of the fireplace and quickly warned Bob I was going to cry a wee bit. After all these years he's very understanding when I'm hit with a bout of homesickness.

We just love the presents you sent. Mommie, I'm telling you, Robin and Jenni squealed and ran around like crazy when they opened the box filled with doll clothes you made. They kept saying, "Oh, oh!" as they threw miniature size clothes up in the air and dug deeper to see what else was there.

The children are on vacation this week – oh woe is me! Isn't that an awful comment? But they need school; I need them in school. Nobody naps anymore and the days can seem lo-o-ng. Right now they're wrecking the living room. Earlier there was milk spilled all over the place not once, but three times. Then Skip christened the kitchen floor with sugar … and his hair with my new Chanel No. 5!

We love you,
Pat

When you lose simplicity,
you lose drama.
                              Andrew Wyeth

Chapter Twelve
Life's Routines
1962-63

Dressed and ready for Robin's birthday party

February 27, 1962
Hamden, Connecticut

Prichard, Alabama
Dearest Folks,

Today I had plans with friends to enjoy a spree in Springfield, Massachusetts, but Robin has been quite sick and I didn't want to be away. Her illness started suddenly with a terrible headache and high fever, and she was delirious during the night. That was scary, as was the fact that she didn't eat a bite of food for 56 hours! She still has eaten only two small servings of soup but, thank goodness, she's definitely better.

Jenni has been in Suffield for "special time" with Nana Kitty and Granddad. Their report this morning was that she has been a happy girl, behaving well, sleeping late and making no sour faces. And following her routine at home, each morning she asks the grandparents, "Hey, what are the arrangements for the day?" Jenni told them today she was ready to go home, adding, "I had a good time, but I want to see how they all look again."

Skippy has really missed her and said last night, "I hate Jenni to go off!" By the way, he has become fascinated with magic tricks and at any time during the day will make the announcement, "Everbody, I do magic now, watch dis disapeeoo!" Then he grins and hides the item behind his back, anything from a toy to a piece of toast.

Yesterday the weather was cold, rainy, and raw, and Bob was scheduled to work into the evening, so I knew I'd be facing a long day, but an unexpected nap really helped. Skip doesn't like napping nowadays, but he fell asleep sitting in my lap having his back tickled. I wasted no time in grabbing a blanket to settle on the sofa for a doze, nice-a-cozy, as Robin would say. I have been SO cold for days. I'd been following on TV the events honoring Colonel John Glenn and, before sleep overtook him, even Skip liked watching the exciting parade from the White House to Capitol Hill. What must it feel like to Colonel Glenn to be the very first American to orbit the Earth? Wasn't it exciting last week when he went rocketing into space from Cape Canaveral and then splashed down in the Atlantic? Wow!

We were thrilled with the wonderful news that John made the dean's list. Both boys have done so well in college, and that makes all your efforts worthwhile. We called this week to wish Sam a happy 25th birthday.

Love you so much,
Pat

March 19, 1962
Hamden, Connecticut

Prichard, Alabama

Hi, Mommie and Daddy,

Get ready for one of the best "Robin stories" yet. I wanted to put everything down in writing while it's fresh. I bet we'll still be laughing over this one years from now.

During the children's regular night bath routine recently Robin was tired and cranky and being completely uncooperative. Nothing seemed to suit her, and I must say, soon my mood matched hers. She was *really* angry with me and started talking about running away from home. I stayed calm, commenting agreeably, "Well ... if that's what you want to do. ..." Hearing that Jenni quickly glanced up at me with a questioning look, but then went back to drying herself off. Still paying not a whit of attention to Robin, I lifted Skip from the tub, wrapped him in a towel, and we continued with the evening ritual.

Meanwhile Robin went to her room and put on her footed Dr. Denton pajamas, packed a few things into a small play suitcase, and came back to the bathroom doorway, where she posed and very dramatically proclaimed, "Goodbye! I'm leaving." I had just about had it with her and decided to call her bluff, so I simply ignored the threat and kept on with Jenni and Skip's bath routine.

When we finished and went downstairs, there stood Miss Robin, waiting in the hallway, still threatening to leave. As soon as she saw us she picked up her toy bag and kind of flounced over toward the front door, flung it open and yelled, "GOODBYE." I gave her a casual goodbye wave. And little sister Jenni, watching wide-eyed, sucking her favorite two fingers, lisped around the fingers, "Don't fowget you schooss, Wobin."

It was 20 degrees outside, but Bob was due to be walking up the hill from the bus stop any second, so I knew she wouldn't get far from the house. And hoped she wouldn't get pneumonia! So, off she went into the cold night, coatless, hatless, shoeless, clutching that little doll's suitcase, which obviously wasn't holding much for her future needs. After the door slammed shut, suddenly it was eerily quiet. Jenni just looked at me and kept sucking her fingers with obvious enjoyment. Skippy, content, unconcerned with all the high drama taking place, ran his little Matchbox car along the bottom step of the stairs. ... I took a few deep breaths, getting myself prepared for whatever was coming next.

After just two or three minutes, sure enough, Missy Robin managed to get herself out of the situation without entirely losing face. She opened the door with a flourish, pranced back inside, boldly shaking her finger at me with this warning, "*All right*, I'll give you *one* more chance!"

I'm not at all sure I'll be able to keep up with her. Any suggestions greatly appreciated. ...

Have a good laugh!
Love you,
Pat

May 15, 1962
Hamden, Connecticut

Prichard, Alabama
Dearest Folks,

We miss you, Mommie – hope you had a great flight back to Mobile after that really smooth takeoff from La Guardia.

I am sitting under the dryer at Michael's Beauty Shop – getting a soft permanent today – writing on a lined pad so I don't have to think about keeping a straight line. Michael just raved over you, Mom, thinks you are quite a gal. He said when you left the shop the other day all the other customers were talking about your beautiful hair.

Yesterday was rainy and dreary, and to perk myself up I got a sitter and went into New Haven to the hospital to see Ruth. She looked absolutely beautiful and little Barbara is one of the prettiest newborns I've ever seen – jet-black hair, soft pink skin and fine features, cute as a button! I could hardly stand not being able to get my hands on her.

Our best love to you – all 5.
Pat and gang

May 27, 1962
Hamden, Connecticut

Prichard, Alabama
Dearest Folks,

We're in the car on our way home from Suffield and I brought my dandy little tablet and a ballpoint pen to dash off a few lines.

All of us enjoyed a nice day together, visiting while we relaxed outdoors in the gorgeous 70-degree sunny weather. We got into bathing suits to get a bit of color. The folks could hardly believe it, though, when I soon had goose pimples and had to cover up!

Mother Kitty has been feeling very poorly for a week or more. She thinks it's caused by a rise in her blood pressure, which is always high anyway. She has an appointment for a physical exam tomorrow.

I'm just getting over another one of my frequent bouts of sore throat, cold and sinus infection. Oh, and all five of us went to the doctor yesterday for our first dose of the Sabin oral polio vaccine. The dose consisted of a plain cube of sugar containing a few drops of pink fluid – live polio virus! Isn't that amazing? In a month, we'll have a second dose, for the next most serious type of polio, then later on another one.

Love you all,
Pat

June 1, 1962
Hamden, Connecticut
Under the hair dryer

Prichard, Alabama
Dearest Folks,

I think we're going to have a hot summer. For days it has been 85 and 90 degrees and humid, but I haven't been uncomfortable. I'm thriving on a spell of warm weather while all the Yankees are sweltering.

Monday evening Bob called to me, fairly urgently, to look at a sizeable lump he'd found on Skippy's neck. We were both worried as to what it might be, but the doctor thought it was a swollen gland, not mumps, and the swelling did subside the next day.

Then Jenni looked as if she was getting the mumps and I called the doctor again. He wanted to see Jenni *and Bob*. He said it was important to check on whether Bob was immune. Evidently many fathers land in the hospital with mumps as the illness affects adults a lot more seriously than it does kids. It turned out Jenni didn't have the mumps, but Bob apparently is not immune and will need to be careful about future exposure.

Meanwhile, I'm still battling this sinus infection I've had for well over a week. I keep having a tickly throat and awful coughing fits.

We have a new kitty, and it was quite a challenge to get her home. She hated the car ride and kept crying and scratching the box, trying to get out. Time and again Skip would shout, "She's out!" and I would hold my breath, afraid she'd jump on my neck while I was driving. We made it here safely, though, and are already attached to little "Twinkles."

Guess what I did today? A real first for me – I planted about three dozen seedlings of marigolds, zinnias, asters and petunias in the front yard. I was so proud of myself! You know, for me, a "green thumb" might just as easily indicate a disease, so we'll see how (if) these plants thrive. All that squatting sure was good exercise, but now I'm sore.

Take care, of all of you.

Much love,
Pat and brood

P.S. – I've been meaning to tell you what Bob is doing as a kind of special remembrance of my big 3-0 birthday coming up. Most evenings, if I'm still in one piece from the busy day, he works on a profile sketch of me – you know, he has a real talent for drawing. I'm tickled about this ... can't wait to see the end result.

June 23, 1962
Hamden, Connecticut

Prichard, Alabama
My dearest family,

It is another dark, heavy, dreary day – too many of them this past week. The thunderstorms remind me of the scary Mississippi weather when little Patsy would be petrified! Remember how I'd shut my eyes, cover my ears, and try to burrow myself between my Mommie and Daddy for protection? Well, Skip, our little man, is also awfully afraid of "dose funder stoims." When they wake him up at night he usually jumps out of his bed and runs the few steps to Robin's room to crawl in with big sister for protection and comfort against the storm. I'm glad I have my protector right next to me.

Love you all so much,
Pat

August 23, 1962
Hamden, Connecticut

Prichard, Alabama
Dearest Folks,

Here I am, 30 years old, just going about my usual routine. I'm sitting under the hair dryer and will soon see the results of my new "Page Boy" set. My hair is longer in the back now, and I've skipped the French twist and worn it down for a week. Everyone says I look much younger so maybe I'll keep it loose till I get adjusted to being this age.

Bob and I had a spree last week when we went into New York to see the Broadway play, *No Strings*, with Richard Kiley and Diahann Carroll. Wow, is she beautiful, and she plays the part of a black fashion model in Paris so the costumes are incredible. There are some new, unusual things about the play, too. First, the love interest is between an interracial couple – a "first" for Broadway … *and* for us. The orchestra is on the stage instead of in the pit, and there are no violins, etc. ("no strings"). Also different, the audience is allowed to see members of the cast moving the props around. Of course, the music is lovely and our favorite is a song titled "The Sweetest Sounds."

Jenni had a nice birthday number 5 – she loves the bracelet you sent. I took her and three of her little friends to Howard Johnson's for lunch. It was an easy way to give a party – the whole thing cost $4, and included my lunch, a pretty cake and a small favor for each child. You've never seen four more beautiful, dolled-up little girls or heard more chattering and giggling.

What drama in the neighborhood yesterday. … I was outside and happened to look up just as the baby carriage of our neighbor's infant daughter came barreling down the steep hill from their back yard. As I watched, disbelieving, the carriage hit a low pipe or something, which brought it to a sudden stop, and it overturned a little way up from our house. Time seemed to stand still for me – it was so quiet, no one else around. I guess for a few seconds I stood paralyzed, scared stiff of what I might find, but then the adrenaline kicked in and I went running up the hill as fast as my legs would carry me. As I got closer I could hear crying – a good sign – and I scrambled to get to the baby. Miraculously, the mattress and bedding had tumbled out with little Susie so what I found was a tangle of netting, sheets, blanket and baby lying on the soft grass. She was screaming her head off, obviously not injured but mad as could be – it *was* quite an abrupt ending to her pleasant morning nap. I just gathered baby and bedding up in my arms and sank down onto the ground, shaking mightily!

In the meantime Betty looked out her back door to check on the baby, saw that something had happened and *she* came barreling down the hill, screaming hysterically. I was able to convince her that the baby was fine but she couldn't stop crying (the mommy, that is – Susie had already quieted down). From across the street Ruth heard the commotion and ran over. She lifted the baby from my arms and held her – I felt so weak and trembly I couldn't get up, and Betty was still crying uncontrollably! After a few more minutes, though, I recovered my strength and she, her composure. There wasn't much question in our minds that Little Susie's guardian angel definitely was on duty that day.

Tell Sam the wedding gift may be late (we can't decide yet). Had a lovely note from sister-in-law-to-be Carolyn today – I like her from the letter.

Love you loads,

Pat

September 6, 1962
Hamden, Connecticut

Prichard, Alabama

Hi, Folks,

Oh, there must be 200 things to tell you since I wrote last. Of course, it only takes about two days around here to have 100 incidents occur! Especially during the first week of September when the calls begin: those to remind me of various jobs I blithely signed up for last spring and others asking me to commit to new ones – and nobody wants "No" for an answer. This year, with the complications from the iritis in my eye, I was tempted to bow out of everything. Keeping all the doctor's appointments plus managing for many weeks with one normal eye and one fully dilated eye has been challenging. Skip's funny about the dilated eye, wants to see it close up and says, "It's a BIG black eye, Mommy!"

First, I know you'll want a report on school news. Our little Skippy went to nursery school this morning for the first time. He cried, but just a little bit. I think he'll adjust quickly and enjoy the two mornings away with new playmates.

And yesterday was a big day for the girls. We started out in the morning in a torrential rainstorm and dropped Robin off at Mount Carmel School for her first day in second grade. In the mass confusion of cars, parents, kids and teachers I inadvertently disobeyed the traffic policewoman, which almost threw me out of commission for the day! Directly from there we, and scads of others, went to the nursery school for Skippy's registration and get-acquainted session. Then I headed home to fix lunch and get Jenni ready for the new experience of (afternoon) kindergarten, where, again, there was bedlam – hordes of parents and a goodly number of crying kiddos, but, hallelujah, Jenni not among them! Continuing … I got back home at 12:45, did a few chores, settled Skippy to rest, and crawled into my still unmade bed, hoping a brief lie-down would rejuvenate me.

At 2:45, it was back to the school to pick up both girls, making it a jolly total of six trips in one day. I'm not sure yet about Jenni – she was okay yesterday, but then not too eager to go this afternoon. I hope she's going to be a happy kindergartner. Robin is delighted with her teacher and everything else about school so far. She's up and dressed with her bed made first thing every morning.

This weekend I am beginning a stint as a Sunday school teacher for a class of 3-year-olds. What, am I nuts?

Got to go, will write again soon. Dying to hear all about the wedding – I bet it was beautiful!

All love to everybody,
Pat

October 10, 1962
Hamden, Connecticut

Prichard, Alabama
Dearest Folks,

A quick note before it's time to round up the children, feed them, give baths, read bedtime stories, say prayers and goodnight-please-do-not-call-Mommy!

It's another busy week, as usual, and I have specific jobs lined up for each day. Today I cleaned most of the house, made piecrusts and polished silver. Tomorrow evening there's a farewell bridge party for a friend who's moving to the Virgin Islands. Friday night we're hosting a dessert and "Tripoley" party for a few couples we've never entertained before. And on Saturday, we go across the street to Ruth and Jack's where each couple is bringing one course of the meal, plus travel gifts, for a surprise "Bon Voyage" for Fred and Florence, who leave next week on their restaurant tour of Europe. Last Saturday night we went to a dance and met lots of new people. Oh my, aren't we the social butterflies?!!

There *is* a down side to all this flitting around into the late hours, though, particularly for Church School teachers. I am slightly weary on Sunday mornings and almost feel I should explain myself to the class of wee, perky 3-year-olds. Oh, cute story – during the class group time I encourage the kids to share something interesting that happened during the week. Recently, after one little guy said his sister had chicken pox, I asked the others, "Did anybody in your family have chicken pox, too?" Little Billy thought a moment then chirped, "No, we usually have *beef* pot pies at our house."

Did I remember to tell you the pathetically funny comment Skippy made about chicken pox when he had them and was so awfully miserable? Nana Kitty as a young mother had caught a terrible case from little Bob. Trying to comfort Skip, she said, "When your daddy was a little boy and had the chicken pox, he gave them to me." Skippy brightened momentarily, "You mean you can *give dem away*?"

So much love to each one of you, dearest family. ...

Pat

November 26, 1962
Hamden, Connecticut

Prichard, Alabama
Dearest family,

I miss you this morning, and my coffee doesn't taste half as good as yours. The flight back was okay – as good as it could be with so many stops – and I wasn't afraid after a bit, but it was long and tiring.

I had an awful time in the car during the ride from La Guardia and after we got home. I kept choking up, trying not to let the tears start, and my eyes burned so badly I could hardly stand it. Actually I was right here when you called, Mommie, but knew I couldn't talk to you right then. Bob knew it, too, and handled it well. I think I might've needed just a few more days in Alabama! It was so good to be with all of you and feel close as a family unit, Mom, Daddy, John, Rickey, Sam and Carolyn. And certainly I relished the wonderful relaxing vacation, the welcome respite from real or imagined cares, worries and responsibilities.

Oh, Skip said, "No, I didn't miss you," and when I asked what he did while I was gone, he said "Ate cereal!" He stayed with Florence one afternoon while Bob took our girls and Laurie to see a movie, *Lady and the Tramp*, which they loved. Our friends were wonderful to Bob and the kids – who ate dinner at home only three times while I was away.

Love to all of you,
Pat

December 12, 1962
Hamden, Connecticut

Prichard, Alabama
Dearest Folks,

Dating this letter I realized it was 10 years ago today that Bob and I met. Naturally, things are not like they were way back then. The road is not always smooth in marriage, huh? Especially when two personalities are as different as ours. Neither of us seems able to change, though, and so we constantly have to work at agreeing on so many little things. Oh, well, enough about that. ...

Christmas is just around the corner and my shopping has already ended, fairly abruptly, in fact. I ran out of cash – and knew the charge accounts were "overdone," too. Luckily I had nearly finished buying all the presents on the list.

Bob gave me my gift early and I've enjoyed wearing it a couple of times. It's a pretty cloth jacket with a fake fur collar. When we saw it and both

206

liked it, the problem of what he could get me for Christmas was quickly and easily solved.

Of course, I wouldn't be able to wear a short cloth jacket anywhere today in the 18-degree temperature! Over the weekend, along with the cold, we also had snow, sleet, and thunder. The weather may be atrocious but there's variety and it's never boring, huh? *Scary*, though, as when the car skidded on a patch of ice yesterday while I was driving all around the neighborhood hills picking up children for school.

A lot has gone on or, to be more specific, gone wrong. I decided to get my hair lightened a bit and the process was another scary experience. Nearly four hours, and near heart failure. First the hair turned the egg-yolk yellow of a Barbie doll's mane, next a Halloween-orange hue, and finally – after my poor scalp was slightly cooked, and following the application of the toner – a beautiful ash blond shade, which I'll enjoy for a few weeks only. Then I'll happily go back to the *no* pre-bleaching one-step "Topaz" coloring! Oh my gracious, what women won't go through for beauty, huh?

Yesterday I dropped the pretty mantel clock I'd bought for Bob's Christmas present and it broke into many pieces. Bad timing. (Good pun!). And last night, when I perched on the sofa to watch a few minutes of the news while eating my bedtime bowl of Wheaties and milk, I accidentally hit the spoon handle. It flipped out, landed on the floor, and then the bowl went flying after. I just groaned at the mess that both saturated and decorated a large portion of the carpet.

Robin is home again with a cold – she has missed two days of school – and, as usual, I have a sore throat, hoarseness, and sinus drainage.

Take care of all of you now – we love you ever so much.

Pat and brood

DEAR NANA GEEGEE

I SAID I WOULD CRY WHEN MOMMY LEFT. I DID NOT GO TO SCHOOL FOR 2 DAYS BECAUSE I HAD A COLD AND THAT IS WHEN I WROTE THIS LETTER.

LOVE ROBIN

February 4, 1963
Hamden, Connecticut

Prichard, Alabama
Dearest Folks,

How quickly the house fills up – Robin came home bringing two little friends. And with this weather, it's more complicated when children come to visit because I have to meet them at the door and help get boots, snowsuits and hats off before they wade in on the carpet. It's pure mud and ice outside, just miserable since an ice storm Saturday.

I can't imagine Mobile with 8-degree weather. You could join in with all of us up here in Yankee-land as we wish to be way down south in Florida right now!

Hey, Mommie, if you looked at a clock last Tuesday after we hung up, you probably thought I was crazy. I was so worried we had talked 35 minutes, but I hadn't set the timer correctly and it was 25, which is what I had planned for in the telephone budget. Bob told me a change is coming soon and that after 9 p.m. any three-minute call will be a dollar, with 25 cents for each extra minute. That means we can talk 25 minutes for $6.50 instead of $8 – nice!

Last week was not so great. Bob worked all day and every night until 10, plus all day Saturday and Sunday. And he has the same schedule this week. I really miss him when he's gone that much.

Bob's folks have been lucky with the sale of their house. Three prospective buyers were fighting over it, and in less than a week, without a real estate agent, it was sold to the Episcopal Church to be used as the parsonage. It was a lucky break that a member of the church's house finding committee happened to be serving on a jury with Bob's mother.

By the way, report cards came out last Friday and Robin got eight A's and a B, and Jenni got many S's (for "satisfactory") and a few I's (for "improvement shown"). We're proud of them!

Love you all,
Pat

February 12, 1963
Hamden, Connecticut

Prichard, Alabama
Dearest Folks,

I'm at the beauty shop for the works and while I'm under the dryer I'll try to fill you in since I wrote last. … Land sakes, much has happened. Our group of six couples started the series of dancing lessons last week with the

208

cha-cha step. It's going to be great fun – the men will probably never admit it, but we gals are pretty sure they are enjoying the whole experience!

Wednesday, I made dozens of cupcakes for Robin to take to school for a birthday celebration, put together nibbles for the party on Sunday, and did some hemming of skirts. That night, with the proud grandparents joining us, we went to Howard Johnson's for a very nice party in early honor of Robin's turning 8.

We noticed during dinner Robin looked pale and didn't seem to feel quite right. Sure enough, the next morning chicken pox began appearing, lots of them. She has been out of school, of course, and was in agony on her birthday. She fretted about the cupcakes but I froze them so she can take them to her class later. She feels better but is still covered with pox.

Friday afternoon, Bob and I had a spree. He took the day off and a neighbor babysat, and we went out to lunch and a movie. It felt really good to see each other quietly and be able to talk a bit. After we got home he left for Hartford to attend a Naval Alumni Association dinner meeting. It was zero degrees and windy. I spent the evening writing a long letter to Bob's brother Dave and his girls and finishing up various chores. About 11:30, just after I had gone to bed, Skip had a sudden attack of croup – scared me out of my wits. Bob came in about that time, and he got the vaporizer going and then slept in Skip's room the rest of the night. And what a night, with Skip coughing so much and Jenni restlessly wandering around thinking it was morning.

Saturday was a real busy day and we were all tired and sleepy. I cleaned part of the house, dabbed calamine lotion on Robin's itchy chicken pox spots off and on, went to the plaza for needed items, cooked a roast chicken dinner – fell apart soon afterward. Luckily, there were no plans to go out and we enjoyed a quiet evening by a beautiful fire.

Sunday was a rat race. Bob stayed home with Robin and Skip, and did some vacuuming for me, and Jenni and I went to church. I was running late, and it was a day I was scheduled to take my class into the sanctuary. The kids were all *wild*. One little girl got completely away from me and crawled under a pew, yelled, and kept letting one hymnal after another drop with a loud thud. It was frustrating – I was tired and fed up with both the noise and the kids. Couldn't wait to get home.

Once there, I fixed lunch, dusted the living room, and set up for a gathering at 4 p.m. We had 18 here for a party and the opportunity to become acquainted with Ruth and Jack, who want to get on the waiting list for the High Lane Club. One of the requirements is that prospective members meet the members of the Board of Governors. We didn't know most of the people, but everyone said what a wonderful time they were having and stayed on and on even after we stopped offering drinks, which we did when we ran plumb out of spirits! Guess that's the sign of a good party. I was still getting thank-you calls the next day.

There's so much sickness in the neighborhood, and I have been elected (I'm the last resort) to do most of the driving for kindergarten. On one of the days, what with one thing and another, I was up and down this hill a dozen times.

I had signed up to give blood yesterday, so I dropped the girls off at a friend's house and took Skip with me. He's so easy to take anywhere – with his carrying case full of Matchbox cars – and is always a hit with everyone. After checking my blood pressure and finding it fairly low, one of the older volunteers said, "Young little mothers like you shouldn't be giving blood." I told her I'd been a Red Cross volunteer caller for donors the past two years, and only recently had reached the minimum weight for donating blood myself, and I really wanted to do it. So I was set up for the procedure. The two nurses saw the low blood pressure reading and decided to take only half of a unit. I was doing fine, though, and gave almost a whole unit – before I began shaking violently and started to pass out.

And then, well, goodness gracious, I haven't had so much attention in a long time. Told the group around me that I had thoroughly enjoyed ill health for those 45 minutes! Of course, all the while both nurses and volunteers were looking out for Skippy, loving every minute of it – and he was having a ball eating doughnuts and drinking milk. There was concern about my being able to drive, so I stayed quite a while longer and then had a snack before going home. The rest of the day I felt trembly, terribly cold, weak and sore all over from the shaking. I think that's my first and last time to give blood. I'll just keep calling others to donate.

I did have to go out that evening to try on dresses for the fashion show the church women's group is putting on next week. I was a grateful gal when I got home and could finally crawl into bed with a long sigh and a weary goodnight.

All love,
Pat and brood

P.S. – By the way, we had a letter from John last week, thanking us for the briefcase. Written during his visit to meet Kathie's family, he proudly proclaimed, "I am being treated like a king!"

*A warm sunny Florida morning can bring on
something like a cosmic feeling of happiness.*
David Fairchild

Chapter Thirteen
Relocating
1963-64

Pat, kids and new VW Beetle in sunny Florida

April 15, 1963
Hamden, Connecticut

Prichard, Alabama
Dear Folks,

We've thought about it from every angle and have finally come to a decision about vacation plans this summer. We're going to Florida. It'll mean we don't get to see all of you, but our first priority is to look over the eastern part of the state to see whether we want to consider moving there. I hope you aren't too disappointed we won't be coming to Mobile. Anyway, we're still hoping you can join us in Fort Pierce.

We went up to Woodbury yesterday afternoon, about an hour's drive, to see Bob's parents' new house. It's beautiful, with lots of big closets and useful built-ins.

Must go. I have rehearsal almost every night for the next two weeks – busy!

Love,
Pat

April 23, 1963
Hamden, Connecticut

Prichard, Alabama
Dearest Folks,

This is a dilly of a week. With the play and Bob's overtime at work, we'll be out late and need to get a sitter every night. *Guys and Dolls* is such a great show, and my talented friend Florence is wonderful at directing, so all of us in the cast are enjoying the experience. But would you believe I have the beginnings of a sore throat and cold – again? Darn, of all weeks.

We were eager to get your letter this week, and so tickled with your decision to join us for the vacation in Florida. You should be getting the picture postcard anytime. The place in Fort Pierce sounds divine, doesn't it? We received the nicest note from the owner the other day. Evidently, there are only the two connecting apartments, so we should have plenty of privacy. He said a deposit of $50 each would be fine, so Bob is sending a $100 check this week.

Love you,
Pat and gang

May 1, 1963
Hamden, Connecticut

Prichard, Alabama
Dearest Folks,

Now that my musical comedy run is over, life seems a bit less hectic! The play was a success. People enjoyed it, and $1,600 was cleared for the scholarship fund.

Saturday, we got a sitter for the children and drove Bob's folks to Hartford to catch the bus for the first leg of their trip to Europe. After they left at 4 o'clock we couldn't decide what to do with our limited amount of time. We wanted to visit with each other, so decided to enjoy a leisurely drive back on the country roads and stop for dinner at an inexpensive restaurant in one of the small towns. It was a nice little spree.

For our anniversary dinner I prepared ahead of time a scrumptious seafood casserole, those special shredded wheat rolls from Judy's recipe, a salad, and a dip and nibbles for snacking. A bottle of champagne was chilling in the fridge, awaiting only the popping of the cork – and a delicious gooey dessert was ready in the freezer weeks ago.

During Happy Hour, we exchanged small gifts and opened lots of cards. The children shared that part of the celebration with us before their bedtime, and then we enjoyed our quiet dinner for two. Bob said the meal was as good as any served at the finest restaurant.

Bob was pleased with the card he chose for me, a beautiful love poem, which I will treasure. Thanks for your card, Mommie and Daddy. And Rickey, one of the best surprises of the evening was the clever card you sent, "To Sister and the Mister who couldn't resist her." We *adored* it and loved having you remember our day. Thanks ever so much, honey!

Oh yes, Auntie Bussie enclosed in her card the note Bob and I wrote to her on our honeymoon in Sea Island 10 years ago. It's cute … *we* were cute. We're going to mark it special and keep it for posterity.

Much love,
Pat and crew

May 24, 1963
Hamden, Connecticut

Prichard, Alabama
Hi, dear family,

We had a letter this week from Auntie Bussie with details of the exciting plans for a reunion in Devon the weekend of June 15, in honor of Bob's parents' 36th wedding anniversary. It will be the last time for all of us to

213

be together before Dave and his little family leave Connecticut to settle in Hawaii. No one up here knows yet of our thoughts of moving to Florida and the possibility that after this year we'll all be separated by even more miles – in even more directions. All the moves will mean real adjustments for everybody. ...

And, of course, soon after the Devon trip we'll be heading to the Deep South for a reunion with our Alabama gang! Exactly five weeks from today we start out on our trek to check out the Sunshine State. We've had a couple of warm days this month but last night the temperature was in the 20s – in the merry month of MAY – and we were all back into our winter jammies.

I had a terrible scare last week that no doubt aged me another few years. Skip fell off the gym-set glider just as it reached the highest point. He was knocked almost unconscious. He didn't breathe for what seemed like minutes, then started to turn blue and looked as if he might vomit – I was petrified.

Pretty soon I realized he'd hurt his lower back, too, and that really scared me. Thank the Lord, he wasn't seriously injured, but later there were awful bruises on his back. I had immediately called the doctor, who first calmed my near-hysteria and then told me what to do for Skip: let him sleep for a while if he wanted to, then rouse him and check his level of alertness.

Bless his heart, after such a trauma Skip did soon fall asleep. I hovered, watching him sleep, and then waked him to be sure he knew me. Whew! He knew me.

Pat, Bob and kids

June 7, 1963
Hamden, Connecticut

Prichard, Alabama
Dearest Folks,

In three weeks we'll be on our way to Florida. I don't know if I can remember everything I'm supposed to do before departure day. But we have started to make our lists of chores and odds and ends that need to be taken care of ... Bob has enough material on his for a book. He's mapped out each day, almost each hour, and wants us to cover a lot of ground in a relatively short period. And that's what we'll do!

Love,
Pat and gang

October 5, 1963
Orlando, Florida

Prichard, Alabama
Dearest Folks,

I've had kind of a bad day, feeling very unsettled and definitely not a "permanent" part of Florida yet. I'm lonely for something familiar.

Poor Bob is out like a light this evening. He awoke early with an upset stomach, which has happened so many times these past few months as we struggled with the decision of whether or not to make the move to Florida. Each time I worry that the cause is emotional distress, and I can't help being a little depressed thinking maybe we shouldn't have gone through with this big change. Bob has lost weight, is trim as can be – I am feeling a little lost and seeking solace by nibbling.

Today we had tentatively planned a trip to the beach and a cookout there with some neighbors who were also going, but it didn't work out. You may wonder if we were slightly nuts to consider going off for the day when there are still moving boxes stacked all over the house, things in need of repair, and errands and shopping to be done, but we decided that along with our move we would make new, more lenient rules for ourselves. And one is to take off and do things for pleasure sometimes even when we think we ought to be working.

Well, it's afternoon and a day at the beach would've been so much more fun than the day we had here. A serviceman from Sears had come Friday to connect the washer and dryer but couldn't finish the dryer because of a missing part. Even without the use of the dryer I needed to do laundry, though, so today I gathered up the dirty clothes, put them in the washing machine, turned it on, the tub filled up with near-boiling water, and the clothes churned around and around – in the original tubful of water – while the machine clicked through the entire cycle before finally stopping at Off, *still* full of the same soapy water.

I had to fish the clothes out, rinse, wring, and hang them on the line outside. But before they were dry there was a sudden shower, so I brought everything back inside and draped the damn (oops, I meant to spell "damp") clothes all over the stacks of boxes. My one consolation: at least the clothes weren't *frozen* this time!

That was a small matter, but there are more disturbances around here that are unsettling. For instance, our street, as shown on a map, seems to be a continuation of the runway for jet planes from McCoy Air Force Base, no exaggeration. The noise is deafening – and mainly for that reason, we won't buy in this area where we're renting. It sounds and feels like the planes are coming right through the house. The day the movers were here we had our first experience with the jets. One of the fellows was on his way in the door with a mattress on his back when a plane seemed to skim the roof. We all froze in place temporarily, and when it was gone and we realized we had survived the terrifying invasion, out of the sudden profound quiet came a drawled, "You want I should put all this stuff back on the van, Ma'am?" We considered a Yes. ...

The first night, three different times when a big plane came booming over the house, we quaked in our beds. There's also a streetlight that shines in our bedroom window and tends to interfere with restful slumber, as did the loud nocturnal argument from the people living next door. So, between the planes, the bright light and the domestic disturbance, we were exhausted, still dozing at 5:30 – when yet another "player" came into the picture: the truck collecting garbage from the dumpster behind a nearby grocery store. About that time, hearing the loud sounds of hauling and grinding and backing-up beeping, Skippy and Jenni woke up and just started giggling and screeching!

On Tuesday morning, Skip and I escorted the girls to school and the walk was longer and more tiring than I had expected. By the time we got back to the house I was weary and feeling low, and when Skip, poor little guy, started to whine that he wanted a playmate, I began to weep!

I sat down amid all the boxes and cried through a cup of coffee, then dried my eyes, got up and worked for a couple of hours. Soon there was a knock on the door and a bright spot to the morning. The Welcome Wagon hostess arrived with her smiling face and great basket of goodies! After her visit she insisted on driving Skip and me back to the school to pick up the girls. On the way she stopped at a house just down the street and introduced me to a nice young woman with whom I exchanged phone numbers and made plans for getting together for coffee. I have a feeling the neighbor, "lovely Linda," as I already think of her, and "lonesome Pat" will become good friends.

We have looked at a few more houses but haven't found our dream home yet. I'm not sure we will at the price we want to pay. We haven't yet made any decisions about which nice area to choose, what price range to consider, how much money to put down, and all the advice from everyone.

Love from Pat, et al

November 1, 1963
Orlando, Florida

Prichard, Alabama
Hi, Folks,

I just noticed Robin used the other side of the page to begin her grocery list:

1 loaf Pep. Fram B.
(2 jar creamy p.Butter.

Translation: Pepperidge Farm bread and creamy peanut butter. She *loves* to make a list and walk to the grocery store at the end of our street – "It makes me feel like a big mommy!" Both the butcher and store manager have told me how cute she is doing her shopping. She's quite a gal, all right.

Yum, speaking of food, the other evening Bob and I and two neighborhood couples went to "Skyline," the airport restaurant, where the specialty is an unlimited buffet meal with everything imaginable for $2.95. The food was delicious and we were almost too stuffed afterward to concentrate on playing a game of cards.

Robin is in the accelerated third-grade class so no wonder she studies some things I don't know! There's a lot of homework, and it's not easy. She made 2 A's and the rest B's on her report card and was simply crushed. We had to try to convince her a B was really a good grade, too. Jenni made all "Goods" with added comments about her definite talent in art. We are truly blessed that the children are bright and healthy and free of complicated problems of any kind. ...

Love, always,
Pat, Bob and kids

November 9, 1963
Orlando, Florida

Prichard, Alabama
Dearest Folks,

Disappointing news last weekend when Sam and Carolyn called to say they couldn't come for Thanksgiving. We were eagerly looking forward to their visit but understand it might have been a hard trip for an expectant mother.

What wonderful weather ... the days are beautifully warm so far, with cool nights and mornings. It's funny, here Bob keeps commenting on the weather, whereas up North I was the one who kept up a running tirade on the subject.

Did I tell you what the children have said about living in Florida? As you know, during the winter in Connecticut they were used to having full, all-over baths only once a week because they didn't get that dirty and they had such dry skin the doctor advised fewer baths. Here they play outside and have a ball and get filthy. So now each night when I mention baths, they wail, "WHY did we have to move to Florida where people take a bath *every day?*"

Speaking of the children, Skippy has changed. Just a phase, no doubt, but he acts wild, screeches, disobeys with real determination, runs away to the store by himself, and often rides his bike down the middle of the street … shocking behavior for our usually agreeable, serene little guy! Jenni is much changed the other way. She mothers Skip and tries to calm him down when he acts up. What a switch. One never knows with kids, huh?

Robin is brighter, sassier, with more of a mind of her own now than before. I try to stay on her good side – ha ha! She is an intriguing "child-woman," so babyish one minute, amazingly adult the next.

Oh, Jenni loves being able to read, and does so at all hours – she had the light on one night at 2 a.m., reading a "Dick and Jane" book. Says a sleepy-eyed Skippy the next morning, "Dat Jenni, she waked me up to weed to me!" She enjoys practicing her reading and printing at home, plus her beloved drawing and coloring. Next week is visiting week at school, and the teacher has asked Jenni to draw all the pictures for their classroom. (The school is still on half-day sessions because the new building isn't finished.)

That reminds me, I wrote you about the family across the street – the beautiful mother, three children, father overseas in the military. Well, the 9½-year-old, Johnny, has captured my heart! His mother works and feels terrible that Johnny doesn't have a mama to wave him off to school at noon. I told her not to worry another moment about his being taken care of – only that I might steal him from her for good!

Johnny comes over at 9:30 a.m. and he and my little man Skip and I mess around (went bowling Tuesday, to the store one day, walking another, etc.), then I give him lunch and send him on his way. Believe me, it is my pleasure. He is sweet, thoughtful and lovable. Reminds me of Rickey at that age. He's a deep thinker, worries about big problems, doesn't want to upset his mother for anything, and is wonderful with Skippy.

Sunday afternoon, I invited Johnny's mother Doris and some other neighbors for coffee and pie. And that night Bob and the kids and I had a ball – at church! There's a United Church near our house where a family social was held: a potluck supper with delicious food, friendly people, and loads of children. Everyone made us feel like our presence there was the best thing that had ever happened at their new little church. We ate, visited, and watched a magic show for half an hour, after which there was a variety of games for the kids and the parents. The social ended with a great "community sing" – "Yankee Doodle," "My Bonnie," "In the Garden" (my favorite hymn). I'm not sure when Bob has enjoyed anything so much.

Each day we find it harder to think of settling in another area of Orlando. The low-flying, loud planes were the main drawback, and they haven't been quite so bad lately, so now we're at least considering looking at new homes near here. We are still confused as to what we want – darn it. We love the lakes, but lakes and pools scare us because of having young children. We saw a lakefront last week in Maitland, 30 minutes away, that was lovely but the house was small for our family, and especially for having guests, too.

We'll have to sacrifice something – don't know whether it will be room space or lake or beach. Still hoping we'll find our dream home – for $25,000 or under! You'll know as soon as we do. We'll be so excited.

Love you all,
Pat

November 23, 1963
Orlando, Florida

Prichard, Alabama
My dearest family,

We know y'all are as stunned and saddened as everyone else over the assassination of President Kennedy. It is such a tragedy. Oh, for it *not* to have happened. I was at the dentist's office having a tooth filled when the receptionist burst into the room with the news. The doctor and I stared at her as if she'd gone absolutely crazy, we were so disbelieving at such an announcement. No doubt this is one of those terrible events about which people will always remember in detail where they were and what they were doing when they first heard. You know, like Pearl Harbor. ... Of course, Bob and I are staying glued to the television, united in grief with most of the world.

Thinking of Christmas and gifts seems frivolous, almost irreverent, but we all will go on with plans. And I do have a question that needs a quick answer, Mommie. Does Daddy have a tackle box for his fishing trips? If not, I want to get him one for Christmas. If he does, can you give me another idea? Also, Rickey told me he'd like a billfold. I'd be happy to get that, or is there anything else he wants that might be more of a surprise?

We had breakfast this morning with our dear old friend and former Hamden neighbor Jack, who was in Orlando on business. Afterward, we took him to the airport and watched him take off in a beautiful jet, carrying our love to Ruth and the kids. But there's lots left for you, too.

Pat

December 1, 1963
Orlando, Florida

Prichard, Alabama
Dear Nana GeeGee,

We just got in a new Addition in school. My teacher is very nice. If I had all the money in the world I would buy her anything she wanted. When I send this letter to you please send back a letter of my own. I'll always keep it. I have a boy friend, and his name is Jonny. I've always been trying to kiss, but he doesn't like me, he likes a girl named Donna. Please give Uncle John, Sammie and Rickey a kiss for me. Let Granddaddy read this letter. I love you.

Love,
Robin

December 14, 1963
Orlando, Florida

Prichard, Alabama
Dearest Folks,

Sitting here in summery clothes, windows open, looking out at a brilliant blue sky, basking in 80-degree weather ... honestly, we can't believe it! Watching the weather report on TV last night – Chicago 0 degrees, New England sub-freezing temperatures with snow, ice, blizzard conditions – we just giggled and reminded ourselves how smart we were to move in a southern direction! Bob can't get over it and said yesterday, "I wouldn't live back up north for *anything*!" Imagine. ...

Great news – we have decided on a house. The builder was here last night to discuss details. (Bob is drawing you a sketch right now.) It's lovely, with four bedrooms, two baths, living room, dining room, family room, kitchen, patio, fruit trees – and a lake with a beach at the end of the street. Since the house isn't completely finished yet, we can choose colors, flooring, light fixtures, etc. It should be ready about March 8.

Got a letter from John yesterday, and we're excited about their planned trip to Florida. It'll be wonderful to see him and to meet Kathie at last.

Sounds like you're having a ball, Daddy, with that beauty of a boat and such successful fishing trips over in Bayou la Batre. Keep it up. We can fish in *our* Lake Margaret pretty soon – you, too, when you come to see us.

I have another "boarder." Johnny is back in school all day, but a neighbor asked me to keep her 5½-year-old son temporarily, until she finds a housekeeper, and I couldn't say no. There are a few small problems, but most of the time Billy and Skip play well.

Enclosed is Bob's sketch of the house and, from Jenni, a self-portrait just for you. How do you like her pigtails? We send much love to all.

Pat

December 27, 1963
Orlando, Florida

Prichard, Alabama
Dear Nana GeeGee and Granddaddy,

Thank you for the red sweater from John and Rickey. I love the holly suit. At first the pockets itched. But now it's ok, I guess?

Love,
Robin

February 9, 1964
Orlando, Florida

Waterbury, Connecticut
Dear Mother Kitty and Dad,

Can you believe our birthday girl turns 9 today? Seems only yesterday she was just learning to walk and talk – although she talked almost like an adult from the start, didn't she? These days the most exciting part of her life is her crush on that adorable Johnny! Completely understandable, we all love him.

Work on the house is going along on schedule and we should be able to move around the first of next month. We can hardly wait to get in it … and for you to see it!

Now that I've had time to recover, I can give you a few details about the trip to Gadsden, Alabama, for my brother's wedding. The ceremony on January 28 was beautiful – John and Kathie looked so sweet – and the pre-wedding parties and the reception were fun. Of course, it was a bonus to see my folks, including parents-to-be Sammie and Carolyn, whose first baby is due next week.

221

All that was just great ... but getting to the town of Gadsden from Orlando (and back) on a crowded Greyhound bus, 17 hours each way, was a test of faith and endurance. And to make the challenge really interesting, throw in a large picture hatbox to contend with! I'll explain. For the wedding I'd found the prettiest outfit, a long-sleeved pink wool dress with a softly rolled collar and matching long mohair vest. My very fashionable neighbor (Johnny's mom) saw it and said I *must* complete the ensemble with her special "Mr. John" chapeau, that I would look stunning. I believed her. I borrowed the hat. I reveled in the many compliments I received. And on and off for a total of 34 hours, as I grappled with that darn hatbox on the Greyhound, I was ready to shoot both of us!

Must scoot. Take care of each other. We miss you. We love you.

Pat

March 4, 1964
Orlando, Florida

Prichard, Alabama
Dearest Folks,

We are in the new house after three days of moving and a few mishaps – the rugs were delivered soiled and not fitting properly and the antique three-quarter-bed headboard, circa 1795, got dropped and split right in half. It was hard not to shed tears over the damage to that special antique.

Our kitty has been and is still a nervous wreck with all the commotion. She looked lost, paced, and didn't eat the first day, and that night went to a neighbor's bedroom window and meowed from 3 a.m. on. Then last night another neighbor called at 8 o'clock to tell me Trixie was sitting on *her* window crying, and so off I went to retrieve the fickle feline. Roaming around in the dark, calling, "Here, kitty, kitty," I struggled to get hold of her as she wildly resisted my every effort. Had to chuckle at the picture that must have made!

Robin and Jenni got registered at Pershing Elementary and met their teachers, whom they liked immediately. Both teachers are such attractive, bubbly young women. Jenni still loves her former teacher, too, and called her last evening. The two of them chatted like girlfriends, so cute.

My little helper, as Skip calls himself, is fine, and yesterday wondered aloud, "What you gonna do when I go off to school, Mommy, and you all alone?" He is such a sensitive, thoughtful little fellow. I told him I would miss him a lot, but I would be okay. Another thing that is so sweet, Skip says the other twin bed in his room is Johnny's bed. We do miss Johnny and will have him come for overnight soon.

It was exciting to get the letter written while you were in Tuscaloosa, Mommie. What fun to be there helping the new parents and getting acquainted with baby Griff, your newest grandson – my first nephew! Does he remind you more of Sam or of Carolyn? Oh, I just know I would squeeze him good and give him lots of sugar if I could get hold of him. So would the kids.

Lots of love,
Pat plus 4

March 24, 1964
Orlando, Florida

Prichard, Alabama
Hi, whole gang!

Bob got his new car, the beige Beetle-buggy. He's so cute with it, just like a kid with a toy. And wait till you hear this: Skip comes in each day and goes to the bathroom sink to wash his hands all by himself, then says proudly, "NOW I can touch the buggy, huh, Mom?" Bob has given the word … wish I could train the children that well about touching the woodwork in the new house!

Take care, we send much love.
Pat

April 9, 1964
Orlando, Florida

Prichard, Alabama
Dearest Folks,

When you wrote recently you'd been enjoying communing with Mother Nature in the early mornings, it reminded me to describe the daily scene at our new home.

The master bedroom is off the patio where we can look into the backyard and see four tangerine trees and the field beyond. We usually awake to the caress of a lovely morning breeze wafting in through the open windows, the serenade of birds tweet-tweeting, and the aroma of orange blossoms or, I suppose, tangerine blossoms – something that smells good! Ah, it's a heavenly way to start the day. Oh, and there's a bright red daddy cardinal we enjoy seeing on his frequent flybys right outside the window.

I was so glad Jenni recovered from the mumps fairly quickly and got back to school in time to participate in her class talent show. Skippy and I went to see it and had so much fun. Jenni was one of four ladybugs dressed in a black wig and leotards, doing the twist and mouthing the words to a jazzy record!

Sunday morning in the early hours, quite a procession began in our bedroom, which we have decided to call "Grand Central," by the way. First came Robin, sort of moaning that her ear and jaw hurt. Bob and I each opened an eye and murmured, "maybe mumps" and dozed off momentarily. In a couple of minutes Skip appeared, with a rather sad look and a groan, saying his ear hurt. Yep, mumps – the two of them – and both were feverish and sore and miserable for a few days but are much better now.

Trixie the cat, though, that's another matter. She started wailing, making weird sounds and acting a bit crazy, so Skip and I proceeded to go through the ordeal of getting her into the car for the "joy ride" to the vet. I do hate driving with an animal in the car!

The diagnosis was not only a bladder infection, but also an infestation of fleas. Oh, dear me. But the worst part was yet to come. The vet began to tell me how to give a pill to a cat. I listened, groaned inwardly (as you know, I am *not* really a pet person) and hoped there might be an easier method. So later ... I opened Trixie's very favorite food, snuck a pill in it, covered it well, and watched with glee as she gobbled everything up. "YES!" A minute went by and don't you know she spit out that danged little black pill!

I am not, repeat, NOT good with animals, but I am trying to be a good parent because the kids want a pet. I did find a taker for the little white mouse – oh, goody! – for the price of the cage!

Received the first snapshots of Baby Griff. What a sweet-looking cutie. Carolyn wrote, "I sure was naïve about babies." Probably the lament of most brand-new parents!

Love,
Pat

April 15, 1964
Orlando, Florida

Prichard, Alabama
Dearest Folks,

Here are a few more snapshots of the new house. Maybe you could show them to Sam and John, too.

We've been homebound for quite a long period. Just as Robin and Skip recovered from the mumps, Jenni got another bad sore throat. So after a visit to our new, highly recommended pediatrician, we are again staying in. We liked him, but oh, do we ever miss our doctor in Connecticut. Where else could you find a pediatrician who, in the middle of the night, picked up his phone on the first ring – as if he'd been waiting for your call – soothed your fears and calmly explained what you should do for your sick child? You know, on our last visit to him before we left, I told him I thought it might almost be easier to leave a husband than a beloved pediatrician ... he just chuckled.

We invited some new friends for a party meal last Friday, and everything was a success. I always enjoy entertaining. It feels good to plan company meals and use our nice things again after the "renting spree." Saturday evening we enjoyed going out with a couple down the street for hamburgers and to a drive-in movie.

Last night was fun, too, with Jenni's former teacher here for dinner. I think I told you about her. She's 26, single, so sweet, and was a godsend when Jenni was upset over the move South, the rented house and starting a new school. Elaine and I got along as if we'd known each other all our lives, which amazed both of us. She checked Jenni's workbook with a red pencil, at Jenni's request. Skip began printing and she gave him a nice big red "A." Then she played Barbie dolls with the girls and tucked Jenni in for the night. After that she and I had a grand time talking until 11 o'clock. All of us like her so much and want to see her again. History repeating itself, huh, Mom ... doesn't this remind you of how my teachers used to invite me to their homes or come to ours?

Guess what, I sewed today – not from scratch, but I cut off and hemmed the sleeves of lots of shirts for Bob and Skip and turned some of Skip's long pants into shorts. Both "men" like the clothes I fix for them better than any others, which spurs me on a bit, in spite of the fact that sewing definitely is not my favorite task.

Bye for now, and loads of love from all five of us. Skip says he will print you a "letta" soon.

Pat

Prichard, Alabama

Dearest Mommie and Daddy,

I want this to be a special letter, not only because Mother's Day is near, but because I so often think of my wonderful parents and don't tell *you* what I think.

I have experienced being a parent only nine years, whereas you two have been at it nearly 32, quite a difference. I've had my eyes opened just a bit since I've been on the job, believe me, and I know that future years will probably leave me pop-eyed because I have a lot to learn yet from our three children as they grow up and become more independent.

This age we live in now is different from the one of over 30 years ago when you started out as parents, but I'm sure you felt just as we do, and as every conscientious mother and father does: We hope to do the best for our children, always, and in all ways. And what a huge responsibility each child is. ...

The main thing I want to say is that I think you have been very successful in your role as parents. In fact, to me you represent true, marvelous parents in every way. Without certain advantages – enough money, good medical care, books on guiding and caring for children, so many of the things we now have to help – you worked long, hard hours at making a living and giving your four children the necessities, plus a few extras.

And so importantly, you gave us yourselves: your unconditional love, your time, understanding, and example. In our home there was such a definite feeling of love and warmth, and security, and fun. Others obviously felt all those things, too, as all ages liked to congregate at our house! The boys' and my friends always felt at home there.

Since I've been out in the big wide world and met people from all over, I have been struck more than once by a feeling of thankfulness at the upbringing you gave me. It is believed that as children we have to be taught hate and prejudice and intolerance – and I have met those who were. I'm so grateful that didn't happen in our home, and it didn't because you two prevented it by being such good examples of kind, loving people.

Of course, each of you has (just!) a few faults, naturally, as do we all. Let me say, though, that as a parent I hope to have as few faults as you. I'm afraid Bob and I already have more, and we haven't even begun to cope with the teens and the problems thereof.

Now, Mommie, on Thursday you will pass another milestone, so let your (and Daddy's) new motto be "Life really begins in the 50s!" Throughout the years you have weathered many trials together with your children, and now it's time for a little less responsibility in that area and a little more fun for just the two of you.

I'll just say again how much I appreciate all that you both have given to me, all you have done for me. I love you both very dearly.

Pat

May 9, 1964
Orlando, Florida

Prichard, Alabama

Dear ones,

Just a note to explain the enclosures from Jenni. She wanted me to send you her artwork and the school paper with an "A" in writing and a "100" for content. You gave her the book *Rebecca of Sunnybrook Farm,* and if you'll look closely, she has told the story well by the picture she drew, just as Sleeping Beauty's plight pops right out of the second beautifully colored drawing! Our Jenni is quite artistic, and her teachers have commented on it since she was in nursery school. Enjoy!

Much love,
Pat

BY JENNI

THE CAT SAYS MEW-MEW. FATHER IS A MAN. I RAN TO THE STORE. A PIG IS FAT. I LIKE TO PLAY WITH BALL AND BAT. ALICE SAT DOWN. I CAN RIDE A BICYCLE.

June 23, 1964
Orlando, Florida

Prichard, Alabama

Waterbury, Connecticut

Devon, Pennsylvania

Honolulu, Hawaii

Dearest loved ones,

Please forgive my including everyone with copies of a typewritten letter, but there's much to tell and time has a way of getting away from me.

Believe it or not, at this moment, for a change, I am in the house *alone.* The quiet sounds awfully loud … and is wonderful.

A few minutes ago I walked through the playroom and did a double-take: There were seven kids, seven puzzles, scattered, at least 35 little cars and trucks, the play gas station, two parachutes with men, numerous books and crayons – plus, of course, the regular furniture – and a very noisy TV program blaring forth. Wading through all that, I proceeded on my way to the washing machine in the garage, where I stumbled over the cat's dish, Bob's sneakers, the lawn mower, and six bicycles, in that order!

Skip and Frankie just came in with a handful of Coke bottle tops, wanting a place to save them – "We goin' to win a Wuls Fair twip!" – so I cleared out a corner of one kitchen drawer for their treasures and was gifted with two great big smiles from two adorable little faces.

That gorgeous Doris, Johnny's mom, former neighbor from the rental house, and a friend came for dinner last night. I served beef stroganoff over steamed rice, tossed salad, Judy's shredded wheat rolls, and peppermint stick ice cream with chocolate sauce. Mmm.

Our friends Jim and Shirley moved into their new home, and late in the afternoon we went to see them, bearing housewarming cold beer and iced tea, lots of my Southern fried chicken, tomato and lettuce sandwiches, brownies, and punch for the children. We sat among the boxes of all their belongings – Bob and I so thankful we weren't in that situation now – enjoying supper and a rundown of their hectic moving day.

Theirs is definitely an energetic family and something wild is usually in progress even on a non-moving day! Besides the three active kids, there's a large German shepherd pup, a mother cat with two kittens, and a pet rabbit. That day, just before the movers arrived, the rabbit got away. All the kids were bawling, and the whole family was in a state. Then Shirley had the idea of a hunt for the hare, offering one dollar to the finder of the rabbit. All 30-something kids on the street quickly scattered and the bunny rabbit was found in a matter of minutes!

You should hear Bob describe his Father's Day. It was supposed to be a day when he could decide what he wanted to do. First of all he wanted to sleep late, so at 7 a.m. Jenni came in with cards the kids had made and insisted he see and appreciate them that very minute. Said he to me later, "I tried not to be mad at them for wishing me such a Happy Father's Day." He felt better after I gave him my present, an extra-special breakfast of his favorites.

I knew he would want us to go to the beach, but during breakfast my monthly visitor arrived, ruling out a nice day at New Smyrna. I ventured a meek, "Is there anything *else* you would like to do, dear?" Well, he guessed he would just paint the fence, then maybe in the afternoon we could all walk down to the lake and he could have a swim. (In my head I quickly rearranged the dinner schedule to fit this new plan.)

As it turned out, when we were ready to go to the lake, Skip was really upset at having to leave his friend Frankie in the middle of the game they were playing, but I whispered a reminder that it was Daddy's day. So he looked back and shouted, "I *have* to go with him, Frank, 'cause it's *Father's Day!*"

Now, for the real highlight story of the day: We have been saying I should learn to drive the new Volkswagen. When I fetch and deliver various playmates, the kids always want to ride in the little beige Beetle.

Saturday, while in the car with Bob, I watched carefully as he shifted gears, and I felt confident I could manage the little bug. So ... the next morning I was going to pick up one of Jenni's playmates and decided it would be a good time to get the practice. I walked outside where Bob was painting the fence and casually voiced this idea, adding that I'd be driving a short distance on a quiet Sunday with no traffic, a perfect opportunity.

He was standing there, paintbrush in hand, wearing my old straw sun hat, a scream of a picture. Well, on hearing my idea, his eyes popped out, the paintbrush started to quiver, and a trembly voice squeaked, "Wh-h-h-at?"

He pleaded that I had been in the driver's seat only five minutes, *once*, that the shift was *very* different, and so forth ... on to the final, bordering-on-desperate appeal, "You *know* how much I think of that little car."

Well, yes, I answered, yes, I knew it was my rival for his affections! You see, what made this so darn funny to me was that I knew exactly what his reaction was going to be, and it was like watching a movie plot unfold.

Anyway, I smiled, said that was fine, another time would be better, I was sure – knowing he would feel guilty. I went back inside to get my key for the station wagon, and he soon followed, relenting, telling me that it really *was* the perfect opportunity and he would get the key to the VW.

So then, back to the garage, where I slipped behind the wheel of the Beetle. He was already nervous. As I began to readjust the seat position and the rear view mirror and both side mirrors, he openly cringed, and with a pathetic little smile said how nice it had been, never having to make any such changes when he got into the car. I told him I understood. I also told him I would turn around and come right back up the next street if I didn't feel perfectly confident.

He still hung onto the car. Jenni tried to tell him she was sure Mommy could drive it just fine. Finally, I asked him to get in and ride over with me if he was so scared. He grabbed the car door and shouted, "Oh, NO-O-O,

I couldn't stand *that!*" "Okay, then," said I, "let go of the car. And *try* to relax."

So, off we went, Jenni and I both grinning. Needless to say, I loved driving the cute little Bug and had no problems. About a half hour later we arrived back home to find Bob grinning widely, waving a white handkerchief – I haven't had the heart to put him through such an ordeal again.

As you know, our firstborn has been away from us visiting her Alabama grandparents for pert-nigh *three* weeks, and we are really missing her. It has gotten to the point now that every night I lie in bed and decide I am going to call and tell Robin she *must* get on the next plane! I think she misses us, too, but is not really homesick. ...

Dave, Joni and Lynnie, we all feel terribly guilty about our neglect of you three (and the three-quarter little one on the way) and hope this letter will make up somewhat. We think of you often. I did get a box off to Honolulu recently and hope it arrives okay.

Mommie and Daddy and you boys in Alabama, we think about all of you a lot, too. But I just don't write as much as I should.

Sam, we enjoyed your note last week and the enclosed articles.

John and Kathie, I hope you are settled at Mercer, at least for the short while before Louisiana State beckons.

And we hope all the older folk (oops, now I've done it, my name will be Mud!) are having a good summer. Auntie Bussie, I still think you should step onto a jet and scoot down here!

Gee, our family is "reely beeg," as Ed Sullivan would say. We love all of you dearly and wish we could see you much more often than we do. Everybody take care and write to us whenever you can. We love hearing news from all. Know that we love you.

Pat

And Life, that sets all things in rhyme.
May make you poet, too, in time –
But there were days, o tender elf,
When you were poetry itself.
                    Christopher Morley

Chapter Fourteen
Little Bits of Literature
1964-69

Skip and Lady in Prichard, Alabama

August 24, 1964
Orlando, Florida

Prichard, Alabama
Dearest Folks,

Another wild week! Honestly, there's so much going on I'm gonna flip before school starts. Beginning today and for the next two weeks, I'm keeping three children for our neighbor who is working at Woolworth's. And to help ease Betty's first day on the job, I decided to cook her family's supper in the oven along with ours tonight.

By the time you get this, Dave will be a daddy again. Joni's Caesarean is scheduled for tomorrow, and we can hardly wait to hear the news from Hawaii that baby is here and he or she and mother are fine.

It was birthday week at our house. Five of Jenni's little girlfriends were here on the 21st for supper and a fun party. She thoroughly enjoyed helping me prepare the balloons, hats and favors. I'll convey Jenni's thanks to you for the sweet card, the money, and cute purse, which she adored. The little pipsqueak, fresh as a daisy, witty and smart, bounced in the other day with this bulletin: "Well, two boys just went behind a tree and fought over me!" And on another day, in a more serious vein, this verbal gift: "Mommy, the three most precious things to me are you and Daddy and God ... also Mary and all those holy people."

Very early Sunday morning the children woke me up to start my birthday celebration. We had all gone shopping in downtown Orlando, where the girls bought presents with their own money, so they couldn't wait to have me open the gifts. Jenni evidently spent quite a bit of her own birthday cash on a very colorful, richly decorated souvenir-type napkin holder, which she, and every child who has seen it, thinks is the most beautiful thing in the world. It's a bit flashy, but I was *so* pleased over her idea – it has a special place on the table. Robin chose a pretty pin with a green stone, very appropriate for my August birthday.

We went to the beach Sunday afternoon, planning to stay late and build a bonfire, but suddenly swarms of mosquitoes invaded and nearly carried us off. We fled fast, heading for the car, all ten of our arms waving frantically to swat them away! Last week when we wanted to stay and enjoy the cool and calm of early evening on the beach, a terrible storm sent us scurrying.

Will try to write more soon, though I do have a lot of thank-you notes to send. Daddy, I certainly did enjoy your call, it was a real treat!

Much love to all,
Pat

November 2, 1964
Orlando, Florida
Prichard, Alabama
To Nana GeeGee and Granddaddy,

I was sick on Monday, November 2, 1964. I had a sore throat. I hope Granddaddy feels better. Yesterday I was in church school and I was a slave girl in a play. The playhouse is finished all except the door and the painting. My frend Pattie got bit by blackie, Frankie's dog. Me and Robin got dressed up in Mommy's old clothes. I was a bride and Robin was a Mexican girl. Robin was much prettyer then me. And Skippy was a Skeleton on halloween. I think I'm going to be a Brownie and I thought I was to go on Monday, and Mommy talked to my Brownie teacher and I am to go on Friday Night. And Robin is going to be a cheerleader. Good Night and Good Morning to all of your family.

Love,
Jenni

January 3, 1965
Orlando, Florida
Prichard, Alabama
Hi, Mommie and Daddy,

This priceless little poem written by Jenni for Skippy will ensure you have at least one good chuckle on the day you receive it. I'm also sending a copy to Bob's parents and to Auntie Bussie. It's too cute not to share.

Love you,
Pat

My Brother

My brother's name is Skippy
And he has strep throat,
He's pale with fever,
So he looks like a goat.
Today he's a little better
He doesn't feel as sick,
Today he has more color,
Now he looks like a chick.
I think he'll be better,
On Saturday,
So he'll be able
To go out and play!

233

February 14, 1965
Orlando, Florida

Prichard, Alabama
Dear Mommie and Daddy,

I hope you two sweethearts are having a Happy Valentine's Day. I've had a warm spot in my heart for the special "love day" as long as I can remember. But then you know what an ol' sentimentalist I am, always have been and probably always will be.

And speaking of a warm spot, I think you'll get one or two in your hearts when you read the short story I've enclosed, my contribution to a church circle booklet on faith. It's about our little Skip and his big faith.

Much love,
Pat

"Ask and it will be given you; seek and you will find." – Matthew 7:7

Among my 5-year-old son's most prized possessions was a small black wallet "just like Daddy's." He played with it, proudly showed it off at every opportunity, and carried it everywhere, even to bed. Alas, one day the wallet went missing and there was a very sad little boy at our house. We searched every room, all around the yard, in the car. I felt certain it was gone forever and consoled Skip with the promise of another. Suddenly, though, a sweet smile broke through his tears and he announced, "No, Mommy, I can say prayers and GOD will let me find it!"

A week or so later, during which he said prayers of such simple, complete faith, we went to a grocery store where I occasionally shopped and Skip reminded me to ask at the counter about his wallet. I was hurried, a bit harried, somewhat impatient – and sadly lacking in the faith department – but we went to check.

Imagine my wide-eyed surprise when the clerk reached under the counter and pulled out the wayward wallet. Not so Skip. He beamed at the lady and affirmed, "I knew God would find it cause I asked Him!"

March 22, 1965
Devon, Pennsylvania

Orlando, Florida
Dear Pat, et al,

Here goes for my March letter, and there is absolutely nothing of interest to report. Sincerely yours.

Thanks so much for your nice letter and for the darling snapshots. Those kids certainly are growing up! What a handsome brood. When are you going to have another?

Glad Bob is getting along so well in his course work, but then I'm not surprised. It could be a case of slight prejudice, but nothing great he ever does surprises me.

The story of my life is still the revision of the book. Having vowed two years ago I would never again bring work home from school with me, I have been doing just that for a long time now. This is the biggest job I've ever done all by myself and is taking more time than I had anticipated. It was duck soup when Dr. Jim and I did it together.

I've talked to my friend Sally on the telephone only because I won't let her come up till the book is finished. I've got to get it done before long because the house is filthy, all my clothes need mending, I need badly to go to the dentist, and I don't have a speck of permanent left in my hair. But first things first.

Two of my other friends have been cagey about coming over, and once in a while they peer into the window to see if I've finished writing for the day. If so, they come in for Cokes and cocktails. So I'm not a complete hermit.

I do appreciate your warm invitations to Florida. At the moment all I can do is say "thank you" and laugh a rueful laugh. Spring vacation is over. My first session of summer school begins immediately after the spring term ends.

Well, I must get back to the book. Be good to each other and much love to all.

Auntie Bussie

April 20, 1965
Devon, Pennsylvania

Orlando, Florida
Honolulu, Hawaii
Dear nephews and nieces,

Last week because of Easter, I had a four-day release from campus. Every one of the four, I went to bed at an ungodly early hour and got up similarly. I didn't stir out of the house, and by the end of Sunday I was a quarter way into the last chapter of the revision! I expect to finish all the writing this weekend and then spend one more week in careful proofreading, pagination, etc., and send the thing off on Monday, May 3. I already feel slightly lightheaded in anticipation.

This week I am immersed in master's and doctor's examinations. It's that time of year at University of Pennsylvania. It means some late days for me, which is kind of scary because I have to walk from class to parking lot in the dark. We're seeing signs of violence between races in dear old West Philly.

One recent evening, I passed a white policeman who had three dark-skinned men lined up against a building at gunpoint. Believe me, I walked by as fast as I could without appearing to be running.

On another evening, I walked up a street completely deserted except for two black teen-agers who were tossing back and forth one of the most lethal-looking knives I have ever seen. Since I learned in some ancient psychology class that fear can be smelled, I told myself I was not afraid. Huh! I also decided that fear could probably be seen. So I did not cross the street, or run pell-mell: I just walked right between them. I was lucky. We have had students and faculty members both slugged and killed.

On another note a real series of bright spots in my life is all the cards, notes and snapshots from all of you. Pat, one of your letters was so delectable Maggie actually ate it up. I came home one day to find small bits of it all over the living room rug.

Maggie had her 13th birthday last Sunday, for which she got two extra dog biscuits. This means she is the human equivalent of 91 years! She is so loving, so undemanding and so cooperative with a working mother. It's nice to come home every day and have her jump two feet into the air in ecstasy at having this wonderful person come back to her. No human ever did that for me!

A whole lot of love to everyone.
Auntie Bussie

236

July 10, 1965
Orlando, Florida

Prichard, Alabama

Dear "Parents of the New President" ...

... of the "Welcome Wagonettes Club of Orlando," that is! Isn't it exciting?

I can see that the job is going to keep me pretty busy – as if I weren't already. I'm enclosing the notice and picture from the Orlando newspaper. And from the cover page of our monthly Welcome Wagon Newsletter, where "Pat's Prologue" is featured, I'll quote part of my message for July:

"Happy July! This month many of us will be dusting off the suitcases, finding someone to care for the lawn, the mail, the cat ... and insisting at the last minute "But we may *need* them" when our husbands look aghast at the huge stacks of clothes we plan to take! VACATION – a magic mood – one that can be captured at home, too, by relaxing our schedules a bit.

"But even though we think of July as a carefree time, let's not forget that during this and every month we, as Welcome Wagonettes, have a responsibility toward the newcomers of Orlando."

Sound okay? You know your daughter – I am sure I'll enjoy writing these monthly messages.

I love you!
Pat

September 10, 1965
Orlando, Florida

Prichard, Alabama

Dear Mommie and Daddy,

Thought you might like another sample of my words to the Welcome Wagonettes in the September issue of the newsletter. Bob is proud of my association and accomplishments in the club and asked me to send the original of this month's newsletter to his folks.

Love from Pat

"School begins! Can't you just hear the exclamations of 'hurray' from mothers and the sighs of 'Alas, it's our turn again' from the teachers?

"It seems that, along with the opening of school, every single organization goes into action, and each year when I turn my calendar to the month of September, I am panic-stricken because it looks as if I have managed to acquire a job in nearly all of them!

"I am exaggerating a bit, of course, but those innocent-looking calendar pages do hold a full schedule for me, as I'm sure they do for most of you. But even as we are worrying about our new duties, old chores and busy days in general, let's sneak in a pleasant thought by Mr. Longfellow for this particular month. ...

> The morrow was a bright, September morn;
> The earth was beautiful, as if newborn;
> There was that nameless splendor everywhere,
> That wild exhilaration in the air,
> Which makes the passers in the city streets
> Congratulate each other as they meet!"

October 30, 1965
Orlando, Florida

Prichard, Alabama
Dear Granddaddy and Nana GeeGee,

I will get you a good present for Christmas. It will be the best present ever in the hole world.

Tomorrow is Halloween you know. I wish I was there and I hope you have a lot of candy. I give you all my love.

From Skipper to you
Xoxoxoxoxoxoxoxoxox

Hi, folks,

Just a quick note I'll slip into the envelope with Skip's cute letter to bring y'all up-to-date on the exciting news in and around Orlando these days. For months there've been all sorts of rumors in the newspaper and among business people about what *really* big company is coming to this area. Property of more than 30,000 acres has been purchased by a "secret" buyer. Lots of speculation, of course, and we've read that evidence points to Howard Hughes being behind the "mystery plant," or Douglas Aircraft, with some connection to the space industry for the development of a Manned Orbiting Laboratory to be launched from Cape Kennedy. But at the top of the list is some form of Walt Disney operation, which is by far the most fun possibility! Just the other day the *Orlando Sentinel* headline read "We Say It's Disney." You know how much we love Orlando so anything's okay with us. Whoever, or whatever company it is, it'll probably be years before a business is up and running, anyway.

I'm staying unbelievably busy – it's a "full fall." My schedule this whole year has been that way, though – as evidenced by how few letters I've written to you, huh?

> Love you,
> Pat

> December 23, 1965
> Orlando, Florida

Prichard, Alabama
Dear Nana GeeGee and Granddaddy,

I think you know about my broken wrist and my cast and sling. All my friends say I'm lucky because I don't have to do my work! That old playhouse we had before was torn down. In school I made a clay pot for my mommy for Christmas. I like Florida very much.

I hope you come down some day. How is John? How is Sammie? How is everybody? Say hello to them all. Will you?

> Love,
> Jenni

P.S. – I love you!
P.S. – I am sending you my picture of a tree and presents and fireplace. I am writing this with my cast on.

> December 26, 1965
> Orlando, Florida

Prichard, Alabama
Dear Nana GeeGee
>   Thank you and Granddaddy
>   For all my Presents
>   I like the darts wallet
>   and really like
>   the cowboy
>   suit. I
>   got some
>   boots too
>   Come to see us
>   Love,
>   Skipper

January 1, 1966
Dear Diary,

I was cheerful this New Year's morning and said rather saucily to Bob, "Good morning, darling!" He thought he was in the wrong bed. Hope I can keep having a better disposition in the early morning (and at other times).

Pat

January 3, 1966
Orlando, Florida

Prichard Alabama
Dear Nana GeeGee and Granddaddy,

Thank you for the red dress. It's just a tiny bit too big! Some things I got for Christmas were a globe, a human eye set, lots of jewelry, two dresses and a super ball. I hope you had a very Merry Christmas? I love you!

Love,
Robin

January 10, 1966
Dear Diary,

It's so nice to have Mommie down for a visit while Bob is away at Clemson. The children are having a great time with their Nana GeeGee, as always. We'll all be glad to see the end of Bob's schedule of working one month in Orlando and the next month studying at Clemson in South Carolina. Cutest comment from Jenni the morning after Bob's latest homecoming, waiting to see what her daddy had brought or what fun thing he was going to do for her – "You did things for *all* the others. You drew a picture for Robin, you gave Skippy a piggyback ride, you slept with Mommy. ..."

February 16, 1966
Orlando, Florida

Prichard, Alabama
Dear Nana GeeGee,

Thank you very much for the record. You know, I didn't get to hear the record until three days after my birthday! I got a microscope for my birthday and it is NEATO! I had a real happy birthday!

Love,
Robin

April 30, 1966
Orlando, Florida

Honolulu, Hawaii
Dear Uncle Dave and Aunt Joni and Lynnie,

We have missed you, and we want to visit you but we can't. When Lynnie made the gift and sent it to us, I read it and I never knew Lynnie could spell hard words like me, and draw so good too. I guessed one night how to spell extremely. Daddy wanted me to say this, When he got through with his school he would write.

After Easter we had a play, Hansel & Gretel. Robin and Debbie and Susan, Sharon, Cathie, Cindy, and I all had parts in the play. Some neighbors came and we made 80 cents.

We wish we could see Kimi but we can't. Daddy said he was aching to see her. She is a cute baby in the pictures we see of her. In school we are studying about dinosaurs and fishes. I made a report of dinosaurs and I brought in seven books and one fish book. I asked my mommy one night how do we know that the men who found the first dinosaurs put them together the right way.

We were reading about the rain in Hawaii and we haven't had rain but sunshine for three months now. We need rain, because our grass is dying. Except we water it every day to keep it from dying. Aunt Joni, Mommy said that she was sending your long book letters to Nana GeeGee and Granddaddy in Alabama. We hope we can visit you some day. Good-by!
Love,
Jenni

P.S. – Skippy loves you too and says he is mad because his name is on peanut butter jars.
P.P.S. – This picture is for Lynnie. She is dancing a hula in a grass Hawaii skirt.

May 2, 1966
Prichard, Alabama

Orlando, Florida
Dear Pat,

Here is the last letter from my dear friend Margaret in Hawaii. She writes such interesting letters. I sure wish you and Margaret could be in Mobile at the same time one of these years. But even if you just know each other thru me, you still have a strong connection. I was thinking Margaret and Bob's brother Dave might like to meet each other while he's living in Hawaii. You think we ought to check and see if they want to?

I am real busy so I won't write much this time. A bushel of love.

Mommie

Dearest Wilba,

Hallelujah! Dearest friend, you just can't imagine how I long for a "feather tick," which is, indeed, a feather mattress. There is no such thing in this part of the world. Hereabouts people buy nothing but stone-hard mattresses, and even then they put plyboard between the mattresses and springs. I can't begin to tell you how much I appreciate your helping hand in locating the feather mattress and taking care of having it shipped to Hawaii. Thank the good God for a friend like you.

For the past week, we in Honolulu have not known which end of the pond to fish, which channel to tune in, or much of anything else, due to the excitement attendant upon playing host to the "traveling White House." President Johnson, the Vice President, and the Vietnamese have kept the entire city on tenterhooks, for security reasons, and just out of plain curiosity and anxiety regarding the "war decisions" being made in our midst.

Honolulu is a staging area for our operations in the Far East, and the escalation of this terrible Viet Nam situation brings to our memory the conditions that existed in Hawaii during World War II. I cannot bring myself to believe that we are on the threshold of still another Asian conflict. Surely some way can be found to stop the slaughter and honor our commitments before there is another outbreak in Korea, or a new horror to face in Thailand, Laos or Cambodia. It is hard for me to accept wars among nations, families, or neighborhoods. Between black, white or yellow the waste of human life and all that Life implies – hopes, ambitions, progress, health, resources and continuity – constitutes an enigma that defies my understanding. If a war – any war – held out hopes of a final solution to the woes of humanity, then, in that context, it could be borne gloriously, and fought to the gallant end. But, to the contrary, all history teaches but one lesson – that wars breed into each new conflict the same four horsemen – and we still must learn the lesson of the Apocalypse.

As I read back I beg humble forgiveness for getting so carried away. One might think my personal avocation is a criticism of the human race – and I'm sure the human race is in far more knowledgeable hands than mine. Ha!

Now, from such lofty subject matter, back to the matter of the *mattress*, and another big thank you! All our love, as always, to Randolph, Rickey and your own dear self.

Margaret

Happy Mothers Day
May 1966
By Skip
> I am glad for Mothers
> I am glad that Mothers
> Can cook supper so
> that we can eat.
> I thank you for Mothers
> dear god.
> a-Men

June 5, 1966
Dear Diary,

Now, along with my job as Recording Secretary of the Central Florida Council of Welcome Wagon, I've been elected president of the Bowl-a-Bits League. Darn, I *was* going to say no to outside responsibilities starting in the fall and try to carve out a little leisure time just for ME. ... How can I learn to say No?

June 21, 1966
Dear Diary,

We just got home from two weeks' vacation in Connecticut, our first trip back there since moving away nearly three years ago. We all had a wonderful time. Being with Bob's mother and dad was great. They treated us royally.

And in Hamden, dear friends (and old neighbors) Ruth and Jack hosted not one, but *two* parties in our honor, each for a different group of our friends. Everything was perfect, except there was a heat wave – which gave us a chance to really tease the Yankees that it was much hotter up there than in Florida.

Now we have only 10 days at home before the kids and I go to Alabama for another vacation, and poor Bob heads back to Clemson to study.

August 4, 1966
Dear Diary,

Home again. It's hard to get back into the routine after all the vacationing. In Alabama, Skip and Granddaddy became *the best* buddies in the world. Skip would get up at 3:30 or 4 a.m. with Daddy to share the coffee ritual before their fishing trips. Daddy would fix Skip "almost black" coffee (actually liberally laced with milk), and they'd sit at the table in the quiet, dimly lit kitchen drinking coffee while they talked over the plans. I bet Skip will always carry special memories of those pre-dawn hours with his beloved granddaddy. I reminded Daddy to watch his P's and Q's since he is a hero in Skip's eyes.

The folks have a new dog, the first pet since Tartar died, and we all fell in love with sweet, pretty Lady. The kids wanted badly to bring her home with us, naturally. The cutest thing, Lady senses when Daddy is going somewhere and barks to go out, where she heads for the truck to sit patiently and wait for him. Skip says, "Lady's *smart!*"

It was so good to have time to visit with the kin. Saw Aunt Della and her family, and spent hours with Aunt Hazel, with Robin and Jenni thoroughly enjoying her two youngest, Renee and Phyllis. Mom sewed for us, and the girls loved that.

We missed Bob but he had a good final session at Clemson, finishing fourth in the class of 14, so we're quite proud of him! He left South Carolina and came to Alabama to see my folks a couple of days. Then he drove our little family back home to Orlando.

August 4, 1966
Orlando, Florida

Prichard, Alabama
Dear Granddaddy,

I had fun on our fishing trips. I want to come and see you and Nana GeeGee again. Please write me back. I love you both.

From Skip

August 23, 1966
Dear Diary,

My 34th birthday ... and with it there's good news and there's bad news. Bob has been offered a nice promotion with the telephone company, but the position is in Jacksonville. And we really don't want to leave The City Beautiful where we are so content. Oh, dear.

August 25, 1966
Dear Diary,

Today is little Kimberly's second birthday and we've never seen her! They are all flying to the mainland to live after three years in Hawaii. What a change Wisconsin will be for them. Good to have Dave and his family a few thousand miles closer, though! Robin was talking about the family recently and kind of sighed, "I wish we could have a *homemade* aunt, too." Such a cute way to distinguish between an aunt by blood or through marriage, huh?

September 2, 1966
Orlando, Florida

Prichard, Alabama
Dear Nana GeeGee,

I just had to write and tell you about something you said when I was visiting you. Remember you said I had nothing on my breast. Well that's not true any more! One side is about an inch out and the other one is almost as big. In a couple of months or even weeks Mommy will get me a bra!!!!!!!!

Love,
Robin

September 26, 1966
Dear Diary,

Today Robin proclaimed: "Now that I have a belt and a bra, I am almost a woman!" I love it. ...

October 15, 1966
Dear Diary,

So much has happened. Bob took the new job and began working in Jacksonville during the week. Our wonderful house went on the market and the kids, I, and most of our neighbors either cried or felt like crying. We were so torn about leaving. ...

Then Bob decided to investigate the possibility of becoming a stock broker since studying the stock market is already sort of his hobby. Amazingly, everything fell into place quickly. He was interviewed and hired by an investment firm here; he resigned from the telephone company; and our house came off the market. We are staying in Orlando! Everyone is relieved and so-o-o happy. (And to help financially, I signed on as a Welcome Wagon hostess.)

December 25, 1966
Orlando, Florida

Merry Christmas to all from Sunny Florida!

We've never done this before – a letter at Christmas-time instead of the usual cards with notes. But there is just *so* much news to tell this year – and we promise not to make it too long!

All five of us are busy and well. Robin is almost 12 and getting to be quite the young lady. She is doing some baby-sitting already, but oh! those awful rock 'n' roll records she plays! Jenni is 9, in fourth grade, and very nonchalant about her good marks in school. Skip, a happy 7-year-old, is busy these days singing "All I want for Christmas is my *four* front teeth!"

As for Pat and Bob, some big changes have taken place recently and "there just aren't enough hours in the day!" Bob resigned from the telephone company in October after 11 years of service in order to enter the securities business. After six months of training, three in Orlando and three in New York, he will become registered about May 1st (our 14th wedding anniversary) and will be ready to set Wall Street on its ear!

Of course, this means we can live in "The City Beautiful" permanently – and that makes us all *very* happy!

Pat, meanwhile, has become a Welcome Wagon Hostess. It's right up her alley! Although there's some hard work involved, she loves greeting newcomers to Orlando – and making new friends in the process.

So you can see we are busy and happy as we approach Christmas and the New Year. We look forward to the adventures of 1967, while giving thanks for our many blessings. For you, our friends, we sincerely wish the happiest of holiday seasons and a rich and satisfying year ahead. Do let us hear from you and, remember, our door is always open to you.

We love you all – Happy New Year!

Pat and Bob
Robin, Jenni and Skipper

December 26, 1966
Orlando, Florida

Prichard, Alabama
Dear Granddady Nana GeeGee and Lady.

Merry Christmas to you. I hope you all are feeling good. I am feeling fine. I know that Lady is a nana now. I hope that Rickey is OK. I love you. From Skipper.

246

December 26, 1966
Orlando, Florida

Prichard, Alabama
Dear Nana GeeGee and Granddaddy,
    Thank you for the pretty red dress. Tell Rickey that I loved the Barbie furniture. I hope I see you some day.

Love,
Jenni

P.S. – I love you.

January 15, 1967
Orlando, Florida

The *Orlando Sentinel*
Orlando, Florida
Dear Editor:
    Please accept the following essay as my entry in the *Sentinel's* contest:

WHY ORLANDO?

Four years ago, on a cold day in Connecticut, my husband popped the question, "How would you like to move to Florida?" Being an old sun worshipper who had shivered through eight winters, I was thrilled! Talking is always easier than doing, however, and we spent many sleepless nights before we finally made our decision.

"Which part of Florida?" We immediately began to dream of living at the ocean's edge, but when my husband considered all the available positions, everything pointed to Orlando. We had never heard of it! Naturally, we had a few little doubts, especially as our arrival day happened to be on the 13th of the month … a Friday. We know now, of course, that it was our lucky day! Although our choosing Orlando was a happy accident, there's nothing accidental about our plan to stay here forever.

Orlando is a very special place. It captured my heart in just a few weeks, and I quickly felt so at home. It has the peace and security of a small town along with the advantages of a large city.

Its beauty is a story in itself. The citrus trees filled with bright orange and yellow fruit, the lovely parks bursting at the seams with flowers of every color, the fascinating little clouds playing hide-and-seek in the oh-so-blue sky – these are only a few of Orlando's beauty points. Have you ever watched the sunlight playing on a lake, or taken a deep breath and been surprised by the delicious aroma of orange blossoms?

Oh yes, I think you will agree that I am especially lucky in my work: As a Welcome Wagon Hostess, I have the delightful opportunity of introducing "my" lovely city to the newcomers!

Sincerely,
Pat
A Happy Orlandoan

January 20, 1967
By Jenni

My Prayer

Things to Remember in My Prayer to Thank the LORD for What He Gave to Us

1. Always remember to thank the LORD for what he has given us.
2. Always remember to say heal the sick and help the poor and heal the people with birth defects.
3. Always say help me to stop sucking my fingers and biting my fingernails.
4. Please make me beautiful now, beautiful when I am an adult.
5. Watch over everyone and keep everyone safe and healthy.
6. Always let us have wonderful, beautiful dreams.
7. When we see scary and horror and the bloody-type movies, please, please, let us forget to dream and think about them.
8. When somebody in the world dies, let them go into heaven.
9. Always say I LOVE YOU ALL.
10. At the greeting of my prayer I shall say DEAR LORD.
11. At the end of my prayer I shall say IN JESUS NAME I PRAY.

P.S. – Please forgive us of our sins, and I must respect people.
And I hope I don't get any cavities and my teeth stay in good shape.

February 15, 1967
New York City

Orlando, Florida
Dearest Pat,

Just a note to let you know I got back fine. The plane was ready and I boarded about five minutes after you left me, so you couldn't have been with me much more anyhow. We were about 15 minutes late landing at JFK, which isn't bad. The temperature was 32 degrees, and I was back at the apartment by 10.

It's the understatement of the year to say that I enjoyed the weekend! Everything about it was great! Especially you. I am becoming more impressed with you all the time, honey. It may be that our frequent separations over the past couple of years have matured you even more, but you're quite a gal! You're a top-notch Welcome Wagon Hostess, well-liked by your friends, a loving and loved mother, and a thoughtful and patient and loving wife. I'm more proud of you these days than I've ever been before. ...

Thanks again for a wonderful weekend – and remember, it's all downhill from here on.

All my love,
Your Bob

April 23, 1967
Orlando, Florida

Prichard, Alabama
Dear Nana GeeGee and Granddaddy,

As you know I have had my tonsils out! For being good I got a stuffed animal from Mommy and seven cards and 34 homemade cards from my school class! The present from my teacher was a lovely bouquet of roses and baby's breath! The vase is a woman and she looks like my teacher! She is Wow Wow!!! I got some notes from more of my friends, too. When we come up to your house I want to ride the horses!!! I won't be scared to either!!! Skippy really wants a dog now! He's bothering Mommy about it! Mommy enjoyed your telephone call. It was meant for me but I couldn't talk then! I bought some Super-Stuff! It's crazy! Be seeing ya!!! Bye-bye!!!

Love and hugs and kisses,
Jenni

P.S. – xoxoxo
xxxxxxx I love ya!

May 1967
By Skippy

My Skates

One day I borrowed roller
       skates,
And I skated till it was
       very late.
I hope for my birthday
       in May
A pair of skates come
       my way.

June 17, 1967
Prichard, Alabama

Orlando, Florida
Dear Mommy and Dad,

Almost every day Nana GeeGee says, do you miss your mommy and daddy, and I always say NO! One time at breakfast Nana GeeGee said, do you miss your mommy and daddy yet, and I said, I do a little crumb. And then I said, when I begin to go home I will miss you a big toast. I love you very, very much. I told Nana and Granddaddy when my dad went to N.Y. I was daddy sick. But after he got home he still smelld the same.

I hope dolly is all right. You had better not sold dolly yet. Please don't give her away till I see her again

I Love You,
I miss you a little bit.
Skippy

July 12, 1967
Orlando, Florida

Prichard, Alabama
Dear Nana GeeGee & Granddaddy,

I've started doing something that I know you'll be glad of. I am taking sewing lessons. A lady in the neighborhood is giving them.

There are five girls in the group, including her daughter, and I'm the oldest. We're making ourselves a dress and a skirt. My material is just GORGEOUS!

My skirt is almost finished except for the hem and waistband. I had already measured it with my pattern, cut it, sewed it, put in darts, and even put in a zipper! Pretty soon I'll start making my dress. Instead of the teacher showing me how to make shorts, Nana GeeGee, I want you to.

We've been doing well down here but still missing you. How's everything? Good-bye and I love you.

Yours truly,
Robin

P.S. – XOXOXOXOXOXOXOXOXOXOXOXO – AND MORE!

July 20, 1967
Dear Mommy,

I am sorry that you had a bad day today, and I will try to be better tomorrow. OK? OK! I love you so very much!

Maybe if you get a good sleep tonight you will feel better tomorrow. When I was in my room I was crying because you were unhappy, and I wanted so much for you to come into my room and hug and kiss me. That was the only thing I wanted. I love you so much, I don't want you to be sad.

Yours always,
Robin

P.S. – Kiss! .... Hug! ....

August 22, 1967
Orlando, Florida

Prichard, Alabama
Dear Nana GeeGee!

Hi! How are you and Granddaddy?

Well, I had a nice birthday. I got a full-length mirror from Mom and Dad! Thank you for the money! I can buy "Love's Fresh Lemon Body Mist" with it. Thank you!

Skippy, how are you? Having fun in Alabama? I miss you so much. Please hurry home. Okay?

Love,
Jenni

September 12, 1967
Orlando, Florida

Prichard, Alabama
Nana GeeGee,

It seems like every time I write, I tell you my problems. Well, that's the reason for this one. I've been so depressed lately, mostly because I don't have a boyfriend. And my hair is too short – I hate it!

Love,
Robin

November 16, 1967
Orlando, Florida

Prichard, Alabama
Dear Nana GeeGee and Granddaddy,

I have missed you very much. I am looking forward to coming. Youd better have some clothes ready for me. I would of put some exclamation points but I dont know how on a typewriter. Oooh, I just cannot wait. I cant write on a typewriter very well so my letter wont be very long. Well, so long. I love you!

Love,
Jenni

December 27, 1967
Orlando, Florida

Prichard, Alabama
Dear Nana GeeGee & Granddaddy,

I sure wish you could have come to our house for Christmas. I really did like comeing to your house. Right now I am writing a letter to you and telling you how fun it was to come to your house.

I love you.
Skippy

January 1, 1968

Mom,

I am outside riding my bike. I won't go far so if you want me just call me. Happy New Year.

Skip

February 17, 1968
Orlando, Florida

Prichard, Alabama

Dearest Mommie and Daddy,

Well, here I am between guests, with only three days to get ready for more – Jack and Ruth, our friends from Connecticut. Bob's parents drove off about 8:30 this morning into bad weather, I'm afraid. Evidently there was lots of snow in the Carolinas and we're not sure how they will manage.

Of course, if necessary, they could simply stay over somewhere along the way, but they were anxious to get home soon. Dave is due back in Woodbury on Friday, and they really want to be there for him. He called the other evening with unsettling news concerning the status of the divorce proceedings. Apparently the granting of a final decree will be delayed.

We certainly did enjoy being with Bob's folks again during their visit. They are so easy to have around, and since they were here longer than usual this time, we all went ahead with our work and/or reading, and no one was ever inconvenienced.

We four grownups went to a Naval Academy Alumni Association luncheon on Valentine's Day and had great fun. Five of Dad's classmates from the Class of 1925 were there with their wives, so it was a well-represented class, which tickled Dad. I always enjoy myself, chatting with everybody! That night all seven of us – the kids, Bob's parents, Bob and I – went out for our favorite Arby's roast beef sandwiches and mocha milkshakes for supper.

All three children had their regular dental checkups last week. No cavities for the girls and they were ecstatic. Ol' Skippy had two small ones. My foot is still not completely healed, it hurts off and on, swells, and I can't wear regular shoes yet.

Must scoot now. Much love from Bob and me and your three desserts.

Pat

Dear Nana GeeGee and Granddaddy,

I am sending this in Mom's envelope. Thank you so much for the $5.00. It really helped my "kitty." I have about 30 dollars. I had 40, but spent 10 on a scarab watchband.

Nana, you probably don't know this, but lately I've been buying "16" (a magazine for teenagers). I just love it! Well, anyway, I've seen this guy, he's probably about 16, in some Walt Disney shows. He's just a doll, his name is Kurt Russell, and I'm writing to the magazine and asking for his address and for them to tell me something about him.

I have pictures of real handsome stars all over my closet door! Mom and Dad were kinda shocked when I put them up, but I guess they don't realize I love to do that kind of thing.

I just finished making two more dresses. I'm enclosing a drawing of one of them. It has short sleeves and no collar. And Mom just bought me a set of electric hair curlers! I absolutely love them!!!

Well, I love you and bye for now. Kiss and hug!

Robin

March 23, 1968
Orlando, Florida

Woodbury, Connecticut
Dear Nana Kitty and Granddad,

I told you I would send a letter about little league. Today on March 23, 1968 we played the Metts. We won them by 4 runs. The score was 5 to 1 and I made a run. We are going to play the Metts again. On April 4, 1968 we are playing the Metts. On April 9, 1968 we are playing the White Socks. And after that we are playing the Astros. Well I better get going and do my dutys.

I love you,
Skippy

March 28, 1968
Orlando, Florida

Prichard, Alabama
Dear Nana GeeGee and Granddaddy,

I will send you a poem I wrote because I had to stay home and did not feel good.

Having a cold is being sick
so you can't go outside
and get yourself licked.

It's not very fun to stay in bed,
because after a little while
you start to hurt in your head.

So be brave and bold and
wait till tomorrow
to be told!
By Skippy

May 11, 1968
Orlando, Florida

Prichard, Alabama
Dear Nana GeeGee,

I sure hope I get to come up for a while by myself this summer!!! I'm really looking forward to it! I miss you so much. Nana Kitty and Granddad left day before yesterday, but we all had the most wonderful time! I wish you and Granddaddy could have been here also!

My contacts have been doing wonderfully! I have them in now. (I'm watching TV, too! Haha.) It's almost 10 o'clock so I'd better hurry and finish this letter before the mailman comes!

The enclosed picture is of me and two friends joining the church. It's not really a good picture but at least I have one. Well, toodles!
Love,
Robin

P.S. – I love you! And please write!

August 23, 1968
Mom,

Happy Birthday! Your present will unfortunately be delayed. Something didn't turn out perfect. Sorry!
Love, Love, Love,
Jenni

September 1, 1968

My list to do.
By Jenni
1. Ask someone to iron my dress.
2. Change clothes.
3. Call Sharon.
4. Ask Dad if I can chalk on driveway or patio.
5. Maybe change socks.
6. Write letter to Susan.
7. Get baton ready to take to school.
8. Play, Outside!
9. Get allowance.

December 25, 1968
DEAR ROBIN, JENNI AND SKIP,
    BECAUSE YOU ARE ALL SO GROWN-UP NOW, I LEFT YOUR PRESENTS WRAPPED, UNDER THE TREE, TO BE OPENED LATER. BUT ENJOY THE STOCKING GIFTS I LEFT AS SOON AS YOU GET UP!

MERRY CHRISTMAS,
FROM SANTA CLAUS

December 25, 1968
Orlando, Florida

Prichard, Alabama
Dear Nana GeeGee and Granddaddy,
    I can't thank you enough for the nightgown and robe. I just love the color! Some of the other things I got are a camera, purse, jewelry box, jewelry, and some games. Well I miss you!

Love, your granddaughter
Jenni

January 27, 1969
Dear Diary,

So happy for John and Kathie – they now have a bouncing 3-week-old baby boy! He was born January 7th and they've named him Mark. It's kind of a funny story. They were on the waiting list with an adoption agency in New Orleans, where John happened to be attending the National Math Convention when Kathie, at their home in Mississippi, got a call from the agency that there was a baby for them. Of course, she asked if John could just pick up the baby right then, and was told, not surprisingly, that both parents had to appear! So John took off for Starkville to fetch Kathie and they turned around and drove back to New Orleans, picked up their baby and headed back home to Mississippi – a family! Now two of my brothers each have a son – and we have two nephews to go with the two nieces from Bob's brother.

April 21, 1969
Orlando, Florida

Prichard, Alabama
Dear Grandparents,

I miss you a lot! I just can't wait until this summer when Mom drives us to Alabama.

I am planting a garden and I'm going to use a flower called "Bachelor's Buttons." I got them off a corn chips package.

We kids think that Mom and Dad are going to take us to play bingo on Wednesday night. Do you remember when I won ten dollars there? I'm hoping to win more than ten dollars this time.

I heard that my Uncle Dave is on a business trip to Alabama now. If you see him would you tell him "hello" for me? Thanks. Well, this is just a note, but good-bye!

Tons of love,
Jenni

May 30, 1969
Orlando, Florida

Prichard, Alabama
Dearest Nana GeeGee,

Last night I'd have given anything if you could have been with me. There was a party at the pool and I wanted to go, but I couldn't find anyone to go with me. It wasn't because the two girls I called didn't want to go (they really did) but one had a sprained ankle and the other had to babysit.

Most of the girls I know who were going had boys to go with them. It made me all depressed. Sometimes I don't think my parents understand how I feel. … Isn't it funny that every time I have big trouble I come to you, Nana? You must be tired of it, but you can't imagine how much it helps even to write to you!

I'm back now. I was just gone about three hours – went to church with Holly, a good friend of mine. Afterward we walked around Lake Eola, then went for a rowboat ride on the lake. Two boys were rowing, too, and showing off to us like you wouldn't believe! We really had a great time and I'm in a better mood now! (Aren't you glad?)

Well, Nana, thanks so-o-o-o much for listening. I love you so very much!

Robin

P.S. – Can't wait to see you!

June 2, 1969
Orlando, Florida

Prichard, Alabama
Dear Granddaddy and Nana GeeGee,

Thank you for the five dollar bill. I bought two baseballs with it. If you would like to know, baseball is my favorite sport right now. I am going to join the summer baseball camp. Right now in Little League we are doing terrible. Our record is 5 wins, 12 losses, and we only have THREE MORE GAMES! I have been getting beautiful hits, so I am going to be in the All Star game.

Jenni has a boy friend. He has the same last name as us. I have a girl friend. I must be going now. By, by.

I love you,
Skippy

July 20, 1969
Prichard, Alabama

Orlando, Florida

Hi, Bob, honey,

Just a few lines to share my feelings about the historic event that took place tonight. Mommie, Daddy and I watched on television as the Apollo 11 Lunar Module *Eagle* landed on the moon.

Landed on the moon?!? Incredible. ... When Neil Armstrong touched the moon's surface and declared, "One small step for man, one giant leap for mankind," I just got goosepimples. A few minutes later, outside, looking up into the heavens at the actual moon, realizing there was a human being on its surface at that moment ... well, we simply, quietly, tried to absorb it all.

Standing there, I cradled the precious little one already growing inside, silently acknowledging the momentous event of this night-to-remember, and wondered at all the fantastic things this baby will be witness to in his or her lifetime.

G'night for now, sweetheart. We are all looking forward to seeing you next week, especially me. I *miss* you.

All love,
Your Pat

P.S. – I always think of more, don't I? Tell Dave and Dorothy the kinfolk here are so happy for them and have really enjoyed hearing the story of how we first met sweet Dorothy, felt certain she and our Dave would be absolutely *perfect* for each other, then set out as matchmakers – and watched the two of them fall in love.

You know, honey, just thinking ... if the new baby is a boy, maybe he could be David, too (David II, in fact). It's such a wonderful name, with the special meaning of "beloved." Let's ask Dave how he'd feel about a namesake nephew.

The family is one of nature's masterpieces.
George Santanyana

Chapter Fifteen
Life's Travels
1969-73

Pat, David and "Sleepy" at Walt Disney World

August 11, 1969
Orlando, Florida

Prichard, Alabama
Dearest Mommie and Daddy,

What a happy "accident" happened today! It meant that along with our card for your 38th anniversary I can gift you with a wonderful little story.

As you know, when I was in Alabama last month my waist was already expanding, so today I bought maternity shorts. I left the pairs of shorts on the bed while I went to the bathroom, and in just those few minutes Robin and Jenni discovered my secret purchase.

Their questions were quite discreet as they probed, but they admitted having wondered about it before because "we thought you looked bigger." They asked if Skippy knew and I told them Daddy and I had already decided we were going to tell them about the baby that night at dinner, so we should keep the secret a few hours longer.

Fast forward to dinnertime: We were all seated around the dining room table and Bob said the blessing, at the end of which, following a dramatic pause, he closed with "And God please bless the *six* of us. Amen." Of course, Robin and Jenni were beside themselves with anticipation, but we all stayed quiet and kept our eyes on Skippy, waiting for a reaction … but he looked interested only in what was for dinner!

Finally I ventured, "Skip, what was that Daddy said? Bless the six of us?" After a moment his eyes lit up and a huge grin spread all the way across that sweet little face as he joyfully cried out, "ARE WE GONNA GET A DOG?!!!"

Happy Anniversary!
Pat and the gang

August 21, 1969
Orlando, Florida

Prichard, Alabama
Dear Nana GeeGee, Granddaddy and Lady,

Thanks so much for the nightie. It's so pretty! The one you gave me last year is kinda wearing out! Besides, I'd rather have a change of color.

I got so many nice presents! I'm happy with all of 'em! Tell Lady I love her!

Mucho love,
Jenni

September 5, 1969
By Skippy

My Code

1. I will study my hardest this year.
2. I will not get mad at my friends.
3. If my big sister sings again I will keep my temper.
4. When my mother and father go out at night I will not play rough.
5. I will come to school on time, and not any earlier.
6. I will not fuss if we get a lot of work.
7. I will keep my school books in good condition.

December 26, 1969
Orlando, Florida

Woodbury, Connecticut
Dear Nana Kitty and Granddad,

Thank you for the speedometer you gave me. This is the day after Christmas, so we have not put it on my bike. By the way I got a new bike. We will put it on my bike tomorrow. My bike is a sting-ray Renegade. It doesn't have a lot of fancy things but I like it a lot anyway. I got a pretty lot of things, and I'll name them now.

Bicycle
Blow Whistle
Hot Wheel Tracks
A lot of Shirts
An ant Farm
Hoppity-hop
And some other things.

Yours Truly,
Skippy

P.S. – Write me back please.

December 31, 1969
Orlando, Florida

Prichard, Alabama,

Happy New Year, my dearest family!

　　We have all fared quite well in 1969, haven't we? In the hours between the closing of one year and the beginning of another, I always find myself filled with a strange mixture of emotions: half happy and half inexplicably sad. But I am going to zero in on happy thoughts for 1970, especially those of the eagerly anticipated arrival of our fourth blessed event. ...

　　　　　　　　　　　Much love – Happy 1970!
　　　　　　　　　　　Pat and crew

P.S. – I saw the enclosed poem in the newspaper recently. Doesn't it sound *just* like my life?

　　　　　The alarm bell rings at six, you're off at a run,
　　　　　The race doesn't end when the day is done.
　　　　　You wake the youngsters, begin to dress.
　　　　　Hope nothing is lost or needs a press.

　　　　　It's into the kitchen and you start to cook.
　　　　　Then you stop to find a child's lost book.
　　　　　It's your day to drive for the neighborhood pool,
　　　　　And 'midst childish chatter you get to school.

　　　　　The running continues at a faster pace,
　　　　　As you work at home, or some other place.
　　　　　There's always laundry, cleaning and such.
　　　　　Sewing, sorting; it seems too much.

　　　　　There are errands to run and shopping to do,
　　　　　Sometimes, it seems you'd never get through.
　　　　　Meetings and projects, they keep you a-hop,
　　　　　Demands on your time seem never to stop.

　　　　　You freshen up for the breadwinner.
　　　　　Then bathe children and get the dinner.
　　　　　Later it's homework and dishes to wash,
　　　　　And mending and letters and ... but by gosh ...

Although in leisure you'd like to revel,
Here is the pitch – and it's on the level:
You'd rather have this job than any other –
It's such a challenge being a mother.

Author Unknown

February 10, 1970
IMPORTANT NOTICE OF EXTRA DIVIDEND

Management is very pleased to announce an extra dividend delivered at Orlando, Florida, on February 10, 1970.

Name of dividend: David
Amount of dividend: 6 lbs., 5 oz.
Condition of parent company: Sound
Production Manager: Pat
Treasurer: Bob

February 11, 1970
Orlando, Florida

Orange Memorial Hospital
Orlando, Florida
Dear Mommy,

I miss you so much, and I hope you can come home Saturday. I'm so glad the baby came alright and I'm glad it's a boy since Daddy wanted one so bad. He says he's gorgeous and really perfect, has sandy hair and hasn't got one bruise or blemish. Will we name it Christopher? That's a cute name.

I know Nana Kitty's here and all but I really wish you didn't have to stay gone so long. Is it okay if I go to the dance this Friday? I may not feel like it since I haven't been feeling good this last week, especially today.

Well, bye, please hurry home. I love the baby. I love you so much. I miss you.

Jenni

P.S. – I would be afraid to ask Nana Kitty if I could stay home because she and Granddad would think I'm taking advantage of your being gone. Think about it. I love you.

February 13, 1970
Orlando, Florida

Orange Memorial Hospital
Orlando, Florida

Happy Valentine's Day, Mommy – we can't wait for you and baby David to come home!

Love from Robin (The Greatest), Jenni (The Beautiful and Powerful Sweetheart of the Year), Skip (The Masterful) and DAVEY (me, too!)

February 14, 1970
Orlando, Florida

Orlando, Florida
Dear Nana Kitty and Granddad,

Thank you for taking such good care of my daddy and sisters and brother while Mommy and I were in the hospital.

Happy Valentine's Day – I love you.
Your newest grandson, David II
(With help from Daddy)

February 15, 1970
White Sails Apartments
Pompano Beach, Florida

Orlando, Florida
Dear David,

It was good to see you come home yesterday with flying colors. You have a great family there and they were all so wonderful to us. Our special thanks to all five. Our trip down (200 miles) was easy and uneventful. We were in town by 4 p.m. after a steak-and-cheese sandwich on the way. Weather is great – water temp 68 degrees, pool 80.

Love,
Granddad and Nana Kitty

February 23, 1970
Orlando, Florida

Prichard, Alabama
Dear ones,

Everything is going so well. David is a dream baby. Having three older children to help is a dream, too! We're all just dippy over him, of course! Just think, David's almost two weeks old and wasn't even due for another ten days. I'm lucky that everything is fine but without those final uncomfortable weeks of pregnancy.

I want to share Skippy's beautiful comment as he held David for the first time. The baby lay in his big brother's arms, gazing serenely up at his face. After observing David quietly for a few seconds, Skippy said, "He looks like he's wise and knows everything already, like he's been here before." There they were, the two brothers, one a little under age 11 and the other less than one week from my womb into this world. It was quite an amazing scene to witness.

We can't wait for y'all to head down Orlando way and meet your newest precious grandchild.

Bushels of love,
Pat and Bob, Robin, Jenni, Skip
and David (wow!)

P.S. – My friends had planned a baby shower February 19, but with David's early appearance there has been a slight postponement. The clever invitation Linda designed shows Pooh Bear holding a colorful balloon, with the words "Pooh invites you to his party for pregnant Pat. ... Pooh presents preferred."

April 27, 1970
Orlando, Florida

Prichard, Alabama
My dearest family,

Just a couple of lines this evening before I have my bowl of cereal and say goodnight to the world for a few hours. My hope is that Wheaties at bedtime will make me a champion at breakfast!

The wonderful news is that Dave and Dorothy are united in marriage at last. I believe I can truthfully say the whole family is *almost* as ecstatic over the marital blessing of this love story as the bride and groom! It was a sweetly simple, beautiful ceremony. Dorothy was radiant, Dave in seventh heaven, and their combined quintet of daughters completely charming.

With love in the air,
Pat

May 5, 1970
Orlando, Florida

Prichard, Alabama
Dear Nana GeeGee and Granddaddy,

How are ya? I'm fine. Just 23 more school days! Isn't that great? Nana, before I forget, I want to wish you a Happy Mother's Day! (Mother's Day goes for grandmas, too!)

I've been doing well in school. On my last report card my grades were:

Math – A
Physical Education – A! (as always)
English – A! (been making B's)
Geography – B! (been making C's)
Science – A! (been making B's)
Health – A

And I got all 1's in conduct. 1 is the best you can make.

How's Lady? I miss her. I really wish Mom would let us have a dog!

David coos and smiles now. He can even roll over when he's on the floor.

Well, that's all the "Super Six's" news!

Bye,
Jenni

P.S. – I LOVE YOU!
WBSP (Write Back Soon Please)
Love-n-Peace!

May 23, 1970
Orlando, Florida

Prichard, Alabama
Dear Nana GeeGee and Granddaddy,

How are you? I'm just fine. When will you write me? Soon, I hope. How's Lady? Probably she's ok. Is she as sweet as always? I wish (Skip, too) that Mom would allow us to get a dog. We really need one. Skip will probably write you and thank you for his $3. I won't tell you what he spent it on, ok? He got some other things like balls, tennis balls, baseball, a pitch-back (a doohicky that bounces the baseball back to you). I think it's real swift. Also he got a tetherball and we've played it so much that our wrists and pinky fingers are real sore.

Last nite a girl named Annette spent the night with me. It was sort of fun.

Right now David's crying and fussing for no reason at all. Dad says he's spoiled but Mom and I don't think so. I don't know what Robin and Skippy think. I tape-recorded some of his coos, and when he "talked" to all of us. It was real cute only the tape didn't sound too great. It was all fuzzy. Well, I love you! Bye!

Luv,
Jenni

P.S. – Mom told us John and Kathie are going to have a baby. Congratulations, you will have another grandchild! Do you hope it's a girl or a boy?

May 24, 1970
Orlando, Florida

Prichard, Alabama
Dear Nana GeeGee and Granddaddy,

Thank you very much for your 3 dollars. At first I couldn't decide what to get with it. Then I decided to get a tetherball.

I also got 10 more dollars, a baseball, three tennis balls, a kickball, and best of all, a Pitch-back net. With the ten dollars I got a baseball glove.

I am glad you gave me money, because I like it better.

If you can, hurry and come down here or try to talk my Mom and Dad into letting me come up there on a bus, airplane or train.

I love you.
Skippy

May 25, 1970
Orlando, Florida

Prichard, Alabama
Dearest Mommie and Perky Daddy!

Great to hear that you're feeling so well, Daddy. I bet you're back to dancing the "Bugaloo" and the "Teaberry Shuffle" by now! I could hardly stand not getting on the phone Friday night, but Robin wanted to tell y'all about the honor she received. Isn't it great? She credits you, Mom, with starting her out on the Home-Ec road. You should see her creation for the 9th grade party coming up soon – a very pretty white dress with scallops around the neck and hem.

Robin was away part of the weekend with a girlfriend. They had a good time even though an all-day rain yesterday messed up their planned boat trip and picnic. While she was gone Jenni and Skip did such a great job with David. I really have built-in help right down the line! Sunday morning they got him up and changed him, then brought him in to our bed, all three looking so cute. Skip fed David last night when we had some friends here for drinks – and Jen, who is very proud of herself when she takes care of the baby, does a fine job and is getting better at it all the time. David's as sweet as ever, really a very happy little guy most of the time.

Skip had a fun birthday – a ball game, a pizza supper, cake and ice cream, then "goodies" from the family. And he loves that money you sent!

It looks like the stock market is about finished, huh? Oh dear, we sure are hanging on these days, hoping for a recovery real soon. ... Bob's morale is pretty good, though, considering the state of the business.

I'll bet Rickey is getting excited about his trip to Yugoslavia. It's nice that he'll get to see England, too. What an adventure! Must run now. We all send much love!

Pat and the rest of The Super Six

June 18, 1970
London, England

Prichard, Alabama

Dear Mom and Dad,

Greetings from merry England – and now I know why they're so merry here. All the young ladies wear short skirts. Dad, you would love it.

Things were fairly uneventful until I caught a city bus to the airport in Tampa. A girl who finished at Louisiana State University with me got on the same bus with her boyfriend, who I like very much. They were on the same plane I was and we helped each other get set up here in London. Tonight and tomorrow I'll stay at a Quaker youth hotel, which is very nice and inexpensive – $3 a day including breakfast, and a full dinner for 75 cents more. I also have to help wash dishes, but I think I'll like it.

I'll probably take a train to Yugoslavia – it costs $40 and takes two days, but a plane flight is $100.

Rickey

June 24, 1970
Belgrade, Yugoslavia

Prichard, Alabama

Dear Mom and Dad,

I've been very busy traveling and enjoying myself this past week. Saw the play *Hair,* it was very good – they change the jokes to keep it contemporary.

I left London last Wednesday on a student train and met many very nice people. Seven of us stayed in a private home in Rijeckn (Yugoslavia) Thursday night. Getting to Yugoslavia was great – the train ride through the Alps was indescribable. I finally realize why people get so hung up on the Alps.

Friday, five of the "group" caught a boat from Rijeckn to Dubrovnic – a 22-hour ride down the Adriatic Sea, never more than a couple hundred yards from the coast. That also was beautiful. The Adriatic water is very clear and mountains rise up from the coast all the way down. I slept on the deck of the boat wrapped in my sheet – I looked like a mummy.

Three students from North Dakota and I shared a room in a private apartment home in Dubrovnic. We were three stories up, and it had a terrace overlooking the bay. I've really been roughing it. I slept on a sleeping bag on the terrace. It was really nice until it rained at 7 a.m. The room was $1.20 a day each, with a private bath.

I flew from Dubrovnic to Belgrade today on a jet for $12. The economy section somehow filled up, so I was given first-class accommodations. The view from the plane was beautiful. It was a cloudless day.

I was two days late getting here for school, but no one was upset since several of us had been delayed because of travel difficulties. One couple had stood for 12 hours on a train. I've really been lucky.

I had the worst cold of my life last week, but I'm recovering now. The lectures are quite good and given by some of the highest officials in the Yugoslav government. I must say this country impresses me more each day. It is rapidly becoming a very democratic but still socialist country.

How is life in Alabama? I miss the family, but I find the people here, in general, nice and easygoing. I hope Dad can slow down and spend some time with Skip while he's visiting. Please freeze some of that good food for me.

Love,
Rickey

July 13, 1970
Belgrade, Yugoslavia

Prichard, Alabama
Dear Mom and Dad,

I've been busy lately with academics instead of tourist activities. I finally got over my cold after 11 days, and our academic pace has slowed down. We made a short trip (1½ hours each way) to a famous old fort in Novi Sad, Yugoslavia, that was completed in 1697 after 82 years of work. It was quite interesting. Tomorrow we're going to a *really* old monastery two or three hours south of here. The official program is completed on July 29 in Zagreb, Yugoslavia, but I'm not sure when I'll finish my "incomplete" from last quarter – probably here in Belgrade the first week in August as my room is paid through then and I'll be able to study, I think.

I ordered a pair of sunglasses today for $11.46 – not bad, huh! Hated to hear of Dad's timber-cutting misfortune. Will he come out OK financially? How is he doing with his cold? Hope it wasn't as bad as mine.

Mom, it might be better for all concerned if you asked one of my friends to drive my car every two or three weeks.

Tell Skip hello for me – I hope he appreciates the peace and quiet of your house. I certainly miss it. The doctor's three kids (ages 3, 5 and 7) live 10 feet from me. I've really met some interesting people here. I'll definitely return next year if given the chance.

Rickey

July 23, 1970
Belgrade, Yugoslavia

Prichard, Alabama
Dear Mom and Dad,

I leave Belgrade Monday to go with the group to Zagreb for two days and then I'm free – and I'm not returning to Belgrade. It has been very depressing here. It's a big relief to know the program is almost over. I'm supposed to hook up with my friend if he gets military leave like we planned, and then I'll arrive back in Tampa around noon on September 11. If I have enough money, I'll fly to Mobile.

I'm having to watch my spending closely now – no souvenirs, only beds and food – but I'm not complaining. The less money one has here, it seems, the "closer" he lives with the people. For example, I'm good at finding "workingmen's" cafes – good food, cheap, and a lot of atmosphere.

Love,
Rickey

271

July 24, 1970
Orlando, Florida

Prichard, Alabama
Dear Nana GeeGee,

I wanted so much to come along with Skippy, and he said he wanted me to. We both like to watch a lot of TV and we wouldn't get bored with both of us there.

Oh, guess what? Aunt Dorothy is getting applications for my friend Debbie and me to be candy stripers at the hospital next school year!

One night a few weeks ago, Mom and Dad and I were sitting together, and we started talking about dating. After a bit, Mom said, "Oh, yes, we'll have to have a little talk about that soon." Well, a few days later, just Mom and me were together and she asked me how much I knew about dating. I said (get this), "Oh, probably a lot more than you think I know!" She said, "That's what I thought you'd say!" So that was the end of that, for now anyway.

Nana, how long can you stay when you drive down here to bring Skip back? Try to stay at least three to five days. Okay?

I finished my room yesterday, and it's so pretty. The yellow takes on a green shade when I have this green rug in here and it's lovely. I want you to see it soon.

Do you think next summer, if Jenni doesn't, maybe I could come up alone for a few weeks like I did so many years ago? Think about it, okay?

Well, that's all I wanted to tell you, for now! Write back soon.

Robin

P.S. – I love you.

August 10, 1970
Prichard, Alabama

Orlando, Florida
Dear Mom and family,

How are you all doing without me? I'm having fun up here. Nana GeeGee and I went to play nine holes of golf this morning. We're going tomorrow for 18 holes. We'll probably play on the weekend and again next week, too!

Boy, when I get home, I sure am going to miss my nightly helping of pink-eyed purple-hull peas! I do love them so. I'm making a cake for

Granddaddy on the day before I go. Nana GeeGee said I could, and I want to do something for him. You should see the scab on his head. It's dreadfully ugly! He says it doesn't hurt and will soon go away.

Jenni, I found out who came through the door on "Dark Shadows." It was Carolyn, huh? But how is she alive now? Roger killed her.

Mommy, *Gone with the Wind* was so good! I cried so much. I wish I could see that movie a million more times.

Well, see you soon. Please write!

All my love,
Robin

August 23, 1970
Orlando, Florida

Orlando, Florida
Dear Mom,

For the *nicest, kindest, prettiest,* and *most loving* woman on earth!! Happy Birthday.

Your children – all four of them

October 13, 1970
Dear Diary,

John and Kathie's baby boy arrived okay on the 8th but he developed a massive infection within the first day or so. Treatment was started there in Starkville – for probable pneumonia – but it was soon decided he should be moved to a larger hospital in Memphis. I know it was hard for Kathie when John, with Mom, left with the sick baby. Her doctor was reluctant to discharge her when she wanted to go home, but Kathie told him her father-in-law would take good care of her. She was right, of course, Daddy is the world's best at tenderly tending to someone. We are keeping all of them in our prayers.

March 26, 1971
Orlando, Florida

Prichard, Alabama
Dear Nana GeeGee and Granddaddy,

Hi! How are you? We're all fine. Well, except that David is a bit cranky today. He skipped a nap! He used to go to bed so well, not crying a bit, but just relaxing with Iggy, his little Eskimo doll. But this week he's changed.

He's finally realized that it's more fun to romp around on the floor and visit with Nana Kitty than it is to go to bed with Iggy!

My other grandparents leave next week. They're finally going back to Woodbury. I wish they would stay at least a few days longer, but after all the vacationing they've done in Pompano, St. Croix and everywhere else, you can guess that they're very anxious to get home! I guess I would be, too! You should see them. They are so tan.

Well, Nana GeeGee, I'm starting to get more and more baby-sitting jobs! Just last night, I had to refuse one. It's nice to have an income other than my allowance! Tonight I'm sitting for my "baby brovver."

Yesterday I made a cake. I used a mix for the cake part, but I made the chocolate butter icing from scratch. It was pretty good! It was my first layer cake. Can I make some food when I come up there to visit? I have a few good dessert recipes!

Mom will be glad when March is over. She dislikes the wind so much! And I do sometimes (even though I usually love it) because the dirt blows! It gets all over you. Ugh!

Granddaddy, you like to go to bed early, don't you, so I guess you wouldn't like to watch "The Late Show" with Nana GeeGee and me? Oh well, too bad!

Well, I'd better go help Mom or something. Also I have to finish a crossword puzzle. I love word puzzles. Do you? Bye, bye!
Love ya,
Jenni

P.S. – Please write back soon! Love you all! Mom says she didn't get a chance to write you this week so this letter helps take its place!

April 25, 1971
Dear Diary,

Little Adam is so much on my mind. John and Kathie realized one of his legs is longer and bigger around than the other and his head seems larger than normal, and they decided to take him back to the Memphis hospital where he'd been treated as a newborn. As they were waiting in the hallway, Adam being held in Kathie's lap, the most amazing thing occurred. A doctor just walking past – not the pediatrician they were to see, not anyone they knew – stopped suddenly, looked at Adam and asked, "How long have his eyes been this way?" He called the phenomenon "sunset gaze," when only half the pupils are showing … and there on the spot diagnosed hydrocephalus.

It's been determined that it was possibly the infection and/or treatment, or a combination, that Adam had six months ago which somehow caused a problem with the brain getting rid of water. Now a shunt has been inserted from his brain to drain fluid into his heart. It will probably need to be lengthened as he grows and, later, surgery to make some adjustments to his leg is also likely. So, more prayers – but he's doing all right.

April 26, 1971
Orlando, Florida

Prichard, Alabama
Dear Nana GeeGee,

Hi! How are you? And Granddaddy? Lady? Hope you're all just fine!

Every time I think of summer I get so excited! I can't wait to drive a golf cart. And also something else that's very important. It's this – would you help me learn how to sew? I really want to so much! I know I'd enjoy it thoroughly, and I envy people who can make clothes for themselves.

Every once in awhile I go to the back room and sew something by hand. I don't know how to start the machine or even cut out a pattern!! I really need help! Please? Did you say you were going to make me a knit pant-suit (!) and a dress? That's great! You remember the blue no-sleeved dress you made me last time you were here? Well, I've already outgrown it in the bust. Yep, it's just too tight!

Well, it's getting on to 9:30 so I'd better get to bed!

Love,
Jen

P.S. – Give my love to Granddaddy and tell Lady "Jenni's comin'!"

May 19, 1971
Orlando, Florida

Prichard, Alabama
Dearest Nana GeeGee,

How have you and Granddaddy been lately? I'm really looking forward to this summer. School is getting to me. Some girlfriends and I have been selling stationery to help raise money for a camp we want to go to over the summer.

You know, Nana, I pray every night that within the next few months I'll meet the most fantastic guy that ever lived! I sure hope my prayers are answered, don't you?

By the way, am I having a ball with my driver's license! Mom's really letting me go places now.

I'll write again soon, okay?

Love always,
Robin

May 24, 1971
Orlando, Florida

Prichard, Alabama

Dear Nana GeeGee and Granddaddy,

How are you? I'm fine. I am writing to you to thank you for giving me three dollars. Now I have 63 dollars and 25 cents!

I am looking forward to coming up to Alabama this summer. With all the money I have, I can buy golf clubs! And other things too. I want you to help me pick out a set of clubs because next year I'm taking golf lessons in junior high school.

I have to be going now.

Love,
Skippy

June 29, 1971
Prichard, Alabama

Orlando, Florida

Dear *famille* (is that correct for family, Robin? French, ya know?),

Hi! Well, I guess I'll get the bad news over with first, then the other stuff. Uncle Bill had a severe heart attack this afternoon and he's in critical condition. They won't know much yet until 48 hours.

GOOD NEWS! I'm slowly learning the basics of the art of sewing. We've bought one pattern so far – a7jp. We hope it fits, and we're making hot pants.

Little Griff has long hair, you know how independent he is! Right now it's almost as long as mine, so we really look more like sisters than like cousins. Haha. And you should see Uncle Rickey's long hair – wow!!

Mommy, you'll be glad to know I'm helping but there isn't that much to do with just three people. It's mostly dishes!

Nana GeeGee and I talk about EVERYTHING! From family matters and how you got married to boys and sex. Nana does the talking – I do the listening!

Skippy, you'll love Granddaddy's cows, calves and bull. I took some pictures and I'm gonna milk the Jersey cow in the morning.

Pretty soon Nana is going to take me golfing and we'll walk about nine or so holes.

Sorry Mom, but I bought some more Maybelline eyeshadow for $1.59 here instead of $2.00 at home! I'm drinking tea 10 times a day and 10 x 10 times a day I have to go to the bathroom!

Every once in awhile I kiss little David's shirt and Nana gets a kick out of that. She says, "Only you would have thought to bring that!" Oh well! Nana said she is putting a letter to you in with mine so I will let her tell you more about that.

Tonight at supper Lady was getting pieces of chicken from me under the table! Oh yeah, also at supper Granddaddy made some remark (you know the way he talks!) about the cow's titties, and that was the end of me! I laughed so hard!!

Now I'll tell you about the plane trip then I'll say goodbye.

Well, after I got on there was a guy about my age and I took notice of him! The plane arrived in Tampa on time and that guy and I got off. This man came up and said to me "Are you Karen?" I said "No" But it turned out that he led this little girl Karen and me and that guy, his name was Jim, to another gate.

Jim and I kept rolling our eyes around because we didn't expect to be led like babies around a huge airport! It was funny, though. We understood how each other felt! We sat together on the next plane and he got off in Pensacola and I said "Rats!" under my breath.

Well, when we got to Alabama, the stewardess was gonna lead me and about six little kids off the plane to make sure we were met but I told her I would go myself. Man! They lead you around like kindergartners till you're 16!! But I thought the Tampa airport was pretty, and the stewardesses were nice. It was a fun trip, and Dad, I'm glad I had a long-sleeved dress because I was cold!

Any new "pool developments?" Well, I'd better go now. The television is great!

Love to everyone!
Jenni

P.S. – Kiss David 1,000,000,000,000 times for me!

Hi, Pat and Bob,

Wanted to send a hello note along with Jenni's letter and tell you how much we've been enjoying our second granddaughter. She really is something. We've had some good talks about different things – she's smart, very wise and so very, very interesting.

Don't think I've ever seen anything so sweet as Jenni bringing along David's shirt with his baby smell on it – we take turns kissing it.

We've heard from Hazel twice since Bill's heart attack and each time the news is even worse. Naturally we're upset and anxious. We'll talk about this more by phone.

Again, Jenni is a perfect delight – thanks for having such beautiful grandchildren for us.

Love,
Mom

July 12, 1971
Orlando, Florida

Prichard, Alabama
Hi, Nana GeeGee!

I just wanted to tell you I really enjoyed my visit and I thank you and Granddaddy so much for having me! The plane trip was fine, but I sure wish we could have driven so you could see David now! He is the sweetest thing in the whole world! I wish I had given you the shirt for keeps so you could kiss it often! Lots and lots of love!

Jenni

July 30, 1971
Prichard, Alabama

Orlando, Florida
DEAR AUNT PAT,

I WOULD LOVE TO COME DOWN. I WISH YOU COULD COME UP. HOW OLD ARE YOU – ALL OF YOU? HERE IS A ART PAPER. I AM A ARTIST.

WILL YOU COME DOWN FOR CHRISTMAS. PLEASE WRITE BACK. THANK YOU FOR THE PICTURES. I AM AT NANA GEEGEE HOUSE.

LOVE GRIFF

August 2, 1971
Woodbury, Connecticut

Orlando, Florida
Dearest Pat and Bob,

The boys have gone off to play golf, and I only hope they get in nine holes before it rains. Have you had any rain since we left? We think we brought it along with us, for after 50-some days of drought, it has rained most of the time since we touched down at Bradley Field in Hartford. The weather prophecy is "more of the same for Tuesday and Wednesday." It wouldn't bother us except for Skip, but it certainly limits our outdoor activities.

The flight from Orlando was fine – on time and seats together on both planes. The 17 Dutch people on board with us were good entertainment. During World War II their village in Holland had been liberated by our 101st Airborne Division and they were here 80 strong (some in California, some in Chicago, etc.) to pay tribute to their heroes. More than one said they and their countrymen from every village liberated by Americans and Canadians would never forget and would be forever grateful.

We arrived home in a downpour so bad that I suggested Dad take off his pants and open the garage door in his shirt and underwear. Skip got a big kick out of that.

We had lunch Friday at the Friendly, and I had a cup of clam chowder. Skip asked what it tasted like, and I gave him a spoonful. "Boy, that's good," he said, so we ordered him some, which he ate to the last drop. He said, "Mom and Dad have this for dinner sometimes, but Robin told me I wouldn't like it."

Saturday Auntie Bussie and her friend Frank picked us up to go to the lake. It rained on and off, so we couldn't be outdoors, but in between showers several of the men went swimming, and Skip also went sailing around for a tour on the martini barge. I'm sure he never attended such a party and may never again. There were 19 of us, and after dinner we played some sing-along records to the accompaniment of Dad's and Art's slide whistles and Skip on the coffee tables as bongo drums.

Now I must go to the village for a few things – Skip is eating as if food were going out of style and drinking two and three glasses of milk at each meal. I promised him we would have pancakes this morning, and as he went off to bed last night he asked, "*What time* tomorrow morning are we going to have pancakes?" We are so delighted with his appetite!

It was a happy, wonderful visit with you all in Orlando, and as always we thank you for the kindness and hospitality. Give David a special kiss from Nana Kitty and love to each and every one.

Mother Kitty

August 3, 1971
Woodbury, Connecticut

Orlando, Florida

Dear family,

How are you? I'm having a great time here in Connecticut! All the mountains make me want to live here again.

I have been visiting different people all during my stay here. Today we went swimming in a neighbor's pool even though she is in Africa. Plus we had dinner with Auntie Bussie.

Nana Kitty has probably told you I have been eating well and sleeping 10, 11 and even 12 hours a day.

Tell David I'll be calling him Thursday or Friday night. Well so long.

Love you,
"Tip-pur," as David would say

August 9, 1971
Woodbury, Connecticut

Orlando, Florida

Dear Super Six,

Right now I am marinating a flank steak a la Dorothy – hope it's as good as hers. We had planned to go out to a steak place for Skip's farewell dinner, but we have had to cancel yesterday's and today's plans because of Skip's sore throat.

He spoke of it after we came home from the boat Saturday, so I started him gargling right away. Yesterday we skipped church and swimming and stayed here quietly, still gargling. When I took Skip's temperature, he had some fever, so I started him on aspirin.

He seems to feel fine today but we thought we ought to have a quiet day with much excitement and busyness tomorrow. He seems perfectly happy. We have both played games with him almost constantly, and Dad has shown some slides, too.

Skip will probably tell you about his faint spell in church last week. All was fine until the final hymn, and I looked at him and he was as white as a sheet. I asked him if he was all right and he didn't answer, so I asked Dad to take him out. By the time I got out, probably five minutes later, he was in the car and all right again, so we made nothing of it. Dad told him he was probably tired.

I was so sorry the night Skip called you that I didn't know David was on the phone saying "Nana Kitty." I was getting dinner, and didn't get the message until later.

Last Monday, Skip and Dad played golf and hurried home after nine holes to watch the moonwalk. It was special to see it with Skip since together we had watched the televised blast off of Apollo 15 *Endeavor* and its crew from Kennedy Space Center while we were still in Orlando – and the splashdown two days ago during our boat excursion on Long Island Sound! Thrilling, all of it, including the moonwalk coverage, with astronauts David Scott and James Irwin in the "Falcon" lunar rover exploring the Hadley Rille-Apennine Mountain area and collecting some of the oldest ever "Genesis Rock." Easy to understand the depth of the experience when Commander Scott said of the mountains and plains: "Their majesty overwhelms me. They loom still and serene, a tableau of forever." These grandchildren of ours, growing up in the "space age," will have many exciting events to relate to their children and grandchildren.

I know how glad you will all be to have your boy back tomorrow for a short time before he heads to Alabama to see his other grandparents. What a busy guy! He has been good and we will miss him. Much love to everyone.

Mother Kitty

August 22, 1971
Orlando, Florida

Prichard, Alabama
Hi, Skip,

Just a short note with Jenni's birthday thank-you note to Nana GeeGee to say good morning to y'all. Jen had a really good swim party, even though three girls couldn't come. The fun pool activities went on about five hours.

David is doing better and better in the pool. He will lean over in the water now and try to blow bubbles, sometimes getting water in his nose. Yesterday he kept saying "gick" and finally Robin asked him to *show* her the gick because we couldn't figure out what he meant. He stopped what he was doing, went over to his toys, found the box of blocks, looked at different ones, picked one up and came running over with it, saying, "Ere's the gick" – it was the "C" block with a picture of a "chick!" Smart, huh?

Hey, Skipper, your garden is growing! Daddy weeded and watered it last night. Maybe soon we'll have vegetables.

Love to everyone there from the gang here!

Mommy (or "Ba," as David says)

P.S. – Your card to Jen was *so* sweet, Skip!

October 22, 1971
Orlando, Florida

Prichard, Alabama

Dear Nana GeeGee,

Hello! How are you? I am fine, and so is everyone else around here.

I'm sending you my school picture. I'm wearing the yellow shorts outfit you made me. I got lots of nice comments on it.

Well, now I'm making a dress again. I got the material at TG&Y, and the total, with zipper, was $3.93! Cheap! The material is that silky, slinky kind, and if I remember correctly you said that kind was hard to sew on! To me it's easy!

I'm making the dress from the same pattern we used for the yellow outfit. I just finished putting in the darts a while ago. Robin's going to help me with the sleeves, which are short, and I'll wear a gold chain belt. The color of the material is a design of red, black, gray, white, brown, and beige. Real pretty!

I'm joining Future Homemakers of America and tomorrow I'm going to a convention in the Tupperware Auditorium for half of my initiation. The other half is this: I have to wear a dress backwards and inside-out, red lipstick in two big bright circles on my cheeks, three ponytails, a tape-measure for a belt, and knee-socks, and then I have to carry a doll and wear white lipstick on one half of my lips and red on the other half! Isn't that crazy!? I have to do it Monday. Yuck!!

Well, I'd better go now. I have to baby sit. I love you!

Jenni

December 30, 1971
Woodbury, Connecticut

Orlando, Florida

Dear Pat, Bob and kids,

Thank you so much for a wonderful Christmas visit with the best of "Southern hospitality." It was very good to see all of you again, and very

282

good to be treated so well and taken care of even when I felt like a bloomin' hypochondriac! I was so mad!!

Pat and Bob: I read the cookbook all the way home on both planes. It is really fun, but it also has some good old-fashioned recipes that I don't have and aren't easy to come by anymore. The "bird server" is just darling and has already been used for salted nuts for happy hour when Frank came on Tuesday. We'll use it again on New Year's Day at a friend's house where we'll be watching three football games. Three! No kidding!

Robin: Can't tell you how much I appreciate your artistry, time and effort that were put into that attractive wall panel. The colors are lovely for my study-guest room (I've changed that room since you were here), and the panel is already hanging there. Come see it soon!

Jenni: My "bird by pond" is so sweet, and I had a hard time deciding where to put it because I wanted it in every room. However, I spend most of my time awake in the living room, so it's atop of the television, where I can see it all waking hours.

Skip: At the risk of breaking my neck, I got out the tall ladder and put the chimes on that beam that runs through the center of my living room. It's a good place. Nobody gets conked on the head, and when I air the room I hear a very pretty tinkle! I love them, Skip, and will use them for many years to come.

To one and all: Thank you, thank you! And a very Happy New Year.

Love,
Auntie Bussie

January 28, 1972
Dear Diary,

Thinking about John and Kathie and the things of note this month. Today is their 8th anniversary – and oh my goodness, I can still recall the memorable bus rides I took (I and the borrowed Mr. John hat!) to attend their wedding. ... On the 7th Mark turned 3 – and Adam, 16 months, recently had surgery to lengthen the shunt implanted to drain fluid from his brain to his heart. He's doing well, and they are encouraged by the likely possibility that the problem will be cleared up before the shunt would need to be changed again ... the kind of news that's good to hear!

February 5, 1972
Orlando, Florida

Prichard, Alabama

Dear Nana GeeGee,

Mom said you and Granddaddy wanted to hear about Disney World so I guess I'm the best one to tell you.

When we went out there last week it was the second trip for me and Mom and Robin, and the third for Dad and Skip since it opened last October. Robin took her friends Jan, Dianne and Gail. Since her birthday is coming up it was her "party." David stayed behind and had fun with his playmates, Kathy and Tripp. Mom and Dad said we're probably going to take him to Disney later this year.

Well, first, you get to the main gate to Disney World where you pay your 50-cent parking fee. Right after that we had to stop at the Disney Service Station outside the other gates because our car had trouble. We were all ohing and booing so a man at the station drove us to the entrance – and into the park, just like VIPs! Dad got our tickets. They cost $5.75 for each person and we got a little book with colored passes for different kinds of rides. Then we separated. Robin and her friends went off alone, Skip and I did, and Mom and Dad stayed together.

Skip and I went to the Haunted Mansion, everyone's favorite. We went through it two times. First you go into a gallery, the doors close behind you and a voice explains about the owner – whose portrait on the wall slowly turns from man into skeleton. Then you go down a dark hall into a room with a conveyor belt thing and get into big black cars. There you go! It's SO neat! It's pitch dark and all these ghostly projections are floating around. You see different scenes, and everything is so real. Just wait'll you see it all. Outside the mansion it looks like an old rundown estate run by an eccentric old man. Oooh, it's so cool, Nana and Granddaddy! The ride lasts about 15 to 20 minutes.

We went on the Grand Prix Raceway three times. It's lots of fun. There are millions of cars, all striped and painted. You go really fast in them. There's a huge track and you go around once and the men flag you as you pass. There is even a grandstand for the onlookers.

After that we went into the Country Bear Jamboree. It's cute, and like the Mickey Mouse Revue in every way. The bears dance and sing and give a great show. They seem so real but they're just robots.

We went to the Mad Hatter's Tea Party next. It's just a ride with little cars shaped like teacups. The big platform moves around and the teacups move, too. You can make the teacups go around faster by turning the wheel inside. I made the car go so fast and that was fun!

Nana GeeGee, you and Granddaddy would like Monsanto's America the Beautiful exhibit. There are eight screens that show different places in America. Like in one big screen you see in front of you, on both sides and in back. It's cool.

Now I'll describe Flight to the Moon. You see Mission Control, and then you go into a capsule with seats enough for everyone. As you blast off you feel like your stomach has been left behind!

Some of the other rides and stuff I've been on are: Mr. Toad's Wild Ride, Peter Pan's Flight, Jungle Boat Cruise, Skyride, the Tiki Room and the Hall of Presidents.

When can y'all come down and see it? It's a fantastic place!

Love,
Jenni

February 28, 1972
Orlando, Florida

Prichard, Alabama
Dearest Folks,

Seems ages since I last wrote – I just don't know where the time goes. Do you know that tomorrow it will be eight years to the day that we moved into this house? I must say they have been really happy years.

Since we got home from our visit in Pompano Beach with the Connecticut "Snowbirds" a week ago, the weather has been simply gorgeous. But the three days we were at the beach with Mother Kitty and Dad were very cold and windy, and we mostly stayed inside their small apartment, huddled by a little electric heater!

Bob and his dad did play nine holes of golf two days, and the four of us went meandering through a beautiful shopping plaza one afternoon – and, of course, we went out for delicious meals each night. But not once did we even consider putting on a swimsuit!

I didn't feel very perky while we were there, had a burning pain in my upper back. The doctor had diagnosed "a probable nerve-ending injury or irritation" and prescribed medicine to help ease the pain. Even with my discomfort, the change of pace was good for Bob and me – and, as always, we so enjoyed being with his parents.

The children had problems, too. The morning before we were due to leave, Skip woke up with diarrhea, vomiting, and a slight fever. I was afraid David would get sick too, since he and Skip had shared an "Icee Drink" during haircuts earlier in the week, and that it might be more serious for a small child. Turned out he escaped the "bug" but Robin and Jen got it on Saturday – so somebody was sick the whole weekend. Everyone is fine again now.

Both girls are on a sewing kick after a long rest from it. Jenni whipped up the cutest little shift over the weekend – it cost $1.00! And Robin is working on a dress of lovely material, with full sleeves. It's too large for her through the shoulders and she's not happy with it, but I bet she can fix it. I am so glad both girls like to sew. I still don't like sewing even a hem or a single button. I'd rather read, or write!

This week Robin plans to apply for work at Walt Disney World, and soon we hope to check into some colleges. If a job should prevent her from coming to visit you this summer we've suggested the time between Christmas and New Year's as another possibility. She really wants that visit with you after missing last year.

The little peanut David has turned into a typical 2-year-old, full of mischief, quick with the NO, and a bit silly and show-offy at times, but oh so cute with it all. He says "Mommy spank-a hand!" but isn't the least bit affected by it if I do.

Last night Bob, David and I had supper at McDonald's and we laughed so hard at David saying "am-bur-bur-bur-bur-burg." He doesn't know when to stop! He speaks with a kind of musical lilt, always adding extra syllables on the last word. In fact he can speak the letter "O" in six syllables! The other night during a family dinner of meat loaf, baked potatoes, green beans and sliced tomatoes, David ate silently for a few minutes and then volunteered, "Isn't dis go-o-o-o-o-d?"

Well, I must go on to more chores – what busy days I have, never catching up!

Much love from all six here to two dear ones there.

Pat

March 4, 1972
Orlando, Florida

Prichard, Alabama
Dearest Nana GeeGee,

Hi! How's Granddaddy, and Lady? And everyone else? We're all fine here.

I'm so mad! The pool is broken! Daddy is going to try to fix the pump or we'll have to call someone.

Well, Mom took me to Penney's today to get sewing stuff for Home Ec class. For my home project I'm making a pantsuit.

David is as sweet as ever. But he does say "no" a lot. The sweetest thing he does is put his hands on your cheeks and give you a big smack!

Well, hug everyone for me!

Love,
Jenni

April 16, 1972
Woodbury, Connecticut

Orlando, Florida
Dearest Pat and Bob,

You two will never know till you are aged parents having visited your children how much it means to receive notes like you each wrote last week. We thank you!

Do keep us posted on Skip's modeling career – and the progress of yours, Pat!

We came into the house on Thursday to find a huge vase full of forsythia – so bright, "springy" and welcoming. Our neighbor was in Williamsburg, but she had asked her husband to bring it over. Such thoughtful gestures make arriving home even happier, and it really is good to be here again.

When Dave called yesterday we were sitting on the patio having lunch and the weather was as beautiful as it was last Sunday in Orlando, so we hope spring has sprung.

With my fingers crossed, I report that there has not been a trace of gallbladder pain since the Tuesday before we left the beach, and I am slipping back gradually to butter, cheese, mayonnaise, etc.

Auntie Bussie stopped in on her way home from school Friday and wouldn't even take off her coat. She said she was so tired she didn't want to talk or listen. So the visit was brief.

Well, I have things to do so will stop and just send lots of love to you all. And always thanks for being you.

Mother Kitty

April 29, 1972
Orlando, Florida

Prichard, Alabama
Dearest Folks,

Skip had an 8 o'clock baseball game scheduled today and we got up-and-at-'em real early only to have it rain. David and I rode over to the field and picked up Skip and two buddies, all soaked and covered with red mud. I had to laugh when Skip, ever the eternal optimist, even though disappointed and a soggy mess, commented, "Oh, well, the coach gave us some free gum!" He's beautiful!

Robin stayed overnight with a girlfriend whose parents are at a convention in Chicago. Don't you know they're having fun all alone. I'd like to be a fly on the wall and hear the talk. Jenni got to fill in at Robin's favorite sitting job last night and was very late getting in, so she's still asleep.

I've been going to bed early this week – once at 9:45, before the kids. I have an appointment for a regular check-up Wednesday. The doctor told me he would do an "estrogen count test," figuring that, with no more periods, and the hot flashes, my hormone production has decreased over the past few months. I re-read the chapter on menopause in the book we talked about, Mommie, and it's scary to read how the ol' body begins to atrophy with age. I don't know, so far this 40th year is not my favorite.

Robin had an interview at Disney World last week and is scheduled to report to her new job on May 20. We don't know what she'll be doing yet. She's supposed to work weekends till school is out, then five days a week during the summer.

David is still quite a character, just amazing us with his conversational comments. He has slowed down on his eating and gotten finicky – normal, but frustrating. Once in a while, when I try to get him to eat one more bite, he'll say, "No, Mom. I sorry, don't bother me." One morning he was cranky and finally, as I pulled him away from some "no-no," he said, "I can't stand it!"

Did I tell you we're taking Dave and Dorothy out for dinner at the Citrus Club tonight to celebrate their second and our 19th anniversary? I'm looking forward to it.

Take care of you two – we all send lots of love.

Pat, Bob and kids

May 1, 1972
Woodbury, Connecticut

Orlando, Florida
Dearest bride and groom!

Happy anniversary! We are thinking of you today and wishing you many more of the same! We thought of you and Dave and Dorothy celebrating together and could picture you at the Citrus Club since Bob had treated us to lunch there one day.

Spring has really come with beautiful, mild weather. Our daffodils and forsythia are out and we have sat on the terrace until dinnertime the last two days.

Last Monday night we went to a town meeting, which was a budget hearing. We didn't want to go and it didn't prove anything that we did, but we feel we should put in an appearance once in awhile.

We were up early the next morning so Dad could go to the clinic for his "medical summary" – it used to be a physical check-up! Somebody said they can charge more with the fancy name. Anyway it's worth whatever they charge because again Dad is a perfect specimen.

Heaps of love to all,
Mother Kitty

May 7, 1972
Orlando, Florida

Prichard, Alabama

Hi ... and we hope your Mother's Day and birthday are great, Mother-Mommie!

Jenni stayed home with David today while a few of us went to church, and not only did she take good care of him, she spruced up the house beautifully on her own initiative so that everything looks nice and neat, *and* she baked a delicious cake.

It is quite sticky and thunder-showery today, so no swimming or sunbathing, which we had planned to do. Ol' Skip is most upset about the weather because he had planned to mow a lawn this afternoon. Right now, with baseball practices and games and school, he has trouble doing his lawn work if the weather interferes. He has four mowing jobs for the summer and we hope they won't be too much for him. He is so conscientious about his responsibilities. So are the girls.

By the way, Skip had a report card of all A's this week, and Jen got her usual good report also – though with a couple of B's, which she doesn't like. No word on Robin's grades yet, but she is looking forward to finishing her junior year and working at Disney World a lot more during the summer.

Bob and I talked last night about a possible vacation, maybe three or four days at some pleasant, cool resort area in the mountains, either in northern Georgia or the Carolinas. It's been hot and very humid, with scattered thunderstorms all day, and our air conditioner has konked out, darn it.

Speaking of being hot, I really am having hot flashes often. All of a sudden my whole body will just start to steam, I'll feel unbearably warm for a few seconds and then it'll go away. I did have my check-up last week, and the doctor said even though I'm young, I'm evidently menopausal. It's almost funny sometimes when I feel so hot I just take off out the back door, across the patio, walk into the shallow end of the pool and begin splashing water over myself, clothes and all! And a couple of times I've gone out there in the middle of the night when I've waked up just drenched – occasionally I've had to change my nightgown twice in one night. Uh, miserable.

Now I'm gonna run. Maybe I'll flop for a while and read the paper while David is still sleeping. Mommie, we sent you a little gift package for your special days. Know we're thinking of you and loving you. You, too, Daddy!

Pat and gang

P.S. – For our anniversary last week we celebrated with a family "fondue party" – fun!

May 19, 1972
Orlando, Florida

Prichard, Alabama
Hi, Folks,

I've got myself hemmed in the playroom with David, with the gate across the kitchen entrance. Right now he is trying to knock the gate down with this little bike! He wore me out by 10 o'clock this morning. We took a walk, came back in and had some scrambled eggs and toast, and he went to bed for an early nap. Later I'll probably take him over to play with his friends, which he simply loves to do.

He has come into his own, often answering us with "I don't want to," "Wet's not," or "No!" and getting into one thing after another. I don't know that I'm going to make it through this stage as I am feeling a mite weary.

On the other hand he is such a joy to us all. He is now learning to say "The Lord's Prayer," and some of the words are priceless – just like the "pugness" for republic and "weirty" for liberty in the "Pwedge of A-weegance" that he recites.

It has been another week on the run – grocery shopping a couple of times, family underwear shopping at Sears, haircuts for the boys, baseball practices and games, a dentist appointment for Skip, a doctor's appointment for me to get my foot callous removed again, plus endless chores and loads of laundry, cooking, bridge group here Tuesday, etc. Is it any wonder I can't stay awake much past 9:30 at night? I am so tired.

Robin is to report to Disney World for work at 7 a.m. tomorrow. Bob is going to take her to the employee entrance and then go to the main gate to drop off Skip and two friends and Jenni and a girlfriend to spend the day at the theme park. It's sure to be a big day for Robin – hope all goes well for her.

For Mother's Day, the three older children took me to church, where the service was so inspirational I cried off and on the entire hour. And the kids teased me about it the next hour. I felt like I could come home and be the best person who ever lived – for that day, anyway! Alas, I knew my good intentions would likely fall by the wayside.

Robin gave me one of those really big, cute cards and then surprised me completely with a large box of cut spring flowers, enough for huge bouquets in two or three rooms, so we all enjoyed their beauty. Jenni's gift was one of those funny "World's Greatest Mom" statues of a woman with her mop and bucket and gold cup. That morning Skip said, "Oh, is it Mother's Day?" So we went to the store, where he chose eye shadow and a pretty card "For Someone Nice!" plus a cute card for David to give me. The kids went out and got hamburgers for our supper that evening.

Can you believe our Skip is 13 today? The kids in one of his classes made and signed a card, "Happy Birthday to a Sweet but Cool Guy!" And he is.

Jenni's news: she was inducted into the Junior National Honor Society last Friday evening. Remember how excited I was when that happened to me at Murphy?

We're just tickled pink that you're beginning to talk about a visit! It will take some doing, trying to fit schedules – especially for Robin to fly there first and drive back to Orlando with you.

> Take care, love you!
> Pat and the rest of the Super Six

> May 29, 1972
> Orlando, Florida

Prichard, Alabama
Dearest Nana GeeGee,

I'm so happy! I absolutely love my job! I know my summer schedule now so I've devised a suggested plan for me to come up there. I would leave Orlando on June 12 and stay with you until June 15 or 16. It will be an awfully short visit, but at least I'll get to come, huh? Oh, Nana GeeGee, I want to see you and Granddaddy so bad. I've got so much to tell you!

> Gobs of love,
> Robin

June 25, 1972
Orlando, Florida

Prichard, Alabama
Dearest Mommie,

We already miss you terribly after having such a good visit together, but I know Daddy was happy to see you. Maybe you'll both come down next time, and soon. By the way, Mom, Disney World reported an attendance of 60,000 people at the park the day you and I went. Can you believe that many bodies? Where are they coming from?

A lot has transpired since you left! I gave Bob an okay signal at noon to talk "man-boy-dog" to Skip. Skip called the lady with the toy collies, there was only one left and she'd already had calls about it. Skip was panicky so I suggested they pass on that one and visit the animal shelter. Such excitement – Bob, Jenni and Skip took off immediately and very soon came home with their prize, a precious little puppy. (Okay, I give you permission to laugh and say "I told you so!")

She looks like your Lady, only with a lovely golden coat instead of black – but the same white markings on all four feet and the diamond on her forehead, face and the tip of her tail. She hasn't uttered a peep yet and was so well behaved during a bath (she was so smelly when they brought her home) that we couldn't believe it. Since she looks and acts like a "Little Lady," that's what we christened her.

Right now Little Lady is sleeping peacefully in her box, just like David used to do as a baby. David, meanwhile, is leaping through the playroom, from couch to floor, from table to floor, wild as a bear. Our fear is that the little canine will follow in his footsteps and also become wild one day – that's when I'll call on you!

Much love from all.
Pat and Bob + 4 + 1 dog

July 15, 1972
Orlando, Florida

Prichard, Alabama
Dearest Mommie and Daddy,

I hardly remember when I wrote last, or what. As you can imagine, we are still in profound shock over the accidental death of our neighbor's son, Robin's special friend. Bob is having an especially hard time, plagued as he is with the memory of pulling Allen's body from the bottom of their pool. We don't know how the family is bearing the sorrow. There seems so little we can do, but I've taken dinner over a few times and Skip has mowed their lawn. One day when I went to see Jean, she gave me a book and picture of Allen for Robin and one of his shirts for Skip. They are in our prayers every day and in our thoughts constantly. ...

Robin is still gone from early morning until late at night, working her shift at Disney, then enjoying the after-work social life among the teenage crews. Oh, Mom and Daddy, you'll appreciate this. Every day Robin tells us everything she and her new teenage friends say and do. And it just simply amazes Bob that she's so open, but he's cute about it with her.

We went to New Smyrna Beach last Sunday to see one of our neighbors in the brand new condominium apartment they bought for vacation/rental, and we liked the set-up so much we are going to rent it for two weeks in August. Bob will take off from work one week and commute some days in the second week.

Oh, dear, and then there's the puppy. What did I say about her sleeping peacefully? One recent night when for a change all the children were home and safe in their beds at a decent hour, I c-c-c-rawled into bed with a long sigh after a particularly hectic day. And at that instant, during my long sigh, the puppy started crying. It was awful. All night she cried. Next night, same thing, and I was up, sitting in the den at 1:45 a.m., wondering what in the heck to do. She makes so many messes, Jenni and Skip are sick of cleaning up after her. "Wittle Wady," as David says, stays outside most of the day but in the garage at night and on the porch during the daily Florida thunderstorms.

Next week Bob and I are going to the Tampa-St. Petersburg-Clearwater area for *four* days of relaxation – no chores, no kids, no puppy, just us chickens! Ah, a taste of paradise.

In the meantime, though, a few hours from now Sally and Jack, our dear friends who moved to North Carolina, and are in town visiting, and two neighborhood couples are coming for dinner. Already prepared is a new dish, "Red Snapper Rolls Elegante!"

Love ya,

Pat and gang

August 23, 1972
Prichard, Alabama

Orlando, Florida
Dear little Orlando family,

Sure do miss y'all. Have just finished reading your long, sweet letter from the beach and can picture you lovely golden tan people in that heavenly place. Maybe we'll get to see it next year.

Yes, we agree with everyone that Jenni is growing more beautiful each day. Hope she had a special 15th birthday.

And Pat, we really hope your big 4-0 is delightful. Wow, at this time 40 years ago, honey, I was so sore you couldn't touch me with a powder puff, and that's no joke. Seriously, my special wish for you on this day is "Learn to roll with the world." Try to be interested in changes, new ways of life. Some of your children will no doubt think and live differently, so try to be as near ready for it as possible. Hope you can feel like I do, Pat. I want to and plan to keep growing up instead of growing old.

A happy Sammie, Carol and Griff got here Sunday just in time for a drink, grilled steaks, baked potatoes and salad. They had a perfect week at the Unitarian summer gathering at Appalachian University.

Must stop and think about what I'll give your daddy for supper. Much love to all.

Love,
Mommie/Nana GeeGee

November 30, 1972
Orlando, Florida

Prichard, Alabama
Hi, Folks,

Just a short note to send this lovely picture of Jenni, who no longer looks like this, with pretty, uncluttered teeth. She spent almost three hours in the chair getting some of the bands put on yesterday and burst into sobs as soon as she got out of the office. I hate this procedure for her – so unfortunate at her age, so uncomfortable, too. We've had to go back to have "spacers" put between the teeth and next Tuesday she has another real long appointment. Hope the dentist and orthodontist don't break us – wow!

Robin is busy this week going out to school functions and meeting new people. She may ask a new boy to the December 26 dance. Wish her luck! Skip is feeling under the weather – a sore throat again. But David is feeling perky. He says when I frown, "Be *happy*, Mom – some sings are funny!" He's a mess – smart, witty and tough!

All week I've been preparing food ahead to put in the freezer for the holidays – casseroles and special desserts, plus hors d'oeuvres, including185 tiny meatballs for a pre-Christmas party.

The Army-Navy game party is at the Officers Club Saturday – then dinner with Dave and Dorothy that night. A busy weekend it seems.

Must run now. Take care of yourselves, you two!

Much love,

Pat and the rest of the Super Six

P.S. – Hey, I bowled a 189 game yesterday!

December 2, 1972

Woodbury, Connecticut

Orlando, Florida

Dear Pat,

Bob issued a very gracious invitation from you both yesterday, and we accept with pleasure – and gratitude for thinking of it. After the usual flak from Dad about "do you suppose they felt they had to ask us because we hadn't heard from the manager about the rental apartment," and, "won't it upset their living arrangements?" he agreed that it would be most enjoyable. Thanks for wanting us! We look forward to spending the Christmas holidays with you in your home.

Love,

Mother Kitty

December 22, 1972

Orlando, Florida

Prichard, Alabama

Dearest Mommie, Daddy and boys,

We are a bunch of busy bees, buzzing around and enjoying everything about this special time of the year. Bob's folks have arrived, and we've had the usual fun holiday cocktail party here and gone to Happy Hour treats at some of the neighbors' homes. I hope y'all are having fun, too.

The best comment of the week came from our precious little David. When he first looked upon the gaily ornamented, silver-tinseled, magically glowing Christmas tree, he stood awestruck for a few moments before reverently addressing it: "Twee, you are so bew-tee-ful."

Much love from all the gang here – Merry, Merry Christmas!

Pat

295

January 8, 1973
Sea Aire Apartments
Delray Beach, Florida

Orlando, Florida

Dearest Pat and Bob,

We love it here. It's such a nice change from Connecticut this time of year! My only complaint is that the refrigerator is under the sink counter and too small, but everything else is great. It's a beautiful spot, well-kept, good maid service, a handyman who will wash our car every other day for $1, and such nice residents. Our apartment is most attractive – all greens, blues and white, and very comfortable. It's the type of place that has the nice touches – a complimentary newspaper at our door every morning, a large pot of chrysanthemums here when we arrived.

The weather has been heavenly, in the 80s every day, with the ocean temperature 72 degrees and the water as calm as a lake. Just my cup of tea. The pool is heated, but I only use that to wash off the salt water and get in an extra swim. I am really trying to get my exercise that way.

Our daily schedule is pretty much the same – arise around 9 a.m., putter around the apartment, then down to the beach, where we are in and out of the sea half a dozen times. About 1 o'clock we dress and go out for dinner and errands, and then back and into bathing suits and on the beach until 5 p.m. or after. We have drinks on our porch with a beautiful view of lawn, palms, beach and ocean, and then we come in for our bite of supper whenever we feel hungry. The evenings are for reading, knitting, TV and puzzles. Then we both give up after the 11 o'clock news and cry that another day is gone. I beat Dad at Scrabble last night, Pat, which started us reminiscing about the ongoing good-natured rivalry between you and our next door neighbor in Riverside when we played the game during your long visit with us in 1954. Dad and I were always pleased as punch each time you beat "Champion Jack!"

We speak of you all many times a day. What a happy, happy holiday season we had with you and how good you are to us. We love you very much! Dad sends thanks to Bob for the letters and enclosures. We are thinking of him and wishing him well in his first weeks at his new job.

Much love to all,
Mother Kitty

March 9, 1973
Mobile, Alabama

Orlando, Florida
Dearest Pat and gang,

Had my nice spend-the-night with Rickey in Tallahassee – a good way to break up the trip between Orlando and Mobile. We went to a Chinese restaurant for dinner – my first and I loved it. The only trouble coming home was that the air conditioner in the car broke again and I didn't have air for the whole trip. Belts were broken and they had to put a new compressor in when I got back to Mobile.

I arrived home about 1:30 p.m. Tuesday, and that sweet daddy of yours was cooking and had Sammie here working on the house – what a man, huh? John and Mark came from Starkville a couple hours later to spend a few days with us during spring break at Mississippi State. John has been doing lots of little jobs for us – he's great to have around. Sammie has rented a house in Chapel Hill and will be moving to North Carolina soon. (The notice of his and Carolyn's divorce was in this morning's paper.)

Just got home from our team play golf and visiting with lots of gals at the club.

They were so glad I had brought you out to meet them, Pat, and each one told me just what a wonderful person they think you are and how easy and delightful to be with, and of course I agree wholeheartedly. I can never say enough about how much all of us loved your visit, and I enjoyed driving you back home and seeing the rest of the family
Mommie

P.S. – Give all my love especially to my Robin and tell her I'm still counting on that visit she talked about. Also, Skip will surely want to catch some fish out of the lake. Tell him his cousin Mark caught a 12-inch trout plus several more.

April 25, 1973
Mobile, Alabama

Orlando, Florida
Dearest loved ones,

My golf game has been shot to pieces today because of rain, so I'm closed in with this chasing dirty old man. Ha. Boy his brain is working overtime with all the things he comes out with. Having a "fistula" was not fun, but you know your daddy, now he's making getting well from the

297

minor surgery *into* fun. Seriously he is really doing great – feels so good. In his words, "I can't hardly stand it."

I think we are going to like living in this nice area of Mobile. It's real pretty and the people seem to be friendly. Dad takes several short walks each day and has already met some of our neighbors. John spent a few days down here last week and we sure did enjoy him. The two of us went to the lake for an hour's fishing one evening while Dad napped.

That was a good chat with you Sunday, Pat. John said about the 3-minute egg timer you use for our phone calls, "I'm going to get me one of those."

Honestly, I'm just so happy about Robin getting ready for college. I have much faith in her.

Love,
Mommie

Hi to all,

I'm looking forward to seeing all of you soon. I am doing fine. Went to the doctor yesterday and he asked how I was doing. I told him fine – but my wife was having much trouble because she was closed in from the rain and I had been chasing her. He chuckled.

Monday morning the TV repairman was working on our TV. I was laying on the couch. I got up, and he said, "What seems to be your trouble?" I just unsnapped my pajama bottoms and let them fall to the floor. He said, "I see." There was no more explaining to do.

Love,
Daddy

Pat -

The weather is so awful. If it doesn't stop raining soon, I'm afraid we'll all be washed away.

I found Dad's note and his joke about the TV repairman – I told you he was a dirty old man. Ha.

Mommie

Education is an admirable thing,
but it is well to remember from time to time
that nothing that is worth learning can be taught.
Oscar Wilde

Chapter Sixteen
Leaving the Nest
1973

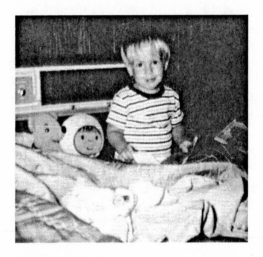

David in his nest with Iggy and Pooh

June 10, 1973
Orlando, Florida

Auburn University
Auburn, Alabama
Hi, Robin,

Little Lady is in the house with me, nosing around, yipping occasionally and looking very puzzled, wondering where the family went. Soon after you, Dad, Jenni and Skip left this morning, David wandered into your room, then came out to find me and asked, "Mom, *where* is all Wobin's sings?" Right away, though, he remembered, "Oh yeah, she's gone to Auburn!"

If you thought we did a lot of laundry last Friday, Robin, you should've been here today. I washed six or seven loads of pillow covers, mattress pads, sheets and towels. But aside from that, and cleaning out the refrigerator and straightening up the house a bit, I didn't really work too hard. I wanted to spend a lot of time talking and playing with David while we swam and sunbathed, which the little peanut and I both enjoyed immensely. By the way, guess what he likes to listen to now – Skip's 8-track of "Dead Skunk in the Road."

Well, honey, you know how much my prayers and hopes for a fabulous start are with you right now, don't you? I feel positive this is the beginning of a wonderful phase of your life. This morning I almost wished that I, too, was just starting out at a great college!

I shed a few tears and will no doubt weep some more during the summer because you are going to be missed by your mom (and everyone else). Here's keeping my fingers crossed that your roommate will be just right, all your classes will be perfect, and you'll get adjusted and be happy from the very first week. I love you so much!
Mom

June 11, 1973
Auburn University
Auburn, Alabama

Orlando, Florida
Dearest family,

Can you believe it? I already miss you! I was so upset that I couldn't say goodbye to Dad and Jenni and Skip the way I wanted to. My roommate is home visiting her family here in Auburn, so I'm all alone in the dorm room and it's kinda desolate. The room does feel homey, though, with all my stuff in it.

My "suitemates," as they're called because we share the same bathroom, are really nice. One of them has a sister who's a senior here, and she has a car, so all of us went to Western Sizzler for a dinner of steak-and-potatoes. The thing I've noticed most is how friendly and quick to smile everyone is here. Even the teachers and administrators. At the restaurant four guys saw us, said hi, and sat down with us! We all ate together. They were really funny and we had a good time.

Do y'all think we should set up a schedule for telephoning? I do – how about something like every two or three weeks? But make the first one soon, because I miss you. Write and let me know.

I love you so much,
Robin

June 12, 1973
Orlando, Florida

Auburn, Alabama
Dear Robin,

How's it going? I wish I could have gotten to say goodbye but I guess Dad did it for me. You should have seen him! He and Skip went ape over all the cute girls. (Don't worry, I told Mom.) But really, what a lot of pretty girls! You'll have some stiff competition, Sis!

Coming back in the car, I have never felt so tired in my life. It seemed like we drove all night but got home around 12:15. Were we glad to get to bed!

I've got your furniture in my room and everyone says it looks great! They like it lots better in my room than in yours. Sorry!

It's weird not having you around. Do you miss David? Spotted anybody up there you like yet? Tell me about your new friends so far. I don't know what I'm gonna do this summer. I'm so bored. Oh well – I have to get David ready for bed. Bye! Write back.

Love,
Jenni

June 12, 1973
Auburn University
Auburn, Alabama

Orlando, Florida
Hi, everyone!

Boy did I have a hectic day today! I think I lost four pounds walking and starving to death. We didn't eat breakfast but went straight to the registration office. It's about a mile and a half away from our dorm, and then we had to wait in so many lines. I had a lot of trouble finding out about my CLEP credits. My advisor is gone, so another counselor helped me arrange a schedule. I've attached it here so you can see it.

I will call you on Sunday if you haven't already called me. Please do call – I've answered three calls tonight from other people's parents!

It's beginning to seem like home here. I did cry a lot last night, but not for long. I miss you all. Write me soon!

Love,
Robin

June 16, 1973
Orlando, Florida

Auburn, Alabama
Hey, Robin!

Sorry you won't be able to come to New Smyrna Beach when we go for two weeks. Too bad, huh?

I sure wish you hadn't taken Carly Simon, I miss it. My records are so dull. I get tired of all the same music.

Do you save all of your letters or throw them away or what?

Wow, our house is really getting into shape. Your bed is gone (sold) and we're in the process of selling both sofas, two big chairs, a coffee table, a refrigerator, etc. Your ex-room is painted Autumn Wheat – yuck! – and Skip is moving in.

I fixed your halter top. Mom is gonna send it to you soon.

David tells everyone where you are, and he's got a new belt that he wants "to show Wobin when she comes home from cowege in August."

Tell me all about things. And write back!

Love,
Jenni

June 17, 1973
Woodbury, Connecticut

Orlando, Florida
Dear Pat and Bob,

You two were certainly nice to your "old folks" for our 46th anniversary. We loved the cards, and the snazzy green necktie will set me off as hot stuff with all my friends. We have enjoyed all the stories from Orlando about the goings-on, graduations, trips, visits and parties. And we hope Robin is off to a great start in college!

Mother keeps you up to date on us so I will not trespass there – she does better than I could anyway. I am still enjoying golf and grass cutting once a week. When we come down in August, I'll take on Skip, Bob and Dave for a golf game, hopefully.

My love to all your great gang.

Dad

June 17, 1763
Orlando, Florida

Auburn, Alabama
Hi, Robin,

I'm sorry, I thought I'd write at least three times this week and I wrote once. Thank goodness for your great letter-writing sister, huh? Both of your letters came, and the family enjoyed them immensely. So did the neighbors – some will probably be writing to you. Edith said Doc wanted her to call us or come down the street at 11 o'clock last Friday night to see whether we had heard from you and if you were okay. Thought that was kind of cute.

The big move is going on at this very moment. Skip's things are being transferred into the middle room, which he and Dad painted this weekend. The new curtains against the "Autumn Wheat" walls really look perfect.

I just asked David what he wanted to tell you. He said, "I tell Wobin, say Wobin you're bew-tee-ful." Oh, remember I bought him a belt to wear with his Pooh short pants? Well, the darn belt has changed his whole personality – into a real rough, tough and swaggering big boy! He looks and feels almost "too big for his britches."

Before I forget, honey, would you mind saving all the letters you get from us? Even Skip and Dad have mentioned they plan to write.

We all miss you and love you, Robin. Good luck each day!

Mom and crew

Hi, Robin!

I'll write this week. Hope everything is 100 percent fine. Thanks for the Father's Day card.

Love,
Dad

June 18, 1973
Orlando, Florida

Auburn, Alabama

Dear Robin,

Well, young lady, we miss you around the neighborhood. We hope you are liking your new home and especially your new friends by now. Your mother let me read your first true letter written home. Although you sounded a little homesick, time will pass quickly when you get involved with your classes.

Jenni let me see her yearbook. Both of you girls are very photogenic. David rides over almost every day in his little red car to see Doc and usually leaves with a stick or two of chewing gum. However, the latest craze is pink peppermint, and he likes to have about five in a paper towel to take home. Your mother is trying to discourage that.

Hope it's cooler up in Auburn than here. It's 96 degrees again today and has been about that all week.

Now do have fun this summer, and we hope you will find a nice Romeo to help while away the evenings.

Our love to you,
Edith and Doc

June 19, 1973
Orlando, Florida

Auburn, Alabama

Dear Robin,

Hi! I just now got your letter. Thanks a lot. I did just what you said and gave David a big hug! You already sound more grown-up from your letters. Mom and Dad even noticed it too.

I sure hope your blind date was a smash! Did you go to a movie? Did he kiss you goodnight?

I'll bet it's fun shopping and stuff in that little town. Have you been to the clothes stores yet? What is a dorm meeting? It did sound funny, with everyone being in curlers and old robes. I'll bet your classes are tough. Are your professors nice? I guess they're mostly women since your major is Home Ec.

Everybody asks, "How's Robin?" You know everybody misses you. Well, have fun and see you in August!

Love,
Jenni

June 20, 1973
Orlando, Florida

Auburn, Alabama
Dear Robin,

Well, here's the first letter I've written you since you've been in college! You better keep it for your memoirs. Ha! I have so much to say and so little time to say it in, because I'm so tired. My room is finally complete and you wouldn't know it used to be your room! I got an eight-track stereo player, which is great, you'll have to see it. Today Jenni and I did all of YOUR clipping in the yard – yuck! When we finally finished it looked good, even with our blisters.

Little Lady is getting better at being inside, and very soon she will be housetrained! I bet you're excited about that.

Well, must be going now but I will write and send a picture of my room. *I miss you.* Write back.

Love,
Skip

June 20, 1973
Auburn University
Auburn, Alabama

Orlando, Florida
Dear family,

I am now in the "fun center" of Auburn University – Haley Center Lounge. It's the only place where I can socialize with boys! All my classes are filled with girls since I'm majoring in Home Economics, you know. It gets kind of boring after awhile.

You know what our darling dorm mother did to us on Monday night? I had gotten to bed early – 11:25 – and at 12:05 we had a fire drill. Scared me to death, I'll have you know! I was asleep. Had to get up, put on a bathrobe, grab a towel and dash down four flights of stairs out into a wet, yucky night. We were all so furious.

305

I especially wanted to tell Jen how the classes and teachers are here. We get to leave classes whenever the professor finishes, which is very often 20 or 30 minutes early. Three of my teachers asked us to call them by their first names. Oh, and one of my teachers looks exactly like Tiny Tim with black glasses. He came to class in jeans, an old shirt and moccasins. I couldn't believe my eyes. He's cool. We should have a good time in there.

I wish you knew how boring it gets up here. Everyone keeps saying how summer quarter is awful compared to fall. I hope they are right. There's nothing to do except write letters, listen to records and read. I don't have much homework. Did I mention that I signed up for women's intramural tennis? It will give me something fun and active to do.

Well, gotta go. I love you all, and write me PLEASE!

Robin

June 20, 1973
Orlando, Florida

Auburn, Alabama
Hi, Robin,

Even though we talked with you on the phone earlier this evening, I thought I'd write a note. I should have done it before now. I'm sorry we left you at Auburn as we did, but Jen and Skip were getting bored, Jen didn't feel well, and it looked like you were busy, so I felt it was best that we take off for home. Our trip home was uneventful, just long. It took us nine hours with the stops but the old station wagon performed magnificently!

It's not surprising you're bored, Robin. Sounds like your classes don't take up enough of your time, plus not enough other activities yet. And your roommate being from Auburn doesn't help. How about scouting around the fourth floor for other girls you might spend time with? The more friends you have, the less bored you'll be. Also, the right job somewhere would be nice – not too many hours, but just enough to fill in the time gaps, be a good experience, and provide a little spending money.

We want you to be happy at Auburn. Keep your chin up, gal. Send us some happy reports, okay? We love you.

Dad

June 22, 1973
Orlando, Florida

Auburn, Alabama
Dearest Robin,

Your old mom is feeling "rheumatic" this morning. We got our new bed and I have been sleeping on two pillows because the mattress doesn't give an inch.

Jenni and David just left to walk down the street where Jenni is to babysit. She asked to take the peanut so he could play with the kids until lunchtime, and I heartily agreed. He has been wilder, more bored and crankier of late, and I have been, too. This morning at breakfast, he asked "Hey, where's Wobin's chair?" (We've moved one to the dining room for a while.) He keeps up with everything concerning you, never fear!

We had a crazy few hours of indecision yesterday. Dad called from work to tell me he had been asked to go to New York for a business meeting Monday and was wondering if I should go along, and then both of us could go on to Woodbury afterward to visit Nana Kitty and Granddad. All the complications that would be involved came to mind immediately, though, and we decided it probably wasn't such a good idea.

I'm glad you called Wednesday when you were feeling homesick, and I only hope you felt better instead of worse after talking to us, honey. You know, I can still vividly remember times in Hamden, already married and a mother, when I felt literally sick from wanting so badly to see my family back in Alabama. It'll be better for you to get through that first awful ache for home while you're young and single, I believe. It's very normal, a part of growing up and finding real independence.

Guess what? I had my horoscope done by a serene, long-haired young man who interpreted my natal chart. It was most interesting. I might consider taking a course in astrology from him – wild thing for a mother to do, huh? One of the most fascinating points shown in my chart was that I could and should be a writer, which has long been a secret desire of mine. We'll talk more about it sometime, okay?

I'll try to catch the postman, so bye for now, Robin. You know we think of you SO much, miss you a lot – and most of all, hope for great happiness for our firstborn!

Love you,
Mom

June 25, 1973
Orlando, Florida

Auburn, Alabama

Hi, Robin!

Kind of quiet around here right now. David is napping and Jenni and Skip are playing cards. I was going to swim, but it's overcast. Dad did fly to New York yesterday and is due home at 9 tonight.

Today Jen went for a dental check and cleaning and I took David along to start getting him acquainted with that procedure. He was so good – climbed right up in the chair and talked to the hygienist. He'll go for a regular checkup in a few months.

We're all getting excited about going to the beach. Nana GeeGee and Granddaddy plan to come down from Alabama for our second week there. Did they visit you in Auburn over the weekend? Nana said they might, and I really hope they made it.

Take care, and know we love you. David told me to send you a kiss in a letter!

Mom and crew

June 25, 1973
Woodbury, Connecticut

Auburn, Alabama

Dear Robin,

Hello there, College Gal. Thought I would give you a break by typing this so you could read it easily. We talked to your Pa last night when he was in New York, and I hope by this time he is safely home in Orlando. It was just too bad that he was so close, within 90 miles, and yet we did not get to see him. But he did have a busy schedule, and so did we, unfortunately.

I told him about my new car, a beautiful Wedgwood Blue Olds '88 Royale, pretty much like the white and black one you and Jenni liked so much. This one is a bit more sumptuous and we love it. When Christmas comes around, in about six months, you will get a chance to ride with me. The time will come awfully fast, too!

Nana Kitty and I wish you all sorts of success at Auburn. That includes not only studies, but good friends, fun and especially good health. Try to get some pleasure out of everything you do, and the first thing you know, even work will be fun. I have enjoyed every job I've had through the years, even though some were not as rewarding as others.

We love you and want nothing but the best for our Robin.

Granddad

June 26, 1973
Auburn University
Auburn, Alabama

Orlando, Florida
Dearest Mother,

Last night as I lay in bed, I remembered the talk we had about how you wished your children realized that you are also an individual, not just a mother. I want to tell you I finally know how it feels to think of you that way, as a person and a friend, and I am so glad. It feels good!

When you told me you had seen an astrologer who stressed your capabilities as a writer, it hit me; you have wants and dreams just as I do. Somehow I never could see that before. But Mom, I'm so glad you went – and having an astrological chart done, or taking an astrology course, is not a wild thing for a mother to do at all!

In thinking back, I can remember hearing you say someday you would like to write a book. There's nothing in the world I think you should do more than that. It is a grand idea, and I know you could do a wonderful job. You have a way with words – I am sure of that from all the times you have helped me with assignments. And you feel things so deeply and are so sensitive and wonderful that I know you could write a bestseller, especially one about family relations and love and everything. Mom, PLEASE do it, it would be so GOOD.

I am sad when I think of the times I have disappointed you in any way, Mom. I love you more than any person in the world and would do anything for you. Always try to remember that even when I am not being loving, okay?

All my love to my wonderful mother,
Your Robin

June 27, 1973
Woodbury, Connecticut

Auburn, Alabama
Dear Robin,

Well, you have been a college girl for two weeks now and we think of you a lot and hope you are adjusting happily to a very different life from the one you led at home. We are so glad you like your roommate. Your classes

309

sound really interesting, the sorts of courses I would like, and I shall be glad to talk to you about them.

When will we see you again? Granddad and I are going to Orlando for about 10 days in August.

Too bad you didn't like your blind date, but don't be too fussy for a while until you get to know more people. One thing can lead to another if you keep on circulating.

Granddad sends love and so do I. Keep busy and happy!

Nana Kitty

June 27, 1973
Woodbury, Connecticut

Orlando, Florida
Dear Bob,

Stockbrokering certainly must be tough right now. I cannot help but feel so many things in our country are being let slide, due to Watergate, lack of Congressional leadership and correct action, the strength of the loudmouths, prices and costs, the downgrading of the dollar, and other factors.

I think things will be better when Americans can once again feel more secure in their leadership and its honesty, and not be so stricken by inflation. That's a big order to accomplish – I hope Nixon is up to leading the way. Enough of that!

Have a great vacation. We enjoyed our talks with you and hope the New York City trip was productive. Looks like we'll be in Florida in August. You'll see my beautiful new car.

I wrote to Robin yesterday, and Mother wrote today.

Love from us both,
Dad

June 30, 1973
Orlando, Florida

Auburn, Alabama
Dearest Robin,

Just a quick note to let you know I *so* much appreciate your expressing how you feel about me after this separation. It seems to be part of the life process that we usually don't learn to really, fully know and appreciate our parents until we grow up and go away. I'll expand on that later either in person or in another letter, okay? We just loved talking to you and especially hearing your enthusiasm and happiness, honey.

Love you,
Mom

July 2, 1973
New Smyrna Beach, Florida

Auburn, Alabama
Dear Robin,

Please pardon the Snoopy stationery, but it's the only notepaper we have over here at the beach. So far the weather has been perfect. We have all gotten sun but have been careful not to get too much too fast.

David has been difficult at times, finding it hard to stay interested in any one thing too long. And getting up early, which means your mother and I are up early too!

You should have seen the car coming over here – really packed, including David's crib. I didn't think we'd get it all in.

We're glad to hear you sounding much happier and at home at Auburn. I am proud of you for going to see teachers, professors and others when necessary to straighten things out and not being bashful about it. Keep it up, gal, we're very pleased.

I heard a radio program about Southeast Conference football, and the experts picked either Alabama or Auburn to be the top team! So it looks like you should have an exciting autumn there.

Lots of love,
Dad

July 4, 1973
Fishers Island, New York

Auburn, Alabama
Hi, Robin,

We're here for a few days at Isabella Beach off New London, Connecticut, in Long Island Sound. You can see from the postcard how beautiful it is. Weather foggy but fun swimming in surf, eating, playing games with our friends. All the yachts in the harbor are "full dressed" with their flags and pennants flying.

Love from Granddad and Nana Kitty

July 8, 1973
New Smyrna Beach, Florida

Auburn, Alabama
Hi, Robin!

We were really tickled you had a special Fourth of July with some of your new girlfriends. We had a great day here at the beach. Rode the waves awhile, sunned, had cocktails, ate a good dinner and finished off with ice cream cake.

Nana GeeGee and Granddaddy like Chateau-by-the-Sea a lot. We wish you could have come down from Alabama with them. I'll bet you've loved reading the family letters Nana sent you, huh? She brought me a bunch and we've had a great time reading them. Some of the funniest are from when you and Jenni were little.

Skip suddenly seems much older over here! He and his buddies have been girl-watching and met some girls – stayed out talking to them till after 11 p.m. two or three nights.

It was good to hear your voice last night, honey! Much love from all your family.

Mom

TO ROBIN
I LOVE YOU! WE MISS YOU SO MUCH.
LOVE DAVID

July 13, 1973
Orlando, Florida

Auburn, Alabama
Dear Robin,

Hi! Well, I guess I've cheered up some since last week so I'm in the mood to write you.

Mom and Dad finally decided to let me go home from the beach with Dad because he was leaving early to go back to work. Dad got a couple of good meals out of it because I cooked for him this week!

So today is Friday and Dad went back to New Smyrna and I get to stay here by myself for three days. Hooray! My friend Sharon is coming over tonight to keep me company, and tomorrow night I'll stay at her house.

You know, it's surprising how if you change your appearance it can change your mood as well. I was sick of my hair, so I took Mom's advice and used this really cheap stuff (33 cents!) called "Clairoxide." She said it wouldn't hurt my hair at all. Now I can really say that my hair is blond, not dishwater blond or dirty blond but blond. I like it.

I baby-sat a little girl named Jennifer two nights this week. She is so cute and sweet! She's 6 or 7 months old and it's really a change from David now that he's growing up. You know, little babies are so helpless – you have to do everything for them.

Who are you going to room with this fall? Are you going to change dormitories? When in August are you coming?

Well, write me soon!

Love,
Jenni

July 14, 1973
Auburn University
Auburn, Alabama

Orlando, Florida

Hi, everyone!

I'm sitting in the laundry room at the moment. I guess you all are home from the beach by now. I hope you had a good time. Even though it can get boring here at times, overall it's a fun experience. I just wish I could have been at the beach with you for even one day! Oh, and I never knew how much I could miss our beautiful pool at home.

Things seem to be going well for me. I've made up my schedule for the fall. I'm sending you a list of my classes and the schedule. And I have met so many nice people!

My roommate and I made a red velvet cake yesterday to take to her boyfriend. We took about two hours in the lobby kitchen, and people kept coming up to say how good it smelled. Then we drove over to her boyfriend's house and left it with his mother – me carrying the cake the whole way on my lap! My roommate was so afraid I'd drop it.

Well, I think my laundry is almost dry, so I'll close for now. I love you all. Take care and write soon. How about another great letter from my Skip? David, sweetie, thank you for your note! Jenni, I'm glad all's A-OK. Keep the letters coming!

Hugs and kisses,
Robin

July 16, 1973
Orlando, Florida

Auburn, Florida

Dear Robin,

Enclosed is a check for $50 to add to your account. Hope this will hold you alright, but let me know again if you get low.

Your fall schedule sounds good. What is the normal number of hours to take in a quarter? Does this mean you will be a sophomore by the end of the winter quarter? How many credits (hours) do you need to graduate? With college costs what they are today, gaining a quarter would be very helpful!

Sure hope your blind date Saturday worked out well. Let us know. I'm proud you've had several dates. One of these times you'll meet a guy you click with (although we don't really want you to get steady with anyone yet either!).

I'm also proud of your attitude about college life, proud of the friends you've made, proud of your marks, and just generally pleased with your first month at college. Keep up the good work, Robin!

Lots of love,
Dad

July 17, 1973
Holiday Inn
Seymour, Indiana

Auburn, Alabama

Hi, Robin,

You can see we are on our way to Minnesota and Wisconsin. Just hope we will be back in Orlando to say Hi to you the last part of September. Hope everything is going along OK at school. Our best, always.

Your favorite old neighbors,
Edith and Doc

July 23, 1973
Auburn University
Auburn, Alabama

Orlando, Florida

Dear family,

Hey, everyone! I hope you're all doing fine. I'm sitting in the Haley Center Lounge right now with my suitemate. It's been so vacant down here

314

lately – not nearly as many cute guys as usual. Rats! But maybe business will pick up soon!

Guess what? Miss Edith and Doc sent me a Holiday Inn postcard from Indiana. Wasn't that sweet of them? I feel like their granddaughter or something!

I'm almost positive I'm going to be able to go to Mobile and see Nana GeeGee and Granddaddy – a guy I know has offered me a ride when he goes in a couple of weeks.

Not long till the end of the summer term. The time has gone so fast. I'm anxious to get home. I love you all so much!

Robin

July 23, 1973
Orlando, Florida

Auburn, Alabama
Dearest Robin,

I'll say again, honey, it is just wonderful you are getting along so well, sound so happy and well-adjusted, keep meeting new friends, and going out on blind dates. Dad and I are *so* glad your college career has begun on such a positive note. We'd be crushed if you really weren't happy at Auburn.

Jenni and David played in the pool this morning and had such fun with an 88-cent raft that has become everyone's favorite water toy. But then at lunchtime little David said, "You wanna see my sore froat, Mommy?" Just like that, he was sick – feverish, no appetite, wanted only to lie down in his "house" behind Dad's big chair. He is so darn precious, always creating a cozy nest, with his blanket for comfort and stuffed toys Iggie and Pooh for company. How blessed our family is to have this special little guy, huh?

We send lots of love,
Mom

July 26, 1973
Mobile, Alabama

Orlando, Florida
Hi, Pat,

I'm washing and drying the last of Skip's dirty clothes while he is packing his suitcase and getting ready to leave. The two of us played golf this morning, and on the way home we talked about how he sure had lived to the hilt during this vacation with his old grandparents! He really is a good golfer and I wish he could have the chance to play and practice a lot.

315

Everyone who sees him swing and hit the ball comments on how well he does, especially for a 14-year-old.

We've enjoyed Skip so much. Yesterday while we were playing golf, he said something priceless to me: "Nana GeeGee, I want you to be living 10 years and more from now cause I want my wife to see and know you, and you to know her." Isn't that the most precious thing a grandmother could ever hear?

I talked on the phone to Robin and made plans to drive up to Auburn to pick her up, maybe next weekend.

Now, Skip and Granddaddy are standing on either side of me ready to leave for the airport. I will give this letter to Skip to bring home to you on the plane.

Lots of love to all,
Mom

July 28, 1973
Orlando, Florida

Mobile, Alabama
Dear Nana GeeGee and Granddaddy,

How's it been up there without your oldest grandson? Pretty boring, huh! I didn't tell anybody, but I kind of wish I was still there. I really had a great time and I enjoyed watching Watergate with you (Haha).

Nana, I've been talking to my Dad and Mom and it's almost decided that I will join Alhambra Golf Club. It would cost I think $250 a year, but I might get a discount because of my age. I will write back after it's for sure.

Granddaddy, you'd better get better in golf because when I come back next year I'll whip your butt!

Well, must be going. Love you both.

Skip

July 28, 1973
Orlando, Florida

Auburn, Alabama
Dear Robin,

How is college going lately? I'm fine here and I hope it's the same there. Thursday I got back from Alabama on a plane and guess what!! The person I sat next to was the mother of your friend Jan. We talked about you, and it was fun.

Last night was the first night Lady slept inside, and she made it all the way through safely – in other words, no messes. She is such a great dog.

So you're going to be home in August, huh! I'll be looking forward to it. I really hope everything is all right up in "War Eagle" country. Well, got to be going now. (I really don't have to, but I have never been a good letter writer.)

Love,
Skip

July 30, 1973
Orlando, Florida

Auburn, Alabama
Dear Robin,

How are you? Well, everybody loved my hair. I mean everybody!

Yesterday I went over to Uncle Dave and Aunt Dorothy's new house. They just bought it and have to absolutely redo it. Washing, painting, lighting, plumbing, carpeting, landscaping, everything.

I asked them if I could help. We worked all day – I mean hard work – till 7:30 at night and then, dead beat, stinky, sweaty, plastered with paint, we dragged ourselves into Taco Tico and had a good supper. I had so much fun, and they really appreciated my help. Robin, they are so happy with each other and so much in love! And fun to be with.

I can't wait till school starts – really. I also can't wait for my birthday, because then I get my license!

Well, I'll see you later. Write me!

Love,
Jenni

August 6, 1973
Auburn University
Auburn, Alabama

Orlando, Florida
Hey, all!

It was not the best time to go visit Nana GeeGee and Granddaddy, with finals coming and all, but then anytime would be difficult. And I really wanted to see them.

I like their new house a lot. It's not quite the same, because the old one was part of my childhood, you know, but they seem really happy with it and that's all that matters.

317

While I was there, I saw Uncle John, Uncle Rickey and their friends. Of course, Nana Gee cooked me peas, okra and cornbread – positively the best meal this quarter! I ate so much, I'm surprised I didn't get sick.

Nana said she thought I'd changed a lot. I think I have, too – quite a lot in a lot of ways. I do so hope you see it in me when I get home.

Gotta go! Love and hugs,
Your Robin

P.S. – Remember, Mom, I told you I had written to Allen's mother on the first anniversary of his drowning and just filled the letter with my memories of him? Well, she answered and at the end wrote, "Robin, thank you for talking about Allen. So many people seem to try to forget he ever existed. And I don't want to forget anything about him. I miss him so much." I cried, but at least now I can be sure how she feels and not ever be afraid to talk more about him.

August 6, 1973
Mobile, Alabama

Auburn, Alabama
My Robin,

Loved our telephone visit last night. You made me feel soooo good because you sound very happy! Not every Nana is lucky like I am in having a granddaughter like you.

Just wanted to send this old letter on to you so you can see how your daddy felt about his new baby girl when you were born. He called you "Miss America 1973" – and that would be this year, huh? I bet you remember hearing many times about the signs he made to welcome you and your mommy home from the hospital, especially "Robin's Nest" for over the door to your tiny room. And later your mommy wrote that in your baby book he had noted: "Cord fell off 2:00 p.m. 16 Feb. 1955." Isn't it such a sweet letter? I can still remember how it warmed the cockles of my heart more than 18 years ago, and I read it over and over.

You may have this one to keep, and I hope you will enjoy it as much as I have. There are lots more letters with many, many cute, sweet things you did and said – just like you've seen in David since he came.

We'll think of you and be speaking of you often.

Love,
Nana GeeGee

August 6, 1973
Orlando, Florida

Auburn, Alabama
Dearest Robin,

Well, I guess you're back in the old school routine today. Hope you had a swell time in Mobile with some of your very favorite people. How was the ride? Did you take a bus back to Auburn?

We put another ad in the paper today, still trying to sell the old green sofa, and it worked! Wait till you see the house. It's going to be quite different. Dad and I went shopping all day Saturday and ordered a swivel rocker to match the new sofa – wow, is it elegant. We bought a few wall decorations and have put them up already. Still haven't found tables and lamps that are just right for the living room. We have to keep looking.

Must run now. I've been so bad about writing – not in the mood, I guess. Come on home so we can talk. Much love from all your family, Robin.

Mom

August 13, 1973
Ormond Beach, Florida

Auburn, Alabama
Robin,

Granddad and I flew to Orlando from Connecticut Friday and had a nice visit with your parents before heading over here to this beautiful apartment in Ormond Beach. All of Dave and Dorothy's gang visited us yesterday and we had a great time. This is living!

Love,
Nana Kitty

August 14, 1973
Orlando, Florida

Auburn, Alabama
Dear Robin,

I miss you. I have a super idea for when you get home. Let's you and me go to Disney World. Skip, sorry to say, is not included this time.

I'm not going to write again before you get home since it's a week from tomorrow and then I'll see you for almost a month.

Robin, I know I told you, I did get my ears pierced two or three weeks ago. I absolutely love them, but I can't change the earrings for another two weeks!

See you soon, Sis!

Love,
Jenni

August 16, 1973
Orlando, Florida

Auburn, Alabama
Dearest Robin,

Just a short note to say hi and I'm sorry I haven't written. You'll be home in less than a week, though. All of us are so eager to see you! We've enjoyed your letters, and Nana Kitty and Granddaddy, who are down from Connecticut, have read all your college mail to catch up on your news.

We stay busy every moment around here – wow! You probably won't recognize the house with all the new stuff.

Now I must collapse again and rest awhile.

Love you,
Mom

September 17, 1973
Orlando, Florida

Mobile, Alabama
Dearest Folks,

Robin and I are waiting at the designated spot for the "friend of a friend" who's giving her a ride back to Auburn. It's early and we're sleepily quiet. ...

Skip and Jenni have the school schedule again this year where they need to get up before 6 a.m., so ours is an early rising household each day. David just started sleeping in a big bed, and he wants to get up pretty early, too. This morning he went off to nursery school – after first hiding for a couple of minutes, saying he shouldn't go. He and his daddy were kinda cute driving off, both waving happily. My plan for the three hours of freedom on Monday and Tuesday mornings is to do errands and then just be quiet and relax. But I wonder if it'll ever come off that way?

We are getting a bit weary of hot weather and rain and are really looking forward to some coolish nights along with the warm, dry days of fall. Bet y'all are, too.

Skip still goes out to Alhambra for golf one or two afternoons during the week and one weekend day. Bob will meet him there for a game this evening if it doesn't rain. Oh, Skip's Sears television commercial is scheduled to air next week! Since I registered all of us with the agency, he and David and I have had a few still photo sessions, but this is the first TV work and it's very exciting.

By the way, I began a six-week models workshop on Thursday afternoons. I've already learned a couple of tricks about walking, sitting and standing gracefully. But nothing, particularly perfection, ever comes without hours of that old practice, I guess!

You two take care. We all send love to you. And Skip said, "Tell Nana GeeGee I've gotta get her down here to play golf with me!" How 'bout it?

Pat and crew

September 17, 1973

TO NANA GEEGE
I LOVE YOU. I HOPE I CAN SEE YOU SOON.
LOVE, DAVID

September 24, 1973
Orlando, Florida

Auburn, Alabama

Hi, Robin!

I just called about Skip's television commercial schedule – it's going to be shown numerous times on Wednesday, Thursday and Friday during the "Mike Douglas Show," "Bonanza," "Sanford and Son," and the news on two different channels! Very exciting – wish you could see it.

Skip's got a bad cold now and hasn't felt well. He did a few chores but spent most of the weekend resting or doing homework. Jenni went to the big football game Friday night – your old Boone High got skunked! The next day she helped paint bathrooms at the high school as part of a civics group project. Oh, we saw a report of Auburn's win on Saturday with 46,500 fans in attendance – gracious!

David, who was a little pill most of the weekend, woke up being an angel this morning, eager to go to school. The other day I asked him, "How would you like it if we got you a Big Wheel to ride? He looked up with a delighted, "By MARX?" He remembers all the brand names just the way you did when you were little.

Dad and I had a pretty quiet weekend here, mostly doing a lot of rearranging in a couple of the bedrooms. He took the crib down and the back room is shaping up nicely.

Much love from all,
Mom

September 27, 1973
Auburn University
Auburn, Alabama

Orlando, Florida
Dearest Mom,

Well, life at Auburn seems to be settling into a routine this second day of classes. One bit of news is that I'll be working part time at the radio station – typing, filing, etc. No pay, but contact with nice people. Couldn't hurt! At least I'll have another group of friends.

Thanks again for the astrology books, Mom. They have been extremely popular since my return. Everyone wants to know about the zodiac sign of the guy they like!

The enclosed poem is the one I mentioned that reminded me of you.

I love you!
Robin

The Green Place

Lord, may there be a still, green place
For everyone ... a little pool
Within a forest where the lace
Of ferns is delicate and cool;
A meadow where across the grass
Small clover-scented breezes pass.

And Lord, if there are those for whom
There is no quiet retreat,
Oh, let a healing memory bloom
To bring a refreshment deep and sweet
And please, Lord, keep it very green
However long the years between.

Grace Watkins

October 14, 1973
Orlando, Florida

Auburn, Alabama
Dear Robin,

I am sorry I haven't written sooner. You know how busy things always are around here, plus the stock market has perked up lately and business has improved at the same time, which, of course, is the kind of "busyness" that I like! Incidentally, I'm writing out on the pool patio. The pool water is refreshing now – about 75 degrees – because the nights here have cooled off somewhat.

I see where Auburn got beaten by LSU yesterday. I guess Auburn doesn't have one of its best teams this year. Maybe next year! Of course, the competition is very good – LSU, Tennessee and Alabama are all in the top 10 in the country.

Sorry I missed your call yesterday. I was playing golf with Skip before I brought him home from the course. He hasn't gone over to Alhambra very often since school resumed, but he was there all day yesterday and Jenni just took him back today. One thing that made it more attractive for him was that they are going to pay him $3.20 any day he puts in an appearance to work. Seems like a strange amount, but since he likes it anyway, it's just gravy.

Well, bye for now. Study hard, eat properly, watch your pennies. I'm enclosing some money for you, so please make it last – and did I say have fun? Take care of yourself.

Much love,
Dad

October 28, 1973
Orlando, Florida

Auburn, Alabama
Dear Robin,

Sorry I missed another call from you. Maybe I'll be here for the next one.

I'll bet there was joy in Auburn after beating Houston 7-0 Saturday. I was wondering if you saw the game. We saw brief highlights of the action today on TV.

Hope to see you in about a month. Thanks for your letters to me alone – makes me feel kind of special!

Love,
Dad

October 31, 1973
Halloween – Boo!
Orlando, Florida

Auburn, Alabama
Hi, Robin,

Jen is out with David, alias Casper the Friendly Ghost, to trick-or-treat the neighborhood, and Skip is at a friend's house to help scare the tricksters with a rigged-up skeleton.

Dad and I actually had a quiet supper of soup and turkey sandwiches before the first peal of the doorbell. But now the onslaught has begun, as I knew it would when I started a letter. Lots of little goblins on our street tonight. What goes on at college on Halloween night?

Hello again. Now the hubbub is over, I've showered – "cleanest one in the house," as Granddad teases! – and will soon head for bed. Skip and his friend brought their stuffed dummy to our porch, hooked it up with a walkie-talkie, and from inside the house talked to kids as they came up to the door. Funny reactions ... and David was cutest of all, going outside to have a conversation with the scary man.

The first neighborhood newspaper came out today, and it could well be called "The Skip Gazette." His name's all over the place, and he's also the circulation manager.

Jenni, along with so many other students, attended today's funeral service for the pilot of the small plane that crashed and killed those four boys from your old Boone High School. She said it was so sad. It was a tragic accident.

Better sign off now. Take care, study hard, and have fun! We all send much love, honey.

Mom and crew

November 5, 1973
Orlando, Florida

Auburn, Alabama
Dear Robin,

We've had two newsy, upbeat letters from you since I wrote last. One of your wonderful attributes, Robin, is an optimistic outlook. I know you get down occasionally, as we all do, but you always bounce right back with more enthusiasm than ever! That is something not everyone has. Feel proud of it. A positive attitude will carry you far. And remember, when you do feel hurt so acutely, it means you can also experience joy very deeply – and how much better to be able to really feel both than to be in any way blasé about either. So keep having a strong faith about everything – yourself, your college career, your romantic future – and you'll be A-OK. Amen … end of sermonette!

I'm sorry you have to work Thanksgiving weekend, honey. But even though you can't come home, Dad and I will see you the following weekend when we come up. We're really looking forward to it.

Oh, I want to tell you how David astounded us during a quick stop at your dad's office after church Sunday. He walked all around just looking at everything and soon noticed the large map on the wall in the manager's office. He stopped to study it and then very seriously inquired, "Mom, do you know the word CAM-BO-DEE-A?" We all nearly fainted. We assume he heard it used on the news, probably in connection with a map being shown, and was spurred to remember it when he saw the map in the office.

So glad you had a fun time at the Halloween party, and we'll be eager to see the pictures. And yep, you're right, it is possible to have loads of fun without alcoholic drinks. I remember what absolutely great, roaring good times we and our friends in Connecticut used to have at our parties, when Black Cherry soda was apt to be the most potent libation.

You can imagine how my heart sank when you mentioned possibly flying home sometime in a small plane with a young pilot. I know we'd worry, especially in light of the tragic deaths of the four Boone High students I wrote you about. Keep looking around for other rides, too, will you, honey?

Must close and go make a turkey casserole for dinner. We all send much love!

Mom and crew

P.S. – Hey, we're sorry your War Eagles didn't win against the University of Florida on Saturday. There were a lot of happy Gators, though!

November 18, 1973
Orlando, Florida

Auburn, Alabama
Hi, Robin!

Thought I'd best get a note off to you today so you'll get it before the Thanksgiving holidays. Hope I can get everything ready for our trip to

Alabama, although it seems I hardly have time to organize my thoughts, much less the packing.

The most exciting event of the week occurred yesterday when your dad, the boys and I went to the airport to see if we could catch a glimpse of President Nixon as he arrived for his appearance at Walt Disney World last night. After we saw Air Force One land at McCoy we took a chance on the route the entourage would take and drove down the road a short distance to wait and watch. There was just our little foursome standing beside the road when suddenly the limousine appeared and President Nixon was waving to us! Of course, he was inside the thick-glassed car, which passed by quickly, but it was still thrilling!

Uncle Dave and Aunt Dorothy came on the spur-of-the-moment last night and had supper with us. We tried out my new chicken salad recipe, which was delicious, if I do say so! Had such a good time – you know how much we always enjoy being together.

Little ol' David had very swollen, bright red tonsils last week, but no fever, and he's better now. I did take him in to be checked and on the way home from the doctor's office, we stopped by the Orange County Agricultural Center to see all the animals at the Farm City Week Exhibit. David loved that. He really wanted to take one of the free baby chicks home, and I questioned where it would stay and how he would take care of it. "Well," he assured me, "we could keep it for a *while*, and when it grows too big, we can just let him out, to go out in the future, to seek his fortune!"

We'll catch up on all the rest of the news just one week from now when we see you in person, okay, sweetie?

Much love from your family,
Mom

And the day came
when the risk to remain tight in the bud
was more painful than the risk it took to blossom.
Anais Nin

Chapter Seventeen
Liberation
1974

Pat and kids in Pine Mountain, Georgia

January 6, 1974
Auburn University
Auburn, Alabama

Orlando, Florida
Dear Jenni,

Man, have I got a lot to tell you! I'm having a ball up here. Friday night Linda and I were sitting around bored to death and she suggested we go over to the guys' dorm. Well, they were having a party and we dove right in! I never had so much fun! We all danced for three hours straight.

You've got to come up next fall for a football game, okay? Well, better go, love you.

Your sis,
Robin

February 9, 1974
Auburn University
Auburn, Alabama

Mobile, Alabama
Dear Nana GeeGee,

I sent away for information about a job on a cruise ship for spring and summer. Wouldn't that be fantastic? Think of the people I would meet, especially rich young bachelors, and the great pay!

Imagine, I'm 19 today – but I don't feel anything different. Not exactly the same disappointment it was on my 5th birthday when I ran to look in the mirror and couldn't believe I hadn't changed a bit, that I still looked 4! Mom said when she and David were talking about his 4th birthday coming up tomorrow, he asked, "*Which day* am I going to grow up?"

I'll write again soon. I love you.

Your greatest receiver of advice,
Robin

February 28, 1974
Auburn University
Auburn, Alabama

Orlando, Florida
Dearest Skip,

How about this stationery – is it your first scented letter? Aren't you privileged?

Skip, that's great about the golf team! I'm so proud of my brother. You're really accomplishing a lot nowadays in school and in golf. I wouldn't be at all surprised if you became a famous pro before you're 30!

Hey, did you hear about Elvis Presley coming to Auburn? I'm going to see him – and wow, am I excited! Imagine, The King in Auburn! I'll tell you all about it later.

I love my art courses. I can't wait to show you and the rest of the family some of my stuff. Several things are really good, I think. It's mostly modern art, which I never even liked before.

I gave blood for the Red Cross yesterday – a whole pint! It wasn't exactly what you'd call a W.E. (wonderful experience), but I'm glad I did it. Besides, anyone in our family can get free blood for a year if anything happens. That's good because blood is expensive.

I wish I knew how I was gonna get home! I don't have a ride yet and I'm getting worried. Wish me luck!

Better go. I'm expecting a long letter from you soon. I love you, hon. See you soon.

Robin

March 6, 1974
Mobile, Alabama

Orlando, Florida

Dearest Pat and gang,

I just got home from my golf day with the ladies group. I played pretty good and sure enjoyed all the girls. Glory be, tho, your daddy and I are having the bestest time – I still can hardly believe it, that he's going to the golf course with me and really playing! I hope Bob and David will join us, too, when we come down to Florida and go golfing with Skip.

It goes without saying we loved every minute of Robin's visit. She's someone I'll never worry about. She's truly a wonderful and good person, can make up her own mind, won't be swayed by people. Whatever she does or don't do in living her life she'll really think about it beforehand. Just hope the guy that gets her will be worthy. She was so happy and excited after your call Saturday, just kept talking about you two. One statement was, "Mom and Dad sounded like they were happy and pleased with me!"

We had the nicest day yesterday. About 15 neighbor families got together at one house for a potluck dinner. So glad Robin got to go.

There were several boys and girls her age who are in college here at the University of South Alabama.

Daddy and I send lots of love.

Mommie

March 7, 1974
Auburn University
Auburn, Alabama

Orlando, Florida
Dear Jen,

What I would have given if you could have been here last night. I know you've heard all about "streaking," right? Well last night from about 11 o'clock till morning we had a "mass streak." There were guys in huge groups, *all nude*, running through the quad with an estimated 3,000 people following – screaming their heads off and having a blast!!

The Auburn police, the university police and all the fire engines were out chasing the streakers with sirens blaring. It's all so much fun. I wish you were here with me – you'd love it.

I've got sunburn from yesterday. The weather is gorgeous, especially after our dreary winter, and the kids here are going crazy with Spring Fever. College is a gas!

Be sure to start saving your money to come up here fall quarter. I'll save some too. I want you to have the privilege of seeing college life firsthand before you get out of high school. You'd have such a good time – I promise!

I hear things haven't been going too well for you lately. Why don't you write and tell me, hon? You know how much I want to give you the help of a more experienced older sister that I never had.

Take care – see you soon,
Robin

P.S. – I might go on a movie date this weekend to see *The Sting*.

March 12, 1974
Orlando, Florida

Mobile, Alabama
Dear Nana GeeGee and Granddaddy,

Well, I bet you never thought you'd see the day I'd write to you on my own. As a matter of fact I probably wouldn't of but I'm still home from

330

school. This is the 11th day I've been home in bed, but I think I'll be going back tomorrow. I miss my golf so much. It's been almost two weeks since I've picked up a club.

Granddaddy, I hear you've been playing a lot of golf lately. You're going to have to get *real* good to beat me. I'm going to want some competition from both you and Nana.

When Dad and I went to the Citrus Open golf tournament we saw all the pros. Boy, I hope someday I can get as good as they are.

Last weekend my other grandparents came here for the day and then went back to the place they are renting in New Smyrna Beach.

Something funny happened with David last Sunday. Mom says you never know what's gonna come out of the mouth of a 4-year-old. I was sitting on the couch and David was looking at his calendar. I asked him to find my birthday so he looked through the pages and eventually found it. Then I asked him if he could find his birthday so he looked and looked, but finally he said, "Dammit, I can't find my birthday!"

Well, I'm out of space and I've got some other work to do. Hope to see you soon.

Love you both,
Skip

March 12, 1974

TO DAD	I LOVE YOU	FROM DAVID
TO SKIP	I LOVE YOU	FROM DAVID
TO MOM	I LOVE YOU	FROM DAVID

March 28, 1974
Callaway Gardens
Pine Mountain, Georgia

Orlando, Florida
Mom,

Got y'all a room at White Columns Motel, pictured on the postcard, for April 9, 10 & 11. It's small, but nice and close to everything. Waitress job still back-breaking but okay. Miss you and the family so very much. Can't wait to see you. Love you always and think of you all the time.

Your Robin

April 14, 1974
Mobile, Alabama

Orlando, Florida
Pat and gang,

Hi to all. We are fine here, hope every one is ok there. Have a Eggy Easter.

Love you,
Daddy

May 5, 1974
Orlando, Florida

Woodbury, Connecticut
Dearest Mother Kitty and Dad,

Hello, very neglected ones! We borrowed a typewriter from some neighbors for business purposes and I decided to try typing a letter. I don't know if I'm going to be able to keep up my longstanding habit of writing fairly lengthy letters to both families. I'd feel so-o-o guilty, but if any of you followed me around a few days you would easily understand why I'm sometimes pert nigh incapable of composing a coherent letter. My physical energy level is often low and my mind at times a muddled mass of brain tissue.

Along these lines – and this is *not* just talk – I am going to stop all my outside activities for a year, except for possibly a once-a-month bridge club. I had a good test on my new resolution this week when I declined the presidency and later the secretary-treasurer position in the American Field Service club. Then I gave a firm *no* to working at the Friends of the Library Book Sale this month and another to being on the Rules Committee of the bowling league. It's hard for me to turn people down, but I did it.

Now, for what I plan to be doing. Of course, after a long hiatus, I'll be back to school carpooling, a sometimes confining, slightly confusing activity. But, thank heaven, it won't be as bad as it used to be in Hamden when there were three kids going in different directions and winter weather was my nemesis! I anticipate, too, being more involved in David's class activities. I think he'll like having me go on field trips and participate in class parties. (A fun field trip soon is to see the peacocks on Genius Drive.)

I want to have time to rest more, dabble in my writing, invite friends in for a visit without feeling I have to steal the time from something more important, to read the morning paper before 9 p.m., or sit quietly and daydream, or just plain be lazy every so often. An occasional modeling job would be fun, and I'd like the freedom to try other little things that might help me to enjoy life more.

Maybe it's "women's lib" or a touch of selfishness, or the fear that my life is passing by in a flurry of frenetic activity, but I have to make some changes. In the past I've half-teased about resigning from my job as wife and mother, but in all seriousness I'm afraid if I don't alter my schedule, I won't be much good at *any* job. I admit I am disenchanted about a lot of things – maybe (hopefully) it's temporary, all part of the "menopausal mania" that seems to have afflicted me and affected my outlook on life – and my goal is to create more time just for myself, time needed to get Pat restored.

Unfortunately some schedules won't change, and will even get worse! Jenni finally found a job at a new local meat market. Starting tomorrow her hours will be from 3:30 to 7:15 p.m. on Mondays, Tuesdays, Thursdays and Fridays, and 10 a.m. to 8 p.m. on Saturdays, at $2.20 an hour. Can you imagine Jen suddenly making that kind of money? I've threatened her with her life if she tries to spend it all. So … I'm open to any suggestions as to how I should try to handle serving dinner under these new hours!

Robin called the other evening and told us everything was going pretty smoothly. We drove up to Callaway Gardens to see her recently. It's a beautiful resort set at the foothills of the Appalachian Mountains, a good place for temporary/seasonal work for a college girl. Soon after our visit, my parents also went for a few days and the three of them had a good time together. Mom and Daddy liked the area so much they are going back again the middle of this month to play some golf. Robin borrowed a car and drove over to Auburn one weekend – said she was so glad to be back there for even a short while and couldn't wait to return to classes in the fall.

Skip still works at Alhambra Country Club most of his waking hours, when not in school. We did get him to stay home yesterday and help his dad in the yard, after which we all enjoyed a swim in the pool. Actually, David stayed in the water the whole afternoon, so long that we discovered the bottoms of both big toes were worn raw! Now today he's a mess with his very sore toes – but he has a really pretty suntan.

We had planned to take Skip to Lee's Lakeside for dinner Saturday and when Dave and Dorothy called to invite us to have tacos with their gang, we asked them to join us instead. Turned out to be a great evening with yummy food and lots of laughs.

I can't possibly fit all the details of our moviemaking into a letter, but enclosed is a copy of some notes I wrote about it. I will say, it was an interesting, unique experience! We met so many fascinating people (great, nice, so-so and weird) and, not surprisingly, were most "star-struck" over the gracious and very beautiful Dina Merrill. Bob and I held up reasonably well during the hectic schedule but were glad when it was over. The last week was difficult, on the set five nights in a row – all night. The rest of the world didn't exist for us during that time and, feeling chronically sleepy and tired, we actually found it a bit reminiscent of those first weeks with a newborn!

There was a call from the modeling agency recently to see if I would do a freebie television commercial on race relations for the Chamber of Commerce. Naturally I wanted the experience, and a nice one it was. Two of us gals did a short spot and the photographer complimented us on a good job, adding, "I do a lot of TV work and I'll remember you for some work for which you'll get paid next time." Hope he does.

For the first time, after eight years, I lost a contact lens the other morning. Still not sure exactly what happened. Leaning over the bathroom sink, I went through the motions of placing the lens in one eye but evidently missed, and it disappeared – at first camouflaged by soap bubbles, where combs and brushes were soaking in the sink, before being swept down the drain. A good lesson for following the instructions to lean over a towel and look into a mirror on the counter *next* to the sink when inserting and removing contact lenses. It was only a couple of days before a replacement arrived by special delivery, but I was lost without the good vision in my right eye. First mishap was a near-spritzing of my whole body with Style hairspray instead of after-bath refresher – uh oh!

Must close now. I've been sitting here a while and need to do a few chores before we go out to bowl in our league this evening.
All my love,
Pat

May 3, 1974
PAT'S NOTES ON MOVIEMAKING

Bob and I reported to the temporary set, a local hotel lounge, for first-day filming of *The Meal*, in which we will be extras. Running late, we dropped off David at his friend's home and rushed to the hotel – where we could then "hurry up and wait," a favorite phrase in the business, we soon discovered.

We met the producer, director, assistant director, casting person, makeup artist and assistants, wardrobe mistress, and assorted gofers. A big thrill when, alone in the corridor, I saw the fabulous Dina Merrill walking toward me. What did I do but gush

"You *are* Dina Merrill." Really, how embarrassing, but she smiled graciously and continued on her way.

The extras got extra makeup and presented quite a sight: many masked-looking faces, each framed by a high fluffy white tissue collar to protect clothing. As each extra's makeup was done the perky young assistant to the wardrobe mistress recorded in minute detail that person's attire and accessories, from the color, and whether frosted or plain nail polish, to jewelry, hair ornaments and what hue of hosiery. Of course, makeup brands and shades had already been meticulously noted. All of this in case of re-shooting scenes later.

Done to perfection and ready for stardom, we waited two hours to begin because Miss Merrill's costume didn't fit properly. But we received more coaching about lighting, our positions, the actions desired. Much of our work as extras consisted of pretending to listen to a piano player as we sipped our virgin cocktails of water-with-ice-and-slice-of-lime and smiled and chatted among ourselves. Just moving lips, though, NO sound since music and background noise would be dubbed in later.

During lunch breaks we all milled around getting better acquainted while enjoying a real meal. (During the weeks of filming, the "set meal," in the form of a huge banquet, appeared perfect on camera and perfectly gross in reality!) At noon on the first day, we met the male lead, Carl Betz, and the fine supporting actor, Mr. Leon Ames, a personal favorite of mine and a peach of a guy. Everyone was very friendly, even to us lowly extras.

The first time the whole cast and all extras had a rehearsal our group almost preened when the director said, "Extras, you look good!" This was followed by, "Let's make movies." There was a thrill along with the hint of nervousness on first hearing the familiar "QUIET – ACTION – CAMERA ROLLING." We knew it was time to look alive and animated for our debuts!

At the end of each day we signed releases and listened as the director called out our names with a hearty "Thank You!" Then we happily accepted the crisp new bills he doled out. Bob and I would quickly gather our belongings and head home, still excited and full of grease paint – which required a lot of elbow grease to remove!

The majority of the filming was done in a lovely old local mansion with all sorts of rooms into which we were herded and requested to stay. The powers-that-be didn't want us roaming all over; when they needed bodies, we were supposed to be right there, at their beck and call. As soon as we female extras saw the men's domain, and then our quarters, we considered rising up in arms like women's libbers because our dorm area was quite stripped of amenities while the men were treated to comfy sofas and television!

Numerous incidents served to lighten moods and relieve moments of tension or boredom. One scene being shot around 3 a.m. had been troublesome from the start. With a weary crew, 30 tired, restless extras, a few neighborhood dogs barking on and off at the unusual night activity in their area, and the occasional sound of a car engine or a low-flying plane, there was valid cause for frustration. Four aborted takes – the fifth nearly at a successful conclusion – and suddenly a moving object/shadow and an uncommonly loud fluttering sound interrupted the filming once again. At this, we wondered if tempers finally would blow. But after a few seconds of pregnant silence, followed only by the sound of a long sigh, there came the director's quiet plea, "Cu-u-u-t ... will ... somebody ... kill ... the ... moth?"

And the drama during another scene being filmed late one evening in the gun room. Emotions in the movie scene were intentionally volatile for the action buildup to a fight; emotions in the room were running high because it was crowded with cast and extras, actors were flubbing lines, and the filming had gone on for hours. All the tension was released unexpectedly, though, when one character, after erring in his lines numerous times, finally delivered them superbly, only to take the scripted manly swig of his drink and get a toothpick up his nose – followed by lots of sputtering!

At about 4 o'clock one morning, a couple of behind-the-scenes tricks came to light. In the quiet I kept hearing a rhythmic "psssee, psssee – psssee, psssee." As the sound became more distinct I saw the origin: a young member of the crew re-spritzing all the palm plants to make them glisten for the camera. I'd have asked for a quick spraying myself but that night we weren't supposed to look fresh. Instead, to prepare for the last party scene in the movie, when we guests/extras needed to realistically show the ill effects of the trauma surrounding the "The Meal," the call was, "MAKEUP ... *Mess up these people!*"

A few prize comments out of the many voiced by various extras: "I didn't come to be in this movie to be put in the back row." "At a real party, if I got stuck with a couple of girls and no man, I'd

336

leave." And for about the 50th time, from a prima donna to any and all, "Does my hair look all right?" "Ravishing, dear," assured a nonchalant chorus of extras lounging nearby. But my favorite was the slightly complaining-but-tinged-with-pride, "Do you think they put me in the back because I have too much bosom?"

And then finally, at the end of our three weeks in the world of movie make-believe, the three magic words – "IT'S A WRAP!"

May 7, 1974
Orlando, Florida

Dear Parent,

David is a very bright, well-adjusted little boy. He tries to think things out before speaking. He is very pleasant and adjusts to most situations immediately. He loves both indoor and outdoor activities. I have enjoyed having him in my class this year.

He also draws all the girls just like a magnet. They love him and want to sit beside him or hold his hand!

Sincerely,
Miss Peggy

May 7, 1974
Orlando, Florida

Mobile, Alabama
Dearest Mommie,

Happy Birthday and Mother's Day to the best mom ever! I sent the enclosed story to a magazine's "Out of the Mouths of Babes" section, but whether or not it's published, it will be appreciated by you and Daddy, I know! Enjoy. ...

Love you both,
Pat

The neighborhood carpool for my 4-year-old son David's nursery school class provides many amusing stories, but my favorite involves a conversation about birthdays.

One day Greg, super active and nearly always over-the-top excited, scrambled into the car shouting "Tomorrow is my birthday – AND it's Halloween!"

Right away Kathy offered that her birthday was close to Halloween, too. And Darryl, whose birthday I knew to be March 17, beamed when I reminded him that was also St. Patrick's Day.

There was a quiet moment before shy Jennifer broke her usual silence to whisper, "My birthday is December the 25th."

So pleased that she had joined in, I practically gushed, "Oh, children, did you hear? Isn't that wonderful? Jennifer has the same birthday as Jesus!"

"Jesus?" queried David in a perplexed tone as he scanned all the faces in the car. "*He's* not in our carpool."

May 9, 1974
Mobile, Alabama

Orlando, Florida
Dear Pat,

Hi to all. I read your letter yesterday Pat. You are right, it has been a long time since I saw you. I am looking forward to seeing all there.

Your Mother is out of town. I am sending a check for her birthday gift that you paid for. You may need it before I see you. If there is any change left from the check, give it to David for me. Tell him he does good school work.

Love you,
Daddy

July 23, 1974
Dear Diary,

I wish I had started this "book" long ago, but here goes. Of course, I did keep diaries in my teens, and sporadically over the years, but now I am serious about journal-keeping. Does everyone tend to put off things, I wonder? Especially fulfilling dreams? I want to write a book, a real book, but have doubts that I possess enough talent, training or self-discipline to do it. So, in the meantime, I dabble in haiku poetry, which I enjoy, and write various little articles, mostly just for myself, and always scores of letters. Recently I began the practice of Transcendental Meditation, and once in awhile an almost fully formed haiku will just pop out of the quietness. You suppose a whole *book* might pop out if I meditated long enough?

Seriously, sometimes now, in my "depressed 40s," I feel I've frittered away any bit of creativity I might've had. I know that's not the way to look at it, though. I've put my energies into family and friends – marriage, motherhood, social and community involvement. Still I have a desire to create something … but even more than that, I want to shed the destructive habit I've developed lately of regretting past events and harboring resentments. I want to find serenity and more joy about little and big parts of my life. And stop dreading getting old – wonder if that stems from my Leo nature, not wanting my "reign" to end? Maybe I ought to just create a new *me*.

Pat

July 26, 1974
Callaway Gardens
Pine Mountain, Georgia

Orlando, Florida
Daddy, dear,

Just got your letter and was kinda pleased at most of what you said. I'm glad you're glad that I'm excited about returning to school in the fall. I guess I'll work here until Labor Day, but I'd rather come home.

I was very depressed last week, much more than at any other time in my life, I think. I don't know why, except that sometimes I just feel mad at the world. I'm lucky the feelings don't last long, though, and then I'm okay again.

I've been going to the plays that are performed here at the Inn. I really enjoy them and get so caught up in the stories. I've seen four so far: *I Do! I Do! – See How They Run – Black Comedy – How to Succeed in Business Without Really Trying.*

Thank you for being so loyal, Daddy, in writing as well as in your love and your wishes for the best for me. What would I do without you?

Love,
Your Robin

August 25, 1974
Callaway Gardens
Pine Mountain, Georgia

Orlando, Florida
Dear Mom,

It's so special to get a letter from you these days. I went out to dinner after picking it up at the post office and must have read it three times.

Life has become humdrum lately. Everyone's ready to quit and go home. I've been either staying home and having gobs of people over playing

339

guitars and singing or going to the Fireside Lounge to dance and have a beer. They turned the room we ate in into a lounge and it has become the local hangout. It seems I have been elected best (or only) girl dancer in Pine Mountain, Georgia! I've mastered "The Bump" with one guy especially and am having the time of my life dancing for three hours at a time.

I must sign off now but will be *home* soon. My, does that word sound warm and inviting! I love my family so much.

Take care, Mom, I love you,
Robin

September 10, 1974
Orlando, Florida

Auburn, Alabama

Hi, Robin,

In your letter to Jenni awhile back, you told about the streakers, and we got such a kick out of the story. Well, just to let you know there are no laggards in your family. ...

First there's your brother – no, not Skip, your baby brother. The other evening we entertained new friends who hadn't yet met David. He was his usual cute, bright, relaxed self, naturally, and even as we all were enjoying him, Jen and Skip said they'd take him for a while and let us grownups visit. So we settled back with cocktails and canapés and continued our casual chatting. Suddenly we heard a slight commotion and saw the flash of a small body streaking past in the hall, through the dining room, into the living room where we were, back out across the hall, and out of sight: little David, clad only in red-and-white Keds! Sneaky Skip and Jenni planned the surprise, David performed perfectly, and all of us had such a good laugh.

Now, that was really cute, but Robin, you will be flabbergasted over the next tale! The other night Nana GeeGee called with the following "news flash" and was still so tickled she could hardly get it told.

She and Granddaddy had an impromptu gathering of assorted friends who were milling around in the kitchen and dining room having drinks and snacks, enjoying the party. Daddy suddenly had an inspired idea and decided to share it with one of the fellows and enlist his help in carrying it out. The friend's job was to create a diversion, if necessary, but primarily to make sure the pre-planned path for Daddy's daring mad dash was kept open. The way Mom told it, everybody *knew* something had taken place, they'd *seen* it, but they didn't *believe* what they'd seen: my daddy, your granddaddy – dressed only in jockey shorts and sneakers – streaking through the crowd!

She said they all were laughing so hysterically she thought the rescue squad might need to be called, in case of apoplexy, especially in some of the rowdy mid-60-year-olds. We always knew Daddy could be clever and funny. I'd say that little caper rates as the *piece de resistance*, wouldn't you? Chuckling, I wrote this haiku:

> Happy partying –
> Young and old were there
> Swoosh, streak,
> Look, one … BARELY there!
> We love you lots,
> Mom

October 10, 1974
Auburn University
Auburn, Alabama

Orlando, Florida
Dear Jen,

Hey sis! Just got your letter today and I knew I'd better write now while I was in the mood. I'm so glad to hear about the car. I'm not really jealous – just happy for you because I know you really needed one.

I'm excited about working at the art gallery during Christmas. I haven't yet decided just how much I really like school, but I believe studying and training in art is worth anything. I just love it and am so glad I decided to change my major from Home Ec.

Speaking of love, I love you so much! I miss you. Keep writing and be sure you read all my letters home even if they're not addressed to you, okay?

> Your loving sis,
> Robin

October 17, 1974
Auburn University
Auburn, Alabama

Orlando, Florida
Dear Mom and Daddy, and family,

Just got Mom's letter today and I enjoyed it tremendously! Everything's going well here. The only bad thing is that this dull social life is getting to me. There are so many gorgeous men around, but I don't know any of them.

I don't know whether I mentioned how much I love the dorm mother. She's just a doll and we're real good friends, and guess what? She's going to try to get me a desk-girl job for next quarter. She has a definite pull – and she wants me! It would pay $2 an hour for 10 to 12 hours a week. That's $20+ a week spending money. Hotcha!

My studio courses are going very well – A's in perspective drawing and B's in design. English is as dull as ever but grades are so-so. Test next week in Art History, which I plan to ACE. Wish me luck!

Dad, let me know how much I have in my account next time you write just so I'll know, okay?

I love you all,
Robin

P.S. – I've spread my-mother-the-writer's beautiful haiku "endeavors" all through the dorm. Feel proud, Pat!

October 26, 1974
Dear Diary,

I have the treat of a weekend at the beach by myself. I'm still trying to "find myself." What will I find? What the heck does that *mean*, anyway? Does it mean experiencing life to the fullest, all of it – the good and bad, joy, sorrow, guilt, excitement, boredom? I looked long at the ocean today. How endless it is, not like life. Or, *is* life endless, will my soul float about in the ether, perhaps inhabit another being when I no longer exist here on earth? I can't figure out these deep mysteries now; will I be able to when I am older? I thought I'd know everything by the time I reached this age. Now, I vacillate between thinking I'm wise and suspecting I must be the most naïve woman alive.

November 18, 1974
Auburn University
Auburn, Alabama

Orlando, Florida
Dear Daddy,

I got your letter today and was so pleased at the way you feel. I read it to a very close friend who is very much like me and has loving parents too, and she actually cried! It means more than the world to me for you to be proud of me. I hope you realize how much I love you and how much your praise means to me.

I had a big Art History test after I read your letter and it really did spur me on to make good!

All my love to my favorite Daddy!
Your eldest lil' girl, Robin

November 22, 1974
Dear Diary,

I haven't wanted (haven't felt able) to write about it, it's too unsettling and I feel sad and confused, but a lot is happening concerning our marriage. It seems to just keep slowly deteriorating. Bob and I have gone to a psychiatrist, who advised counseling with a family therapist, and during five sessions so far we've aired and explored a lot of our feelings. We know we still care about each other, and we are going to try harder, but we both are beginning to feel unsure of our future as husband and wife. *I* feel unsure about my whole self, period.

November 29, 1974
Orlando, Florida

Mobile, Alabama
Dear Mom and Pop,

Thanks for being so easy to talk to and understanding about our problems. Not all in-laws would be as supportive as you are. I do appreciate your offer of help. Pat and I will do our best to get things back on track again, a *new* track. I think you're right, a lot of our problems are the result of the changes in Pat due to "the change." And sometimes good things grow out of difficult times.

It was great to celebrate Thanksgiving with you all at the condo in New Smyrna Beach. The turkey was delicious! Take care of yourselves, and I hope to see you again soon. In the meantime, don't worry. We'll do the best we know how.

Much love,
Bob

December 20, 1974
Orlando, Florida

Mobile, Alabama
Dear Pop,

Thanks for the clippings you sent. They are interesting. Please send any others that are important.

Sorry it took so long to get this check to you. And thanks for taking care of the battery replacement in the car for Pat during the week she and David were at the beach with you.

Our "situation" sort of goes warm and cool. Pat doesn't seem to have warmed up any in her feelings toward me yet, but I keep hoping. I don't want a separation unless it just has to be.

Merry, merry Christmas to you both,
Bob

December 25, 1974
Orlando, Florida

Orlando, Florida
Merry Christmas, Mom and Dad,

You two are the nicest present anybody could ask for on Christmas. You're both just great and I love you both for being you.

I love you,
Skip

P.S. – This card entitles you to a lifetime subscription to ME!

January 1, 1975
Orlando, Florida

Mobile, Alabama,
Dear Nana GeeGee and Granddad,

#1 Grandson here. I'm just writing to let you know I'm still around and kicking. How's it going with you two? Nana, has that old man been bugging you? If he has, let me know. Haha.

Say, I've been talking to my parents about flying up to Mobile for spring vacation. How's it sound to you?

You probably know I'm saving my money to buy a car this summer. I figure I'll have around $1,400 by then. The car I want to buy costs around $1,800 to $2,000 plus the insurance, which would be about $250. If all goes well with your oil well, I may ask to borrow a little money until I can pay

344

it off, that is, if you don't mind giving up some dough temporarily. I know you wouldn't mind, Nana, but old what's-his-name might get upset. (Just kidding!)

I got my report card from school, and my semester average was 3 A's and 3 B's. I was really happy because that will help me get a scholarship for college.

Nana GeeGee, I hope you really liked my putter and I hope you're putting every green. Granddaddy, I never could find you a good Christmas present, but I've got one now and you'll get it when I see you.

I haven't been playing much golf, but I've made a resolution to really start playing so I'll be at my best to play you two, hopefully in March! I also got my hair styled and I really think you'll both like it.

I'll talk to you on the phone or write real soon. I love you both,

Skip

P.S. – You two both know when I cut you down a bit (especially Granddaddy) I don't mean any of it. I really love you both and I feel more fortunate than anyone else to have such wise, understanding, and all-around cool cats for grandparents. Hope to see you both soon!

February 9, 1975
Orlando, Florida

Auburn, Alabama
To Robin
From David
Have a nice birthday and a nice valintin's. I love you.

P.S. – Thanks for my card.

March 31, 1975
Orlando, Florida

Mobile, Alabama
Dear Nana GeeGee and Grandaddy,
Well, here I am writing just one day after I left and I already miss being around you and having fun. I stayed up last night and thought about summer school and decided to go for just three weeks instead of seven so I can visit with you at New Smyrna Beach and play lots of golf! On the plane ride home, I sat next to a college girl and talked to her about the University

of West Florida at Pensacola. I might go there or to Auburn so I can be around you.

I have some homework to do so I'd better go.

I love you both,
Skip

My joy, my grief, my hopes, my love,
did all within this circle move.
Edmund Waller

Chapter Eighteen
Leaning on Others
1975-76

David learning to swim in Orlando, Florida

April 20, 1975
Dear Diary,

Alone in New Smyrna Beach for a few days, temporarily even without my little David. Bob and I have decided to try a "creative separation" this summer, a time for each of us to reflect on how we are going to handle our ongoing unsettled situation. More often than not lately we are like two acquaintances, amiable, but emotionally removed.

I'm reading the thought-provoking book *Shifting Gears*. That title seems apropos for what I'm doing – or endeavoring to do. It is a painful process, this growing and trying to make decisions about possible huge changes in my life. I wish there were a way I could change gears without hurting anyone, just snap my fingers and have the people I love be uninvolved in all the complexities of my "identity crisis." Often I am so confused I actually feel physically ill. And sometimes I wish for a small peek into the future to see if I am going to come through this still intact and sane – and more open to life with all its joys *and* stresses.

Pat

May 8, 1975
Woodbury, Connecticut

Orlando, Florida
Pat dear,

While feeling nostalgic – as I reach 65 tomorrow – and going through my file of "treasures" tonight, I came across the first letter you ever wrote to me. Since I couldn't part with it for the world, I decided I'd make a copy at school tomorrow and send it to you. Thought you might treasure it, too.

I just can't afford copies of all the letters I've saved from Bob since year one and from Robin, from then to now. (I just finished writing to her.) Wish you could travel to Woodbury sometime and review the past with me.

Much love,
Auntie Bussie

May 17, 1975
Auburn University
Auburn, Alabama

Orlando, Florida

Dearest Mom,

It only took two days for me to get your letter – record time! I always feel so close to you when I read your letters. I know they are from the heart.

I sent a birthday card and note to Auntie Bussie, and yesterday got a long letter from her. She is so sweet. The letter was very encouraging to me as far as setting my future goals and working hard for what I want. My immediate goal is to do well on final exams and leave here to come home the first week in June.

I won't go into it much in a letter, Mom, but I hope we can really "get to know each other" this summer and in the coming months. I so much want to help you over this crisis, and I don't really know what I can do except be there when you need me. I want to, and hope we can establish a closeness like we've never had before. I plan to spend as much time in New Smyrna with you as possible.

Uncle Rickey was here this week and we went out for dinner and a drink. He's going to see you this weekend – I'm sure he'll tell you all about it. He's sure a good guy!

I'd better go now. I love you, Mom, and think of you constantly.

Your big girl,
Robin

May 17, 1975
Auburn University
Auburn, Alabama

Orlando, Florida

Dear David,

Hi! Thank you very much for the lovely picture you made for me. I put it on my wall with all the other pictures you've sent. My friends think you are a very sweet boy for sending Robin so many pretty pictures.

I'll be home soon now, and I can't wait to see my David. You can mark on your calendar that you'll see me before June 5.

Be an extra good boy for Mom, and have lots of fun over at Chateau-by-the-Sea.

I love you oodles and oodles.

Your big sister,
Robin

June 1975

daddy,

i love you so much becaus your my daddy. happy fathers day!

love,

david

June 25, 1975
Maitland, Florida

New Smyrna Beach, Florida
Dear Pat,

Enjoyed so much seeing you Monday, but I'm afraid that night was a sleepless one with my brain insisting on pondering. And this time, since you have asked for my opinions, I am writing down my thoughts.

My dear sister-in-law, I am both troubled and disturbed that you don't feel a close relationship with Christ and God. I feel strongly this is the key to all your unhappiness – your puzzlement about who you are in your marriage and family. "All things are possible to those that love and trust the Lord." Read 1st Corinthians Chapter 13. Yes, that is an order!

Sometimes I felt you were saying what you thought I wanted to hear, really what you wanted to hear, but your real self was missing. I noticed this when you talked about the children. They don't need you as a pal yet. They need a mother – not always the most fun, I know. I question why you feel your life at home is so unhappy.

"Actions speak so loud I can't hear what you say," courtesy of ye ol' philosopher and oh so true. Children are a tremendous responsibility, the most important job entrusted by God, and it falls very squarely on a mother's shoulders.

So Pat, be careful with your priorities. Be careful that real happiness isn't right under your nose. To me you are basically a giving person. Don't stifle a natural ability to love and trust. It will come back a thousand-fold.

I just reread this and am tempted not to send it. I just don't know if it can be of help. I pray so. It's not meant to criticize.

But I pray the Lord will speak to you as you read – and then if you want we can talk again.

Love,
Dorothy

June 27, 1975
Callaway Gardens
Pine Mountain, Georgia

Orlando, Florida
Dearest Daddy,

The mix-up with the bank was caused by a check I didn't record, but I'm really only $5 overdrawn. I get my paycheck tomorrow and will send it to the bank in Auburn. I hope this teaches me once and for all to pay close attention to my account!

There've been some changes in the living arrangements here. I have a new roommate and am much happier.

My friend Dan wrote me another letter, which boosts my spirits – he wants me to visit him. The best thing is, he knows I'm not ready for a physical relationship and says he really respects and would never take advantage of me. Aren't you pleased at my choice in men?!

Daddy, I'm so proud of you. I love you so much and want the best for you just as you want it for me. I almost cried when I read in your letter that you do realize I have my own attitudes and ideals in life. It made me feel so good, thank you for saying that.

Give my warmest love to the family. And I send special love to my prestigious and handsome daddy!

Robin

July 7, 1975
Dear Diary,

David and I have been in New Smyrna nearly two months and were joined by Mommie and Daddy three weeks ago. Bob, Jenni and Skip have come over a few times, and other family members have visited. Sam and Rickey were here four days, Griff stayed two weeks (he's 11 now, delightful, adored by all), and cousin Katie drove down from Savannah for the Fourth of July holiday weekend. She has gone through a terrible divorce involving betrayal and much heartbreak – our hearts ache for her.

July 9, 1975
Dear Diary,

Mom and I met the loveliest, most enchanting young woman. On our way back to the condo the other evening from an errand in New Smyrna, we decided (well, Mom decided!) that we should stop by the lounge in the hotel on the beach and have ourselves a little drink. Daddy was home with David, we figured thoroughly enjoying each other. And Daddy always wants Mom to go and do as she pleases – just don't make him go along! Anyhow, Terri and Ernie are the entertainers at the club: Terri sings and he plays the organ and sings. They're Filipinos, so attractive and talented, and on stage they appear to be having the time of their lives. Terri looks like a little doll, a miniature person, really. At the break, having already noticed her impossibly high-heeled shoes, I asked, "*How* tall are you, really? And that was the start of our getting to know each other.

We introduced ourselves, she sat down at our table, and we three had a nice visit. Before we said goodbye Mom and I invited her to come to the condo sometime and meet Daddy and have a good homestyle Southern meal. I hope she will. There's just something so appealing about her. ...

July 13, 1975
Dear Diary,

Various Orlando friends vacationing in New Smyrna Beach often invite David to visit with them, so I have plenty of uninterrupted time to try and sort out my confusion. I walk miles on the beach, my tears mingling with the salty sea, feeling as if I'm drowning in them and in the awful uncertainty plaguing me. I see the ocean, so vast and eternal, and think how small and transient I am, wonder how important am I in the overall "plan."

Back and forth, pro and con ... how to decide on the next step, if and when to take a next step? I can't explain, I don't even know exactly what's wrong. Why I feel like whoever I was originally has disappeared – and in her place has surfaced someone who looks the same and for the most part acts the same but is a kind of stranger to me. I'm keenly aware of the wonderful blessings in my life – and so guilt-ridden that despite all the good things, still, deep down inside I feel lost and alone and unhappy.

July 14, 1975
New Smyrna Beach, Florida

Mobile, Alabama
Dearest Folks,

It was one of those gorgeous, sparkly days here at the beach, prompting David's breakfast blessing: "The sun rising over the ocean is beautiful. The morning is so pretty." No matter what goes on, he is a constant bright spot. … He *really* loves being at the beach.

We've missed you since you went back to Alabama. David talks about both of you often. I know I'm lucky to have this cozy condo available to retreat to this summer. (The manager is very optimistic about winter rental prospects, Daddy, so it should prove to be a good investment for y'all, although I know you prefer owning real estate closer to home.) This is a tough time for me and for all the family. As always you two are such loving listeners and staunch supporters, and I thank you.

I know you'll enjoy being perked up by some recent "David-isms." His cute, funny comments continue to surprise and delight. Nowadays they're apt to be centered around his main curiosity, the reproduction process. Oh yeah … and so he and I have had a little "birds and bees" talk. I attempted to go from A to Z in fairly brief, simple terms and he quickly summed up the whole sex subject pretty well and to his complete satisfaction. After just a few thoughtful moments he exclaimed, with a hint of relief, "Mom, I *sure* am glad you had *four* eggs! If you only had three you wouldn't know *me*!"

Ever since you and he observed the two birds on the wire, Daddy, he is even more interested in the concept of mating. David retells the story: "Granddaddy told me to watch the birds bill and coo, that's when they kiss with their beaks. So I looked and looked, and then I saw one bird just hop on top of the other bird. They mated!" Following that incident, and keeping his interest piqued, he discovered two lizards on the balcony ledge, mating – so vigorously in fact they soon fell off! Dismayed, he tore down the three flights of stairs to check on whether they'd stayed together. Of course, they hadn't, and he couldn't find them, and he came back up with such a sad little face.

When Bob came over for the weekend, things were about half and half, good and not-quite-so-good between us. We both agree it's important to keep at least some connection between us during this period – we aren't sure how things are going to turn out eventually. Neither of us is ready yet to make any kind of final decision, or to stay completely apart and not see each other. And the plan, we know, is that I will be going back home in a few weeks. Anyhow, right away little David intended to get the situation straight in his mind and, greeting Bob with a big hug, he asked, "Where you gonna sleep, Daddy?" Bob's clever response, "Wherever Mommy tells me to, David."

And … Bob and I did share the big bed and were cuddled in sleep Sunday morning when David came in to wake me for his breakfast. Later in the kitchen, between bites of cereal, he enthusiastically shared this tidbit on his favorite fascinating subject: "*Well*, Mommy, I thought you and Daddy were *mating*!" To which Bob muttered, "No such luck, boy." A really funny, light moment that both cleared *and* cheered the air.

I'll sign off tonight but write a few more lines tomorrow before the postman picks up outgoing mail.

(10:30 a.m.) As David said, "Today we first watched 'the Russia's' space shot!" Then we walked two miles along the ocean, he in the shallow water and I in the cool, soft sand, waving to each other every minute or so. On the way back I got hit with a wayward Frisbee. It startled me, and smarted, but luckily just glanced off my sunglasses, leaving only a red mark on the cheek.

Bob reported that the kids are fine in Orlando, working hard. Jenni made a 98 on her first chemistry exam, and Skip an A on his first half of summer school American History.

Thank you both again for your help in so many ways this summer. I send much love to very wonderful parents. A big hug from David.

Pat

P.S. – David and I plan to watch the launch of *Apollo* from Cape Kennedy at 3:50 today. It will be exciting to view it from here, a clear shot straight down the beach.

August 4, 1975
New Smyrna Beach, Florida

Mobile, Alabama
Dearest Folks,

I hope you received the gift I arranged to have sent from Jordan Marsh in Orlando. It's for your anniversary but please open it whenever it's most convenient, depending on your plans and where you'll be on August 15.

Jenni and two girlfriends arrived at 11:30 Saturday night, stayed an hour and then went to The Islander hotel to spend the night with two more friends. They came back here the next morning for sunning and swimming, and I fixed a spaghetti dinner for all of us at 3 p.m. before they headed back to Orlando.

I sent a note by Jenni to let Bob know I miss him. ... I'm going to give my best efforts to "a new start" this weekend when he comes over again. I'll work on convincing myself it's going to be a good time together, that even though I might find it hard to soon go back to the hectic routine of regular home life, I'll do my best. Wish me (us) luck.

Take care. We love you ever so dearly. And, again, thank you many times over for all you've done for me this summer. David sends hugs and kisses to you both. ...

Pat

P.S. – One evening David and I went to the Islander for an early light supper and to enjoy the music and see our lil' Terri-doll. He was so cute, wanted to dance, and we did. Terri sent her love to "Mama and Papa Gee" – said to tell y'all she'd cook you some "cabbeege" the Filipino way the next time you come down!

October 13, 1975
Orlando, Florida

University of Central Florida
Orlando, Florida
Dear Madam,

Recently I became interested in the Japanese haiku form of poetry. I've found that once aware of haiku, it can almost become a way of life, with the tiniest sight or experience opening the mind to the idea of a poem.

Each 17-syllable haiku specifies or intimates a season, evokes some kind of emotion, and by the power of suggestion depicts a scene – possibly a different one for each reader.

I have spent many enjoyable, sometimes painful, moments creating poems, and am enclosing a few for consideration in the Florida State Poets Association contest.

Sincerely,
Pat, aspiring poetess

"In the beginning ..."
creation, faith,
wonder, love –
lesson for today

Tangled seaweed, tossed
ashore, freed by
autumn's storm – a
prisoner still

Joy abounds, sorrow
lurks ...walking the beach
recollecting
secret dreams

Swinging hand-in-hand
with springtime,
young lovers
immune to heaven's tears

Butterflies flitting
around the
lovely lily –
wedding festival!

Ethereal froth –
Angels? Whitecaps
in heaven?
Blending sea and sky

Sand – soft, cool, inviting
toes wiggling down deep –
balmy beach-bumming day!

Tilted gold canoe
adrift on a
midnight sea –
silent crescent moon

Behold:
nature's palette –
breathtaking, lifegiving
glorious sunrise!

November 1, 1975
Orlando, Florida

Orlando, Florida
Dear Pat,

Haiku is a very special category, and the contest is for lyrics. Maybe someday we can sponsor a haiku contest. Your lovely haikus certainly prove you a poetess.

Sincerely,
Florida State Poets Association

November 10, 1975
Dear Diary,

Days go by, weeks pass, an ingrained family routine is adhered to – eat, sleep, school, work, play. Bob and I, agreeing there'll be no big decision made about separation or divorce for the time being, have unwittingly become established in our own unwritten "couple code," according to which we are pleasant to each other, show interest in daily doings, manage children and household affairs as a team … and avoid true intimacy and in-depth discussions about our future. Honestly, I think we are just so tired of continually trying to "work things out" and now are reluctant to release the feelings of relief at this kind of reprieve. So, we'll continue as we are now until such time as it ceases to be the answer. Then, who knows?

November 12, 1975
Wayne, New Jersey

Orlando, Florida
Dear Pat,

I was very happy to hear from you. Think about you lots and miss you, and wish you weren't so far away. It is strange how some paths are meant to cross, as ours did during that week we were both staying at the same apartment complex in New Smyrna Beach. Meeting a true and beautiful human being like you means a great deal to me. And even if we shouldn't see each other again, I know we shared a special connection.

Hang in there, Pat. Life is not simple these days. It seems we all have to put forth so much extra time and effort regardless of the task or situation. I am an optimist and I *know* you are going to make it.

How is David, and the rest of the family? Please give that sweet little guy a hug and kiss from me. Take care and have a happy Thanksgiving.

Love,
Bette

357

November 20, 1975
Mobile, Alabama

Orlando, Florida
Hi, Pat and Bob and children,

A little card to say Happy Thanksgiving! And pass on this funny line of your daddy's. When the air conditioner broke last week in the middle of a real hot spell, I called the repairman. Dad said, "Sugar, did you tell him to hurry up and come fix it so we can turn it off for the energy crisis?" Sounds just like him, don't it?

We love you and are thankful for all of you.

Mom

February 17, 1976
Orlando, Florida

Mobile, Alabama
Dearest Folks,

I'm in a hurry, as usual, but would like to mail this today so I'm going to rush through my note. I'm sending these snapshots and the folder with Skip's picture for you to see. If you will, please send everything on to Robin. If you want any of the pictures, just mark on the back and I'll have reprints made.

David took your birthday gift of $5 plus $5 from Auntie and bought a Holiday Inn – no, not a real one (we wish, huh?) but the cutest toy version. He sends his very own thank-you note, too. Oh, he came out with this thank-you prayer the other night:

> Thank You for the flowers
> Thank You for the bees
> Thank You for Christmas
> Thank You for trees – Amen
> Thank You for birds
> Thank You for bees
> Thank You for us
> Thank You for the bus – Amen

After the second Amen, his eyes flew open, and with a giggle and just a hint of surprise, he whispered, "Rhyming turns me on!"

Thank goodness Skip feels so much better and is almost back to his regular routine. He is still taking cortisone, on that crazy, confusing tapering-off schedule. The doctor warned of possible bad headaches while

358

"coming down" off the cortisone, and Skip has had them. He had a physical exam this week and is to have another in March to check his spleen, the organ most apt to be damaged by mononucleosis. You know, it's usually referred to as "the kissing disease" with humorous comments, but it is a serious illness, and ol' sweet Skip can tell you there's nothing funny about it. He was really *sick*.

Bob drove Jenni to St. Petersburg yesterday for her personal interview with the doctor who is head of the dental hygiene school. They said he was the greatest guy and spent lots of time with them. St. Pete is fourth out of 155 schools in the country, and there are 800 applicants for 34 spaces! Jenni likes Palm Beach Junior College, too, and I feel sure she'll get into one of them. Will write more soon. So much love to you dear ones!

Pat and gang

March 29, 1976
TO: NaNa GeEGEe
I MISS YOU   I WISH I COULD SEE YOU   I LOVE YOU
THANK YOU FOR THE MONEY
LOVE, DAVID

March 29, 1976
TO ROBIN
I MISS YOU.   I WISH I COULD SEE YOU   I LOVE YOU
LOVE, DAVID

April 1, 1976
Auburn University
Auburn, Alabama

Orlando, Florida
Dear Mom and Dad,

Got your letter today, Mom, and David's note was so cute. Tell him "I love you and miss you."

Daddy, if you have time, please try to write me a note. I miss your letters with news and compliments! Okay?

Love to all,
Robin

P.S. – Thank you for your prayers, Mom. I really noticed a difference in my attitude since our talk. I've been praying for you, too.

April 10, 1976
Auburn University
Auburn, Alabama

Orlando, Florida
Dear Mom,

I really like oil painting and seem to be doing fine at my first few attempts. Wish me further luck! I've been thinking of you and hoping all is well (emotionally, especially). This may sound strange, but I'll be here whenever you might need me. You're a very special lady – do you know that?

Much, much love,
Your very own oldest daughter
Robin

May 2, 1976
Orlando, Florida

Auburn, Alabama
Dear Robin,

Thanks so much for that good letter of explanation after talking with your dean. I think I understand pretty well now what you have to accomplish from here on. As your dad, I feel your letter was well written, clear and very mature, and I'm proud of you.

As I said on the phone, Robin, I feel strongly there is nothing very much more important to me right now than for you to have the opportunity to complete college successfully. How about if you and I make a deal? You do the school work as well as you can. Do the best job possible from now until graduation. Don't worry about outside jobs unless you can definitely do it without interfering with your studies, and don't feel guilty about not providing money yourself. That's your part of the deal, besides continuing to keep your head on straight and maturing the way you have, and going on being the daughter we can be proud of.

My part of the deal is to provide the dollars needed from now until graduation. Also the best guidance and support I can offer. Is that a deal? Together, we can finish strong.

Finally, I would like to help you get your first car next summer, a new or relatively new one, with me making a substantial down payment and you making the monthly payments thereafter.

Enclosed is a check for $100. You'll have to keep me posted in advance of your need, okay? Try to give me an idea of your total costs for the summer.

Take care of Robin, and know that we love you very much.

Dad

Auburn, Alabama

Dearest Robin,

I loved my Mother's Day card. I saw the same one and almost got it for *my* mom! So enjoyed your note to me, and then your sweet letter to Dad, which came today. Jenni and I had read Dad's letter to you before he mailed it and we both said, "Robin will cry when she gets this letter!" I thought it was a good letter, and, as you said, really from his heart. So you do as he suggested and get through school well, happily and guilt-free.

Dad and I had a meeting with the minister in Maitland last week, with another scheduled for next week. Our problems are far from solved, and I guess we still don't know what the outcome will be, but we are usually cheerful with each other these days.

The most exciting news is about David. He has had six swimming lessons and is just like a fish, under the water more than on top of it. The first day he fussed slightly but the next he rushed in saying, "Omigosh, I can't believe myself!" Other recent funny comments: "Jen, you know, dental hygienists take care of me. They're so pretty. But in bed you don't look that pretty." And when she accidentally sat down too close to him, this calmly delivered admonishment, "Jen, you squished the hell out of me."

Jenni received a list of available apartments and possible future classmates from Palm Beach Junior College this week and is really excited. Skip and a date went to the prom the Saturday evening before we came home from the beach – we were sorry to miss seeing that handsome guy in his ruffled shirt and white tux with tails.

Must run now. I'm sleepy, can't think straight. Take care, we all send lots of love.

Mom and the gang

June 10, 1976
Orlando, Florida

Woodbury, Connecticut

Dearest Mother Kitty and Dad,

Today was a big day for Skip. He bought a car. He and his dad had our mechanic friend check it over really well and decided it was okay. It's a brown 1973 Capri with 23,000 miles. He has worked hard for the money and this is his purchase alone.

Instead of selling or trading both Pontiacs, Jenni is going to use one and we'll let Robin, who's home this week for summer break, take one back to Auburn. She got a ride to Orlando at the last possible moment, but the guys turned out to be undependable and really messed her up about going back – one of the reasons we decided to let her use the other old Pontiac for a while.

I wish y'all could see Robin. She looks stunning! She'll be home again for two or three weeks in late August. In fact, that break is going to be just right for our trip to Bob's 25th reunion in Annapolis. David will have started first grade and Skip will be in school and at his job, and Robin's going to be the mama while we're away. She'll need to be prepared for handling *any* situation, but we don't worry – she can.

Here's the latest funny incident with David. But some background first. During a bath one night David mentioned how big he is getting to be now, but that he probably had been very little when he was in my tummy. He wanted to hear "the egg story" again, then asked if *all* little girls had eggs. I explained that when girls are older, maybe teenagers, their bodies begin to produce and release eggs but the girls usually wait until they're all grown up and married before they have babies from the eggs. Not many days after the conversation we were in the car – Skip and his shy, quiet girlfriend, too – and David suddenly proclaimed in a most serious tone, "Well, Nancy, I guess you are gonna get *pregnant*." Our mouths were agape, and the poor teenagers aghast and sputtering. But even as Nancy feebly protested, David stressed, "*Oh yes,* you are, cause God made you that way, with *eggs*!"

Would you mind saving my letters to return to me? Thanks in advance. I don't write my folks much these days because they've been calling more often, so I've lost my chain of letters, which serves as a partial diary. Mom has saved all my letters for more than 20 years!

Take care. Love to you both from all of us here.

Pat

June 14, 1976
Orlando, Florida

Auburn, Alabama
Hi, girl-with-a-car!

Robin, we certainly did enjoy having you home last week. You really do have a sunny disposition and are easy to get along with – and very nice!

Need I say again – heck, why not? – how beautiful we all thought you looked? Simply stunning! I'm glad everything went so smoothly during your visit and am just delighted you are able to have a car at last.

Love,

Mom

Hi, gal,

Sure loved seeing you last week. I'll write you soon, but I wanted to remind you to keep a check on the following:

Water in radiator – check when engine cold – fill to arrow on side of radiator.

Oil – should be between "add" and "full."

Battery – water levels to neck rings at bottom of necks.

Tires – keep inflated to 28 inches when cool.

It's a good idea to check them all except tires once a week – especially now after a long trip.

I love you,

Dad

July 12, 1976

Orlando, Florida

Woodbury, Connecticut

Dear Mother Kitty and Dad,

Three of us have the sore throat-cold virus right now (Bob and Skip are free of signs as yet), and I'm so mad because this is my high school reunion week. Skip and I plan to leave early Wednesday, drive to Tallahassee for a late lunch with my brother Rickey, and arrive in Mobile that evening.

The reunion festivities take place Friday evening, Saturday and Saturday night, and naturally I would like to feel and *look* great! This is the first Murphy High School Class of 1949 reunion, 27 years after graduation. Don't you know it will be fascinating to see classmates who've metamorphosed from teenagers to mid-lifers?

We'll probably go to see Robin at Auburn on Tuesday the 20th and head home the following day. Then Bob and I can look forward to his reunion in Annapolis.

Before I forget, Mother Kitty, could you advise me on the type of dresses I should have for the festivities at the Naval Academy, especially the main

363

formal dinner dance? How dressy are the banquets? You two have attended many reunions, but this is our *first*.

Love from all of us,
Pat

July 15, 1976
Mobile, Alabama

Orlando, Florida
My dear David,

Skip and I had a fine trip yesterday. We got to your Uncle Rickey's house at 12:30 and had a delicious lunch. We left there at 2:15 and arrived at Nana GeeGee and Granddaddy's house at 6 o'clock.

Nana and Granddaddy have been sick but feel better now. Granddaddy asked me to send you this dollar bill and tell you he will give you some allowance when he is with you at the beach.

Guess what? Nana bought a beautiful new car. Skip drove it home today. It is a light silver-colored Pontiac with dark red floors and white seats. Wow, it looks like a Cadillac!

Skip and I miss you and Dad and Jenni. Be a good boy, and all of you have a nice week. We'll see you soon. We send lots of love, and Nana and Granddaddy do, too.

Mommy

July 18, 1976
Starkville, Mississippi

Woodbury, Connecticut
Mother Kitty and Dad,

Hi from a pretty spot in Starkville, Mississippi. I'm sitting on the deck of my brother John and Kathie's house enjoying the beauty of the woods and the music of birds.

Skip and I had a fine trip to Alabama. We stopped to have lunch with Rickey in Tallahassee and had a good visit with my parents in Mobile. Tomorrow we'll go back to Mobile by way of Stonewall and Quitman, where we'll see Mississippi kin and friends.

I *loved* everything connected with the 27th Murphy High School reunion. It was as great as I'd hoped it would be, and even more fun than I could've imagined. The most amazing thing of all, I think, was seeing people I actually remembered quite well from 1949 now with gray hair and grandkids! Of the many good stories from the reunion, one of the best was

364

recognizing two guys who had been through school with me from the fifth grade on – and our mutual delight at rediscovering each other. Charlie must have exclaimed "Patsy! Patsy! Patsy!" at least 100 times Friday evening, and his jolly, spontaneous delivery each time seemed to tickle everyone within earshot. Oh, such fun, and the sweet memories will linger with me.

Now, in addition to battling a sore throat, I'm tired and need to rest a day before we go on to Auburn to see Robin, meet her roommate and tour the campus. We plan to drive back to Orlando on Thursday. I haven't traveled so much in years. Skip is missing his girlfriend but probably can hold out a few more days.

I called home today, and Jen said all's well and that David has been so good. She told me his latest prayer, which I'll quote at the end. What a treasure that little guy is.

Hope you're well and happy. Take care.

Love,

Pat

By David
> Thank You for night
> Thank You for day
> *And*
> Thank You for the day
> That is far away.
> Thank You for the food we're eatin'
> Thank You for our money
> Thank You for the happy day we had.

July 28, 1976
Orlando, Florida

Woodbury, Connecticut
Dear Mother Kitty and Dad,

Hi from home – Skip and I returned late last Thursday and have been busy adjusting to our work routines.

On the last leg of our trip, before the full day's drive home to Orlando, Robin took us on a tour of Auburn's campus. The highlight for us, of course, was seeing Robin's watercolors hanging in a huge painting studio! Afterward we had lunch, and then enjoyed shopping for small gifts for Jenni and David.

The girls' apartment seemed entirely too small for four, so Skip and I stayed at a nearby motel, where Robin, her roommate and a few other friends dropped in to visit with us during the evening. The next morning Robin met us for breakfast before we left. She does love Auburn and her art! Let's hope Jenni will be as happy in her dental hygiene studies at Palm Beach Junior College. She starts in about 10 days.

Love from all,
Pat

August 5, 1976
Mobile, Alabama

New Smyrna Beach, Florida

Dear David,

I hear you are at our apartment at the Chateau for two weeks. I will depend on you to take care of everything, such as taking out the garbage and picking up your toys so no one will trip over them and fall. Enclosed is your pay for two weeks. Have a good stay. Tell all hello from me and Nana GeeGee.

Love,
Granddaddy

Change is the only evidence of life.
Evelyn Waugh

Chapter Nineteen
New Launches
1976-77

Pat, Wilba and Skip at high school graduation

August 9, 1976
Palm Beach Junior College
Lake Worth, Florida

Orlando, Florida

Dear Mom and Dad,

I wanted to write you this little note to say thank you for all you've done, especially for helping me get organized and move down here. Thank you also for your support, both financially and psychologically. I'm sorry, I know a lot of the time I'm moody and uncooperative. I don't know what makes me that way. But I really appreciate all your help. And I am *really* glad and proud to have parents like you.

Well, I've lived in this town almost two days, and it's gonna take a lot more getting used to. The kitchen in the apartment is real cute but unfortunately there are little ants that get all over everywhere if a teeny crumb is left out. Yuck! And the water has sulfur in it. It stinks! I'll never get used to it. I'm having trouble sleeping, too, because it's a strange bed and all. Oh well, I'll have to go around school with dark circles for a while.

I opened my checking account today at the bank down the street. My checks will be here in about a week.

Give David a kiss for me!

Love to you all,
Jenni

August 16, 1976
New Smyrna Beach, Florida

Lake Worth, Florida

Dearest second-born-who-has-flown-the-nest!

I can't get used to that yet, Jenni, especially since I came to Nana GeeGee and Granddaddy's beach condo after you left and haven't been at home with a regular schedule. It'll be October before I realize how different life will be with our two daughters gone. Until then, there's the beach, Dad's and my trip to Annapolis, Robin's visit home, Labor Day, and your visits home. Your dad is tentatively planning to go to Connecticut for a few days in early October, so still no regular routine, even then.

I've thought about you so much, hoping everything is going along smoothly. Now, tomorrow's the big day when your classes begin, and I'm sure you'll be happier when you're well into the school swing. I understand how last week could've been a bit boring for you.

The card and sweet note really pleased us, Jenni. It seems that young people do feel differently about their parents as soon as they leave home.

As you grow older, you'll find yourself feeling even more of that and understanding your parents better, too. It's all in the process of LIFE, sweetie!

Take care, and have a good week! David and I send love and kisses.

Mom

August 16, 1976
New Smyrna Beach, Florida

Auburn, Alabama

Dear Robin,

Well, I just wrote the first letter to the second daughter who has gone away to college. Oh my gracious, do you realize that now and in the coming years I'll need to write even more letters than before?

Thanks for writing to me here, honey. It was fun to receive notes from both you and Jenni on Friday. While I'm here to do some deep and serious thinking, with no car or telephone, I feel more out of touch with everyone, but it has been okay. Last week I read Catherine Marshall's book *Beyond Ourselves*, about her search for faith, and it really helped. Her words inspired me to not give up on myself but to keep trying to seek guidance from God in all matters large and small.

Your dad was here for the weekend and we did some planning for our trip north September 9-19. We'll attend the reunion at Annapolis and then drive up to New Jersey to spend a few days with old friends Ruth and Jack. After we leave there and head back home we'll stop to see Shirl and Bill in Wilmington, Delaware, your Uncle Sam and cousin Griff in Chapel Hill and dear cousin Katie in Savannah. Will you mind being the substitute mommy for that long? We hope to visit with you some before we leave, so hurry home as soon as classes are over.

The first week back in Orlando after this beach stay will be a really busy time, getting everything ready for launching both our high school senior and our first-grader! David sends a kiss and a hug to his Robin. And we send you lots of love.

Mom

369

August 24, 1976
Palm Beach Junior College
Lake Worth, Florida

Orlando, Florida
Dear Mom and Dad,

I finally got back here Sunday night, but wait till you hear what happened. I was told at the bus station in Orlando that I'd get to Palm Beach at 10 o'clock. But the bus arrived at 8:55. I was the only one who got off, and the station was empty. It closed at 9, so I had to wait outside till the girls got here from our apartment in Lake Worth, a half-hour drive away.

This part of town was deserted and I was pretty scared. I got in a phone booth and pretended to talk on the phone until Kathy and Carrie got here. Then, after we got all the way home, I realized I had left my makeup bag in the phone booth. So back we went, another hour of driving.

In clinic yesterday, we started working with our dental instruments. Everything has to be just perfect and it's really hard. But everyone is helping everyone else, so it works out OK. We have tests or quizzes almost every day and all the instructors are PICKY. We have to know EVERYTHING. So all we do is study, study, study.

Dad, you will be interested in seeing my sketch pad. We are doing tooth drawings. They have to be shaded and not more than 1 millimeter off in measurement. I'll be sure to bring it home and let you see my artwork.

I'm doing fine on money. I have about $275 in the checking account and no big expenses expected. So is that good news, or is that good news?

Thanks for your letter, Mom. Just keep those cards and letters coming.

Well, I need to go to bed now. I'm pooped. Give David a big hug for me. Mom, I hope you had a happy birthday yesterday.

Love to you all,
Jenni

August 29, 1976
Palm Beach Junior College
Lake Worth, Florida

Orlando, Florida
Dear David,

Hi! Have you started first grade yet? Mom said you can't wait to learn to read "kerchief" writing! My school is hard, but it is fun. Do you miss me? I miss you a lot. When I come home I want to look at your teeth. In two years I will clean them for you. I am coming home Friday so I will see you then. Have a kiss and a hug ready for me.

I love you,
Jenni

September 5, 1976
Orlando, Florida

Woodbury, Connecticut

Hello, Mother Kitty and Dad,

Seems so long since I wrote, will you please forgive me? First, a big thank-you for the set of John Jakes novels for my birthday. I look forward to indulging in some good reading soon.

As you can guess, we are getting more and more excited about our trip. I am as tickled over Bob's 25th Naval Academy reunion as I was over my 27th at Murphy High! This is definitely our year of reunions. We plan to leave here early Thursday – what a great trip it promises to be!

I still haven't figured out what to wear for the formal dinner dance – although more of a worry now than clothes is my *skin*. My summer tan is fading, skin is shedding in uneven layers, and I'm looking a little leopard-like. Have been oiling myself like mad, hoping to get rid of the dead skin and smooth out what's left. After each application I carry an old sheet around to wrap myself in to protect the furniture – what a mess!

Skip has started back to school and also has a full work schedule, but took a couple of days off for a Labor Day spree at the beach. He and a friend stopped in last night after work before driving to New Smyrna. I gave them a full spaghetti supper at 10:45! Skip was exhausted – me, too – but he never presses me about meals. He is so good in every way and enjoys food so much that I like to fix meals for him no matter the time of day or night.

Jenni is home for the weekend, looking pretty as a picture! Everything is going just fine for her. She rattles off big medical words and is so excited about the dental hygiene course. She loves checking David's teeth – and he's a perfect little practice patient. Oh, she needs 14 particular types of extracted teeth for the course, so I've gone with my jar of alcohol to track down an oral surgeon who's willing to save them for her. (That particular chore is a new one on my "to do" list!)

Much love from us to you,
Pat

September 9, 1976
Fayetteville, North Carolina

Orlando, Florida

Hi, Davey – and Robin and Skip,

We had a pleasant 530-mile trip to the motel shown on this postcard. Got fish for supper, walked around for exercise, and now are going to bed soon. Hope you had a good day at school today, David. We think of all of you, miss you, and love you very much!

Mommy and Daddy

September 9, 1976
Fayetteville, North Carolina

Lake Worth, Florida

Hi, Jen,

We're here after a pretty easy 530-mile drive today, with about 350 more to go. We're really excited about all the reunion festivities and seeing old friends. Enjoyed you and your roommates a lot during the Labor Day visit home, Jenni. Y'all were so darned cute as you left Monday. We kept chuckling all evening. Keep having fun and doing good work. Good luck with your plants!

Love to you and your "roomies,"
Mom and Dad

September 14, 1976
Cherry Hill, New Jersey

Orlando, Florida

Dearest David, Robin and Skip,

Aren't the young cadets pictured on this Annapolis postcard handsome? You know, Skip, we used to wonder if you might follow in your granddad and dad's Naval Academy footsteps (sealegs!).

I'm writing this while at Ruth and Jack's. What fun to see them and John and Barbara again. We've told them all about y'all, naturally. You'd love their dog, Ginger – so cute, thinks she is a person!

We still have more friends and some kinfolk to see and miles to drive but will be home soon. We love you!

Mom and Dad

September 15, 1976
Cherry Hill, New Jersey

Woodbury, Connecticut
Hi, Mother Kitty and Dad,

We are at Ruth and Jack's home and, to quote Lawrence Welk, having a "wunnerful, wunnerful" time catching up with these dearest old friends. The 25th reunion in Annapolis was such fun. I don't recall Bob ever being more excited and talkative! And no surprise, just as I had predicted he won the prize for being the youngest-looking classmate of the class of 1951. There are so many stories to tell you about the comments on his youthful appearance. *I* was feeling older by the minute! Of course, seeing and having lots of good visiting time with old friend Al and his lovely wife Sarah was a highlight of the weekend.

A telephone call to Orlando reassured us that all was AOK there. Robin said little David has been so good she's accomplishing all sorts of extra chores, and sweet Skip is working hard in his regular routine.

Later today we'll be on our way to Wilmington for an eagerly anticipated brief reunion with Shirl and Bill. I called on Shirley back when I was a Welcome Wagon Hostess and our families became instant friends, but they soon moved back to Delaware and we haven't seen each other in nine years. After that stop it's on to Chapel Hill, then Savannah, and home Saturday. I must say, having been so royally wined and dined everywhere, we're afraid we'll soon resemble blimps!

Much love,
Pat

September 24, 1976
Auburn University
Auburn, Alabama

Orlando, Florida
Dearest Mom,

Good news! I got a job working at the Holiday Inn as a cocktail waitress. Not exactly what I wanted but at least it's money, huh? I'll be working two or three weeknights and sometimes weekends from about 7 at night till 1:30 in the morning. I got my schedule worked out perfectly and should have plenty of time to take care of school work, so don't worry about that. I'm so glad I'll be busy. I love a full life!

Please write back soon. It may be an effort for you to write sometimes, but the joy it brings me really makes it worth your time, I hope.

All the news about little doll David makes me homesick. Tell him his letter goes on the refrigerator and all will see it. Give him some lovin' for it!

Write soon,
Robin

October 5, 1976
Orlando, Florida

Woodbury, Connecticut

Dearest Mother Kitty, Dad – and Bob,

Since you left for your visit in Connecticut, I've written 15 notes and letters – to our friends, both of our girls, and my folks – about our trip to the USNA reunion. And here's letter #16!

David has developed a cough but seems to feel okay. I'll call the doctor if he has a fever or more symptoms later. Oh, I want to tell y'all about another of those amazing conversations with David. Twice he mentioned his heart "tickling" and I asked him to explain what that meant. He said, "Well, it doesn't feel very good, like when I stick my fingers in oil, and it makes me feel sick." Then he tried a couple more ways to describe it, but finally shrugged a shoulder in exasperation and admitted, "I don't think I can *answer* that question!"

We both laughed over that, but awhile later he continued more seriously, "Mom, do you know how your heart feels when you're *so, so* scared, or when you're sorry so, so much you can't stand it? Well, that's almost like it feels when my heart tickles." I am keeping an eagle eye on him so I don't want you worry, okay?

You were missed at league bowling this week, Bob – I had games of 151, 133 and 147. At the moment you and I have the same 144 average. Better watch out!

Mother Kitty, I'll be thinking of you celebrating a birthday Saturday. I'm betting it'll be special this year with "your boy" there. Just make sure he gets on the plane to Orlando in time to attend our friends' wedding reception that evening!

Much love to you three,
Pat

October 22, 1976
Woodbury, Connecticut

Orlando, Florida
Dear Robin,

It was nice to receive your letter while your dad was here. His visit was my best birthday gift and a treat for Granddad as well. We really celebrated, too. We went to the matinee in New Haven of Ice Capades with Dorothy Hamill – she is adorable and the show was spectacular. In the evening Auntie Bussie had a dinner party, complete with a German chocolate cake with candles for me.

We are always glad to hear you love your artwork and glad, too, you were able to find a job. Your dad did tell us about the paintings you brought home in September and in such glowing terms that we are eager to see them at Christmastime.

Love from us both,
Nana Kitty

October 31, 1976
Orlando, Florida

Auburn, Alabama
Hi, Robin,

Every year Halloween makes me think back to when you were about 9 months old and your enthusiastic but inexperienced parents took you to the door to see the your first "Trick-or-Treaters." You quickly became pert nigh hysterical! And all evening, even when you were safely back upstairs in your little crib, you would SCREAM each time the doorbell rang. Ah me, we learned a lot with you, honey, before your sister and brothers came along.

"Disney" David is dressed as Mickey Mouse this year and is out collecting candy with a new little friend from his class. He said one of his big words in such a cute way yesterday. He was up in the tangerine tree when it started sprinkling. Dad called to him that it was raining and asked if he was getting wet. "No-o-o," came the little voice, "I think its just viperating." (Evaporating!)

I got an early morning call from Jenni yesterday with big news: She met a great guy last week and really enjoyed a couple of dates with him – said he's gorgeous. Then today, an early morning call of a different nature. At 4 a.m. someone had smashed into the back of her car parked in front of the apartment. She said the damage looked pretty extensive. Just hope the other person's insurance carrier takes care of it quickly without a hassle.

Dad might have to go down there, but he has told her what to do in the meantime.

Jenni asked me if I could be her patient later this month and I hope to do it. She's doing great in clinic – all A's each session.

Take care, honey, much love from all your family.

Mom

November 16, 1976
Orlando, Florida

Auburn, Alabama
Dear Robin,

See, I told you your dear old dad would write you sometime. And I decided that if I'm going to do it before you come home, I'd better get on the ball.

We just got a check for the Grand Prix today from the insurance company. Unfortunately, they only give what the book value of the car is and don't take into consideration what good shape the car was in. But we did luck out on the other side because Uncle Dave bought a one-year-old Chevette and sold us his old 1968 Chevy for $300. It has 85,000 miles on it but is really in pretty good condition, especially the engine. I guess Jenni will take it back to Lake Worth when she comes home for Thanksgiving.

Skip is talking more and more about wanting to go to Auburn and we are going to apply. Wouldn't that be something to have our family represented at Auburn for eight straight years!

Keep having fun and studying hard. We'll see you in less than a month now.

Loads of love,
Dad

November 17, 1976
Orlando, Florida

Mobile, Alabama
Dearest Folks,

Tomorrow is the beginning of a new schedule for me. Your little Pat is starting a part-time job as newspaper reader and researcher from 8:30 a.m. to 12:30 p.m., Monday through Friday, in an office just 10 minutes or so from home. Awhile back I answered an ad with a letter, explaining why I thought I should be considered for the job even though I lacked the required minimum two years of college. I was told the letter got me the job!

David was cute on hearing about my job, as he is about everything. He wanted to be sure of these things: Would I be here when he got home from school? What would happen if he was sick one morning? What would happen if he got sick at school and "the nurse wouldn't know the phone number where you work?" After I explained everything in detail he was perfectly content.

I love you two. Take care.

Pat

December 5, 1976
Orlando, Florida

Auburn, Alabama

Hi, Robin, honey,

You may be home before this gets to Auburn. It would serve me right since I've waited so long to write. You can't believe how far behind I stay with everything now that I have the job.

Don't know whether you're planning to look for part-time work during Christmas break – probably not, huh? To tell the truth, I'm going to need help here at home. I have to keep working at the newspaper right through the holidays except for Christmas Eve day. And with all six of us around, plus Nana Kitty and Granddad here from Connecticut, and friends dropping in, there'll be chores galore.

I'm going to ask you and Jenni to be especially thoughtful about keeping your "dorm area" picked up and neat, and helping out in all the other areas of homemaking. Okay, honey? You know there are many times when I not only feel tired, but "down," and it'll give me a lift to have the gift of my two lovely daughters' smiling faces and helping hands!

I know you'll enjoy spending time with your baby – and David can't wait to see you! Jenni got a big kick out of him when she was home Thanksgiving weekend.

Maybe Skip will open up a bit for you girls, too. It's a little difficult to communicate with him these days, but I don't have a fit about it as I probably did when you and Jen had those spells. Poor guy, he does work hard (and *has* since he was 11 years old), first, mowing lawns, then at Alhambra Golf course, and later at TJ Murphy's and Publix Market. Oh, Robin, he's getting really interested in the possibility of joining you at Auburn next year. A few of his friends are planning on going there, too.

Take care. We love you and are looking forward to having you home real soon!

Mom

December 7, 1976
Palm Beach Junior College
Lake Worth, Florida

Orlando, Florida
Daddy,

Thanks so much for the money! It came right when I needed it. This is just to let you know I'll be home probably Friday night, after my last final exam.

I doubt you were worried, but I want to reassure you that I have passed clinic. We had our test yesterday, which I'll tell you about later. I don't know how well I did, but six girls failed.

I have to go study now.

All my love,
Jen

December 24, 1976
To Santa,

I want some m and ms in my stoking. But thas not all in my stoking. I want some crayollns. I want a super man colring book. I want a skunk. These are for David.

December 25, 1976
Dear David –

Your note was a little late for getting you just what you wanted. I hope you like the Star Trek and other things I have left wrapped for you. Thank you for the cookies. Merry Christmas!

Santa Claus

December 30, 1976
Dear Diary,

Robin and Jenni have been home for the Christmas holidays, and Mother Kitty and Dad are here, too, making a full house. The atmosphere is not tense, but actually pretty festive – our façade is still in place – which makes little David's keen observation more startling. The folks, Dave and Dorothy, and Bob and I went out to dinner for our annual early celebration of New Year's Eve. David was at a friend's house when we left but at home later, as the girls helped him with his bath, he asked where we were. When they told him he got very still, looked up intently and said in a kind of puzzled voice, "Wonder why did they go out to dinner. You know Mommy and Daddy don't love each other anymore." Shocked, Robin and Jenni asked why he thought that. "Cause I never have saw them kissin' since a long time when we went to Disney World."

Oh, I hope my heart won't break. Or anyone else's.

Pat

January 6, 1977
Delray Beach, Florida

Orlando, Florida
Dear Bob and Pat,

This letter is to tell you again what we said when with you, that we certainly appreciate all the nice things, the good food and the whole gang. It was fun being around everyone for an extended period, and I think we got to know our grandchildren better than ever. Our Christmas presents were a source of pleasure, too, and we thank you all.

Our trip down on Sunday was easy and most of the traffic seemed to be going north after the Orange Bowl. Anyway, we are now well organized and have been in the ocean. We're enjoying this great weather and planning to go for She Crab Soup today.

Love to you both and your young'uns,

Dad and Mother Kitty

January 10, 1977
Orlando, Florida

Mobile, Alabama
Dearest Mommie and Daddy,

Gracious, it has been a long time since I've written, thanks to your great phone calls. My work as a newspaper reader is going well, but so much sitting really affects the circulation in my legs. I've brought in a padded chair from home, plus a little stool, and I never cross my legs but they still hurt at times. Of course, in my adult life when have I ever before had the luxury of sitting for such lengthy periods? My body is just not used to it! So I took the step today and placed my ad for a position as "home manager" in two local newspapers. And have crossed my fingers. …

Love from the gang here,

Pat

379

January 12, 1977
Palm Beach Junior College
Lake Worth, Florida

Orlando, Florida
Dear Mom and Dad,

Hi there! Thank you so much for your letters. When I got them I just started to cry. I don't know why. Silly, I guess. Thanks for the check, too. It will come in handy as we just got hit with a bill for some liability insurance.

We had a real interesting experience today. A nurse came to our clinic class to teach us CPR (cardiopulmonary resuscitation) so we'll know what to do in an emergency. It's pretty complicated to learn. There are a lot of things to remember, and the techniques are different for adults and children. Next week we'll take our test and demonstrate on a very lifelike mannequin. Then if we pass we get a certificate good for two years, after which time it's supposed to be renewed. Isn't that neat? I'm so glad to know I might be able to save someone's life.

Dad, next weekend when you're down to visit Nana Kitty and Granddad at their Sea Aire apartment, I'll be coming to spend Saturday with them, too. So I'll see you there.

Well, say "love ya" to Skip and David for me.

All my love,
Jenni

January 17, 1977
Orlando, Florida

Auburn, Alabama
Dear Robin,

We have been having cold weather here. It's supposed to get down to 25 degrees tonight, so I know it's much colder at Auburn! Hope you don't have to go out tonight. I think the car might be hard to start in real cold weather – hard on the battery if you have to crank it over and over.

Thanks for the good information you sent Skip on housing at Auburn. Make a note of any other good but inexpensive housing you hear of for him. And thanks in advance for your help.

How is the job going? You'll have to weigh your having a job against how much cash you're really saving, the time involved, interference with school, etc. Use your judgment, okay? Take care of Robin.

Much love, kiddo,
Dad

380

January 19, 1977
Auburn University
Auburn, Alabama

Mobile, Alabama

Dearest Nana GeeGee and Grandaddy,

It's midnight and snowing outside, as it has been all day. It's so pretty, but since I'm here by myself it's a little lonely.

I am now working only on Friday and Saturday nights, which I hate but can't change. I'm looking around for another job, but nothing has come up yet, so I guess I'll stick with this until I can afford to quit. I am still looking forward to your visit, Nana GeeGee. You know I really need your company and good advice frequently! Be sure to give me enough notice to be able to get off work, okay?

I want a change of scenery, too. Maybe graduating and moving to a new place will be really good for me. A new job, a new life, new friends, the whole bit, all in only about eight months. Kinda scary but also exciting. I guess deep down I'm really anxious for the change.

Well, better go to sleep. Please call more often even just for short talks. I really need them – and you!

All my love,
Robin

January 24, 1977
Orlando, Florida

Auburn, Alabama

Dear Robin,

A Realtor came to see and take measurements of the house in preparation for putting it on the market. I get so depressed thinking about all that's connected with leaving this beautiful home I have loved living in for so many years. But then again, there comes a time to make a change. Whatever happens between your dad and me, whether we separate or not, we would need to sell the house. It'll be too big for us three, with three of you kids gone after Skip leaves. So now it's time to begin looking around. I wonder, where do we start?

Skip appreciated all the housing information you sent. He and his friend Robert plan to visit Auburn during spring break. Skip and David had off school Tuesday and Wednesday in addition to the days last week because their schools don't have heat. We were cold, and I know you were! Jen wrote to us in bold red letters, "IT SNOWED HERE!" In South Florida!

Dad went down to Delray Beach to see his parents during the weekend and then attend Jenni's capping ceremony and be her patient today.

We've been wondering about your job situation, honey. Let us know what you decide. Take care – love you lots.

Mom

January 26, 1977
Orlando, Florida

Mobile, Alabama
Dear Nana GeeGee and Granddaddy,

How are y'all doing? I'm just fine, but I'm getting real anxious to be able to be with both of you some in the summer. I can hardly wait till I'm all done with work and can relax and shoot the bull with some of my favorite relatives. On my calendar in my room, I'm counting the days till then. I've got some real good jokes. Some of them are just right for the dirty old man!

By the way, I have been swinging my golf clubs around and I feel as loose as ever. I just know I'll be taking up golf when I get to Auburn.

My graduation from Boone High will be on June 10. If you all are planning on driving down anytime around then, I would be honored if you would come. It will be exciting for my parents to see me graduating *with honors* with a 3.8 grade-point average. I have been working my butt off to get into and stay in the Honor Society because I know it means a lot to my dad. I'm happy with my grades, but I think the encouragement my dad gave me inspired me to work extra hard.

I love you both,
Skip

January 31, 1977
Orlando, Florida

Auburn, Alabama
Dearest Robin,

We have put the house up for sale. I'm holding back a river of unshed tears, there's a lump lodged in my throat, and my heart seemed to plummet to my feet when I saw the actual sign out front. But we feel it's the right step. We're telling other people we don't need as much room now, which is true, but in fact we'll no doubt go separate ways.

I'm hoping to get you a "Package ala Birthday" on the way soon, honey. I'm so busy, but you know I think of my gal every day, pray for all good things for you and love you ever so much.

Mom

February 12, 1977
Auburn University
Auburn, Alabama

Orlando, Florida
Dearest Mom,

It was so good to talk to you on the phone this morning. It sure does make me feel good just to know you're getting along okay. I do think about you a lot, and worry. I can't help it.

I finally bought a parakeet! He's a lovely light sky blue and white, but I don't have a name yet. I want a medieval or old-fashioned one like "Count of Monte Cristo" or something neat like that. I'll let you know. He won't chirp yet. I guess he's still scared in his new home. But I'm hoping to train him to perch on my finger and talk.

Special love to my mom, whom I think about all the time and miss very much!

Your Robin

February 15, 1977
Dear Diary,

Bob and I talked to David about our separation, which now is inevitable. "Will you have a divorce?" he asked, and we told him that might come later. I used his relationship with his friend Kathy as an example of how you can still love somebody and just want to see them sometimes even though before you wanted to spend *lots* of time together, and always liked to play the same games, etc. I said that could happen to a husband and wife, too. But Bob and I both reassured David over and over how much *we love him*. When his dad asked how he felt about everything we'd discussed, his cautious but wise answer was "I don't know, I'll have to *test* it first." We mentioned what he'd said to Robin and Jenni at Christmas about our not loving each other and asked why he felt that was true. He told us the same: "Well, I haven't ever saw you kiss each other anymore but that time when Daddy and me left to go to Disney World." More than I ever realized, a child senses what's beyond the "happy face" facade.

The most important change in me the past six months is that I feel a close connection to God again and can pray earnestly for guidance in all my decisions. Last August when I felt so desperate and read Catherine Marshall's book *Beyond Ourselves*, I began to admit I could not go it alone any longer. Since then, even with the deep sadness I feel over the breakup, I've gained at least a small measure of inner peace. Maybe I'll become a better person because of all the "creative suffering" I've already experienced – and have yet to face as the family circle is fractured.

February 15, 1977
Delray Beach, Florida

Orlando, Florida
Dear Pat and Bob,

Pat, believe me, my heart is heavy over the sad situation in your family and I understand the grief you are feeling. Dad and I have never given up hoping and praying that somehow you would come to a happier ending, and it is heartbreaking for us to watch your beloved family break up.

In spite of this, I do feel that both you and Bob deserve more than the half a life you have been living and we wish for you both the chance for years ahead of true happiness. If there were anything on earth I could say or do to keep your dear family happily together I would do so, but I think a talk as you suggested would only repeat the heartaches we both feel and do nothing to ease them.

Dad and I have felt very close to you, Pat, and are always grateful for the many kind and thoughtful things you have done for us.

Our love to you all,
Mother Kitty

February 28, 1977
Orlando, Florida

Auburn, Alabama
Dear girls,

I'm going to write one letter for you both and have the letter passed around this time. Otherwise, you may not hear from your old mom for another long spell. I really am sorry my letters have fallen off so badly, Robin and Jenni. Of course, you know it has been a tremendously difficult period for your dad and me. I feel physically and mentally and emotionally drained. But even as I write that statement I can tell you I also feel some peace and relief and, at times, even the barest touch of excitement about the future.

I can't believe I have gone through so many different phases, stages, or whatever, in the past few years. I do feel I have grown as a person – as Pat – and in some ways like myself more now. The growth has been accompanied by pain – at times waves of grief over all the losses pierce my heart like arrows – yet I think it has been healing, too.

For a long while I felt so full of bitterness, resentment, regret for "a wasted life" and other negative emotions. Now I feel as if I'm at least starting to get well. I'm sure there will be more pain involved, along with fear and loneliness, but I'm counting on coming through it all and being a better person because of it, or in spite of it, or something. ...

Many people here know about the separation now. The word got out at bowling as acquaintances began putting two and two together.

As it stands, if and when I find the right place for David and me, we'll move out. Your dad will stay at the house and keep it in good shape for selling and Skip will stay with him until he heads to Auburn.

I've taken one step toward trying to find some direction in my "professional" life. The Center for Continuing Education for Women offers a battery of tests, evaluations, and guidance counselors to bring it all together, and I went for the first time last Wednesday right after work. When I dragged in at 4:15 I was wrung out, but the tests were interesting, and I left there feeling very hopeful. I'm eagerly awaiting the results.

Skip decided to leave his job at Publix Market. He and a friend are starting a lawn maintenance and pool cleaning business for the summer. They are excited, and I'm sure will do well. Both young men are so dependable and conscientious about responsibilities.

Cousin Katie and her gentleman friend were down from Savannah for a weekend at Disney World and came for dinner Friday. She's such a doll – wow, did she look stunning in a gorgeous hand-sewn red dress.

I loved "letter-talking" to my girls tonight. Y'all be sweet, hear? And have fun – and all good days

Best love from your family,
Mom

385

Living is a form of not being sure,
not knowing what, next or how.
The artist never entirely knows.
We guess. We may be wrong,
but we take leap after leap in the dark.
                                        Agnes de Mille

Chapter Twenty
Letting it Flow
1977

Pat's dad Randolph in the Alabama oil field

March 7, 1977
Orlando, Florida

Woodbury, Connecticut
Dear Auntie Bussie,

I have had a recurring strong urge to write to you, composing many letters in my head, but tonight I'm going to sit down and let this one flow onto paper. My schedule is so exhausting now that I usually have little energy left to write.

I've hoped we could talk when you come to Florida but am afraid there won't be an opportunity. I did tell Bob's folks I thought it would be good if I could talk with them, but they preferred not to – and maybe you would, too. So there are no strings to this letter. I've been in the family for over half of my life, though, and my nature rebels against just sliding out of it without a few words from my heart and a goodbye of some kind.

Twenty-four years ago I would have sworn on 24 Bibles that the situation which now exists would never happen to us. I remember so well a letter from you at that time, Auntie Bussie, when love was new and exciting and untested. In it you cautioned that every couple thinks their love is different, that they won't have the problems others have. And I thought, "Oh, but she just doesn't know, *ours will be* different!" Ah, the innocence of youth.

Of course, at that time I think both families were concerned about the dissimilarity in our family backgrounds, but I honestly believe our problems weren't caused so much by that fact as by the differences in our very basic natures. You may feel – and be right – that those differences are formed by background, too. All I remember is how I looked forward to marriage as a marvelous, warm, sharing, very close relationship. Now, looking back with that always-keen 20/20 hindsight, I realize I was floating about in a rose-colored bubble of romance – with absolutely no idea how to be an independent person – fully expecting that Bob would fulfill my every need … forever.

Oh my, so naive, and my expectations were completely unrealistic, although I didn't know or admit the truth of that for many years. It was the onset of menopause, approaching my 40th birthday, more and deeper feelings of "Is this all there is?" and "Who am I, anyway?" It was the shattering of the dream of what I thought my life would be and the things I had always held dear – wifehood and motherhood. I became convinced that I had given the best years of my life and, even after that magnanimous offering, I was still so little appreciated. What awful, mixed-up feelings assailed me. I didn't like myself much. And I didn't know how to handle myself – as a person, a wife or a mother – in the face of such disappointments and questions and confusion.

Bob and I talked over the problems in several sessions with a marriage and family therapist and during counseling from a wonderful minister, but I think help came too late. Now we agree that our bond as husband and wife is broken. It's the death of a marriage. And it is a terrible loss. Any relationship has to be carefully and consistently nurtured or it will die. It's understandable. After a certain point, though, we just couldn't seem to give each other what the other one needed.

A decision has been made on an apartment nearby, and David and I will be moving within the next two weeks. Bob preferred to continue living at the house while it is on the market. It seems best for Skip to stay there, too, for the few months until he goes away to Auburn.

I have really loved all of Bob's family. Y'all have been my family, too. But I guess it's only natural the ties we had will change when he and I are no longer a couple.

I'll see you in April. I love you.

Pat

March 10, 1977
Orlando, Florida

Mobile, Alabama
Dearest Folks,

Robin and Jenni are due home tomorrow and Bob's parents will be in Orlando and probably call to see about coming over for a while. Dave and Dorothy are still in town as well, so we'll be pretty busy around here.

Dorothy and I had a good visit over dinner at our favorite restaurant last Saturday. She's supportive and as dear as ever. I had job counseling two afternoons this week, and another interview today. The career tests were interesting and reaffirmed what I've thought all along about myself. Personality-wise, I'm high in extroversion, intuition and feeling, and right in the middle in judgment and perception. People who are extremely high in the judgment area don't like to leave their little rut, and people high in the perception area are flighty, so the counselor said the middle is a neat place to be.

The tests showed I am very enterprising, especially for a woman. A few occupational themes that kept cropping up were: (1) Advertising Executive, (2) Chamber of Commerce Executive, and (3) Flight Attendant. Indications were that I should be in the center of a lot of activity, have decision-making powers, and work on an interpersonal level helping people. Writing came out strong, too.

Another revelation was that I didn't necessarily need college for college's sake. Instead, some training and "let me at it to learn and do" would be appropriate. One of the counselors said, "You know where I can just see you, Pat? In a hotel, as the banquet director or as a convention hostess." But I can see potential problems with that and so many other jobs, of course, especially ones with unusual hours – what would I be able to arrange for David's care?

Re apartments, I'm holding my breath on one I really want. It's in a pleasant complex, La Costa Brava, only a couple of miles from the house and still in David's school district. The setting is pretty, with a nice courtyard, plenty of giant oak trees, two pools, one by the lake – and on the lot next to the complex is a Lutheran church surrounded by a huge grassy area, a great place for kids to play and me to walk. Everything about the apartment and the grounds feels so "homey."

Last Friday I had a wonderful visit with David's teacher, who said, "I love David. If he wanted it and I could get it for him, I'd give him the moon!" She thinks he will be fine and do well wherever he goes to school – and suggested, "David is such a thinker and has such good sense and is so perceptive, maybe you could take him to visit both public and private schools and see what he thinks."

Daddy, David's teacher also said he's good with money. He tells her about a granddaddy at the beach who pays him, teaches him about money and takes him lots of places!

Got to go "beddie-bye" – TGIF tomorrow! Getting hungry to see y'all. Hope you'll plan a trip down to see us before long. Love you – and love from the boys, too.

Pat

March 21, 1977
Mobile, Alabama

Orlando, Florida
Dear David,

I have been thinking of you very much lately, also all of your family. I know you will like your new place, just you and your mother there. I can see you helping her do things there like you did at our condo at Chateau-by-the-Sea.

When you get all used to everything there Nana GeeGee and I hope to come see you. Say hello to all for me. We love you much.

Granddaddy

March 23, 1977
Orlando, Florida

Mobile, Alabama
Dearest Mom and Daddy,

Isn't the note from David cute? It's all his own. He decided to write and then composed the letter and spelled everything himself. Wait till you hear him tell you whatever you want to know about the solar system. He can reel off facts and figures about each planet, the equator, the axis, the asteroids, etc. We found him reading Robin's college astronomy book one day.

David's class is going to put on the play "Jack and the Beanstalk" and he's playing the lead of Jack. I got a note from his teacher, who wrote, "He's my joy! Thank you for sharing him."

I need to really buckle down to packing. I did a tiny bit today. Movers will come to help us with the big furniture on April Fool's Day.

Love you,
Pat

March 24, 1977
Auburn University
Auburn, Alabama

Mobile, Alabama
Dearest Nana GeeGee and Granddaddy,

Hi, most beloved grandparents. I have some good news – at least I hope you'll think so! It looks like I might be job-hunting in Mobile come August. I've heard lots of good things about the job market there. I'm hoping to talk to y'all about staying with you a few days while I'm looking for a job and later, if everything works out, a small apartment.

Well, school starts Monday. I'll be glad to get moving again. And Skip's coming up sometime in the next few weeks. I'm so excited!

Much love to you both!

Your big girl (next to Mom!),
Robin

March 27, 1977
Woodbury, Connecticut

Orlando, Florida
Pat dear,

The fact that you wanted to write to me was very much appreciated – and the letter made me heartsick. Not that I haven't known, but this made it seem more real. The breakup of a family is such a serious and sad thing.

Now that it is happening, about all I can say is I hope both of you find whatever it is that has been lacking in your lives – and soon. Soon, because it is a great adjustment and change from "we" to "I" in a world that seems to have been built like the ark, for twosomes. It's hard to realize how true that is until you get there. Freedom is wonderful, but it also brings pain and from unexpected quarters. Believe me, I know.

I am sorry, sorry, sorry that you and Bob and the children have to go through this.

Love,
Auntie Bussie

March 28, 1977
Palm Beach Junior College
Lake Worth, Florida

Orlando, Florida
Dear Mom and Dad,

I've been thinking of you both constantly, especially this week. There really aren't words to say how I feel. I just want both of you to find happiness. This whole thing has really affected me much more than I thought it would. I wish I could help somehow.

I guess it's a good thing I didn't come home this weekend – I've been sick. I had a fever of 100 degrees Saturday and Sunday. It's gone today but my throat is *sore*.

Please call me soon so I'll know what's happened. I love both of you so much.

Jenni

March 28, 1977
Auburn University
Auburn, Alabama

Orlando, Florida
Dearest Mom,

How's moving going? I'm glad you got the apartment you really wanted near David's school and our old familiar shopping center. I remember seeing La Costa Brava, it's pretty. I believe you'll be happy there. Anyway, I'll be counting on some good news soon, so keep me informed now, you hear?

Well, it appears as if Mobile is my first job-hunting city! I've heard many good things about the town and the job market, and the location is very close to what I've had in mind, as you know.

My bird Rudy has developed an amusing talent. He sings to jazzy records and stops at the pauses between each song. His favorite record is "Lowdown" by Boz Scaggs. Wish you could hear him.

Better go. Much love to my mommy!

Your big girl,
Robin

March 29, 1977
Orlando, Florida

Lake Worth, Florida
Auburn, Alabama
Hi, Jenni and Robin,

I'm overwhelmed with moving and all it involves, and regular chores don't lessen during this particularly busy time. So – not much time for letters, even to my dearest daughters away at college. Thanks, Jen, for passing this along to your sister. …

Jenni, I'm sure you're looking forward to spending a few hours at Nana Kitty and Granddad's vacation apartment in Delray Beach when Auntie Bussie and your cousins Lynnie and Kimi are there for a visit next month. I wish you could go, too, Robin.

Have you thought more about your summer plans, Jenni-Jewel? In many ways it might be better for you to stay and work at a temporary job in Lake Worth since everything here is so uncertain, but I'm sure whatever decision you make will be fine. Tell you one thing – *I* certainly have made a bunch of decisions in the past few weeks

One is that after April I'm going to be on a leave of absence from my job. I need time to regain physical and emotional strength for whatever the future holds – and to be a more attentive mother to all of you, in person and/or by letter.

You know, girls, we may have to make a date to ever see your big brother again! Skip started working at Disney, supposedly part-time, but he has worked nearly every day. He drives a submarine at "20,000 Leagues Under the Sea." Likes it so far.

A funny story for y'all: I put an ad in the newspaper to sell my bed and a nice young man came to look at it – he liked it, paid for it, and planned to pick it up a few days later. In the meantime, I was looking at new beds, getting more discouraged by the minute over the terribly high prices. Then I saw another classified ad describing a bed that sounded like mine, so I called the young man and asked if he'd let me have my bed back and buy the other one instead. It wasn't quite as nice as mine but was the same price, so I offered to pay him $15 to offset the difference in condition – and I got to keep my bed!

Robin, your letter was most welcome today. You know, honey, I hesitate to give an opinion on the possibility of your periodically staying with and/ or living near Nana GeeGee and Granddaddy in Mobile. We all know they love you dearly, but they are used to their own routine and might not be sure about such an arrangement. Let's wait and see if you find a job there, then everyone can discuss the pros and cons. Okay, honey?

Oh, Granddaddy sent David a note with a picture of himself near an oil field and a $2 bill "for helping your mom out." So David wrote back, "Dear Randy – I liked your not (note), the picture was fine. I really needed the $2!" It was so cute, and all on his own.

Oh, gracious, you girls will love the conversation David and I had on the subject of reincarnation the other night after watching the TV special "Tut, The Boy King." David asked if I thought people really lived again somewhere after they died. I told him I believe we have a soul that lives on, after which came this dissertation on reincarnation by our 7-year-old little old soul: "A soul is a god, I think, but do you think we come back alive and *know* what heaven is? I wonder if we come back and *be* somebody else? I wonder if I could have been George Washington, or maybe the first man, Adam – NAKED (with a chuckle here!) – or even King Tut. I wonder if we live in heaven for a while *before* we go back in another lady's tummy? I always wished I knew what it felt like to be a girl. And especially how it feels just before you have a baby. I *think* it probably hurts, huh? I wish I could *know* how everything feels." Isn't he the most fascinating small person?

Something interesting ... I've been contacted by a team of people putting together a television film series, "Goodbye, Hello," about the possibility of your dad and me participating. Couples who are saying goodbye through

393

separation or divorce so often aren't friendly enough to even talk, so I was told we are a rare find for them.

I love you both so much. Take care of yourselves.

Mom

April 1, 1977
Orlando, Florida

Marietta, Georgia

Dear Katie,

Hello, my beloved cousin. I need a good listener right about now – may I pour out my thoughts to you?

I wonder, will this day prove to be prophetic and I a fool to have moved from our home of 14 years to this nearby apartment complex? So civilized are we, Bob coming by to do the "manly" chores he has always taken care of: setting up the stereo and television sets; hanging pictures so perfectly; rearranging several pieces of furniture; replacing the ceiling light bulb; double-checking the windows and the sliding glass and front door locks to be sure all are in working order and will keep David and me safe. And, naturally, before leaving the house, I had cleaned it thoroughly, put fresh sheets on his bed, and Skip's, and brought favorite foods in for them – the regular wifely jobs.

As he said goodbye, with a chaste kiss to my cheek, Bob smiled and gave a small shrug when little David inquired, "Will you go to the liberry now, Daddy, and get a big book to tell you how to cook?"

Surprisingly, I haven't shed any tears today, though how could there be any left if truth be told? Such a wild jumble of emotions, Kate, as you well know, having been through the breakup of a marriage. There is a touch of excitement at embarking on a life as a single person for the first time in a home not headed by a father or a husband. And untold sadness for the loss of my marriage, the love of that special someone, the young-girl dream of "happily ever after." And fear bordering on panic at being on my own.

As exhausted as my mind is, though, trying to make sense of all the crazy feelings, tonight it is my body I don't know how to soothe for it is weary to the bone. And I am soon going to lay it down to rest – on my old familiar bed, in a strange room, alone.

Among the many jumbled thoughts of every description that I had today, Katie, was an obscure flash of memory from the time we were little girls. When I was brushing my hair I suddenly got a mental picture of those gosh-awful electric-curler permanents we used to get so we could have

394

curls just like Shirley Temple's? Heavens to betsy, surely that process ranked up there with other methods of medieval torture – remember?

I'll close on a bit lighter note with a couple more of my precious David's comments. At his bedtime, as we discussed the adventures of our busy, out-of-the-ordinary day, he asked if Robin and Jenni and Skip knew where our home is now. I assured him they know and have our address and telephone number, too. He said, longingly, he really wished *he* had been "borned, too, when they were little." Then, after a moment of silence, came this attention-getter: "Mommy, do you think we could have another baby soon?"

I love you,
Pat

April 4, 1977
Orlando, Florida

Mobile, Alabama,
Dear Nana GeeGee and Granddaddy,

I just talked with mom about y'all coming down here for my graduation ceremony in June. I mentioned it because it was just an idea and I thought it would be nice if you were going to be here anyway. I would be just as happy to see you both in a week or two if you would rather come down now. I am getting kind of anxious to see you. So I'll leave it up to you.

I love you both,
Skip

April 10, 1977
Dear Easter Bunny
Do you have a spare Chocolate Bunny? Well if you do could you please give me one.
Could you possibly give me a real Bunny. Well if you do put it right inside my door.
Could you please hide me the eggs with candy in them. And if you can I'd like you to do more things.

LOVE,
DAVID

April 12, 1977
Auburn University
Auburn, Alabama

Orlando, Florida
Dearest Mom,

I had kind of a meltdown over everything that's happened, but I don't want you to worry because I figured stuff out and I feel better after a *really* good cry. I'd felt sad and lonely and got to thinking what if someday when I'm married, the same thing happened. But I told myself that your separation didn't mean I would have one, too.

Mom, I do know that deep in my heart you are my major concern these days. I feel so close to you that I've been taking on some of your pain, I think. I want you to know how *very much* I love and respect you and your courage and strength. I only hope I can be half the woman you are.

I was surprised and pleased when Dad called this week and asked if the separation had affected me personally in any way and if I was doing okay. And I got a sweet letter from Auntie Bussie, concerned for the separation's effect on us kids. She said she understood that you and Dad had decided you both personally would be happier apart, but she knew it was hard and she was feeling for us. I wrote to thank her and tell her we *would* be okay – and we will be, Mom, all of us.

Your loving daughter,
Robin

P.S. – As you once wrote to me, "Let the good times roll." This can be a marvelous time in your life – you're on the brink of so much happiness. That's my wish for you.

April 15, 1977
Orlando, Florida

Auburn, Alabama
Dearest Robin,

David and I went to New Smyrna Beach on Saturday. We saw the entire gang for a while, but I felt sort of a strain and I guess maybe it was my goodbye to your dad's side of the family, really. Only Dorothy asked how I was – nobody else made a personal remark to me. I was sad, but now feel it was another step forward and am okay. In fact, I feel sure my life will get better and better.

When your last letter came, I read and re-read it. I think you have good insight in realizing you're scared for yourself and your own future along with feeling the pain for me and the present. I can understand that your sobbing session was therapeutic. I know this separation is affecting all of you – there's no way around that. But we'll all get stronger, I think.

Right now I wish the house would sell so we could begin to finalize the agreements/property settlement, etc.

Oh, I almost forgot to tell you – David and I were called last Thursday for a television commercial. I'm only in it for a second but he's in quite a bit. He got to work three hours at $25 per hour and I worked one for $40.

Take care of you. I hope classes are going along well. Love you, gal!

Mom

P.S. – A kiss from David

Mobile, Alabama
May 10, 1977

Orlando, Florida
Dearest Pat,

I want you to see this letter we got from your Aunt Hester out in Texas. It's so sad and sweet and it near about broke my heart. You know Hester and Esther was twins and always felt real close but they never did get to see each other much after they married. Honestly they both had such hard lives, specially compared to mine with Daddy and you children. Anyway, I was sure you would appreciate her words.

Love,
Mommie

Dear Wilba and Randolph,

Have to let you know how much I want to thank you both for being so good to Esther. She was always writing me what you two had done for her and how good you were to her. She is gone now, you will miss her a lot, so will I. She was a dear sister to me and I loved her so much. I told her so several times through life that going to her house was like going back home after Papa and Mama had passed away. I would have loved to be there, but I got so choked up until I was afraid to try to make it. I am doing very well, but I have my bad times too, but just don't say anything about it. I just try to keep going on and do all I can to get some exercise, that's what the Dr. told me to do. Wilba if you can, write me how they put her away, what kind of dress they buried her in and how she looked after they fixed her and did many go to see her? I know you don't like to write but maybe you can spare a little time to do so. I am sending you eleven dollars so you wont have to pay all the tax. I love you, Wilba, you are so good and Randolph too. Let me hear from you.

Love from your sister,
Hester

May 11, 1977
Woodbury, Connecticut

Orlando, Florida
Dear Pat,

Thanks for the lovely Mother's Day card. It reflects the same thoughtfulness that you have always shown us and I truly appreciate it. It was a happy day – a combination of Mother's Day and Auntie Bussie's birthday.

It's been a busy, busy time since our return and a happy one getting back to all our friends again, and even the weather has cooperated. It was like Florida for a while, then it cooled and Monday we awoke to find the ground covered with snow! It didn't last, of course, but it was a surprise.

Our thoughts are with you and David and best wishes for your future.

Love to you both,
Mother Kitty

May 11, 1977
Orlando, Florida

Auburn, Alabama
Dearest Robin,

Thank you so much, honey, for your sweet Mother's Day card and newsy letter. Knowing how much it means to you, I'm very glad your dad called to check on your feelings. It was good of Auntie Bussie to write a concerned letter, too. I guess you children will have to take on the responsibility of keeping in touch with Dad's family now.

The weekend was a LOW point for me emotionally. I didn't feel very perky physically, either, which probably made things seem even worse. But, really, we're getting along okay.

Looking forward to having you home in early June for a few days, sweetie. We'll talk a bunch then, okay? I love you.

Mom

May 11, 1977
Orlando, Florida

Mobile, Alabama

Dearest Mommie and Daddy,

The appointment with the divorce attorney tomorrow has me organizing my list of notes and questions, not to mention gathering my thoughts for such a meeting. Frankly, I don't know if I can make any sense out of either in my present state of mind – sad over the whole situation, confused by the logistics of working everything out and anxious about whether things *will* work out and, if so, exactly what I will do then. I have felt so low. I suppose I'll have to expect all the hurt to surface anew every once in a while and just believe I'll be able to do whatever is needed and emerge a little stronger.

I don't know, though, I certainly was no pillar of strength during a recent Saturday afternoon incident when David was with Bob and I was feeling sort of lonely and blue. I decided to go mosey around the local mall, just to be out among people, hoping the hustle and bustle would take my mind off problems and give my spirit a lift. On the spur of the moment I called Skip from a pay phone there to see if he could join me for a quick supper, but he had other plans … so I moseyed on … and soon caught the aroma of delicious freshly brewed coffee and perked up a bit. I fetched a cup of café latte and went to a nearby bench to sit and savor it and lose myself in the pleasure of people-watching.

As always there were crowds of interesting looking people of all sizes, shapes and colors. Before long my eye was drawn to a couple about your age, mid-60s, strolling along, window-shopping, holding hands so tenderly. I began to feel kind of mushy just watching them. A few minutes after they passed by, there came two more sweethearts, a young man and woman walking leisurely, talking, pausing now and then for a lovely, light "kiss stop." And, well, that did it. I just started to dissolve. With tears already streaming down my face, I went out the nearest exit and headed back home, trying to hold my heart together.

I was torn by the conflicting emotions of feeling happy and hopeful, and angry and afraid. Happy for both couples, and for myself that I had once had sweet young love; angry that it was gone; hopeful about the possibility of a new love someday, but terribly afraid I mightn't ever know again, even in my "golden years," the joy of holding hands and sharing those knowing, gentle smiles with my own special someone.

Well, I guess maybe I emerged from that unexpected painful episode okay after all because following that day and evening of feeling loss and sadness so acutely, I slept well and woke up the next morning, Mother's Day, to plenty of bright spots. There were loving, sentimental cards from Robin, Jenni and Skip, and David gave me a dear little card and school-made present. Then, wonder of wonders, that very old sad-looking orchid plant on the patio burst forth with three perfect blooms, prompting David to come running in, shouting, "Mom, Mom, look, you've got *violets* for Mother's Day!"

I love you, dear ones,
Pat

May 22, 1977
Cherry Hill, New Jersey

Orlando, Florida
Dear Pat,

Forgive me for not writing sooner. I think of you each day and hope and pray that your separation has helped you physically. Without your health you are not able to cope with the emotional strain, which must have been so great with such a decision. We feel so badly that all of this has happened. As your friends and former neighbors, Jack and I felt so close to you as a family for some 20 years and so hoped it wouldn't end in separation. So glad you and Bob were here to visit us last fall. Although you did mention a problem, you both seemed so compatible and happy that I couldn't believe the end would come.

Jack is writing to Bob because we love you both and want you to know how badly we feel that things won't be quite the same. My wish is that you will be better friends with each other as time heals the hurts and the next time we visit Orlando I do hope the four of us can be together as we were so many times in the past.

If there is any way we can help we would be more than happy to do so. Please let us know how you are and what the girls will be doing now after graduation.

Our love and best to you.

Friends as always,
Ruth and Jack

June 19, 1977
Orlando, Florida

Mobile, Alabama
Dear Folks,

Happy Father's Day to you, Daddy dear. ... David did a labor of love for Bob, a poem done in fancy letters all colored in with a variety of colors. He made so many mistakes at first, and cried over them, that I nearly had to stop the project! Skip came over to get David so he could deliver the card to his dad at the house.

Jenni stopped by for a short visit this afternoon. She brought *me* a small gift of cologne for Father's Day. She's a cool character! I think David and I will take a trip down to Lake Worth soon to visit Jen, see the apartment and meet her roommates.

Robin called briefly Friday night to check on me. She said she'd had very good comments on the beginnings of her thesis work. One professor called her ideas refreshing, which pleased her a lot.

We miss you already Mom, and are so glad you came. Thank you, from Skip, for braving the "graduation bleacher exercises." Think you'll be up to another round in 1988 when it's David's turn? I'm not at all sure I will be.

You two take care of each other. I love you so much. Kisses from David and me.

Pat

June 20, 1977
Dear Diary,

I felt both shock and a touch of humiliation today when I tried to pay for two items at Jordan Marsh with a $10 personal check. I've been so proud of my very-first-ever bank account, small though it may be; now I discover a credit card is needed to *cash* my check. And even though the credit history Bob and I have together is impeccable, so far I haven't been able to get one in my own name. But, darn it all, I won't give up – till one day I convince somebody I *am* a good risk.

Orlando, Florida
June 25, 1977

Auburn, Alabama
Dearest Robin,

Skip did something really special this week. He gave me a card with such heartwarming words written inside, thanking me "for your love and

TLC for my 18 years," and enclosed $50 for me to buy a gift for myself. I just fell apart and cried on his shoulder. It meant so much to me during this particular time.

While he was here, he helped me move the sofas around, as per your suggestion, and I like the new arrangement. Thanks, my personal decorator.

Much love to you from David and me.

Mom

June 28, 1977
Norwich, Vermont

Orlando, Florida
Dear Pat,

You must think I'm a terrible friend for not answering your letter sooner, but the truth is I just didn't know what to say to you and still don't, for that matter. Should I say what I feel or what I think you'd like to hear? Maybe some of both, so here goes.

I wasn't completely shocked at the news of the separation because when Jack and Ruth were here last fall they hinted that all was not well between you and Bob. But – and this may hurt – I was angry!

And so I read and reread the letter and then tried to analyze my anger, and the only reason I could come up with and still come back to is this one: You and Bob were our first friends as couples back in Hamden, Connecticut, and even though we haven't seen each other for 10 years I still regard you as our dear friends. Do you remember how we used to laugh at how much alike Gobe and Bob were?

To try to understand, I got the book *Passages* out of the library. Have you read it? If not, I recommend it although the author is a real women's-libber, some of which I agree with and some I don't. But it talks about mid-life crises and the one thing that impressed me was that the author refers to the differences between men and women being the greatest between the ages of 42 and 48. She refers to life as shaped like a diamond and says a wife is the farthest removed from her husband at that age and that eventually they can grow back together. But there are ifs.

You spoke about being sad and sick with grief but didn't say whether it's because your marriage is over or that you were separated. Do you hope to get back together? Gobe has talked to Bob several times the last month or so for business and Bob has said no more than you have.

The book gave me some insight to what I think happened to you and Bob, but I can't really relate because I'm more content with my life now

402

than ever. The kids are, for all intents and purposes, on their own except for occasional visits and emergencies and Gobe and I do pretty much as we please, together or separately.

I don't mean to imply that life is a big bed of roses. We have some problems now and then but we seem to weather them and still enjoy common interests. If you haven't read the book, please do. And before leaving the subject I'd like to say I hope that whatever happens, it's the best for you and for Bob, too. I love you both, you see, and thereby hangs my dilemma.

Pat, I hope we're still friends in spite of what I've said. Write me again very soon and let me know how you're getting along – please.

Love,
Judy

June 29, 1977
Palm Beach Junior College
Lake Worth, Florida

Orlando, Florida
Dear David,

Hi, how are you? Are you taking good care of Mom? I talked to Daddy today on the phone and he said you and Skip and he ate supper at Uncle Dave and Aunt Dorothy's the other night. He said you were a very good boy at dinner. I hope you have a good Fourth of July weekend. How is your summer? I hope you're not too bored. Have fun!

I love you,
Your sis,
Jen

July 6, 1977
Newport News, Virginia

Orlando, Florida
Dear Pat,

Please know that our not writing has not been because we haven't been thinking about you all. The reason, frankly, is that we don't know what to say.

Our first thoughts were that you shouldn't act in haste – it's only normal to have ups and downs in marriage and in life. After reading your letter many times, it doesn't seem like you are acting hastily, though. You are both such dear people, different certainly, but you always seemed to complement each other. Please weigh all possibilities and tread carefully. Don't put yourself in a worse situation and find that you can't turn back. Keep the communication going between the two of you.

If I had to list the most important feeling in my relationship with Allen, loving him, liking him and being able to communicate with him would top the list.

Pat, we think so much of both of you. We know you'll make the right decision.

Love,
Sarah and Al

July 26, 1977
Orlando, Florida

Auburn, Alabama
Dearest Robin,

Gracious, your old mom is way behind ... I hope this phase soon passes and I can again find letter-writing a pleasure and not an almost insurmountable task.

Skip is coming by at 7:30 a.m. tomorrow for breakfast before he heads for Auburn and hand-carries this letter to you. Oh dear, we're going to miss him – but he seems ready for college. He has worked hard and made good money this summer.

David and I drove down to Lake Worth to spend last weekend with Jenni. She has been lonely there this summer. Her job has paid only enough for expenses, and she wishes now she had stayed in Orlando ... it's clearer in hindsight, of course.

Nana GeeGee called yesterday and said you and she had a nice phone visit earlier. I'm planning our trip to Mobile from August 12-22. Is there any possibility you could catch the bus and join us there for a day or two?

Hey, I'm getting new carpet in the apartment. I was pleasant, but strong and assertive with the manager – and got what I asked for. I wish I had known about this behavior before!

This Friday I'm going with friends to see Helen Reddy in concert here at the Sea World Auditorium. That should be a nice treat, huh?

And last Friday, well, I'm sure Skip will tell you about the interview I had at a beautiful estate in Winter Park. I was told there were many applicants, but I'm still hoping to get the position or at least a second interview. Haven't been this excited over anything in a long time, honey. Wow, for this, too, your prayers would help!

Take care – I love you,
Mom

August 10, 1977
Woodbury, Connecticut

Orlando, Florida
Dear Pat,

Your letter to Dad and me last month was comforting in that you spoke of recently found "peacefulness" and "a more healing effect on your mental health." We wish for you in the days ahead only your contentedness and happiness. Friends and family would be so willing to do anything to help, but it is only you ultimately who can help yourself, and it has to take time.

Our affection for you all these years has been rewarded by your countless acts of thoughtfulness and kindness and we certainly expect to keep in touch. This breaking up of your family is heartbreaking for us, and when Bob told us of the sale of the house I had mixed emotions. I'm so very glad for him to have one less problem, but also sad because of no more of the many happy times we have had together there. Our hope for you now is that you will soon find an interesting job – new interests, new friends, a worthwhile life.

Our summer is passing all too quickly while we are enjoying all the usual things – theater, swimming, cookouts, etc., with short trips now and then.

Robin's invitation to her commencement ceremony at Auburn came yesterday and we wish it were easier for us to make that trip. We would like to be with her on the "Big Day" and will be thinking of her. She is to be congratulated on her accomplishment and we sincerely hope she can find a place in business that will keep her busy and happy.

I hope Jenni's weeks at home have been a help to both you and Bob – with some pleasure and some help physically in cleaning out the house.

Bob keeps us up on Skip's activities and it is hard to believe he and his cousin Lynnie both start college next month. And David seems to be as happy as ever. I hope his schooling for this next year works out to your satisfaction.

We both send love and good luck wishes to you all.

Mother Kitty

Nobody who has not been in the interior of a family
can say what the difficulties
of any individual of that family may be.
Jane Austen

Chapter Twenty-One
Labyrinths
1977

Pat at the Peachtree Plaza in Atlanta, Georgia

August 23, 1977
Palm Beach Junior College
Lake Worth, Florida

Orlando, Florida
Dear Mom,

I've come to like you more and more, and I enjoy being around you. I love you. Happy Birthday!

Jenni

September 5, 1977
Orlando, Florida

Auburn, Alabama
Hi, Robin,

I'm sitting here in the midst of utter chaos, wondering what to do next to be prepared for my "Park Avenue Premiere" tomorrow. I can't believe all the stuff I need to take to the mansion. It'll probably scare my new employer when he sees so many cartons, suitcases, toys, books, etc. He called yesterday after arriving from Chicago to see if I was all set to move in tomorrow. David and I will probably come back to the apartment to sleep Tuesday night and then take more things to Winter Park on Wednesday when Skip can help. I'm a bit nervous but that'll no doubt subside after I get there – I hope!

Was just thinking today what a sweet person you are, Robin. You know I love you very much and pray for your health, contentment and all good things.

Take care, honey. I wish you luck. And you wish me luck, okay?

Mom

September 7, 1977
Mobile, Alabama

Orlando, Florida
Hi Pat,

Just a line to say hi. We have been thinking of you moving and all. I hope you and David are all settled in by now.

Love,
Daddy

September 16, 1977
Winter Park, Florida

Auburn, Alabama
Dearest Robin – and Skip, too!

I'm taking a lunch break and short rest before going grocery shopping. So far today I've cleaned two bathrooms, dust-mopped a large floor area and scrubbed one air-conditioning vent. Yesterday I vacuumed a *big* area and cleaned two more of the dozen-plus bathrooms. And that's only the tiniest beginning in this huge place. Gads! Good thing I bought some support-type shoes; my feet cover miles in this mansion.

One frustration I'm suffering through now is trying to adjust to "one for reading, one for distance" contact lenses during parts of the days and *bifocals* during the evenings. It's enough to drive me up the wall.

I know you can guess how much David and I are going to miss having you around, ol' sweet Skipper Doodle. But I wish you the very best possible first year at college. It's comforting to think of you and Robin there together. How scattered one little family can become, huh?

I'll keep my fingers crossed for the best job situation for you, Robin. ... Skip, please send your address to Jenni and me soon. Jen called last night and is okay except for a terrible cold.

You two take special care of yourselves and each other. I love you both so much

Mom and David

September 18, 1977
Auburn University
Auburn, Alabama

Winter Park, Florida
Hi, Mom,

How are ya doin? I'm just fine, although I miss Orlando and everybody there. I have really been busy here getting all settled and trying to fit in all the fraternity parties. I have never been to more parties in my life. I'm averaging about five or six parties a day, but I'm really getting to know a lot of guys (and girls). I'll keep you informed about where I decide to pledge.

Classes start in four days, and I'm looking forward to meeting more people and seeing what college is all about! I went to the football game yesterday – we lost 24-13.

I'd better sign off. I will call you when our phone is fixed. Give David my love! I miss you both.

Love,
Skip

September 24, 1977
Orlando, Florida

Auburn, Alabama
Dear Robin,

Thanks for Happy Birthday wishes to your old dad. I like the letter better than a present. Sorry to say I'll be 49 on the 26th – next year is the big 50!

David is with me this weekend, though he's spending as much time with his little friend Jorge as he is with me. But David is as dear as ever.

I think you're approaching Skip's situation in the right way – being helpful and available, but not pushy or doting. I know it's very comforting to him to have you there, whether he voices that or not.

I'm very happy in the apartment. It's such a pleasant change for me after 22 years of caring for a house and lawn and garden.

Robin, take good care of yourself, please, and all my sincerest good luck wishes on your coming job-seeking adventures.

Much, much love,
Dad

October 2, 1977
Winter Park, Florida

Auburn, Alabama
Dearest Skip,

Hey, today is your Granddaddy's 65th birthday – but he's still a young one, isn't he? I wish we could all be in Mobile celebrating with him.

It's 6 o'clock and the mansion's family members are off in different directions. I'm sitting here in the beautiful Florida room sipping a Bloody Mary, listening to nice stereo music and pretending I've got the world by a string! David is playing pool in one of the many rooms in the mansion. We're expecting Jenni soon for dinner and an overnight visit before she heads back to South Florida in the morning for school. I continue to keep incredibly busy in my job as chief cleaner, cook, laundress, friend, mother, confidante, psychiatrist, a bit of everything – a long way from being Miz Scarlett (in her pre-war life, anyway).

I worked thoughtfully and prayerfully on a proposal for your dad last weekend but haven't received a counter-proposal yet. It will be good when all of our formal papers and agreements are finalized, whatever the

409

outcome, because when all is settled I'll know what's going to be necessary and will learn to accept and adjust.

For the first time now I'm beginning to feel an interest and be open to at least a casual dinner date with a male. Hope I can meet some possible companions before long!

I asked David yesterday if he was okay and whether he had any worrisome things on his mind. He answered, "No, but I would like to see my brother and sisters and Dad more." He seems very well-adjusted yet I know he does feel the difference.

Skip, I've saved the last part of the letter to discuss the problems you're having adjusting to Auburn. First I want you to know that I do empathize with you so much because it's always hard to decide what is the "right" thing to do when one has differing notions and feelings about a certain situation. It's even more difficult when trying not to disappoint others in the process. You know I'll pray for you to be able to arrive at a decision that will be the best one for you.

Since I didn't go to college I can't speak from that experience, but I do know what pain homesickness can cause. I had so much adjusting to contend with upon first settling in Connecticut – feeling like I didn't belong there, the culture, people, weather, everything was alien to what I had known all my life. And I had been so close to my family that not seeing them but once a year nearly undid me. It was hard.

I couldn't change the situation, and I'm afraid I didn't know how to accept it with enough serenity or graciousness, either, so I suffered with it. Anyhow, I feel for you, Skip, and hope you'll soon be able to work out all the pros and cons of this in your mind so you'll feel more at ease. It could be this is just such a huge step in your life and that within a few weeks you'll be content at Auburn.

Often, time does take care of problems – but not always. You know I'll be with you in spirit during this period of indecision, and I will give you all the moral and any financial support I possibly can.

You have been a wonderful "shoulder" for me during the recent trying months, now I can be one for you, okay? I love you, Skip. David and I miss you.

Mom

October 25, 1977
Auburn University
Auburn, Alabama

Winter Park, Florida
Dear Mom,

It was nice to receive your letter today. I haven't written because I've been so busy pledging in the fraternity and doing homework. I want to keep my grades up because my goal is to get on the dean's list next quarter – *if* I decide to stay. I am joining in, trying to adjust.

We just finished with Derby Week, and was it ever fun. The sorority sisters dressed me up like a hot dog, and then got me a little drunk. By the way, I got my "big sister" in the fraternity, the girl I'd asked for. She's beautiful! She won the "Derby Darling" contest last year.

Next Saturday is the Auburn-Florida football game and a lot of friends are coming up from Orlando. I'm really looking forward to seeing old high school classmates. The week after is Homecoming and I'm going to ask a cute girl I've just met.

I've got to go over to the Sigma Chi House now and play cards in a tournament. There's always something going on! How are you and David doing at the mansion? I hope all right.

I love you, you're the greatest.

Skip

October 29, 1977
Woodbury, Connecticut

Winter Park, Florida
Dear Pat,

In spite of the advanced age, my birthday was a very happy one. We had a dinner party at Auntie Bussie's, lots of nice gifts, 23 cards to display and a visit on the phone from both sons.

By now we hope you have been able to adjust more to the job and are finding it the best solution under the circumstances. Glad to hear that David's school is a good one and that he is happy there. My sincere hope is that before too long you will find you are gradually picking up some of the things you feel have been missing in your life and will again be the contented, happy person that I remember so well.

We are eagerly awaiting word from Robin and are hoping so very much she will find a job in which she can be happy. At the moment, I don't know where to write her.

Haven't heard from Jenni since she wrote asking if she could wear my wedding dress, but Bob reports she is thinking now of a summer wedding instead of fall. I'm sure they are a happy pair and I wish them only the best!

Skip's first letter from Auburn was enthusiastic, after which the word was that he wasn't very happy. He did say "I miss the family and my girlfriend," and now a letter yesterday seems to show all is well with him again. I hope so. I'd be sorry not to have him stick it out.

Dad is raking leaves but the weather is lovely. We have a cookout planned for tomorrow.

Love to you and David,
Mother Kitty

November 6, 1977
Auburn University
Auburn, Alabama

Winter Park, Florida
Dear Mom,

So, how is the "old lady" doing? Good, I hope! Sorry I haven't written you lately, but as you know I am so busy with pledging that even my days off are not free time. Pledging is hard but I think it will be worth the time and work in the long run.

Nothing much has been going on up here besides pledging and studying. I think I will be able to pull out about a 2.0 average (3.0 scale) this quarter, which is fairly good.

How is everything with you and David? I hope you're not having to work too hard. I was really happy to hear about your male friends and I'm glad it was a morale booster for you. I know the right person will come along after awhile because you are a pretty woman, and most men won't be able to resist your beauty and personality.

I think you are the greatest mom anyone could have. It's funny it takes a young man to move away from home before he realizes how much his parents mean to him and how much he loves them. I miss you very much and I love you so much, if not more than I ever have. Please take care of yourself and keep being optimistic on men and dating because, in my opinion, you have nothing to worry about!

I love you,
Skip

P.S. – I'll see you in about one month! Can't wait.

November 9, 1977
Winter Park, Florida

Mobile, Alabama
Dear Folks,

Remember when I came here, Daddy, you referred to me as Scarlett? Well, Miz Scarlett's gonna have to leave the mansion now cause the job's done "gone with the wind." Of course, I am being *quite* flip, and funny, but only after having felt sick in heart and body, losing four pounds and crying buckets of tears, day and night, during the past week. But I've decided I might as well try to find any possible little tidbits of humor to help myself survive this latest sudden and unexpected upheaval.

I thought everything was going along just beautifully, but it seems the master of the mansion has asked his new wife for a divorce … and his new housekeeper for a resignation. I was shocked, angry and sad, but I "resigned" as requested.

I called Bob, who, as you know, has been happily ensconced in my old apartment since the house was sold and David and I moved to the mansion. I asked if he would *please* let me have the apartment back. Bless him, he said he would, albeit reluctantly. But we both thought it important that David quickly get back to a familiar place, and his old school, where he is known and loved. With that the case, we knew it made more sense for Bob to find another apartment.

So, incredibly, we'll all be moving again, and I just can't *wait* to see the reactions of the young moving crew as they attempt to deal with the records of our moves: #1, Pat and David, from the house to the apartment; #2, Pat and David, from the apartment to the mansion; #3, Bob, from the house to the apartment; #4, Bob, from the apartment to another rental place; #5, Pat and David, from the mansion back to the apartment. All relocations within an eight-month period. And to make matters even more interesting, with each move various pieces of furniture are "reassigned" to Pat and/or Bob.

I ask you: Does this daughter keep enough drama in your lives? Wish me luck. I love you. A kiss from David.

"Miz PityPat"

P.S. – The ex-mistress of the mansion, Ann, and her daughter Susie, whom David and I like so much, want us to stay in touch and I'm sure we will.

413

November 20, 1977
Atlanta, Georgia

Orlando, Florida
My dearest David,

I have thought about my little brother and missed you so much lately. I can't wait until Christmastime when I can see you! During Mom and Nana GeeGee's visit we have had so much fun at my new home and in Atlanta. Someday you can come up and spend some time with me on vacation. Okay?

Write me a letter soon and tell me what you would like for Christmas. Also, think of a place you would like me to take you while I'm home.

Be a good boy for Mommy and I'll see you in about one month! Many kisses and hugs to my favorite little man.

Your big sister,
Robin

November 29, 1977
Orlando, Florida

Mobile, Alabama
Dearest Mom and Daddy,

I want to tell you again, Mommie, what a simply wonderful treat it was to have the weekend – well, 24 hours – at Atlanta's Peachtree Plaza Hotel with you and Robin. Thanks to you, Daddy, for financially backing the trip – I hope you and Mom will go together someday. What a beautiful, gracious place, what great memories of our time together sharing love and good soul talks and hearty belly laughs. Will we ever forget the funny incident involving my revolving purse? There we gals were, sipping especially fine wine, lingering over a delicious dinner, thoroughly enjoying a panoramic view of Atlanta from the fabulous Sundial Restaurant, 73 stories up, when I casually reached for my purse to get a tissue … and there *was* no purse. I had placed it on the "window sill" beside me when we sat down, not realizing it would travel in a 360-degree turn for an hour before it got back to the spot where we were sitting!

I'm thrilled Robin is getting along so well in her after-college life with a new career and new apartment home in the Atlanta area. She called to tell me about a boy who had just asked her out. Good, I want her to meet nice young men!

I had a great visit with Jenni and Skip before they both left Orlando Sunday. We talked about Christmas plans, but I'm having trouble getting into the spirit. I remembered that all of the family Christmas decorations

414

from 24 years are still in the apartment complex storage area and will need to be divided. Another "division," each one, even the smallest, hurts.

I picked up the separation agreement from the lawyer's office yesterday and gave a copy to Bob. It looks close enough so we believe the final papers can be written up without much delay.

Must hit the hay now. Take care, much love to you. I'll send a kiss from David, who's feeling all the upheavals pretty deeply right now. I'm giving him extra TLC.

Pat

December 7, 1977
Mobile, Alabama

Orlando, Florida
Dear Pat,

It gives me Christmas spirit to share some of my mad money with you, makes me feel good. Maybe you can go to after-Christmas sales for things needed.

Love you,
Mom

December 10, 1977
Orlando, Florida

Mobile, Alabama
Dearest Mom and Daddy,

I meant to write a bit earlier but then decided to wait for these reprints. The picture of my new "fella" isn't really a good likeness, much too posed. Age-wise he can look anywhere from teens to 50s, a little tricky since he's nine years younger than I am.

Well, wow, the apartment has filled up. Skip arrived at midnight Tuesday and Jenni yesterday, and we got a big, live Christmas tree today. All the holiday decorations are in boxes scattered around the living room and dining area, and we have stuck suitcases and assorted things in every imaginable nook. When Robin arrives late on December 22, Skip will move over to his dad's place, only because we can't all fit here. Guess we're lucky Bob borrowed my large suitcase for a trip this weekend – at least that cleared one spot!

I received your Christmas gift check – thanks. The children all need money so instead of choosing presents to come from you, I'm going to give them the cash, except for David, okay? We've all decided that a lot of gifts

under the tree is especially not important this year – being together is. …
I'm at a loss for ideas for you two – help!

Guess what, Skippy took his Mommy to register at college this week!
He and I laughed and laughed about it driving out to Valencia Community
College. I'm signed up for classes in general psychology and English
composition on Tuesdays and Thursdays during the January through April
session. A college gal, whaddaya know?!

Guess I'll sign off for now. Hope you two are feeling pretty perky these
days. Take care of each other, hear? I love you very much.

Pat

December 24, 1977
Atlanta, Georgia

Orlando, Florida

Thanks, Mom, for being *you*! I love you. Merry Christmas.

Robin

December 24, 1977

Dear Diary,

How different this first Christmas of separation with so many missing
treasured traditions: The large gaily decorated home filled to overflowing
with mom and dad and kids and grandparents, cousins and kin; the usual
teasing as to whether or not we could open just one present before Christmas
morning (I always voted yes and had to be appeased if it was decided no!);
the bustling around the kitchen – the aromas – while preparing a huge
turkey-and-trimmings feast; the lovely night scene of hundreds of lit
candles-in-sacks-and-sand lining the sidewalks and driveways throughout
the neighborhood. No … it doesn't seem like Christmas – no turkey, even,
but the kids will be here for a roast beef dinner later.

It's hard, though, not to dwell on what all this means. *Separate*: to part,
disconnect, divide, to go in different directions – such a common verb to
hold such heartbreak.

Earlier today I went by the motel where Mother Kitty and Dad are
staying during the holidays this year. We visited about an hour and when
I got up to leave Mother Kitty held out her arms to me. We hugged, both
of us choked up and tearful. She said, "Dad and I love you and wish
you happiness. Everything you did for us was always loving, kind and
thoughtful. It's hard to let go, but we have wonderful memories of a lot
of years together." The three of us realized it can never be the same, but
we want to keep in touch. She and Dad told me they will always want to

416

know about me and how I am, and without question I feel the same about them. Sixty minutes with two people dear to me, years of memories … a bittersweet Christmas gift to myself.

Life is what we make it – always has been, always will be.
Grandma Moses

Chapter Twenty-Two
Looking Up
1978-79

David with kitty Spunky and teddy bear

January 11, 1978
Smyrna, Georgia

Orlando, Florida
My very dearest Mom,

First of all, I want to thank you for your supportive letter in response to my idea about moving to Orlando. I will think about it wisely and whatever I decide, knowing I have your support will help a lot. I *sure* do love you, Mom.

Now the bad news. My car has been giving me trouble for weeks, but yesterday the gas line broke and the carburetor is shot and will have to be rebuilt. Not only does the repair eat into my budget, but being without the car is a problem all around. I wrote Dad a long letter and asked his advice. The mechanic said I should trade in the car soon, especially with the snow and 10-degree temperatures lately. I'm scared to death of it going out again. I've missed some working hours already, and all this anxiety is driving me crazy.

Nana GeeGee called last night and fed me some loving encouragement, which helps a lot. And, Mom, even with all this "stuff" I don't want you to worry. I'll survive – I always do!

Good luck at school, I'll be thinking about you! Much love to my *very* best friend.

Robin

My *dear* David,

I just wanted to tell you I love you very much and I miss you. I hope you are happy in school and everything else. I think about you all the time. It could be a long time from now, but I may be coming home to Orlando to live, and if I do then we can spend a lot of time together and do lots of fun things. Would you like that?

Please write to me soon. It makes me SO happy to get letters from you!

I love you,
Your big sister,
Robin

January 12, 1978
Orlando, Florida

Lake Worth, Florida
Dear Jenni,

Really enjoyed you while you were home during Christmas break, sweetie. We miss you … but are excited to hear you're into masks and rubber gloves these days! I know how you hate wearing both – but whatever you have to do for a few more months to become a full-fledged dental hygienist, huh? The end is in sight, so perk up for this final semester.

Ye old mama has entered the classroom with a bang this week. Tuesday I had two classes plus a qualifying test in English Composition. You'll laugh, I was already in trouble even before the test began – couldn't figure out where in the mass of teeny-weeny fill-in squares to record my Social Security number. Two classes today, also, including a long chapter and workbook section in Psychology. Getting educated is going to keep me busy!

Take care – I love you very much. David sends you a kiss.

Mom

January 17, 1978
Orlando, Florida

Valencia Community College
Dear Professor,

I am going to take the liberty of writing my first English Composition class paper in letter form, which I hope will be agreeable with you. I have written literally hundreds of letters during the past 35 years or so and, since I am nervous about the writing sample you have requested, I believe I will feel more comfortable with a letter.

The most exciting thing for me right now is LIFE – finding joy in life again after a few years of too much time spent regretting the past, ignoring and/or wasting the present, and dreading the future. There were many "growing pains" along the way to this new-found enjoyment of life, but they have been constructive growing pains.

During the last seven or eight months I have read a number of self-help books, attended various seminars, and learned to practice TM, TA, and IPM – all those interesting techniques identified by initials. I made a discovery that has been invaluable to my present happiness: *I* can control my life to a great degree. Amazingly, I never realized that before. I had always been a very trusting and dependent person, allowing myself to be easily influenced by the people in my life. It's fantastic to know I have power within myself strong enough to change conditions outside myself. Sometimes I feel like a child with a new, magic toy!

My refrigerator door is covered with favorite philosophical sayings, and there is one with which I would like to close this letter, although at the moment I can remember only the last line, "And to be open to the newness of each new day." That's my motto!

I am a little afraid of but looking forward to this class, Professor. And I am very eager to learn everything I can.

Sincerely,
Your new student,
Pat

January 27, 1978
Dear Diary,

As of today I am a divorced woman. What an emotional time. I woke up irritable and weepy. At the courthouse I met my dear friend Betty Sue, my witness, who gave me a hug ... and my attorney, who enveloped me in a warm embrace and also boosted my morale somewhat with his praise for the person I am and the way I've handled myself and the situation.

The proceeding was brief. The judge granted the "Dissolution of Marriage" and wished me a happy life. Back at the apartment, Mom, who is visiting from Alabama, held me in her arms when I needed to cry one more time "for all the old times."

February 14, 1978
Louisville, Kentucky

Orlando, Florida
Dear Pat,

My friend, I pause every now and then to reflect on my progress in learning about life. Recently this thought surfaced that I had not thoroughly pondered previously: I learned a lesson about accepting and loving people for what they are, no more, no less. Really loving people in the variety of forms God created them. I have not always had that capacity and now, thank heaven, I do. It erases much selfishness. It reminds me to make allowances for human error. It makes my eyes smile at strangers as well as friends. I feel good about the way I feel toward people, proud even. I probably appreciate this feeling more because I had to learn it. It also makes me aware of others who have not yet found this simple secret to life's inner happiness.

My lesson came from watching a friend live her daily life. It began in 1963 with our introduction by the Welcome Wagon hostess – when we were both new to Orlando, renting houses on the same street – and continued through the years in our new homes, where we were again neighbors. What I learned from her still benefits me today, and will forever.

The friend's name is Pat. Thank you, Pat!

Love,

Linda

February 15, 1978

Orlando, Florida

Smyrna, Georgia

Dearest Robin,

Sorry I haven't written in a while but I've been swamped with work, both at home and at school. Up until late today I thought I might actually fail the English Composition assignment due tomorrow because I could not come up with one creative idea. But finally I decided on the subject of maturity. (I'll enclose a copy of the essay as it is now, although I may read it again tonight and still make a few changes.) Now I should be studying the next chapter in psychology: "The Brain and Nervous System." After just skimming the pages, though, I'm not at all sure my brain or my nervous system can handle all that information. But I'm going to practice what I learned about memory retention in last week's chapter – read it thoroughly and then *sleep*, so there'll be less interference.

My new friend Ernie came over Monday and we celebrated Valentine's Day with an evening of dining and dancing. I'm thinking of having a small party next week to introduce him to a few friends. Of course, I haven't entertained in so long I'd better brush up on my rusty skills if I am to live up to my former "hostess with the mostest" title!

I've put together a resume, which your Aunt Dorothy typed for me. Now I need to pick it up and get copies made. And decide where to send them.

I must close, honey, and study a little while before I go to bed, and I'm already so tired. You take care of *you*, okay? I love you very much. We miss you.

Love and kisses,

Mom

A LOOK AT MATURITY

From my vantage point of age 45, I have two distinctly different views of the meaning of maturity. When I was 16, I believed it was a destination at which I would someday magically arrive, serene and secure, but at 40 I began to realize it was an ongoing journey – along a road often bumpy and filled with curves and detours. Let me explain. ...

There was a definite "once upon a time" quality to my destination theory. The fairy tale, briefly: A young girl dreamed of growing up, falling in love, getting married and having babies. After high school, a secretarial job and pleasant social life with friends filled the waiting time until a handsome Prince Charming charged up and, without a hitch, quickly romanced and swept her off her feet. Soon, the traditional, virginal white wedding, bliss in a honeymoon cottage and, after a year or two, the knitting of baby booties. Through some years, Mr. Stork delivered four precious baby bundles, the Prince scaled the corporate ladder, the family settled in bigger and better castles. The couple's love, the children, and the bank account grew. There was laughter and fun and travel. They lived fully, happily ... ever after. In other words, events flowed along on the dream schedule, the couple matured, and life was a cliché – just a bowl of cherries, a bed of roses.

Oh, dear, the pure innocence that gave birth to such fantasies. Only dewey-eyed youth could envision such perfection.

Actually, though, in my case, reality paralleled the fairy tale for a few years – and, ultimately, made the ending of the real-life version more shocking. I aspired to no career, wanted only to be wife and mother. My prince, a dreamy Navy ensign, drove up in a 1952 baby blue Pontiac convertible and, in just weeks, wooed and won me. We were radiant at our wedding, reveled in honeymoon heaven and newly married life (this marred only by military separations), eagerly welcomed each of four wonderful children, enjoyed rewarding promotions, and resettled into larger and nicer homes.

So far, so good. Then, at 40, an overwhelming disenchantment descended upon me, engulfed me. I hadn't realized the sheer amount and the constancy of physical, emotional and mental energy that would be required of me as a mother and homemaker; the difficulty of building the bank account in the face of myriad family needs; the necessity of deferring travel plans. I never imagined a scarcity of intimacy, of fun and laughter and, especially, the possibility that love would not deepen, but die. I certainly hadn't pictured myself menopausal, growing old and dried up, dealing with depression and crazily behaving hormones – grieving the loss of the very essence of my feelings of femaleness. *What* had gone wrong? Forty – at my destination, but far from being serenely mature, I was a mess. ...

In my dilemma I began searching for answers to the dichotomy between all those glorious expectations and the disappointing reality. I found one convincing explanation in *Shifting Gears*, a powerful study by Gail Sheehy. In a chapter entitled "The Maturity Myth" the author writes, "Maturity, according to the myth, is a set condition. It puts all its emphasis on being grown-up and leaves no room for growing. It promises that we will be grown-up once we settle down, and that after a few years of consolidating our material position in the world, we will be home safe at about the age of forty." Ah, the destination I pictured as a youth.

But my belief now coincides with that of one of the women interviewed by the author, who stated, "If you define maturity as being fully developed, as a peak that you reach and then drop off from, then thank God I will never be mature in that sense. Maturity for me is a process, the process of becoming more of myself and continually growing." In other words the ongoing journey theory I came to believe in.

So, now when I hear young people discussing what they're going to be or do when they grow up, I chuckle and remind myself, "*I* am not *ever* going to grow up – I'm just going to GROW!"

February 23, 1978
Orlando, Florida

Orlando, Florida
DEAR DADDY,
I WISH I COULD SEE YOU MORE. AND I LIKE TO DO THINGS WITH YOU. I LOVE YOU.
LOVE,
DAVID

424

March 3, 1978
Orlando, Florida

Mobile, Alabama
Dearest Mom and Daddy,

Let's see what news there is for you today. ... Skip and his friend found a small house to rent and will move in next week. Last night Skip said, "Well, Mom, I'm going to miss the good dinners you always have waiting for me when I get home. I'll have to get to cooking now." And tonight he was so cute imitating Archie Bunker having a fit when he came in and dinner wasn't ready! Later Skip came up to hug me, say thanks again, and tell me he was glad I'd have less work to do with him gone. Maybe ... but I think I'd druther have the work. David and I loved having Skip with us these few months.

I talked to Robin earlier, mostly about interviews and her worries concerning a job. I told her I believe everything will turn out just great for her. When I brought my friend Ernie up to date on her situation, he was sweet, said, "I hope everything will be good with Robin. Does she need anything? Tell her we are willing to help. You know I care about your kids. I hate it if they have problems ... same way I feel about you."

A letter from Jenni had good news. Last week on midterm finals in clinic (working on a patient) she made the highest mark of anyone in the class. Great, huh? Oh, you know how David loves to play Superman – well, Jenni thrilled him by making Superman outfits for him and his friend. They wear them in action and I'm often dodging little supermen in flying capes!

Finally got an English Composition paper together at 10:30 the other night, and the next morning I studied psychology in the laundry room while I washed and dried three loads of clothes. About the chapter coming up titled "Emotion" – my comment: "What do you want to know? I've run the gamut, been through every one!" All the subjects covered in the psychology class are really interesting and I've learned and relearned *so* much. Keeps me busy, keeps me growing. ...

I love you,
Pat

April 10, 1978
Orlando, Florida

Mobile, Alabama

Dear Mom,

I sure do wish you were still here with me in Orlando. I still cry at some point every day, but the stream of tears seems to dwindle a bit more each time.

I know you and Daddy will want to read the enclosed essay I wrote as an English assignment. When I received the paper back from the professor, I was immensely pleased to see four letters: "WOW – A!" And he told me he thought it worthy of publication.

Love,
Pat

COPING WITH UNCOUPLING

The divorce rate in America has been climbing steadily and is now at an all-time high, with nearly a million divorces each year. This divorce boom might suggest that ending a marriage is an easy matter, but nothing could be further from the truth. No matter how good or bad a marriage has been, terminating it is almost always an extremely painful, wrenching experience.

When marriage partners begin to sense that divorce is a distinct possibility, they also realize how complex are the bonds that have been formed in the relationship. There are physical, emotional and economic ties. The partners have shared the passion of love, the birthing of children, the building of houses, the struggle of business, and the joys and difficulties of intimate daily life.

Unfortunately these bonds are not magically dissolved along with the formal Dissolution of Marriage. One by one they all go through a change in nature. It is unusual for a person to end a relationship with another in one neat, quick slice – though that method would, indeed, be convenient. Instead there must be a step-by-step uncoupling, followed by the creation of a new relationship with the former spouse; and these are arduous, painful processes.

This period of separating and re-creating is a traumatic one when each partner is apt to feel unloved, abandoned, bruised, lonely, scared, and that he or she has failed in some way. It is also a time of distress for children of any age – and even for parents and friends of the couple. The entire process, as in my case, can take years, as shown by a few excerpts from my diaries.

July 1974 – I believed wives and husbands always kept their hearts completely open to one another, but maybe I was wrong. Sometimes it isn't easy for one or the other to share the deepest thoughts, desires, or fears … and a great measure of intimacy is lost.

November 1974 – Our marriage is slowly deteriorating, but we have decided to go to a marriage counselor for help.

April 1975 – We are staying apart this summer, trying a "creative separation" to see if we can build a real marriage again. *So many* people will get hurt if we break up.

August 1975 – Should we just stay together for the sake of our children? Will they be all right if we don't make it?

December 1975 – We have gotten further apart than ever but have decided to try even harder to solve our problems. It's difficult to picture us really happily married in the future, but I guess nothing is impossible. …

June 1976 – We are like two acquaintances. It's strange. I feel so lonely and depressed. I worry about loneliness if we separate, but then I sometimes feel unbearably lonely lying beside this once-beloved husband.

December 1976 – Robin and Jenni are home from college for the holidays, and we all are pretending to be merry and gay. Little David, though, has seen through the pretense. He said matter-of-factly to his sisters, "You know Mommy and Daddy don't love each other anymore." I think I know this will be our last Christmas as a family. *How* can this have happened?

February 1976 – Skip is 18 and I never realized how much this would affect him. The girls have cried openly and I'm sure Skip has shed secret tears. He said, "It hurts, Mom, but I think if you and Dad hated each other and were fighting I just couldn't stand it." At times I am sure I cannot cope with all this. I pray, pray for extra strength.

March 1977 – It's over. And there is some sense of relief in the decision. We have told all the children, our home is up for sale, the die is cast. There's such silent sadness here … but we have worked through a lot of the bitterness, resentments and regrets. We believe we can stay on friendly terms. I feel it is imperative, we must.

April 1977 – Moving day was a terrible physical and emotional ordeal. It felt like claws wrenching my heart apart. I could hardly bear to look at my children's faces of forlorn hope. Even the half-empty house seemed enveloped in an aura of sorrow. The division of material possessions was agonizing.

September 1977 – I wonder what Bob is feeling? He doesn't show his emotions. My emotions continue to go every which way – I'm scared, sad, happy, downhearted, excited – but I *think* I'm getting stronger day by day.

January 1978 – A Dissolution of Marriage has been granted. The divorce is final, three months short of a Silver Wedding Anniversary. We have survived … so far.

February 1978 – Jenni is engaged to be married. I'm happy for her, and glad, too, that I no longer feel disillusioned by love and marriage. That must mean I am on the road to a full recovery. Someday.

Divorce *is* prevalent, and painful. But there's comfort in the fact that eventually most divorced people find satisfactory new attachments. They can learn from experience, and they are not necessarily doomed to make the same mistakes twice.

A haiku poem I wrote after the divorce sums up the contents of this essay and my thoughts on the uncoupling process:

Seasons of Goodbye

December despair
June's sweet mem'ries
Fall's regrets
Spring's hope eternal

April 20, 1978
Dear Diary,
Questions from David: "Mom, are you gonna get married again? I want you to get married again, and Daddy, too. … Mom, if Daddy gets married again, will he be my stepfather?" Bless his wonderful little self. He is so earnestly trying to keep things straight.

April 20, 1978
Palm Beach Junior College
Lake Worth, Florida

Mobile, Alabama
Dear Nana GeeGee and Granddaddy,

Hi! I'm sure you probably can't make it for my graduation but I wanted to send you the invitation anyway. I'm finally out. And now the wedding plans are keeping me busy!

Nana, Happy Birthday to you next month and, remember, you're not getting older, you're just getting better!

Much love,
Jenni

May 7, 1978
Dear Diary,

Mom's birthday, gee, I wonder how it feels to be 64? Sometimes I'm sure I have the age thing licked, and other times I know I still dread getting old. If only I can *think* young no matter what. Not like this week, when I've not been "young thinking" at all, but have succumbed to feeling tired, old and more-than-slightly worn.

I need to heed Skip's new motto: "Don't take life too seriously – you'll never get out of it alive!" Amen. ...

July 9, 1978
Dear Diary,

David and I are staying at Chateau-by-the-Sea in New Smyrna Beach this week with Mom and Daddy who are down from Mobile for a vacation. Little Sis (my name for Filipina doll Terri ever since she adopted us as her American family) comes by to visit every chance she gets. She loves to help "Papa" cook – and we put music on and dance and sing and just have a ball. She has such serenity and wisdom along with her great capacity to uplift and spread joy!

I asked Daddy if he and I could have an appointment to really visit. We talked about the oil business, which has brought him great excitement and financial rewards at age 66. I told him I'd be a Kelly Girl starting after this vacation and he thought that was a good (temporary) decision – and might prove to be a great way to make contacts for a possible full-time job in the future. I confessed my fears, and he told me to try hard not to panic and get to feeling so low but to keep looking up. I shared my English composition paper on divorce – I, reading and crying, he, listening and crying – then we hugged and cried some more together.

Mom and I had time to talk over things, too. She says time will take care of so much, and no doubt it's true. (I remember she and Daddy gave me that "time-will-take-care-of-it" promise when I was in teenage turmoil over having said goodbye to both of my first loves. Of course, they chose not to tell me back then how much time it would take and how deeply it might hurt! Now they don't have to go into detail, I *know*.) Mom said she and Bob had had a good talk at Jenni's wedding reception, that he was friendly, warm and open. He told her he certainly had done a lot of thinking and realizes now he "should have spent more time taking care of Pat's needs." She thinks we might get back together, but I don't see how that could happen. …

All I know is each day I pray I can think positively about my life, all the areas of my life. That I can live fully, live freely, that is, without doubts, resentment or guilt. I do know I'm loved by so many dear people, who are always supportive, and I am deeply thankful.

One day that sweet Robin teased me, "All that matters is that *I love you!*" I told her if that would work, I surely would be the most secure being in the world. All four children show their love in beautiful ways and words. I need to try harder to hide my sadness because I know it's a terrible burden for them. And the mother-daughter talk this week with my mom, "Wise Wilba," firmly reminded me of it.

July 17, 1978
Mobile, Alabama

Orlando, Florida
Dear Mom,

I am in Alabama now. How are you? I am fine. I had fun on the plane. We went through clouds. Got to sit by the window. I stayed one week in Mississippi. It was fun. We went to see *Grease*, and we went to K-mart. It was fun. Give Skip and Robin and Ernie a kiss. I love you.

Love,
David

July 26, 1978
Orlando, Florida

Mobile, Alabama
Dearest Mom and Daddy,

Well, I've got my sweet little boy home again. He seems older. That's what happens with a visit to really cool grandparents!

Wasn't it interesting that two of our Orlando friends were on the same plane? David was thrilled when the pilot let him visit the cockpit for a few minutes. He liked the whole flight.

When I asked if everything went well on the trip to Starkville to see Uncle John and family he grinned and answered, "Yes, except for just a few minor difficulties."

He certainly had a good vacation, and I thank you for it. Also I want to thank you both for treating us to the beach vacation at The Chateau in New Smyrna Beach.

David said you were feeling a lot better, Daddy. Good, I hope you're up to acting devilishly perky again soon! Skip and Robin are coming for dinner in a few minutes for David's Welcome Home party. I baked a cake! Take care of each other. We send you two lots of love.

Pat and David

July 28, 1978
Mobile, Alabama

Orlando, Florida
Dearest Pat,

Thanks so much for the letter and pictures from Jenni's wedding – they are good. We're so proud of that shot of Daddy and me. Would you please have about four or five prints of it made? I'd like one for Sam, John and Rickey – I'll give you money for them. Did any pictures turn out of you singing at the organ with Ernie?

We certainly enjoyed David – he is truly beautiful. Boy is he ever ready to know about everything, just like Robin was at age 8 or 9. Now we're super happy that our Skip will be arriving in a few days for his visit with us. We're planning to do some traveling since Skip loves to drive and we love being together.

Must run to get this in the mail to you. Love and kisses to you and David.

Mom

July 29, 1978
Richmond, Virginia

Orlando, Florida
Dear Mom,

It was nice to hear from you so quickly! When you mentioned you were having the old standby dinner of meatloaf, baked potatoes and green beans, I had to run out and buy the makings for the same dinner. The power of suggestion – how I wish we all could have been together to eat.

I've just finished reading a book, Mom – *The Best Place to Be* by Helen Van Slyke – and it really got me thinking. It's a tear-jerker about a 47-year-old woman who goes through a lot of trauma and loss. She and her mother have never been close, so the daughter arranges a reunion because she realizes her mother, or she herself, could be gone at any time and her mother would never have known what love and respect her daughter felt for her. It sounds kind of mixed-up, but in a way that's what I'd like to say to you because if something were to happen to either of us, I'd want it said.

For one thing, I love you very much. I admire you, your strength and your kindness for everyone around you. I'm really proud of you, not only because you're my mother but because I'm proud of the person you are. I want so much to be more like you, but maybe that will come with the years. I not only love you as a mother but also as a woman and a friend. And I'm proud to be your daughter. I love you, Mom, and miss you so badly – David, too.

All my love,
Jenni

July 31, 1978
Richmond, Virginia

Orlando, Florida
Dearest Mom,

I miss you so much I can hardly stand it! And my boy, David, too! But I'm trying to keep busy, which helps. Being homesick is no fun.

The townhouse is shaping up pretty well and I really like the kitchen. Tonight for dinner I made beef stew in the crockpot, salad, rolls and an interesting cucumber dish. Yum! That reminds me, Mom, please send me some of our favorite recipes: Fu Man Chu casserole, curried chicken salad, Ernie's Filipino pansit, banana nut bread, that fish with the tomatoey sauce, Robin's baked chicken, and any others you think I'd like. Also, can you tell me how you cook a turkey?

Kitty is fine, although she's at the vet's today for a second worming treatment and rabies shot. She has already adjusted to her new home and is really good company.

Keep me informed on your life, Mom, and take care of yourself. I love you and miss you. Hug and kiss David for me.

Jenni

August 5, 1978
Dear Diary,

This is the ad I placed in two small neighborhood newspapers today:

Personable lady desires position with refined widow or couple who needs all-around Home Manager. Twenty years' experience as cook, hostess, shopper, personal/social secretary. Prefer private quarters.

August 16, 1978
Orlando, Florida

Mobile, Alabama
Dearest Mom and Daddy,

Do you have Jenni's new address in Virginia? Her 21st birthday is Monday. I splurged on two more crystal wine glasses so they'll have four and be prepared to invite another couple over for dinner. David just dictated a letter to Jenni while I typed it. I helped him to see how to compose an interesting letter, and he was so cute with his words.

Hope y'all had a really nice anniversary yesterday. I was thinking about you and how wonderful it is, particularly in this day and age of such a high divorce rate, to have a good 47-years-long marriage like yours. We'll have a *blast* in 1981 for your Golden Anniversary!

I have felt so low and blah the past couple of days, like I'm fighting off a virus or something, but no doubt I'll perk up again soon. Robin called this afternoon and asked to keep her baby brother overnight. She and David will have fun – they like to watch the TV show "Starsky and Hutch" together. David informed us recently that he loves Robin's bed because "it's so good for thinking, especially with the fan humming!" He is so adorable. Oh, this was cute – awhile back he mentioned maybe he should start using Ban deodorant so I bought a bottle for him. The first time he tried it he came to show me. He had put some under his arms *and* on his neck. Today after his letter to Jenni was already in the mail, he realized, "Oh, I forgot to tell Jen that I use Ban now!"

Well, I must say goodnight. I still plan to write Jenni a long letter – and I want to take a leisurely bath before going to bed, too. Take care of your dear selves. I love you,

Pat

September 6, 1978
Dear Diary,

David said this morning, "I hope you don't get a job, Mom, 'cause I'm kinda scared to come home and stay here when you're gone." Now that mixes me up more than ever. *What* am I going to do about my situation?

September 21, 1978
Dear Diary,

Darn, I am so gullible and soft-hearted and naïve and vulnerable. I've discovered things are not as they seemed with Ernie. (Thinking about the situation, I jotted down a few lines of haiku: Perfect prey for love's pain, my warm heart – When sweet words belie all is well.) I must not pretend, fool myself too long. I have to face reality about the future of the relationship – the *lack* of a future of the relationship. Somewhere, isn't there someone willing to love me with all his heart and let me do the same? And have honesty and trust and intimacy and no games between us?

September 25, 1978
Dear Diary,

We had a family dinner the other evening. Bob was included and, always the true gentleman, arrived at the apartment with a bottle of wine for me. Being together felt a bit unusual, but it was pleasant and, all in all, successful.

Robin and I had a great trip to Savannah for Cousin Katie's remarriage and all the festivities beforehand. I loved the city. We went to lunch, browsed in the interesting gift shops, watched huge ships passing each other on the river. Enjoyed a pre-wedding shower and meeting scads of Katie's friends. Wedding day was wild: shampoos, hairdos, helping the bride into her finery, drying her few nervous tears. Katie looked beautiful, and so much like Grandma Jennie I couldn't get over it. At the reception we were tickled when so many people thought Katie and I were really sisters – as we've always felt we are.

October 16, 1978
Dear Diary,

A special someone I loved long ago reappeared unexpectedly. Seeing a heartbreaker from my teen-age years at age 46 was a fascinating experience. Each of us seemed greatly changed – and exactly the same. Amazingly, we immediately felt a spark between us still. But too many complications and possibilities of people being hurt, so it was only a brief, poignant reunion. With many bittersweet moments since, wondering what might have been.

November 14, 1978
Orlando, Florida

Richmond, Virginia
Dear Jenni,

Last night I said hell I wish Jenni was back. I even cryed becaus I wished you would come back. I went to bed around a quarter of ten and I didn't get to sleep until eleven thirty. I hope you come back to Florida. What do you want for Christmas? I have about $14.50.

David

November 15, 1978
Richmond, Virginia

Orlando, Florida
Dear David,

Thank you for your beautiful letters in cursive writing. I think you write better than me!

I wish I were in Florida, too. I miss everyone very much. It is getting pretty cold up here, and I hope it will snow when you come to Virginia for a visit.

Our new puppy is so cute! I'll send you some pictures as soon as they are developed. We named him Christian. He weighs only one pound. You can hold him in one hand. Sometimes at night he will cry for his mommy. He still pees on the floor sometimes, but he is learning to go outside. He has a little bed. Kitty is trying hard to like him!

Kitty and Christian say meow and woof to you and Mom. I love you and miss you very much!

Jenni

Mobile, Alabama
Dearest Folks,

Well, here I am at another temporary assignment after receiving a 9:30 a.m. call that Red Lobster Restaurant company headquarters in Orlando needed a receptionist in the main lobby today. It's a beautiful office complex with a slew of people coming and going continuously and phones ringing off the hook, with callers asking so many questions, some of which are just like Greek to me. Keeping up with a switchboard is *wild*. I'm slowly catching on, though, and am considering filling out an application for full-time work here.

I really enjoyed my stint demonstrating cameras last weekend at K-Mart and did quite well as far as sales went. Kodak assumes the demo person is not doing a good job unless she sells five cameras within a five-hour period; any amount over that earns a 50-cent bonus per camera. I worked 14 hours and sold 46 cameras, so I'll get about $15 plus my $3.20 per hour.

Thank you both very much for the generous check for Christmas presents. I went shopping yesterday and quickly spent it. I chose for Skip one of the neat cameras I was selling, plus battery and film, as a combined gift from you and me. I ordered the oval platter of Jenni's china for her gift from you, found a nifty Dallas Cowboys travel bag for David, and I'll give Robin $25 toward new frames for her glasses. The gift I chose for myself is a pretty nightgown, the type that can be used as a pool/beach dress, too. I'll wrap the gifts (and attach the signed tags you sent) for under the tree – and you'll receive thank-you notes from the kids later.

Well, it's almost 5 o'clock, the place is clearing out, and I'll be leaving, too. Take care of each other and know that much love is coming your way.

Pat

Orlando, Florida
Pat dear,

Thanks for your card and the snapshots. I am *so* glad to have them to add to the "rogues gallery" in my album. My pictures of Robin, Jenni and Skip go back to babyhood and I like to keep the snaps up to date.

Jenni is really beautiful and it is hard to believe this is the kid who used to suck index and ring fingers and twirl a strand of hair!

Have a good Christmas and Happy New Year.

Love,
Auntie Bussie

December 20, 1978
Auburn University
Auburn, Alabama

Orlando, Florida

Mom,

You're the best "mommy" a boy could ever have. Not only that, you are a great friend and advisor. Have a wonderful Christmas.

I love you,
Skip

January 2, 1979

Dear Diary,

Well, what am I thinking as another new year begins? Mainly that I simply cannot believe the quick passage of time. I've had lots of thoughts these past few days, pondering the years ahead. Wondering what in the world my future holds. Whatever is ahead, though, my motto is going to be: "Chin up, Pat!"

Sweet David arrives home from Virginia tomorrow and I can't wait to see him. I miss that little guy so much but am happy he got this chance to visit Jenni. And to see snow!

I was pleased by the note Bob sent along with the January child support check, in which he thanked me for my Christmas card and my words of reflection about our relationship. He said friends and family had commented that we "must be doing something right." We're trying. ...

Now, to end this day's musings with a touch of humor – Skip and Robin were here for dinner, during which she wanted to talk over all the fears and questions she's wrestling with concerning her possible future with Terry, the new man in her life. At a pivotal moment, while she was relating serious thoughts, Skip bit into his meat and a piece of it flew right out over the table. She groaned, "SKI-I-P, I'm talking about my *life* here and you're playing with your chicken!" It was one of those funny little incidents that had the three of us laughing until we were just plain silly!

January 2, 1979
Richmond, Virginia

Orlando, Florida

Dear Mom,

We had a wonderful time with David. He is a sweetheart. But you know that! I'll tell you on the phone a few cute things he said. He wants me to tell you he likes Pepperidge Farm white toast with honey for breakfast, and Manwich sloppy joes for supper.

I just came downstairs from tucking David in. I knew something was bothering him and when I asked him about it he started crying and said he didn't want to leave. It just about broke my heart, Mom. But I know he misses you. He kept wanting to call you. It was so sweet.

Talk to you soon.

Much love,
Jenni

February 18, 1979
Richmond, Virginia

Orlando, Florida

Dear Mom,

Hi, it's 5 p.m. and has been snowing heavily since about 10 this morning. The snow is at least a foot deep already. What a nuisance – and driving is so dangerous. I never appreciated Florida winters until I had to experience one up here. It's reported that this is one of the worst winters ever in Virginia. I had to pick this one! I'm so tired of being cold and having the heater dry out my sinuses at night

Tomorrow at work there will probably be tons of cancellations. There have been every time it snows. And a day without dental hygiene patients is dull. But I do like the atmosphere at the office very much, and the women I work with are a lot of fun.

Take care – I love you!

Your Jenni

March 21, 1979
Orlando, Florida

Orlando, Florida
Dear Coach,

Thank you for being my coach this year. I realy am glad you toght me. You're the best! I am sorry that I missed half of the year because I had a flamed atendent.

Your friend,
David

DAVID'S ESSAY OF FOOTBALL

A football game is a rough game. A football is a leather ball shaped like no other ball. It is usely brown. If you want 6 points then you have to get a touchdown. If your kicker is really good you might try from fifty yards away to kick a field goal. A field goal is 3 points.

April 12, 1979
Woodbury, Connecticut

Orlando, Florida
Robin dear,

I am sure you've heard some of the news accounts of the nuclear power accident on Three Mile Island. There have been such conflicting reports about the degree of danger to the surrounding area from the "meltdown" and whether evacuation was necessary, but I can tell you if I still lived in Pennsylvania, *I* would have gotten out of there.

I was really tickled to get a letter from you so soon after I had asked you to "keep in touch." Five years is a very long time for me to go without seeing my dear first grand-niece, and I for sure don't want that much time to pass again. If we can't "commune" in the flesh, we can at least do it on paper.

Your comments on getting together soon again, and wanting to see New England "if finances ever permit" gave me a great idea, and then gave me pause. I'd love to have you, if only for a weekend, and would be very willing to foot the bill for your flight. However, I'm not sure your Nana Kitty would be happy about you staying with me! She's my sister, I love her, and I'm not about to do anything to hurt her. I'm also not about to buy a plane ticket so you can stay with your grandparents! See my dilemma? If you have a solution let me know.

I'm glad if I struck a few chords of "things I hadn't thought of before." I never give advice unless I'm asked for it and even then seldom attempt to do anything but bring up ideas to be thought out – which you apparently understand. So, since you did ask, I feel I just have to add one more thing.

It's this: You said the only difference between living together and getting married is a little piece of paper. Then later you said you wanted to be with Terry all the time but you felt you weren't ready for marriage. In my mind these two statements didn't quite agree. If marriage is just a little piece of paper, what's so big about it that you're not ready for it? Will you give that some thought, too? Whatever you do won't affect my feelings for you, Robin, but I hate to have you do anything at all about which you are uncertain and conflicted. I think you are, but I also think you've made up your mind. Am I right?

Much love,
Auntie Bussie

P.S. – I have a lot of snapshots from very way back that I'd like to show you, including some of you in the altogether. You were a beautiful baby – and I was excited over my first grand-niece.

April 21, 1979
Woodbury, Connecticut

Orlando, Florida
Robin dear,

It was good to hear from you again so soon and that you are considering a trip to New England. We can talk about all of the other things then. But before that, I feel I must say something to you about your Nana Kitty and Granddad.

Honey, don't sell them short. They may "live in their own little world," but it is in a world of a very good and sound marriage and of having and rearing your father and your Uncle Dave. Of all of us, they are the only ones who "made it" together. Your father, Dave, and I failed and only Uncle Dave has been able to re-establish what your grandparents have and what I believe most of us really wanted. Perhaps your grandparents' sense of right and wrong and not swerving from it was a help in accomplishing what they have.

And about their judging you, that I can't believe. My sister has talked a lot about you to me. She has always said there is something special about a first grandchild even though the others are loved, too. At every stage of your development, she has shown me snapshots of you and said how pretty you are. You are very special to her.

Also, Robin, she has an image of her family as being just about "right." When things went wrong, such as divorces, she was shaken but she quickly recovered with some rationalization. Nothing any of her children or grandchildren (or, I am sure, future great-grandchildren) do can be "wrong."

This may be fantasy but it's a nice one, and it includes you, whatever you do.

About herself, she feels like a good mother and grandmother, who is loved by all. True! She does not like other people to know anything that is going wrong with any member of the family and tries to hide it, even from me. I'm kind of hard to fool, though!

So I am sure she would be terribly hurt to know there are things you would confide in me that you wouldn't confide in her or things you would tell me that she wouldn't want me to know.

Robin, dear, do you see the spot I'm in? Your Nana Kitty is my sister. I love her dearly and am determined never to let anything get between us. I'm not a bit sure she could understand why you are coming to visit me when it's been a long time since you've visited your grandparents. I think it would be best if you did not tell anyone else I'm paying "air freight." How about if you split the visit and say you'd like to spend Thursday and Friday with your grandparents and then go to Auntie's on Saturday and Sunday. That way we'd have a lot of time to talk, plus all day Monday while I drove you to the airport.

Let me know how you feel about this.

Much love,
Auntie Bussie

April 27, 1979
Dear Diary,

Grieving is so hard. It hurts to lose the warm, tender feeling that comes with caring for a certain person. For a while I have seen – and tried vainly to ignore – sure signs of the romantic relationship between Ernie and me drawing slowly, inexorably to an end. Visits have become few and far between and emotional distance separates us even when we're together. I know it's over, but neither of us has said the words yet.

I don't doubt we'll still see each other occasionally in the future, but once more as friends, like we were in years past when each of us was still married. But now … I just feel lover-less. Don't know why I am ever surprised … things change, I grieve, life goes on.

May 13, 1979
Dear Mom,
    I just want to say, you're a great mom on Mother's day.
Your son,
David

June 4, 1979
Richmond, Virginia

Orlando, Florida
Dear David,
    What have you been doing since school let out, just playing? Mom said the new arrangement for her to keep your friend part-time is going to be great since you and Chris really like playing together. You and Mom are going to be staying in New Smyrna Beach in August, and that will be a lot of fun for you, little beach lover! David, can you still remember when you used to lie on your tummy and talk down the holes to the crabs? You were very serious about it and amazed us with your own special language for them.
    Kitty is just fine, she is so pretty. We were thinking about letting her have a litter of kittens, but I am afraid I'd want to keep them all! She had to go the vet the other day for some booster shots and to be wormed but she's okay. She gets in bed with me every night and if it's chilly outside she curls up under the covers next to me and keeps me company. She sends her love to you!
    In a month from now we will be deciding which clothes to pack for our trip. I can't wait to see you and the rest of the family. Maybe when we leave you can fit in my suitcase and come up here to live! I do have an idea, though. At the end of the summer or in the fall we'll see if you can fly up here again. If I can afford it we'll do it!
    Well David, you take care of Mom, and I know you're a good boy so I don't have to tell you to be one. All my love to you. I miss you so much!!
Jenni

July 4, 1979
Dear Diary,
    A low-key day, certainly not one bursting with fireworks of any kind. I spent it alone, slept late, and throughout the day enjoyed a few long-distance phone visits with family and friends. Also puttered around in the

kitchen, which sometimes brings a measure of comfort when I'm on the verge of feeling blue.

I got the sad news that our former neighbor, Jean, finally came to the end of her valiant battle against breast cancer. When I went to calling hours at the funeral home and saw her frail, ravaged body, I hoped her soul and gentle spirit had already been reunited with her beloved Allen, the son from whose tragic drowning six years ago she was never able to recover. And what mother could?

August 15, 1979
Dear Diary,

I called Mom and Daddy who were cute as could be teasing each other and having fun on their 48th anniversary. What a pair, those two!

Enjoying these few days in New Smyrna Beach ... refreshing swims in the pool and ocean and great walks along the beach, sometimes at a brisk pace, sometimes strolling and collecting shells. Yesterday, looking at nature's masterpieces of sea and sky, I realized how happy I felt at that precise moment. I vowed to store the joy for times when my worries intrude.

September 3, 1979
Orlando, Florida

Richmond, Virginia
Dear Jenni,

I can't wait till Christmas. I hope it snows in Virginia. How big is Kitty now? We like the apartment. What's your house like? What does kitty do? Guess where I am going next month. We are going to a Bucs game. I love you. I miss you.

Your little brother,
David

September 4, 1979
Woodbury, Connecticut

Orlando, Florida
Dear Robin,

Granddad and I are glad to hear you were finally offered the job you wanted and we do wish you luck! We will be interested to hear how it is going and how you like it.

The summer has gone so quickly and it has been a busy one for us visiting different friends in various places. We have been away five times already with one more to go this coming weekend. Then we are looking forward to the end of the month when your dad and David fly up for too short a time.

I am glad to hear you are happy with Terry. You are my first grandchild and very dear to me, so perhaps you can understand that it is difficult for me to see why, when you love each other so much, an "arrangement" like this is necessary. Only because I do care for you am I sorry to have you miss the normal, exciting things that go along with engagement and marriage – and I think of you as a sentimental girl to whom all that would mean a lot.

Now it's lunchtime – come join us for a grilled cheese and bacon sandwich!

We both send love,
Nana Kitty

September 9, 1979
Orlando, Florida

Mobile, Alabama
Dear Mom and Daddy,

I have fantastic news! I decided to keep quiet about everything until I knew the outcome, and today I got a call that I have the job. So, here's the story: While still at the beach I wrote a letter explaining my background in answer to an Orlando newspaper ad for a sitter/housekeeper. The young woman phoned and said she and her husband were very impressed with my letter and wanted to meet me as soon as I was back in Orlando.

I went to their home for the interview and we immediately liked each other. Annette, a high school math teacher, and Neill, who's in the commercial real estate business, have been married about 10 years and are expecting their first baby early next month. They live in a large, lovely old home just one mile from the apartment and only a few blocks from David's school. The best part of the job, besides caring for a precious baby, is that my hours and days of work will be based on the school schedule; I'll be off when David is not in school. David can walk from the house to and from school, and if he can't be in class for any reason he'll be able to stay with me at work. Perfect, huh? The position won't be regular full-time until the first of the year so I'll continue with various part-time jobs until then.

During this time my friend Tom called (remember, my divorce attorney, teacher of the Transactional Analysis course I took, young Chris's stepdad?). First he boosted my morale sky-high with compliments on all my wonderful attributes! Then he asked if I'd like to work for him, re-train,

444

after almost 30 years, to be his legal secretary. I admire Tom so much and felt honored that he approached me about the position, but I told him honestly that on my pros and cons list for regular daily life baby care beat out the business world. For instance, before-and-after school, and sick care for David won't be a problem. Neither will there be the need for a dressier wardrobe (or wearing panty hose, which I detest!). No money going out for lunches and downtown parking fees. I can take care of my Davey, wear comfy clothes, eat homecooked treats and park in the driveway. And as an added bonus I can continue to watch Chris part-time for Tom and his wife Patricia, who spends weekdays in Tallahassee attending law school. I think it'll be a win-win-win situation – for *three* families.

Now I can relax my worried mind a bit, and so can you two for me!

Lots of love,
Pat

P.S. – Please tell Sam, John and Rickey about my job the next time you write or call them. I know they'll be happy for me … and maybe even halfway envious of my good fortune in having a baby to love on most every day!

September 19, 1979
Orlando, Florida

Mobile, Alabama
Dear Folks,

Isn't this note cute? I found it on the kitchen table when I got home tonight. I couldn't resist my boys. So now we have Spunky II, not an outside, but an inside cat. I think Skip had the idea, too, that a kitty would help David adjust to Skip's leaving for Auburn again.

Love,
Pat

Mom,

David and I found a little kitten on Saturday. We both fell in love with it so I brought it over to the apartment. I was worried it would get hit by a car if it stayed out by the road. Anyway, would you consider just keeping it outside and letting David feed it? Once he starts feeding it, it will be his cat but he can have it outside. David said he would buy the food. Well, at least consider it.

I love you,
Skip

September 19, 1979
Auburn University
Auburn, Alabama

Orlando, Florida
Dear Mom,

I am sitting here in the Sigma Chi House right now. The first chapter meeting is going on so they make all the pledges sit in one room until the meeting is over. The funny thing is, there are only two pledges as of now. Next week rush starts and there will be about 30-35 more.

I'm getting to know most of the brothers who are new since I was here. There are about 30 of them, several more than I expected. When we first arrived I really felt out of place because so many faces looked unfamiliar. The first thing I wanted to do when I drove up was to turn around and go back to the security of my mommy! But I knew things would work out soon, and they have.

By the way, all my credits transferred from University of Central Florida, so I haven't lost any class time. In fact, I took a two-hour English proficiency exam this morning, and if I pass it I won't have to take an English course, which would save me three hours.

I've got to go to bed now – we have a work party tomorrow morning and it's late.

I love you,
Skip

P.S. – Our trip up was terrible, pouring rain for the last 250 miles.
P.P.S. – Keep this! It's my first letter from school.

October 2, 1979
Monterey, California

Mobile, Alabama
Happy Birthday, Dad!

Wish you were here with us on our little jaunt – it's a beautiful setting. Let's see now, born 1912, it's 1979 – 67, huh? Who would have thought it? Not me.

There are two things I want to do at 67: 1) Look back on a life rich in love, variety, and satisfaction as yours is; and 2) look ahead to you again for a new 25-year model. It's good to share life with you. See you around.

Love,
Sam

October 5, 1979
Dear Diary,

The baby arrived! Mama Annette and Papa Neill called from the hospital with the news of a fine, healthy girl, Saralyn. I already feel as if she's part my baby, too, even though I won't start keeping her on a regular basis for a while yet. David is very excited!

October 7, 1979
Dear Diary,

A couple of friends and I went for readings by a medium in the spiritual community of Cassadega on this lovely, bright autumn day. I was told I radiate love, have a beautiful aura, and am intelligent, very spiritual and somewhat lonely … and that much happiness lies ahead. Also, that I could write a book about how to love and show care to one another and the book would be a great help to people. No wonder I have the feeling writing a book is going to be a part of my destiny. Interesting, huh? And uplifting to hear myself described in such a positive way.

October 11, 1979
Orlando, Florida

Mobile, Alabama
Dearest Mom and Daddy,

David had a great time in Connecticut and loved the day of sightseeing in New York. Bob raved about how *good* he'd been – didn't surprise me. He learned to play "solitairy" and "crochet" (solitaire and croquet).

I had dreaded, and hesitated to tell David on the phone about the little kitty dying so suddenly but decided that was best. Let's face it, there *was* no easy way. As soon as he got home we visited Spunky's grave and he just sobbed, asking, "*Why* did she have to die?" I cried, too. He went back to the grave alone Tuesday. I know he shed more tears but it's good for him to let the sadness out.

Now a funny little story – David told me his friend Laurie had called and asked him to go out. "Mom, I just don't know *what* to do." With serious attention, I commented, "Wow – go out, where would you go out to at age 9?" His quick reply, "Beats me, that's why I'm asking you."

Oh, Daddy, I thought perhaps by sending this check now, everything could be arranged to begin the new interest rate the first of next month. Thanks so much. I appreciate being able to invest my little "nest egg" from the house sale with you.

Y'all take care of each other – we love you so much.

Pat

447

October 12, 1979
Orlando, Florida

Woodbury, Connecticut
Dear Granddad and Nana Kitty,

I just wanted to thank you for letting me come to Connecticut. Dad and I had fun in New York! We saw the Statue of Liberty. We went on the top of the Empire State Building and we saw everything in NYC and everything around it. Dad said when Skip was little he called it the ENTIRE State Building.

School is going great now. My class is going to Sea World in December on a field trip. Well, I guess I will see you later in December.

Love,
David

October 19, 1979
Dear Diary,

It's midnight and I'm sitting here feeling lonely. Oh, dear Lord, I am so lonely. The longest day. I'm almost obsessed with the desire to fill the hollowness I am feeling. I so want an intimate companion, not just for cuddling or making love, but one with whom I can share my thoughts and dreams and fears and wildest fantasies.

I see poor Abraham, David's old goldfish, forever confined, able only to look out at the world beyond his miniature ocean in a bowl. I don't want that, to be bound in a space, with a limited view. There are too many beautiful visions in my mind, beyond my present ken, that I want revealed as realities in my future.

November 29, 1979
Dear Diary,

The highlight of this day was attending the surprise birthday party Tom gave for his wife and meeting some of their lovely friends. David and Chris were so cute. They were excited and felt quite grown-up. I'm in awe of Patricia, who is an accomplished pianist, singer, artist and a soon-to-be lawyer. As I was feeling so untalented, though, she hugged me tightly and praised, "Pat, you are the *best* substitute mother with your warmth and love and hugs for Chris. I thank you."

December 2, 1979

Dear Diary,

After being in the fun and warmth of the birthday party circle and then today with my new baby's family where love is rampant, I was overcome with such forlorn feelings – like I might never have those wonderful things again. I'm sad ... Bob came to get David and, as sometimes happens, I suddenly had this terrible heartache for all that had been but is no more. I feel as if I might choke on this pain.

December 5, 1979
Richmond, Virginia

Orlando, Florida

Dear Mom and David,

We have a new addition to our family, another cat! A little stray black kitten was left out in the cold last week and he was crying so pitifully that I brought him in. He's very sweet, pitch black all over except one white spot under his chin. I named him Lucifer, and he lives up to his name, believe me. I took him for a checkup and shots and the vet said he is 12 to14 weeks old. Kitty likes him although she pretends she doesn't sometimes. He sleeps with me and so does Kitty, so there's a bedful. David, you'd love him!

Well, gotta run.

Much love,
Jenni

December 12, 1979

1979 CHRISTMAS LIST
By David

1) A little baby kitten (two or three if possible)
2) A football that won't go flat on me
3) A "T" shirt of the great Tampa Bay's Doug Williams #12
4) A lamp for my big, beautiful desk
5) Loads and loads of stuffed animals
6) A fish tank for my fish and some more (I hope)
7) One of those lazer printed pictures of a tiger

December 20, 1979
Mobile, Alabama

Orlando, Florida
Hi Pat,

Enclosed is interest check for January 1980. Things are moving so fast I could forget it during the holidays. Hope things are OK with you.

Hoping you and all the family have a real Happy Xmas and New Year.

Love you,
Daddy

December 20, 1979
Mobile, Alabama

Orlando, Florida
Dear Pat,

Hope this bit of my mad money will give you a little boost, as it gives me one to send it.

You and the children share a lot of love with each other – after all that's the very best thing to have at Christmas time and always. Give my Skip and David a big hug for me!

Love you so much,
Mom

December 23, 1979
Dear Diary,

God, could You please make a house call today? I need some company and some loving care. Yes, I know … I guess I ought to go to *Your* house. It seems I am going to be plagued with loneliness this holiday season, so I went to my friendly library and stocked up on books to help me get through it.

For many years we had the most pert-nigh-perfect holidays. Now those memories bring smiles and tears, all jumbled together.

December 25, 1979
Mom,

Have a wonderful Christmas. You really do make many lives much fuller. You are a wise woman!

I love you,
Skip

December 31, 1979
Dear Diary,

Well, here it is New Year's Eve and I'm doing a pretty good job of treating it like an ordinary day. No plans, no date, no celebration – except the pizza and popcorn party-for-two David and I had before he went to bed. Can't help picturing the festive scene at the club in New Smyrna Beach and reminiscing about the past two years when I celebrated with Ernie and his great music, and dancing, and the camaraderie of friends there. …

My wishes for next year: Good health for my loved ones and me; the ability to support myself and not always feel overwhelmed with money worries; a nice social life; maybe a charming new man or two to date … and more strength and serenity to face all of life with a good, positive attitude. Happy New Year, Pat!

Life is not measured by years,
but by anniversaries of the heart.
Flavia Weedn

Chapter Twenty-Three
Little Bundles
1980

David and Saralyn in Orlando, Florida

January 1, 1980
Dear Diary,

A sunny, blue-sky, crispy-cool New Year's Day, pleasant in every way. So enjoyed a Happy New Year phone call from Mom, who's out in Arizona visiting John and family. And at noontime, to launch 1980 in proper Southern tradition, the kids and I relished a dinner of ham-hock-seasoned black-eyed peas (cooked with a dime in the water for good luck) and hot-from-the-iron-skillet crusty cornbread. Yum, delicious fare.

Skip left for Auburn and is looking forward to a good quarter. David was sweet, so sad, though, crying because he knew he would miss his big brother and buddy.

Pat

January 10, 1980
Dear Diary,

Neill brought over Saralyn's crib, swing, stroller, diapers, and boxes of milk. The apartment looks baby-ready! David and I will have fun keeping her here while Annette and Neill enjoy their spree in The Crescent City.

January 11, 1980
Dear Diary,

Lovely day, lovely baby – contentment. How sweet Saralyn is. Robin came by to enjoy her, too ... said I looked like a young girl with the baby. David wishes Saralyn *was* ours!

Wonderful news: Jenni will soon be moving back to Orlando. She's coming home and we're thrilled.

January 16, 1980
Dear Diary,

We said bye-bye to our baby and miss her terribly but her mama and papa were happy to see and have Saralyn back.

In a kind of reverie this afternoon I suddenly realized that gradually over time two important changes are occurring in my thinking: I truly don't "want" so much, as I used to, and I am adjusting a bit better to growing older. *That* has not been easy.

January 19, 1980
Dear Diary,

Today I took a giant step forward on the path of independence, maturity and wisdom when I wrote to Ernie, formally ending our relationship. Good for me.

January 23, 1980
Orlando, Florida

Tempe, Arizona
Dear "Mama,"

Remember I used to call you that when I was really young. ... Don't recall when or why I stopped, but I know I dropped many typically Southern sayings after Bob and I were married and living in Connecticut, when I'd see that those damnyankees were baffled over certain of my expressions. For instance: sweet milk (versus buttermilk); light bread (not cornbread); "own and own and own" (on and on, a long time); bucket, or rocks (in Yankee talk, pail or stones).

It's interesting, now I'm more aware of my heritage each day and long to express it as I once did. I'm even craving lots of the soul food I seldom served in past years. Suddenly I feel like cooking messes of cabbage and turnips, big pots of peas or butter beans with okra and, my favorite, cornbread. Along with these foods tasting so delicious to me, I seem to be gaining from them a sense of security and of a stronger identity. I accept this as a good sign I am shedding any and all cloaks, real and/or superficial, I might have wrapped around myself over the years and that I am going to find, to know, to be more *me*. And be especially proud of my roots. One note here: You and Daddy – our family – are way up high on the list of my life's best blessings.

Take care, keep enjoying Arizona. Daddy will be finished with his business in Alabama and back with you soon so you both can enjoy a few more weeks out West! Love to John and Kathie, Adam and Mark – and much to you.

Pat

P.S. – Sunday we were at Robin and Terry's for a spaghetti supper, and at Jenni's Tuesday for her delicious chili. Such fun, and a lot of laughing goes on. I just sit with a grin on my face, waited on by these two daughters – reaping the harvest, enjoying "the fruits of my labor."

January 27, 1980
Dear Diary,

Two-year anniversary of the divorce ... and it feels like the start of motherhood again! Baby-sat two kids all day and am ready to start my regular job taking care of Saralyn. I'm happy, looking forward to it.

January 30, 1980
Dear Diary,

First day on the job yesterday, and I was sick. Made it till Annette got home at 4 p.m., when I sped home to bed with 101-degree fever, chills and aches and pains. David and Chris enjoyed their day on the job with me and were so helpful. Saralyn is such a good baby, too, which was a blessing. Fortunately, I felt much better today.

February 1, 1980
Dear Diary,

Daddy and Rickey called from Mobile and I sure did enjoy visiting with each one. Particularly happy to speak with my little brother after so long a time. He is doing well, enjoying life, and Daddy's fine, so cute.

February 3, 1980
Dear Diary,

I felt a sense of fulfillment at the end of my first week of work as a nanny, knowing I did a good job. I'm tired by the end of my workday, but I do enjoy caring for sweet Saralyn. David wrote to Skip, "Saralyn is growing rapidly. She's eating her solids now." My little man. Skip called yesterday to tell us he tied a guy for the highest test score in the history of Sigma Chi Fraternity – wow!

February 9, 1980
Dear Diary,

We celebrated the two Aquarian birthdays with a special dinner. First baby Robin was born 25 years ago today and David, the "family baby" who came along 15 years later, will be 10 tomorrow. All four children are *so* great. I'm a lucky mom!

February 10, 1980
Mobile, Alabama

Orlando, Florida
Dear David,

Hope you have a great 10th birthday. Wish I could be there to celebrate with you! I'm spending a few days in Mississippi with Uncle John's family and it's coooooooold here. I'm enclosing some dollar bills to spend on something you would like. Have fun and know that Granddaddy and I love you a whole bunch.

Nana GeeGee

February 10, 1980
Winter Park, Florida

Orlando, Florida
Dear David,

In honor of your birthday, here is a poem about you and our New Smyrna Beach vacations with you and your mom and the rest of the gang.

D – Dashing down to the ocean, first one in!
A – Attentive to wee ones – no food throwing!
V – Visiting the hot dog stand for a Coke!
I – Is it time for dinner?
D – Delighted to play Tripoly, all night, all of us!

See you this summer! Love ya lots!

"Auntie Ann" and Susie

February 14, 1980
Dear Diary,

I've always loved Valentine's Day, sentimental, romantic gal that I am. A wonderful surprise – Mom tucked a $100 bill inside a card for me.

February 16, 1980
Dear Diary,

David got a bigger aquarium for his birthday and we went shopping for goldfish. Old Abraham likes the roomier quarters and fit right in with the new residents.

February 24, 1980
Dear Diary,

Uh oh, David found one of the new water babies belly-up in the bowl and cried so sadly when we buried it out back. (I can still recall the first time Robin got fish as pets and her little playmate warned, "The only thing is, Robin, goldfish die a *lot*.")

The kids and I all got together for delicious spaghetti at Robin's. We heard from Skip that he was elected to an office in Sigma Chi. Quite a guy, our Skip.

February 25, 1980
Dear Diary,

Gray, rainy Monday, another week beginning, a smiling baby to greet me at work! And a super supper this evening – Jenni fixed her special chili for Robin, Terry, David and me. Then we laughed through two or three hours of playing Boggle. It's such *fun* having "the gang" around.

February 27, 1980
Orlando, Florida

Tempe, Arizona
Dear Nana GeeGee and Granddaddy,

Hear you are having a good time in Arizona. I'm having a nice time down here. I wish I saw the Grand Canyon. It must have been fastenating. And I wish I went to Las Vegas too!

Thank you for the nice card you sent me and the $5.00. I really needed it.

I got an aquarium for my birthday and I got some fish for it. I got 7 at the store to go with Abraham. One was not strong enough and died. But the others are still living and healthy.

I am so glad that Jenni moved back down here right next to Robin's place.

Everybody says Hi. Tell everybody hi.
Love,
David

March 6, 1980
Dear Diary,

Another fish died, and poor David feels really sad about it. But on the happier side, he told me recently he thinks I have the *best* job in the world! He always enjoys Saralyn, is just great with her – and she adores him. I'm so glad my job allows me to still be a "present" mother for my Davey.

March 11, 1980
Dear Diary,

No cigarette since Saturday night when I'd smoked too many and right then made a commitment to myself that I would no longer indulge in that habit. It will help that I've begun practicing Transcendental Meditation again. I can tell I don't feel as relaxed or content without it.

March 16, 1980
Dear Diary,

David has been sick – a fever, no appetite, lies on the couch all day. He has been checked twice for a strep infection, but evidently has just one of the various unnamed viruses. We have been extremely careful to keep him isolated from Saralyn, who has remained germ free and pretty perky. She was so cute today I nearly ate her up!

Heard from the folks, back home in Mobile after the extended period in Arizona. Great news is that Mom may come to visit in two or three weeks.

March 24, 1980
Dear Diary,

My boy has missed almost two weeks of school, still looks peaked and tires easily. He slept 3½ hours today. The doctor checked for mononucleosis, but that's not the problem. David did perk up enough yesterday to act a bit smart-alecky and as much as I dislike scolding him, I did. As usual, though, my anger was defused pretty quickly by David's reaction. He says when I get upset with him I look really mean, but really funny, and he just *can't* help laughing!

March 27, 1980
Auburn University
Auburn, Alabama

Orlando, Florida
Dear Mom,

I had a fantastic time over the spring break. It was the busiest I've been in a while. It was great seeing you and the rest of the family even though it was only for a short time. My friend Jerry was really impressed with my family, probably because we all get along so well. That is really rare nowadays – to see a family without personality clashes.

I'm going to have a tough quarter. I'm only taking 15 hours, but they are going to be harder than my 20 last quarter. Besides that, I have to do another initiation at the fraternity and am in charge of the whole thing. Also, the fraternity has a big event planned for almost every weekend.

Take care of yourself and keep on truckin'! I love you.

Skip

March 31, 1980
Dear Diary,

David is well again. He went to school for a full day the end of last week, and now is back to skating, too. Excitement on the baby front: Saralyn got her first tooth!

April 3, 1980
Dear Diary,

I heard the whole gang – Bob, his parents, Dave and Dorothy and Auntie Bussie, who's down from Connecticut for a visit – had gathered for dinner. I always feel extra sad knowing those occasions are gone forever for me. But perhaps someday I'll have someone special again, with a big new family, too.

April 15, 1980
Dear Diary,

Mom left early this morning, heading back to Mobile and her honey. She was here the week I had off work, and we stayed so busy and had such a great time. We talked non-stop, of course, as always, even staying up too late most nights. Robin and Jenni joined us for supper and yakking a few times. Mom and I went shopping – drove over to the Daytona Beach Mall one day. She knows my budget is slim and very generously bought me a few cute items of clothing on sale. I am blessed with a special mother. ...

April 30, 1980
Dear Diary,

The Adult Education Public Relations course I began a few weeks ago is not all I had hoped for, but I'll continue and maybe learn something I can use someday. ... A recent inquiry about keeping a second baby in the fall got me to thinking. I've had 25 years of extensive experience in my field, with the earned equivalent of a Ph.D. (Actually I already claim two degrees, my M.A.M.A. and N.A.N.N.Y.) So I should be able to quadruple my pay, right? Think big, Pat!

May 1, 1980
Dear Diary,

Anniversary of Bob's and my wedding today, and it would have been 27 years. I was telling a friend last week that I'm now three years down the lonely road of divorce, and it isn't a joyful journey. But I'm feeling pretty good about myself and my life.

May is, I think, my very favorite month of the year. The weather is beautiful and I so enjoy my daily strolls through the peaceful neighborhood with Saralyn. She jabbers and smiles and squeals, so happy with life. Me, too, I'm content.

May 6, 1980
Dear Diary,

Two years after the professor's comment that he thought my English Composition essay "Coping With Uncoupling" worthy of publication, I sent a slightly revised copy of it to two magazines. Better now than never, I decided. How I'd love to have it accepted.

I'm reading a variety of books on meditation. I want to seek The Truth in serious meditation and have it affect my life in every way. I *am* living more in the *now*. ...

May 7, 1980
Orlando, Florida

Mobile, Alabama
Dearest Folks,

Along with my Happy Birthday wishes for you, Mom, I'm enclosing a copy of two notes I know you and Daddy will enjoy reading. One is to David, written by the student teacher for his class at Blankner Elementary this year, and the other is his response. On first reading Miss Julie's note, David, already missing her, cried and said with feeling, "She made *magic!*"

Much love,
Pat

To David

Oh, David! I'm going to miss you so much. I hope I have more students like you! Thank you so much for the pretty necklace. You helped me more than you will ever know... I am giving you and the other students a story I wrote about your fourth-grade class. Good luck always. I'll just bet someday you will be at Auburn. Take care!

Love,
Miss Julie

Dear Miss Julie,

I miss you! I didn't think I would miss you so much so soon. After I read your story a few times I started to cry because I knew I would not be seeing you anymore so my mom said maybe we could meet somewhere for dinner or you could come over to our house.

Love,
David

May 11, 1980
Orlando, Florida

Orlando, Florida
Happy Mother's Day!

You are a treasure, you are wonderful, you're the best mom ever! I know all your dreams will come true – they wouldn't dare not for such a terrific lady! I love you!

Did I say "Thanks for everything you do for me?"

Robin

May 11, 1980
Blankner Elementary School
By David

IT'S MOTHER'S DAY

My Mother loves me when ... I am good.
My Mother looks prettiest when ... she puts on her makeup.
If I could give my Mother something special from me, it would be ... everything I could.
My favorite thing about my Mother is ... when she is nice and happy.
The funniest thing about my Mother is ... when she's mad.
I want to say, "Thank you, Mother" for ... everything you've done for me.

May 11, 1980
Winter Park, Florida

Orlando, Florida
My dearest Pat,

I enjoy our chats so much. If everyone could have a dear friend like you there would be no need for therapy in this world. Someday all our lives will straighten out. The future will be brighter. At present we have to be patient. We all have so much to look forward to if we stay "up" and talk about what we'd like to see happen. We have to make our own lives, as no one will do it for us, right?

461

Thank you for being the kind, wonderful friend you are.

Love ya always,

Ann

May 15, 1980

Dear Diary,

Started an extra sitting job for three teens while the parents are vacationing in Rome, Italy. Takes me back a few years being "mother" to a 16-year-old girl and 12- and 14-year-old boys. And then there's the mama dog and her eight puppies!

May 20, 1980

Dear Diary,

This moonlighting job is keeping me hopping. All the running back and forth is wearing me out, watching Saralyn during the day and the other three kids at night.

My ol' sweet Skip is 21 years old today. Wish I could've seen him. I got the idea to put together a "21-year baby book" with his birth certificate, notes about his babyhood, a little blond curl from his first haircut, some drawings, school papers, remembrances from sports activities, various awards, pictures of him at different ages … all sorts of goodies. I was so busy after he was born I didn't keep records in a baby book like I did for the other three kids. I'll surprise him with it at Christmas.

May 23, 1980

Dear Diary,

Jenni fixed her first-ever pot roast when David and I went for dinner tonight, and it was delicious. She's such a good cook. I feel so very blessed with my super children. Thank you, God! Skip called and will soon be coming home for 10 days.

May 25, 1980

Woodbury, Connecticut

Orlando, Florida

Robin dear,

It's very remiss of me not to have acknowledged your nice birthday card and note sooner than this.

Fact is, I've been in Pennsylvania having a ball with a lot of my old friends. You wouldn't know, of course, but when you live someplace for over 50 years and then move, it is as though you were born the day you moved! Nobody up here (except your Nana Kitty and Granddad) knows anything about me before 1966. It is a great comfort to me to go back to Pennsylvania whenever I can and be with people who have known me from about Day One.

I'm glad you have your mother and dad and Uncle Dave to talk to, and I'm sure they have been a help. Wish I were close enough to get in on it, too. However, I guess we'll have to do it by U.S. Post Office!

Without more details than I have, about all I can say is this: From my own experience, I can't help but feel that when you are uncertain – don't. The trouble with advice from older people is that it tends to make one stubborn. It did me. Almost everyone warned me that I was making a mistake in marrying Ted. It *was* a dreadful mistake and I wasted 23 years trying hard to make a go of it. Once I saw the score, I just picked up and moved out. By then I was well-established in my career, was able to support myself, and found that life was very good, with lots of good friends, and I really didn't need to be a "twosome" in order to achieve and be happy. By now I *really* like that state.

You are very young (pardon me for that!). You have a great career ahead of you. You can support yourself well and can be completely independent. I'm not sure you can realize what a great situation that is. In spite of the "Noah's Ark" concept, it is no longer true that people are acceptable only in pairs. A *lot* of women are finding that out – and enjoying it.

However, Robin, you are a lot younger than I was when I discovered that, and you have your whole life ahead of you. I hate to give advice, but you asked for it. Don't contract yourself to anything of which you are not absolutely sure. You have lots of time and lots of people who love you. Somewhere out there in the future there may be something for you of which you are very sure. That happened to me – but I'd put it off till too late. I was almost 50! Now I'm 70!

I think of you so much and want to help you so much. Do keep in touch, and fill me in on a lot of your feeling and thinking – if you wish. Then maybe I could help more.

Very much love,
Auntie Bussie

May 29, 1980
Dear Diary,

This has been "Pat's Poop Week!" Papa Neill and I took Saralyn to the doctor. She has had diarrhea, but is doing okay since she drinks Gatorade really well and hasn't become dehydrated. What a precious little person – I love her so much and am so glad I have this job.

In keeping with the theme for the week, the mama dog at my temporary night job left piles of presents outside my bedroom door a couple of mornings. The vacationing family arrived home safely this evening, though, so my moonlighting job is finished. Hurray, lots of work accomplished.

June 3, 1980
Dear Diary,

Went to the Scholastic Awards Night at David's school, where he received an award with a star for an A average. Bob, Robin and Jenni were there, too. Skip got home later. He looks great!

June 4, 1980
Dear Diary,

A "truth" (for me) revealed itself today: Once the desire for things – that is, material possessions, glamour, excitement, even to some extent love, attachments, and sexual expression – lessens, and one is content with one's inner being, then fear of death also lessens.

June 5, 1980
Dear Diary,

Skip fetched Saralyn and me and we three went to my apartment for lunch. Just like David and the girls, Skip's very sweet with the baby. While he fed her baby food squash she flirted shamelessly with him and he loved it. I think my boys are going to be wonderful daddies someday.

June 5, 1980
Woodbury, Connecticut

Orlando, Florida
Robin dear,

I was glad to get your letter and know you are feeling better about things.

In a way, it was so much easier to grow up as long ago as I did. There *were* no acceptable "alternatives." Therefore, they didn't even have to be considered, and one didn't have to put oneself on the rack to try to find the right one. Yet, a lot of us made mistakes without even having to think about it. Now, it seems, young people have to intellectualize and rationalize because of all the choices – and sometimes I wonder if this process doesn't cloud very deep-seated and emotional feelings. It's impossible for me to assess what the total results of the two "systems" are because it seems there's just about as much "relationship misery" in the world now as there was then. I'm pouring this out because I think a lot about it. I really care about young people – then and now. Wish I had the answers. I'd for sure give them to you.

Let me tell you about a relationship I had …

I don't talk about this to many people, but you have always been my "special" first great-niece. I've told you more about me than I've told anyone else. If there is anything in it that helps, I'm glad.

It's great to hear your jobs are going so well. Hope David gets his award. Glad your mother is doing well. Give her my love. And reserve a lot for yourself!

Auntie Bussie

June 9, 1980
Dear Diary,

All four kids and I were together for my lasagna dinner, and we sure had fun. David, so cute and enthusiastic, had cleaned the apartment for the party and said he wished we had an even bigger family, *all living at home with us.*

June 14, 1980
Dear Diary,

Skip left for Auburn today. We'll miss having him around. … After attending an introductory lecture on Transcendental Meditation recently and having it feel "right," David and I were formally initiated into TM and given our mantras. When I find it hard to meditate I'm encouraged to not *try,* just let it happen. Ol' Davey is doing beautifully with his "walking meditation."

June 15, 1980
Berkeley, California

Mobile, Alabama
Dear Dad,

I'm sure you and Mom are saying "Why would Sammie write a letter instead of picking up the phone? That's not like him," but I want to share with you my good fortune in life: I have lived long enough to have an experience of you – to "get" you.

I don't think a day goes by that I fail to remember you, to see something marvelous about you. During the past weeks, my realizations have frequently been about the way you have organized your life, including the physical space around yourself, to support you in being effective and powerful in

465

what you do. Right now I am appreciating what you do with your intellect (which several of us share), which is that you have trained yourself to focus it down to a concentrated beam of very high energy (which skill few of us share).

In the same vein, I think of your skill in setting objectives and going for them. Somehow this reminds me of your fantastic powers of imagination. I have the answer to my question, How did you achieve so much? You just did.

Wonderful as these traits/accomplishments are, though, my most basic sense of you comes to me as though from a secret place we share. It's not really a secret place; it's more the result of letting myself just behold you.

I behold your gentleness and goodwill, your love of your family, of me. I behold your generosity of spirit, the absence of meanness about you. I behold your playfulness, your inquisitiveness, your quickness. And above all else, I behold your love and your courage.

I want you to know of my pride and my happiness that you are my father. Happy Father's Day. I hope it's a good one.

Love,
Sam

June 17, 1980
Dear Diary,

My TM teacher said she has no doubt I will reach enlightenment in my lifetime. Of course I am not exactly sure what that means (!) but it is my aim, with better and better real living each day along the way. David has decided he doesn't want to continue meditating after all. That's okay, he knows the technique should he ever want to practice it again.

June 18, 1980
Dear Diary,

A surprise awaited me on this last regular day of work until school reopens and Annette returns to teaching. Cleverly hidden inside the box of diapers was a sweet thank-you card with my paycheck and a generous bonus. I'll miss the daily contact with the baby. But David and I are looking forward to sharing a few days with Annette, Neill and Saralyn in New Smyrna Beach – and later, with the kids, our friends Ann and Susan, and various others who'll be coming and going in a merry-go-round fashion!

June 24, 1980
Dear Diary,

Fine day on the beach. Saralyn is adorable in her swimsuit and hat, and she loves the ocean. David and I baby-sat so Annette and Neill could enjoy a night out before they head back home tomorrow.

June 28, 1980
Dear Diary,

Nice vacation ... old and new friends have been in and out all week enjoying relaxed time with the kids and me – playing Scrabble, Tripoley, Crazy Eights and Gin Rummy, joining us for lunch and/or dinner, swimming, and fun on the beach.

July 6, 1980
Dear Diary,

David and I are kind of sad today with everybody leaving and the beach house so tidy. I'd much rather have it messy and filled to the brim with people having fun! The Fourth of July was a real celebration with lots of loved ones over for a cookout and a spectacular fireworks show on the beach. Vacation ends tomorrow, but it has been great.

July 10, 1980
Dear Diary,

Cleaned up the beach house, packed and drove home three days ago. Unpacked, straightened up the apartment, got a few groceries in, then re-packed for the hospital. I went in yesterday to have foot surgery for the "Morton's neuroma." I woke up as the last two stitches were being placed, and that was *awful*. I dozed on and off all day. Received beautiful potted plants from my girls and some friends.

July 25, 1980
Dear Diary,

Recovery has been slow, with my foot swollen and "throbby" much of the last couple of weeks. But the stitches were removed today and it feels much better.

July 31, 1980
Dear Diary,

Excitement over knowing we'd be Alabamy-bound kept both David and me from sleeping well last night. But we had a fine flight (three legs to the trip, actually) to Mobile and were met by Mom and Daddy, who look great. Lots of talking and eating went on the rest of the day.

August 5, 1980
Dear Diary,

The gang has gathered! John and Kathie and their boys drove down from Starkville, Mississippi, a couple of days ago. David and his cousins, Adam and Mark, seem happy to be together. Rickey is in and out from his home across town, and today Sam flew in from California, and nephew Griff arrived by bus from North Carolina, where he's spending part of the summer with old friends in Chapel Hill. It's just great to see all these beautiful people and be in the middle of such activity – yep, much of which is in the kitchen! We do love to *eat*. We've had fun looking at the old picture albums, reminiscing and chuckling over various poses and crazy hairstyles and such.

Daddy told us more about the oil business and took us on a drive out to see the processing plant. Such a lucrative venture, and Daddy's so smart about it.

August 7, 1980
Dear Diary,

Boo hoo, goodbye time, the end of a special visit with all the family. We promised we'll congregate next August for Mom and Daddy's 50th wedding anniversary.

August 14, 1980
Orlando, Florida

Mobile, Alabama
Dear Nana GeeGee and Granddaddy,

Thank you for letting me come over. I just hope we can come again. Thanks for the good ice cream and all the other food. I am really busy now. I am going to a garage sale tomorrow. I'll probably make $40.00. My car wash business is swell. I just made $5. Tell everybody hi.
Love,
David

Hi, Y'all!

David and I made a *drastic* change from our wonderful, restful vacation with you to a week so filled with work that we are exhausted. We're joining our friends in a garage sale and you know how much work that entails, but it's a good chance for us to make some money.

Three sitting jobs this week – not only with Saralyn, but also 2- and 5-year-old boys. Saturday I have to tag and pack all items for David to take to summer camp.

Foot still tender, but every so often I'll prop it up for a few minutes and then continue with chores.

Love you so much,
Pat

P.S. – I heard two great similar sayings this week: "The trick in life is to die young as late as possible." And the other, when asked by a child if she were young or old, an elderly lady answered, "My dear, I have been young a very long time." I want to proclaim that at 100!

August 17, 1980
Orlando, Florida

YMCA Camp Wewa
Apopka, Florida
Dear David,

You just left this afternoon, but I want you to receive some mail real quickly so I'm sending a letter today. I know I am going to miss you all week, but I'll think about the good times you are having at camp and that will make me feel okay! I'll take care of your pets for you – also any business calls you get for car washes. I love you, David. Say hi to Chris for me.

Mom

August 18, 1980
Orlando, Florida

YMCA Camp Wewa
Apopka, Florida
Dear David,

Hi! How was it sleeping on the top bunk last night? You didn't roll off or anything, did you? How did your friend Chris sleep?

I'm doing okay. Kitty and Lucy are helping me pretty much – they send you meows! Well, have fun. Stick to the buddy system!

Love,
Jen, Lucy and Kitty

August 18, 1980
Orlando, Florida

YMCA Camp Wewa
Apopka, Florida
Dear David,

How are you doing? I sure hope you are enjoying your very first camping experience. I ate dinner with Robin and Terry last night and am going to see Jenni later today. Also, Skip called me yesterday from Lubbock, Texas, where he is at a meeting for his fraternity. He'll be coming home to see us pretty soon, maybe in 10 days.

Everything is okay here except that I miss you! I love you!!!
Mom

August 19, 1980
Orlando, Florida

YMCA Camp Wewa
Apopka, Florida
Hi, David!

How's my boy? I bet you will look older and bigger to me when you get home Saturday. You think so? I saw Jenni Monday and the cats – Lucy was just wild! She almost flew across the room chasing a fly. I will be eager to hear everything about camp, okay?
I love you,
Mom

August 19, 1980
Orlando, Florida

YMCA Camp Wewa
Apopka, Florida
Dear David,

I'm still at work now, but I thought you'd be happy if I wrote you a letter. Are you having a good time? I hope so. I went to camp when I was as old as you and we had fun. We even had to walk all the way across the park to go to the bathroom! And we had something called apple butter on our toast every morning. Do you have that?

Well, I miss you and so does Terry. Be a good boy and have fun. I hope you make lots of new friends!

Love,
Robin

August 20, 1980
Orlando, Florida

YMCA Camp Wewa
Apopka, Florida
Hi, David,

Hope you and your friend Chris are having a real good time. Be sure to do all the things you want to do there. I want to hear all about it after Saturday. Chris's dad will pick you up about 11 o'clock on Saturday morning. Have fun!

Love,
Dad

August 23, 1980
Dear Diary,

My 48th birthday, and a nice one, with both long-distance and local calls from all kinds of family members and friends. Best of all, my David came home from camp today! I was *so* glad to see him. Poor little guy, though: He said he was so homesick at camp he couldn't read the letters we all sent him because it would make him too sad. He tried to write one postcard to me while he was away but couldn't even finish it. So today he handed it to me, and I read his bravely written, "Dear Mom, Camp is fun. I am shooting BBs, canoeing and archery. I just got back from lunch and I saw a snake." Tom and Chris brought him home and we visited a bit over juice and cookies. But the minute they left David burst into tears, pleading, "Oh, Mom, I don't *ever* want to go to camp again!" Then he sat down and opened the little bundle and enjoyed all of his camp mail.

August 23, 1980
Auburn University
Auburn, Alabama

Orlando, Florida
Mom,

I don't plan on trying to tell you how good a mother you've been to all of us because I can't put it into words. If I had to go back and live life all over again, I wouldn't change a darn thing – especially you!

Happy Birthday! I love you,
Skip

August 27, 1980
Dear Diary,

David is such a big help to me at work. We took Saralyn to her baby swim class, then shopping, and later met Robin at her office and all went out to lunch. During spare time in the evenings I'm having fun working on sorting and selecting pictures, etc., to make the "baby book" for Skip.

August 30, 1980
Dear Diary,

One week after my 48th birthday and I am feeling about 90. Tired and depressed and weepy describes me today. I hardly care about anything. I must perk up.

September 3, 1980
Dear Diary,

I've climbed up from the despairing depths I wallowed in over the weekend – so glad! I cleaned the apartment and cooked a bit ahead for Skip's visit. He arrived really late, right after I had decided I might have to start worrying. He's fine – sporting a cute little mustache – and brought home some very impressive grades. David started fifth grade and got the teacher he had wished for.

September 12, 1980
Dear Diary,

Mom called, and in an almost casual tone as we talked about the crazy ups and downs of my life and what might the future hold, she mentioned the possibility of David and me moving to Mobile next year. They're thinking I could do part-time secretarial work to help Daddy in his oil dealings. Plus they would pay my tuition for college classes! That *could be* just the right move for David and me in 1981, but it would be a big decision … I don't know.

September 27, 1980
Dear Diary,

There are three important pieces of news to record: Jenni is going to get a divorce. These past months have been a very sad and difficult time for her, and I'm glad she's starting to feel better about everything. Another change in our lives and situations: Robin and Terry will be moving to Fort Lauderdale next year. After those two announcements the last one doesn't sound like such big news, but I have not smoked in three weeks.

September 30, 1980
Dear Diary,

Just thinking today how beautiful David is, in every way … and how blessed I am to have Robin and Jenni and Skip and David. I love each one so very much. They were precious babies and have just continued to become even more dear.

October 5, 1980
Dear Diary,

A birthday week – Daddy turns 68, my cousin Katie 48, Rickey 33, nephew Adam 10, Mother Kitty 76, and our baby celebrated her very first. David and I joined Annette and Neill's kin and friends for Saralyn's baptism and birthday party brunch. We just love that whole big family and always have a good time at their gatherings.

October 13, 1980
Dear Diary,

Reading earlier today I was struck by the statement "Be the space at the center and you will have everything to give to others." Although I'm not sure if I could explain it, I understand the meaning of that kind of space. I think.

Haven't had a cigarette in over a month, yippee, I am getting there this time. Let's see, I've registered with Kelly Temporary Services again, mainly for convention work on the weekends David is with his dad. Oh, and I must record this first for me: I went to a movie *by myself* and did okay.

October 18, 1980
Dear Diary,

Knowing I was scheduled to take the CLEP tests today, last night I programmed myself to fall asleep early, awake feeling refreshed and alert, and then do *very* well. So … I sat from 8 a.m. to 12:15 taking the exams for English, with essay, and Humanities. Glad that's done – though if I do well, I might consider taking others.

Good news: Mom and Daddy are coming down from Alabama for Thanksgiving!

October 24, 1980
Dear Diary,

I did it, signed up for "est." There are training sessions in Miami during two weekends next month. What a huge decision for me – not only because I have to figure out how I can arrange to spend two weekends in Miami (to take a course I've heard scary things about), but because I'll have to rearrange my budget to come up with a few hundred dollars. But with pounding heart and trembling hands I declared, "Darn, I'm doing it." Just one more step in Pat's learning-about-life series. I am sure it will be an adventure filled with invaluable experiences.

November 4, 1980
Dear Diary,

Election Day, and Republican Ronald Wilson Reagan is the new president of the United States of America, the 40th president to hold office.

I have been making travel plans for the first "est" training weekend. I am excited and oh-so apprehensive. David is thrilled about his weekend plans, a trip to Tampa with his dad to see a Bucs game. I'll miss him, but from Miami.

Saralyn reminded me of a kissing parrot today – she kept kissing me and repeating so many of my words. Such an affectionate tiny sweet person – I adore her.

November 9, 1980
Dear Diary,

Oh my gracious, not quite as long a day in "est," but even more in depth, and so utterly exhausting. I'm not going to *attempt* a written description of "est" processes, or of the trainers and helpers or even the extremely strict rules. But from all of those I *am* going to transform the quality of my life!

November 16, 1980
Dear Diary,

When Bob came to pick up David, I asked him for a hug and he complied. It's good to feel comfortable with him.

The final "est" session went from 9:30 a.m. Sunday to 3:30 a.m. Monday, by which time not only had I "got" it, I didn't like it – and I had *had* it! It seems there is no magic formula for life except to choose whatever happens and just let it be. At this point my feelings about the training are mixed: I know it was worthwhile; *and* I was disappointed in it. I was completely exhausted, too, remember. With the passing of a little time, and some reflection, I might view the whole "est" experience in a different light.

November 26, 1980
Dear Diary,

David and I had a talk about self-confidence today. I want to guide him in the *best* possible way, and I want to always spend enough quality time with him to do so. I've noticed that he seems to be going through a mildly withdrawn stage. I think he needs more male adults to interact with. (I wouldn't mind a male adult or two to interact with myself!)

November 27, 1980 – Thanksgiving Day
Dear Diary,

The first year Mom and Daddy and I have spent this holiday together in about 28 years! Jenni, Robin and Terry joined the folks, David and me for a grand turkey-'n'-trimmings feast. We had a fine time. The folks will drive back to Mobile after a couple more days. Daddy doesn't really enjoy traveling or long visits, he likes to be at home, in his regular routine, keeping his eye on everything.

December 1, 1980
Dear Diary,

A fantastic beginning to December with news of the results of my CLEP tests: English Composition and Essay – 694, and Humanities – 522. Those scores give me full credit of six hours in each subject, except that since I have already taken English Composition I, only three of those six hours will be used from CLEP.

December 3, 1980
Dear Diary,

Busy poring over college catalogue to see what courses are available. I had a counseling session at Valencia Community College with a wonderful woman who inspired enthusiasm, gave me ideas, filled out the financial aid sheet, etc. Family and friends are excited for me to be registering for classes.

December 6, 1980
Dear Diary,

The apartment is decorated and looks festive and very Christmasy. David and I are really in the holiday spirit! Bob took David shopping and that little guy selected the best, most thoughtful gifts for family members.

Daddy surprised me with a phone call to say he's so proud of my CLEP scores and my decision to start college courses.

December 11, 1980
Dear Diary,

Mother Kitty called to invite me to lunch soon. Christmas Day will be here before we know it and David is ready, with presents bought and wrapped, but not I. Skip will be coming in the next few days, and we're so eager to see that dear guy!

December 14, 1980
Dear Diary,

So many friends dropped by yesterday as I was wrapping presents, Skip got home in the afternoon, and Annette and Neill brought Saralyn to stay overnight. A busy, happy house!

We were up early with sweetie-pie Saralyn. I'd almost forgotten how precious a baby is the very first thing in the morning – so fresh! I cooked a chicken dinner for my boys (and me – I ate the most). Had a real good visit with Jenni today. She seems to be enjoying dating again. I like seeing my kiddos happy.

December 16, 1980
Dear Diary,

Robin and Terry and Skip and I attended PTA at Blankner Elementary for the chorus performance of Christmas music. It was well done and entertaining. Our David looked handsome and proud … and his family proud of him.

Being in the atmosphere of elementary school never fails to bring back memories of how much I loved school and my teachers. My favorite, from seventh grade, I've kept in touch with since 1944!

December 17, 1980

I've registered for Philosophy on Tuesday evenings and an American Government class conducted on television. It'll be helpful to take that course via TV and save on the number of trips to and from campus and the hours spent away from home. And I have no problem keeping up or studying on my own. Skip drove out to Valencia and picked up the books for me – and later picked a big bagful of sweet, juicy oranges from the neighbor's tree. For those two favors I fixed him a favorite dinner of tasty marinated flank steak!

December 18, 1980
Dear Diary,

Took my darling Saralyn to the Blankner chorus performance for young audiences this morning. She danced, she threw kisses to David – and he's not a bit embarrassed to acknowledge and return her adoration. The music teacher spoke to me with praise for David and his beautiful voice.

December 19, 1980
Orlando, Florida

Mobile, Alabama
Dear Nana GeeGee and Granddaddy,

I hope you receive this card before you head off to California for Christmas with Uncle Sam, but if not, you'll have it when you get back. I wish I could have seen you in Orlando over Thanksgiving, but I had a good time in Nashville with my friend Jerry. I'll try to get to Mobile sometime next quarter – that is, if that old fart will say it's all right. What about it, Granddaddy?

Have a safe trip, and Merry Christmas.

Love,
Skip

December 23, 1980
Orlando, Florida

Winter Park, Florida
Dear Mr. Manager,

I like working at my daddy's office. Thank you for giving me the McDonald's gift certificates. I am sure going to use them. (With inflation

you can't buy anything.) Merry Christmas and a Happy New Year!
                    Sincerely,
                    David

December 25, 1980 – Christmas Day
Dear Diary,
    The kids spent the morning at Bob's, and then all of them were here at
the apartment from early afternoon on to open presents. A really fun gift
from my friend Ann: *For Ladies Only*, a book of photos and information
about 85 eligible bachelors in the Orlando area! But the best gift of all,
given or received, was Skip's "baby album." I had gathered all the material
and Robin put it together so artistically. He was completely surprised, and
touched, I think. My introductory poem to him read:

MY SON

You were born
Gift-wrapped in joy …
Tiny sweet angel boy.

And grew into
A winsome child
Loving, innocent, mild.

Came the teens,
For others, prime time big scenes.
What a blessing – your congenial genes!

Now unfolding is the man,
Paragon
of a Master Plan.

And I still see in the man
The boy,
Feel anew that first joy!

December 29, 1980

Dear Diary,

Skip went along to help when Robin and Terry moved to Fort Lauderdale the day after Christmas. We are going to miss having them near us in the same city.

I'm so glad I went to Dave and Dorothy's to see loved ones. Everybody was there except Bob and his lady friend, Joanne. I think Dave's youngest, Kimi, had changed the most in two years. She's such a lovely young lady – all five of the girls are. Wonderful visit … I felt comfortable and much loved.

December 31, 1980

Dear Diary,

Up early to get Skip off to Atlanta to visit a friend for a few days. David and I went to Jenni's for a spaghetti supper and stayed through midnight to watch the televised celebration in Times Square. Pretty exciting for David – first time he ever stayed awake and welcomed in a new year.

For everything there is a season,
and a time for every matter under heaven.
Ecclesiastes 3:1

Chapter Twenty-Four
Landmarks
1981-82

Wilba, Randolph and Griff at 50th anniversary

January 3, 1981
Louisville, Kentucky

Mobile, Alabama
Dear Pat,

What a Christmas gift you gave me! To hear you sound so "up" again after a long time was completely wonderful. And you quit smoking – that is the richest of all toppings. I wish for you continued strength and offer any help I can give. Even though I'm out of the state, I am not out of reach by phone or postman.

Don't know how you heard of "est," the program you attended, but certainly it must have been an answer to prayer. You also had to have been ready to receive all that inspiration and knowledge for it to have been so effective. Perhaps a year ago it would have meant nothing. So give credit to yourself, dear friend. Pat, you did it. You got your strength back. You've got a lot of living to make up for. I'm excited for you. Keep me posted. Say hi to all your kids.

Love,
Linda

February 10, 1981
Orlando, Florida

Orlando, Florida
Hey, Dad,

Thanks for the bike! I really like it!
Love,
David

February 17, 1981
Orlando, Florida

Mobile, Alabama
Dear Mom and Daddy,

I am feeling excited about the decision to move to Mobile. So far David is not adjusting to the idea as well, but we are discussing all sorts of possibilities.

Yesterday when I told Annette and Neill I won't be with them next school year tears welled up in Annette's eyes immediately and Neill said they sure will hate to lose me. Both are happy for the wonderful opportunity for me, though. Annette said, "We'll just have to find a second-best, I guess."

Sunday was a dreary-looking day and I brightened it by getting all decked out in a new pink ensemble to go to the Unity Church service. I tell you, I looked like a dish ... of strawberry ice cream, that is! The sermon topic was marriage, and the minister's message inspirational. One of the talented Unity members sang "The Hawaiian Wedding Song" and another offered a beautiful clarinet solo of "Stardust," both quite different from traditional church music, but so enjoyable. .

You remember Edith and Doc who lived next door to us here in Orlando when the kids were growing up? Doc died a few years ago and Edith moved back to Kansas to be near a niece, her only relative. Edith was in town last week and we spent a lovely afternoon together. I picked her up at noon and we had such a good time talking and looking at old pictures, seeing Jenni and David, eating supper out. I'd almost forgotten how much I enjoy her. At 79 she is still beautiful, so lively and interested in everybody and everything, and has the cutest sense of humor.

I hope you're feeling chipper again, Daddy, you, too, Mommie. Thanks to you sweethearts for my pretty valentine!

> Love you,
> Pat

February 17, 1981
Orlando, Florida

Mobile, Alabama
Dear Nana GeeGee and Granddaddy,

Thank you so much for the 10 dollars. I put it towards my bike. It is real neat. It's red and it has funny black wheels. I will see you in August.

> Love,
> David

February 18, 1981
Orlando, Florida

Winter Park, Florida
Dear Joanne,

Thank you very much for the preppie shirt. I wore it yesterday and I got a couple of compliments.

As you know, I got a bike and I sure love it.

Next week I am going to Fort Lauderdale to see Robin and Terry and I will stay until Sunday. I am real excited. It will be my first bus trip.

You are the travel agent in our family. Do you want to make my travel arrangements?

Love,
David

February 20, 1981
Fort Lauderdale, Florida

Orlando, Florida

We do not know who first gave love
or who first took love
or where it all began.
But we are happy that it did.
We are happy that it is.
We are happy as it is.
We are in short
in long
in love
and happy!
Robin and Terry
joyfully announce their marriage

March 12, 1981
New Smyrna Beach, Florida

Orlando, Florida
Dear Pat,

Dad asked me to thank you for his very nice birthday card and note. He truly appreciated receiving 19 cards at his ripe old age of 78. We had the usual party with birthday cake and candles – never too old for that!

Auntie Bussie arrives on the 25th. The days of that week are already full of plans and Dave and Dorothy want to spend the weekend. Others will come for the day Saturday and Sunday. Bussie is leaving on Thursday, so maybe you can drive over and have lunch with us Monday, Tuesday or Wednesday.

We were happy to have Robin call with the news that she and Terry had been married. Our wish for them is to have as happy a life together as Dad and I have.

483

I am sure your decision to move to Mobile was a difficult one but it does seem wise in many respects, and Dad and I surely wish you happiness and success in the years to come. We will miss the visits from David that we enjoy while we are here. Tell him we are eager to hear about his trip to Fort Lauderdale.

It's too beautiful a day to stay indoors – so it's out to my chaise in the sun.

Love,
Mother Kitty

April 6, 1981
Woodbury, Connecticut

Orlando, Florida
Pat dear,

Just wanted to tell you again how much I appreciated and enjoyed your taking time out for the trip to New Smyrna Beach. It was a nice visit, after four or five years. My trip home was as uneventful as the one down. And somehow it is always good to be in my own little nest again.

Please don't leave for Mobile without sending me your new address. We can correspond even when we can't visit.

Good luck with your college career – and everything else.

With love,
Auntie Bussie

May 1, 1981
Dear Diary,

I suppose this day will always bring memories of marriage and Bob. We did, after all, celebrate our anniversary on May 1st for nearly a quarter of a century. I wonder if I'll ever get married again. ... Of course, so far, in the past 1½ years I haven't even had a lunch date, never mind marriage!

May 10, 1981
Auburn University
Auburn, Alabama

Orlando, Florida
Mom,

I wanted to write a short note to let you know I wasn't upset you couldn't make it to the fraternity Mothers' Club, just disappointed. It was nice to meet the mothers of all my Sigma Chi friends, and I wish I could have had you to show off to everyone.

I think you're the greatest person, as well as the greatest mother, of anyone I know. I think of you often and regret not being able to see more of you during my school breaks. It's just that I have so many people to say hello to, and so much to do. I'll see more of you during my next break and I know we'll be able to get together when you're in Mobile.

Take care. Happy Mother's Day!

I love you,
Skip

May 30, 1981
Dear Diary,

I read a wonderful book this week – *A Woman of Independent Means*, by Elizabeth Forsythe Hailey. It's a novel composed of letters written by a woman to family members and friends. That's somewhat the idea of what *I* aim to do one day. ...

June 14, 1981
Orlando, Florida

Mobile, Alabama
Funny Daddy,

What a great big bunch of laughs I had this morning when I called you in the hospital. You are incredible! So witty ... but let's hope you have no more fistulas, even though this one proved to be fodder for your funny one-liners!

I'm sure you'll be feeling 100% better by the time you read this, when you are back home with your lady love.

Take care and we'll see y'all *very* soon.

Love you,
Pat

June 26, 1981
Orlando, Florida

Tucker, Georgia
Hi, Robin,

While repacking the china and the books, I found and have mailed both favorite books you asked for. Now you'll have something else to unpack. Have you settled in and gotten oriented to the new surroundings? The Atlanta area must seem quite different to you from South Florida.

How I, too, wish you could be here for a couple of days – for purely selfish reasons. This job of packing is overwhelming.

So glad you found a pleasant job situation, honey, and that you and Terry are doing okay.

Much love,
Mom

June 30, 1981
Dear Diary,

The packers worked five hours and everything is now stowed either in the moving truck or our station wagon. ... David and I went to say goodbye to Annette, Neill and Saralyn and were enveloped in warm wishes and hugs and given special going-away gifts. (We're all happy about the new arrangement for Saralyn's care. There is a wonderful "oma" who can keep Saralyn in her home along with two or three other children.) After that tearful farewell, we then joined Bob and Jenni at Red Lobster where Bob treated us to dinner, which I thought was so sweet. Afterward, just as he would've done in the past, he gave my car a "pre-trip check." He had also offered the use of his apartment so David and I came back here to spend our last night in Orlando before heading to Alabama early tomorrow. It feels somewhat unsettling to be in this strange apartment surrounded by familiar furnishings that used to be mine/ours. Yes ... but now it's time to quit mulling over the conundrum of my life and go to sleep – I'll need to be rested to begin this next adventure.

June 30, 1981
Dear "Day-Day" (David),

Thank you for being so kind and loving with Saralyn. You are so special to us all and always will be!

Hope you can use this little travel clock on your many trips to Atlanta and Orlando. We'll miss you and can't wait for you to come back and visit us. Please take care and write us when you have time.

Love,
Neill, Annette and Saralyn
(bow-wow from Tux!)

Dearest "Pat-Pat,"

We hope every time you wear this necklace you'll remember Saralyn, "Pat's sweetheart."

We all love you and will miss you so, but there's one thing you've taught us to believe and so we will. There is a reason for things working out the way they do.

You've shared our most wonderful experience, Saralyn, with us. Now we must share you with others elsewhere. Please take care and let us know if there's ever anything we can do for you.

Love,
Neill and Annette

July 3, 1981
Woodbury, Connecticut

Mobile, Alabama

Dear David,

Now that we are not going to hear about you so often from your dad I hope you will write us a letter once in a while. Granddad and I are interested in all you will be doing. Did you get into St. Paul's school? They will be making a mistake if they don't take our David with such a good record at your old school in Orlando.

We love you and hope you will be very happy in your new home.

Nana Kitty

July 3, 1981
Tucker, Georgia

Mobile, Alabama

Dear Nana GeeGee,

Mom told me you wanted suggestions on an invitation for the 50th anniversary party. We talked about several ideas but the favorite is a sepia colored fold-over card and your old black and white wedding photograph on front in cameo, with the words of Kahlil Gibran's treatise on marriage printed across the picture and information about the party inside.

We can't wait to see all of you at the party. I wish we could come down sooner, but we probably won't be able to.

All is well with us, but really busy. So I'll cut this short. Take good care of yourselves and Mom and David.

We love you,
Robin

July 4, 1981
Orlando, Florida

Mobile, Alabama
Dear David,

I wonder what you're doing this 4th of July. Hope you're having a fun cookout or picnic to celebrate the holiday. Joanne and I watched the men's tennis finals from Wimbledon, England, on TV, and soon we're going to visit some friends in Winter Park for a small Independence Day celebration.

Yesterday was a holiday for me as the stock market was closed. A three-day weekend is very nice!

Was your trip to Mobile fun? Did you stop overnight near Tallahassee? I hope the whole drive was successful, with no problems. I'll call you, but you should write me a letter once in awhile, too.

Please say Hi to Mom and Nana GeeGee and Granddaddy. Tell your mom she still has my back door key, and ask her to mail it back to me, okay? Thank her for the clever note on my July 1st calendar page.

This is only the fourth day you've been gone, but I really miss you already. I wish you could be here to see *Raiders of the Lost Ark* with me – Joanne won't go to "wet-palm" movies!

Take care, I love you.
Dad

July 8, 1981
Mobile, Alabama

Tucker, Georgia
Dear Robin and Terry,

Guess what happened to me the other day. When me and Granddaddy went out to the pizza place I found a one hundred dollar bill. Granddaddy had to hold me down because I was so excited. I put $90 in the money market and I kept $10. We really had fun on that trip.

Mom and I had a nice trip on the way up, we stopped in Tallahassee and stayed on the 3rd floor of a hotel on a hill that was two stories high and only as long as a couple of Station Wagons. Speaking about Station Wagons – I named our Station Wagon Old Yeller as we passed a Porche.

I love you,
David

July 8, 1981
Mobile, Alabama

Tucker, Georgia
Dear Robin and Terry,

We may talk by phone before you receive this so I won't go into detail of news here. Our furniture is still in a warehouse in Orlando, but the word is that it probably will arrive Saturday or Sunday. The apartment the folks found for us looks nice, spacious for a one-bedroom, but if it had been available a two-bedroom would have been even better.

So far David and I feel as if we're on vacation, just visiting the folks. We are okay about the move most of the time, although once in awhile we get really lonesome for everything about Orlando, which is natural, huh?

Hope your jobs are going great, and everything else, too. Talk to you soon.

I love you,
Mom

July 16, 1981
Mobile, Alabama

Orlando, Florida
Dear Dad,

Well, I haven't found any more one hundred dollar bills lately. I guess my money tree has died! The movers came yesterday with all of our furniture but it is in bad shape. All of it got wet. It is SOAKED. We will probably get our money back and more. I think I will get a waterbed or a bunk bed instead of two ordinary single beds. I have some more money to put in the money market – 20 smackeroos! On the second hand, I guess my money tree isn't totally dead yet.

There is a neat tree fort in back of a house we are looking at. That is a pretty house too. Four bedrooms, 2½ bathrooms, a big, big den, living room, laundry room, porch, two stories and there is even an intercom in the kitchen that you can hear people at the front door, two car garage and a 150x200 yard.

Nana GeeGee and I went golfing today and I did pretty good, one shot went about one hundred yards. I should be called "The one hundred man."

Everybody says hi. Tell Jenni hi. I love you.

Love,
David

P.S. – I hope we don't have to take this wet stuff to the Supreme Court!

489

July 20, 1981
Dear Diary,

So much negative energy I've felt today. All this mess about our damaged possessions, working on the insurance claim, and wondering where we'll live now that we let the apartment go, even car trouble. And Daddy and I had a heated discussion over what I should do at this point about the moving company's responsibility. I realize he wants to guide and protect me during this ordeal, yet I need to make "grown-up" decisions, too. But disagreeing with Daddy is something entirely new for both of us, and not relished!

A bit of a lift to my mood, though, knowing the 50th anniversary party is planned and preparations are in order, except that I haven't quite finished composing my tribute for Mommie and Daddy.

July 21, 1981
Tucker, Georgia

Mobile, Alabama
Dear Mom and David,

I still don't have any ideas for a gift for Nana GeeGee and Granddaddy – help! I am going to look for a new dress for the party. Mom, your black and white gown sounds perfect! I'm so looking forward to the party and especially getting to see your brothers and, of course, cousin Renee and all her family. I'm dying to get together after all these years!

Everything else is going pretty well and we like the Atlanta area. There are so many nice little "homey" houses near where we'll be living. Maybe before too long we can be in one of them.

Well, gotta go. I love and miss you both so much.

Robin

July 22, 1981
Orlando, Florida

Mobile, Alabama
Dear David,

Thanks for your letter, my boy – it was GREAT! Please keep it up – why not try to write me every two weeks or more if you can?

I hope the business of the movers letting all of your things get wet has straightened out some. They should really make it up to you and Mom, plus the inconvenience and aggravation. It's really good that you have Granddaddy and Nana GeeGee there to help you out.

The 20 "smackeroos" you sent me are already invested. The current rate of interest is 17.15%. Save up until you have $20 or more to deposit, okay?

Keep up your golfing! Skip could be really good if he played more often. Maybe you'll be even better.

Do you know if you're going up to Auburn for Skip's graduation? Ask Mom what the outlook is. I believe I'll be going, but I'd like to know who else is going.

It has been very hot here since you left, between 90° and 100°, and thunderstorms almost every day, too. It will stay like this till October.

News from Central Florida is that Universal Studios is going to build a $200 million entertainment park between Orlando and Disney, to be ready by 1983. So you'll have that to see, plus Little England and Epcot when they are finished.

Say hello to Mom and your grandparents. Take good care of David. I love you and miss you.

Dad

July 25, 1981
Dear Diary,

David cried at bedtime during our nightly "review" of our experiences and thoughts of the day. He said so poignantly, "Talking about when I was real little makes me sad that I can't ever go back and live it over." I was thinking, there's some of my life I'd like to live over, too, but maybe not the last few years. (And definitely not these present days of upheaval.)

July 28, 1981
Orlando, Florida

Mobile, Alabama
Dear Pat and David,

I received the unique invitation to the Golden Anniversary party. I thought it was clever and very touching. Who thought up the idea? It would be fun to be there, but I think I would be a little out of place. However, I appreciate the invitation and seeing the actual announcement. Thanks.

I've decided to go to Skip's graduation by car – it's so much cheaper. I hope you come, because I believe it would mean a lot to Skip. And I want my little boy there.

I trust your horrible mess is getting straightened out gradually. Certainly was inexcusable!

Love to you both,
Bob/Dad

August 1, 1981
Mobile, Alabama

Orlando, Florida

Dear Dad,

Did you see that wedding last Wednesday of Prince Charles and Lady Diana? It was a blast, but I wonder why all of those British people go crazy over two normal people getting married.

Nothing exciting has happened. In fact it's been pretty boring – that is if it hadn't been for Legos. I've been playing with my Legos all day. (It's the only thing to do.) I got a new one yesterday and it's real expensive. Oops (I ought to keep my mouth shut) I mean neat!

I read your letter. It was nice except if we thought you were going to be out of place we wouldn't of sent you an invitation. I hope you can come. If I don't see you at the party I will see you at the graduation.

I love you,
David

August 2, 1981
Orlando, Florida

Mobile, Alabama

Dear David,

I'm sure you have wondered if Joanne and I would get married someday. Well, we have decided to be married on September 18 in Annapolis. We will be there for my 30th reunion of graduation from the Naval Academy. It will be a very simple wedding, and we are not going to have any of our children attend.

After the reunion ends, we will drive back to Orlando. Then I will move out of my apartment and live with Joanne in hers.

I am going to have to give some of my furniture to Skip and the girls because there just isn't enough room in Joanne's apartment. So if there are any of my belongings that you can remember and want for yourself, let me know soon.

We can talk more about this the end of this month at Skip's graduation. I'm really looking forward to seeing you – it's been a month already!

David, I know you're happy about Joanne and me getting married. It will be a new experience for you to have a stepmother. Joanne is very fond of you and we look forward to your visits in our home. You have accepted your mom's and my separation and divorce so well, and I thank

492

you for that. I know it isn't easy for a little guy, but these things do happen, unfortunately. And when they do, we all have to make the best of it and try to make our lives happy again.

> Lots of love,
> Dad

> August 2, 1981
> Orlando, Florida

Mobile, Alabama
Dear Pat,

My letter to David will fill you in on my "news." Probably not a big surprise to anyone – just the where and when. We can discuss it further in Alabama if you want to.

Our almost 25 years of marriage have many, many happy memories for me, and I will always care about you and want your well-being. But we do move on. ... I hope your Mobile change, although off to an unfortunate beginning, will make you very happy, just as I'm sure my coming marriage will receive your best wishes.

Please relay my news to your parents. Now you can see, with my news plus my trip to Auburn, why I just don't think I should attend the Golden Anniversary celebration. Perhaps now you all will better understand my not coming.

> Love,
> Bob

> August 5, 198
> Woodbury, Connecticut

Mobile, Alabama
Dear David,

After I sent you that card from Fishers Island we came home to find your nice letter awaiting us. Granddad and I just loved it and all the interesting news.

We will have to call you our rich grandson! I never heard of anyone finding a hundred dollar bill!

I'm glad you're beginning to play golf. You will enjoy that all your life. I know what fun it is riding around in a golf cart.

That was a mess about all your belongings getting wet. I hope the moving company will take care of it satisfactorily.

Good luck in your new home and love to you and Mom. We will miss seeing you at the beach this winter.

Nana Kitty

August 6, 1981
Mobile, Alabama

Orlando, Florida

Dear Dad,

Congradulations that you and Joanne are getting married! I am so glad, now I will have a Step-Mother. I hope you live happily ever after.

Guess what! Granddaddy and I bought that house I told you about. (It is for Mom, Nana GeeGee, Granddaddy and me). Since we are moving into a big house we can use a lot of furniture so don't sell anything.

I LOVE you. And I still want you to come to the party!

Love,
David

P.S. – Have fun in Annapolis!

August 6, 1981
Mobile, Alabama

Orlando, Florida

Dear Bob,

My reaction to your news was a sudden burst of tears, which surprised me, for of course, I wish you and Joanne happiness. Your marriage, though, marks the ending to anything and everything we ever had or were together, and there is still a lot of sadness. Somehow, it seems more final, with me right back here in Alabama, living with my mother and father again, almost as if our life together never happened. I mean, those are some of the thoughts and feelings that surfaced. Someone told Mom recently they had heard Mobile is the deadest place in the United States for meeting people. Just my luck.

Since our move to Alabama, everything has gone haywire, and I have felt so unsettled and uncertain I've had to fight feelings of regret over the decision to come back. (My positive attitude is having a hard time keeping on top.) The changes involved in an out-of-state move are many, and not always easy, even without such a mess as we've been thrown into.

The hassle is beginning to take its toll. I have even suffered – and I mean that literally – phlebitis, a blood clot in the upper arm. It began Saturday

494

and by early Monday morning when I got to a doctor, I was in bad shape. Should have gone to the emergency room, I suppose, but that's usually a horrible experience, too. Three doctors concurred in the diagnosis of phlebitis, so blood thinning medications and codeine were started – and worked quickly and very well, leaving just soreness by today.

Instinct, experience, and everything else tell me all will be well again at some point in time. Right? I hope.

I'm sure you will find special meaning in being married at Annapolis, Bob. So many of your friends were married there back in 1951, and your parents, too, in 1927.

About furniture and other items, please advise what is available and what's up in the air among the kids. I am interested, now more than ever because of the extensive damage to our furnishings and the fact that we're moving to a larger home. And I still have sentimental feelings about all the furnishings that once graced our homes – which I realized the night David and I stayed in your apartment while you were away before we drove to Alabama.

Talk to you before long – see you in Auburn.

Love,
Pat

August 6, 1981
Auburn University
Auburn, Alabama

Mobile, Alabama
Dear Mom,

The big day is almost here! I'll be seeing you soon and we'll have a lot of talking to do! Thanks for all your moral support!

I love you,
Skip

Auburn University
requests the honor of your presence
at Summer Commencement
Friday afternoon, August twenty-eighth
Nineteen hundred and eighty-one
two-thirty o'clock
Auburn Memorial Coliseum
Auburn, Alabama

August 10, 1981
Mobile, Alabama

Orlando, Florida
Dear Stepmother,

Congratulations! I'm glad you finally will get married. Now I guess I will be staying at your house when I come down.

A lot is going on up here. We are getting set for the party. It is going to be a blast! I wish you could come.

Did you hear that I found a one hundred dollar bill? I put it in the money market. Dad probably told you about that.

Did you hear about our furniture? It's a mess! The movers put it out in the rain. We might have to go to court. I'll call you and tell you about that. (It's a long story.)

Me, my mom and my grandparents are moving into a big house in October. It has a tree fort in the back.

I love you.
Love, David

August 15, 1981
Mobile, Alabama

Orlando, Florida

Congratulations on your Golden Wedding Anniversary!

That's quite an achievement – 50 happy years together. Hope you have 50 more! I will be with you in spirit as you celebrate.

Best wishes, and love,
Bob

August 15, 1981
The White House
Washington, D.C.

Mobile, Alabama
Dear Wilba and Randolph,

Nancy and I send our warm congratulations as you commemorate your 50th Wedding Anniversary. This is indeed a special occasion to be celebrated with much pride and happiness. We wish you every shared joy in the future.

Ronald Reagan

August 15, 1981

THE SWEETHEARTS
By Pat

He first saw her in the mill
and thought she looked right fine.
'Course she already had an eye for him
and a secret vow – "*he* is mine!"

Ah, so young she was, and fair,
and he, dashing and debonair.
Soon they courted – and fell in love.

In August 1931 there came a day
that would always be remembered
in a very special way. …

A few dollars he paid for a license,
the preacher, and a ride to
Enterprise to claim his bride.
There were no frills, fineries or bows,
just one sweet, simple wedding pose.

He gave her a ring …
not then, but one year later – a
$5.50 prize bought on time
from the local Five and Dime.

Their love blossomed, so did she –
and in the year '32, baby made three!
A daughter, who started the family,
soon asked for a little brother … so
along came three, one after the other!

The family grew and hard times, too. …
During lean years, in sickness or in strife,
their love did not perish but grew stronger
as young husband and wife
continued to love and to cherish.

497

Time marched on, the family
increased even more.
The children grew up, dated, mated,
added in-laws and grandbabies galore!

In mid-life, when it's so easy
to fall into a rut, there came a lull …
to fill it she learned to swing, chip and putt
while he played the field (in oil, that is!).

Now the $5.50 ring has long been replaced
with oil and diamonds and gold,
but the sweethearts still stand face to face
vowing once again to have and to hold.

(P.S. – When her anniversary party dress was
unveiled, revealing its sexy front slit,
he sailed right into his now-famous line:
"Sugar, I 'spect we'd better plan on leaving that
party 'bout a quarter-to-nine!")

August 17, 1981
Orlando, Florida

Mobile, Alabama
Dear David,

Thank you for your letter. Gosh! I hope you are not going to start calling me "Stepmother" instead of Joanne! We are both very excited about the wedding plans. Your dad will tell you all about them when he sees you at Skip's graduation.

In exactly one month, two days and 15 minutes, this will no longer be my whole house. You should see your room. It looks like a storeroom. We have had new bookcases, cupboards, and drawers built all across the end of the sitting room area of the big bedroom. So while the new wood is being painted, all the books, stereo, etc., are all over the floor in the other bedroom.

We are going to meet Jenni at the airport tonight, so I will hear all about the party. It must have been fun to have your sisters and brother all together in your new hometown where you could show them around.

I felt so sorry for the mess that you and your mom had to go through with the moves. I just hope all of the irreplaceables like scrapbooks and photo albums were not damaged – for those there can be no compensation.

We miss you and will look forward to a visit as soon as possible.

Love,
Joanne

August 18, 1981
Woodbury, Connecticut

Mobile, Alabama
Dear Pat,

Along with our best birthday greetings to you, I shall cheat Uncle Sam and send along a note too. We thought of you all on Saturday and are sure it was a successful anniversary party and happy time for everyone.

Now I hope you can get straightened out. The moving situation was truly an awful experience, and then for you to have a painful phlebitis seems like too much. I do hope the problems are clearing up.

With Dorothy and Dave's marriage such a solid, happy one we are delighted that Bob has found someone to care for him. At our age it is a good feeling to have one's children settled so satisfactorily. The wedding being held in the chapel at Annapolis is a dividend for us and a great chance for a brief visit with our four dear ones.

David's letter to us was darling and I hope he will keep it up.

There have been and are still to be too many visits this summer. I guess as we grow older we are more and more content at home together.

We do wish you good luck in your new life!

With our love,
Mother Kitty

August 18, 1981
Blankner Elementary School
Orlando, Florida

Mobile, Alabama
To Whom It May Concern,

It is a pleasure to commend David to you. He is a straight A student, working on and above grade level. He is also a good athlete and sings in the school chorus. David does beautifully neat work, regularly receives an A in conduct, and maintains the affection and respect of his classmates. He will be a joy to the teacher fortunate enough to have him in her class. If he remained at Blankner Elementary, he would be chosen for the school safety patrol. I sincerely hope you will consider him for your patrol if that is feasible.

Sincerely yours,
Miss Joan
Fifth-Grade Classroom Teacher

August 18, 1981
Office of Financial Aid
University of South Alabama
Mobile, Alabama

Mobile, Alabama
Dear Pat,

Congratulations! Because of your outstanding academic record, you have been selected to receive one of a limited number of Presidential Scholarships available to entering transfers of exceptional academic merit.

This award covers the $12 registration fee in addition to tuition charges for 12 to 16 hours of credit each quarter. The award is for the 1981-1982 academic year beginning with the fall quarter. Renewal of the award for subsequent years will be based on your cumulative grade-point average and will require the filing of a Financial Aid Application.

Please accept my congratulations for your superior academic record. May every success be yours as you continue your educational endeavors.

Sincerely,
Director,
Office of Financial Aid

500

August 20, 1981
Tucker, Georgia

Mobile, Alabama
Dearest Mom,

Wasn't the party fun? I've been remembering it all week. Nana and Granddaddy smiled more than I've ever seen them smile and they both looked so cute. And you looked poised and stunning. Don't we have a great family?

Ever since seeing Renee's baby girl, we have been talking a lot about children. I *know* you'll be happy to be a grandmother someday, right?

Even though we knew we wouldn't have much time together, I still feel cheated out of a good visit. Can't wait for you, Nana GeeGee and David to come to Georgia. Maybe David could take the bus for a weekend, or would it be too long a trip?

I love you,
Robin

August 22, 1981
Martha's Vineyard
Nantucket, Massachusetts

Mobile, Alabama
Hello David,

Doesn't the picture on this postcard look like you feeding the sea gulls in Florida a few years ago? Yesterday Nana Kitty and I had a nice four-hour drive from Woodbury to Cape Cod and then a half-hour trip on the ferry pictured to get here. We have enjoyed seeing all the people, young and old, riding their bikes, just hundreds of them. Today we will spend the day at the beach in Chappaquidic after another little ferry ride near us. Wish we could be with you for Skip's graduation next week.

Love,
Granddad and Nana Kitty

August 22, 1981
Harrisonville, Missouri

Mobile, Alabama
Dear Wilba and Randolph,

It was a great anniversary party and reunion, and it couldn't have honored a finer couple. You two have always been special to me since 1945 when Bill and I were married. You have been not only family, you have

501

been more than a sister and brother – you have been my friends, and I want to take this opportunity to say THANKS for always being there.

It was wonderful renewing acquaintances with relatives and friends that might never have happened otherwise, and the whole occasion fills several pages in my mind's book of memories.

Love,
Hazel

September 8, 1981
Winter Park, Florida

Mobile, Alabama
My dearest Pat,

Thanks for your letter. We were wondering how things were since you moved. That's terrible about your furniture. I hope there's a good settlement with the moving company. Nice, though, that you and David and your parents are moving into a new home. I certainly hope all goes well from here on. And, oh, I am so proud of you with school. You deserve a lot of credit for all you've done.

How is my David? Tell him his picture is on Susie's bulletin board at Florida State University. He will be seen by lots of gals! Good to hear that your girls are okay, and Skip. I know Skip will go a long way with his life. He has looks, personality and brains – what more could a guy have? I hope he finds someone who really appreciates him.

Well, my dear, take care, and keep us posted. Give a big hug to David – also to the "golden sweethearts!"

Love and miss you,
Ann ("Ex-Mistress of the Mansion")

September 20, 1981
Annapolis, Maryland

Mobile, Alabama
Dear David,

Joanne is now your official stepmother. We had a very nice wedding on the 18th. Then we had my 30th Reunion at the Naval Academy during the weekend. Now we are resting up at an inn in Oxford, Maryland, before starting back to Winter Park tomorrow.

Much love,
Dad

October 1, 1981
Woodbury, Connecticut

Tucker, Georgia
Dear Robin,

This is a lovely rainy morning, a good time to write a letter to my granddaughter and later go out for lunch and bridge.

I know you want to hear my version of the wedding. Our brief time in Annapolis was one of the special, happy times for Granddad and me – pure joy! We had a dinner party for 10 Thursday evening at the Officers Club – and even before that it was wonderful to have your dad and Joanne and Dorothy and Dave with us. Also, we liked Joanne's brother and his wife so very much, and it was an added dividend to see two of your dad's classmates and one wife whom we have known for 30 years. The noon wedding was short and simple – such good taste when it was a second marriage for both – so lovely in that beautiful, historic chapel. Joanne's luncheon at a nearby inn was done so perfectly, as she does everything, and the 11 of us enjoyed every minute of it. It is a warm, contented feeling for Granddad and me to have your dad cared for by such a thoughtful, generous person as Joanne. We have been so thankful for the solid marriage of Dave and Dorothy.

By the way, Granddad took pictures, but we have sent one set plus all the negatives to the "bride and groom" – not knowing what or how many copies they might want – so put your bid in to them.

Good news that you are enjoying Atlanta and by the time you receive this Skip will be there too, which will be nice for you both. Jenni writes that they had such a good time together in Orlando, and we talked to Skip on the phone this week.

Christmas will surely be different this year – Skip, David, you and Terry, Lynn and Mike, and Kimi will all be missing – and Joanne's three sons plus one wife will be on hand. We will still hope to see some of you later in the winter.

So glad you are enjoying domesticity – it has always been a happy part of my life. Are you doing anything in the line of art?

We are going to New Haven to the Navy-Yale game on Saturday with three other couples. We'll have a tailgate picnic first and dinner at one couple's house later. So we are still having fun.

Love,
Nana Kitty

October 14, 1981
Starkville, Mississippi

Mobile, Alabama
Dear Aunt Pat and David and Nana GeeGee and Granddaddy,

Dearies, my mom said I had 56 dollars in the bank. I have put every cent in the bank. I'm doing good in school. Thank you for the money. Thank you for remembering my birthday. It was fun. I am 11 years old now.

Sincerely,
Adam

October 12, 1981
Tucker, Georgia

Mobile, Alabama
Dear Mom,

Please keep us up to date on how David is doing. We're so worried about him being sick. What is the doctor saying about how long it might take David to recover? I guess mononucleosis is more serious than most people think.

Everything's fine with me – I may have found an additional freelance client. Skip will be leaving for Chicago tomorrow on business for two weeks. I'm already getting used to him being here and am going to miss him.

Looks like Dad, Joanne and Jenni will be coming up for Thanksgiving weekend, and we'll be able to spend Friday night till Sunday morning together. We will be visiting Terry's folks in Savannah Wednesday night through Friday morning. This way we'll get to see almost everybody between now and Christmas.

Well, better run. I love you and David and Nana GeeGee and Granddaddy.

Love,
Robin

P.S. – Hope your classes are going great!

October 26, 1981
Winter Park, Florida

Mobile, Alabama
Dear Pat,

Here is a check for David's bills. I will have enough to get reimbursed in part on my medical insurance. And I will submit them as soon as I get all the bills for him through the present illness.

We'll hold David's reservations the way I gave them to you, leaving Atlanta for Orlando Sunday afternoon, December 27, after you two have had Christmas with Robin, Terry and Skip. Then leaving Orlando for Mobile early a.m. on Sunday, January 3. That is the best schedule for me as far as having the guest bedroom free and for the best airfares.

Thanks for helping our boy through this long siege. I know it's been tough to go through it "alone." But it's also bad for me to be so far away from him.

Love,
Bob

November 7, 1981
Tucker, Georgia

Mobile, Alabama
Dear David,

I can't believe you're still not feeling well. I'll bet you're tired of being sick. I really wanted to drive down to see y'all this weekend but since it didn't work out, I'm going to try and plan to come next weekend. Okay? Sure wish I could have helped with the garage sale. Please ask Mom to keep the stuff I might want.

I need you to give me an idea of what you want for Christmas. So be thinking about it. Tell Mom we can set up a single bed here for someone to sleep on at Christmas – maybe she can sleep there and we'll set you up on the couch or a pallet on the floor. Anyway we'll work it out between us and Skip.

I love you very, very much, my David. See you soon!

Love,
Robin

November 17, 1981
Woodbury, Connecticut

Mobile, Alabama
Hi, David,

How about that, you get a letter from your old Granddad! Some surprise!

Anyway, it proves we are thinking about you and hoping you will be well again and full of pep. We have been sorry too that you are missing so much of your new school.

Just think, we expect to be arriving in Winter Park only three weeks from today. It takes a lot of preparation, getting out the right things, including my golf clubs, swimming gear, etc., and we have a smaller car than before to fill up with all our stuff for our five months in Florida. We are hoping to get out of Connecticut before the first snowfall.

Enclosed is a kind of electronic word game I used to send to your cousin Kimi for her to play with when she had to be alone now and then. I thought you might try it.

Have a happy Thanksgiving and maybe Nana Kitty and I will get a look at you again one of these days.

We love you, boy,
Granddad

November 25, 1981
Mobile, Alabama

Tucker, Georgia
Dear Robin,

I thought you kids would like to see a sample of work from your old college mom's Drama Class. This earned a very nice mark and great comments from my professor. Please show it to Skip, and ask him to pass it on to Jenni.

Love,
Mom

November 18, 1981
Drama 110 – 12:00 Class

THE COMEDY OF ERRORS – CRITIQUE

Seldom have I seen an actor exhibit more *joie de vivre* than did Erik/Dromio during a recent presentation of William Shakespeare's The Comedy of Errors at Seaman's Bethel Theatre on the campus of the University of South Alabama. I feel that of all the students who participated in the Department of Dramatic Arts' production, Erik deserves kudos for his excellent performance.

In portraying Dromio of Syracuse, the young actor fairly exuded mental and physical energy. The role demanded much – he gave all. Whether leaping through the air or curled under a bench, or graphically describing a very fat lady, or gracefully executing, with Antiphobus, a delightful "dialogue dance" – all the while articulating Shakespeare's verbiage without a hitch – Erik appeared to be having the time of his young life. Real or role, his enthusiasm was highly infectious. (Bravo, Dromio!)

This infection, alas, did not spread to the abbey. ...

December 24, 1981
Dear Diary,

Late Christmas Eve at Robin and Terry's apartment in Atlanta – weather, wet, raw, cold. Our darling David is just as sick as can be again and tonight we took him to the Emergency Center when he suddenly developed a really high fever and a full body rash. There he was examined by a soft-spoken, gentle female physician. She and the nurses were so kind to David – and comforting to me. He has swollen lymph nodes, and red ears and tonsils, and a blood count indicated a viral infection. Large doses of Vitamin C and penicillin were prescribed to try and ward off bacterial infection. I described David's recent medical history to the doctor and told her how afraid I am that he has leukemia, but she assured me otherwise. I am terribly concerned, though, and feel *so* sorry for my sweet Davey. How I wish I could make him well.

December 25, 1981
Dear Diary,

We set David up comfortably on the sofa where he could watch, participate or just doze while we opened the oodles of presents under the tree. As in Christmases past we took almost all day with that delightful chore – with breaks for eating, of course. Skip was here, too, so I had three of my four kids with me. And we all enjoyed Jenni's call from Orlando – she was feeling very "ho-ho-ho-ish!"

December 27, 1981
Mobile, Alabama

Tucker, Georgia
Hi, Robin,

We made it home safely in a little over six hours, with two stops and two hours of night driving – so I did well. The Nova just sailed along.

The little nest of pillows and blankets we made for David in the back seat was perfect for the trip. He felt miserable but didn't complain. He's so good, really. He has been in bed ever since we got home. He even had quite a severe upset stomach last night. It's unbelievable how the ailments keep coming.

We enjoyed being with you in your home this Christmas – such a nice gathering place. Too bad David's sickness prevented even more fun for him, for all of us.

The house, and Mobile, felt more like home to us after the trip, and that's good. Mom and Daddy were waiting for us with open arms.

All this afternoon I've been catching up on paying bills, balancing the checkbook, writing notes, and doing laundry.

Be sure to hug Skip for me when he comes over and tell him David did grin and say to Granddaddy last night, "Oh, I forgot to kick Skip's butt for you."

Y'all take care of each other. We send much love to you sweet ones.

Mom

December 28, 1981
Office of the President
University of South Alabama
Mobile, Alabama

Mobile, Alabama
Dear Pat,

Welcome to the ranks of those rare scholars who have achieved the perfect scholastic grade average of 4.0. Your name is now on the list of "President's Scholars." May I extend to you my most sincere congratulations and my personal acknowledgement of the high respect I hold for you.

508

This achievement, I know, has not been an easy one. It requires courage, hard work and a high sense of responsibility to yourself and to your fellow man. It is to you and those like you that the toils of a troubled and complex civilization will be granted as a reward. You will not find all the answers, but you will find some. That is all we need and all we ask.

My warmest good wishes go with you wherever and always.

Sincerely,
The President
University of South Alabama

December 28, 1981
Winter Park, Florida

Mobile, Alabama
Dear David,

Here we are in Florida, a long way from Connecticut. And although we have had several Christmas parties and openings of gifts, we have missed you and wished you could be in two places at the same time. I am going to enjoy my great little perpetual calendar for a long time, moving it around with us in the days ahead. It was just right for my needs. Thanks a lot for sending it.

Happy New Year to our youngest grandson from Nana Kitty and me.

With love,
Granddad

December 28, 1981
Orlando, Florida

Mobile, Alabama
Dear David,

Hi there! I miss you so much, and I know how disappointed you are not to be able to come to Orlando yet. But it would be no fun for you anyway until you're feeling better.

I couldn't get the headphones for your Christmas present, but I got something else, which Dad will bring next month when he visits you. We'll find some headphones for your birthday, okay?

The cats are fine and send their love. David, we love and miss you!

Your sister,
Jenni

December 29, 1981
Tucker, Georgia

Mobile, Alabama
Dearest Mom and David,

I don't think I've thought of anything much except you two since you left. I want to just jump in the car and come down there. David, I look at the little statue of the couple in the swing all the time. It was one of my favorite presents. You always pick good ones!

I love you both with all my heart!

Robin

December 31, 1981
Orlando, Florida

Mobile, Alabama
Dear Mom and David,

I miss you! Next Christmas we *have* to be together – I didn't like this separation at all. Any changes in how you feel, David? Dad keeps me posted on your condition.

Thank you, David, for the memo board – I *love* it! It's really me isn't it? I'm going to hang it in the kitchen where I do my lists. You picked a *great* gift, little brother.

And Mom, thank you for the sweater and book, and the little goodies box – that makeup is the right color for me. And thank you very much for the money you sent a couple of weeks ago. You're so thoughtful to do that, Mom. I love you and David so much. I wish you were closer than Mobile.

I want 1982 to be a good one for you two. Know that I'm thinking of you and wishing I could be there to kiss you.

Much love,
Jenni

January 3, 1982
Winter Park, Florida

Mobile, Alabama
Dear David,

A week from today you and your dad probably will be watching two football games together there in Mobile and I can watch HBO here. There really have been a lot of games, but none as exciting as the Dolphins game last night. I hope you were watching.

Thank you very much for my happy Turtle Tile, he really is darling. Your dad loved his trip book and has been busy writing in it to recap our trips.

We had a really nice Christmas. My three boys and your cousin Kimi were here as well as Jenni and your Nana Kitty and Granddad. It went on for hours! We have a big box of your gifts packed and ready to travel to Mobile so you'll be the first person in Mobile, I'll bet, to have Christmas in 1982.

I'll be waiting to hear all about your weekend with your dad. I hope you are feeling better and have lots planned to do while he's there.

Much love,
Joanne

January 6, 1982
University of South Alabama
Mobile, Alabama

Mobile, Alabama
Dear Pat,

Please accept my earnest congratulations for achieving the Dean's List for Fall Quarter 1981. This is an accomplishment of which you should be proud.

On behalf of your professors, I wish you continued success. If I or other members of this office can assist you in any way, please let me know.

Sincerely,
Office of the Dean
Arts and Sciences

January 7, 1982
Mobile, Alabama
Director, Office of Financial Aid
University of South Alabama

Mobile, Alabama
Dear Sir,

In accordance with our telephone conversation yesterday, please be advised that I am not going to attend the University of South Alabama during Winter Quarter due to my young son's illness. I hope to return to my studies in March and hereby request that the Financial Aid Office reserve my Presidential Scholarship, BEOG Grant, and student loan for use during Spring Quarter. Thank you for your help, and for your personal concern.

Sincerely,
Pat

January 9, 1982
Woodbury, Connecticut

Mobile, Alabama

Pat dear,

Thanks for your pretty Christmas card. It's always good to hear from you. Notes from Robin, Jenni, Skip and David were much enjoyed too.

I'm so concerned about David. None of the news sounds good. Wish the doctors would get off their duffs and *do* something for him.

How's college going? Are you still enjoying your classes? I often found that my adult students got a lot more out of any courses than did the undergrads. Maybe it pays off to wait some years.

Again, I hope 1982 improves things for you.

Much love,
Auntie Bussie

Chapter Twenty-Five
Longing for Family
1982-83

Randolph and first great-grandchild, Nicholas

January 10, 1982
Dear Diary,

Bob flew into Mobile from Orlando today. He brought a large box of Christmas presents for David – lots of nice toys – and David stayed up almost all day playing games with his dad even though he kept saying how bad he felt. He was happy to see his daddy. Bob had appointments to see the psychologist and the physician, both of whom believe much of David's illness is of a psychological nature and that he *will* be fine again.

Pat

January 12, 1982
Dear Diary,

Big news! Our boy went out to a movie with Bob this afternoon and then all of us played games in the evening. David was really tearful at bedtime, though, and confessed to his daddy he's afraid he's never going to get better.

January 15, 1982
Dear Diary,

I'm certainly not getting many chores of a personal nature accomplished since I began devoting myself completely to David's recovery. But I am getting in a lot of practice playing games – Bonkerz, Backgammon, Connect 4. It might sound like the job is easy, but it's not, it is a challenge. David is not his normal self now, so my staying neutral, standing firm, and insisting he behave in certain ways takes much patience.

I can see David improving in some ways and regressing in others. When his home teacher called unexpectedly and wanted to come for a lesson, David threw a fit, cried and said he felt too bad. But I stood firm and the teacher came. David seems to be getting more dependent on me, and that's not good because the goal is to get him back to doing more things on his own. But the psychologist complimented me for the way I'm handling the somewhat delicate situation. I'm sure glad he's involved now to guide me.

January 15, 1982
Winter Park, Florida

Mobile, Alabama
Dear Pop and Mom,

As I flew home on Sunday night, I felt a great deal of satisfaction that the three days I spent in Mobile with you and David and Pat had gone very well. I suppose things really went better than I had anticipated, because I

514

was well prepared for the worst. In any event, the weekend with David was extremely beneficial to everyone. I only hope we are on the road back to a normal, completely well David.

You both helped to make my visit a successful one. There was no feeling of being uncomfortable, no uneasiness that I felt while in your home, although it might have been so with *other* families. I think we all got along famously, and I thank you for that, as well as putting me up for the weekend. I appreciate your kindness and generosity.

Thanks again, very much.

Love,
Bob

January 15, 1982
Tucker, Georgia

Mobile, Alabama
Dearest David,

I would give anything if you could be here in the snow season. It has been so pretty, especially today because it was sunny and just pleasantly cold. Skip and Terry and I have gone for walks in the snow every day, and it's lots of fun! I took pictures and will send you some when they're developed.

Dad said he had a great time with you and Mom, Nana GeeGee and Granddaddy in Mobile. I'm so glad. And also that you got to see *Raiders of the Lost Ark* – wasn't it great? Be sure Mom gets to see it too.

Well, I'm getting fatter every day. David, I think by the next time you see me, you'll be able to pretty much tell I'm expecting a baby.

I have a chance for another job, and I'll find out on Tuesday. I am really ready to start work again so wish me luck. Write to me soon, okay?

We *love* you,
Robin

January 23, 1982
Maitland, Florida

Mobile, Alabama
Dear David,

It was so good to receive your letter! Aunt Dorothy and I both thank you.

515

We are delighted you like the electronic baseball game. You seemed to enjoy the football game we gave you last year so much we thought a similar game might be fun for you.

Did your father tell you that your Christmas tree ornament hung proudly on our tree? That was a nice idea for a gift, and we appreciate it. You shall see it shining on our tree again in just 11 months.

We missed Skip here over the holidays, but we did get to see Jenni twice. She looks and seems great. Both are doing well in their jobs. Skip called twice to say "Hello."

Kimi will come here from Wisconsin for her spring break from school just as she did last year. We hope you can do the same. What week will you have off from school?

We missed you at Christmas, but you did not miss the annual family Decathlon! Toward the end of the vacation when we have the Decathlon, everyone got the 24-hour bug and no one felt like competing in the events except for putt-putt golf and darts. So we saved the new trophies for next year, and *you* can help with being a referee and equipment manager. Soon you will be able to be a contestant, like your brother was a few years back, so get good exercise and enjoy your physical education classes at school.

(I am going to enclose a copy of the funny letter about the contest that Skip wrote five years ago when he missed the Decathlon because he had been sick.)

Write again soon, David, because we miss you. Get well.

We love you,
Uncle Dave and Aunt Dorothy

Re: Renewal of Consideration by Alabama-Florida Invitational Decathlon Championships III Selection Committee

July 17, 1976
Mobile, Alabama

Maitland, Florida

Dear "Dr. Dave,"

Regarding your March 25, 1976, Notice of Rejection by the above-named selection committee, I hereby respectfully re-submit my application to your honorable (?) selection committee. I am presently visiting in Alabama where I've had the opportunity to discuss this whole situation with my Granddaddy, who is in agreement with me that I should be given special permission to compete in the Decathlon with you and your sons-in-law since:

l) I am your beloved firstborn nephew; and 2) I don't believe you would want to risk having me possibly scarred for life by such a rejection.

In reference to the March memo, I have corrected the three factors listed for my rejection, namely:

I. Youthful age has been rectified due to the passing of 58 days, at which time I reached a very mature 17 years of age.

II. With the advice of my personal physician, certain expensive medication, the absence of oral contact with any member of the opposite sex, and, not to be overlooked, the Tender Loving Care of my mommy, my unhealthy condition of mononucleosis has been cured.

III. Lastly, quoting from the memo another one of your reasons for my rejection, "Your failure to appear before the committee at the appointment time scheduled," I offer this explanation: My failure to appear before the selection committee was, in fact, due to the failure of your notification of any such scheduled appointment time.

IV. In addition to your mistake, I believe there was an underlying discriminatory factor present which should be brought to the attention of the International Olympic Committee.

In closing, I am prepared to appear before the selection committee and to compete with the athletes of the great states of Florida and Alabama. I firmly believe my superb physical and mental capacities will be a great asset to the Alabama-Florida Invitational Decathlon Championships III.

Thanking you for your consideration in this matter, I remain

> Your nephew,
> Skip,
> Head, Beverage Department
> Publix Supermarket

P.S. – Have you ever considered shortening the name of the event?

January 23, 1982
Mobile, Alabama

Winter Park, Florida
Dear Dad and Joanne,
    Thank you for the sweater
    That made me look fine –
    And thank you for the radio
    I listen to it all the time.
    Thank you for the puzzle
    That I have yet to put together –
    And thank you for the laughing thing –
    I think it made me better!
            Love,
            David

P.S. – Thank you for the Connect Four game also. I couldn't fit that in the poem.

January 27, 1982
New Smyrna Beach, Florida

Mobile, Alabama
Dear David,
    I wish I could write as beautifully as you do! Granddad and I enjoyed your letter so much and thought it looked neater than those we have received from many grownups.
    We were so glad to hear what fun you and your dad had when he was in Mobile recently. Now we are hoping to see you here during spring break.
    Granddad and I are having a lovely, lazy time here at the apartment on the beach, and the weekends are always fun when your dad and Joanne or Aunt Dorothy and Uncle Dave come over. Granddad has played golf once a week and he rides his bicycle on the beach every day when the tide is low.
    Next week we are going to visit friends in a place south of here called Tequesta. And the next week we are invited to spend a couple of days at your dad's. One of the plans is to attend a movie, our first in about five years.
    It is cold and windy today but mostly the weather has been great.
    We both send much love. Our best to the rest of the family.
            Nana Kitty

February 1, 1982
Mobile, Alabama

Orlando, Florida
Winter Park, Florida
New Smyrna Beach, Florida
Woodbury, Connecticut
Tucker, Georgia
Atlanta, Georgia
Hello friends and family members,

The holiday mail brought pretty cards and newsy notes from so many dear ones, and, as always, I appreciated and enjoyed them. Since I didn't write at Christmas and don't want to be out of touch another year, I decided to send a "February News Report."

Some of you don't know David and I moved to Alabama last summer. It was hard for us to leave Orlando, but there was in Mobile an opportunity for me to combine flexible part-time work for Daddy with a full-time college career at the University of South Alabama, where I had been accepted and awarded a Presidential Scholarship. I am one quarter-hour away from being a sophomore and, so far, don't know what I want to be when I grow up. Actually, I have a lot in common with many other students who haven't decided on a career – except that I'm going to have less time to *pursue* one, being nearly a half-century old already!

Unfortunately, soon after we arrived in Mobile in July, we were beset with problems, and it has been chaotic ever since. Our troubles began as a result of a very unwise decision made by a warehouseman in Orlando and the driver of the moving van. All of our furnishings and personal belongings were placed outside the storage unit, drenched by a drought-breaking rainstorm, *then* packed with wet pads onto the moving van, where for three days and nights they "soaked" and began to rust and mildew. No use trying to fully describe the resulting scene – just use your wildest imagination. But as sodden, disintegrating boxes and broken bits and pieces of assorted items tumbled out of the van onto the driveway, the delivery had more the look of flotsam than furnishings. The case still has not been settled, and I'm not very optimistic of a good outcome because the moving companies seem unbelievably well-protected. Even my regular homeowner's property insurance would not cover that particular kind of damage. What was there to do except pick up the pieces – literally and figuratively – and go on? Three moves since then, and we are presently living with my parents in their new home.

About the time I finished cleaning up from that first move, I developed phlebitis in one arm and was ill for a couple of weeks, recovering just in time to continue with preparations for the family reunion and celebration we'd planned for my parents' Golden Wedding Anniversary on August 15. The party, a smashing success, was the highlight of 1981.

My next step was to proceed with decisions concerning damaged furniture. I arranged for a talented, though not professional acquaintance of my folks to do some refinishing and sent the finest pieces, including a couple of cherished antiques, to be restored. A wise decision, it seemed. Well, I thought so, until those pieces were *stolen* during a warehouse robbery! So much for fretting over material possessions.

Besides, all that was forgotten in September when David had first a sore throat and an ear infection, and then came down with a severe case of mononucleosis. He was very ill for a few weeks, and long before he recovered from the mono, he began to have myriad other problems – acute sinusitis, several viral infections, the flu, severe headaches requiring hospitalization/ tests, and a chronic sinus allergy, plus various adverse reactions to a few of the many medications prescribed. He missed all of regular school but has kept up his studies through a Homebound Teacher. It has been such a difficult period, and we are exhausted. He is in therapy for depression – actually I am, too, and even Mom and Daddy went to one session. My role in the treatment of David's depression is one of the hardest things I've had to do as a parent: staying neutral, firm, and not overly solicitous while my "baby" is experiencing the worst time in his young life. It is a slow process, a very delicate one, but we have a good therapist and there has been some improvement within the past two weeks. I dropped out of school this quarter to devote all my energies to David's recovery. Please send your loving thoughts and prayers this way.

Now to some bright spots, and we did have a few, thank goodness. The most exciting news is that a new baby is on the way to the family circle, the first of our fourth generation! Robin and Terry, married early last year, are due to become parents in June and we don't know *who* is the most excited. They live in the Atlanta area, where Skip also settled after he graduated from Auburn in August of last year. The Atlanta gang would like to get Jenni up there, too, but so far she has decided to stay in Florida. Bob remarried last September and he and his wife, Joanne, live in Winter Park.

David and I hope for a *much* happier year in 1982, and we want yours to be super!

Pat

February 4, 1982
Woodbury, Connecticut

Mobile, Alabama
Pat dear,

You don't ever have to have an "excuse" to write me a personal note. I did appreciate the "official report," but you, please, feel free to write to me any time you want to communicate. That's what old aunties are for.

As a matter of fact, I had you on my letter-writing list. I have been so concerned about David.

Honey, I wish you were nearer to me and that we could have some long talks. It's almost impossible to "advise" by mail, and I can't tell you what I would do anyway. Not even a therapist can do that. That has to be your own decision. However, maybe I can say some things about an old lady's experience with a long life.

I understand that right now you are really in the depths. You've had a *rough* time since moving from Orlando. It's been enough to get you very down, and all this trouble with poor little David and the mess with the furniture has come at the time when you say you are "almost 50." That seems to be a crisis in many women's lives – and just where I was when my beloved Jim died, and I thought life was really over. Now I'm "almost 72" and it isn't over yet!

I can understand, too, that you are lonely. Ever since you got to Mobile you have been absorbed in furniture and David. You haven't had time to make friends. The most important thing to do is to get David well and feeling secure again. After that, and I'm sure the therapist will help, you will have time to get un-lonely. You've never had trouble making friends. You are a dear, warm, attractive, woman. Five minutes after I met you, you had me in the palm of your hand! So don't doubt that decision to move. It may not have been wrong. I ran to my family in Connecticut, too, when I was 56. It didn't work out too badly. Of course, I never fulfilled my youthful romantic dreams, but life is not just a big romantic dream – at least not for most of us. How I do wish you were nearer and we could talk!

Well, I am proud of your grades. You say you don't know what you can do with them, but they, for sure, won't hurt you if you look for a job. I don't know if your therapist would approve, but I'm going to say it anyway. Once you get David squared away I'd suggest you look for one. It doesn't have to be a "career." I think that for people like us it's good to be out in the world, knowing people, making friends – which shouldn't be hard for you.

Don't ever apologize for "spouting off." Look what I've done! Anytime, Pat.

Much love to you and David,
Auntie Bussie

February 6, 1982
Orlando, Florida

Mobile, Alabama
Dear Pat,

I was concerned when there was no news at Christmas and called Bob to check on you. I am so sorry about the troubles you and David have been having, and do hope David is getting better by now. It's hard to understand what goes on in anyone's mind. Perhaps there were just too many problems, people, changes, relationships and illnesses for one child to manage or cope with. It must be difficult for all of you. Just know that your friends are thinking of you.

Bob said both Jenni and Skip are doing fine and that Robin is expecting a baby this summer. I know that's exciting, happy news for the family!

Please tell your parents hello and give David a hug for me. Hope you can come for a visit soon.

Love,
Betty Sue

February 6, 1982
Orlando, Florida

Mobile, Alabama
Dear Pat and David,

You really know how to cure someone else's feeling sorry for herself! Here I was griping 'cause my car keeps falling apart, no money for a new one, no time for things I want to do and scared to death of the things I have to do. I just didn't know how good I had it as a single mom with a young son until I read your last letter. I did pass my Bar exams and am now a full-fledged lawyer – whatever that means.

We really care about you two. Chris was delighted when he thought David would be visiting here after Christmas – and would be just as delighted to see you, David, *whenever* you can visit. For that matter, we have room for both of you comfortably and would be glad if we could contribute to cheering y'all up. Please keep the option in mind, and believe that I mean it.

I'm glad the boys made a pact to keep in touch by phone. I moved a lot until I was 13 and I sure remember how neat it was to keep a few close friends I could talk to no matter how long we had been apart.

Pat, I feel your discouragement. I think it was about this time last year I decided that if I could make it through next October without a nervous breakdown, I would never ever have one. And you won't either, although I'm sure you doubt it sometimes.

We'd like to give both of you a big hug, but this will have to do for now.

Love,
Patricia and Chris

February 8, 1982
Dear Diary,

This week the mail brought all kinds of good thoughts from friends in Orlando in response to my February report. My friend Patricia and her son Chris want us to stay with them near our old apartment complex so the boys can play together like they did after school and at summer camp. She and I spoke by phone after she sent me a lovely letter, and she said Chris told his teacher about David being sick so the teacher is planning to ask the students to send notes to David to cheer him up for his 12th birthday this week.

I'm still so darned confused about what to do in the near future and find myself wishing so much that David and I were still in Orlando or moving back. But what a big undertaking that would be. I'm praying for guidance in this matter.

February 8, 1982
Blankner Elementary School
Orlando, Florida

Mobile, Alabama
Dear David,

My name is Judy. You probably don't know me. I wasn't in any of your classes. Our teacher told us about your illness and your birthday coming up. I hope you have a happy birthday. I also hope you'll get better soon.

Sincerely,
Judy

Dear David,

Do you remember me? We were in 4th grade together. I'm fine. I hope you'll get well soon. When you get well, please write me. I miss you, too.

Sincerely,
Viet

Dear David,

I hope you get better soon. I was a classmate of yours in 5th grade. I liked you alright you were very funny. Happy birthday.

Sincerely,
Darice

Dear David,

Hi, I know you probably don't remember me 'cause I don't know you at all. Well the teacher told my class you were sick so I thought I'd write you to tell you I hope you feel better and Happy Birthday!

Sincerely,
Shelly

Dear David,

I wish you were here this year. You were very good on your states and capitals. And you could draw real good. I hope you feel better.

Your friend,
Jim

February 12, 1982
Dear Diary,

Having Robin here visiting this weekend makes me want her nearby all the time. She definitely looks pregnant now. I can't believe my first grandchild is on the way!

I called Patricia yesterday and asked her to think carefully, be candid, and tell me whether it would be possible for David and me to stay with her and Chris temporarily should we move back to Orlando. That would help us get settled while I find a job. Her quick response was a phone call today to let us know she and Chris are excited and want us to come right away! She said we could stay up to three months, at least, more if necessary. Over the phone it sounded like Chris was jumping up and down behind his mom. I feel really optimistic. ...

February 22, 1982
Mobile, Alabama

Orlando, Florida
Dear Counselor,

Please see the enclosed evaluation I completed on a former young patient. David's mother Pat tells me they will be coming to you to continue in therapy when they return to Orlando.

David and his mother were referred to me on December 14. Since that time I've met with them on a weekly basis. The focus of our work has been to deal with David's depression and get him back in school. I note that David's medical problems began in the fall of 1981, and although this may be coincidental, his father also remarried at that time. A move in July 1981, from Florida to Alabama, which took David away from his father and all things familiar, probably has contributed to David's problems.

It is interesting to note also that since David's continued illness and all the difficulties related to it, his father has shown considerable concern for his symptoms with frequent phone calls and a trip to Mobile to visit David.

I believe it is not too far off to make an educated guess that part of the reason David needs to maintain his symptoms is to maintain this type of contact with his father. I also believe David more than likely still has some reconciliation fantasies that he is fighting very hard to hold onto.

Sincerely,
Dr. Bob

February 22, 1982
Tucker, Georgia

Mobile, Alabama
Dear Mom,

I've felt *so* good about *everything* since talking to you this morning. I hope Orlando welcomes you and David back with open arms!

Hope the trip to Florida is not too bad. I'll send up a prayer for your protection.

I went to a maternity shop this afternoon and found some light cotton slacks that fit like a dream and cost only $12.99 so I got white, red and blue. They should take me through the whole time, I think.

We'll talk about trying to come down to Orlando on Easter weekend – it would be wonderful to see everyone.

Give Jen and everyone a big hug.

We love you very much!
Robin

February 23, 1982
Mobile, Alabama

Tucker, Georgia
Dear Robin and Terry,

Thank you for the model ship. I will wait till I come up there to put it together with y'all. Did you have a nice anniversary? I am sorry I didn't send you a card.

I love all 3 of you. Take care of my little niece/nephew in your tummy, Robin!

Love,
David

February 24, 1982
Dear Diary

David and I drove off about noon, in tears. Mom and Daddy were crying a little bit, too. Goodbyes are always, always painful. Of course, we're all wondering just what is in store for David and me in Orlando. Hopefully only all good things. I continue to pray for direction and enthusiasm through yet another period of change.

February 25, 1982
Dear Diary,

We stayed overnight in Tallahassee and I had to buy new tires because all four on the old yellow station wagon had cracks in them. The new ones cost $150.

Today David and I were nervous as we entered our old home area, but Patricia and Chris made us feel welcome when we got to their condo. Jenni came by tonight and a couple of friends have called already. We could hardly wait, and went to see Annette, Neill and little 3-year-old Saralyn today. Saralyn ran right into my arms calling me "Pat-Pat" just like old times. I loved it!

Bob took Chris and David out to supper tonight, and Patricia is still at work … and the first thing I did when I was alone was to let go and burst into tears. I'm feeling so down and very concerned about my future right now. Maybe I'm just extra tired from all the packing and activity and the trip down. I'm sure I'll be better able to cope in a few days after we've settled in.

February 25, 1982
Charlotte, North Carolina

Orlando, Florida
(Forwarded from Mobile, Alabama)
Dear Pat,

It was a pleasant surprise to receive your long letter. As Jack and I read it, your many problems made us really sad. Life seemed to be on the upswing for you in your quest back into the education field. Pat, I can imagine how discouraged and depressed you must be. I would be also. Right now you're going to have to take one day at a time, but I know you and David will be alright. Please know you both are in our prayers.

How marvelous that your parents celebrated a Golden Wedding Anniversary! They certainly seem to have remained young in spirit. Your mother always impressed me. I know how much help she and your dad have been to you – and you've needed it.

Pat, you must be absolutely thrilled at the prospect of being a grandmother! Please tell Robin how happy we are for her. I bet Jenni and Skip and David are excited, too, about soon being aunt and uncles.

Keep your chin up!

Love,
Sally

March 1, 1982
Dear Diary,

The welcome David received at Blankner Elementary today was warm and wonderful. Friends called out to him and stood up and applauded as he entered the classroom, and he got the teacher he had looked forward to having when he was in school here before we moved to Alabama. David stayed at school all day and walked home. He looked exhausted – and he cried at bedtime. But I think he's going to be all right.

I spent the day calling about Help Wanted ads in the newspaper and even went to a few places to fill out job applications. I also checked on apartments at our old complex but there are none available.

Mom and Dad called to check on David's progress tonight and were so pleased he's doing well. They miss us.

March 2, 1982
Mobile, Alabama

Blankner Elementary School
Orlando, Florida

Enclosed is the summary of David's third-quarter grades and attendance. I am also enclosing the score sheet for the I.Q. test I administered to David on February 24, 1982. Judging by my work with David and the results of this test, I would definitely recommend he be enrolled in a special program for bright and gifted students.

The complete record for David's other school work can be obtained by a formal request to Hillsdale Middle School. If I can be of further assistance, please feel free to call upon me.

Homebound TeacherProgram
Mobile County, Alabama

March 7, 1982
Tucker, Georgia

Orlando, Florida
Dearest Mom and David,

I sure do hope this letter finds you both *HAPPY* in Orlando again! As I sit here right now the baby is pushing on my stomach really hard and kicking from time to time. I'm really beginning to think I'll have a *boxer*. In the last two weeks he/she has really gotten going. I feel kicking several times a day, usually after I've eaten and at night. Terry's only felt a kick slightly one time, but it won't be long before it will be stronger. Last night he/she kicked once so hard that I literally jumped up off the couch.

My job is just okay – but maybe I can stick it out while it's serving its purpose. Mom, I want you to find something you really like, too.

It's so nice to picture you all in Orlando. Have I mentioned that Skip and I may be coming April 15? Don't tell anyone but I think deep down, secretly, I want to live there for good someday. I really miss being able to see you all often, and especially when the baby's growing up. Oh well, I can wish, can't I?

I love you both very much.
Robin

March 9, 1982
Woodbury, Connecticut

Orlando, Florida
Pat dear,

I'd already heard you were back in Orlando, and all (including me) are glad. Twice when you wrote me you said you wanted to "crawl" back. You didn't crawl, you had a big decision to make, and I think you made the right one for both you and David. Bless him.

Thanks for letting me know.

Always,
Your Auntie Bussie

March 10, 1982
Orlando, Florida

Tucker, Georgia
Dearest Robin and Terry,

I was just ready to write you when the postman came and brought a nice letter from the little mommy-to-be! I'm so excited Baby is pushing and kicking these days. There may be times you'll think you're going to produce a whole team instead of a tiny single person. David and I are also excited we're going to see our Atlanta branch next month. What a treat! Why doesn't everybody just move back to Orlando, for Pete's sake, or for *Pat*'s sake!

Before I forget, I want to tell you my Aunt Dot died. You remember, she was the gentlest, sweetest lady. David and I always enjoyed visiting with her in Mobile and we feel really sad she's gone.

Mom and Dad, John, and Sam called during the week. They all asked what baby furnishings you have and I said not much. John and Kathie have one or two of everything imaginable that you're absolutely welcome to use – crib, stroller, highchair, swing. To pick up any of the items would mean a five-hour drive from Atlanta to Starkville but might be worth it. Just let them know if you want anything.

David has been going to school all right but doesn't have much pep left for playing or going out to eat with his dad, etc. Now, unbelievably, he has the flu and feels just rotten again. It's discouraging.

I've checked out a few job possibilities and have an interview tomorrow that I'm excited about. Still haven't contacted friends here – I'm using my energy to get adjusted and look for opportunities. The temporary living arrangement with our friends Patricia and young Chris is okay. I am so thankful it's working out well. David and I have no desire to move back to

Alabama. We feel more "right" in Orlando. Our hearts are here. I guess it really *is home.*

We send *much* love to you.

Mom

March 15, 1982
Mobile, Alabama

Orlando, Florida
Dear Pat,

I hope things are going well for you and David. I talked with Bob on the phone yesterday and he states that David did quite well in school prior to coming down with an illness. I encourage you to not let this slow him down and to get him back into school as soon as possible.

Tell David hello for me, and I hope he enjoys playing with the football I sent. Please write and let me know of David's progress as I am still very interested in how things are going for the two of you.

Sincerely,
Dr. Bob

March 20, 1982
Dear Diary,

A red-letter day! News that I got the job as nanny and executive home manager for one of the most prominent families in Orlando. The well-known business owner/husband/father told me my references were so good he wasn't sure whether to believe them. Everyone he called raved about me. (A couple of my friends and former employers later told me how surprised they were, how *they* didn't at first believe the person calling was who he said he was!)

David is excited because we will live in the same school district – on a beautiful estate. He's also thrilled to have been chosen "Student of the Week" for all the sixth grades at Blankner – a red-letter day for him, too.

March 24, 1982
Newport News, Virginia

Orlando, Florida
(Forwarded from Mobile, Alabama)
Dear Pat,

Please know our delay in writing since receiving your letter in no way reflects a lack of thoughts Al and I have sent to you during this time. We are truly so sorry to hear about your many misfortunes, and we're very concerned about David. Hopefully by now things are looking up.

What great news that you're a student – we're proud of you! And going to be a *grandmother*! That's wonderful. Al said to tell you he can still remember when you were with Bob's parents in Connecticut back in 1954 and he visited one weekend. He teased you about *when* you were going to have a baby. Imagine, now that first baby of yours is going to have one.

Much love to you,
Sarah and Al

March 24, 1982
Prairie Village, Kansas

Orlando, Florida
(Forwarded from Mobile, Alabama)
Dear Pat and David,

Just reread your February letter and so, what next? Bet you feel nothing is left in the books! But I do hope, David, that you are well again and able to be in school, which has always come first with you.

I am delighted to hear Robin is expecting. Do you have a preference, Pat, girl or boy? You will be a doting grandmother. And David, I bet you and Skip and Jenni are excited about the baby.

I have been in very good health this past winter, had my first flu shot last fall so did not even have a sniffle. For my 80th birthday two weeks ago I received 17 cards – many from Florida friends – five long-distance calls and a lovely orchid plant. I was taken out to three different dinners and a luncheon at one of our finest hotels, so that will have to be the last big birthday celebration.

Do hope everything is looking up for you by now. Please give my regards to your mother and dad.

Lots of love to you and David,
Edith, your old Orlando neighbor

P.S. – Come see me!

April 5, 1982
Dear Diary,

Second week on the new job and I'm feeling more comfortable but it's still like Grand Central Station on the estate. "The boss" is getting ready to open a new business, so there's a lot of activity: vehicles being fixed, out-of-town visitors coming and going, late-night meetings and parties, electricians, plumbers, you name it. The hours are really long and I can see how flexible I'll need to be. But I'm sure I can establish a routine of sorts someday.

The baby is so precious and has a special place in Nanny Pat's heart already. His mommy took a picture of us to send to her family.

David is feeling better every day. He's starting to get a little fresh and sassy with me, really normal for a 12-year-old … it's a good sign.

April 7, 1982
Mobile, Alabama

Orlando, Florida
Dear Pat,

Thanks for your recent letter. It really sounds like things are beginning to go well for you and David. I'm certainly pleased, for I can't think of two people who deserve it more.

I hope David keeps up the good work in going to school. I was excited about the news he gave me in his letter. Sounds like things are really looking up for him. I'll look forward to receiving a call from you when you come to Mobile. Again, I'm glad things are going well for the two of you.
Sincerely,
Dr. Bob

April 7, 1982
Mobile, Alabama

Orlando, Florida
Dear David,

Thanks for your letter. I'm sorry you haven't gotten a chance to play with your football, but anyway, it's baseball season! Maybe in the fall when you drag it out of the closet you will think about me. Congratulations on being elected for Student Council and being selected as Student of the Week for the sixth grades. It sounds like the new job your mother has is really going to work out fine for the two of you.

Keep riding that bike to school. Good luck and keep letting me hear from you!
Sincerely,
Dr. Bob

April 20, 1982
Tucker, Georgia

Orlando, Florida
Dear Mom,

Well, after spending all that time with you, it only made it extra hard to leave you! I miss you already.

We had a pretty good time when we visited Nana Kitty and Granddad at the beach. The weather was great, but I got *very* burned in the first 2½ hours I sat outside on Friday. I heard that the hormone level during pregnancy is different so the skin is ultra-sensitive, but it was too late by that time.

Nana Kitty gave me the sweetest baby gifts. She knitted a sacque and matching booties and blanket. They're white with turquoise ribbons interwoven around the edges, really beautiful. And she gave me her sterling silver baby cup from 1904.

The trip back home was a little less comfortable for me, but we made good time. My ankles have remained swollen off and on since that day with you. I thought the much cooler weather here would help, but it really hasn't. I saw the doctor yesterday and he just said the same as you did, "Dr. Pat" – keep the feet up as much as possible. All else is fine with me and Little One.

I feel very good about your house on the estate property and the whole set-up. It's "home" in my mind already. I'm so glad we could see each other a lot and I could help you fix it up. I hope so much that this is a very happy period for you, Mom.

Write when you can. I know how busy you'll be. Love to Baby Christopher – what a precious little one for you to be able to take care of, "Nanny Pat"!

Love,
Robin

May 9, 1982
Tucker, Georgia

Orlando, Florida

My mother is loving.
My mother is sweet.
My mother is perfect
From her head to her feet!

533

I know I've said this a hundred times before – but now I'm really sure – you are the best mom ever! I'm so proud of you and your life, Mom. You've really pulled it all together. HAPPY MOTHER'S DAY!

We love you!
Robin and Terry and Little One

May 9, 1982
Woodbury, Connecticut

Orlando, Florida
Pat dear,

So glad to hear about David and that you are happy in your new situation. I'd heard similar reports from both Robin and Dave, so I guess I can relax from the concern I've been feeling. You'll be pleased to know Robin said, "With Mom there, it already feels like home base."

My Florida wintering family and friends are back in Connecticut, so I've been busy house cleaning after a fairly lazy winter. Pretty soon the every-weekend house parties at Mount Snow begin and they keep on hopping until after Labor Day. Looks as if the summer is short already.

Keep me posted on how things are going.

Much love to you and David,
Auntie Bussie

May 14, 1982
Tucker, Georgia

Orlando, Florida
Dear Mom and David,

We went to our first baby class last night. Can you imagine the sight of about 20 pregnant women, with husbands, in one room. It was quite a spectacle for visitors to the hospital who didn't know it was planned. The class was so big the instructor had to stagger the exercise hour so we could all fit on the floor.

The classes will cover breathing and exercising, breastfeeding, and hospital routine, plus a doctor and pediatrician will speak. On the way home last night, it all suddenly began to feel *very* real. I felt a little scare spread through me, considering the *awesome* responsibility that's about to turn our lives upside down. But then the baby moved and I was sure it would be hard but perfectly wonderful.

I hope you two made it to New Smyrna Beach. I'll be picturing you there this weekend. Enjoy, enjoy, as we wish we could!

I love you both *very much*!

Robin

June 11, 1982
Sheraton Inn
Madison, Wisconsin

Orlando, Florida
Hi, David,

Your dad certainly surprised us today! It is so good to have him here. There are 14 members of our family together for your cousin Lynnie's wedding, and it is lots of fun. We all arrived at the airport within 20 minutes of each other.

Love,
Nana Kitty

June 15, 1982
Yosemite National Park
Yosemite, California

Orlando, Florida
Hi, David,

Wish you were here! Your Uncle Sam and I stayed in this beautiful place two nights and I thought of you when I saw this postcard. Nevada Fall drops 594 feet over a cliff. I'm having great fun here in California. Now it's on to Hawaii with your mom's Aunt Hazel and your Aunt Kathie and cousin Mark.

Love,
Nana GeeGee

June 19, 1982
Honolulu, Hawaii

Orlando, Florida
Aloha, David,

We are having so much fun in our lovely 50th state. On an 80-mile trip yesterday, we saw the pineapple harvesting just like on this postcard. Very interesting. Also spent five hours at the Polynesian Cultural Center. You would have loved it. Saw two great shows and lots more.

Love,
Nana GeeGee

June 30, 1982
Orlando, Florida

Mobile, Alabama

Woodbury, Connecticut

Dear *Greats* – Nana GeeGee and Granddaddy and Nana Kitty and Granddad!

Well, aren't we blessed with the arrival of little Nicholas today? At 6 pounds, 13 ½ ounces, he weighed in just a few ounces less than his mommy weighed at birth. It feels wonderful to be a grandmother, and it must be extra special for y'all to welcome your first *great*-grandchild. Nicholas is a very lucky little guy to have *two* sets of great grandparents.

I'm sure Robin will send pictures to all of us soon. She couldn't be more proud if she had just given birth to the future king of England. And it *is* neat that both Robin and Princess Diana gave birth to firstborn sons the same week.

Much, much love,
"Nanny Pat"

P.S. – Jenni, Skip and David are so tickled to be aunt and uncles!

July 7, 1982

Dear Diary,

There has been a lot of joyous sharing of love during these past few days in Georgia getting acquainted with the newest member of our family circle. Nicholas is so beautiful, a serene baby, sweet as he can possibly be. David is thrilled with him, though he thinks the baby sure sleeps a lot.

I'm in awe, experiencing the feelings involved in having become a grandparent. All the while aware of my own self and my contribution, I am compelled – and content – to gaze at Robin, and at newborn Nicholas. We seem, to me, a vignette of LIFE itself unfolding in slow motion in precious, tangible form … and I feel proud and humble and immensely grateful to be a part of the miraculous circle.

Orlando, Florida
Dear Mom,

Hi! You've just left us to go back home and I miss you so much already. I really would give just about *anything* for you to live close by your new grandson and me.

Little Nicholas has been on a pretty rigid three-hour eating schedule. Sometimes between feedings he stays awake, just looking around and moving his arms and legs. We finally put a mobile on the bassinet and also a mirror so he can see himself. Both of those things keep his attention for at least a while. He's so alert.

His hair is lightening somewhat and also seems to be thinning out a bit. I can't see him changing because I see him every day. But Terry's sister Ann visited last night and she thinks he is slowly fattening up.

Thanks again for all the help and goodies while you were here. Also, thank you *very* much for the first deposit in Nicholas' new savings account!

Wish me luck getting back into my clothes before August 19 when I'm scheduled to go back to work.

I love you and David lots and lots!
Robin

July 22, 1982
Woodbury, Connecticut

Orlando, Florida
Dear Nanny Pat,

Granddad and I were just delighted yesterday to get your card, note and the snapshot of Nicholas – what a distinguished name! He is just adorable. The two of us had a great time passing the picture back and forth, oohing and aahing over him.

What did Uncle David think of the baby? And Uncle Skip? I'm sure his Aunt Jenni is eager to see him. She had a hard time even believing he was coming.

We both send love to David and will be glad when we can see him more often.

Thanks again for your usual thoughtfulness.

Love,
Great-Nana Kitty

July 27, 1982
Norwich, Vermont

Orlando, Florida
Dear Pat,

How relieved we were to hear all is well again with you and David and that you are happily resettled in Orlando. The nanny position with living quarters located so near David's school sounds like an ideal situation for you both.

And how exciting about your new grandson! I am sure Robin is thrilled.

Here's a shocker for you. Did you ever think you'd see the day when your old friend Judy would have to go on a diet? I've been packing it in and on for a couple of years and when the scales hit 131, I realized I didn't want to be fat and fifty! Fifty (ye gods), I can't do a thing about, but fat I can. I've already lost a few pounds and hopefully will be a fit and trim mother of the groom in September when my firstborn is married.

I'll try my best to remember your birthday next month – the big five-oh, right? If I don't, forgive, it'll be because I'm wrapped up in wedding do's and house showings. We've decided it's time to sell this big old house and build a new one to suit our needs for the future. That's why I'm writing now, just in case.

I'm happy for you, Pat. It's just such a shame you had to go through that rough siege to get where you are now. Sometimes we are tested beyond endurance. But it has turned out well for you and David. Thank goodness!

Love to all,
Judy

July 28, 1982
Woodbury, Connecticut

Orlando, Florida
Pat dear,

We are now having an electrical outage in Woodbury. So if you can't read this, blame Connecticut Light and Power. A kerosene lamp doesn't do too much for my old eyes.

You must know how I love snapshots and I'm so grateful for the ones you sent. I got three from Robin the day before, so I now have 13 new ones. Nicholas is a darling and I can imagine how proud you all are. I'm so happy for Robin. I know how she wanted that baby. She will make a very loving mother. It was also good to catch up on the current looks of the rest of the family and to see a picture of the baby of whom you are taking care. Do congratulate David for me on his grades. I found the therapist's reports most interesting.

538

Give David a hug and kiss from me and tell him to do the same for you.

Much love,

Auntie Bussie

July 30, 1982

Mobile, Alabama

Orlando, Florida

Hi Pat and all,

We are doing nothing one day, then piling it up the next day so you see we are okay. Your cousin Katie and her daughter stopped by yesterday on the way from Georgia to Mississippi. We had a good visit with them before they drove on to Stonewall to see more kin.

We received pictures from you and Robin. The baby is precious.

Love,

Daddy

P.S. – David, save all that money that your making, the South will rise again.

August 5, 1982

Woodbury, Connecticut

Orlando, Florida

Dear Pat,

Writing that date makes me realize that four months from today we hope to be leaving for Florida!

You were very generous sending us the pictures of Nicholas. We love them, have exhibited them to one and all and framed the sweet one of David holding the baby. We enjoyed hearing the reactions of Uncle Skip and Uncle David. Thanks again for remembering us so thoughtfully.

All reports of David's being so well, busy and happy are good news to us. Tell him the enclosed magazine article is so he will know our state of Connecticut better.

This is my "day off" after a rather special dinner party last night. I'm off to lunch and bridge with dinner out tonight.

Give David a squeeze for me.

Love,

Mother Kitty

August 17, 1982
Tucker, Georgia

Orlando, Florida
Dearest Mom,

First of all – Happy Birthday on the 23rd! I sure wish you could be here to share a birthday cake with Jenni but don't worry, we'll put on a candle for you too, okay? Your gift from me is coming via Jen when she goes back to Orlando.

I know it's just killing you not to be seeing Nicholas, so let me catch you up on the latest. Last week he rolled himself over for the first time. He was on the floor watching me pack and I took my eyes away for an instant, and when I looked back he was lying there with his eyes *wide* open like, "*What* was *that!*"

His schedule has gotten pretty good the last few weeks. He has a bottle about 8-9 a.m., stays up two hours or longer, has a bottle 12-1 p.m., sleeps till 5 or so, has another bottle and is awake for a while, then he has a bath and bottle around 8-9, then – *get this*—sleeps till 4, 5 or 6 the next morning. He's slept as much as nine hours a night! It's really been great. I don't know if or how it may change when he starts going to the babysitter, but she really seems like you, Mom, as far as helping with schedules and all, so I have high hopes.

He has cooed a few times, little ones that you almost miss, and he makes the most hilarious faces! Honestly, he really is *beautiful* – I hope to have pictures for you soon.

We received something interesting in the mail today – a letter from Granddad containing a lot of genealogy information about Nicholas' ancestors and the previous Nicholases (there were two). He's having it researched further and will send us a more complete history later. I guess he's *really* pleased about our choice of names.

Gotta run – time is precious these days!
I love you so much,
Robin

August 21, 1982
Dear Diary,

I talked to the girls on the phone today long distance. Jenni said Nicholas opened a part of her heart she didn't even know she had. She fell in love with her little nephew. The depth of her feelings surprised her – and Robin too. The sisters are thoroughly enjoying their time together.

August 23, 1982
Dear Diary,

Well, here it is, the big five-oh. I'm not as upset by aging today as I've been in the past, just thankful for my good health and well-being, pleasant work and, most of all, my loved ones. You know, all those wonderful things that can't be bought. Nice bosses Linda and Bob opened a special bottle of champagne to toast my VIP day, and Jenni came by to see me.

September 1, 1982
By David

MY FIRST DAY AT JUNIOR HIGH

On August 30 I woke up to the sound of my alarm. I ate and caught the bus and saw a lot of familiar faces. At school, I wandered around trying to remember where everything was. In homeroom, I got my locker and stuff. Then I went to geography, math and English to see more familiar faces. Lunch was good and so were my next classes. So I went home happy, yet tired, from my first day at Middle School.

October 2, 1982
Orlando, Florida

Mobile, Alabama
Happy Birthday, Daddy!

I am thinking about you. Turning *70* is pretty much a milestone, wow! Just keep perking along, Daddy, hear?
Much love,
Pat

Orlando, Florida
October 2, 1982

Marietta, Georgia
Dear Katie,

Happy Birthday, my sweet cousin! How does it feel to be a half-century old? Simply unbelievable is what I thought on my 50th a few weeks ago. ...

Well, I've been at my new nanny job over six months now and it's going well. I have never worked harder or longer hours, but I adore the baby and he's a joy to take care of, and there are always unusual or exciting happenings and interesting people coming and going, sort of like Grand Central Station. David and I are settled in our own place on the property, though most of my time is spent at the big house.

David is just so tickled to be in sixth grade at his old school, with his favorite teacher, and a job as a school patrol. Those horrific days of his illness are only a distant memory now. It's good to feel that we faced, persevered, and overcame all the problems that beset us and for now at least can enjoy soaring along on a more upbeat note.

And speaking of soaring, Katie, have you ever heard of hot air balloon racing? I wasn't familiar with it before, but here in Orlando David and I have met a couple of champions of the sport. In fact one is Joe Kittinger, a sweet, very personable man who is quite famous, having set a world record in 1960 with a 102,000-foot parachute jump as an Air Force test pilot. He wore an electrically heated pressure suit, rode a balloon up more than 19 miles high, and then bailed out. He fell at about 700 miles an hour and broke the sound barrier, the first person ever to do that, *not* in a plane. Can you imagine? His picture was on the cover of *Life* magazine with that leap. He also flew many bombing missions in Vietnam and was then captured and held as a prisoner of war.

Joe is so modest and unassuming, so just plain *nice*. He flies the banner plane for Orlando's popular entertainment center "Rosie O'Grady's" and has already given David a ride, which was just about the most exciting thing that had ever happened in David's young life! Joe placed David's and my name on the special list to receive "balloon mail" from the races – a dated postcard that has traveled on the balloon, with the names of the starting point and the destination, how many miles and for what number of hours the balloon was aloft, and the signatures of the crew.

I hope you are feeling well and not swamped with work, Katie. I can't wait for our trip to Las Vegas. We'll celebrate our 50th birthdays a bit late but in high style. What kinds of clothes are you bringing? I just splurged on a new sweater and blouse from Lillie Rubin, the ritziest shop in Orlando. Of course I got them on sale and I won't tell you what I paid, but let's just say I'd better win some hands of black jack.

In our family's true fashion, I am bringing a survival kit of tea bags, instant coffee and the hot pot for boiling water. I'll also bring nuts, granola bars, peanut butter, small cans of tuna and Vienna sausages. Oh, and crackers.

Much love,
Pat

October 17, 1982
MY TO-DO LIST
By David

Wednesday
- Turn lights on
- Bring in cat
- Feed swans, cat, bird
- Get things to go to stay with Chris

Friday
- Come over at 12:00 to help Jen with cat
- 4:00 pack, feed swans and bird (cat gone to vet)
- Wait for Dad
- Turn on lights

Saturday
- Epcot

Sunday
- Late afternoon Jen will be here
- Feed swans, bird

Monday
- Come home 3:00 orthodontist
- Mom comes home late afternoon

Tuesday
- Cat home

October 21, 1982
Woodbury, Connecticut

Orlando, Florida
Dear Pat,

If I am correct you are making merry in Las Vegas this week and I hope it is a real fun time for you. Thanks for your very nice birthday card and the more recent snapshots of our baby Nicholas. He really is a darling and we are proud to show him off. Just between you and me, I was amused the other day when the plumber was checking the furnace for the winter and Dad showed him the pictures.

Also glad to hear tidbits about David and that he is fine and acting like a normal teenager.

Love to David and tell him we will be so glad to see him in less than two months.

Love,
Mother Kitty

October 23, 1982
Dear Diary,

Well, I went to Las Vegas with $400, hoping not to spend it all, and came back with $200, so no complaints. We won a $100 jackpot and a $200 jackpot, which would have been $600 if only I had put *three* coins in instead of one – typical gambler's lament. Katie turned into a frantic gambler, wide-eyed when winning and depressed when losing. We ate a lot of breakfast specials and had free drinks day and night, and never did use all our coupons. We loved the sounds of the coins falling out of those one-armed bandits. I played with nickels so even a little win made a big racket. My right arm got so weak pulling the lever on the slot machines, I had to hold it up with my left hand to keep going.

November 22, 1982
Tucker, Georgia

Orlando, Florida
Dear Mom and David,

We love the picture of you, David. I think you're beginning to look a lot like Skip, especially around the eyes. You sure are growing up – not really my little baby anymore but still "my boy!"

Nicholas has another little cold but the vaporizer at night and some Tempra seem to take care of it pretty well. He's so beautiful – sometimes I can't believe he's really mine, you know?

Love to you both and Jen, too,
Robin

November 25, 1982
Dear Diary,

Happy Thanksgiving! Began the day lying abed an hour or so after awakening, just thinking about all the hours I've worked in my 50 years. It's no wonder I look and feel older and more tired some mornings.

Then I had to hit the kitchen at the big house to finish preparing for today's feast. The bosses had asked a few people over, along with Jenni and

David and me. The funniest part of the holiday was that the roaster pan for the turkey wouldn't fit in either of the two modern, top-of-the-line ovens at the big house, so I brought the turkey back across the estate grounds to cook it in my old modest-but-larger oven! When it was done Jenni and I took it back across the lawn in a wheelbarrow, being very careful not to tip it over! The guests came outside to watch the two-woman turkey operation, laughing and taking pictures.

January 1, 1983
Dear Diary,

I got way behind in my journal the week after Christmas with working so many hours and having all the kids here for the holidays. The house was filled to the brim. By the time Skip's girlfriend arrived, there was only one set of towels left and nowhere to hang them. But all the kids had a good time, so much so that Robin and her family delayed their trip back to Georgia to stay a couple of days longer.

Nicholas is a doll-baby, such a good boy, with a wonderfully happy disposition. Even with strep throat and diarrhea recently, he didn't fuss. I kept the playpen (where he slept) in my room and got up when I heard him stir. He has a cute little happy squeal and a soft talking voice, and the perkiest eyes shaped like almonds and turned up at the corners. The cutest things about Nicholas are the way he puts his thumb into his mouth and sucks it so contentedly, and how he rubs his feet together the whole time he's taking a bottle. He's a precious little person and I love him wholeheartedly.

Robin said this visit made her know for sure she'd like to live here in Orlando again. Meanwhile, Jenni and her boyfriend are getting along well and talking about moving in together. I'm so blessed with the wonderful children I have, and my grandson.

After everyone left, I got the big house and my house straightened up and celebrated New Year's Eve with a nice bath, a pedicure, a bit of relaxation and a bowl of Wheaties. Goodbye to 1982 and hello to 1983.

January 1, 1983
Tucker, Georgia

Orlando, Florida
Dear Mom,

We had such a good time with you last week – you're *such* good company for me, you know! We got back fine. Nicholas slept 13 hours Saturday night and has napped pretty well, so he's getting better. Skip came over Sunday for TV football games and dinner. He says he wants to come over more often to spend time with Nicholas – isn't that cute?

I love you, Mom, and thanks for all the gifts! Talk to you soon.
Robin

January 27, 1983
Tucker, Georgia

Orlando, Florida
Dear Mom,

We received the box of goodies the other day – thanks! All the baby stuff is so cute, and thanks for the presents, too. Nicholas is all better but did pass at least the cold part on to me, so I was out of work on Tuesday. The house is *so* empty without him, so I kept him home, too.

He's really getting more active, Mom. He scoots around in the walker and will not leave the coffee table alone. And his eyes and face are becoming so much more expressive – especially the look of "questioning" when he doesn't understand something. He loves to peek around furniture when we play "Hide and Seek" with him.

I've given him Jell-O several times lately, and he seems to really like it but has a terrible time keeping it in his mouth. It just melts and dribbles down his chin. I tried instant mashed potatoes, but he kind of choked on those, so I'll wait awhile before trying again.

I love you very much,
Robin

February 10, 1983
Dear Diary,

My baby turned 13 today! David celebrated last night with his dad and stepmother, who surprised him by taking him and two of his friends for a pizza dinner and birthday cake, and tonight Jenni brought over another cake. Poor David was supposed to take a flight with our pilot friend Joe Kittinger but got sick and had to postpone it. So his favorite present was the camouflage suit from me.

Robin turned 28 yesterday. David and I called and sang Happy Birthday to her and in the background we could hear Nicholas softly banging on a table.

February 14, 1983
Orlando, Florida

Orlando, Florida
Pat-Pat,

Neill was talking with Saralyn the other day and he asked her what love was. Her answer: "Pat-Pat is love!" Happy Valentine's Day!
Love you,
Annette, Neill and Saralyn

February 14, 1983
Tucker, Georgia

Orlando, Florida
Dear Mom,

Knowing now what being a mother is like really makes me know how very lucky I am to have you! Happy Valentine's Day. I love you.
Robin

February 17, 1983
Dear Diary,

Robin and I talked on the phone tonight about the possibility of their moving back to Orlando. I'm picturing the little family living here on the estate, renting the apartment below ours, which will be available after April. We are keeping our fingers crossed that somehow everything will fall into place. David and I get to see Jenni often – we have dinner together a couple times a week – and always say we wish we had Skip and Robin and her family right here with us, too.

February 24, 1983
Tucker, Georgia

Orlando, Florida
Dear Dad,

You asked about our current plans. Our apartment lease expires this month and if we stay where we are the rent will increase to almost $500 a month, not including utilities. The cost of living here is much higher than in Florida. I feel at this rate we're just getting worse off by the day.

The ground floor of the house where Mom lives has been offered to us at an unbelievably low rent for possibly a year or more. With that monumental savings on rent and in several other areas, we should be able to save a few thousand dollars to match your offer toward the down payment on a house

547

within a year or two. I feel the time has come for us to step back, re-assess, scrimp a little and begin again.

Much love,
Robin

P.S. – We so appreciate the check for the new dishes – thank you!

February 28, 1983
Dear Diary,

Judy and Gobe came today from New England and we enjoyed a fine reunion, ending 16 years without a personal visit. It is amazing how easily really old close friends can pick up again and enjoy being together. Bob and Joanne saw them last night. Judy looks cute at 128 pounds. She used to weigh only 90!

March 9, 1983
Dear Diary,

Bob's dad turned 80 today and he celebrated by being discharged from the hospital after a hip replacement. I hope my card reached him before he left. Auntie Bussie is still in the hospital in Connecticut with pneumonia. I *hope* she will still be able to come to Florida for a visit later this month as planned.

March 11, 1983
Dear Diary,

My kiddos are heading for Mobile today – Robin and Nicholas from Atlanta and Skip from Tallahassee, where he's wrapping up an on-site job. Wish I could go too. I'm feeling listless, chilled and achy today, like I might be getting a virus.

March 15, 1983
Tucker, Georgia

Orlando, Florida
Dearest Mom,

I'm in pretty good spirits this past week or so. The weekend visit in Mobile was really nice and relaxing. Nana GeeGee and Granddaddy enjoyed Nicholas so much.

He talks constantly! He ate two Lorna Doone cookies and loves them, and then on the trip he had French fries from McDonald's. And the cutest thing of all was when Granddaddy gave him a spoonful of pot likker from the peas and then, a little later, appeared with a gallon of ice cream and announced "This is just for Nicholas and me!" He loved both! Oh, Mom, I wish you'd been there.

I've been picturing Orlando a lot lately, seeing myself puttering around the downstairs kitchen, with Nicholas trailing behind, and having coffee on Saturday mornings with you ... think that's a good sign? I miss being near you more than just about anything I know. ...

> I love you, Mom.
> Robin

March 15, 1983
Dear Diary,

Robin called with exciting news. A former beloved boss here told her the job market in Orlando is good and that he'd look around for job openings for her, so she's preparing her resume. She's really eager to move back to sunny Florida, especially now that there's nearly a foot of snow on the ground in Atlanta and Nicholas is sick again.

> March 18, 1983
> Woodbury, Connecticut

Orlando, Florida
Pat dear,

You've no idea how much I appreciated your card and telephone call nor how I enjoyed our talk. You are a lamb and I love you – always have.

Since my bout with pneumonia, it's heaven to be home from the hospital. I'm getting a little better every day. I'm being good and not even impatient. It actually feels great to be lazy – something new for me. People are being very good to me. My friend Sally wanted to take me out to lunch today and I had to turn her down because I'd already said I'd go out to supper with Frank. I've had three phone calls this morning with offers of help and there is a dear little family right next door who would help me in any emergency, so I'm a very lucky gal.

Take care of yourself, Pat. Don't work too hard. Much love to you and David.

> Auntie Bussie

April 1, 1983
Dear Diary,

I have started re-reading *Joy's Way* – A Map for the Transformational Journey, by Dr. Brugh Joy, the spiritual mentor of my favorite actor, Richard

Chamberlain. I really want to experience one of his retreats. I wrote a letter requesting a scholarship to a 10-day retreat/transformational conference at Sky High Ranch in Lucerne Valley, California, in the Mojave Desert. Right now I can't manage both airfare and the conference fee.

April 28, 1983
Dear Diary,

My brother John-boy's 42 today! Gosh, we are all getting up there in years. ... I am so excited about life nowadays and that's a great feeling. I remember well times when I felt I certainly ought to be excited about each day but in reality was not. So if the good feeling about daily life has come about only as I've aged, then I'm less unhappy about aging.

May 1, 1983
Dear Diary,

Thirty years ago, Bob and I were married in Prichard, Alabama, and began what turned out to be a long marriage, but not a 30-year one. Now that we've been apart six years, I'm a little less nostalgic over anniversaries. Jenni is bringing dinner tonight for an early Mother's Day treat since she'll be on vacation next week.

Orlando, Florida
David and Pat
Rosie O'Grady's Balloon Mail – From Vadito, New Mexico, to Levy, New Mexico. May 2, 1983, 3.5 hours.

May 8, 1983
Atlanta, Georgia

Orlando, Florida
Mom,

I'm sure you know by now, you are THE GREATEST! I'm so happy to see your life going so well now, because when you're happy I'm ecstatic! Happy Mother's Day.

I love you, Mom,
Skip

May 12, 1983
Dear Diary,

David and I went to pick up his passport – now he's all set for serious travel. ... We went to the mall yesterday after school to do some shopping, and he was all decked out in his new clothes this morning – a lilac Izod shirt, regular pants and the wild-looking black-and-white-checkered Van's shoes. David pointed to each and clocked off, "Preppie ... normal ... punk." His hair is that beautiful light blond again – good-looking kid! Good kid, too, although these days I notice there's a certain amount of back talk with sassy retorts and attitude. I don't like it, but unfortunately it truly is normal for teen-agers.

May 15, 1983
Dear Diary,

Another busy day, one filled with a lot of parenting for David. We had long talks about life, behavior, growing up – everything except sex, which we ran out of energy and time for. It was successful because we communicated well, which is the most important thing of all. We discussed one friend of his who seems to me to be a bad influence. David believed that friends don't influence a person and I think I helped him see otherwise.

May 18, 1983
Dear Diary,

Tonight Robin and her little family are on their way to Florida. I remember having the idea then "thinking positive" about the possibility, and look how it worked out. With Nicholas here, and my job caring for Christopher, David and I will be in baby heaven, and he's looking forward to it as much as I am.

May 22, 1983
Dear Diary,

Robin, Terry and Nicholas pulled up to the estate and unloaded their moving truck the other day to begin their new adventure. Jenni came over to help and I fixed dinner for everybody. Then we all got packed up to head to New Smyrna Beach for this week.

Nicholas is a precious baby, so appealing, with the most pleasant little personality. I took him down to the beach early today and thought how, with all the times I've been at New Smyrna and all the events in my life that I've pondered over in front of this big old ocean, I guess I never once thought about standing here holding my young grandson. He smiled at me, patted my chest, tucked his head under my chin and promptly fell asleep. I simply cherished the special moment that seemed carved out of time in a world gone still. ...

Skip got here late yesterday, looking as handsome as ever – no, more so! He brought good news that he's getting a promotion and a raise soon. For a belated 24th birthday celebration we had his favorite spaghetti dinner. Then Robin put a candle in a brownie and we all serenaded our sweet Skip as he made his wish.

Meanwhile, Jenni and her fiancé announced their plan to move to Cocoa Beach, an hour's drive from Orlando. Darn, I can't believe Robin just got here and now we're losing Jenni.

Go and grow – increase.
It furthers one to undertake something.
It furthers one to cross the great water.
The I Ching

Chapter Twenty-Six
Lands Far Away
1983-85

Hazel, Wilba, Pat and Katie on European tour

June 6, 1983

Dear Diary,

Sunday in a phone conversation Bob and I talked for two hours about the children and what's going on in their lives. David seemed to be the main topic as we discussed possible plans and goals for his summer vacation, which begins in a week.

Can't believe David's latest surprise: He wants to have his left ear pierced! Nobody else in the family likes the idea at all except for broadminded Nana GeeGee. Isn't she amazing, my mom? I'm okay with it, too, and look at it this way – as long as something David wants to do won't harm him or others, why fuss over it?

Pat

June 25, 1983

Dear Diary,

The morning began with real excitement at the big house. Little Christopher toddled into the kitchen trying to tell me something, and even though I couldn't quite make out his 16-month-old version of the story, I realized he was frightened and asked him to show me what was wrong. A few steps out of the kitchen, suddenly there it was: a large dove or pigeon had come down the chimney and was frantically flying all around the den and foyer! Christopher, poor little guy, became nearly hysterical as we ducked and covered our heads and tried to stay out of the way of the bird's flapping wings. As soon as I could reach it, I flung open the front door and the bird flew out, leaving behind a couple of limp, much-too-close-to-the-scene bird watchers. Christopher stayed right next to me and waved "Bye-bye, birdie" at all the doors the rest of the day.

Orlando, Florida
David and Pat
Rosie O'Grady's Balloon Mail - From Paris, France, to Pfitzhof, West Germany. June 26-27, 1983, 27 hours.

June 30, 1983

Dear Diary,

It's Nicholas' first birthday! I had the day off from work, spent a few hours shopping and running errands, and later the whole family and a bunch of friends and my bosses got together to celebrate. The birthday boy had a banged-up face from a fall earlier, but he was in high spirits this evening enjoying the company, his new toys and delicious ice cream cake.

July 4, 1983
Dear Diary,

Today I said special prayers of thankfulness for freedom. Freedom in this wonderful country and also my own personal sense of freedom, both very important. I have gone slightly mad this week, spending money like it was going out of style – on sale bargains, of course. I think I have more new shoes and new pants than I've ever had at one time. I'm okay financially, though, and it's fun to be able to stretch my budget once in a while and buy for myself with a certain (small) amount of freedom. Actually a bit of guilt creeps in when I purchase quite a few items – a leftover from married days.

July 5, 1983
Dear Diary,

We had a cookout in the garage off the west portico of the big house last night and later watched the fireworks in downtown Orlando from the back yard. Tonight Robin is doing some sewing and hemming for me, helping me get ready for my big trip to Sky High Ranch. David is going to stay with Bob and Joanne part of the time while I'm gone, and he and his dad are going to Atlanta, where they'll hook up with Skip to see a Braves baseball game. When they get back he'll stay with his sisters and his friend Chris.

I'll miss all the kids, big and little. ... Christopher is finally saying Mama! He calls me Na-Na and Nicholas is Nick-Nick. Nicholas has christened him Titifur.

July 14, 1983
Mobile, Alabama

Orlando, Florida
Hi to all,

Thought you would like to have this story from the paper, Pat. I think it is like your writing.

We are ok here. Hope you and all the boys and babys are ok.
Love,
Daddy

July 15, 1983
Woodbury, Connecticut

Orlando, Florida

Pat, dear,

Loved the latest snapshots! Everyone is so good-looking and it's the first I've seen of Bill. He and Jenni look like a couple of models. Do you remember the snapshot of you, spread out on a chaise, with Jenni bulging up your middle? One day I'll never forget is when we all went to my swimming club and Jenni got sand in her suit. Nothing consoled her, and we all had to go home.

When Robin came to spend the weekend with me, too long ago, we looked at my photograph albums from the time I was a baby to the current one. She really seemed to enjoy it.

Yes, I am better, slowly but surely. The cough, the hacking and the wheezing are completely gone. The appetite is still not as it was, which would be great, except that lowers the energy. The breathing is still not normal but is manageable as long as I'm in moving air. I need the windows open, the air conditioner running, or the air from an electric or hand-held fan.

Dave called today and we talked for 42 minutes! I'm so grateful to my nephew for keeping me up to date on most of the family news.

Glad to hear about your impending vacation. You deserve it, and I hope you have a real wonderful, relaxing time.

My love to you and your offspring.

Auntie Bussie

July 22, 1983

Dear Diary,

I am in Lucerne Valley, California, right smack in the middle of the desert, where it's hot, dry, windy, quiet and quite beautiful. Some of the group here named me director since I got busy at the airport yesterday and hired a van to bring what eventually totaled nine people out here to the ranch. We arrived a lot earlier that way instead of waiting hours for the next shuttle.

Sky High Ranch is an interesting place. Some long buildings, a few mobile homes scattered about. Six of us are housed in a building called the Taj, a five-room mobile home. All buildings are near the main conference room, kitchen and dining room with the pool and sauna close by. (Uh ... wearing swimsuits is optional – my fantasy is to feel free enough to be able to go to the pool nude by the time the conference ends!)

The food is different and delicious. Mostly vegetarian meals served with lots of seeds and nuts and sprouts. Yummy, but gave my tummy the golly-wobbles last night.

I'm disappointed that Brugh Joy no longer conducts the Sky High conferences. I so wanted to meet him after reading *Joy's Way*. But having the experience with the present leader is going to be just fine, I'm positive. Richard radiates love and a deep caring in the most quiet-spoken, humorous manner. Entering the room on first meeting, he gave each person a warm hug of welcome.

July 26, 1983
Dear Diary,

There's a sense of timelessness here. The 30 of us have experienced quite a few exercises together and now are in a period of fasting and silence for 2½ days. My first two days here, I had an upset stomach and I cried a lot. It seems my ego is being broken down in stages, starting with having to battle a runny nose in public – something I've always disliked. I've discovered glaring truths about myself: I like to control most everything. I enjoy power. I enjoy praise. "Let go and let God" is my mantra during this conference – and I already feel different. I'll probably try to write more in depth about the unusual experiences, exercises and feelings I've had after some time has passed. But if so, I doubt they can be described in the same way because I'll be looking at them from another level of consciousness.

During today and tomorrow the group leader and the staff will be sharing energy with each person. I'm the last one in the final session. Richard must sense I need time to become more open to giving up my controlling ego. A few people already have started to have revealing experiences, but we are continually asked not to have expectations of what can happen, just to "be" and to trust.

I find it incredibly difficult to describe the activities at the retreat and the effect they have on me, and yet I want to try to capture in words something of the experiences with music. To begin each morning session, we lie on the floor while a classical selection plays at a *very* high volume. I don't have a wide repertoire of classical music, and with my sensitive hearing, have always preferred listening to music at a low volume. And I have never listened even at a low volume while lying on a floor that seemed to have metamorphosed into a drum, with vibrations stemming from the bowels of the earth. The initial moments of that first time I felt overwhelmed, as though I were being assaulted from every angle, and I battled the urge to get up and run screaming from the room. But some deep breaths calmed me down from my panicky state and I began to feel another world open up deep within my being. Oh, I wish there could be a recording of my every thought and sensation during each of the musical "interludes."

At times it seemed I would soar out into the universe, all the way to a heaven on angelic wings, only to then descend into a hell, back and forth, over and over, pierced with a feeling of indescribable joy, then of ineffable sorrow, each exquisite. Often, with a sudden intensity, only the feeling of sorrow and sadness remained, and it was the whole world's, and the tears flowed from so deep a place within me I didn't know it was there. This happened again and again. Another mystery ... I am not certain I will *ever* know what takes place inside my soul, or wherever, when the strains of Pachelbel Canon reach me. I know I never before understood the sheer power of music in this way.

A few individuals sleep out in the desert. I wish I were brave enough. Some also hike off alone, but I've decided I'm not going to force or beat myself up for not doing certain things that are truly scary to me. I did have an acupressure massage, which was uncomfortable at first and indescribably relaxing afterward. The masseuse, like all the staff members, just let love flow out through her fingers. She shared a few things about what she felt from my body, wise observations and then gentle suggestions for possible change. She said perhaps I was strong-willed because I had needed to be before, and that now I could just let everything soften. I'd like that, less adamant, a softer will.

August 1, 1983
Dear Diary,

On a plane, somewhere between Houston, Texas, and Orlando, Florida. ... The conference is over. I left Sky High Ranch this afternoon and am back in "this world" again. I want to catch up with the recording of the past few days.

Except for a couple of trials close to the end, the 2½ days of silence and fasting were easier for me than I ever would have believed. In the final part of that experience, we gathered at 4:30 a.m. to climb the nearby mountain, a true challenge every step of the way for unathletic me. At the top we watched the spectacular fiery sunrise and then spent a half hour in meditation before proceeding back down. Oh my goodness, and I'd thought trekking up the mountain was my biggest challenge ... but coming down went *way* beyond that. My only saving grace was the strong, steady fellow climber behind me grabbing hold of big wads of my clothing so I didn't just take off sliding nonstop ALL the way to the bottom.

Back at the ranch – extremely grateful to be there – we disrobed and crawled into the sweat lodge for the purifying ritual. I found the Indian sweat ceremony to be a bit daunting: 15 naked and near-naked bodies scrunched up together in a low hut, around (and *very* close to) the mound of hot stones in the center, onto which water was thrown following each person's prayer, producing *lots* of steam. Sprigs of fresh sage helped us breathe more easily as we sweated profusely. It *was* purifying, no question. So then, probably still in the process of purifying, we ran from the lodge, sweating and shouting, and leapt into the cold pool water. I tell you, by the time I crawled out of that water, I felt like I had dreamed the impossible and conquered the unconquerable.

After that refreshing dip, to completely separate us from our recent realm of silence-without-food, we were served the most delicious, colorful, fresh-tasting, hearty breakfast by the ever-radiant staff members. And while replenishing our bodies with such fare, we received nourishment for our souls with the sharing of more of the daily life-altering experiences.

The following three days were filled with more exercises, energy sharing, healing, learning and performing the Sacred Meditation, and personal meetings with the group leader. On the last night we were eagerly anticipating the dinner party, the one guaranteed to bring us back to the regular world, with steak and champagne and music and dancing. On the way to the dining room, I tripped on the rocks lining the sidewalk and fell forward, flat, bruising my chest, ribs, arms and hands. It hurt like the very dickens. Friends were solicitous and I went on in to dinner, subdued and maybe a little bit in shock. Of course, I didn't get to dance and enjoy the party and I felt really sad – but at least I started wanting to go home. I had thought at one point I might never want to leave Sky High.

On Sunday, feeling as if I'd been hit by a Mack truck, I teasingly shared during the final group session that although I'd heard all week we definitely would be brought down from our "high" before we left, I didn't suspect I'd be grounded in quite so literal a fashion!

After the conference I stayed on an additional three days to work, as part of my scholarship, but as a result of that spectacular grounding experience could manage only limited chores, mostly helping out with laundry. Unfortunately, now I'm returning to home and work, hurting every time I move and breathe. Oh, I wish I hadn't tripped.

August 3, 1983
Dear Diary,

David is happy to have me home, and my bosses are now calling me "Nanny Guru." It sure is good to see everyone again. I had X-rays taken and got a special rib belt to wear, but the doctor says only time will heal this, which I already knew … darn it.

August 18, 1983
Dear Diary,

I had the most unique experience this morning. I suddenly awoke, unaware of a dream or of any thought, and simply erupted into gales of laughter that just bubbled up from my toes so spontaneously and spread throughout my whole body. It lasted some few minutes, then gradually subsided, only to start up anew! I still feel absolutely *full* of joy – never experienced anything like it before. I wonder if it was an aftereffect of some of the transforming of my self and my spirit that began at Sky High, perhaps a release of Kundalini energy? Or maybe simply a gift of grace.

Oh, here's a loosely constructed haiku recalling my time in the desert:

Sky High
Dawn breaks, soft bells ring
Rousing sleepy desert souls –
The awakening!

August 23, 1983
Dear Diary,

Today's my 51st birthday. Oh my goodness, how incredible that seems. I still feel like that young girl I used to be. She must still be down within my being somewhere. I'm feeling joyful, happy with living.

August 28, 1983
Dear Diary,

David starts back to school tomorrow and is ready for eighth grade. We talked about a few school-time rules concerning homework, using the telephone, having friends come by and so forth. It went very well. He agreed that my requests are reasonable and we sealed the deal with a big hug. How proud I am to have him as my son.

Orlando, Florida
David and Pat
   Rosie O'Grady's Balloon Mail - From Colorado Springs, Colorado, to Concordia, Kansas. September 5-6, 1983, 31 hours.

October 2, 1983
Dear Diary,

Today is Daddy's 71st birthday and cousin Katie's 51st – and baby brother Rickey turns 36 this week! At this time of my life, the minutes, days, weeks, months and years all seem to fly by, but every day is a joyous new beginning. … Jenni and I had a good visit at her apartment today, just relaxing and chatting.

October 15, 1983
Dear Diary,

Got a letter from one of my Sky High friends, a "soul sis," who wrote: "There have been times recently when I would have given all my worldly possessions for one of your hugs. You are such a complete and total expression of love and acceptance, a living example of what it's all about." Such praise for what I aspire to is an exquisite gift. …

November 1, 1983
Dear Diary,

Jenni and Bill were married over the weekend – a lovely simple ceremony in a chapel in Cocoa. There was a dinner for 30 people afterward in Cocoa Beach at Gatsby's restaurant, a favorite of NASA's astronauts. Everyone was so dressed up and good-looking. David executed his "duties" with his usual aplomb – he first took Robin to her seat and then filled in for his dad and escorted Jenni down the aisle.

November 2, 1983
Prichard, Alabama

Orlando, Florida
Dear Pat,

Well you have a new member in the family. From what everyone says Bill must be a fine young man. We wish them much happiness. Don't work too hard.

David, I'm sorry about the Cowboys, also the Cowgirls having to cover up.

Love,
Daddy

November 5, 1983
Dear Diary,

Called Mobile today, where Skip is visiting the grandparents, and was dismayed to hear Daddy has suffered some kind of problem with his heart and is in the hospital for tests.

November 9, 1983
Dear Diary,

This morning as I write, Daddy is undergoing quadruple bypass surgery. The doctors said he is in good general health and should do well. I've sent much positive energy and prayer up that way today. John drove down from Mississippi to help take care of everything. He's great at that. Since Daddy was ill, Skip's weekend in Mobile was not at all the visit he had planned, but his being there was a comfort to the folks.

November 11, 1983
Dear Diary,

Over a week has flown by since Daddy had the surgery. He has progressed well and we're all very thankful. I'm glad my brothers are able to help out the folks. Sam is arriving in Mobile from California tomorrow.

November 15, 1983
Marietta, Georgia

Prichard, Alabama
Good morning, Uncle Randolph!

Thinking of you since Pat informed me of your surgery. She said you were doing fine. My prayers are for a speedy recovery for you. You have always meant so much to my life, although our paths don't cross often. I would like to thank you for your love and concern through the years for Daddy and my family and me.

A big hug to Aunt Wilba. Love you both!
Katie

Orlando, Florida
David and Pat
Rosie O'Grady's Balloon Mail – From Las Vegas, Nevada, to Franklinville, New York. November 15-18, 1983, 2,001 miles (World Record for Distance).

562

December 4, 1983

Dear Diary,

Panic is setting in! So much needs to be done before the holidays. And it's beginning to smell like Christmas already, with Robin baking all kinds of goodies downstairs to give for presents.

Speaking of smells, David and I brought our decorations from the cellar, where they had picked up a musty odor, so we sprayed everything liberally with Christmas tree scent. We then put tiny white lights and a few small balls and ornaments on the little three-foot artificial tree. Meanwhile, the big house has been decked out with an old-fashioned flair that is simply breathtaking. From the foyer, you can see the gaily festooned curving staircase, the fresh Christmasey floral arrangements on both entrance tables, and off to the right the huge tree decorated with one-of-a-kind ornaments, rows of bows and garlands and what seems like a thousand lights. It'll surely rival the tree at The White House!

December 20, 1983

Dear Diary,

We've laughed over our tiny tree with about a hundred presents under it. What fun we'll have opening all of them. I don't remember ever enjoying buying presents or anticipating each person's pleasure as much as I have this year. I feel like Santa Claus!

December 21, 1983

Dear Diary,

Daddy had a setback and has been having some problems. He lost his balance during a walk and fell down and cut his face. He's been very depressed, cries easily, and wonders whether he'll ever be normal again, but the doctors tell us this is expected after heart surgery. I want to go to see him and Mom after the holidays.

December 25, 1983
Orlando, Florida

Orlando, Florida

Mom,

For finding us this house and making it a home, for being the world's best nanny, not to mention the world's best mom, we are forever grateful and give you this Christmas our most precious love.

These coupons are good for:

- All the chicken-and-rice dinners you can eat for a year.

- Replacing all the light bulbs you can buy in one year.
- All the mending for "ripped" or "bought-too-long" clothes you can muster up in a year.
- All the "can you do one little job for me" jobs you can think of in the next year.
- One of whatever your little heart desires (within reason of course).

Much love,
Robin

December 28, 1983
Dear Diary,

What a good Christmas gathering the children and I had here at my modest abode – with so many presents and a delicious dinner. After a few hours with me the "kids" then continued on to various homes for two or three more celebrations. Yesterday Skip and I went to Maitland to visit Dave and Dorothy and their gang and spent a warm, enjoyable hour with loved ones we seldom see.

It was incredibly cold all weekend, with record-breaking temperatures freezing us, plants and citrus. We could keep the first floor warm, but upstairs was awful so we stayed at Robin's for the most part. It warmed up yesterday, there was a tornado watch today and the forecast for the New Year's weekend is another freeze.

December 28, 1983
Woodbury, Connecticut

Orlando, Florida
Pat dear,

What nice packages I did get from you all! I have already sampled Robin's cookery, and the notepaper and crossword calendar are waiting for me. You must've remembered my penchant for crossword puzzles. My sister sends me the one from the Sunday paper every week, a friend gives me a couple of books of them every Christmas, and I still have to buy extras because I run out. So thanks very much!

Love,
Auntie Bussie

David dear,

Thanks so much for the notepaper. I always need it, and the notes with the shells are so pretty and Florida-ish. Robin sent me some snapshots and you are getting pretty big and handsome, aren't you? Hope to see you in March and check up on that.

Love to both of you,
Auntie Bussie

January 1, 1984
Dear Diary,

This first day of a brand-New Year was spent with Skip and two of his friends on the road between Orlando and Mobile, where we arrived about 5:30 – with me as a complete surprise since Mom and Daddy had no idea I was coming along on the guys' trip to New Orleans to attend the Sugar Bowl game. The surprise worked beautifully. I got out of the car a block from the house and walked up to the front door and rang the bell. When Mom answered the door, she didn't say a word, just kept looking at me, unable to make the connection between the person standing there and her own daughter!

January 4, 1984
Dear Diary,

A beautiful day here in Mobile, nippy but with lots of sunshine. Daddy and I just got in from our daily walk. He looks older and is still uncomfortable from the heart surgery but once in awhile there's a glimpse of his former perky self. His illness has been difficult for both parents and I hope the worst is over.

Mommie and I have enjoyed a couple of little shopping jaunts at the mall and visits with other kin. Rickey came bearing a big pan of delicious lasagna for our supper one evening – plus two batches of his delectable homemade cookies, one for us to eat and the other for me to take back to Orlando.

January 7, 1984
Dear Diary,

Home again … and just about everybody is sick. Hope I escape whatever germs have invaded because I have lots of work to catch up on and keep up with. David and I took down our Christmas decorations, and this year for the first time the dismantling didn't make him feel as sad. Guess he's growing up. Oh, his next science project involves little white mice – they're here and I hope they don't get loose!

January 27, 1984
Dear Diary,

Oh my, it has been like General Hospital at both our house and the big house. I've been up a lot at night and spent the days wildly running back and forth nannying, nursing and home-keeping. Then *I* woke up sick, and also had my back go partway out, so I had to call in a friend to help take care of us. Reminded me of the times in Connecticut when germs would get to bouncing around and we'd hardly know what to do.

February 10, 1984
Dear Diary,

A week of birthdays. On the 8th we had children and parents, food, drink, and presents for Christopher's second, with much fun had by all. And a couple of days later, a combination celebration for Robin and David, again with lots of fun, gifts, and my spaghetti supper, topped off with brownies-with-candles.

February 23, 1984
Dear Diary,

Two big news flashes: David's science project – mice and their diet – won the second-place ribbon at school and will be entered in the county fair. And he was tapped into the Junior National Honor Society. We are all *so* proud of him.

March 4, 1984
Dear Diary,

Yippee, Jenni and Bill have moved back to town. The past 10 days, while looking for a place to rent, they and their two cats and one fish lived with us! It was a full house and everybody has been really busy. ... Update: At the county fair David's science project took second place for eighth grades in the biological/health division.

March 21, 1984
Dear Diary,

I had a lazy morning before getting dressed for my luncheon date with Nana Kitty and Granddad at their new condominium in Winter Park. Their place is really lovely and suits them well. Auntie Bussie had just arrived from Connecticut and it was great to see her again. She is still having breathing problems, I noticed. We had a few good chuckles reminiscing about when the kids were small. They said Bob had come for dinner with them last night while Joanne is on a trip to China.

March 21, 1984
Qin Shi Huang Mausoleum
Xi'an, China

Orlando, Florida
Dear David,

I thought you'd enjoy this postcard. A fascinating "dig" full of warriors made of terra cotta buried near the emperor's tomb to protect him when he died. You probably saw this in the movie about China at EPCOT. See you soon.

Love,
Joanne

March 25, 1984
Dear Diary,

Robin, Jenni and I took Auntie Bussie out for a delicious brunch at Lili Marlene's Restaurant at Church Street Station and had a great "just girls" visit. I'm so glad the plan worked out for us to have some time together before Auntie goes back to Woodbury. We all felt really close and Auntie had tears in her eyes as she hugged me goodbye. She's a sweetie.

April 1, 1984
Woodbury, Connecticut

Orlando, Florida
Pat dear,

This was such a very special trip. I saw more of you than I have for years and did appreciate so much the time alone with you and Robin and Jenni at such an attractive place. Glad I flew back when I did, though. The next day Frank couldn't get out of his driveway because of the snow and I wouldn't have been able to get up mine! What a narrow squeak.

Much love,
Auntie Bussie

April 3, 1984
Dear Diary,

David and I cleaned up the place today in anticipation of Mom's visit. I'm doing some cooking ahead so we'll have plenty of time to spend together. I've been working hard at the big house too – boy, am I pooped.

April 10, 1984
Dear Diary,

Nicholas is sick with an ear infection, and Mom and I kept him this morning while Robin went to work a half-day. He slept over three hours. He has really taken to his Great-Nana GeeGee.

Daddy sounds so good on the phone this week. It has been five months since his bypass operation and he's recuperating well.

David came home this afternoon with a beautiful report card – he's on the honor roll and the dean's list. We've started to discuss possible career choices. There are so many! I want him to be happy in whatever he chooses to do.

April 17, 1984
Dear Diary,

David and his dad and Joanne are going on a cruise to the Bahamas this weekend. I took him out shopping for a new swimsuit, shirts, and a couple of sport coats and ties for the formal meals. We ate dinner at Red Lobster to get him in the mood. During dinner David suddenly said to me, "I think you're going to meet somebody soon, Mom." It was strange, because today I felt especially lonely.

April 21, 1984
Dear Diary,

I'm off this weekend! Enjoyed a quiet day puttering around my little nest with occasional visits from Nicholas who would come to the bottom of the stairs and call, "Nanny!" Robin had coffee with me and said how much it means to her to be close – physically and spiritually. Tonight Jenni and I saw *Terms of Endearment* together at the movies – cried our eyes out – and then went for a drink at Church Street Station.

May 1, 1984
Dear Diary,

Another 1st of May ... I remember vividly the one 31 years ago, so happy as Bob's bride. I'm happy in a different way now. I've been single for a few years – some of them not as pleasant as the latest ones.

Mom, Aunt Hazel, Katie and I are starting to plan our trip to Europe this August. I'm already thinking about what clothes to take. Meanwhile, the Rosie O'Grady's folks are making plans for the balloon race that starts in California. So exciting.

Orlando, Florida
David and Pat
    Rosie O'Grady's Balloon Mail – From Palm Springs, California, to Hobart, Oklahoma. May 5-7, 1984, 1,300 miles, 46 hours (Winner 1984 Gordon Bennett Balloon Race).

May 9, 1984
Dear Diary,
    Rosie's crew won the big balloon race! Big party tonight in downtown Orlando to celebrate.

May 9, 1984
Woodbury, Connecticut

Orlando, Florida
Pat dear,
    It was a bit on the overwhelming side to open your birthday gift to me. I not only love it but am so appreciative of the amount of trouble you had to go to in order to get all these snapshots and then have them fit into the frame. I am truly thankful. It's one of the nicest birthday gifts ever. But you'll never get it returned for updates! It is on the bachelor chest in my bedroom and will be the first thing I see when I wake up in the morning – my whole family.
    Sally took me out to lunch and was much too generous with gifts. A beautiful coral sweater, a kind of oatmeal that I like and can't get around here, a membership in "The Crossword Puzzle of the Month Club" (!) and two cute cards. Frank wanted to take me to a nice restaurant for dinner, but I asked him to postpone it till tomorrow evening. I've been going like a house afire and really feel the need of a quiet afternoon and evening in comfies by myself.
    Much love to you and the kids and spouses.
Auntie Bussie

May 13, 1984
Dear Diary,
    Had a lovely Mother's Day brunch with the kids today at Lili Marlene's restaurant. We really missed Skip, but he sent a delightful spring bouquet in a copper teapot, and I talked to him on the phone. He says he's having fun dating for a change.

May 14, 1984
Woodbury, Connecticut

Orlando, Florida

Pat dear,

Thanks for the Mother's Day card. It was cute and funny, and I showed it off at the beauty salon while having my hair done.

I'm trying to get my yard in shape after having neglected it all last summer. I work about a half-hour then sit for an equal time and then repeat the process. It's improving slowly.

Dave and Dorothy are expected here for two overnights next week and I am looking forward to that very much. As long as my sister was living nearby, before she and Bob Senior moved to Florida permanently, I never had much chance to house my relatives. Robin was the only one.

Give my love to everyone, and keep a load for yourself.

Auntie Bussie

June 1, 1984

Dear Diary,

Yesterday turned out to be a 16-hour workday and today another wild one. I was worried when overnight David's fever rose and his sore throat worsened. I took him in to be checked and the doctor said it could be either mononucleosis or a strep infection. Having mono twice is rare, though, and there was no swelling in his spleen, so the doctor prescribed penicillin for strep, the more likely culprit.

June 6, 1984

Dear Diary,

Jenni received a postcard today from her fourth-grade teacher, who happened to be on the same luxury barge trip in France as Bob and Joanne. She wrote, "You are my favorite student – always."

June 15, 1984

Dear Diary,

Today is Nana Kitty and Granddad's 57th anniversary. Can you imagine being together as man and wife for 57 years? What an accomplishment! They appear quite frail now at 80.

I've been making a concentrated effort to spend some time in meditation and do a few exercises this week. My "core of serenity" needs a boost – as does my body.

June 24, 1984
Dear Diary,

Talked to Daddy and Mom today. Daddy is still having bladder troubles and needing to get up so much during the night. He seems to have one ailment after another. How I wish he could get hale and hearty again.

July 12, 1984
Dear Diary,

History was made today when Democratic presidential nominee Walter Mondale chose as his running mate Representative Geraldine Ferraro, the first woman ever so named. Times have changed! That's good. But I still had a 17-hour workday and am exhausted, so goodnight!

July 19, 1984
St. Moritz, Switzerland

Orlando, Florida
Dear David,

Today we went to the top of the mountain pictured on this postcard. Diavolezzahutte is 10,000 feet high! It was 36 degrees at the top. Rode in a cable car that held 125 people. Wished you could have been there today just for the ride. Maybe someday – it took me 56 years. We are staying two nights in St. Moritz, a beautiful ski town. Please show this to Mom and Robin – also Jen if you see her.

Love,
Dad

July 19, 1984
Dear Diary,

A second day off, a delightful bonus! It helps to restore my soul, my sanity and my energy. I finished reading about the laws of "Concept Therapy" and recorded two sets, negative and positive. There is a choice in the way we can express ourselves in any situation and my aim is to choose to follow the positive expressions.

These are the positive expressions of the soul and are very beneficial
1. Correctly combined meals
2. Proper muscular exercise
3. Proper recuperation
4. Proper exterior and interior sanitation
5. Faith

6. Hope
7. Generosity – charity
8. Patience
9. Aspiration
10. Sympathy
11. Noninterference
12. Kindness
13. Courage
14. Forgiveness
15. Duty
16. Love

These laws constitute the negative expression of the soul through the senses:
1. Incorrectly combined meals
2. Improper muscular exercise
3. Improper recuperation
4. Improper external and internal sanitation
5. Fear
6. Worry
7. Selfishness
8. Anger
9. Vanity
10. Criticism
11. Envy
12. Greed
13. Hypocrisy
14. Prejudice
15. Jealousy
16. Hate

July 21, 1984
Dear Diary,

I'm reading the *Silva Mind Control Method*. It's fascinating – I am going to make realities out of wishes!

Mom called and we talked over an hour. Good news that Daddy's finally feeling better. My old friend Edith, one of our former neighbors, also called, mistakenly thinking today was my birthday. She sounds cute as ever.

I had a great time playing with precious Nicholas.

July 22, 1984
Mobile, Alabama

Orlando, Florida
Hi to all,

We are ok here now. I am hoping to feel real good again. Got back in to my walk Monday for the first time in a month.

Take care – love you all.

Daddy

July 23, 1984
Dear Diary,

Exciting news of the day is that lil' ol' Spooky became a mother. She had three healthy kittens, one gray and two black. She was under the sofa at the big house, not eager to come out, so six of us in all – my employer and I, Robin, David and toddlers Christopher and Nicholas – lay on the floor, peering underneath to see what we could of the feline birthing process. David was so cute, he finally coaxed Spooky out and she got herself and her kittens into the box we had readied. Then we all hovered, staring and oohing and aahing – Spooky's fan club!

August 15, 1984
Dear Diary,

Well, I'm down to the wire now. The suitcase has stood empty for days but is now packed. It runneth over! My employers and Robin and I shared a nice bottle of champagne in an early celebration of my birthday and upcoming European trip. In the card from the bosses was a check for a splurge in Paris. Skip called this evening to wish me a happy, safe trip.

David had a great time flying with Joe Kittinger in the Rosie O'Grady's banner plane today! Bob and I have discussed David's schedule, and the rules and regulations to be adhered to while I am away, one being that he must report in to the relatives each day.

It's my parents' 53rd wedding anniversary. ... I can't wait to see Mom. We gals have been checking in with each other all week by phone and tomorrow we rendezvous at the Atlanta airport with Katie – Mom from Mobile, Aunt Hazel from Kansas City, me from Orlando. Then off we go on our first trans-Atlantic flight for a whirlwind European tour.

September 3, 1984
Dear Diary,

I haven't written anything since the night before the trip, so there's a lot of recapping to do. The Delta flight to Gatwick Airport in London was smooth and quite enjoyable and didn't seem as long as I'd feared. First day in London we were excited but so tired we just grabbed a quick bite at Wendy's, of all places! Our hotel was in a noisy section (I hardly slept at all), but a neat thing about the Hogarth Hotel was the cozy tea and coffee service in each room. Of course, I had packed my usual large cache of food for the trip but somewhere along the way it was lost.

First full day in London found me propped up in bed with all available pillows, groggy from muscle relaxants. I had reached to get something and pulled my back out. Unbelievable. We had tickets to the musical *Cats* that night and I couldn't bear the thought of missing it. I crawled out of bed to get dressed, moved slowly, and sat in the cab, then in the theater *very* carefully. The Rolls Royce taxicabs are a real experience in London, and so is having the cars on the "wrong" side of the road.

Early Sunday morning the tour bus arrived at the hotel and we began a seven-day whirlwind tour of about that many countries. The tour director, Roberto, was a charming Italian. I was attracted to him, but the whole week was so terribly hectic there was no opportunity for a little flirting over a glass of wine. Darn.

The first day was lo-o-o-ng, with a full-to-overflowing coach, an English Channel crossing – very confusing – and many miles of driving to reach Paris, France. I was terribly uncomfortable with my ailing back. There was a group within the group whose members right from the start were so troublesome and they just got worse by the day. They consistently behaved in such a rude manner. I've never met people quite so aggressive and thoughtless.

What a beautiful city, Paris, with those awe-inspiring old buildings. And at night it's simply breathtaking. "The City of Lights," a perfect name. We toured the city on our own in the evening after dinner and the next day with a local guide. Monday night we took an optional tour, dinner and a show at a small cabaret, followed with champagne and a fantastic show at the Folies Bergere. What a heady experience, no doubt enhanced by the bubbly! I've never seen so many nearly naked bodies, young and not so young, male and female, that I enjoyed looking at so much. They were stunning, and each performance was in such artistic good taste. We sat right in front by the stage and Mom was so cute, reaching up to collect one of the feathers from a scanty costume. We took pictures of her at the table, looking just a bit naughty, surrounded by wine glasses galore and smiling through a long-stemmed flower held in her teeth.

Another long day riding through the French countryside … and I felt awful, with yet another problem besides my back. After such a nice evening in Paris, I had a siege of vomiting and diarrhea during the early morning hours and was weak and dehydrated. I munched on a hard roll for breakfast and sipped spring water during the day. Actually, all of us got a little sick of bread before the tour was over.

We arrived in Lucerne, Switzerland, on Tuesday the 21st and stayed at a small, charming antique-filled Swiss hotel with such a lovely quaint dining room. To bed early that night, exhausted. Aunt Hazel was feeling sick with a cough, chills and fever, but she said she was going to keep going, regardless. The next day, another gorgeous one weather-wise, which it was every single day of our trip, we rode a train up 5,900 feet to Mount Rigi, where the views were spectacular, just like postcard scenes, and then took a harried trip down by cable car. Forgot to mention that I experienced a dream-come-true in Paris when Mom and I sat at a sidewalk café, the Café Rue de la Paries, having coffee and watching the people passing by.

We enjoyed shopping in Lucerne. I chose small gifts for the kids, and Katie bought some nice household items, including a beautiful Swiss clock for her mantel. The optional tour in the evening introduced us to a local fun spot. We had delicious fondue, and then an early celebration of my birthday began with folk singing, music on the jukebox for dancing, good wine flowing, and a few birthday kisses for me!

Next day was again long and tiring, and full of unexpected occurrences in Germany. I thought the Rhine was beautiful and we enjoyed the cruise and seeing the castles. But then there was a scary incident on a narrow street when a German workman pulled our guide inside a building and began to fight with him because our bus was temporarily blocking the street. Our Belgian driver stayed calm and to our great relief was able to soon settle the confrontation. It was in Germany that I turned 52, and with all the hubbub it's a wonder I didn't turn gray!

After the long bus ride to Amsterdam on the 24th, we had a pleasant dinner in the Dutch countryside before our tour of the red light district in the city. Oh, my goodness, unbelievable! The prostitutes are in the windows and out on the street in all stages of dress *and* undress. … Our hotel was not up to par, the night was miserably hot and long, and restful sleep was only in our dreams. The trip back to England the next day was interminable – tired already, Aunt Hazel still ailing, Mom feeling awful, Katie starting with the sniffles, and I, a sore throat, we were a weary quartet crossing the English Channel.

Back in England, we each hugged Roberto goodbye and wondered, hoped, he would survive. The trip had been terribly wearing for him – and us. Then, to top off everything, our three-day stay back in London was a catastrophe. Mom and I were really sick and had to have a "hotel call" by a local doctor, who diagnosed a type of influenza. Fortunately Mom began to feel better within 24 hours, but I got worse. My memories of London involve mainly a bed in two different hotel rooms.

We all felt really low those few days and wished to be home again. On the 29th we left on a long and tiring trip back to the good ol' USA. Mom looked deathly pale and so fragile. Aunt Hazel still had a violent cough. Katie was beyond tired. I was pretty much a wreck – needed a wheelchair at both the Atlanta and Orlando airports. Not one of us could even *think* of traveling again.

Since I've been home I've been depressed along with still feeling terrible physically. I stayed in bed two days before going back to work and am still recuperating. I so want to feel well again and have some happy thoughts. I did dab on a bit of makeup today – a step in the right direction.

September 14, 1984
Dear Diary,

Just heard on the news that our friend Joe Kittinger took off in the Rosie O'Grady's Balloon of Peace at 8:15 p.m. and caught 80 mph winds and is "sailing" across the Atlantic Ocean.

September 18, 1984
Dear Diary,

Joe Kittinger today made the national news … and history! It's great, he is a real hero. The balloon landed near Genoa, Italy, the birthplace of Christopher Columbus. Joe broke a few world records. And his foot!

September 20, 1984
Dear Diary,

Got a trans-Atlantic report on the hot air balloon party in Europe. They are being transported by private jet, staying in suites in the ambassadors' homes in Rome and Paris, and will go to the Vatican, to Maxim's – and then to the White House next week. Joe received a long congratulatory telegram from President Reagan.

Mobile, Alabama

Dear Granddaddy,

You really have been (are!) a success, both in the financial and personal aspects of your life. You're a great person, one I respect immeasurably! I hope you have many, many more birthdays.

Love,

Skip

October 5, 1984

Dear Diary,

Seven astronauts went off into space today in the shuttle Challenger. Meek me, I have no desire for such a journey, no pioneer spirit for space exploration. Shoot, I didn't hold up very well just trying to explore a little portion of Europe!

Thoughts about the future … maybe I should relax about my work for at least four more years. I could try to get more disciplined and do some writing even with a hectic full-time job. In 1988 David will finish high school, my fourth child to accomplish that, and be getting ready to go to college. I'll be 56 and ready to re-evaluate my goals.

October 14, 1984

Dear Diary,

I was up at the crack of dawn yesterday getting ready for the flight to Mobile. Once I arrived the main activity was eating – and cooking. Sam and his friend, and John, Rickey, Daddy, Mom and I had a high adventure in the kitchen all afternoon. Each of us made a certain dish to take to the annual reunion today for Mom's branch of the family at Clarko Park, near Quitman, Mississippi. I saw oodles of first cousins, aunts, uncles and other more distant kinfolk – more than 150 people attended. After 30 years, I even saw Uncle Harmon, Aunt Inez's (first) husband of long, long ago, whose wife's family had a reunion nearby the same day. It felt great to be a part of my roots!

October 21, 1984
Woodbury, Connecticut

Orlando, Florida

Pat dear,

How nice to hear from you, but how awful that you were sick so much on your trip abroad. It seems everyone I know who goes "tripping" comes home absolutely pooped – but for some reason ready to go again and risk the same fate. This makes me so glad I did my traveling in my teens and 20s when I could take it. And now I'm very happy to stay home in my cozy little nest and let other people tell me about their trips. Do hope you are completely recuperated by this time.

I also think you should have some social time for yourself. I've been happy to think of you as having most of your family close by – and obviously appreciating you – but one needs one's own friends, too, and good times with them. You'd better send David to me. Teenagers are my favorites – a bit later teenager than he, but he'll get there. I've always felt that as soon as kids graduate from college they begin to deteriorate! They get opinionated, "set" in their ways and biased. I love most (not all!) of my about 7,000 students.

Had a good phone visit with Dave and Dorothy the other evening. Just got to feeling far away from the family, and Dave is always reliable for getting me up to date on the whole crew. I'll probably have to mortgage the house when the bill comes in. I think we talked about a half-hour.

Tonight Frank and I are having dinner. I had lunch with my friend Sally last week and she brought me a whole load of green tomatoes from her garden. So I'm now making "Old South Green Tomato Lime Pickles." The process goes on for two days. I started yesterday and must finish up today before Frank calls for me at 5.

My best to everyone, and tell Robin I loved her letter. She's next on my list.

Much love,
Auntie Bussie

October 26, 1984
Dear Diary,

I saw a TV program today on Camp Good Times and plan to find out more about it. It's a camp for children with serious illnesses, and "my" greatly admired Richard Chamberlain is a supporter and spokesman.

November 4, 1984
Dear Diary,

We had a "celebration of love" dinner tonight for David, with the original six of us. Bob and I had the idea that a gathering of the family would make David feel more appreciated. I think the older kids thought it was a bit corny but they had a good time. We listened to the tape of David when he was just 2½ years old – so adorable conversing with Jenni and Skip and reciting the Pledge of Allegiance and the Lord's Prayer.

Orlando, Florida
David and Pat
Rosie O'Grady's Balloon Mail – From Phoenix, Arizona to Hatch, New Mexico. November 10-11, 1984.

December 11, 1984
Dear Diary,

I was touched that Bob's mother called and invited me to a Christmas lunch with her and Dad next week whenever I can be off. So far, with everyone's various schedules, we haven't figured out which day our gang can actually celebrate Christmas this year.

December 19, 1984
Dear Diary,

Nephew Griff arrived this afternoon. He's 20 now – adorable and really smart, too. I think we'll all enjoy his visit tremendously. He had fun teasing Robin and me when we were engrossed in watching "Dynasty" on television. We are funny, and Jenni too, keeping up with our nighttime soap operas.

December 22, 1984
Dear Diary,

Skip arrived safely today and Griff departed. We'll miss him – it was hard to say goodbye when his mom and stepfather picked him up. Skip, Robin and I watched the classic Christmas movie *It's a Wonderful Life*. I think it always makes one think about the beauty of having the gift of life.

December 25, 1984
Dear Diary,

All of us celebrated the day, laughing, opening presents and eating. Skip is so cute and funny when our gang is gathered together. Later the kids went to Bob and Joanne's for dinner, and I watched little Nicholas and tucked him in at bedtime.

The girls were pleased with the rings I passed on to them, gifts to me from Bob years ago. I gave the rubies-and-diamonds dinner ring to Robin and the beautiful cluster-of-pearls ring to Jenni.

December 30, 1984
Dear Diary,

Skip got off about 9 a.m. after a tearful goodbye, which really surprised me. He's so gentle and full of love. I think he mostly just wants me to have a special someone in my life and feels sorry that I don't. I tried again to convince him I am definitely okay, that I would welcome a wonderful man, but I'm not pining or waiting for that to happen to the exclusion of enjoying every day. Thank God I have learned how to handle myself in that way because I used to wish time away as I waited for all sorts of other things to happen. And all that time my life was happening.

December 31, 1984
Dear Diary,

David went off for a party and overnight with a friend, and after I watched the New Year come in on TV with Dick Clark via the countdown from Times Square, I had my usual bowl of cereal and went to bed. I guess 1984 has been a pretty good year … I wonder what 1985 holds in store for me?

January 20, 1985
Dear Diary,

On a serious note, it's Inauguration Day. President Ronald Wilson Reagan was sworn in for a second term. Less serious, but important to sports fans, it's also Super Sunday – the Miami Dolphins vs. San Francisco 49ers in the Super Bowl. I had my usual "feeling" about the winner and was correct – San Francisco – to the great disappointment of many here, including David.

February 1, 1985
Dear Diary,

It's the month of love. I always think that because of Valentine's Day. Alas, another year and I have no valentine yet! Robin and Jen both asked me within the past few days whether I had remembered the anniversary of the day Bob and I finalized our divorce. I had not – a turning point. It's hard to believe it's been eight years since we parted. I would like to have someone special again, my dream – and I believe I will.

February 16, 1985
Dear Diary,
Received a response and application from Camp Good Times. I'm going to apply to work there in August – and expect a wonderful experience. Of course, I'm hoping to see Richard Chamberlain if I get to go there! I saw and loved him in both "The Thorn Birds" and "Shogun" television miniseries recently.

Skip is considering taking off work a few months to travel in Europe with two other young men. I am thrilled at the whole idea and have encouraged him to seize such an opportunity for a wonderful, enriching life experience.

February 24, 1985
Dear Diary,
When Nicholas had chicken pox recently, we never gave a thought to David's exposure to them. But this weekend he is quite sick with a severe case – pox all over his body and a fever. He feels awful and I've been trying to help by preparing soda baths and applying Caladryl lotion, keeping his softest shirts washed, and anything else I can think of. This will mean another week of his absence from school. Maybe I'll check into home tutoring because I don't want him to fall behind.

March 4, 1985
Burbank, California

Orlando, Florida
Dear Pat,
Richard is filming in Africa but I know he would want me to thank you very much for your wonderful donation to Camp Good Times. It will certainly be used to help some very courageous children.

By copy of this letter, I am sending your letter to Camp Good Times. The administrator there will be able to tell you more about the volunteer availabilities at the camp and I'm sure will be writing to you.
Kind regards,
Victoria, Assistant to
Richard Chamberlain

March 17, 1985

Dear Diary,

Jenni, Robin and I had dinner at The Olive Garden. I just can't get over how beautiful the girls are. I can sit and look at them, enjoying their physical beauty and knowing they are just as beautiful inside. I feel very blessed that all my children are such special people.

March 26, 1985

Dear Diary,

In between hours of working at the big house and taking care of David, I have rewritten the article for *Ladies' Home Journal* many times by hand. It's still not ready to be typed, but I'm making progress and plan to submit it this week.

I learned that Camp Good Times requires a personal interview before accepting any volunteer, and that means an earlier trip to California should I decide to continue with the idea of consulting there. Along with that possibility, I wrote to Richard Chamberlain's personal assistant and asked if I could contact her in the future for guidance in advertising my services in Southern California, where I might find the ideal nanny, companion or personal assistant position. We'll see.

April 19, 1985
Ladies' Home Journal
New York, New York

Orlando, Florida

Dear Reader,

Thank you for submitting your article entitled "A Matter of Survival." While this is certainly a good topic for an article, the idea does not fit into our editorial needs at this time. Good luck in placing the piece elsewhere, and thank you for thinking of our magazine.

Sincerely,
Editor

May 3, 1985

Dear Diary,

Well, I'm in Los Angeles, actually Brentwood, for my interview with the Camp Good Times staff. I am so excited about the phone visit I had this morning with Richard Chamberlain's assistant, Victoria. She is a doll – so warm and friendly – and suggested that if I come back to work at the camp, we could get together. I told her I admired Richard and she said, "Richard is one who has spiritual beauty." I said his spirituality, which seems to come through in every performance, is what attracts me. She then said, "That's your own spiritual beauty you're seeing." Could it be true? That we actually see our own inner beauty when we find it in another? I hope so.

The trip yesterday went smoothly. Amazing that I could get up at home in Orlando, fly across the country, taxi from Los Angeles airport, check in at the Holiday Inn, freshen up and have dinner, and after another cab ride, walk up to the door at 7:25 for a 7:30 appointment last night. There were six of us to be interviewed by three staffers. We were told about the camp and then each of us shared something of ourselves and our backgrounds with children. We had sessions of interesting role-playing to see how we'd react in various situations that might occur at camp. I should know in three or four weeks whether I'll be invited back.

Orlando, Florida
David and Pat
    Rosie O'Grady's Balloon Mail – From Palm Springs, California, to Alamo, Nevada. May 4-6, 1985 (Winner 1985 Gordon Bennett Balloon Race.)

May 5, 1985
Dear Diary,

I left Los Angeles for the typical hair-raising ride to San Diego on California's freeways. Wild … about 10 lanes of traffic weaving in and out, racing in a continuous stream! Still shocking for this lil' ol' Southern gal who can remember the narrow dirt road with an occasional car in Stonewall, Mississippi. I'd forgotten how pretty the California countryside is and how pleasant the weather. My friend Sharonne, whom I met at the Sky High Ranch conference, welcomed me to her cute apartment with open arms, and we reconnected quickly.

During my few days here we've gone out to dinner with Sharonne's friends and visited the fantastic San Diego zoo. One day we went across the new bridge to Coronado – well new to me since I left 30 years ago – and spent some lovely hours enjoying the beauty and serene atmosphere of the wonderful old Hotel del Coronado. That was nostalgic for me, remembering good times at the beach back in 1954 and '55. And even more nostalgic were the three hours I spent with Alan, the captain of the Diachenko during Bob's Navy days, and his wife Pat who was my "mother-mentor-protector-friend" in Coronado when our husbands were away at sea. The captain has health problems and seemed quite a bit older, but Pat was as cute, perky, warm and caring as I remembered. What a special gift to see them again. …

May 8, 1985
Dear Diary,

When I got back to Orlando Jenni gently broke the news that David had gotten into some trouble while I was gone. Even a week later and after going through so many phases, I am stunned and disbelieving. David, my reliable, dependable, steady son, got into my employer's huge Cadillac station wagon that's for my use and took off with two friends. David got his learner's permit only last month and had never driven this car. There was no licensed driver with him and he was driving at night. A few miles south of home he ran a red light (not by speeding, but cautiously easing through it in his lack of confidence) and was stopped by a policeman. Bob was in Greece, I was in California, and Jenni was in Cocoa, an hour away, but the police officer reached Robin locally and she flew to the scene. My boss and his wife arrived and were very concerned for David's safety, Robin said. But this incident has put my job in jeopardy. Thank God no one was hurt.

David and I went to court, where the judge fined him $27, revoked his restricted license for six months and assigned him to 32 hours of community service. I had already imposed some rules, telling David he can't go to the ninth-grade dance this year or the rock concert he wanted to attend. He can't visit friends, go to Wet 'N' Wild, the movies or anywhere else for a month. And as I explained to him, since I'm not the cause of these consequences he is also not to act resentful or in an angry manner toward me. He has been staying pretty quiet. We're all having a good laugh over his community service assignment, though – shoveling horse waste in the Orlando Mounted Police compound. Thankfully *David* sees the humor and is able to laugh about it, too.

May 12, 1985
NANNY PAT,
HAPPY MOTHER'S DAY! I LOVE YOU.
NICHOLAS

May 12, 1985
Orlando, Florida

Orlando, Florida
Mom,

You are so caring and loving. I hope if and when I ever become a mother I will be very much like you.

Happy Mother's Day!
Jenni

May 12, 1985
Berkeley, California

Mobile, Alabama
Dear Mom – Happy Mother's Day. ...

I love you. I love you for all your supportive and loving acts in my favor over the years – in school, in the army, in and out of marriage, in parenthood, in life. You have shared your time, energy, affection, and resources when they must have felt like scarce commodities what with several others laying just claim to them. Thanks for your generosity over this half-century.

I also thank you for your courageous spirit because I have been bolstered by you, as I know so many others have whose paths have crossed yours. Thanks for the model of vitality that you serve. Your willful insistence to keep moving when moving is long-gone beyond easy inspires me. Thanks for the idea of good health you passed to me. I praise the heavens at my good fortune.

Thanks for sharing your playful spirit over the years. For me, a little fun ranks after only love and health. Finally, as though all this weren't enough, you're a wonderful traveling companion! (And I'm a lucky fellow.)

Love,
Sam

May 13, 1985
Woodbury, Connecticut

Orlando, Florida
Pat dear,

Now that I've read your materials several times, I have finally managed to sit long enough to write to you. First of all, I think you write well and that if rejection slips don't discourage you, you should keep on trying. It isn't easy to break into the publishing bit, and it takes a lot of determination and

585

trying various channels. Had you thought of trying *Cosmopolitan* for the one you sent to *Ladies' Home Journal*?

I loved the family haiku poetry and thought it sensitive and perceptive. I also think your essay could make a good short story. Essays are just not as salable as stories. About the other poetry – don't ask *me*. Find a good poetry critic. As a senior in college, I wrote a long poem on "The Two Soul Sides of Venice" and got it back with the following note from my professor: "This sounds as if you'd had an attack of dyspepsia the night before you wrote it!"

I have only two (I hope constructive) suggestions. One is to try to make your writing a little more colloquial. I mean write the way you talk rather than using words and phrases that are perfectly proper but not common verbiage. The other is to try to separate yourself a bit from your writing – and I don't mean not to use your own experiences and feelings. But for the reader, I would try to make it a little less personal and subjective.

Above all, Pat, don't stop pouring yourself out on paper and always keep a copy of everything you write. You obviously enjoy writing and it's good therapy. And many years from now you will treasure the re-reading.

Good luck. I'm keeping my fingers crossed.

With love,
Auntie Bussie

May 18, 1985

WHAT I HAVE LEARNED FROM MY MISTAKE
By David

Fortunately, there is something good about mistakes – you learn from them. I feel I learned quite a bit from this mistake. It has given me an opportunity to think about what I should and will do in the future. I learned about other things, too, such as legal processes in courts, and working with animals.

In a way, I have enjoyed being around you during my month of being on restriction, Mom, but of course I would rather be free. And next time I have an opportunity to do something not right, I'll definitely think twice so I won't have to go through this again.

For the sake of everyone including me, I am so thankful I am here today. And I am thankful to have a mother who cares enough about me to make sure I learn a lesson from all of this.

May 19, 1985
Cote d'Azur, France

Orlando, Florida
Mom,

How are things? I'm doing just fine here in the French Riviera. Right now I am in Monte Carlo – just finished watching the Grand Prix of Monaco and tomorrow my friends and I are off to Italy for a couple of days, then to Barcelona, Spain, and then (eventually) back to Frankfurt to regroup. We've been biking for about a week solid now. Getting in great shape except for the *fantastic* French food and wine! I'm really having a great time. I miss you.

All my love,
Skip

May 26, 1985
Dear Diary,

Robin and I went to a psychic fair today, where each of us had a reading. The amazing thing to me was that the medium said almost the exact words told me by another psychic several years ago. Each stressed that I have so much love radiating from me – much more than I'm aware of. I liked hearing it both times! She "saw" me in California, connected with an estate, possibly around San Francisco. Hmm, interesting, we'll see.

I've had good phone visits lately with Mom, Daddy, Sam and Katie. Daddy sent me a great picture of himself in a swanky new suit, looking proud as punch.

June 1, 1985
Dear Diary,

Jenni was involved in a car accident today when a woman turned left in front of a stopped truck and into Jen's path. She was bruised and shaken but thank God not seriously injured.

I received a letter this week from Camp Good Times saying they won't be needing me. Oddly enough, I wasn't so disappointed. I guess I had prepared myself well for a "No."

June 11, 1985
Dear Diary,

Just finished a letter to Skip, to be taken by David and his dad when they jet to Zurich, Switzerland, a couple of days from now. My bosses leave the same day for Paris, and they will all be on the same Pan Am flight from Orlando to New York. What a small world.

I told David I was sure he'd enjoy 10 days away from my yelling and that I would try to get hold of myself while he's gone! I've been running back and forth to the big house for several days getting everybody ready to go.

June 15, 1985
Luzern, Switzerland

Orlando, Florida

Hi, Mom! I decided to send you a postcard early so it would beat me home. This is where we were today and yesterday, on Mount Rigi's base. It is beautiful except the weather isn't great – cloudy and some rain. We're hoping it will clear up tomorrow when we go to Zermatt to see the Matterhorn. I am keeping a trip diary and will show you when I get home.

Love,
David.

June 15 – Luzern – Weather prevented us from venturing to the top of Mount Rigi, but we went on lake cruise. Saw very funny-looking German lady who persistently bitched at these other ladies in German. It sounded very strange. Girls look very nice. Stayed at Jlge Hotel.

June 16 – Visp, Zermatt – Left Luzern and drove through many mountain passes. Weather was beautiful. Not a cloud in the sky. Countryside was beautiful. I was in awe. We stopped in Visp for lunch and then went to Tasch. We had to park our rental car and take a train to Zermatt, where there are no gas-run cars. Checked in Elite Hotel. A nice hotel but we were about the only ones around. We strolled through the town and were annoyed by the large number of electricity-run taxis that would sneak up behind us.

June 17 – Zermatt – Woke up early and went to Gornergrat Station. Took about 45 minutes to get to top of mountain. It was cloudy and snowing atop. It was the first time I had been in a substantial amount of snow. We were worried that we wouldn't be able to see the Matterhorn while in Zermatt but the sun burned away the clouds later in the day – all of them! We began our long journey back to Zermatt after GGB took us down past the snow line. We hiked approximately three hours, catching awesome glimpses of dashmatterhorn (as Skip would say) and other things on the way. Ate in a very nice outdoor café that had an unobstructed view of the Matterhorn. Made a few phone calls to Orlando to arrange for Skip to come back from

588

his trip early and stay in the beach house that Mom was going to get later in the summer. The rest of the day was napping and feasting. Also, I seem to be averaging a beer and a couple glasses of wine per day. Mom would probably send me to Alcoholics Anonymous!

June 18 – Zermatt – After eating breakfast, we took cable cars up to about 8,000 feet, where we climbed even farther up to get a better look at the Shmatterhorn. We were actually one peak away from it! We could see Zermatt way, way down in the valley. We went back down to Hotel Schwarzsee and had beer and fries before our short hike down – well, at least we thought it wasn't going to be bad. Dad and Skip said about an hour. I said an hour and a half. We were hiking four hours!!! And through some rough territory. We pigged out at dinner that night. After, we went back to the cemetery to take a picture of "I Chose to Climb." An American who died on the North Face of the Matterhorn had that on his tombstone.

June 18, 1985
Dear Diary,

Over the weekend Robin and I drove to Cassadega, such a quiet place where the quaint ambience, the lovely sounds of birdsong and the absence of modern technology bring a peaceful feeling. We each had a reading by a certified medium. I was told I would not be in my same position at the end of this year and that I would be moving – hard to believe. She also said I could possibly have a problem with my chest or lungs.

Robin was told there'd be a surprise wedding next summer that all the family would be very happy about. Hmmm … Robin's, Skip's, *mine?*

June 19 – Grindelwald, Interlaken – Drove to Interlaken through some high mountain passes. Snow on sides of road was 20 feet high at times! We got out of car to take pictures of all the snow – it was cold! Ate lunch in Interlaken then began driving again. Arrived in Grindelwald at Hotel Alpine, a fairly nice hotel with other guests. Not like Hotel Elite in Zermatt. Rest of day we rested and dined.

June 20 – Grindelwald – Dreary day. We decided to go to Jungfraujoch anyway. It took about 1½ hours to get to top. There were some pretty snow scenes along the way but half an hour of it was through Eiger Mountain. Nothing to see in there but rock. It was a blizzard atop, really. Visibility was a few feet. We went to the Ice Palace, and it lives up to its name. We were totally enclosed in ice and Japanese tourists! There are as many Japanese tourists here as locals. We stopped at Klein Scheidigg for a while. It was pretty chilly.

Ate lunch back in Grindelwald. Hung around in hotel for a while then walked around and ate dinner at the Derby Hotel for the second night in a row. We are thinking about going to Bern tomorrow if it is still cloudy and rainy outside.

June 21 – Grindelwald – A nice day when we awoke. We decided to go hiking. Took Pfingstegg cable car to Phingstegg, hiked about one hour to the Blue Ice Cave in the Upper Glacier. It was awesome! The inside of the cave was glowing blue and it was dripping water very heavily. It seems it would be all gone by the end of summer but it actually grows and moves. They say you can see it move over a period of several hours but we didn't stay that long. We hiked down to Wetterhorn and had lunch. A fairly good hike back to Grindelwald. We went to the hotel and I took a long nap. It felt sooooo good to lie down! Went to dinner and played mini golf later. Skip whipped my butt, but I'll get him back someday.

June 22 – Grindelwald, Luzern, Zurich – After yet another Continental breakfast in Switzerland, we left Grindelwald into the dreary, rainy weather. We drove to Engleberg – at least we almost did. We got halfway up the mountain and couldn't see five meters in front of us because of the clouds. We figured we wouldn't be able to see when we got atop so we turned around and headed for Burgenstock. We almost made it there, too. We got halfway up that mountain and found out we would have to hike the other half. No, we said, let's just go to Luzern and have lunch there. It was raining pretty good there but we found a place. Luzern is a good town. I think I will try to make it back there next time I am in Europe. Luzern has the best-looking girls in Switzerland, definitely! Anyway, we proceeded on to Zurich and had trouble finding a place to stay near the airport due to Swiss Air canceling all the hotel reservations and our seats on the flight. Somehow they thought we weren't going anymore?! They are going to get some hell from someone. We found a place, the Hotel Fischer, a pretty shabby place but okay for one night.

June 23 – Zurich, New York – Left Zurich 12:45 p.m. Flight arrived in New York one hour early. I noticed there was a 4:00 flight to Orlando. We hurried and made it. Thank God. I am already screwed up enough from jet lag. I am thankful to get home safely because of all the hijacking and terrorism going on. Today, an Air India plane blew up near Ireland. How terrible. Anyway, our trip was great. I was glad to see some of Skip and Dad, and I had fun. It's also good to be home.

590

Life is either a daring adventure or nothing.
To keep our faces toward change and behave like free spirits
in the presence of fate is strength undefeatable.
Helen Keller

Chapter Twenty-Seven
Looking Forward
1985

Pat and cousin Katie on Caribbean cruise

June 30, 1985
Dear Diary,

Nicholas is 3! He came in with a little baseball cap perched jauntily askew on his head, looking adorable.

My brother Sam arrived from California yesterday for a brief visit that included plumb orgies in the kitchen! He cooked up a mountain of down-home soul food like cabbage, okra, peas, butterbeans and cornbread – yum yum! Lucky me, company who comes in, buys the food, cooks, and leaves both a fridge and freezer that runneth over.

Pat

July 5, 1985
Prichard, Alabama

Orlando, Florida
Hi, Pat,

Just a line to say Hi to you. Wish you had been here for the Fourth. We had more food than people. The only thing left is a big watermelon.

Enclosed is a check for the birthday present for Nicholas.

Love you,
Daddy

July 20, 1985
Orlando, Florida

The White House
1600 Pennsylvania Avenue
Washington, D.C.
Dear Mrs. Reagan,

I am enclosing a newspaper article from the July 18 edition of the *Orlando Sentinel* in which Mr. George Will pays a lovely tribute to a lovely lady – I didn't want you to miss it!

Being in the public eye and always open to criticism and gossip in every area of life must be distressing, so I would think a word of praise now and then quite an enjoyable bonus. (I work for a prominent Orlando family as a nanny and home manager and, on a smaller scale, am acquainted with some of the strains and stresses that come with being a public figure.)

I agree with Mr. Will that the President has a "talent for happiness" and, very importantly, a wonderful helpmate in you.

With best wishes for your continued happiness and prayers for President Reagan's return to vibrant good health!

Sincerely,
Pat, a friend from Florida

July 21, 1985
Dear Diary,

We can't wait to see our sweet Skip and hear all about his 2½ months in Europe. After Bob and David left for home, Skip hooked up with his friends for a few more weeks of European travel. Now he has arrived back in the USA safely, we've talked on the phone twice, and he will be here Friday to head to the beach with the family for the weekend. Then he's going to spend a few days in Mobile with his Nana GeeGee and Granddaddy – they will really love that.

July 24, 1985
Orlando, Florida

Burbank, California
Dear Victoria,

I have such a happy memory of our telephone visit in May. I had been hesitant to call, fearing you might be cool and intimidating. And then you were on the line – warm, witty, down-to-earth, bubbly, a joy to talk to. Of course, I should have suspected that working with Richard Chamberlain you would be extra special. You made *me* feel special – do you always have such a positive effect on people?

Since May I have looked forward to meeting you in person, but, alas, I won't be returning to California this summer after all for volunteer work at Camp Good Times. Evidently there are a great many extremely qualified applicants eager to serve as camp counselors who live near Los Angeles, not 3,000 miles away.

Hardly any of my plans for this year have worked out, and I've been feeling terribly frustrated. Have you ever had periods in your life when every single new idea is met with delays, snags, dead ends? I am trying to relax about my daily work, my immediate future, even my old age, which I've also brought into the equation to fret over. I'm trying to "Let go and let God," and to believe that with all the closed doors behind me, some others are bound to open soon. Or at least a few windows!

It's nearly birthday time – I'll be 53 on August 23 – and I imagine many people at around the half-century mark do some serious thinking about their dreams and goals. The amount of time ahead for fulfilling dreams seems so much less than it did at 30 or 40 … now I have children near 30 doing their own contemplating.

Please tell me more about yourself. I have enjoyed getting to know you by phone and feel as if we've been friends forever.

Fondly,
Pat

September 1, 1985
Orlando, Florida

Ms. Shirley MacLaine
Wilshire Theatre
Hollywood, California
Dear Miss MacLaine,

I have no idea if this letter will reach you without a complete and proper address, but I'll take a chance on it. If I may be informal, as you seem to be, and impetuous, as you also seem to be, Shirley, I am simply fascinated by what you believe, what you say, what you do, your energy, your positiveness, your down-to-earthness (in spite of your out-of-earth experiences!).

Besides the obvious attributes of talent, beauty, fame and glamour, you exude spiritual beauty – the clear, wise, serene countenance – and a look that says your soul is full of fun and joy! Indeed, I see you as a kind of spiritual swan, and even though I've been on a spiritual quest for a long time, I still feel somewhat the not-so-lovely duckling. No, I don't mean that literally. I think I just need to make a change in my life and work, and connect with people who are questioning and striving to grow spiritually.

Presently I am a nanny, executive home manager and all-around personal secretary/assistant. I'm working on a book about child care – I feel I have something important to say based on 30 "child-educated" years. I might ask if you need a home manager, but I read somewhere that you have a devoted housekeeper; and, of course, I've read about your 28-year-old daughter, Sachi, so you don't need to hire a nanny (though she may someday). But do you happen to have a need for a personal-social-travel-secretary/companion? (I believe I just described my dream job!)

I read somewhere that you rode an elephant when you turned 50 – what must that feel like? I don't mean just riding an elephant, but doing spectacular, crazy, fun-filled things. I was 53 last month and spent the day at a job that has lost some of its challenges, and it has been years since I had a special companion in my life. I do, however, have my fantastic two daughters and two sons, and their families, and lots of shared love.

Shirley, I hope you receive this letter and I hope you answer it and don't think I'm crazy. I am really a very nice lady, with an interesting background

594

and a fascinating future if I am to put any faith in my intuition. I meditate, and many times I can just "see" exciting things happening to me, though I don't know what, how, through whom, or when!

And while I'm waiting ... I have enjoyed this visit with you.

Sincerely,
Pat, an admirer

September 4, 1985
The White House
Washington, D.C.

Orlando, Florida
Dear Pat,

I want you to know how heartening it is to be able to count on the support and friendship of people like you. Thank you so much for your thoughtful message.

With best wishes,
Sincerely,
Nancy Reagan

September 14, 1985
Dear Diary,

With thoughts of investigating future job opportunities in the Los Angeles area, I wrote for a complimentary copy of *Variety* and information regarding placing an ad in the Hollywood magazine. Today I sent this ad, for the "Position Wanted" and/or "Professional Services" column, to appear in the 52nd Anniversary Issue, October 28.

Personal/Social/Travel Assistant. Refined lady, 53, with highest references, considering relocating. Experienced executive home manager and nanny/governess.

September 25, 1985
Orlando, Florida

Child Care Specialists Center
Beverly Hills, California
Dear Madams,

A few days ago I spoke with a member of your agency about the possibility of registering for employment. When I called, I didn't realize a training program was involved. In my case, I've had years of experience and also am in the process of writing a small book on child care, so I don't believe the training would be necessary. However, should I decide to settle in your area in the future I would like to find a good position.

Enclosed is some information on my background.

Sincerely,
"Nanny Pat"

October 19, 1985
Dear Diary,

Well, I might as well record the happy and the sad in one entry – a perfect example of life's ups and downs within a matter of days. ... The first of this month my cousin Katie and I joined four friends for a fabulous week in the Caribbean on the SS Norway, the world's largest cruise ship. Everything about it was wonderful – beautiful ship, fantastic entertainment, delicious food, lovely, congenial people and lots of fun activities. Actor-singer Jim Nabors was our famous shipmate, and one of the guys in our party could have been his twin so we had a special bond with Jim. His nightly shows were great, and during the day he was just his plain ol' everyday friendly self, enjoying the time aboard with fellow passengers.

After the delightful vacation I felt energized, ready to look at working with renewed enthusiasm. On the last night of the cruise, following up on one of my off-the-wall ideas, I even took time in my cabin to write a letter to the president of Norwegian Caribbean Lines inquiring whether the company would ever consider hiring a shipboard nanny. Now that could be an interesting position!

Anyhow, I came home in such a good mood ... and there's no way to describe the shock that awaited me here: My job was over. And even though I had been investigating possibilities for the future because the baby is growing up and I knew I'd need to move on eventually, I never thought this position would end except at a mutually agreeable time, under pleasant circumstances. Oh, but life does have its surprises. ...

I can still barely think of any of it without dissolving into tears. The ready tears, coupled with the ever-present constricting knot in my throat and heavily weighted heart make it hard to function normally. Actually nothing feels normal right now.

I'd heard about the out-of-control parties teenagers sometimes have whenever their parents are away, but I never dreamed of facing such a problem myself. It happened, though, and since it occurred in a house situated on the estate property, my employers, understandably, felt they had no recourse but to let me go. Their decision was made – and my family knew of it – before I came home from the vacation cruise.

When David and I first saw one another, each of us already knowing the far-reaching consequences of what had happened, we were both overcome with emotion – sobbing, hugging, looking at each other, avoiding looking at each other, pleading Forgive me, I'm so sorry, crying How could you? We were near-babbling in our mutual anguish: he in the deepest imaginable kind of remorse and I in equal parts anger and motherly love and concern. I was immediately aware, though, that far greater than any anger I felt at my gentle-natured, sensitive, young/old-soul son was the fear that he wouldn't be able to forgive himself and recover from his deep distress at being responsible for such serious changes in our lives.

His mistake, the catalyst for the resulting catastrophe, was in making the innocent but unwise decision to go by our unoccupied house to pick up some music – and taking a couple of friends along. Young guys who saw a plum opportunity for some forbidden fun and quickly put out the word, which spread with lightening speed until the number of "guests" had mushroomed to party size. David said he first thought he could manage the unexpected situation and keep everyone and everything under control, but in short order he realized the extent of his plight – the behavior of the gathering of guys had escalated beyond any semblance of civility, much less his control, and the whole house was reduced to a shambles. Not surprisingly, a little while later (unfortunately, too late to prevent the damage), neighbors who knew I was away were alerted by the noise and lights and informed my employers of activity at the house.

That's it now, no more details of the debacle. I don't want to record them, to remember them. The past 10 days have been filled with recriminations, regrets, worry and indecision about important changes that have to be made … and emotionally draining farewells. Oh, how am I to get through it? How can I make sure David is going to be all right? How are we both going to move forward with hope and optimism?

October 24, 1985
Dear Diary,

It's evening after a day of sorting, packing, deciding what is going where. I shed tears over many things remembered, like the 31-year-old wedding album, the 1952 "Miss Brookley" photo, Bob's very first letter to me and numerous sentimental cards. Oh, such is life, so many changes over the years. The pictures show that pretty young girl of long ago and Bob *so* handsome. I suppose there'll be more moments of wistfulness as I sift through everything.

So ... what changes there've been in just a matter of weeks. David has moved in with Robin and Nicholas, and tomorrow I'll be going to live temporarily with Jenni and Bill. I'm very grateful for the girls' generosity in sharing their space during this time of upheaval and uncertainty. Neither arrangement is without some difficulties – although we believe David's living with Robin until he finishes high school is going to be a really good all-around solution. I know we'll all do our best to make everything work. And I pray I'll find a new position and home soon.

I had my annual checkup, including a discussion of all the recent problems, with my dear, trusted doctor. I told him my body seemed fairly okay but my *life* was kind of mixed up! He wished me the best, said he was sure something good would come for me.

October 25, 1985
Woodbury, Connecticut

Orlando, Florida
Robin dear,

Just got your long, revealing letter. First let me congratulate you on the big raise. I told your Nana Kitty and all my friends, "I'm so proud of her."

Your mom told me some time ago, via Ma Bell, about David's escapade with the employer's car, and later wrote that there'd been discussion about his living with you if she ever moved from Orlando. Now, in the aftermath of the disastrous party, a decision has been made and David will live with you.

And since you asked for my thoughts, Robin, here they are. From David's point of view I agree the place for him is with you because, as you put it, "David is crying out for a more normal family routine" – and I think he has been for many a year. I have a snapshot I took of him at the beach (he was there with your dad and Joanne to see your grandparents) when he was 8 or so, in his pajamas, curled up in a chair, holding a teddy bear. My heart went out to him right then and I also started worrying about him. I just had the feeling he thought he was in the way everywhere. I think (and it's *only* what I think) he needs a steady home – being shown a lot of love and also given sensible, understandable rules with the discipline to make him stick to them. I do know, from many of my past students, that having fair, limiting rules and being made to adhere to them means that someone loves you enough to care. Time after time I've heard, "My parents didn't want to bother about me enough to set rules and stick to them."

From *your* point of view, I think you may have a job ahead of you, honey. You are busy and young to take this on. But more power to you.

You obviously feel about your little brother the way I do. You *want* to give him what he needs. (Wish I could help.) So, if you have the guts and the strength, more good wishes and luck than I can express. I hope all gets smooth fast. If so you'll be a miracle worker. It usually takes a lot of time for the confidence in self and the feeling of permanence and security – all of which I think are missing for David right now – to come back.

How does Jenni feel about the new arrangements? I'm sure she's much concerned about her brother, too. And I'd love to know Skip's reactions.

I'm really sorry about the mess over the party for your mom and David, for all of you. I can imagine how David might seek the applause of his peers and older boys. He is for sure not the only one – and it is so dangerous. It just makes me sick to remember some of the things that happened when I was Dean of Women at Post College in the late 1960s and early 1970s. It was *awful*.

Tell your mom to call me, or write, anytime she wants to talk. Not that I can do anything, but I can care and share. I hope she finds exactly what she wants in the way of work, soon.

I'd love to have you visit anytime – how we could talk! However, I imagine this is not the best time for you to leave David. When things are more settled – bring him too!

My love (and a lot of it) to you and dear David – and all of the Orlando bunch of the family. OXOXOX

Auntie Bussie

November 2, 1985
Dear Diary,

Although the timing seems "off" now, I went ahead with plans made way back and let David fly to Atlanta to visit with Skip. He has been looking forward to going to Auburn, Skip and Robin's old alma mater, to attend the Auburn-Florida football game today. I know they'll have a good time together being buddies. And I'm sure steady, compassionate older brother Skip will create an opportunity to talk with David about everything that has happened recently and give him wise counsel.

November 23, 1985
Dear Diary,

Leaving my nanny position and the little home I've enjoyed on the estate is really hard. I am trying not to be downhearted or too anxious, but simply to go about doing the things I can do and trust in an eventual positive, fulfilling outcome. I must trust that all things are working toward my good right now.

November 28, 1985 – Thanksgiving Day
Dear Diary,

I am thankful for so many blessings: Robin, Jenni, Skip, David, little Nicholas, Mommie and Daddy and my three brothers, cousin Katie, wonderful friends. And good health. Of course, there are a few things missing from my life, too – a job, a regular home, and for the past nine years no special companion. This year in particular I feel such a terrible sense of aloneness, and yet somehow I still believe my future is going to be filled with fine, happy moments – millions of 'em! Optimistic, that's me. I've got to be.

December 1, 1985
Orlando, Florida

Burbank, California
Dear Victoria,

How are you? I wish I'd hear from you. Yes, I remember you told me earlier this year that it usually takes you a long time to answer letters so I haven't given up hope.

The reason I'm writing now is that my situation has changed and I am trying to decide what to do, specifically whether to pursue my dream of going west. So far I have not felt brave enough to just pack up and move to the Los Angeles area without a definite position there for me – a kink in my pioneer spirit!

I've placed ads in two southern California newspapers but the responses haven't been what I'm really looking for. I have a few other contacts, too, but for some reason I have a strong feeling you may know or have heard of someone who needs me. Perhaps it's just wishful thinking on my part, but you know I tend to follow my hunches!

With that thought in mind, I am sending a copy of my very unconventional resume. After you've had a chance to look it over, would you let me know what you think about my whole situation and tell me if you have any good advice? Please … and thank you!
Sincerely,
Pat

In lieu of a formal resume, the following is a personal "story" detailing my career background and future goals.

Beginning on a humorous note, when I first heard Barbara Mandrell's song, "I Was Country When Country Wasn't Cool," I thought the words a bit apropos of my situation because I was a nanny when nannying wasn't so cool! Now with all the publicity, nanny training schools and placement agencies, I feel sure the position will become a much more prestigious one, and I think more people will recognize the worth of a good nanny.

Actually in my career I have been not just nanny, but executive home manager and sort of an all-around personal and family assistant, three positions which include nearly everything and require many different talents. In addition to the knowledge and skills necessary to accomplish all the work involved, the intimate relationship with the family also calls for other "specialties" – diplomacy, an exquisite sense of timing every day, in every way and in every thing, discretion, social refinement, and care, concern and love in large doses!

My experience spans three decades, through two daughters, now 30 and 28; two sons, 26 and 15; one grandson who's 3; and beloved little charges who have enlightened me along the way. I started to work professionally, though, in 1977 when my marriage of nearly a quarter of a century ended in divorce. I had been a legal secretary at one time but had no desire to take that up again and chose instead to declare myself a Nanny/Executive Home Manager for hire.

The three older children by then were working or in college, but David was only 7, and I felt that not only would I enjoy being a nanny but the position would allow more flexibility as far as his care was concerned – and besides, David loved babies and had been asking for one for years! Many people thought that having a young son might keep me from finding employment as a live-in nanny or home manager, but David has always been an asset. He is very special, as are all of my children; they are the best references I could have.

My first position was that of manager of a local mansion and guardian/governess to two teenagers while the parents spent time in another state for business purposes. I supervised the care of the very large estate, doing much of the work myself, and saw to all the needs of the girls. I shopped, planned and cooked the meals, tended the large number of exotic plants – and made sure that each of the thirteen bathroom toilets got flushed at least once a day because otherwise they developed such unsightly water rings!

I had the opportunity to gain incredible experience even in the short time I was there. Unfortunately there was a sad, very sudden breaking up of the family and, with the changes, the position for which I'd been hired no longer existed. But the former mistress of the mansion and I have remained dear friends since that time. It seems that most of my employers continue to remain almost like family even after our business relationship ends, and I'm so glad that's the case, not only for myself but for my children who have been close to "our" families, too.

My next step was to sign on with Kelly Services, doing temporary marketing, secretarial and public relations assignments, and to care for children on a part-time basis while I looked for another nanny position. That came in 1979 when I went to work for a lovely young local couple. I managed the household and was nanny to their daughter for about two years before what seemed like a golden opportunity appeared.

I had been taking courses at the community college, and discovered that with my record I could attend the University of South Alabama on a Presidential Scholarship and at the same time assist my father in his business. So ... I made decisions and plans and helped interview to find a new nanny for the baby. Our work family gave David and me a send-off dinner and wished us well, and we moved to Mobile, Alabama.

And with the move everything that could go wrong did go wrong. Our troubles ranged from extensively damaged furnishings, to a lawsuit, to the theft of a good many of our possessions, to my having to drop out of college to care for David during a lengthy and severe illness. It was a nine-month nightmare after which we decided to return to sunny Florida!

When we got back to Orlando after the disastrous detour, I found a made-to-order position immediately, truly an answer to prayer. One of the city's busiest and most prominent couples, with a large home and a new baby, needed help – and I fit the bill.

Business, social, and travel commitments kept the couple away much of the time. I had almost full responsibility for the care and training of their son for nearly four years. As manager of the home I planned, coordinated and supervised the care, cleaning and maintenance of the house and grounds, including at times interviewing and hiring. I did the grocery buying and much of the shopping for the home, as well as for the child's needs. I helped to plan, prepare, and hostess social events held in the home, often doing special food preparation, too. I handled some of the household accounts and on occasion social correspondence. On more of a personal assistant level, I oversaw the family's extensive wardrobe, arranging alterations, cleaning and laundry services, and I was lady's dresser, man's valet, and private nurse when necessary. At times I functioned as a secretary in the home where there was a second office for my employer's business affairs. I handled mail and messages and spoke with his associates from around the globe. I stayed incredibly busy and gained invaluable experience in so many areas.

David now makes his home with my oldest daughter and her family, and the arrangement has given me a new kind of freedom. I am 53 – a very young 53, of course! – I know that I can do a superior job, and I am ready for some new challenges and a more varied, exciting lifestyle.

As for being a nanny in the future, I feel a bit like the 56-year-old woman I read about, who, looking to add some glamour to her life and work, had left her job to attend nanny school and said, "I'd like to be a nanny to a child of Meryl Streep's. I could go on location with them." Better yet, I would like to put all my experience and expertise into a dynamite little book for nannies and new parents and then move on to something else.

And as to that "something else," my dream job is to be a personal, social, travel assistant/secretary/friend/companion – quite a mouthful, but descriptive – to a person who leads a busy, exciting life, someone with warmth and generosity of spirit and a good sense of humor. I would be a definite asset (she said modestly!). ...

December 6, 1985
Woodbury, Connecticut

Orlando, Florida
Pat dear,

When, or if, you ever have a few spare minutes, do drop me a line to let me know how things are going with you and the family. I think about you a lot.

Up here everything is okay except for a lousy cold I got from Frank, who got it from his granddaughter, who got it from her baby. However, it's beginning to dry up so I guess I'll live.

It snowed this morning and the world looks pretty – especially since I can stay indoors all day and admire it from a cozy, warm living room.

Frank and I spent Thanksgiving at his daughter's. Sue had a sit-down dinner for 12 with more food than I've ever seen on one table. The kids are a lot of fun and I really enjoy them. We'll go there on Christmas, too.

All our snowbird friends have flown south for the winter so there's little social life up here now. It's a good thing I've always enjoyed my own company and have lots to do to keep me busy.

I expect I'll be coming down again in mid-April and hope to take you and the girls to lunch.

Take good care of yourself.

> Love,
> Auntie Bussie

December 26, 1985
Dear Diary,

Skip and I went on a drive past our old home where we were happy as a family for 15 years. We reminisced about the day he and his dad so tenderly planted the skinny stick that's now a giant tree with mammoth branches overhanging the whole street! As usual I choked up and the tears fell even before we reached the street, talking about when David and I used to go by and look at the house. Skip was so cute, he said okay we won't go there and started to turn the car around, but I dried my tears and convinced him I'd be all right. How easily I cry nowadays ... how hard it is to control my emotional outpourings, being tenderhearted and sentimental as I am.

December 27, 1985
Dear Diary,

Since I launched my voyage of self-discovery, I have come to know myself quite well. That is, what makes me tick, how I feel, why I act and react in the particular ways I do. The journey has been, continues to be and I'm fairly sure will be forever fraught with the perils of uncovering my unknown or at least unacknowledged undesirable traits, and buoyed by little pearls of pleasure when I know without a doubt – and accept – that some qualities I possess, and like, are deeply a part of me, just as I'd always believed.

At this particular year-end assessment I am going to accentuate the positive, as the old song goes. ... I am an eloquent, outgoing, warm-hearted, generous woman. Poised and self-confident, I handle myself well with people. I am often told I have that elusive something called "class," which I hope is true because it's a quality I admire. I remember people, their names, voices, birthdays, telephone numbers even – things I've found most people really appreciate.

I am honest, hopefully not to a fault, though I tend to be direct. And I have integrity. I am a very trusting person and always believe the best in people and situations. I like being needed, respected and appreciated. Recognition is important to me. I am a professional at my work, and it is imperative that I have a good relationship with the people with or for whom I work.

I enjoy writing and reading, music and singing. I definitely prefer spring and summer to fall and winter. I adore babies and young children, and I have a fondness for old folk. But I don't respond well to animals.

I have a positive outlook on life although I always give myself time to grieve over losses, large and small. I cry easily and often, sometimes because I'm sad, sometimes when I am happy. I have a strong personality and a gentle nature and manner.

I know all these things about myself. But I know this, too: "To know how little one knows is to have genuine knowledge." (Lao-tzu)

December 31, 1985
Dear Diary,

Well, it's New Year's Eve and here I am at the home of a wonderful couple for a temporary nanny assignment. I came to work yesterday and was greeted with soft warm hugs and a hearty "Welcome!" Little do they know how much I need the warmth and love they offer.

It's scary coming to a new job in a new household, with unknown schedules and all that, but these young parents certainly are trying to make it easier for me. This afternoon they went out for a couple of hours and came back bearing gifts. A day and a half on the job and I was presented a bouquet of flowers and a box of wonderfully scented soap, bath salts and potpourri with a note that read: "Dear Pat – For however long you are with us, we hope your stay is a joyous one and that this is the start of a wonderful new year."

This young mother, Barbara, and I talked about my future today. She urged me not to settle for something less than my dream and promised to help me in any way she could to find a good position. She praised, "You're too sweet and pretty and capable not to have a wonderful future doing something exciting, finding someone so you're not alone. ..." I'll just dwell on those words.

Barbara asked whether 1985 had been a good year for me. I had been thinking about that earlier when I was working with her baby and remembering the first day of 1985, when I was still caring for little Christopher. Isn't it amazing how much can change in a year? Always things change, always it surprises me. Why, I wonder?

There were telephone calls this evening from two agencies about full-time nanny positions. One that sounds interesting is with a professional baseball player and his wife, their 5-year-old son and 2-year-old twin daughters, a family that divides its time between California and Arizona. I know it's really important that I consider each possibility *very* carefully from every angle. ...

I have certainly learned to adapt to changes in my life better than I ever believed I could. That's a good sign I'll stay mellow as I age (gracefully, of course). But I still have a ways to go. Just being around my own kids this week, I've found it so hard to stay emotionally even. I keep feeling the tears well up. What's that all about?

Guess I'll think about it later. Now I'm going to have my bowl of Wheaties and lay me down to sleep before the official ringing in of 1986 – and its 365 days of possibilities. ...

Epilogue

Don't despair when all seems dark –
In time, once again will appear
A special day, so fair,
Just made for strolling in the park.

There … do you not hear the birdsong,
Feel the sun's warmth upon your face?
Had you forgotten, plodding along,
Those fleecy clouds fashioned of lace?

Listen, and look up when you feel down –
Surely in the balm of beauty all around
You soon will rediscover …
Your cup does, indeed, still runneth over!

Patsy Gilbert,
December 1979

The journey is the reward.
Taoist saying

Postscript

Dear Readers,

Legacy of Letters highlights the first 55 years of Pat's journey. Years in which there came about an amazing leap in communication – from penny postcards to PCs!

The sequel will pick up the family saga in mid-1987 and cover the years following, to present day. At that time, whether or not the storytelling goes on, it is hoped Pat's journey is destined to continue for many more years.

As fellow sojourners, let's cherish our experiences during this leap into the Circle of Life!

Love,
Pat

Acknowledgments

To those who believed in my years-dormant dream and family and friends whose enthusiasm for the project, once begun, has never flagged, to acquaintances and even strangers who heard about the book and gave a thumbs-up, to the typists who input into the computer the contents of hundreds of old, often very-hard-to-read handwritten letters, and to the readers of portions of the manuscript who offered enlightening suggestions laced with lovely-to-my-ears encouragement ... my heartfelt thanks.

A special note of gratitude to Hazel Gilbert (the dear aunt who gifted me with the old letter I'd written to her in 1945, which gave me a jumpstart to get on with writing this book), Christopher Knopf (whose thoughtful critique inspired the idea for an entirely new beginning), Janet de Guehery (typist/editor extraordinaire), Barbara and Jill Shargaa (Jill produced the Lines of Descent diagram), Alice MacMahon, Shirley Casey, Anne and Mary-Slater Linn, Eileen Kupersmith, Shirley Guignard, Fay Wehmeyer and her friends, Margaret Chopra and Janet Morris, Michael Wick, Renee Smith, Sara Sturm, my Robin, and Miss Kathryn and Master Bo, my youngest fans, who frequently delight and uplift with "How is your book coming?" or "Can I help you?"

I wish to lovingly acknowledge my late parents, Wilba and Randolph Gilbert, always my most devoted fans. They supported my every dream and endeavor and would be proud and thrilled to see our story in a book. And I know Auntie Bussie would be so pleased that I accomplished my goal. I would like to recognize other loved ones who have also passed on, especially my former in-laws and my sweet Cousin Katie, for their all-important roles in this family history, and dear friends Judy Wagner and Therese Godfrey, whose love and letters will be sorely missed.

Happily, my children and their families, along with their father and Uncles Sam, John, Rickey and Dave and their families, will be able to read the book and, through the story, discover, relive and cherish parts of their past. Thank you, each one, for all of the priceless letters.

Of utmost importance in the writing of *Legacy of Letters* – and in my life – is Diane Sears. She is "the perfect person" requested in a carefully worded prayer for help that I placed in my Treasure Map. Surely heaven-sent, a writer's angel, this multitalented young woman has been indispensable in bringing together all aspects of the project. She loved the story from the beginning and her belief in this book and its sequel has never wavered. With her wonderfully warm, giving heart and her encouragement every

609

step of the way, she makes each minute of working together a joy. *Thank you*, dear Diane.

Last, but not least, and facetiously, but true ... I am thankful for all of my doctors who have endeavored to keep me perking along as I've worked diligently to complete this first part of the family saga!

About The Author

Born the first of four children in rural Mississippi in 1932, Patsy Gilbert grew up to marry a Naval officer and give birth to four children. After the marriage ended in 1977, Pat became a nanny, caring for the children of prominent families. An aspiring writer all her life, she began *Legacy of Letters* after rediscovering a treasure trove of letters saved by family members throughout the years. Now a grandmother of nine, Pat lives in Orlando, Florida, and is working on her second book, which continues the family saga.

Printed in the United States
26442LVS00001B/376-390